Active Directory

SECOND EDITION

Active Directory

Robbie Allen and
Alistair G. Lowe-Norris

O'REILLY®

Beijing · Cambridge · Farnham · Köln · Paris · Sebastopol · Taipei · Tokyo

Active Directory, Second Edition
by Robbie Allen and Alistair G. Lowe-Norris

Published by O'Reilly Media, Inc., 1005 Gravenstein Highway North, Sebastopol, CA 95472.

O'Reilly & Associates books may be purchased for educational, business, or sales promotional use. Online editions are also available for most titles (*safari.oreilly.com*). For more information, contact our corporate/institutional sales department: (800) 998-9938 or *corporate@oreilly.com*.

Editor:	Robert Denn
Production Editor:	Darren Kelly
Cover Designer:	Hanna Dyer
Interior Designer:	Bret Kerr

Printing History:

January 2000:	First Edition.
April 2003:	Second Edition.

ISBN: 0-596-00466-4
[M]

Table of Contents

Part I.   Active Directory Basics

Part III. Scripting Active Directory with ADSI, ADO, and WMI

Preface

Active Directory is a common repository for information about objects that reside on the network, such as users and groups, computers and printers, and applications and files. The default Active Directory schema supports numerous attributes for each object class that can be used to store a variety of information. Access Control Lists (ACLs) are also stored with objects, which allow you to maintain permissions for who can access and manage them. Having a single source for this information makes it more accessible and easier to manage. However, to accomplish this with Active Directory requires a significant amount of knowledge of such topics as LDAP, Kerberos, DNS, multi-master replication, group policies, and data partitioning, to name a few. This book will be your guide through this maze of technologies, showing you how to deploy a scalable and reliable Active Directory infrastructure.

Windows 2000 Active Directory has proven itself to be very solid in terms of features and reliability, but after several years of real-world deployments, there was much room for improvement. With Windows Server 2003, Microsoft focused on security, manageability, and scalability enhancements that are sure to make even the most recent Windows 2000 deployers consider upgrading. Fortunately, Microsoft has made the upgrade process to Windows Server 2003 Active Directory seamless. You can proceed at your own pace based on how quickly you need to upgrade.

This book is a significant update to the very successful first edition. All of the existing chapters have been brought up to date with Windows Server 2003, and eight additional chapters have been included to explain new features or concepts not covered in the first edition. This second edition describes Active Directory in depth, but not in the traditional way of going through the graphical user interface screen by screen. Instead, the book sets out to tell administrators exactly how to design, manage, and maintain a small, medium, or enterprise Active Directory infrastructure. To this end, the book is split up into three parts.

Part I introduces in general terms much of how Active Directory works, giving you a thorough grounding in its concepts. Some of the topics include Active Directory replication, the schema, application partitions, group policies, and interaction with DNS.

In Part II, we describe in copious detail the issues around properly designing the directory infrastructure. Topics include in-depth looks at designing the namespace, creating a site topology, designing group policies for locking down client settings, auditing, permissions, backup and recovery, and a look at Microsoft's future direction with Directory Services.

Part III is all about managing Active Directory via automation with Active Directory Service Interfaces (ADSI), ActiveX Data Objects (ADO), and Windows Management Instrumentation (WMI). This section covers how to create and manipulate users, groups, printers, and other objects that you may need in your everyday management of Active Directory. It also describes in depth how you can utilize the strengths of WMI and the .NET System.DirectoryServices namespace to manage Active Directory programmatically via those interfaces.

If you're looking for in-depth coverage of how to use the MMC snap-ins or Resource Kit tools, look elsewhere. However, if you want a book that lays bare the design and management of an enterprise or departmental Active Directory, you need look no further.

Intended Audience

This book is intended for all Active Directory administrators, whether you manage a single server or a global multinational with a farm of thousands of servers. Even if you have the first edition, you'll find a considerable amount of new material in this book, which covers many of the new features in Windows Server 2003. To get the most out of the book, you will probably find it useful to have a server running Windows Server 2003 and the Resource Kit tools available so that you can check out various items as we point them out.

If you have no experience with VBScript, the scripting language we use in Part III, don't worry. The syntax is straightforward, and you should have no difficulty grasping the principles of scripting with ADSI, ADO, and WMI. For those who want to learn more about VBScript, we provide links to various Internet sites and other books as appropriate.

Contents of the Book

This book is split into three parts:

Part I, *Active Directory Basics*

- Chapter 1, *A Brief Introduction*, reviews the evolution of the Microsoft NOS and some of the major features and benefits of Active Directory.

- Chapter 2, *Active Directory Fundamentals*, provides a high-level look at how objects are stored in Active Directory and explains some of the internal structures and concepts that it relies on.

- Chapter 3, *Naming Contexts and Application Partitions*, reviews the predefined Naming Contexts within Active Directory, what is contained within each, and the purpose of Application Partitions.

- Chapter 4, *Active Directory Schema*, gives you information on how the blueprint for each object and each object's attributes are stored in Active Directory.

- Chapter 5, *Site Topology and Replication*, details how the actual replication process for data takes place between domain controllers.

- Chapter 6, *Active Directory and DNS*, describes the importance of the Domain Name System (DNS) and what it is used for within Active Directory.

- Chapter 7, *Profiles and Group Policy Primer*, gives you a detailed introduction to the capabilities of both user profiles and Group Policy Objects.

Part II, *Designing an Active Directory Infrastructure*

- Chapter 8, *Designing the Namespace*, introduces the steps and techniques involved in properly preparing a design that reduces the number of domains and increases administrative control through the use of Organizational Units.

- Chapter 9, *Creating a Site Topology*, shows you how to design a representation of your physical infrastructure within Active Directory to gain very fine-grained control over intrasite and intersite replication.

- Chapter 10, *Designing Organization-Wide Group Policies*, explains how Group Policy Objects function in Active Directory and how you can properly design an Active Directory structure to make the most effective use of these functions.

- Chapter 11, *Active Directory Security: Permissions and Auditing*, describes how you can design effective security for all areas of your Active Directory, in terms of both access to objects and their properties; it includes information on how to design effective security access logging in any areas you choose.

- Chapter 12, *Designing and Implementing Schema Extensions*, covers procedures for extending the classes and attributes in the Active Directory schema.

- Chapter 13, *Backup, Recovery, and Maintenance*, describes how you can back up and restore Active Directory down to the object level or the entire directory.

- Chapter 14, *Upgrading to Windows Server 2003*, outlines how you can upgrade your existing Active Directory infrastructure to Windows Server 2003.

- Chapter 15, *Migrating from Windows NT*, gives very basic guidelines on areas to think about when conducting a Windows NT 4.0 migration. This is only an introduction to the subject; readers looking for step-by-step guides or detailed studies of migration will need to look elsewhere.

- Chapter 16, *Integrating Microsoft Exchange*, covers some of the important Active Directory–related issues when implementing Microsoft Exchange.

- Chapter 17, *Interoperability, Integration, and Future Direction*, looks into what methods exist now and will exist in the future for integrating Active Directory with other directories and data stores.

Part III, *Scripting Active Directory with ADSI, ADO, and WMI*

- Chapter 18, *Scripting with ADSI*, introduces ADSI scripting by leading you through a series of step-by-step examples.

- Chapter 19, *IADs and the Property Cache*, delves into the concept of the property cache used extensively by ADSI and shows you how to properly manipulate any attribute of any object within it.

- Chapter 20, *Using ADO for Searching*, demonstrates how to make use of a technology normally reserved for databases and now extended to allow rapid searching for objects in Active Directory.

- Chapter 21, *Users and Groups*, gives you the lowdown on how to rapidly create users and groups, giving them whatever attributes you desire.

- Chapter 22, *Manipulating Persistent and Dynamic Objects*, explains how other persistent objects such as services, shares, and printers may be manipulated; it also looks at dynamic objects, such as print jobs, user sessions, and resources.

- Chapter 23, *Permissions and Auditing*, describes how each object contains its own list of permissions and auditing entries that governs how it can be accessed and how access is logged. The chapter then details how you can create and manipulate permission and auditing entries as you choose.

- Chapter 24, *Extending the Schema and the Active Directory Snap-Ins*, covers creation of new classes and attributes programmatically in the schema, and modification of the existing Active Directory snap-ins to perform additional customized functions.

- Chapter 25, *Using ADSI and ADO from ASP or VB*, goes into how you can extend the scripts that have been written by incorporating them into web pages or even converting them to simple VB programs.

- Chapter 26, *Scripting with WMI*, gives a quick overview of WMI and goes through several examples for managing a system, including services, the registry, and the event log. Accessing AD with WMI is also covered, along with the new TrustMon and Replication WMI Providers.

- Chapter 27, *Manipulating DNS*, describes how to manipulate DNS server configuration, zones, and resource records with the WMI DNS Provider.

- Chapter 28, *Getting Started with VB.NET and System.DirectoryServices*, starts off by providing some background information on the .NET Framework and then dives into several examples using the System.DirectoryServices namespace with VB.NET.

Conventions in This Book

The following typographical conventions are used in this book:

Constant width
> Indicates command-line elements, computer output, and code examples.

Constant width italic
> Indicates variables in examples and registry keys.

Constant width bold
> Indicates user input.

Italic
> Introduces new terms and indicates URLs, commands, file extensions, filenames, directory or folder names, and UNC pathnames.

> Indicates a tip, suggestion, or general note. For example, we'll tell you if you need to use a particular version or if an operation requires certain privileges.

> Indicates a warning or caution. For example, we'll tell you if Active Directory does not behave as you'd expect or if a particular operation has a negative impact on performance.

How to Contact Us

We have tested and verified the information in this book to the best of our ability, but you might find that features have changed (or even that we have made mistakes!). Please let us know about any errors you find, as well as your suggestions for future editions, by writing to:

> O'Reilly & Associates, Inc.
> 1005 Gravenstein Highway North
> Sebastopol, CA 95472
> (800) 998-9938 (in the United States or Canada)
> (707) 829-0515 (international/local)
> (707) 829-0104 (fax)

To ask technical questions or comment on the book, send email to:

> *bookquestions@oreilly.com*

We have a web page for this book where we list examples and any plans for future editions. You can access this information at:

> *http://www.oreilly.com/catalog/actdir2*

For more information about books, conferences, Resource Centers, and the O'Reilly Network, see the O'Reilly web site at:

http://www.oreilly.com

Acknowledgments

For the First Edition (Alistair)

Many people have encouraged me in the writing of this book, principally Vicky Launders, my partner, friend, and fountain of useful information, who has been a pinnacle of understanding during all the late nights and early mornings. Without you my life would not be complete.

My parents Pauline and Peter Norris also have encouraged me at every step of the way; many thanks to you both.

For keeping me sane, my thanks go to my good friend Keith Cooper, a natural polymath, superb scientist, and original skeptic; to Steve Joint, for keeping my enthusiasm for Microsoft in check; to Dave and Sue Peace for "Tuesdays," and the ability to look interested in what I was saying and how the book was going no matter how uninterested they must have felt; and to Mike Felmeri for his interest in this book and his eagerness to read an early draft.

I had a lot of help from my colleagues at Leicester University. To Lee Flight, a true networking guru without peer, many thanks for all the discussions, arguments, suggestions, and solutions. I'll remember forever how one morning very early you took the first draft of my 11-chapter book and spread it all over the floor to produce the 21 chapters that now constitute the book. It's so much better for it. Chris Heaton gave many years of dedicated and enjoyable teamwork; you have my thanks. Brian Kerr, who came onto the fast-moving train at high speed, managed to hold on tight through all the twists and turns along the way, and then finally took over the helm. Thanks to Paul Crow for his remarkable work on the Windows 2000 client rollout and GPOs at Leicester. And thanks to Phil Beesley, Carl Nelson, Paul Youngman, and Peter Burnham for all the discussions and arguments along the way. A special thank you goes to Wendy Ferguson for our chats over the past few years.

To the Cormyr crew: Paul Burke, for his in-depth knowledge across all aspects of technology and databases in particular, who really is without peer, and thanks for being so eager to read the book that you were daft enough to take it on your honeymoon; Simon Williams for discussions on enterprise infrastructure consulting and practices, how you can't get the staff these days, and everything else under the sun that came up; Richard Lang for acting as a sounding board for the most complex parts of replication internals, as I struggled to make sense of what was going on; Jason Norton for his constant ability to cheer me up; Mark Newell for his gadgets and Ian Harcombe for his wit, two of the best analyst programmers that I've ever met; and finally, Paul "Vaguely" Buxton for simply being himself. Many thanks to you all.

To Allan Kelly, another analyst programmer par excellence, for various discussions that he probably doesn't remember but that helped in a number of ways.

At Microsoft: Walter Dickson for his insightful ability to get right to the root of any problem, constant accessibility via email and phone, and his desire to make sure that any job is done to the best of its ability; Bob Wells for his personal enthusiasm and interest in what I was doing; Daniel Turner for his help, enthusiasm, and key role in getting Leicester University involved in the Windows 2000 RDP; Oliver Bell for actually getting Leicester University accepted on the Windows 2000 RDP and taking a chance by allocating free consultancy time to the project; Brad Tipp whose enthusiasm and ability galvanized me into action at the U.K. Professional Developers Conference in 1997; Julius Davies for various discussions but among other things telling me how the auditing and permissions aspects of Active Directory had all changed just after I finished the chapter; Karl Noakes, Steve Douglas, Jonathan Phillips, Stuart Hudman, Stuart Okin, Nick McGrath, and Alan Bennett for various discussions.

To Tony Lees, director of Avantek Computer Ltd., for being attentive, thoughtful, and the best all-round salesman I have ever met, many thanks for taking the time to get Leicester University onto the Windows 2000 RDP.

Thanks to Amit D. Chaudhary and Cricket Liu for reviewing parts of the book.

I also would like to thank everyone at O'Reilly but especially my editor Robert Denn for his encouragement, patience, and keen desire to get this book crafted properly.

For the Second Edition (Robbie)

I would like to thank the people at O'Reilly for giving me the opportunity to work on this book. Special thanks goes to Robert Denn, who was a great editor to work with.

I would like to thank Alistair Lowe-Norris for providing such a solid foundation in the first edition. While there was a lot of new material to include, much of the information in the first edition was still pertinent and useful. He deserves a lot of credit since the first edition was done before Windows 2000 had even been released to the public, and there was virtually no information on Active Directory available.

Thanks to Alistair, Mitch Tulloch, and Paul Turcotte for providing very insightful feedback during the review process. Their comments rounded out the rough edges in the book.

And no acknowledgements section would be complete without recognition to my significant other, Janet. She was supportive during the many late nights and weekends I spent writing. I appreciate everything she does for me.

PART I

Active Directory Basics

This section of the book discusses the basics of Active Directory in order to provide a good grounding in the building blocks and how they function together.

CHAPTER 1

A Brief Introduction

Active Directory (AD) is Microsoft's network operating system (NOS) directory, built on top of Windows 2000 and Windows Server 2003. It enables administrators to manage enterprise-wide information efficiently from a central repository that can be globally distributed. Once information about users and groups, computers and printers, and applications and services has been added to Active Directory, it can be made available for use throughout the entire network to as many or as few people as you like. The structure of the information can match the structure of your organization, and your users can query Active Directory to find the location of a printer or the email address of a colleague. With Organizational Units, you can delegate control and management of the data however you see fit. If you are like most organizations, you may have a significant amount of data (e.g., thousands of employees or computers). This may seem daunting to enter in Active Directory, but fortunately Microsoft has some very robust yet easy-to-use Application Programming Interfaces (APIs) to help facilitate data management programmatically.

This book is an introduction to Active Directory, but an introduction with a broad scope. In Part I, we cover many of the basic concepts within Active Directory to give you a good grounding in some of the fundamentals that every administrator should understand. In Part II, we focus on various design issues and methodologies, to enable you to map your organization's business requirements into your Active Directory infrastructure. Getting the design right the first time around is critical to a successful implementation, but it can be extremely difficult if you have no experience deploying Active Directory. In Part III, we cover in detail management of Active Directory programmatically through scripts based on Active Directory Service Interfaces (ADSI), ActiveX Data Objects (ADO), and Windows Management Instrumentation (WMI). No matter how good your design is, unless you can automate your environment, problems will creep in, causing decreased uniformity and reliability.

Before moving on to some of the basic components within Active Directory, we will now review how Microsoft came to the point of implementing an LDAP-based directory service to support their NOS environment.

Evolution of the Microsoft NOS

"NOS" is the term used to describe a networked environment in which various types of resources, such as user, group, and computer accounts, are stored in a central repository that is controlled and accessible to end users. Typically a NOS environment is comprised of one or more servers that provide NOS services, such as authentication and account manipulation, and multiple end users that access those services.

Microsoft's first integrated NOS environment became available in 1990 with the release of Windows NT 3.0, which combined many features of the LAN Manager protocols and OS/2 operating system. The NT NOS slowly evolved over the next eight years until Active Directory was first released in beta in 1997.

Under Windows NT, the "domain" concept was introduced, providing a way to group resources based on administrative and security boundaries. NT domains are flat structures limited to about 40,000 objects (users, groups, and computers). For large organizations, this limitation imposed superficial boundaries on the design of the domain structure. Often, domains were geographically limited as well because the replication of data between domain controllers (i.e., servers providing the NOS services to end users) performed poorly over high-latency or low-bandwidth links. Another significant problem with the NT NOS was delegation of administration, which typically tended to be an all-or-nothing matter at the domain level.

Microsoft was well aware of these limitations and needed to rearchitect their NOS model into something that would be much more scalable and flexible. For that reason, they looked to LDAP-based directory services as a possible solution.

Brief History of Directories

In generic terms, a directory service is a repository of network, application, or NOS information that is useful to multiple applications or users. Under this definition, the Windows NT NOS is a type of directory service. In fact, there are many different types of directories, including Internet white pages, email systems, and even the Domain Name System (DNS). While each of these systems have characteristics of a directory service, X.500 and the Lightweight Directory Access Protocol (LDAP) define the standards for how a true directory service is implemented and accessed.

In 1988, the International Telecommunication Union (ITU) and International Organization of Standardization (ISO) teamed up to develop a series of standards around directory services, which has come to be known as X.500. While X.500 proved to be a good model for structuring a directory and provided a lot of functionality around advanced operations and security, it was difficult to implement clients to utilize it. One reason is that X.500 is based on the OSI (Open System Interconnection) protocol stack instead of TCP/IP, which had become the standard for the Internet. The X.500 directory access protocol (DAP) was very complex and implemented a lot of features most clients never needed. This prevented large-scale adoption. It is for this reason that a group headed by the University of Michigan started work on a "lightweight" X.500 access protocol that would make X.500 easier to utilize.

The first version of the Lightweight Directory Access Protocol (LDAP) was released in 1993 as RFC 1487, but due to the absence of many features provided by X.500, it never really took off. It wasn't until LDAPv2 was released in 1995 as RFC 1777 that LDAP started to gain popularity. Prior to LDAPv2, the primary use of LDAP was as a gateway between X.500 servers. Simplified clients would interface with the LDAP gateway, which would translate the requests and submit it to the X.500 server. The University of Michigan team thought that if LDAP could provide most of the functionality necessary to most clients, they could remove the middleman (the gateway) and develop an LDAP-enabled directory server. This directory server could use many of the concepts from X.500, including the data model, but would leave out all the overheard provided by the numerous features it implemented. Thus the first LDAP directory server was released in late 1995 by the University of Michigan team, and it turned into the basis for many future directory servers.

In 1997, the last major update to the LDAP specification was described in RFC 2251. It provided several new features and made LDAP robust enough and extensible enough to be suitable for most vendors to implement. Since then, companies such as Netscape, Sun, Novell, and Microsoft have developed LDAP-based directory servers. Most recently, RFC 3377 was released, which summarizes all of the major LDAP RFCs.

Windows NT Versus Active Directory

As we mentioned earlier, Windows NT and Active Directory both provide directory services to clients (Windows NT in a more generic sense). And while both share some common concepts, such as Security Identifiers (SIDs) to identify security principals, they are very different from a feature, scalability, and functionality point of view. Table 1-1 contains a comparison of features between Windows NT and Active Directory.

Table 1-1. A comparison between Windows NT and Active Directory

Windows NT	Active Directory
Single-master replication is used, from the PDC master to the BDC subordinates.	Multimaster replication is used between all domain controllers.
Domain is the smallest unit of partitioning.	Naming Contexts and Application Partitions are the smallest unit of partitioning.
System policies can be used locally on machines or set at the domain level.	Group policies can be managed centrally and used by clients throughout the forest based on domain, site or OU criteria.
Data cannot be stored hierarchically within a domain.	Data can be stored in a hierarchical manner using OUs.

Table 1-1. A comparison between Windows NT and Active Directory (continued)

Windows NT	Active Directory
Domain is the smallest unit of security delegation and administration.	A property of an object is the smallest unit of security delegation/administration.
NetBIOS and WINS used for name resolution.	DNS is used for name resolution.
Object is the smallest unit of replication.	Attribute is the smallest unit of replication.
	In Windows Server 2003 Active Directory, some attributes replicate on a per-value basis (such as the member attribute of group objects).
Maximum recommended database size for SAM is 40 MB.	Recommended maximum database size for Active Directory is 70 TB.
Maximum effective number of users is 40,000 (if you accept the recommended 40 MB maximum).	The maximum number of objects is in the tens of millions.
Four domain models (single, single-master, multimaster, complete-trust) required to solve per-domain admin-boundary and user-limit problems.	No domain models required as the complete-trust model is implemented. One-way trusts can be implemented manually.
Schema is not extensible.	Schema is fully extensible.
Data can only be accessed through a Microsoft API.	Supports LDAP, which is the standard protocol used by directories, applications, and clients that want to access directory data. Allows for cross-platform data access and management.

First, Windows NT Primary Domain Controllers and Backup Domain Controllers have been replaced by Active Directory Domain Controllers. It is possible under Active Directory to promote member servers to Domain Controllers (DCs) and demote DCs to ordinary member servers, all without needing a reinstallation of the operating system; this is not the case under Windows NT. If you want to make a member server a DC, you can promote it using the *dcpromo.exe* wizard. *dcpromo* asks you a number of questions, such as whether you are creating the first domain in a domain tree or joining an existing tree, whether this new tree is part of an existing forest or a new forest to be created, and so on.

Organizational Units are an important change with Active Directory. Under Windows NT, administration was delegated on a per-domain basis, while under Active Directory, both Organizational Units and domains can be used as administration boundaries. This can significantly reduce the number of domains you require.

Windows NT used NetBIOS as its primary network communication mechanism, whereas Active Directory is tightly integrated with DNS and uses TCP/IP. Under previous versions, administrators ended up maintaining two computer lookup databases—DNS for name resolution and WINS for NetBIOS name resolution—but Active Directory no longer does traditional NetBIOS name resolution. Instead, it relies on DNS. You can still install and run a WINS server, but this would be only for backward compatibility until all your machines and applications are upgraded.

The significant difference in replication is that Active Directory will replicate at the attribute rather than object level. With Windows NT, if you changed the full name of a user object, the whole object had to be replicated out. In the same scenario with Active Directory, only the modified attribute will be replicated. Coupled with some very clever changes to the way replication works, this means that you replicate less data for shorter periods, thereby reducing the two most important factors in replication. See Chapters 5 and 9 for more on replication.

The suggested maximum Windows NT SAM was 40 MB, which was roughly equivalent to about 40,000 objects, depending on what proportion of computer, user, and group accounts you had in your domain. Many companies have gone above 75 MB for the SAM for one domain due to the huge number of groups that they were using, so this rule was never hard and fast as long as you understood the problems you were likely to experience if you went past the limit. However, Active Directory is based on the Extensible Storage Engine (ESE) database used by Exchange and developed to hold millions of objects with a maximum database size of 70 TB. This should be enough for most people's needs and is also only a recommended maximum limit. Remember, however, that this new database holds all classes of objects, not just the users, groups, and computers of the previous version's SAM. As more and more Active Directory–enabled applications are developed, more classes of objects will be added to the schema, and more objects will be added to the directory. To bring this into perspective, imagine that one of the world's largest aerospace companies has around half a million computers. Assuming an equivalent number of staff, this still uses only 10% of the maximum database capacity. However, when you begin to consider all the other objects that will be in Active Directory, including file shares, printers, groups, organizational units, domains, contacts, and so on, you can see how that percentage will increase.

For administrators of Windows NT, the significant increase in scalability may be the most important change of all. It was extremely easy to hit the 40 MB SAM limit within an NT domain, forcing you to split the domain. You ended up managing multiple domains when you really didn't want to. It was frustrating. None of the domains were organized into a domain tree or anything of the sort, so they had no automatic trusts between them. This meant that NT administrators had to set up manual trusts between domains, and these had to be initiated at both domains to set up a single one-way trust. As you added more domains, you ended up managing even greater numbers of trusts. To counter this problem, Microsoft introduced four domain models that you could use as templates for your Windows NT design: the single-domain model, the single-master domain model, the multimaster domain model, and the complete-trust domain model. All four are shown in Figure 1-1. The most common model after the single-domain model is probably the multimaster domain model.

Stated very simply, the single-domain model had, as the name implied, only one domain with a SAM smaller than 40 MB and no trusts. Where multiple domains

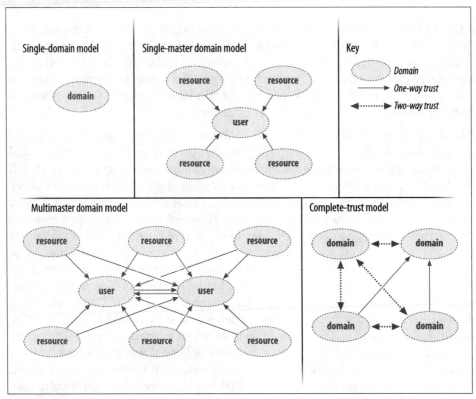

Figure 1-1. The four Windows NT domain models

were needed for resource access but the SAM was still less than 40 MB, the single-master domain model was used. The single-master domain model was made up of one user domain and multiple resource domains. The important point was that the resource domains had one-way trusts with the user domain that held all the accounts. Due to the one-way trusts, the administrators of the resource domains could set permissions as they wished to their own resources for any accounts in the user domain. This meant that one central set of administrators could manage the accounts, while individual departments maintained autonomy over their own resources. When the SAM was going to grow past 40 MB, a multimaster model came into play. The administrators of the user domain split the user accounts into two or more domains, giving them two-way (i.e., complete) trust between each other, and then each resource domain had to have a one-way trust with each user domain. Scaling this up, for a multimaster domain with 10 user domains and 100 resource domains, that's 90 trusts to make up the intra-user trusts and 1,000 separate resource-to-user trusts that must be manually set. Finally, in some cases, the complete-trust model was used where any domain could create accounts and allocate resources to any other domain.

Active Directory acts like a single-master domain model in which the Organizational Units function as the resource domains. As you can see, this eliminates the need for maintaining separate Windows NT resource domains, as these can be converted to Organizational Units in what was the user domain. All Active Directory domains within a forest trust each other via transitive trusts. In Windows Server 2003 Active Directory, transitive forest trusts are also available so that the domains in two different forests can completely trust each other via a single explicit trust between the forest root domains.

Finally, the Windows NT schema was not extensible. No new object types could be added to it, which was a significant limitation for most enterprises. When Microsoft products that extended Windows NT—such as Terminal Server and File and Print for NetWare—were released, each had to store any attribute data that it wanted all together within one existing attribute. Under Active Directory, the schema is fully extensible, so any new products can extend the schema and add in objects and attributes as required.

For more information on moving from Windows NT to Active Directory, take a look at Chapter 15.

Windows 2000 Versus Windows Server 2003

While the first version of Active Directory available with Windows 2000 was very stable and feature-rich, it still had room for improvement, primarily around usability and performance. With Windows Server 2003, Microsoft has addressed many of these issues. To utilize these features you have to upgrade your domain controllers to Windows Server 2003 and raise the domain and forest functional levels as necessary.

The difference between Windows 2000 Active Directory and Windows Server 2003 Active Directory is more evolutionary than revolutionary. The decision to upgrade to Windows Server 2003 is a subjective one, based on your needs. For example, if you have a lot of domain controllers and Active Directory sites, you may want to take advantage of the improvements with replication as soon as possible. Or perhaps you've been dying to rename a domain, a capability available in Windows Server 2003 Active Directory. On the whole, Microsoft added or updated more than 100 features within Active Directory, and we will now discuss some of the more significant ones.

For more information on migrating to Windows Server 2003 from Windows 2000 check out Chapter 14.

Some of the new features are available as soon as you promote the first Windows Server 2003 domain controller into an existing Windows 2000 Active Directory domain. In Table 1-2, the features available when you do so are listed along with descriptions. Note that these features will apply only to the Windows Server 2003 domain controllers in the domain.

Table 1-2. Windows 2000 domain functional level feature list

Feature	Description
Application Partitions	You can create your own partitions to store data separately from the default partitions, and you can configure which DCs in the forest replicate it.
GC not required for logon (i.e., universal group caching)	Under Windows 2000, a DC had to contact a GC to determine universal group membership and subsequently to allow users to logon. This feature allows DCs to cache universal group membership so that it is not necessary to contact a GC for logins.
MMC enhancements and new command-line tools	The new Active Directory Users and Computers allows you to save queries, drag and drop, and edit multiple users at once, and it is much more efficient about scrolling through a large number of objects. In addition, several new command-line tools (*dsadd, dsmod, dsrm, dsquery, dsget,* and *dsmove*) come installed with the server, allowing for greater flexibility in managing Active Directory.
Install from media	Administrators can create new DCs for an existing domain by installing from a backup of an existing DC that resides on media such as a CD or DVD.
WMI Filtering for GPOs	You can apply a WMI filter, which is a query that can utilize any WMI information on a client, to a GPO, and that query will be run against each targeted client. If the query succeeds, the GPO will continue to process; otherwise it will stop processing.

In Table 1-3, the features available in domains running the Windows Server 2003 functional level are listed. A domain can be changed to the Windows Server 2003 functional level when all domain controllers in the domain are running Windows Server 2003.

Table 1-3. Windows Server 2003 domain functional level feature list

Feature	Description
Domain controller rename	With Windows 2000, you had to demote, rename, and repromote a DC if you wanted to rename it. With Windows Server 2003 domains, you can rename DCs, and it only requires a single reboot.
Domain rename	A domain can be renamed, which was not previously possible under Windows 2000. The impact to the environment is pretty significant (i.e., all member computers must be rebooted), so it should be done conservatively.
Logon timestamp replicated	Under Windows 2000, the lastLogon attribute contained a user's last logon timestamp, but that attribute was not replicated among the DCs, thereby forcing you to query every DC to get the effective last logon. With Windows Server 2003, the lastLogonTimeStamp attribute will contain a user's last logon and will be replicated.

Table 1-3. Windows Server 2003 domain functional level feature list (continued)

Feature	Description
Quotas	Users that have write access to AD can cause a Denial of Service (DOS) attack by creating objects until a DC's disk fills up. You can prevent this type of attack using quotas. With a quota you can restrict the number of objects a security principal can create in a partition, container, or OU. Windows Server 2003 DCs can enforce quotas even when not at the Windows Server 2003 domain functional level, but for it to be enforced everywhere, all DCs must be running Windows Server 2003.

In Table 1-4, the features available to forests running the Windows Server 2003 functional level are listed. A forest can be raised to the Windows Server 2003 functional level when all domains contained within the forest are at the Windows Server 2003 domain functional level.

Table 1-4. Windows Server 2003 forest functional level feature list

Feature	Description
GC replication tuning	After an attribute has been added to the GC, a sync of the contents of the GC for every GC server will no longer be performed as it was with Windows 2000.
Reactivation of defunct schema objects	This feature allows deactivated schema classes or attributes to be redefined.
Forest trust	A forest trust is a transitive trust between two forest root domains that allows all domains within the two forests to trust each other. To accomplish the same thing with Windows 2000, you would have to implement trusts for each domain between the two forests.
Per-value replication	This feature allows certain attributes to replicate on a per-value basis instead of a per-attribute basis (i.e., all values). This is vital for group objects because under Windows 2000, a change in the member attribute caused the entire set of values for that attribute to be replicated (unnecessarily).
Improved replication	The Intersite Topology Generator (ISTG) and Knowledge Consistency Checker (KCC) have been greatly improved and will create more efficient replication topologies.
Dynamic auxiliary classes	This feature allows for dynamically assigned per-object auxiliary classes. Under Windows 2000, an object could only utilize auxiliary classes that were statically defined in the schema for its object class.
Dynamic Objects	Dynamic objects have a defined time to live (TTL) after which they will be removed from Active Directory unless the TTL is updated. This can help facilitate data management for short-lived objects.
InetOrgPerson class for users	The InetOrgPerson object class is a standard (RFC 2798) commonly used by directory vendors to represent users. With Windows Server 2003, you can use either the Microsoft defined user object class or the inetOrgPerson object class for user accounts.

In addition to the new features available in Windows Server 2003, Microsoft is developing a lightweight version of Active Directory called Active Directory Application Mode (AD/AM). AD/AM is intended to address certain deployment scenarios related to directory-enabled applications. It runs as a non-operating system service and can be implemented independently or in conjunction with your Active Directory environment. Since it runs as a non–operating system service, you can install multiple instances of AD/AM on a single server, with each instance independently configurable. AD/AM will be similar to a generic LDAP directory, such as OpenLDAP or SunONE Directory Server, with many NOS-specific features and requirements removed. If you are curious about how AD/AM fits into Microsoft's master plan, check out Chapter 17. For more information on AD/AM, check out the following web site:

> *http://www.microsoft.com/windowsserver2003/techinfo/overview/adam.mspx*

Summary

This chapter has been a brief introduction to the origins of Active Directory and some of the new features available in Windows Server 2003. The rest of the chapters in Part I will cover the conceptual introduction to Active Directory and equip you to get the most out of Parts II and III.

CHAPTER 2

Active Directory Fundamentals

This chapter aims to bring you up to speed on the basic concepts and terminology used with Active Directory. It is important to understand each component of Active Directory before embarking on a design, or your design may leave out a critical element.

How Objects Are Stored and Identified

Data is stored within Active Directory in a hierarchical fashion similar to the way data is stored in a filesystem. Each entry is referred to as an object. At the structural level, there are two types of objects: containers and non-containers, also known as leaf nodes. One or more containers branch off in a hierarchical fashion from a root container. Each container may contain leaf nodes or other containers. A leaf node, however, as the name implies, may not contain any other objects.

Consider the parent-child relationships of the containers and leaves in Figure 2-1. The root of this tree has two children, Finance and Sales. Both of these are containers of other objects. Sales has two children of its own, Pre-Sales and Post-Sales. Only the Pre-Sales container is shown as containing additional child objects. The Pre-Sales container holds user, group, and computer objects as an example.[*] Each of these child nodes is said to have the Pre-Sales container as its parent. Figure 2-1 represents what is known in Active Directory as a domain.

The most common type of container you will create in Active Directory is an Organizational Unit, but there are others as well, such as the one called Container. Each of these has its place, as we'll show later, but the one that we will be using most frequently is the Organizational Unit (OU).

---

[*] User, group, and computer objects are actually containers, as they can contain other objects such as printers. However, they are not normally drawn as containers in domain diagrams such as this.

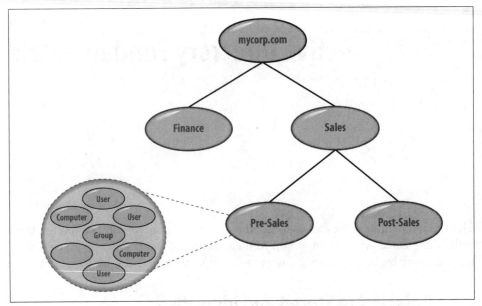

Figure 2-1. A hierarchy of objects

Uniquely Identifying Objects

When you are potentially storing millions of objects in Active Directory, each object has to be uniquely locatable and identifiable. To that end, objects have a Globally Unique Identifier (GUID) assigned to them by the system at creation. This 128-bit number is guaranteed to be unique by Microsoft. The object GUID stays with the object until it is deleted, regardless of whether it is renamed or moved within the Directory Information Tree (DIT).

While an object GUID is unique and resilient, it is not very easy to remember, nor is it based on the directory hierarchy. For that reason, another way to reference objects, called an ADsPath, is more commonly used.

ADsPaths

Hierarchical paths in Active Directory are known as ADsPaths and can be used to uniquely reference an object. In fact, ADsPath is a slightly more general term and is used by Microsoft to apply to any path to any of the major directories: Active Directory, Windows NT, Novell's NDS, and many others.

ADsPaths for Active Directory objects are normally represented using the syntax and rules defined in the LDAP standards. Let's take a look at how a path to the root of Figure 2-1 looks:

```
LDAP://dc=mycorp,dc=com
```

The path starts with a programmatic identifier (progID) of LDAP followed by a colon (:) and a double forward slash (//).

> You probably noted that we said the LDAP progID is most often used in an ADsPath, but that isn't always the case. ADsPaths to other directories can use other progIDs. We go into these other progIDs in more depth in Chapter 18.

In the previous ADsPath, after the progID, you represent the domain root, *mycorp.com*, by separating each part by a comma and prefixing each part with the letters dc. If the domain had been called mydomain.mycorp.com, the ADsPath would have looked like this:

```
LDAP://dc=mydomain,dc=mycorp,dc=com
```

> DC stands for Domain Component and is used to specify domain or application partition objects. Application partitions are covered in Chapter 3.

A distinguished name (DN) is the name used to uniquely reference an object in a DIT. A relative distinguished name (RDN) is the name used to uniquely reference an object within its parent container in a DIT. For example, this is the ADsPath for the default Administrator account in the Users Container in the mycorp.com domain:

```
LDAP://cn=Administrator,cn=Users,dc=mycorp,dc=com
```

This is the DN of the same user (note the absence of the progID):

```
cn=Administrator,cn=Users,dc=mycorp,dc=com
```

This is the RDN of the user:

```
cn=Administrator
```

These paths are made up of names and prefixes separated by the equal sign (=). Another prefix that will become very familiar to you is OU, which stands for Organizational Unit. Here is an example:

```
cn=Keith Cooper,ou=Northlight IT Ltd,dc=mycorp,dc=com
```

All RDNs, DNs, and ADsPaths use a prefix to indicate the class of object that is being referred to. Any object class that does not have a specific letter code uses the default of cn, which stands for Common Name. Table 2-1 provides the complete list of the most common prefixes among the directory server implementations. The list is from RFC 2253, and full text can be found at *http://www.ietf.org/rfc/rfc2253.txt*.

Table 2-1. Key codes From RFC 2253

Key	Attribute
CN	Common Name
L	Locality Name

Table 2-1. Key codes From RFC 2253 (continued)

Key	Attribute
ST	State or Province Name
O	Organization Name
OU	Organizational Unit Name
C	Country Name
STREET	Street Address
DC	Domain Component
UID	Userid

While Microsoft Exchange 5.5 uses the O prefix, Active Directory uses only DC, CN, and OU, with CN being used in the majority of cases.

Examples

Let's take a look at Figure 2-1 again. If all the containers were Organizational Units, the ADsPaths for Pre-Sales and Post-Sales would be as follows:

```
LDAP://ou=Pre-Sales,ou=Sales,dc=mycorp,dc=com
LDAP://ou=Post-Sales,ou=Sales,dc=mycorp,dc=com
```

And if you wanted to specify a user named Richard Lang, a group called My Group, and a computer called Moose in the Pre-Sales OU, you would use the following:

```
LDAP://cn=Richard Lang,ou=Pre-Sales,ou=Sales,dc=mycorp,dc=com
LDAP://cn=My Group,ou=Pre-Sales,ou=Sales,dc=mycorp,dc=com
LDAP://cn=Moose,ou=Pre-Sales,ou=Sales,dc=mycorp,dc=com
```

You can also reference a specific server in the ADsPath as in the following example:

```
LDAP://server1/cn=Moose,ou=Pre-Sales,ou=Sales,dc=mycorp,dc=com
```

When a server is specified, the object referenced in the ADsPath must be contained on that server.

Building Blocks

Now that we've shown how objects are structured and referenced, let's look at the core concepts behind Active Directory.

Domains and Domain Trees

Active Directory's logical structure is built around the concept of domains introduced in Windows NT 3.x and 4.0. However, in Active Directory, domains have been updated significantly from the flat and inflexible structure imposed by Windows NT. An Active Directory domain is made up of the following components:

- An X.500-based hierarchical structure of containers and objects
- A DNS domain name as a unique identifier

- A security service, which authenticates any access to resources via accounts in the domain or trusts with other domains
- One or more policies that dictate how functionality is restricted for users or machines within that domain

A domain controller (DC) can be authoritative for one and only one domain. Currently it is not possible to host multiple domains on a single DC. For example, Mycorp Company has already been allocated a DNS domain name for their company called *mycorp.com*, so they decide that the first Active Directory domain that they are going to build is to be named *mycorp.com*. However, this is only the first domain in a series that needs to be created, and mycorp.com is in fact the root of a domain tree.

The *mycorp.com* domain itself, ignoring its contents, is automatically created as the root node of a hierarchical structure called a domain tree. This is literally a series of domains connected together in a hierarchical fashion, all using a contiguous naming scheme. So, when Finance, Marketing, and Sales each wants its own domain, the names become *finance.mycorp.com*, *mktg.mycorp.com*, and *sales.mycorp.com*. Each domain tree is called by the name given to the root of the tree; hence, this domain tree is known as the *mycorp.com* tree, as illustrated in Figure 2-2. You can also see that we have added further domains below sales, for pre-sales and post-sales.

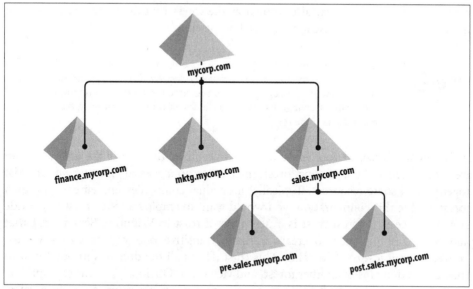

Figure 2-2. The mycorp.com domain tree

You can see that in Mycorp's setup, we now have a contiguous set of domains that all fit into a neat tree. Even if we had only one domain, it would still be a domain tree, albeit with only one domain.

Trees ease management and access to resources, as all the domains in a domain tree trust one another implicitly. Put much more simply, the administrator of *finance.mycorp.com* can allow any user in the tree access to any of the resources in the finance domain that the administrator wishes. The object accessing the resource does not have to be in the same domain. This is equivalent to Windows NT 4.0's complete trust model.

Trust relationships do not compromise security, as they are just setting up the potential to allow access to resources. Actual access permissions still have to be granted by administrators.

Forests

Now lets say that Mycorp also has a subsidiary business called Othercorp. The DNS domain name allocated and used by Othercorp is *othercorp.com*. Remember that when the *mycorp.com* domain was first created, a domain tree was also created with *mycorp.com* as the root. In fact, a new forest was also automatically created with one tree as a member: the *mycorp.com* domain tree. A forest consists of a number of discontinuous domain trees that all trust one another in the same manner that domains in a tree do. In other words, the trusts are transitive: if A trusts B and B trusts C, this implies that A trusts C as well. Forests are named after the domain that is created when creating a new forest, also known as the forest root domain. The forest root domain is important because it has special properties.

In Active Directory, you can never remove the forest root domain. If you try to do so, the forest is irretrievably destroyed. Under Windows Server 2003 Active Directory, you can rename the forest root domain, but you cannot change its status as the forest root domain or make a different domain the root.

In Othercorp's case, all you would need to do is create the root of the *othercorp.com* tree as a member of the existing forest; thus, *othercorp.com* and *mycorp.com* can exist together and share resources. Typically, individual companies implement their own forest, and in this configuration, you would want to employ a forest trust to provide seamless access. A forest trust is a new type of trust in Windows Server 2003 that allows an administrator to create a single transitive one-way or two-way trust between two forest root domains. This trust allows all the domains in one forest to trust all the domains in another forest, and vice versa. Obviously, in this example, we wanted *othercorp.com* to be able to access *mycorp.com*'s resources and vice versa. This doesn't have to be the case; each could have domain trees in its own separate forest with no communication between them. Thus, the forest containing the *mycorp.com* and *othercorp.com* domain trees is known as the *mycorp.com* forest, in which *mycorp.com* is the forest root.

If you have business units that are independent and in fact wish to be isolated from each other, then you must not combine them in a single forest. If you simply give each business unit its own domain, these business units are given the impression that they are autonomous and isolated from each other. However, in Active Directory, this level of autonomy and isolation can be achieved only through separate forests. This is also the case if you need to comply with regulatory or legal isolation requirements.

Organizational Units

Having covered the large-scale (domains, trees, and forests) view of Active Directory, we'll now talk about the small scale. When you look inside an Active Directory domain, you will see a hierarchical structure of objects. This hierarchy is made up of objects that can act as containers and objects that cannot. The primary type of container that you will create to house objects is called an Organizational Unit (OU). There is another type of container that is actually called a Container that can also be used to store a hierarchy of objects and containers.

Organizational Units have domain-like properties, whereas Containers do not. While both can contain huge hierarchies of containers and objects, an Organizational Unit is a security boundary and can have group policies applied to it. This makes Organizational Units the most significant structural component of a domain.

Let's illustrate this with an example. Imagine that you are the administrator of the *pre.sales.mycorp.com* domain from Figure 2-2. You have 500 users and 500 computer accounts in the domain. Most of the day-to-day account and machine management is very simple, but the pre-sales engineers' section is currently undergoing restructuring and an extensive recruitment program; people keep being transferred in or hired. You would like to be able to give that group autonomy, by allowing one of the senior engineers to manage its own section of the tree, but it isn't a large enough requirement to justify creating another domain to manage along with the associated domain controllers. You can instead create an Organizational Unit in your hierarchy called Pre-sales Engineers. You then nominate the senior engineer and give him autonomy over that Organizational Unit to create and delete accounts, change passwords, and create other Organizational Units and hierarchies. Obviously, the permissions that the senior engineer would be given would be properly tailored so that he had control over only that Organizational Unit and not the *pre.sales.mycorp.com* domain tree as a whole. You could do this manually or delegate control using the Delegation of Control wizard, discussed in more depth in Chapter 11.

When you install an Active Directory domain, a number of default Containers (and one Organizational Unit) are created automatically. Some of the Containers include Users, Computers, and so on. If you try to create a new Container, you will find that there is no option to do so from within the Active Directory Users and Computers (ADUC) MMC snap-in. This is intentional; in essentially all cases, you would want to create an Organizational Unit instead of a Container. It is possible to create containers from within scripts, but generally it is not necessary. So, throughout this book, whenever we advocate creating hierarchies within domains, we always use Organizational Units. After all, an Organizational Unit is just a superset of a Container, so there is nothing a Container can do that an Organizational Unit cannot.

Each forest has a child container called Configuration, which itself has a child container called Schema. Both the Configuration and Schema containers are actually hidden from view by default when you view the contents of Active Directory using ADUC. However, you can view a container by specifically connecting to it directly using a tool such as LDP or ADSI Edit, which are available from the Windows Support Tools. These containers are covered in more detail in Chapter 3.

Global Catalog

The Global Catalog (GC) is a very important part of Active Directory because it is used to perform forest-wide searches. As its name implies, the Global Catalog is a catalog of all objects in a forest with a subset of attributes for each object. The GC can be accessed via LDAP over port 3268, and with the GC:// progID in ADSI. The GC is read-only and therefore cannot be updated directly.

In multi-domain forests, typically you first need to perform a query against the GC to locate the objects of interest. Then you can perform a more directed query against a domain controller for the domain the object is in if you want to access all the attributes available on the object.

The attributes that are available in the GC are considered to be members of the partial attribute set (PAS). You can add and remove attributes from the PAS using tools such as the Active Directory Schema snap-in or by modifying the attributeSchema object for the attribute directly in the schema.

 Under Windows 2000, adding an attribute to the PAS caused all GC servers in a forest to resync the contents of the GC. This could have major replication and network traffic implications. Fortunately, this has been resolved with Windows Server 2003, where a GC resync no longer happens after a PAS addition.

Flexible Single Master of Operations (FSMO)

Even though Active Directory is a multi-master directory, there are some situations in which there should only be a single DC that can perform certain functions. In these cases, Active Directory nominates one server to act as the master for those functions. There are five such functions that need to take place on one server only. The server that is the master for a particular function or role is known as the Flexible Single Master Operations (FSMO, pronounced "fizmo") role owner.

Of the five roles, three exist domain-wide, and two apply to the entire forest. If there are 12 domains in your forest, there will be 38 FSMO roles: 12 lots of 3 domain-wide FSMOs and 2 single forest-wide FSMOs. The number of different role owners can vary greatly depending on whether you have domain controllers serving multiple roles, as is often the case.

The different FSMO roles are the following:

Schema Master (forest-wide)

> The Schema Master role owner is the DC that is allowed to make updates to the schema. No other server can process changes to the schema. The default FSMO Schema Master is the first server to be promoted in the forest.

Domain Naming Master (forest-wide)

> The Domain Naming Master role owner is the server that controls changes to the namespace. This server adds and removes domains and is also required to rename or move domains within a forest. Like the Schema Master, this role owner defaults to the first DC you promote in a forest.

PDC Emulator (domain-wide)

> For backward compatibility purposes, one Active Directory DC has to act as the Windows NT Primary Domain Controller (PDC). This server acts as the Windows NT master browser, and it also acts as the PDC for down-level clients and Backup Domain Controllers (BDCs). While doing this, it replicates the Windows NT SAM database to Windows NT 4.0 and Windows 3.51 BDCs. It also propagates down to those BDCs password changes and account lockout requests it receives as a normal DC, in addition to propagating password changes and account lockout requests passed to it from down-level clients out to the other DCs via multi-master replication.

RID Master (domain-wide)

> A Relative-Identifier (RID) Master exists per domain. Every security principal* in a domain has a Security Identifier (SID) that the system uses to uniquely identify that object for security permissions and authentication issues. In a way, this is similar to the GUID that every object has, but the SID is given only to security-enabled objects and is used only for security authentication and verification purposes. While you may log on or authenticate using the SAM account name or Universal Principal Name (UPN) to reference an object, the system will always obtain and authenticate using the SID corresponding to that name.
>
> The server or workstation hosting those objects creates unique SIDs for stand-alone users, groups, and computers on Windows NT/2000/XP workstations and Windows NT/2000/2003 servers in workgroups. In a domain, the SIDs must be

---

* A security principal is a security-enabled object, like a user, group, or computer that can access resources or be specified in ACLs.

unique across the entire domain. As each DC can create security-enabled objects, some mechanism has to exist so that two identical SIDs are never created.

To keep conflicts from occurring, the RID Master maintains a large pool of unique RID values. When a DC is added to the network, it is allocated a subset of 512 values from the RID pool for its own use. Whenever a DC needs to create a SID, it takes the next available value from its own RID pool to create the SID with a unique value.

In this way, the RID Master makes sure that all SIDs in a domain are unique RID values. When a DC's RID pool drops to 100 free values, the DC contacts the RID Master for another set of RID values. The threshold is set to 100 and not 0 to ensure that the RID Master can be unavailable for a brief time without immediately impacting object creations. The RID Master itself is in charge of generating and maintaining a pool of unique values across the entire domain.

Infrastructure Master (domain-wide)

The Infrastructure Master is used to maintain references to objects in other domains, known as phantoms. If three users from Domain B are members of a group in Domain A, the Infrastructure Manager on Domain A is used to maintain references to the phantom Domain B user members.

The Infrastructure FSMO role owner is used to continually maintain the links to phantoms, whenever they are changed or moved on the other domain. When an object in another domain references an object in a domain, it represents that reference by the GUID, the SID (for references to security principals), and the DN of the object being referenced. The Infrastructure FSMO role holder is the DC responsible for updating an object's SID and distinguished name in a cross-domain object reference.

 In a single-domain scenario, the Infrastructure FSMO has nothing to do, so it makes no difference whether the FSMO role owner exists on a server running the GC. As soon as you introduce a second domain, the FSMO role owner should be moved to a non-GC-hosting DC.

The Infrastructure FSMO is responsible for fixing up stale references from objects in its domain to objects in other domains ("stale" means references to objects that have been moved or renamed so that the local copy of the remote object's name is out of date). It does this by comparing its (potentially stale) naming data with that of a GC, which automatically receives regular replication updates for objects in all domains and hence has no stale data. The Infrastructure FSMO writes any updates it finds to its objects and then replicates the updated information around to other DCs in the domain. However, if a GC also holds the Infrastructure role, then by definition, that server hosting the GC will always be up to date and will therefore have no stale references. If it never notices that anything needs changing, it will never update any non-GC servers with Infrastructure updates.

If all DCs in the domain are also GCs, no server will have stale references, and the Infrastructure FSMO role is not significant.

FSMO roles can be transferred between domain controllers. You can transfer the Domain Naming FSMO with the Active Directory Domains and Trusts snap-in, the Schema FSMO with the Active Directory Schema snap-in, and the RID, Infrastructure and PDC Emulator FSMOs using the Active Directory Users and Computers snap-in. Alternatively, you can use the NTDSUTIL utility available on Windows 2000 Server and Windows Server 2003 platforms to perform transfers from a command-line.

While the AD snap-ins and NTDSUTIL can trivially transfer a role from one server to another while both servers are available (and this is the normal method before taking a FSMO role owner down for maintenance), there will be some cases in which a FSMO role owner becomes unavailable without previously transferring the role. In this case, you have to use NTDSUTIL to force an ungraceful transfer of the role to a server. When you do this, you will need to bring the original FSMO role owner back, and for a while you will have two competing FSMO role owners on the network until replication takes place.

 If a server with a role becomes unavailable, another server is not automatically promoted to assume the role. The administrator must move the role to a new owner manually.

One final word of warning: keep NTDSUTIL and other tools nearby on floppies or a mastered CD of utilities in case of problems. Become familiar with the tools on a working network. If you lose one of the FSMO masters for a domain, you should always make sure that you are in control of the situation and are promoting a new DC to be the relevant master or bringing the DC that is the relevant master back swiftly. The last thing that you will want to do is to lose one of these masters and not notice. While at Leicester University on an earlier beta of Active Directory, the entire set of FSMO roles was lost and couldn't be brought back due to a bug. Loss of the FSMO RID Master meant that after each DC had exhausted its pool of RIDs, no more users could be created. While this will more than likely not happen to you, it illustrates the point that you need to have the tools on hand and be familiar with their usage before a disaster occurs. NTDSUTIL and its quirky interface should be very familiar to you as an administrator. You should certainly get familiar with using it to move FSMO role owners around.

The fSMORoleOwner Attribute

The FSMO role owners are stored in Active Directory in different locations depending on the role. The DN of the server holding the role is actually stored as the fSMORoleOwner attribute of various objects. For the mycorp.com domain, here are the containers that hold that attribute in the following order: PDC Role Owner, Infrastructure Master, RID Master, Schema Master, and Domain Naming Master:

```
LDAP://dc=mycorp,dc=com
LDAP://cn=Infrastructure,dc=mycorp,dc=com
LDAP://cn=RID Manager$,cn=System,dc=mycorp,dc=com
LDAP://cn=Schema,cn=Configuration,dc=mycorp,dc=com
LDAP://cn=Partitions,cn=Configuration,dc=mycorp,dc=com
```

The information in the attribute is stored as a DN, representing the NTDS Settings object of the domain controller that is the role owner. So, example contents for this attribute are:

```
CN=NTDS Settings, CN=MYSERVER1, CN=Servers, CN=My Site, CN=Sites,
CN=Configuration, DC=mycorp, DC=com
```

Windows 2000 Domain Mode

Each Windows 2000 Active Directory domain is said to have one of two modes: mixed mode (the default) or native mode. A mixed-mode domain allows servers running previous versions of Windows NT to exist as domain controllers in the domain. A native-mode domain supports only Windows 2000 domain controllers. Supporting a mixed-mode domain was necessary to allow administrators to update Windows NT domains to Active Directory. A mixed-mode Active Directory domain emulates a Windows NT domain. Remember that with previous versions of Windows NT, networks of servers used to have a Primary Domain Controller (PDC) for a domain that held a writeable copy of the accounts database, and zero or more Backup Domain Controllers (BDCs) that held a read-only accounts database copied from the PDC. For an Active Directory network to support older NT servers, one (and only one) of the Active Directory servers has to act as a PDC. That way, the old servers that look for a PDC will find one.

The Windows NT BDCs periodically request a copy of the accounts database to get the relevant user, group, and computer accounts from Active Directory. While all accounts are passed out, the total attributes for each object are a much smaller subset of the total attributes that Active Directory now holds for these types of objects. When requests from member servers come in for authentication, the Active Directory DC acting as the PDC does the authentication and passes a response back in a manner that the older server would understand (i.e., using Windows NT LAN Manager (NTLM) authentication).

Going from mixed mode to native mode is a very trivial operation. You simply connect to a DC with the Active Directory Domains and Trusts snap-in and change the mode under the General tab to native mode.

Going from mixed mode to native mode is a one-way change. Once you have done this, the only way to go back is to wipe the domain and restore from a backup made prior to the upgrade. Never upgrade to native mode unless you are certain that you will not require any BDCs* to exist anywhere in that domain.

Moving any domain from mixed mode to native mode has no bearing in any way on any other domain. It doesn't matter if it is the root domain or a subdomain you are converting, because you are only removing the ability of that domain to replicate data to older Windows NT servers within the domain, not affecting its ability to replicate and interact with Windows 2000 domain controllers in other domains.

The specific differences between mixed mode and native mode are shown in Table 2-2. When you upgrade to native mode, the DCs stop using NTLM protocols to authenticate, the RID pool becomes distributed, and you are allowed for the first time to have a new type of group called "universal" in your Active Directory. The change may be simple to do, but its ramifications are quite wide-ranging.

Table 2-2. The differences between mixed mode and native mode

Action	Mixed mode	Native mode
Replication	PDC FSMO master sends updates to Windows NT BDCs; same DC acts like ordinary Active Directory DC when communicating with other Active Directory DCs. All Active Directory DCs use multimaster replication between themselves.	Only Active Directory DCs allowed, so all DCs use multimaster replication.
Authentication	NT LAN Manager (NTLM) authentication used for communication with Windows NT down-level servers and Kerberos authentication for Active Directory servers.	Kerberos is used when possible and negotiates down to NTLM only when required by the client.
RID Allocation	Forced centralized.	Distributed.
NetBIOS	Can't disable.	Can disable.
Group definitions	Forced; i.e., global groups don't nest, and local groups can exist on individual NT servers.	Allow administrators to create Active Directory-only group definitions, i.e., universal groups and distribution groups.

One important difference between native-mode and mixed-mode domains has to do with groups. We'll go in more detail about those differences later in the chapter.

---

* Windows NT member servers can still exist in native-mode domains; it's BDCs that can't.

Windows Server 2003 Functional Levels

For the Windows Server 2003 release of Active Directory, Microsoft expanded on the domain mode concept by introducing functional levels. Whereas the domain modes applied only to domains, functional levels apply to both forests and domains. Like the domain mode, functional levels dictate what type of operating systems can run on domain controllers in a domain or forest. Each functional level also has an associated list of features that become available when the domain or forest reaches that particular functional level. We covered many of the features that are available for each functional level in Chapter 1.

Functional levels are introduced into a domain and forest when the first domain controller running Windows Server 2003 is added to a domain. By default the domain functional level is set to "Windows 2000 Mixed", and the forest function level is set to "Windows 2000". As with domain modes under Windows 2000, functional levels can be set via the Active Directory Domains and Trusts snap-in. Also like domain mode, once a functional level has been "elevated" to a higher status, it cannot be changed back.

Tables 2-3 and 2-4 show the operating systems that are supported by the various domain and forest functional levels.

Table 2-3. Domain functional levels

Functional level	Supported domain controller OS
Windows 2000 Mixed	Windows NT 4.0
	Windows 2000
	Windows Server 2003
Windows 2000 Native	Windows 2000
	Windows Server 2003
Windows Server 2003 Interim	Windows NT 4.0
	Windows Server 2003
Windows Server 2003	Windows Server 2003

Table 2-4. Forest functional levels

Functional level	Supported domain controller OS
Windows 2000	Windows NT 4.0
	Windows 2000
	Windows Server 2003
Windows Server 2003 Interim	Windows NT 4.0
	Windows Server 2003
Windows Server 2003	Windows Server 2003

For more information on upgrading to Windows Server 2003, check out Chapter 14.

Groups

Active Directory supports three group scopes: domain local, domain global, and universal. Each of these groups behaves slightly differently based on which Windows 2000 domain mode or Windows Server 2003 functional level your forest is at. To complicate matters further, each group scope can have two types, distribution and security.

The type is the easiest bit to define. If the type is distribution, the group can effectively be considered a mailing list (a set of users that you can mail all at once). These are known as Distribution Lists in Exchange, and the concept is identical. Security groups can also act as mailing lists. However, security groups can also have Access Control Lists (ACLs) applied to them for Active Directory objects or files and directories. Distribution groups do not support ACLs. Distribution groups are ignored during a user logon, while security groups that a user is a member of are enumerated and checked during logon. So you can add a user to as many mailing lists as you like without affecting logon speed.

The three different scopes of mailing lists and security groups result from the legacy of Windows NT and the introduction of the GC. Global groups and local groups are the direct descendants of Windows NT groups and are stored in the domains they are created in. Universal groups are a new type of group in Active Directory, which are held in the GC and can be applied forest wide.

In order to fully understand how groups work in Active Directory, we will explain the following items in this section:

- How Windows NT groups have a bearing on Active Directory
- Which groups are available in mixed, native, and Windows Server 2003 functional levels
- Which groups each group may contain in mixed, native, and Windows Server 2003 functional levels
- How you can nest groups across domain boundaries
- What options are available to you for converting between different group scopes in mixed, native, and Windows Server 2003 functional levels

To start with, let's take a look at how Windows NT handles groups.

Groups in Windows NT

Back in Windows NT, domains could have two scopes of groups: local and global. Both were security groups. The local group could contain users and global groups. The global group could contain only users. Both could have permissions assigned to them. Administrators typically took advantage of the fact that global groups could nest in local groups. Users went into global groups, and local groups were given access to resources on local machines, such as file servers. Then you simply put the global groups in the appropriate local groups to assign the permissions.

Windows NT groups are important in Windows 2000 mixed domains, as down-level Windows NT BDCs will need to replicate these groups from the Active Directory FSMO PDC role owner. During an upgrade of a PDC from Windows NT to Active Directory, Windows NT local and global groups are migrated to Active Directory local security groups and global security groups, although they still appear as local and global groups to any Windows NT BDCs.

Group availability in various functional levels

Table 2-5 shows the groups that you can have at the various functional levels.

Table 2-5. Group availability at the various functional levels

Scope of group	Type of group	Available in W2K Mixed	Available in W2K Native	Available in Windows Server 2003
Domain local	Security	Yes	Yes	Yes
Domain global	Security	Yes	Yes	Yes
Universal	Security	No	Yes	Yes
Domain local	Distribution	Yes	Yes	Yes
Domain global	Distribution	Yes	Yes	Yes
Universal	Distribution	Yes	Yes	Yes

At first, the only difference appears to be that universal security groups are not available in Windows 2000 mixed mode. Every other group is available in all domain functional levels. The complexity lies in what each group may contain, and this varies depending on the mode of your domain and which domain the group you wish to add comes from.

Group nesting in different functional levels

You have a Windows 2000 mixed-mode domain and you want to create and then nest some groups. Table 2-6 is the easiest way to describe the available options.

Table 2-6. Windows 2000 mixed-mode restrictions on group membership based on type

Scope	Type	Can contain domain local — Distribution groups	Can contain domain local — Security groups	Can contain domain global — Distribution groups	Can contain domain global — Security groups	Can contain universal — Distribution groups	Can contain universal — Security groups
Domain local	Distribution groups	Yes	Yes	Yes	Yes	Yes	No group access
	Security groups	No	No	Yes	Yes	Yes	No group access

Table 2-6. *Windows 2000 mixed-mode restrictions on group membership based on type (continued)*

		Can contain domain local		Can contain domain global		Can contain universal	
Scope	Type	Distri-bution groups	Security groups	Distri-bution groups	Security groups	Distri-bution groups	Security groups
Domain global	Distribution groups	No	No	Yes	Yes	No	No group access
	Security groups	No	No	No	No	No	No group access
Universal	Distribution groups	No	No	Yes	Yes	Yes	No group access
	Security groups	No group access	No group access	No group access	No group access	No group access	No group access

Two points to note: first, universal security groups are evidently not available in mixed mode, which corresponds with Table 2-5. Second, domain global security groups can contain only users in mixed mode.

When you convert a domain to Windows 2000 native or Windows Server 2003 functional level, certain groups become available, but you do not lose any group nesting options that you had in mixed mode. The new options can be summarized quite easily as follows:

- Domain local security groups can contain domain local security and domain local distribution groups.

- Domain global security groups can contain domain global security and domain global distribution groups.

- Universal security groups become available.

Let's look at this summary using a table. Consider Table 2-7, with the extra options available only in Windows 2000 Native mode and Windows Server 2003 emphasized in bold.

Table 2-7. *Windows 2000 native and Windows Server 2003 restrictions on group membership based on group scope*

		Can contain domain local		Can contain domain global		Can contain universal	
Scope	Type	Distri-bution groups	Security groups	Distri-bution groups	Security groups	Distri-bution groups	Security groups
Domain local	Distribution groups	Yes	Yes	Yes	Yes	Yes	**Yes**
	Security groups	**Yes**	**Yes**	Yes	Yes	Yes	**Yes**

Table 2-7. Windows 2000 native and Windows Server 2003 restrictions on group membership based on group scope (continued)

		Can contain domain local		Can contain domain global		Can contain universal	
Scope	Type	Distri-bution groups	Security groups	Distri-bution groups	Security groups	Distri-bution groups	Security groups
Domain global	Distribution groups	No	No	Yes	Yes	No	No
	Security groups	No	No	**Yes**	**Yes**	No	No
Universal	Distribution groups	No	No	Yes	Yes	Yes	**Yes**
	Security groups	No	No	**Yes**	**Yes**	**Yes**	**Yes**

While these tables are fine, there is one other complicating factor that needs to be taken into account: cross-domain group membership.

Group membership across domain boundaries

Since universal groups are held in the GC, you can add universal groups from one domain to universal groups from another domain. Restrictions are shown in Tables 2-8 and 2-9. Two items are listed as "Special," which signifies distribution groups in Windows 2000 Mixed, and distribution and security groups in Windows 2000 Native and Windows Server 2003.

Table 2-8. Restrictions on group membership based on group scope

Group scope	Can contain users and computers from		Can contain domain local groups from	
	Same domain	Different domain	Same domain	Different domain
Domain local groups	Yes	Yes	Special	No
Domain global groups	Yes	No	No	No
Universal groups	Yes	Yes	No	No

Table 2-9. Restrictions on group membership based on domain

Group scope	Can contain domain global groups from		Can contain universal groups from	
	Same domain	Different domain	Same domain	Different domain
Domain local groups	Yes	Yes	Yes	Yes
Domain global groups	Special	No	No	No
Universal groups	Yes	Yes	Yes	Yes

Tables 2-8 and 2-9 work in conjunction with Tables 2-6 and 2-7. You would normally check which groups may be members from either Table 2-6 or Table 2-7 (if any) and then cross reference with Tables 2-8 and 2-9 to identify what options you have across domain boundaries.

Converting groups

Converting groups from one scope to another is available only in Windows 2000 Native and Windows Server 2003. There are limits on what groups can be converted based on the existing members of the group and the current type and scope of the group. The former should be fairly obvious based on the existing restrictions that we've shown in Table 2-7. The conversion process cannot work if the existing group members would not be valid members of the new group type once the conversion had taken place. However, when you upgrade to Windows 2000 Native or Windows Server 2003, you gain the ability to convert between groups based on these restrictions:

- Security groups can be converted to distribution groups.
- Distribution groups can be converted to security groups.
- A domain local group can be converted to a universal group provided that the domain local group is not already a member of another domain local group.
- A domain global group can be converted to a universal group provided that the domain global group does not contain any other domain global groups.

Wrap-up

While this all looks complicated, using the tables helps a lot. Ultimately you need to decide how long you will be staying in Windows 2000 mixed mode before going to Windows 2000 native or Windows Server 2003 so that you can decide what sort of groups you are looking for. You also have to consider in Windows 2000 native and Windows Server 2003 that the more universal groups you add, the larger the GC, and the longer members of those groups will take to log on. Chapters 8 and 10 explain more about when and how to use groups in your designs.

Summary

In this chapter, we've gone over the groundwork for some of the main internals of Active Directory. We covered such concepts as domains, trees, forests, Organizational Units, the Global Catalog, FSMOs, Windows 2000 domain modes, and Windows Server 2003 functional levels. We then delved into how groups work in Active Directory and what features are available under the various domain modes and functional levels.

With this information under our belts, let's now take a look at how data is organized in Active Directory with Naming Contexts and Application Partitions.

CHAPTER 3
Naming Contexts and Application Partitions

Due to the distributed nature of Active Directory, it is necessary to segregate data into partitions. If data partitioning were not used, every domain controller would have to replicate all the data within a forest. Often it is advantageous to group data based on geographical or political requirements. Think of a domain as a big data partition, which is also referred to as a naming context (NC). Only domain controllers that are authoritative for a domain need to replicate the information within it. On the other hand, there is some Active Directory data that must be replicated to all domain controllers. There are three predefined naming contexts within Active Directory:

- A Domain Naming Context for each domain
- The Configuration Naming Context for the forest
- The Schema Naming Context for the forest

Each of these naming contexts represents a different aspect of Active Directory data. The Configuration NC holds data pertaining to the configuration of the forest, for example, the objects representing naming contexts, LDAP policies, sites, subnets, and so on. The Schema NC contains the set of object class and attribute definitions for the types of data that can be stored in Active Directory. Each domain in a forest also has a Domain NC, which contains data specific to the domain, for example, users, groups, computers, etc.

In Windows Server 2003 Active Directory, Microsoft extended the naming context concept by allowing user-defined partitions called application partitions. Application partitions can contain any type of object except security principals, such as user objects. The major benefit of application partitions is that administrators can define which domain controllers replicate the data contained within them. Application partitions are not restricted by domain boundaries, as is the case with Domain NCs.

You can retrieve a list of the naming contexts and application partitions a specific domain controller maintains by querying its Root DSE entry. You can view the Root DSE by opening the LDP utility, which is available from the Windows Support Tools. Select Connection → Connect from the menu, enter the name of a domain controller, and click OK. The following attributes pertain to naming contexts and application partitions:

namingContexts
    List of DNs of all the naming contexts and application partitions maintained by the DC.

defaultNamingContext
    DN of the Domain NC the DC is authoritative for.

configurationNamingContext
    DN of the Configuration NC.

schemaNamingContext
    DN of the Schema NC.

rootNamingContext
    DN of the Domain NC for the forest root domain.

In this chapter, we will review each of the three predefined naming contexts and describe the data contained within each, and then cover application partitions and example uses.

Domain Naming Context

Each Active Directory domain is represented by a Domain NC, which holds the domain-specific data. The root of this NC is represented by a domain's distinguished name (DN). For example, the mycorp.com domain's DN would be dc=mycorp,dc=com. Each domain controller in the domain replicates a copy of the Domain NC.

Table 3-1 contains a list of the default top-level containers found in a Domain NC. Note that to see all of these containers with the Active Directory Users and Computers (ADUC) snap-in, you must select View → Advanced Features from the menu. Alternatively, you can browse all of these containers with the ADSI Edit tool available in the Windows Support Tools on any Windows Server 2003 or Windows 2000 CD.

Table 3-1. Default top-level containers of a Domain NC

Relative distinguished name	Description
cn=Builtin	Container for predefined built-in local security groups. Examples include Administrators, Users and Account Operators.
cn=Computers	Default container for computer objects representing member servers and workstations.
ou=Domain Controllers	Default organizational unit for computer objects representing domain controllers.
cn=ForeignSecurityPrincipals	Container for placeholder objects representing members of groups in the domain that are from a domain external to the forest.
cn=LostandFound	Container for orphaned objects.

Table 3-1. Default top-level containers of a Domain NC (continued)

Relative distinguished name	Description
cn=NTDS Quotas	Container to store quota objects, which are used to restrict the number of objects a security principal can create in a partition or container. This container is new in Windows Server 2003.
cn=Program Data	Container for applications to store data instead of using a custom top-level container. This container is new in Windows Server 2003.
cn=System	Container for miscellaneous domain configuration objects. Examples include trust objects, DNS objects, and group policy objects.
cn=Users	Default container for user and group objects.

Configuration Naming Context

The Configuration NC is the primary repository for configuration information for a forest. Every domain controller in the forest replicates the Configuration NC, which is why it is considered forest-wide. The root of the Configuration NC is found in the Configuration container, which is a subcontainer of the forest root domain. For example, the mycorp.com forest would have a Configuration NC located at cn=configuration,dc=mycorp,dc=com.

Table 3-2 contains a list of the default top-level containers found in the Configuration NC.

Table 3-2. Default top-level containers of the Configuration NC

Relative Distinguished Name	Description
cn=DisplaySpecifiers	Container that holds display specifier objects, which define various properties and functions of the Active Directory MMC Snap-ins.
cn=Extended-Rights	Container for extended rights (controlAccessRight) objects.
cn=ForestUpdates	Contains objects that are used to represent the state of forest and domain functional level changes. This container is new in Windows Server 2003.
cn=LostandFoundConfig	Container for orphaned objects.
cn=NTDS Quotas	Container to store quota objects, which are used to restrict the number of objects that security principals can create in a partition or container. This container is new in Windows Server 2003.
cn=Partitions	Contains objects for each naming context, application partition, and external reference.
cn=Physical Locations	Contains location objects (physicalLocation), which can be associated with other objects to denote location of the object.
cn=Services	Store of configuration information about services such as FRS, Exchange, and even Active Directory itself.
cn=Sites	Contains all of the site topology and replication objects. This includes site, subnet, siteLink, server and nTDSCconnection objects, to name a few.
cn=WellKnown Security Principals	Holds objects representing commonly used foreign security principals, such as Everyone, Interactive, and Authenticated Users.

Schema Naming Context

The Schema NC contains objects representing the classes and attributes that Active Directory supports. The schema is defined on a forest-wide basis, so the Schema NC is replicated to every domain controller in the forest. The root of the Schema NC can be found in the Schema container, which is a subcontainer of the Configuration container. For example, in the mycorp.com forest, the Schema NC would be located at cn=schema,cn=configuration,dc=mycorp,dc=com.

 Although the Schema container appears to be a child of the Configuration container, it is actually a separate naming context in its own right. Figure 3-1 shows how the Schema and Configuration NCs are segregated in the ADSI Edit tool.

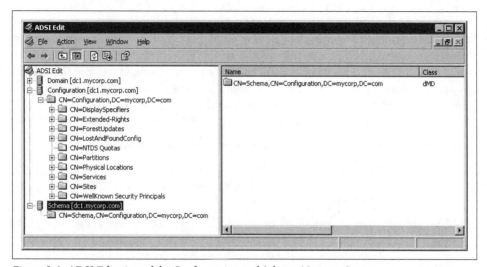

Figure 3-1. ADSI Edit view of the Configuration and Schema Naming Contexts

You may be wondering why the schema isn't just contained within the Configuration NC. As we covered in Chapter 2, there is a Schema FSMO role that is the single master for updates to schema objects. The Schema FSMO role is necessary due to the highly sensitive nature of the schema and the fact that two conflicting schema updates could spell disaster for a forest. Since there is only a single domain controller that schema changes can be made on, the schema must replicate differently from the Configuration NC, which can be updated by any domain controller in the forest.

Unlike the Domain and Configuration NCs, the Schema NC does not contain a hierarchy of containers or organizational units. Instead it is a single container that has classSchema, attributeSchema, and subSchema objects. The classSchema objects define the different types of classes and their associated attributes. The attribute-

Schema objects define all the attributes that are used as part of classSchema definitions. There is also a single subSchema object that represents the abstract schema as defined in the LDAPv3 RFC (*http://www.ietf.org/rfc/rfc2254.txt*).

Chapters 4 and 12 deal with the schema in more depth.

Application Partitions

Application partitions are a new feature in Windows Server 2003. They enable administrators to create areas in Active Directory to store data on DCs they choose rather than on every DC in a domain or forest. You can define which domain controllers hold a copy of the partition, known as a replica. There is no limitation based on domain or site membership, which means you can configure any domain controller in a forest to hold any application partition replica. The existing site topology will be used to automatically create the necessary connection objects to replicate among the servers that hold replicas of an application partition. Domain controllers will also register the necessary SRV records (explained in more detail in Chapter 6), so that clients can use the DC locator process to find the optimal domain controller for an application partition, just as they would for a domain.

There are a few limitations to be aware of with application partitions:

- Application partitions cannot contain security principals, which most notably includes user, group, and computer objects. Any other type of object can be created in an application partition.

- None of the objects contained in an application partition are replicated to the global catalog. Even if a domain controller that holds a replica of an application partition is also a global catalog server, the domain controller will not return any objects from the application partition during a global catalog search.

- Objects in an application partition cannot be moved outside the partition. This is different than objects contained in domains, which can be moved between domains.

- The Domain Naming FSMO must be on a Windows Server 2003 domain controller to create an application partition. After the application partition has been created, you can move the Domain Naming FSMO back to a Windows 2000 domain controller if necessary.

Application partitions are named similarly to domains. For example, if you created an application partition called "apps" directly under the *mycorp.com* domain, the DNS name would be *apps.mycorp.com* and the distinguished name would be dc=apps,dc=mycorp,dc=com. Application partitions can be rooted under domains, as shown in the previous example, nested under other application partitions (for example, dc=sales,dc=apps,dc=mycorp,dc=com) or as part of a new domain tree (for example, dc=apps,dc=local). For more information on creating and managing application partitions, check out the *NTDSUTIL* utility.

Application partitions tend to store dynamic data—data with a limited lifespan. See the next section for more on this. Dynamic data from network services such as DNS, Dynamic Host Configuration Protocol (DHCP), Common Open Policy Service (COPS), Remote Access Service (RAS), and RADIUS can all reside in a partition in AD. This allows uniformity of access from applications via a single methodology. This enables developers to write to a special area only available to specific servers rather than into a domain partition that is replicated to every DC. In fact, application partitions will allow multiple versions of COM+ applications to be installed and configured on the same computer, resulting in more cost-effective management of server applications.

Storing Dynamic Data

While application partitions give administrators more control over how to replicate application data, the problem of data cleanup still exists. That is, applications that add data to Active Directory are not always good about cleaning it up after it is no longer needed. That's why the ability to create dynamic data was also added as a feature in Windows Server 2003 Active Directory. Dynamic objects are objects that have a time-to-live (TTL) value that determines how long the object will exist before being automatically deleted by Active Directory. Dynamic objects typically have a fairly short life span (i.e., days). An example use of dynamic objects is an e-commerce website that needs to store user session information temporarily. Since a directory is likely going to be where the user profile information resides, it can be advantageous to use the same store for session-based information, which is generally short-lived. The default TTL that is set for dynamic objects is 1 day, but can be configured to be as short as 15 minutes. Using a Domain NC to store dynamic objects with a very short TTL can be less than ideal because it may take more than the TTL period to replicate to all the domain controllers within the domain. Instead, you can use an application partition to replicate the data to a subset of domain controllers based on application requirements.

To create a dynamic object, you simply have to add "dynamicObject" to the objectClass attribute when creating the object. This is why you cannot make existing static objects into dynamic objects. The entryTTL attribute can also be set at creation time to set the TTL to something other than the one-day default. To prevent a dynamic object from being automatically deleted, you can "refresh" the object by resetting the entryTTL attribute for the object to a new TTL value (time in seconds).

Summary

In this chapter, we covered how objects are grouped at a high level into naming contexts and application partitions, which are used as replication boundaries. The Domain NC contains domain-specific data such as users, groups, and computers. The Configuration NC contains forest-wide configuration data such as the site topology objects and objects that represent naming contexts and application partitions. The Schema NC contains all the schema objects that define how data is structured and represented in Active Directory. Application partitions were introduced in Windows Server 2003 Active Directory as a way for administrators to define their own grouping of objects and, subsequently, replication boundaries. Storage of DNS data for AD-Integrated DNS zones is the classic example of when it makes sense to use application partitions, due to the increased control they give you over which domain controllers replicate the data. Dynamic objects are also new to Windows Server 2003 Active Directory; they allow you to create objects that have a time-to-live (TTL) value. After the TTL expires, Active Directory automatically deletes the object.

CHAPTER 4

Active Directory Schema

The schema is the blueprint for data storage in Active Directory. Each object in Active Directory is an instance of a class in the schema. A user object, for example, exists as an instance of the user class. Attributes define the pieces of information that a class, and thus an instance of that class, can hold. Syntaxes define the type of data that can be placed into an attribute. As an example, if an attribute is defined with a syntax of Boolean, it can store True or False as its value.

Active Directory contains many attributes and classes in the default schema, some of which are based on standards and some of which Microsoft needed for its own use. However, the Active Directory schema was designed to be extensible, so that administrators could add any classes or attributes they deem necessary. In fact, extending the schema is not a difficult task; it is often more difficult to design the changes that you would like to incorporate. Schema design issues are covered in Chapter 12, and in Chapter 24 we cover how to extend the schema programmatically. In this chapter, we're concerned only with the fundamentals of the schema.

Structure of the Schema

The Schema Container is located in Active Directory under the Configuration Container. For example, the distinguished name of the Schema Container in the mycorp. com forest would be `cn=schema,cn=Configuration,dc=mycorp,dc=com`. You can view the contents of the container directly by pointing an Active Directory viewer such as ADSI Edit or LDP at it. You can also use the Active Directory Schema MMC snap-in, which splits the classes and attributes in separate containers for easy viewing, even though in reality all the schema objects are stored directly in the Schema Container.

The schema itself is made up of two types of Active Directory objects: classes and attributes. In Active Directory, these are known respectively as classSchema (Class-Schema) and attributeSchema (Attribute-Schema) objects. The two distinct forms of the same names result from the fact that the cn (Common-Name) attribute of a class contains the hyphenated easy-to-read name of the class, and the lDAPDisplayName

(LDAP-Display-Name) attribute of a class contains the concatenated string format that is used when querying Active Directory with LDAP or ADSI. In the schema, the lDAPDisplayName attribute of each object is normally made by capitalizing the first letter of each word of the Common-Name, then removing the hyphens and concatenating all the words together. Finally, the first letter is made lowercase.* This creates simple names like user, as well as the more unusual sAMAccountName and lDAP-DisplayName. We'll specify the more commonly used LDAP display name format from now on.

Whenever you need to create new types of objects in Active Directory, you must first create a classSchema object defining the class of the object and the attributes it contains. Once the class is properly designed and added to the schema, you can then create objects in Active Directory that use the class. Alternatively, if you want to add a new attribute to an object, you must first create the attributeSchema object and associate the attribute with whatever classes you want to use it with.

Before we delve into what makes up an Active Directory class or attribute, we need to explain how each class that you create is unique not just within your Active Directory but also throughout the world.

X.500 and the OID Namespace

Active Directory is based on LDAP, which was originally based on the X.500 standard created by the ISO (International Organization for Standardization) and ITU (International Telecommunications Union) organizations in 1988. To properly understand how the Active Directory schema works, you really need to understand the basics of X.500; we'll run through them next.

The X.500 standard specifies that individual object classes in an organization can be uniquely defined using a special identifying process. The process has to be able to take into account the fact that classes can inherit from one another, as well as the potential need for any organization in the world to define and export a class of their own design.

To that end, the X.500 standard defined an Object Identifier (OID) to uniquely identify every schema object. This OID is composed of two parts:

- One to indicate the unique path to the branch holding the object in the X.500 treelike structure
- Another to indicate the object uniquely in that branch

OID notation uses integers for each branch and object, as in the following example OID for an object:

```
1.3.6.1.4.1.3385.12.497
```

---

* Names defined by the X.500 standard don't tend to follow this method. For example, the Common-Name attribute has an LDAP-Display-Name of cn, and the Surname attribute has an LDAP-Display-Name of sn.

This uniquely references object 497 in branch 1.3.6.1.4.1.3385.12. The 1.3.6.1.4.1.3385.12 branch is contained in a branch whose OID is 1.3.6.1.4.1.3385, and so on.

 Each branch within an OID number also corresponds to a name. This means that the dotted notation 1.3.6.1.4.1, for example, is equivalent to *iso.org.dod.internet.private.enterprise*. As the names are of no relevance to us with Active Directory, we don't cover them in this book.

This notation continues today and is used in the Active Directory schema. If you wish to create a schema object, you need to obtain a unique OID branch for your organization. Using this as your root, you can then create further branches and leaf nodes within the root, as your organization requires.

The Internet Assigned Numbers Authority (IANA) maintains the main set of root branches. The IANA says of itself:

> The central coordinator for the assignment of unique parameter values for Internet protocols. The IANA is chartered by the Internet Society (ISOC) and the Federal Network Council (FNC) to act as the clearinghouse to assign and coordinate the use of numerous Internet protocol parameters. The Internet protocol suite, as defined by the Internet Engineering Task Force (IETF) and its steering group (the IESG), contains numerous parameters, such as Internet addresses, domain names, autonomous system numbers (used in some routing protocols), protocol numbers, port numbers, management information base object identifiers, including private enterprise numbers, and many others. The common use of the Internet protocols by the Internet community requires that the particular values used in these parameter fields be assigned uniquely. It is the task of the IANA to make those unique assignments as requested and to maintain a registry of the currently assigned values. The IANA is located at and operated by the Information Sciences Institute (ISI) of the University of Southern California (USC).

You can find the IANA web page at *http://www.iana.org*.

You can request an OID namespace, i.e., a root OID number from which you can create your own branches, directly from the IANA if you like. These numbers are known as Enterprise Numbers. The entire list of Enterprise Numbers assigned by the IANA can be found at *http://www.iana.org/assignments/enterprise-numbers/*. This list of numbers changes every time a new one is added. At the top of the file you can see that the root that the IANA uses is 1.3.6.1.4.1. If you look down the list, you will see that Microsoft has been allocated branch 311 of that part of the tree, so Microsoft's OID namespace is 1.3.6.1.4.1.311. Leicester University's OID namespace is 1.3.6.1.4.1.3385. As each number also has a contact email address alongside it in the list, you can search through the file for any member of your organization that has already been allocated a number. It is likely that large organizations that already have an X.500 directory or that have developed SNMP MIBs will have obtained an OID.

In addition to Enterprise Numbers, country-specific OIDs can be purchased as well. An organization's Enterprise Number registration has no bearing on whether it has obtained a country-based OID namespace to use. If you don't see the company listed in the Enterprise Numbers list, don't be fooled; the organization could still have a number.

For example, Microsoft has been issued the Enterprise Number 1.3.6.1.4.1.311, yet all of its new schema classes use a US-issued OID namespace of 1.2.840.113556 as their root. The 1.2.840 part is uniquely allotted to the United States. In other words, Microsoft has obtained two OID namespaces that it can use but is choosing to use only the US-issued namespace.

If you want to obtain an Enterprise Number, fill in the online form at *http://www.isi. edu/cgi-bin/iana/enterprise.pl*. If this URL changes, you can navigate to it from the main IANA web page.

Once an organization has an OID namespace, it can add unique branches and leaves in any manner desired under the root. For example, Leicester University could decide to have no branches underneath and just give any new object an incrementing integer starting from 1 underneath the 1.3.6.1.4.1.3385 root. Alternatively, they could decide to make a series of numbered branches starting from 1, each corresponding to a certain set of classes or attributes that they wish to create. Thus, the fifth object under the third branch would have an OID of 1.3.6.1.4.1. 3385.3.5.

The range of values in any part of an OID namespace goes from 1 to 268,435,455, i.e., from 2^0 through $2^{28}-1$.

To reinforce this point, let's look at a couple of examples directly from the Active Directory schema. If you open the Active Directory Schema snap-in, you can look at the schema class OIDs very easily. Navigating through the classes when we open the property page for the printQueue class, we get Figure 4-1. You can see that the unique OID is 1.2.840.113556.1.5.23. This tells us that the number is a defined part of Microsoft's object class hierarchy.

Figure 4-2 shows the property page for the organizationalPerson class. Here, you can see that the unique OID 2.5.6.7 is very different, because within the original X.500 standard, a set of original classes was defined. One of these was organizationalPerson, and this is a copy of that class. Microsoft included the entire base X.500 classes within Active Directory.

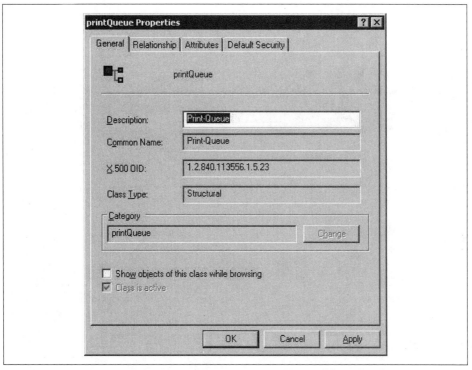

Figure 4-1. printQueue Schema class properties

 The OID numbering notation has nothing to do with inheritance. Numbering a set of objects a certain way does nothing other than create a structure for you to reference the objects. It does not indicate how objects inherit from one another.

Let's dissect an example attribute and class to see what they contain. With that information, you will be able to see what is required when you create a new schema object.

Attributes (attributeSchema Objects)

Just as class information is stored in Active Directory as instances of the class called classSchema, attributes are represented by instances of the class called attributeSchema. As with all objects, the attributeSchema class has a number of attributes that can be set when specifying a new instance. The attributeSchema class inherits attributes from the class called Top. However, most of the Top attributes are not really relevant here. Table 4-1 shows the defining attributes of an instance of the attributeSchema class (i.e., an attribute) that can be set.

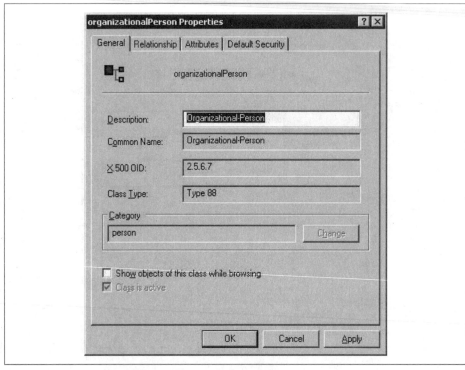

Figure 4-2. organizationalPerson Schema class properties

Table 4-1. The defining attributes of an attributeSchema object instance

Attribute	Syntax	Mandatory	Multivalued	Description
attributeId	OID	Yes	No	The OID that uniquely identifies this attribute.
cn	Unicode string	Yes	No	The Relative Distinguished Name (RDN).
isSingleValued	Boolean	Yes	No	Whether this attribute is multivalued.
lDAPDisplayName	Unicode string	Yes	No	The name by which LDAP clients identify this attribute.
attributeSyntax	OID	Yes	No	Half of a pair of properties that define the syntax of an attribute. This one is an OID.
oMSyntax	Integer	Yes	No	Half of a pair of properties that define the syntax of an attribute. This one is an integer.
schemaIDGUID	Octet string	Yes	No	Globally Unique Identifier (GUID) to uniquely identify this attribute.
objectClass	OID	Yes	Yes	This will hold the values "attribute-Schema" and "Top" to indicate that the value is an instance of those classes.
accessCategory	Integer	No	No	Used by the system.

Attribute	Syntax	Mandatory	Multivalued	Description
attribute-SecurityGUID	GUID	No	No	GUID used by Active Directory to identify the security of this attribute.
classDisplayName	Unicode string	No	No	The name displayed when viewing instances of the attribute.
defaultHidingValue	Boolean	No	No	Whether the object is to be hidden or displayed within tools by default.
description	Unicode string	No	No	A description of the attribute.
extendedChars-Allowed	Boolean	No	No	Whether extended characters are allowed in the value of this attribute.
isDefunct	Boolean	No	No	Whether the attribute is marked as disabled (i.e., unusable) in Active Directory.
isEphemeral	Boolean	No	No	Used by the system.
isMemberOfPartial-AttributeSet	Boolean	No	No	Whether the attribute is held in the GC.
linkID	Integer	No	No	Whether the attribute is linked with another attribute (e.g., memberOf and members).
mAPIDisplayType	Integer	No	No	The integer by which MAPI clients identify this attribute.
oIDType	Integer	No	No	Used by the system.
oMObjectClass	Octet string	No	No	Used by the system.
rangeLower	Integer	No	No	For strings, this is the minimum character length; for integers, it is the minimum value; otherwise, it is unused. It must be less than range- Upper.
rangeUpper	Integer	No	No	For strings, this is the maximum character length; for integers, it is the maximum value; otherwise, it is unused.
schemaFlags	Integer	No	No	Used by the system.
schemaFlagsEx	Integer	No	No	Used by the system.
searchFlags	Integer	No	No	Whether this attribute is indexed: 0=Not Indexed, 1=Indexed.[a]
systemOnly	Boolean	No	No	If true, once the initial value has been set, only the system can create instances of this attribute. Administrators cannot create instances of the attribute if this is set, but they can add this attribute to new or existing classes as required. The default is false.

[a] Indexing an object allows you to locate instances of the object or objects containing a particular value of an attribute by consulting the index rather than looking at each object. As with databases, index-aided searches run much faster than other searches.

The syntax of an attribute indicates the type of data that it holds, which we'll cover in a moment. The "Mandatory" column indicates whether the attribute must be set when initially creating an attributeSchema object. Attributes that are not mandatory do not have to be set when creating the object and can be defined later, if they are needed at all. The "Multi-valued" column indicates whether the particular attribute can accept an array of values or whether it accepts only a single value; there are no multivalued attributes here other than objectClass.

Dissecting an Example Attribute

The userPrincipalName (UPN) attribute is used on user objects to provide a unique method of identifying each user across a forest. Users can log on to a workstation in any domain in the forest using the UPN if they so desire. The UPN attribute, in fact, accepts valid RFC 822 (email) addresses, so the UPN for user *tpood* in the *emea. mycorp.com* domain could be either *tpood@mycorp.com* or *tpood@emea.mycorp. com*. In fact, any UPN suffix, such as *@mycorp.com*, can be used in a forest. The only requirement is that the UPN value for a user is unique across all users in a forest.

Active Directory does not enforce uniqueness of a UPN when it is set. If two different users in the same forest are assigned the same UPN, neither will be able to log on.

To dissect the attribute, we need to find out what values had been set for it. Perhaps the easiest way to do this is to use ADSI Edit from the Windows Support Tools, which can be installed from a Windows Server CD by running *\Support\Tools\setup.exe*. Table 4-2 shows the values of attributes that have been set for the userPrincipalName attribute.

Table 4-2. userPrincipalName's attributes

Attribute IDAPDisplayName	Attribute syntax	Attribute value
adminDescription	CASE_IGNORE_ STRING	User-Principal-Name
adminDisplayName	CASE_IGNORE_ STRING	User-Principal-Name
cn	CASE_IGNORE_ STRING	User-Principal-Name
distinguishedName	DN_STRING	cn=User-Principal-Name, cn=Schema, cn=Configuration,dc=mycorp, dc=com
instanceType	INTEGER	4
name	CASE_IGNORE_ STRING	User-Principal-Name
nTSecurityDescriptor	SECURITY_ DESCRIPTOR	<SID>

Table 4-2. userPrincipalName's attributes (continued)

Attribute IDAPDisplayName	Attribute syntax	Attribute value
objectCategory	DN_STRING	cn=Attribute-Schema, cn=Schema, cn=Configuration, dc=mycorp,dc=com
objectClass	CASE_IGNORE_ STRING	top; attributeSchema (two values of a multi-valued attribute)
objectGUID	OCTET_STRING	<GUID>
showInAdvancedViewOnly	BOOLEAN	True
systemFlags	INTEGER	18
uSNChanged	LARGE_INTEGER	USN when last changed
uSNCreated	LARGE_INTEGER	USN when created
whenChanged	UTC_TIME	Time when last changed
whenCreated	UTC_TIME	Time when created
attributeID	CASE_IGNORE_ STRING	1.2.840.113556.1.4.656
attributeSecurityGUID	OCTET_STRING	<GUID>
attributeSyntax	CASE_IGNORE_ STRING	2.5.5.12
isMemberOfPartialAttributeSet	BOOLEAN	True
isSingleValued	BOOLEAN	True
IDAPDisplayName	CASE_IGNORE_ STRING	userPrincipalName
oMSyntax	INTEGER	64
schemaIDGUID	OCTET_STRING	<GUID>
searchFlags	INTEGER	1
systemOnly	BOOLEAN	False

We can see that the name of the attribute is User-Principal-Name (adminDescription, adminDisplayName, cn, name), that it is an instance of the attributeSchema class (objectCategory and objectClass), that it inherits attributes from both top and attributeSchema (objectClass), and that the UPN attribute is not visible to casual browsing (showInAdvancedViewOnly).

The userPrincipalName attributes show the following:

- It is to be stored in the GC (isMemberOfPartialAttributeSet).
- It is to be indexed (searchFlags).
- It has an OID of 1.2.840.113556.1.4.656 (attributeID).
- When binding to it with ADSI, we should use userPrincipalName (lDAP-DisplayName).
- Instances can be created by anyone (systemOnly).
- It stores single (isSingleValued) Unicode strings (attributeSyntax and oMSyntax).

In Figure 4-3, you can see many of the values for the UPN attribute. We have indicated which attributes are changed by checking or unchecking each checkbox.

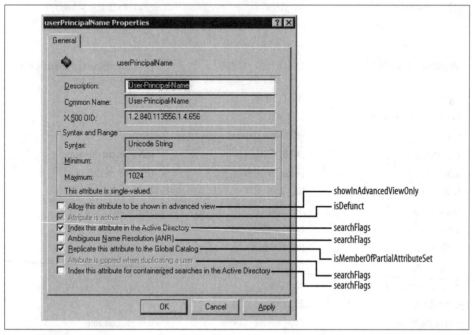

Figure 4-3. The UPN attribute as viewed by the Active Directory Schema snap-in

Attribute Syntax

The syntax of an attribute represents the kind of data it can hold; people with a programming background are probably more familiar with the term "data type." Unlike attributes and classes, the supported syntaxes are not represented as objects in Active Directory. Instead, Microsoft has coded these syntaxes internally into Active Directory itself. Consequently, any new attributes you create in the schema must use one of the predefined syntaxes.

Whenever you create a new attribute, you must specify its syntax. To uniquely identify the syntax among the total set of 21 syntaxes, you must specify 2 pieces of information: the OID of the syntax and a so-called OM syntax. This pair of values must be set together and correctly correlate with Table 4-3. More than one syntax has the same OID, which may seem strange; and to distinguish between different syntaxes uniquely, you thus need a second identifier. This is the result of Microsoft requiring some syntaxes that X.500 did not provide. Table 4-3 shows the 21 expanded syntaxes, including the name of the syntax with alternate names followed in parentheses.

Table 4-3. Syntax definitions

Syntax	OID	OM syntax	Description
Undefined	2.5.5.0	N/A	Not a valid syntax
Distinguished Name	2.5.5.1	127	The Fully Qualified Domain Name (FQDN) of an object in Active Directory
Object ID	2.5.5.2	6	OID
Case-sensitive string	2.5.5.3	20	A string that differentiates between uppercase and lower-case
Case-insensitive string	2.5.5.4	20	A string that does not differentiate between uppercase and lowercase
Print case string (Printable-String)	2.5.5.5	19	A normal printable string
Print case string (IA5- String)	2.5.5.5	22	A normal printable string
Numeric string	2.5.5.6	18	A string of digits
OR name	2.5.5.7	127	An X.400 email address
Boolean	2.5.5.8	1	True or false
Integer (integer)	2.5.5.9	2	A 32-bit number
Integer (enumeration)	2.5.5.9	10	A 32-bit number
Octet string (Octet-String)	2.5.5.10	4	A byte string
Octet string (object)	2.5.5.10	127	A byte string
Time	2.5.5.11	23	The number of seconds elapsed since 1 January 1970
Unicode	2.5.5.12	64	A wide string
Address	2.5.5.13	127	Used internally by the system
Distname-Address	2.5.5.14	127	Used internally by the system
NT Security Descriptor	2.5.5.15	66	A Security Descriptor (SD)
Large integer	2.5.5.16	65	A 64-bit number
SID	2.5.5.17	4	A Security Identifier (SID)

Most of these are standard programming types. If you're not sure which syntax to use, take a look at a preexisting attribute and see if you can find an appropriate syntax for the attribute you wish to create. For example, the userPrincipalName attribute has an attributeSyntax of 2.5.5.12 and an oMSyntax of 64, so it must contain Unicode strings.

Classes (classSchema Objects)

Schema classes are defined as instances of the classSchema class. Table 4-4 shows the most important attributes that you may wish to set.

Table 4-4. The defining attributes of a classSchema object instance

Attribute	Syntax	Mandatory	Multi-valued	Description
cn	Unicode	Yes	No	The Relative Distinguished Name (RDN).
governsID	OID	Yes	No	The OID that uniquely identifies objects of this class.
lDAPDisplayName	Unicode	No	No	The name by which LDAP clients identify this class.
schemaIDGUID	Octet string	Yes	No	Globally Unique Identifier (GUID) to uniquely identify this class.
rDNAttID	OID	No	No	The attribute that indicates what two-letter-prefix (cn=, ou=, dc=) is used to reference the class. You should use only cn here unless you have a very solid idea of what you are doing and why.
description	Unicode string	No	No	A description of the attribute.
subClassOf	OID	Yes	No	The class that this one inherits from; the default is Top.[a]
mustContain	OID	No	Yes	The list of attributes that are mandatory for this class.
systemMustContain	OID	No	Yes	System version of the previous attribute.
mayContain	OID	No	Yes	The list of attributes that are optional for this class.
systemMayContain	OID	No	Yes	System version of the previous attribute.
possSuperiors	OID	No	Yes	The list of Auxiliary (or 88-Class) classes that this object can be created within; e.g., User objects can be created within Organizational Unit objects.
systemPossSuperiors	OID	No	Yes	System version of the previous attribute.
auxiliaryClass	OID	No	Yes	The list of Auxiliary (or 88-Class) classes that this object inherits attributes from.
systemAuxiliaryClass	OID	No	Yes	System version of the previous attribute.
defaultSecurity-Descriptor	Octet string	No	No	The Security Descriptor to assign to new instances of this class. Note that this SD is applied to new instances of the class if and only if an SD is not specifically provided and set during the creation of the instance.
objectClassCategory	Integer	Yes	No	0 = 88-Class 1 = Structural 2 = Abstract 3 = Auxiliary
systemOnly	Boolean	No	No	If True, once the initial value has been set, only the system can create and modify instances of this class. The default is False.

Attribute	Syntax	Mandatory	Multi-valued	Description
objectClass	Object	Yes	Yes	The class that this object is an instance of; i.e., classSchema.
nTSecurityDescriptor	NT-Security-Descriptor	Yes	Yes	Security Descriptor on the classSchema object itself. For example, setting an SD allows you to govern who can actually create instances of the object and who cannot.
defaultHidingValue	Boolean	No	No	Whether the object is to be hidden or displayed within the MMCs by default.

[a] Remember that the X.500 specifications indicate that an auxiliary class cannot inherit from a structural class, and an abstract class can inherit only from another abstract class.

Object Class Category and Inheritance

Classes are special in that they can inherit from one another. For example, let's say that we wanted to store two new types of objects in the schema representing a marketing user and a finance user, respectively. These users both need all the attributes of the existing User class as a base. However, the finance user needs 7 special attributes, while the marketing user needs 3. The extra attributes required by both users do not match in any way. In this example, we can create a Marketing-User class, a Finance-User class, and 10 distinctly new attributes. However, rather than having to specify that the Marketing-User and Finance-User classes have each of the attributes of the original user class individually, all we need to do is specify that the new classes inherit from the user class by setting the subClassOf attribute to user. When we do this, both the new classes inherit every single attribute that the user class had. We can then add the extra attributes to each class and we have two new classes. It really is that simple.

You can think of the Active Directory schema as a treelike structure, with multiple classes branching down or inheriting from one base class at the top that has the attributes all objects need to begin with. This class, unsurprisingly enough, is called top, which was originally defined in the X.500 spec. Some classes inherit directly from top, while others exist much lower down the tree. While each class may have only one parent in this layout, each class may also inherit attributes from other classes. This is possible because there are three categories of classSchema object, known as the objectClassCategory, that you can create: structural, abstract, and auxiliary.

Structural
> If a class is structural, you can directly create objects of its type in Active Directory. The user and group classes are examples of structural classes.

Abstract
> It is possible that you would want to create a class that inherits from other classes and has certain attributes but that is not one you will ever need to create

instances of directly. This type of class is known as abstract. For example, let's say that the Marketing-User and Finance-User were to be the first of a number of structural classes that had a common structure. In that case, you could create an abstract class to be used as the basis of other structural classes. Abstract classes can inherit from other classes, can have attributes defined on them directly, and in all other ways act like structural classes, except that instances of them cannot directly be created as objects in Active Directory.

Auxiliary

An auxiliary class is used to store sets of attributes that other classes can inherit. Auxiliary classes are a way for structural and abstract classes to inherit collections of attributes that do not have to be defined directly within the classes themselves. It is primarily a grouping mechanism.

The X.500 specifications indicate that an auxiliary class cannot inherit from a structural class, and an abstract class can inherit only from another abstract class.

 To comply with the X.500 standards, there are actually four types of objectClassCategory. While objects are required to be classified as one of structural, abstract, or auxiliary by the 1993 X.500 specifications, objects defined before 1993 using the 1988 specifications are not required to comply with these categories. Such objects have no corresponding 1993 category and so are defined in the schema as having a special category known as the 88-Class.

Let's take a look at the user and computer classes, which are used to create user and computer accounts, respectively, in Active Directory. The computer class (OID: 1.2.840.113556.1.3.30) and user class (OID: 1.2.840.113556.1.5.9) are each structural, which means that you can create objects with them directly in Active Directory. The computer class inherits from the user class, so the computer class is a special type of user in a way. The user class inherits from the organizationalPerson abstract class (OID: 2.5.6.7). This means that the total attributes available to objects of class computer include not only the attributes defined specifically on the computer and user classes themselves but also all the attributes that are inherited from the organizationalPerson class. The organizationalPerson class is a subclass of the person abstract class (OID: 2.5.6.6), which is a subclass of the abstract top class (OID: 2.5.6.0). There are no classes above top; it is the root class.

The user class that Microsoft needed to define in Active Directory had to be more than just the sum of the X.500 standard parts. After all, Microsoft uses Security Identifiers (SIDs) to identify users, and these were not contained in the original X.500 standards. So to extend the attributes that make up a user, Microsoft defined some auxiliary classes and included these in the user class makeup. The auxiliary classes are mailRecipient and securityPrincipal. mailRecipient is a collection of attributes that allow a user to hold information relating to the email address and mail account associated with that user. securityPrincipal is used to hold the SID and other user-related security attributes that Microsoft needed.

Figure 4-4 indicates how the computer class is made up from a number of other classes.

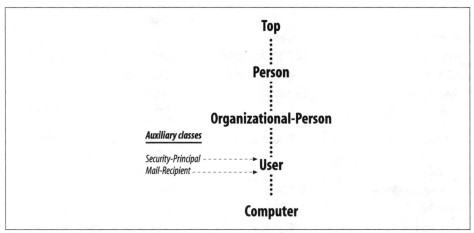

Figure 4-4. The computer class

If you were to use a tool such as ADSI Edit, you could see the inheritance and class relationships quite clearly. For example, looking at the objectClass attribute of any user object, you would see that the values held in this attribute were top, person, organizationalPerson, and user. In other words, this attribute indicates that each user object inherits attributes from all these classes. Similarly, for any computer object, the objectClass attribute holds top, person, organizationalPerson, user, and computer. If you were to look at the subclassOf attribute on the computer class object itself in the schema, you would see the user class. The user class has a subClassOf attribute that indicates organizationalPerson, and so on.

Dissecting an Example Class

Let's now look at the user class in a little more depth. Using a tool like ADSI Edit, we can see the values of each attribute for the user classSchema object. Table 4-5 contains the attributes and values.

Table 4-5. Attributes and values for the user class

User attribute's LDAP-Display-Name	User attribute's syntax	Value contained in user's attribute
adminDescription	CASE_ IGNORE_ STRING	User
adminDisplayName	CASE_ IGNORE_ STRING	User
cn	CASE_ IGNORE_ STRING	User

Table 4-5. Attributes and values for the user class (continued)

User attribute's LDAP-Display-Name	User attribute's syntax	Value contained in user's attribute
defaultHidingValue	BOOLEAN	False
distinguishedName	DN_STRING	cn=User, cn=Schema, cn=Configuration, dc=mycorp, dc=com
instanceType	INTEGER	4
name	CASE_IGNORE_STRING	User
nTSecurityDescriptor	SECURITY_DESCRIPTOR	\<SID\>
objectCategory	DN_STRING	cn=Class-Schema, cn=Schema, cn=Configuration, dc=mycorp, dc=com
objectClass	CASE_IGNORE_STRING	Top; classSchema (2 values of a multivalued attribute)
objectGUID	OCTET_STRING	\<GUID\>
showInAdvancedViewOnly	BOOLEAN	True
systemFlags	INTEGER	16
uSNChanged	LARGE_INTEGER	USN when last changed
uSNCreated	LARGE_INTEGER	USN when created
whenChanged	UTC_TIME	Time when last changed
whenCreated	UTC_TIME	Time when created
governsID	CASE_IGNORE_STRING	1.2.840.113556.1.5.9
defaultObjectCategory	DN_STRING	cn=person, cn=schema, cn=configuration, dc=mycorp, dc=com
defaultSecurityDescriptor	CASE_IGNORE_STRING	Long text-encoded representation of a SID
rDNAttID	CASE_IGNORE_STRING	cn
lDAPDisplayName	CASE_IGNORE_STRING	User
schemaIDGUID	OCTET_STRING	\<GUID\> that uniquely identifies this class
subClassOf	CASE_IGNORE_STRING	organizationalPerson
systemAuxiliaryClass	CASE_IGNORE_STRING	securityPrincipal; mailRecipient
systemMayContain	CASE_IGNORE_STRING	Various attributes[a]
objectClassCategory	INTEGER	1
systemPossSuperiors	CASE_IGNORE_STRING	builtinDomain; organizationalUnit; domain-DNS
systemOnly	BOOLEAN	False

userCertificate; userWorkstations; userSharedFolderOther;userSharedFolder; userPrincipalName; userParameters; userAccount-Control;unicodePwd; terminalServer; servicePrincipalName; scriptPath; pwdLastSet; profilePath; primaryGroupID; preferredOU; other-LoginWorkstations; operatorCount; ntPwdHistory; networkAddress; msRASSavedFramedRoute; msRASSavedFramedIPAddress; msRASSavedCallbackNumber; msRADIUSServiceType; msRADIUSFramedRoute; msRADIUSFramedIPAddress; msRADIUSCallbackNumber; msNPSavedCallingStationID; msNPCallingStationID; msNPAllowDialin; mSMQSignCertificatesMig; mSMQSignCertificates; mSMQ-DigestsMig; mSMQDigests; maxStorage; logonWorkstation; logonHours; logonCount; lockoutTime; localeID; lmPwdHistory; lastLogon; lastLogoff; homeDrive; homeDirectory; groupsToIgnore; groupPriority; groupMembershipSAM; gPOptions; gPLink; dynamicLDAPServer; desktopProfile; defaultClassStore; dBCSPwd; controlAccessRights; codePage; badPwdCount; badPasswordTime; adminCount; aCSPolicy-Name; accountExpires

You can see the following about the user class:

- The name of the class is user (adminDescription, adminDisplayName, cn, name).
- It is an instance of the classSchema class (objectCategory and objectClass).
- It inherits attributes from both top and classSchema (objectClass).
- This object class has a SID governing who can access and manipulate it (nTSecurityDescriptor).
- The instances of the user class are visible in normal browsing (default-HidingValue).
- The user class itself is to be hidden from casual browsing (showInAdvanced-ViewOnly).
- The user class has an OID of 1.2.840.113556.1.5.9 (governsID).
- It can have instances created by anyone (systemOnly).
- It inherits attributes not only from top and classSchema but also from securityPrincipal and mailRecipient (objectClass and systemAuxiliaryClass).
- When connecting to instances of the class via LDAP, the two-letter prefix used should be cn (rDNAttID).
- The user class is a direct subclass of the organizationalPerson class (subClassOf).
- There are a large number of attributes that instances of the user class can have values for (systemMayContain).
- This class can be created directly under only three different parents in Active Directory (systemPossSuperiors).
- The class is structural (objectClassCategory).
- A default Security Descriptor should be applied to new instances of the user class if one is not specified on creation (defaultSecurityDescriptor).

How inheritance affects mustContain, mayContain, possSuperiors, and auxiliaryClass

Let's look at the mustContain, mayContain, auxiliaryClass, possSuperiors, and their system attribute pairs. You can see that the only values that are set are systemPossSuperiors, systemMayContain, and systemAuxiliaryClass. These were the values set on the initial creation of the user class and cannot be changed. Note that there were no mandatory attributes set at the creation of the original class because the systemMustContain attribute is not listed. If you later wished to add an extra set of attributes or a new optional attribute to the user class, you could use auxiliary-Class or mayContain and modify the base definition. This occurs if, for example, you use the Active Directory Connector (ADC) to link your Active Directory and a Microsoft Exchange 5.5 schema. When you install the ADC for the first time in a forest, it extends the schema to include new Exchange objects and attributes, as well as modifying existing Active Directory objects to include new Exchange-relevant attributes. If you were to do this, the user class would be directly modified to include three of these Exchange-related auxiliary classes in the auxiliaryClass attribute: msExchMailStorage, msExchCustomAttributes, and msExchCertificateInformation. The ADC is discussed more fully in Chapter 16.

The attributes that are required when you create a new user are not listed in the mustContain attribute. That's because objectSID, sAMAccountName, and the other attributes are inherited from other classes that make up this one. The mustContain attributes can be defined directly in auxiliaryClass, systemAuxiliaryClass, or sub-ClassOf, or they can be defined on the classes inherited from further up the tree. Both sAMAccountName and objectSID, for example, are defined on the security-Principal class.

The same principle applies to the mayContain attribute. The entire set of these attributes is available only when you recurse back up the tree and identify all the inherited mayContain attributes on all inherited classes.

possSuperiors, on the other hand, can be made up of only those items defined directly on the class, those defined on the class in the subClassOf attribute, or any inherited classes defined on any other subClassOf attributes up the subClassOf tree. If that was too confusing, try this: an instance of the user class can have possSuperiors from itself, from the organizationalPerson class defined in the subClassOf attribute, from the person class (the organizationalPerson class's sub-ClassOf attribute), and from top (the person class's subClassOf attribute).

Viewing the user class with the Active Directory Schema snap-in

Take a look at Figure 4-5. This shows the user class viewed with the Active Directory Schema snap-in. You can see the relevant general user data.

Notice that quite a bit of it is not configurable after the initial configuration, including governsID, schemaIDGUID, rDNAttID, objectClassCategory, systemOnly, objectClass, subClassOf, systemMustContain, systemPossSuperiors, systemMay-Contain, and systemAuxiliaryClass.

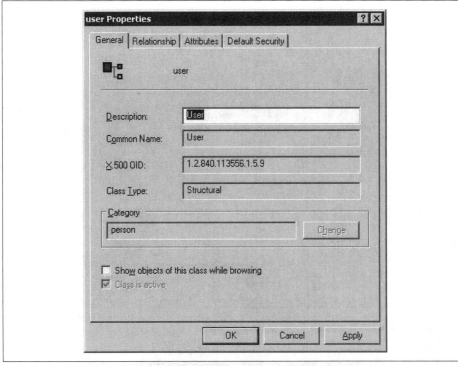

Figure 4-5. User class schema entry general settings

To see the so-called relationship settings (subClassOf, auxiliaryClass, systemAuxiliaryClass, possSuperiors, systemPossSuperiors), look at Figure 4-6. In this screen, you can see that the user class in this schema is inheriting attributes from the two auxiliary classes.

The third and final screen is the Attributes tab for the user class and is displayed in Figure 4-7. This shows the mustContain, systemMustContain, mayContain, and systemMayContain attributes of the user class.

Dynamically Linked Auxiliary Classes

With Windows 2000, auxiliary classes were statically linked to structural classes via the auxiliaryClass and systemAuxiliaryClass attributes. This went against how most directory services implemented auxiliary classes, which typically allowed dynamically assigned auxiliary classes on instances of objects. A new feature in Windows Server 2003 is the ability to do dynamic assignments of auxiliary classes to individual objects instead of to an entire class of objects in the schema. Having the dynamic auxiliary class mechanism provides much more flexibility for application developers who may want to utilize existing structural and auxiliary classes but do not want to extend the schema to define such relationships.

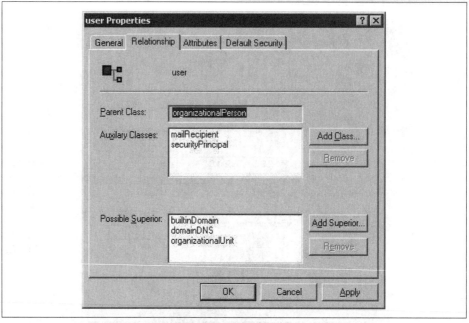

Figure 4-6. User class schema entry relationship settings

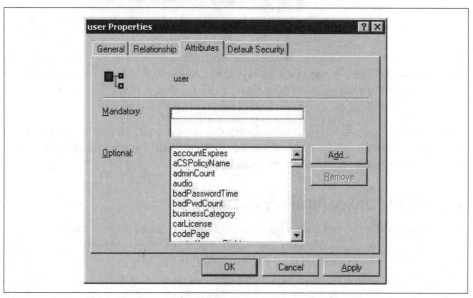

Figure 4-7. User class schema entry attribute settings

To dynamically link an auxiliary class to an object, you only need modify the object-Class attribute of the object to include the name of the auxiliary class. Any auxiliary class can be used, provided that all mustContain and systemMustContain attributes contained within the auxiliary class are set at the same time. You can also remove a dynamically linked auxiliary class by clearing any values that have been set for attributes defined by the auxiliary class and then removing the auxiliary class name from the object's objectClass attribute.

Now let's illustrate why dynamically linking auxiliary classes is a good idea. Assume we have a forest with several domains, each representing divisions within a company. Each division manages its own user objects. One of the divisions, named Toasters, wants to assign additional attributes to their user objects. These new attributes would only apply to employees within the Toasters division. Under Windows 2000, the only way to accomplish this would be to create the new attributes in the schema, create a new auxiliary class, and include the new attributes in the auxiliary class. At that point the new auxiliary class could be added to the auxiliaryClass of the user classSchema object. That means every user object contained within the forest would then have the new attributes. If each division wanted to do something similar, you can see how the number of attributes on all user objects within the forest could grow very quickly and unnecessarily. With Windows Server 2003, you would still create the new attributes and auxiliary classes in the schema, but you would not modify the auxiliaryClass of the user object. Instead, each division would dynamically link their auxiliary class to *their* user objects. This provides for a much more efficient and clean implementation than was possible under Windows 2000.

Summary

In this chapter we've shown you how the internal blueprint for all objects in Active Directory, known as the schema, was derived from the X.500 directory service. We explained the purpose of the OID numbering system and how it can be used. We then detailed how an attribute and its syntax is structured in the schema as attributeSchema objects, using the userPrincipalName attribute as an example. We showed how attributes are added to classes by detailing how classes are stored in the schema as instances of classSchema objects. To make this clearer, we dug into the details of the user class to see how it was constructed. Finally, we covered how auxiliary classes can be dynamically linked in Windows Server 2003 and why it is significant.

Chapter 12 builds on what you've learned here to demonstrate how you can design and implement schema extensions.

CHAPTER 5

Site Topology and Replication

This chapter introduces a major feature of Active Directory: multi-master replication. Active Directory was one of the first LDAP-based directories to offer multi-master replication. Most directories replicate data from a single master server to subordinate servers. This is how replication worked in Windows NT 4.0 as an example. Obviously, there are several problems with a single-master replication scheme, including single point of failure for updates, geographic distance from master to clients performing the updates, and less efficient replication due to single originating location of updates. Active Directory replication addresses these issues, but with a price. To get the benefit of a multi-master replication, you must first create a site topology that defines how domain controllers should replicate with each other. Especially in large environments, maintaining a site topology can be a significant amount of overhead.

This chapter looks at the basics of how sites and replication work in Active Directory. In Chapter 9, we'll describe the physical infrastructure of a network layout using sites. We'll also discuss in that chapter how the Knowledge Consistency Checker (KCC) sets up and manages the replication connections and details on how to effectively design and tailor sites, site links, and replication in Active Directory.

Site Topology

Active Directory uses the term *site* to mean a collection of subnets that coexist on a local area network (LAN) or metropolitan area network (MAN), i.e., a physical network in a particular location with good connectivity between all sections of that network. Active Directory uses sites to define boundaries of replication around the physical network.

Active Directory replication is very efficient. Only changed attributes are replicated, rather than entire objects, as was the case in Windows NT. And with Windows Server 2003, link-value replication is available for some attributes, so only changed values for a multi-valued attribute are replicated instead of all values. Link-value replication is a much needed feature which was not available in Windows 2000 Active Directory; it is intended to address issues such as the 5,000 member limitation for group objects. Replication also can take place over multiple TCP/IP transports, so that you can find a replication protocol to suit the environment a particular site requires.

 The recommended minimum speed for a well-connected network is 1.5 Mbps (i.e., a T1 link). You will see this actual value vary from article to article and book to book, as different people find that their network runs fine over a slower connection speed. We'll cover this later, but the absolute true minimum is around 128 Kbps of available replication bandwidth out of a 256 Kbps total available bandwidth. Your mileage may vary; the only way to determine the best solution in your environment is by testing.

Administrators must create the site topology in Active Directory, as the process is not automatic. The main site-topology objects of interest include the site objects, subnet objects, and site link objects. One of the major uses of the site topology is for clients to find their closest DC. That is why subnet information must be associated with sites. Clients use their IP address to determine which Active Directory subnet they belong to and subsequently which site. The site information can then be used to determine the closest DC.

Once you've set up a site, an Active Directory process called the Knowledge Consistency Checker (KCC) automatically creates and dynamically manages a replication schedule and a set of intrasite (i.e., within a site) replication links among DCs in the site. As you add more DCs, more intrasite links are added automatically. If you were to do nothing more, data would be effectively replicated by Active Directory around your site. When you add your second site, the same automatic intrasite creation mechanisms spring into action, creating links and a replication schedule among the various DCs in this second site. The algorithm that is used adapts as more sites and DCs are added, so that certain built-in criteria are never breached; this assures that the network is always properly replicated. Note, however, that creating a second site does not trigger the system to also automatically create intersite (i.e., between sites) replication links and a replication schedule. Instead, site links that connect two sites have to be created manually. We'll cover the KCC in greater depth later in Chapter 9.

Site and Replication Management Tools

Obviously, as more sites and connections are created, the topology can get very large. Microsoft provides the Active Directory Sites and Services snap-in to help manage the topology. It actually allows you to get right into the guts of the Sites Container, which holds all the site topology objects and connection objects. The Sites

Container is located directly under the Configuration Container in the Configuration NC. It would be located in cn=sites,cn=configuration,dc=mycorp,dc=com in the mycorp.com forest. You can create new sites, subnets, and links, set replication schedules for each link, and so on.

Other replication-related tools are available in the Windows Support Tools:

RepAdmin
> A command-line tool for administering replication.

ReplMon
> A graphical utility for managing and monitoring replication.

Why Have Active Directory Sites?

Sites exist to allow clients to find the closest DC, GC, DFS share point, or even an application distribution point (via SMS). Sites don't even have to have any DCs at all in them; a site can be composed entirely of subnets. In this case, clients need to find a DC, preferably in the nearest site. The client actually queries both Active Directory (for cost-based selection of the nearest site) and DNS (using site records that we will go through in Chapter 6). While the details on sites are held in the DNS, the actual topology is held in Active Directory. This topology uses site link costs to determine the proximity of other sites.

With cost-assigned ratings to links and the fact that Active Directory replicates only updated properties rather than entire objects, Active Directory has improved Windows NT's attempts to span domains across WAN links. While under Windows NT, creating a domain across very slow links was next to impossible; with Active Directory it is possible to span domains across very slow links or even links that do not have synchronous connections at all but instead receive and send changes asynchronously via email. In fact, while Active Directory domains can easily be defined to span sites, sites also can hold multiple domains. Remember that a site literally represents an area of good connectivity, but it doesn't dictate how you arrange your domains; the connections between sites do that.

The First Site

When you create the first domain controller of the first domain in a new forest, a default site called Default-First-Site-Name is created, and the domain controller is assigned to it. Subsequently, installed domain controllers are added to this site automatically. Even if you then create multiple sites, new servers are always added to the first site. To change that, you need to assign one or more subnets to each site. That way, any server on a specified subnet is automatically added to the appropriate site.

Adding Subnets to a Site in the Sites and Services Snap-In

When adding subnets to sites via the Sites and Services snap-in, you must enter the name of the subnet in the form network/bits masked; e.g., 10.186.149.0/24 is network 10.186.149.0 with subnet mask 255.255.255.0.

The bits masked in the subnet name are the number of bits set in the subnet mask for that subnet. It can be between 0 and 31. The subnet mask is made up of 4 octets or bytes (4 sets of 8 bits). To convert the subnet mask to bits, convert each octet from the subnet mask to binary. The subnet mask 255.255.255.0 is 11111111.11111111. 11111111.00000000 in binary, which uses 8+8+8 bits (i.e., 24) to define the subnet mask. A subnet mask of 255.255.248.0 would be 11111111.11111111.11111000. 00000000, which is 8+8+5 or 21.

If subnets and IP addresses mean very little to you, check out Chuck Semeria's article "Understanding IP Addressing: Everything You Ever Wanted To Know" at *http:// www.3com.com/other/pdfs/infra/corpinfo/en_US/501302.pdf*.

The Default-First-Site-Name site can be renamed if you wish, but note that site names cannot exceed 63 characters or contain dot (.) or space characters.

Data Replication

Microsoft has introduced a number of new terms for Active Directory replication, and most of them will be completely unfamiliar to anyone new to Active Directory. To properly design replication, you need to understand how replication works, but more to the point, you need to understand how replication works using these new terms, which are used throughout both Microsoft's documentation and its management tools. Here is the list of the terms you'll encounter as we explain replication. These definitions will make more sense later.

Update Sequence Number (USN)
> This 64-bit value, which is assigned to each object, increments every time a change takes place.

Originating write/update and replicated write/update
> A change made to an object on a specific DC is an originating write; replication of that change to all other DCs is a replicated write.

High-Watermark Vector
> This USN represents the maximum number of changes ever to occur on a particular NC.

Up-To-Date Vector
>This is the USN on a specific server that represents the last originating write for an NC on that server.

Tombstone
>Because of the complex replication available in Active Directory, simply deleting an object could result in it being re-created at the next replication interval, so deleted objects are tombstoned instead. This basically marks them as deleted. Objects marked as tombstoned are actually deleted 60 days after their original tombstone status setting; however, this time can be changed by modifying the tombstoneLifetime attribute of cn=DirectoryServices,cn=WindowsNT, cn=Services,cn=Configuration,dc=mycorp,dc=com for the mycorp.com forest.

Property version number
>This number indicates how often this particular property has been updated.

Timestamp
>This time and date are stored on an object for comparison checking.

Globally Unique Identifier (GUID)
>This system-generated alphanumeric string represents a unique identifier for an object within an enterprise.

Flexible Single Master Operations (FSMO)
>This term designates a server that performs one of the following roles: PDC Emulator, Infrastructure Master, RID Master, Schema Master, or Domain Naming Master.

A Background to Metadata—Data That Governs the Replication Process

Active Directory replication enables data transfer between NCs on different servers without ending up in a continuous replication loop or missing any data. To make this process work, each NC holds a number of pieces of information that specifically relate to replication within that particular NC. So the replication data for the Schema NC is held in the Schema NC and is separate from the replication data for the Configuration NC, which is held in the Configuration NC.

 To minimize the use of abbreviations, we will refer to DCs from now on simply as servers. The terms property and attribute are also used interchangeably.

The High-Watermark Vector and orginating/replicated updates

Each server has a separate Update Sequence Number (USN) for each NC. The USN is stored as a 64-bit value in the Active Directory database and is indexed for rapid searching. This value is used to indicate how many updates have actually taken place to an NC on a particular server and is known as the High-Watermark Vector. Each server also maintains a record of the updates that it made to its NC for a particular USN. This allows other servers to request individual changes based on particular USNs. Replication distinguishes between two types of update:

Originating update
> Occurs when the server itself or an application connected to that server makes a change to its own copy of the NC.

Replicated update
> Occurs when the server receives a change it needs to make to its own NC from another server.

So if you use the Active Directory Users and Computers snap-in to create five users on Server A, Server A's USN is incremented five times, once for each originating update. If Server A receives six more changes from Server B, Server A's USN is incremented six more times, once for each of the six replicated updates.

 If an Active Directory database transaction is aborted, i.e., fails to complete, the associated USN value is ignored from then on by Active Directory. It is not assigned to any object or reused in any way. The USN continues incrementing as changes occur, but that value is considered unusable.

To summarize, each server in a forest holds at least three NCs (Domain, Configuration, and Schema), and each of these has a High-Watermark Vector USN.

High-Watermark Vector table

Each server also maintains a list of the High-Watermark Vectors for all its replication partners. This table is updated only during replication. If we have a server with two partners, each partner maintains the High-Watermark Vector for my server. If a change occurs on my server, the High-Watermark Vector on my server is updated, but the High-Watermark Vectors on my partners are not updated until the next replication cycle.

Up-To-Date Vector

Each server also maintains the USN that represents the last originating write for the NC on itself. This is known as the Up-To-Date Vector. If the USN on a server for a particular NC was 2000, and the server made an originating write to that NC, both the High-Watermark Vector and the Up-To-Date Vector USN would become 2001. If, subsequently, the server received five replicated writes, the Up-To-Date Vector would stay at 2001, while the High-Watermark Vector would become 2006. Obviously, if a server never has an originating write, the Up-To-Date Vector USN is never set for that server.

Up-To-Date Vector table

Each server also maintains a list of the Up-To-Date Vectors for every server that has ever made an originating write. This is known as the Up-To-Date Vector table. If Server A makes an originating write, it creates an Up-To-Date Vector for itself and adds it to the Up-To-Date Vector table. When it next replicates with all of its partners, it passes its Up-To-Date Vector table to those partners. The highest originating write value for a server is thus passed around to all servers in an NC.

> If you are replicating a domain NC, the maximum number of entries in an Up-To-Date Vector table has to be the total number of servers that make up the domain. If you are replicating the Configuration or Schema NCs, which are replicated enterprise-wide, the maximum number of entries in the table would be the number of servers in the entire forest.

As the tables have to uniquely identify the server in addition to the USN, each entry in both sets of tables stores the GUID of the server along with the USN value.

Recap

The following list summarizes the important points of this section:

- Active Directory is split into separate Naming Contexts, each of which replicates independently.
- Within each NC, a variety of metadata is held:
  - Each NC on a server has a unique USN for itself. This USN is incremented whenever a change occurs on that server by any means. This is known as the High-Watermark Vector for that server within this NC.
  - For each NC on a server, the server records the USN of the last originating write that was made to the NC and the server's identifying GUID. This is known as the Up-To-Date Vector for that server within this NC.
  - For each NC on a server, the server maintains a High-Watermark Vector table that contains one entry for each of its replication partners within this NC. The values a server holds for its replication partners are updated only during a replication cycle.
  - For each NC on a server, the server maintains an Up-To-Date Vector table that contains one vector entry for every server that has ever made an originating write within this NC. Each entry consists of two values: an Originating-DC-GUID and an Originating-USN. These values are updated only during a replication cycle.

While each server has a GUID, so does the Active Directory database (NTDS.DIT). This latter GUID is used to identify the server's Active Directory database in replication calls. The GUID is initially the same as the server GUID but changes if Active Directory is restored on that server.

 This change of GUID makes sure that the other DCs on the network do not immediately replicate all the missing changes to this newly restored version of Active Directory. As the GUIDs are different, the change is detected and Active Directory is left alone.

How an Object's Metadata Is Modified During Replication

To see how the actual data is modified during replication, consider a four-stage example:

Step 1
> An object (a user) is created on Server A.

Step 2
> That object is replicated to Server B.

Step 3
> That object is subsequently modified on Server B.

Step 4
> The new changes to that object are replicated back to Server A.

This four-step process is shown in Figure 5-1. The diagram depicts the status of the user object on both Server A and Server B during the four time periods that represent each of the steps.

Now use Figure 5-1 to follow a discussion of each of the steps.

Step 1—Initial creation of a user on Server A

When you create a user on Server A, Server A is the originating server. During the Active Directory database transaction representing the creation of the new user on Server A, a USN (1000) is assigned to the transaction. The user's uSNCreated and uSNChanged properties are automatically set to 1000 (the USN of the transaction corresponding to the user creation). All of the user's properties are also initialized with a set of data as follows:

- The property's value(s) is/are set according to system defaults or parameters given during user creation.
- The property's USN is set to 1000 (the USN of this transaction).
- The property's version number is set to 1.
- The property's timestamp is set to the time of the object creation.
- The property's originating-server GUID is set to the GUID of Server A.
- The property's originating-server USN is set to 1000 (the USN of this transaction).

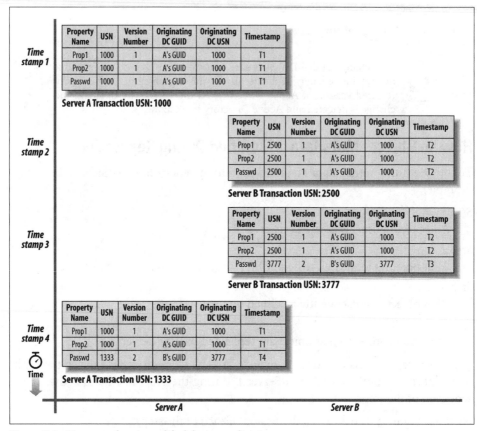

Figure 5-1. How metadata is modified during replication

This tells you that the user was created during transaction 1000 on this server (uSN-Created = 1000). It also tells you that the user was last changed during transaction 1000 (uSNChanged = 1000). You know that the properties for the user have never been modified from their original values (property version numbers = 1), and these values were set at transaction 1000 (property's USN = 1000). Finally, you know that each property was last set by the originating server Server A during transaction 1000 (originating-server GUID and originating-server USN).

The preceding example showed two per-object values and five per-property values being changed. While uSNChanged and uSNCreated are real properties on each object in AD, properties of an object can only have values and cannot hold other properties, like a version number.

In reality, all of the per-property replication metadata (Property Version Number, Time-Changed, Originating-DC-GUID, Originating-USN, Property-USN) for every property of any object is encoded together as a single byte string and stored as repl-PropertyMetaData, a nonreplicated property of the object.

A property's metadata can be seen by using the RepAdmin, ADSI Edit, or LDP tools provided in the Windows Support Tools.

Step 2—Replication of the originating write to Server B

Later, when this object is replicated to Server B, Server B adds the user to its copy of Active Directory as a replicated write. During this transaction, USN 2500 is allocated, and the user's uSNCreated and uSNChanged properties are modified to correspond to Server B's transaction USN (2500).

This tells you that the user was created during transaction 2500 on this server (uSNCreated = 2500). It also tells you that the user was last changed during transaction 2500 (uSNChanged = 2500). You know that the properties for the user have never been modified from their original values (property version numbers = 1), and these values were set at transaction 2500 (property's USN = 2500). Finally, you know that each property was last set by the originating server Server A during transaction 1000 (originating-server GUID and originating-server USN).

Step 3—Password change for the user on Server B

Now an originating write (a password change) occurs on Server B's replicated-write user. Some time has passed since the user was originally created, so the USN assigned to the password change transaction is 3777. When the password is changed, the user's uSNChanged property is modified to become 3777. In addition, the password property (and only the password property) is modified in the following way:

- The password value is set.
- The password's USN is set to 3777 (the USN of this transaction).
- The property's version number is set to 2.
- The property's timestamp is set to the time that transaction 3777 occurred.
- The property's originating-server GUID is set to the GUID of Server B.
- The property's originating-server USN is set to 3777 (the USN of this transaction).

Looking at the user object, you can now see that the object was last changed during transaction 3777 and that that transaction represented a password change that originated on Server B.

Step 4—Password change replication to Server A

This step is similar to Step 2. When Server A receives the password update during replication, it allocates the change transaction a USN of 1333.

Remember that updates occur at the property level and not the object level, so only the password is sent and not the whole user object.

During transaction 1333, the user's uSNChanged property is modified to correspond to Server A's transaction USN.

This tells you that the user was created during transaction 1000 on this server (uSN-Created = 1000). It also tells you that the user was last changed during transaction 1333 (uSNChanged = 1333). You know that all but one of the properties for the user have retained their original values (property version numbers = 1), and these values were set at transaction 1000 (property's USN = 1000). Finally, you know that all but one of the properties were last set by the originating server Server A during transaction 1000 (originating-server GUID and originating-server USN). The password was modified for the first time since its creation (password version number = 2) during transaction 1333 (password's USN = 1333), and it was modified on Server B during transaction 3777 (originating-server GUID and originating-server USN).

That's how object and property metadata is modified during replication. Let's now take a look at exactly how replication occurs.

The Replication of a Naming Context Between Two Servers

In the following examples, there are five servers in a domain: Server A, Server B, Server C, Server D, and Server E. It doesn't matter what NC they are replicating or which servers replicate with which other servers (as they do not all have to inter-replicate), because the replication process for any two servers will be the same nonetheless. Replication is a five-step process:

Step 1
    Replication with a partner is initiated.

Step 2
    The partner works out what updates to send.

Step 3
    The partner sends the updates to the initiating server.

Step 4
    The initiating server processes the updates.

Step 5
    The initiating server checks whether it is up to date.

Step 1—Replication with a partner is initiated

Replication occurs between only two servers at any time, so let's consider Server A and Server B, which are replication partners. At a certain point in time indicated by the replication schedule on Server A, Server A initiates replication for a particular NC with Server B and requests any updates that it doesn't have. This is a one-way update transfer from Server B to Server A. No new updates will be passed to Server B in this replication cycle, as this would require Server B to initiate the replication.

Server A initiates the replication by sending Server B a request to replicate along with five pieces of important replication metadata, i.e., data relating to the replication process itself. The five pieces are:

- The name of the NC that Server A wishes to receive updates for
- The maximum number of object updates that Server A wishes to receive during this replication cycle
- The maximum number of values that Server A wishes to receive during this replication cycle
- Server A's High-Watermark Vector for Server B in this NC
- Server A's Up-To-Date Vector table for this NC

The maximum object updates and property values are very important in limiting network bandwidth. If one server has had a huge volume of updates since the last replication cycle, limiting the number of objects replicated out in one go means that network bandwidth is not inordinately taken up by replicating those objects in one huge sweep. Instead, the replication is broken down into smaller chunks over multiple replication cycles.

This step is illustrated in Figure 5-2, which shows that while the initiation of the replication occurs from an NC denoted as xxxx on Server A (where xxxx could represent the Schema, the Configuration, or any domain), the actual replication will occur later from Server B to Server A. High-Watermark Vector is abbreviated as HWMV and Up-To-Date Vector as UTDV.

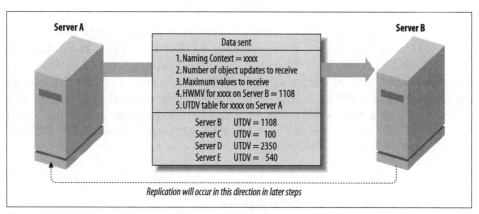

Figure 5-2. Initiating replication with Server B for NC xxxx

Step 2—The partner works out what updates to send

Server B receives all this metadata and works out which updates it needs to send back for this NC. First, Server B finds its own High-Watermark Vector for its copy of the NC and then compares the two High-Watermark Vectors. Assuming that there have been some updates, Server B instantly knows how many updates have happened since Server A last replicated with Server B. This has to be true, as Server A would have been updated with Server B's High-Watermark Vector during the last replication cycle. So, any difference between the two vectors now must represent changes on Server B since the last replication, and Server B knows which individual USNs Server A is missing. Assuming also for now that the number of updates does not exceed the maximums specified by Server A in its metadata, Server B can supply all of the missing updates to Server A.

However, this entire set of updates may not need to go to Server A if Server A has had some of them replicated already from other servers. Server B now needs some way of knowing which updates Server A has already seen, so that it can remove those items from the list of updates to send. That's where the Up-To-Date Vector table comes in. For each update that could potentially be sent, Server B checks two pieces of data attached to the object that was updated: the GUID of the server that originated the update (the Originating-DC-GUID) and the USN associated with that update on the originating server (the Originating-USN). For example, a password change to a user may have been replicated to Server B and recorded as USN 1112, but it may in fact have originated on Server D as USN 2345. Server B cross-references the originating server's GUID with Server A's Up-To-Date Vector table to find Server A's Up-To-Date Vector for the originating server. If the Up-To-Date Vector recorded in the table for the originating server is equal to or higher than the USN attached to the update on Server B, Server A must have already seen the update. This has to be true, because Server A's Up-To-Date Vector table is used to indicate the highest originating-writes that Server A has received.

Let's say that Server B has four updates for Server A: one originating write (Server B USN: 1111) and three replicated writes (Server B USNs 1109, 1110, and 1112). The reason there are four is that 1112 is the last update made on Server B in this example, and Server A's HWMV for xxxx on Server B from Figure 5-1 is 1108. So, look for updates starting at 1109 up to the last update on Server B, which is 1112. The first two replicated writes (Server B USNs 1109 and 1110) originated on Server E (Server E USNs 567 and 788), and one (Server B USN 1112) originated on Server D (Server D USN 2345). This is shown in Table 5-1.

Table 5-1. Potential updates to be sent

Server B USN	Originating DC GUID	Originating DC USN
1109	Server E's GUID	567
1110	Server E's GUID	788

Table 5-1. Potential updates to be sent (continued)

Server B USN	Originating DC GUID	Originating DC USN
1111	Server B's GUID	1111
1112	Server D's GUID	2345

According to Figure 5-2, Server A already has Server D's 2345 update because Server A's Up-To-Date Vector for Server D is 2350. So, both Server A and Server B already have Server D's 2345 update, and there is no need to waste bandwidth sending it over the network again. The act of filtering updates that have already been seen to keep them from being continually sent between the servers is known as propagation dampening.

Now that you know how the High-Watermark Vector table and Up-To-Date Vector table help Server B to work out what updates need to be sent, let's look at the exact process that Server B uses to work out what data is required.

When Server B receives a request for updates from Server A, it starts by making a copy of its Up-To-Date Vector table for Server A. Having done that, it puts the table to one side, so to speak, and does a search of the entire NC for all objects with a uSNChanged value greater than Server A's High-Watermark Vector for Server B. This list is then sorted into ascending uSNChanged order.

Next, Server B initializes an empty output buffer to which it will add update entries for sending to Server A. It also initializes a value called Last-Object-USN-Changed. This will be used to represent the USN of the last object sent in that particular replication session. This value is not an attribute of any particular object, just a simple piece of replication metadata. Server B then enumerates the list of objects in ascending uSNChanged order and uses the following algorithm for each object:

- If the object has already been added to the output buffer, Server B sets Last-Object-USN-Changed to the uSNChanged property of the current object. Enumeration continues with the next object.
- If the object has not already been added to the output buffer, Server B tests the object to see if it contains changes that need to be sent to the destination. For each property of the current object, Server B takes the Originating-DC-GUID of that property and locates the Up-To-date Vector entry that corresponds to that GUID from Server A's Up-To-Date Vector table. From that vector entry, Server B looks at the Up-To-Date Vector Originating-USN. If the property's Originating-USN on Server B is greater than Server A's Up-To-Date Vector Originating-USN, the property needs to be sent.

If changes need to be sent, an update entry is added to the output buffer. Server B sets Last-Object-USN-Changed to the uSNChanged property of the current object. Enumeration continues with the next object.

If no changes need to be sent, Server B sets the Last-Object-USN-Changed to the uSNChanged of the current object. Enumeration continues with the next object.

During the enumeration, if the requested limit on object update entries or values is reached, the enumeration terminates early and a flag known as More-Data is set to true. If the enumeration finishes without either limit being hit, then More-Data is set to false.

Step 3—The partner sends the updates to the initiating server

Server B identifies the list of updates that it should send back based on those that Server A has not yet seen from other sources. Server B then sends this data to Server A. In addition, if More-Data is set to false, one extra piece of metadata is sent back as well. The returned information from Server B is:

- The output buffer updates from Server B
- Server B's Last-Object-USN-Changed value (i.e., its own High-Watermark Vector)
- The More-Data flag
- Server B's Up-To-Date Vector table for this NC (sent only when More-Data set to false)

This is shown in Figure 5-3.

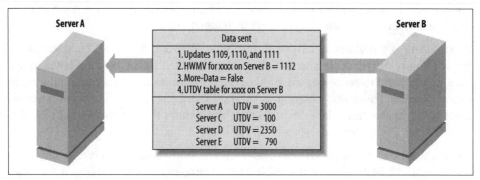

Figure 5-3. Server B sends the updates to Server A for NC xxxx

 If Server B calculates that Server A is already up to date and requires no updates, only the last two pieces of metadata are returned to Server A. This can occur if Server B's High-Watermark Vector is identical to that passed by Server A, i.e., no updates have occurred since the last replication cycle. This also can occur if Server B's High-Watermark Vector has changed but Server A has already seen all the updates. In both cases, just the metadata is returned.

Step 4— The initiating server processes the updates

Server A receives the data. For each update entry it receives, Server A allocates a USN and starts a database transaction to update the relevant object in its own copy of the Active Directory database. If this update represents a change to an object (rather than an object deletion, for example), the object's uSNChanged property is set to the

USN of this transaction. The database transaction is then committed. This process continues for each update entry that was received.

After all the update entries have been processed, Server A's High-Watermark Vector for Server B is set to the Last-Object-USN-Changed received from Server B. In other words, Server A now knows that it is up to date with Server B, up to the last change just sent over.

The Last-Object-USN-Changed that Server A receives allows it to know the last update that Server B has made. This will be used in the next replication cycle. In the previous example, the highest update sent across to Server A is USN 1111. Server B's USN 1112 update is not actually sent since Server A has already seen it. However, the Last-Object-USN-Changed returned by Server B with the data would still be 1112 and not 1111.

Step 5—The initiating server checks whether it is up to date

Server A now checks the More-Data flag. If More-Data is set to true, Server A goes back to step 1 to start replication with Server B again and request more updates. If More-Data is set to false, every update must have been received from Server B, and finally Server A's Up-To-Date Vector table is itself updated.

The Up-To-Date Vector table allows Server A to identify which updates Server B has seen and thus by replication which updates it has now seen. Server A does not replace its Up-To-Date Vector table with the one it was sent. Instead, it checks each entry in the received table and does one of two things. If the entry for a server is not listed in its own Up-To-Date Vector table, it adds that entry to its own table. This allows Server A to know that it has now been updated to a certain level for a new server. If the entry for a server is listed in Server A's Up-To-Date Vector table, and the value received is higher, it modifies its own copy of the table with the higher value. After all, it has now been updated to this new level by Server B, so it had better record that fact.

Table 5-2 shows Server A's Up-To-Date Vector table and High-Watermark Vector for the xxxx Naming Context before Step 1 and after Step 5.

Table 5-2. State of UTDV table and HWMV for Server A before and after updates

	HWMV for Server B	Server B UTDV	Server C UTDV	Server D UTDV	Server E UTDV
Before step 1	1108	1108	100	2350	540
After step 5	1112	1112	100	2350	790

Recap

The following main points summarize replication between Naming Contexts:

- The High-Watermark Vector table is used to detect updates that need to be sent from replication partners.

- The Up-To-Date Vector table is used in propagation dampening to filter the updates so that only updates that the initiating server has not seen are transmitted from a partner.

- The uSNChanged property on each object is used to identify which objects might need to be sent out as updates to the initiating server.

 You can force manual replication of a particular NC on a DC if you choose, using the Sites and Services snap-in. Browse to the connection object that you want to replicate over, right-click it, and select Replicate Now.

How Replication Conflicts Are Reconciled

While the replication process is fine on its own, there are times when conflicts can occur because two servers perform irreconcilable operations between replication cycles. For example, Server A creates an object with a particular name at roughly the same time that Server B creates an object with the same name. Both can't exist at the same time in Active Directory, so what happens to the two objects? Does one get deleted or renamed? Do both get deleted or renamed? What about an administrator moving an object on Server D to a new Organizational Unit while at the same time on Server B that Organizational Unit is being deleted? What happens to the soon-to-be orphaned object? Is it deleted along with the Organizational Unit or moved somewhere else entirely? Consider a final example: if an admin on Server B changes a user's password while the user himself changes his password on Server C, which password does the user get?

All of these conflicts need to be resolved within Active Directory during the next replication cycle. The exact reconciliation process and how the final decision is replicated back out depend on the exact conflict that occurred.

Conflict due to identical property change

In this case, the server starts reconciliation by looking at the version numbers of the two properties. Whichever property has the higher version number wins the conflict. If the property version numbers are equal, the server checks the timestamps of both properties. Whichever property was changed at the later time wins the conflict. If the property timestamps are equal, the originating server GUIDs are checked for both properties. As GUIDs must be unique, these two values have to be unique, so the server arbitrarily takes the property change from the originating server with the higher GUID as canon.

Conflict due to a move of an object under a now deleted parent

This is a fairly easy conflict to resolve. In this case, the parent is deleted, but the object is moved to the Lost and Found Container, which was specially set up for this scenario. The ADsPath of the Lost and Found Container for Mycorp is:

```
LDAP://cn=LostAndFound,dc=mycorp,dc=com
```

Conflict due to creation of objects with names that conflict

The server starts reconciliation by looking at the version numbers of the two objects. Whichever object has the higher version number wins the conflict. If the object version numbers are equal, the server checks the timestamps of both objects. Whichever object was changed at the later time wins the conflict. If both object timestamps are equal, the originating server GUIDs are checked for both objects. The server simply takes the object change from the originating server with the higher GUID as canon.

In this case, however, the object that failed the conflict resolution is not lost or deleted, but is renamed with a unique value. That way, at the end of the resolution, both objects exist, with one having its conflicting name changed to a unique value. The unique name consists of the following format: *<DEFANGED_Object-Name<LineFeed>CNF:<DEFANGED_ObjectGUID>*.

Replicating the conflict resolution

Let's say that Server A starts a replication cycle. First it requests changes from Server B and receives updates. Then Server A requests changes from Server C and receives updates. However, as Server A is applying Server C's updates in order, it determines that a conflict has occurred between the updates recently applied by Server B. Server A resolves the conflict according to the preceding guidelines, and finds in Server C's favor. Now, while Server A and Server C are correct, Server B still needs to be updated with Server C's value.

To do this, when Server B next requests updates from Server A, it receives, among others, the update that originated on Server C. Server B then applies the updates it receives in sequence, and when it gets to the update that originated on Server C, it detects the same conflict. Server B then goes through the same conflict resolution procedure that Server A did and comes to the same result. Server B then modifies its own copy of the relevant NC to accommodate the change.

Additional problems occur when changes are made on a server and it goes down prior to replicating the changes. If the server never comes back up to replicate changes, those changes are lost.

Alternatively, if the server comes back up much later and attempts to replicate those changes back to Active Directory, there is a much greater chance of conflict resolution with that server failing the conflict, if many of the changes that were made on that server have subsequently been made in Active Directory more recently on other servers. This isn't a problem but is something you need to be aware of.

Summary

We've now looked at the importance of the site topology in Active Directory and how that relates to your physical network. We've also considered the metadata that governs the replication process, how the system keeps track of changes to objects and properties automatically, how data is replicated among servers including propagation dampening, and how conflicts are reconciled.

Later on, in Chapter 9, we take this knowledge further and show you how Active Directory manages and automatically generates the replication connections that exist both within and between sites. With that knowledge, we can move on to the design principles for sites and links in Active Directory.

CHAPTER 6

Active Directory and DNS

One of the big advantages of Active Directory over its predecessor, Windows NT, is the reliance on the Domain Name System (DNS) as opposed to the Windows Internet Naming Service (WINS) for name resolution. DNS is the ubiquitous, standards-based naming service used on the Internet. WINS, on the other hand, never garnered industry support and, because it is a proprietary Microsoft offering, was typically used only to support Windows NT NOS environments.

The good news is that with Active Directory the dependencies on WINS have been eliminated, but the potentially bad news is that Active Directory has a lot of dependencies on the DNS infrastructure. It is only potentially bad based on the flexibility of your DNS environment. Often, the groups that manage DNS and Active Directory within an organization are different, and getting the two teams to agree on implementation can be difficult due to political turf battles or technology clashes.

The intent of this chapter is to provide you with a good understanding of how Active Directory uses DNS and a description of some of the options for setting it up within your organization. We will briefly touch on some DNS basics but will not go into much depth on how to configure and administer the Windows DNS server. For more information on those topics, we highly recommend *DNS on Windows 2000* by Matt Larson and Cricket Liu (O'Reilly & Associates).

DNS Fundamentals

DNS is a hierarchical name resolution system. It is also the largest public directory service deployed. Virtually every company uses DNS for name resolution services, including hostname to IP address, IP address to hostname, and hostname to alternate hostname (aliases). DNS is a well-documented standard that has been around since the early days of the Internet. The RFCs in the following list cover some of the basics of DNS:

- RFC 1034, "Domain Names - Concepts and Facilities"
- RFC 1035, "Domain Names - Implementation and Specification"

- RFC 1912, "Common DNS Operational and Configuration Errors"
- RFC 1995, "Incremental Zone Transfer in DNS"
- RFC 1996, "A Mechanism for Prompt Notification of Zone Changes (DNS NOTIFY)"
- RFC 2181, "Clarifications to the DNS Specification"

There are three important DNS concepts that every Active Directory administrator must understand. Zones are delegated portions of the DNS namespace, resource records contain name resolution information, and dynamic DNS allows clients to add and delete resource records dynamically.

Zones

A zone is a collection of hierarchical domain names, the root of which has been delegated to one or more name servers. For example, let's say that the *mycorp.com* DNS namespace was delegated to *ns1.mycorp.com*. All domain names contained under *mycorp.com* that *ns1.mycorp.com* was authoritative for would be considered part of the *mycorp.com* zone. A subset of the *mycorp.com* zone could be delegated to another server, for example, *subdomain1.mycorp.com*, could be delegated to *ns2.mycorp.com*. At that point, *subdomain1.mycorp.com* becomes its own zone for which *ns2.mycorp.com* is authoritative.

The terms zone and domain are often confused in DNS parlance. A domain or domain name can actually be any type of name contained within a zone. The term zone has significance in relation to a portion of the namespace that has been delegated. A subdomain on one server may be a zone on another. The difference is determined by identifying the root of the contiguous namespace that was delegated.

Resource Records

A resource record is the unit of information in DNS. A zone is essentially a collection of resource records. There are various resource record types that define different types of name lookups. Table 6-1 lists some of the more common resource record types.

Table 6-1. Commonly used resource record types

Record type	Name	Description
A	Address Record	Maps a hostname to an IP address
PTR	Pointer Record	Maps an IP address to a hostname
CNAME	Alias Record	Maps an alias to a hostname
MX	Mail Exchanger Record	Specifies a mail route for a domain
NS	Name Server Record	Specifies name servers for a given domain

Table 6-1. Commonly used resource record types (continued)

Record type	Name	Description
SOA	Start of Authority Record	Contains administrative data about a zone, including the primary name server
SRV	Service Record	Maps a particular service (e.g., LDAP) to one or more hostnames

One important resource record to note is the SRV record type. SRV records are used extensively by domain controllers and Active Directory clients to locate servers that have a particular service. We will describe how Active Directory uses these records in more detail later in the chapter.

DDNS

Dynamic DNS, defined in RFC 2136, is a method for clients to send requests to a DNS server to add or delete resource records in a zone. Having this capability has greatly increased the supportability of DNS in large environments. Before DDNS, the primary means to update a zone was either by directly editing a text-based zone file or via a vendor supported GUI, such as the Windows DNS MMC snap-in.

 RFC 2136 can be found at *http://www.ietf.org/rfc/rfc2136.txt*.

Active Directory takes full advantage of DDNS to ease the burden of maintaining all of the resource records it requires. Each domain controller can have anywhere from a few dozen to a few hundred associated resource records depending on the size of the Active Directory site topology. And when the site topology changes, the resource records for a particular domain controller can also change. Because of the dynamic nature of the Active Directory resource records, in a large environment it could easily take a person working full time to manually maintain all the records.

DC Locator

One of the fundamental issues for clients in any NOS environment is finding the most optimal domain controller (DC) to authenticate against. The process under Windows NT was not very efficient and could cause clients to authenticate to domain controllers in the least optimal location. With Active Directory, clients use DNS to locate domain controllers via the DC locator process. To illustrate at a high level how the DC locator process works, we will describe an example where a client has moved from one location to another and needs to find a DC:

1. A client previously located in Site A logs in from Site B.
2. When the client boots up, it thinks it is still in Site A, so it proceeds to contact a DC in Site A using DNS unless the server name was previously cached.

Securing Your Dynamic Updates

The RFC that defined Dynamic DNS, RFC 2136, did not provide for a security model to secure updates from clients. As you might expect, this is a very serious limitation to widescale adoption. To address this problem, RFC 2137, "Secure Dynamic Update," was created. Unfortunately RFC 2137 was not very practical in implementation and tended to be overly complex. Later, RFC 2535, "Domain Name System Security Extensions," defined a public key–based method for securing DNS requests, commonly known as DNSSEC. RFC 3007 was then created, which obsoleted RFC 2137 and updated RFC 2535 to provide a more flexible method to secure update requests. Many DNS server products have only recently started to provide support for these RFCs, and only time will tell whether they will become widely adopted. Check out the following for more information on RFC 2535 and 3007:

> *http://www.ietf.org/rfc/rfc2535.txt*
> *http://www.ietf.org/rfc/rfc3007.txt*

While Windows Server 2003 provides support for some of the resource record types defined in RFC 2535, such as KEY, SIG and NXT, it does not provide full compliance, such as message signing and verification. The approach Microsoft takes to providing secure dynamic updates is by using ACLs in Active Directory. Zones that are Active Directory Integrated (described later in the chapter) store their DNS data in Active Directory. You can then set ACLs on the DNS-related objects in Active Directory to permit or deny users to update records. By default, authenticated computers in a forest can make new entries in a zone, and only the computer that created an entry is allowed to modify the data associated with that entry.

3. The DC in Site A receives the request and realizes that the client should now be talking to a DC in Site B due to its IP address changing. If the server does not cover Site B, it will return the clients new site in the reply.

4. The client will then perform a DNS lookup to find a DC in Site B.

5. The client then contacts the DC in Site B. Three things can happen: the DC responds and authenticates the client; the DC fails to respond (it could be down), and the client attempts to use a different DC in Site B; or the DC fails to respond, and the client searches and fails to find another DC in Site B, instead turning back to the DC in Site A and authenticating with the original server.

The two main things that are needed to support the DC locator process are proper definition of the site topology in Active Directory and containment of all the necessary Active Directory related resource records in DNS. In the next section, we will describe the purpose of the resource records used in Active Directory. For a more detailed description of how the DC locator process works, including the specific resource records that are queried during the process, check out Microsoft Knowlede Base (KB) article 247811 "How Domain Controllers Are Located in Windows" and

Microsoft KB article 314861 "How Domain Controllers Are Located in Windows XP" at *http://support.microsoft.com*.

Resource Records Used by Active Directory

When you promote a domain controller into a domain, a file containing the necessary resource records for it to function correctly within Active Directory is generated in *%SystemRoot%\System32\Config\netlogon.dns*.

The contents of the file will look something like the following for a DC named *moose.mycorp.com* in the *mycorp.com* domain with IP address 10.1.1.1. We've reordered the file a bit to group records of similar purpose together. Note that some lines may wrap due to their length.

```
mycorp.com. 600 IN A 10.1.1.1
ec4caf62-31b2-4773-bcce-7b1e31c04d25._msdcs.mycorp.com. 600 IN CNAME moose.mycorp.
com.
gc._msdcs.mycorp.com. 600 IN A 10.1.1.1
_gc._tcp.mycorp.com. 600 IN SRV 0 100 3268 moose.mycorp.com.
_gc._tcp.Default-First-Site-Name._sites.mycorp.com. 600 IN SRV 0 100 3268 moose.
mycorp.com.
_ldap._tcp.gc._msdcs.mycorp.com. 600 IN SRV 0 100 3268 moose.mycorp.com.
_ldap._tcp.Default-First-Site-Name._sites.gc._msdcs.mycorp.com. 600 IN SRV 0 100 3268
moose.mycorp.com.
_kerberos._tcp.dc._msdcs.mycorp.com. 600 IN SRV 0 100 88 moose.mycorp.com.
_kerberos._tcp.Default-First-Site-Name._sites.dc._msdcs.mycorp.com. 600 IN SRV 0 100
88 moose.mycorp.com.
_kerberos._tcp.mycorp.com. 600 IN SRV 0 100 88 moose.mycorp.com.
_kerberos._tcp.Default-First-Site-Name._sites.mycorp.com. 600 IN SRV 0 100 88 moose.
mycorp.com.
_kerberos._udp.mycorp.com. 600 IN SRV 0 100 88 moose.mycorp.com.
_kpasswd._tcp.mycorp.com. 600 IN SRV 0 100 464 moose.mycorp.com.
_kpasswd._udp.mycorp.com. 600 IN SRV 0 100 464 moose.mycorp.com.
_ldap._tcp.mycorp.com. 600 IN SRV 0 100 389 moose.mycorp.com.
_ldap._tcp.Default-First-Site-Name._sites.mycorp.com. 600 IN SRV 0 100 389 moose.
mycorp.com.
_ldap._tcp.pdc._msdcs.mycorp.com. 600 IN SRV 0 100 389 moose.mycorp.com.
_ldap._tcp.97526bc9-adf7-4ec8-a096-0dbb34a17052.domains._msdcs.mycorp.com. 600 IN SRV
0 100 389 moose.mycorp.com.
_ldap._tcp.dc._msdcs.mycorp.com. 600 IN SRV 0 100 389 moose.mycorp.com.
_ldap._tcp.Default-First-Site-Name._sites.dc._msdcs.mycorp.com. 600 IN SRV 0 100 389
moose.mycorp.com.
```

While it may look complicated, it isn't. Let's go through what these records actually mean, splitting the records up into sections for ease of understanding. To start with, the first record is for the domain itself:

```
mycorp.com. 600 IN A 10.1.1.1
```

Each DC attempts to register an A record for its IP address for the domain it is in. A quick and easy way to get a list of all the domain controllers in a domain is to simply look up the A record for the domain name. We will now walk through that query to show the domain controllers that have registered an A record for the *mycorp.com* domain:

```
> nslookup mycorp.com
Server:  moose.mycorp.com
Address:  10.1.1.1

Name:     mycorp.com
Addresses: 10.1.1.1, 10.1.1.2, 10.1.1.3

> nslookup 10.1.1.1
Server:  moose.mycorp.com
Address:  10.1.1.1

Name:     moose.mycorp.com
Addresses: 10.1.1.1

> nslookup 10.1.1.2
Server:  moose.mycorp.com
Address:  10.1.1.1

Name:     deer.mycorp.com
Addresses: 10.1.1.2

> nslookup 10.1.1.3
Server:  moose.mycorp.com
Address:  10.1.1.1

Name:     elk.mycorp.com
Addresses: 10.1.1.3
```

Next we have the following record:

```
ec4caf62-31b2-4773-bcce-7b1e31c04d25._msdcs.mycorp.com. 600 IN CNAME moose.mycorp.
com.
```

This is an alias or canonical name (CNAME) record. It is contained under the _msdcs subdomain, which is used by domain controllers to intercommunicate. The record is comprised of the GUID for the server, which is an alias for the server itself. DCs use this record if they know the GUID of a server and want to determine its hostname.

Next we have this A record:

```
gc._msdcs.mycorp.com. 600 IN A 10.1.1.1
```

This is registered only if the DC is a Global Catalog server. You can query *gc._msdcs. mycorp.com* to obtain a list of all the Global Catalog servers in the forest in much the same way you could query the domain name to get a list of all the domain controllers for a domain.

The remaining records are of type SRV. The SRV record type was defined in RFC 2052, "A DNS RR for Specifying the Location of Services (DNS SRV)." The full text can be found at *http://www.ietf.org/rfc/rfc2052.txt*. Simply put, SRV records allow you to specify server(s) on your network that should be used for specific protocols. These records also allow you to remap the port numbers for individual protocols or the priority in which certain servers are used.

There a few more Global Catalog specific records shown next:

```
_gc._tcp.mycorp.com. 600 IN SRV 0 100 3268 moose.mycorp.com.
_gc._tcp.Default-First-Site-Name._sites.mycorp.com. 600 IN SRV 0 100 3268 moose.
mycorp.com.
_ldap._tcp.gc._msdcs.mycorp.com. 600 IN SRV 0 100 3268 moose.mycorp.com.
_ldap._tcp.Default-First-Site-Name._sites.gc._msdcs.mycorp.com. 600 IN SRV 0 100 3268
moose.mycorp.com.
```

One interesting thing to note about SRV records is the seventh field, which is used for the port for the service. In every case above, 3268 is used, which corresponds to the Global Catalog port. You may have also noticed the entries that contain Default-First-Site-Name. Each Global Catalog server registers site-specific records so clients can find the optimal Global Catalog based on their site membership. See the "Site Coverage" sidebar for more information.

Site Coverage

You can create sites in the Active Directory site topology that do not have domain controllers that are located in the site. In this situation, the domain controllers that have the best connections as defined by the site links will "cover" for that site. When a DC covers for a site, it will add site-specific SRV records so that it will advertise itself as a DC that can handle queries for clients in the site. To see a list of the sites that a particular DC is covering for, run the following NLTEST command and replace dc01 with the name of the DC you want to query:

```
c:\> nltest /dsgetsitecov /server:dc01
```

NLTEST is part of the Windows Support Tools.

The next few SRV records are for Kerberos authentication (port 88) and the Kpasswd process (port 464), which allows users to change passwords via Kerberos:

```
_kerberos._tcp.dc._msdcs.mycorp.com. 600 IN SRV 0 100 88 moose.mycorp.com.
_kerberos._tcp.Default-First-Site-Name._sites.dc._msdcs.mycorp.com. 600 IN SRV 0 100
88 moose.mycorp.com.
_kerberos._tcp.mycorp.com. 600 IN SRV 0 100 88 moose.mycorp.com.
_kerberos._tcp.Default-First-Site-Name._sites.mycorp.com. 600 IN SRV 0 100 88 moose.
mycorp.com.
_kerberos._udp.mycorp.com. 600 IN SRV 0 100 88 moose.mycorp.com.
_kpasswd._tcp.mycorp.com. 600 IN SRV 0 100 464 moose.mycorp.com.
_kpasswd._udp.mycorp.com. 600 IN SRV 0 100 464 moose.mycorp.com.
```

Just as with the Global Catalog SRV records, there may be more of the site-specific Kerberos records for any additional sites the DC covers.

The rest of the SRV records are used to represent a domain controller for a particular domain and site. One record to note is the _ldap._tcp.pdc._msdcs.mycorp.com._ entry, which is registered by the DC that is acting as the PDC Emulator for the domain. No other FSMO roles are registered in DNS.

```
_ldap._tcp.mycorp.com. 600 IN SRV 0 100 389 moose.mycorp.com.
_ldap._tcp.Default-First-Site-Name._sites.mycorp.com. 600 IN SRV 0 100 389 moose.
mycorp.com.
_ldap._tcp.pdc._msdcs.mycorp.com. 600 IN SRV 0 100 389 moose.mycorp.com.
_ldap._tcp.97526bc9-adf7-4ec8-a096-0dbb34a17052.domains._msdcs.mycorp.com. 600 IN SRV
0 100 389 moose.mycorp.com.
_ldap._tcp.dc._msdcs.mycorp.com. 600 IN SRV 0 100 389 moose.mycorp.com.
_ldap._tcp.Default-First-Site-Name._sites.dc._msdcs.mycorp.com. 600 IN SRV 0 100 389
moose.mycorp.com.
```

Based on all these records, you can obtain a lot of information about an Active Directory environment by doing simple DNS queries. Some of the information you can retrieve includes:

- All Global Catalog servers in a forest or a particular site
- All Kerberos servers in a domain or a particular site
- All domain controllers in a domain or a particular site
- The PDC Emulator for a domain

Delegation Options

Now that we've covered what Active Directory uses DNS for, we will review some of the options for setting up who is authoritative for the Active Directory–related zones. Ultimately, the decision boils down to whether you want to use your existing DNS servers or different servers, such as the domain controllers, to be authoritative for the zones. There are many factors that can affect this decision, including:

- Political turf battles between the AD and DNS teams
- Initial setup and configuration of the zones
- Support and maintenance of the zones
- Integration issues with existing administration software and practices

We will look at each of these factors as they apply to delegating the AD zones. Other slight variations of these options do exist, but we will discuss only the basic cases.

Not Delegating the AD DNS Zones

The first impulse of any cost-conscious organization should be to determine whether the existing DNS servers can be authoritative for the AD zones. That would entail populating all the necessary resource records required by each DC. While this sounds fairly trivial, there are several issues to be aware of.

Political factors

By utilizing the existing DNS servers for the AD DNS zones, the AD administrators will likely not have the same level of control as they would if the zones were delegated and managed by them. While it does limit the scope of control for a crucial service used by Active Directory, some AD administrators may find it a blessing!

Initial setup and configuration

The initial population of the AD resource records can be burdensome depending on how you manage your resource records and how easy it will be for you to inject new ones. The domain controllers try to register their resource records via DDNS on a periodic basis. Most organizations do not allow just any client to make DDNS updates due to the potential security risks. For that reason, you'll need to configure your existing DNS servers to allow the domain controllers to perform DDNS updates. And unless you restrict which zones the domain controllers can send DDNS updates for, it opens a potential security hole. If a domain controller can update any zone, an AD administrator could conceivably perform individual updates for any record in any zone while logged onto that DC. This should not typically be a problem, but depending on how paranoid the DNS administrators are, it could be a point of contention.

Support and maintenance

Assuming the existing DNS servers are stable and well supported (as they tend to be in most organizations), name resolution issues should not be a problem for AD DCs or other clients that are attempting to locate a DC via DNS. Ongoing maintenance of the DC resource records can be an issue, as pointed out previously. Each time you promote a new DC in the forest, you'll need to make sure it is allowed to register all of its records via DDNS. The registration of these records could be done manually, but due to the dynamic nature of the AD resource records, they would have to be updated on a very frequent basis (potentially multiple times a day). Yet another option is to programmatically retrieve the *netlogon.dns* file from each domain controller on a periodic basis and perform the DDNS updates from a script. In large environments, the manual solution will probably not scale, and either DDNS or a programmatic solution will need to be explored.

Integration issues

When Windows 2000 Active Directory was first released in 1999, this was more of a problem than it is today, but if you are running older versions of DNS server or administration software, it may not support SRV records or underscores in zone names (e.g., *_msdcs.mycorp.com*). Upgrading to the latest versions should be a priority in this case.

Figure 6-1 shows how the client request process is straightforward when the AD DNS zones are not delegated. Clients point at the same DNS servers they always have.

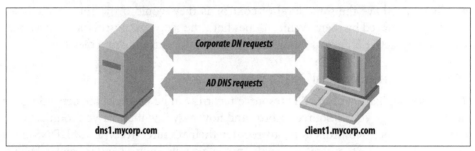

Figure 6-1. Client request flow when the AD DNS zones are not delegated

Delegating the AD DNS Zones

While at first glance it may seem pretty straightforward to support AD DNS zones in your existing DNS infrastructure, it can cause difficulties depending on your environment. Perhaps the most straightforward option is simply to delegate the AD zones to the domain controllers to manage. And if you use AD Integrated DNS zones, the maintenance becomes even easier. After you've done the initial creation of the zones by promoting a DC and adding the DNS service, the records are stored in AD and distributed to the other DCs via replication.

Political factors

These days most organizations have a central DNS team that manages and supports name resolution. If you make the decision to delegate the AD DNS zones to domain controllers, for example, a significant part of name resolution for your clients will not be done on the existing corporate servers. This can make the DNS administrators uncomfortable and rightly so.

Initial setup and configuration

The initial setup to delegate the AD DNS zones is straightforward. An NS record and any necessary glue records—for example, an A record for the server to which you're delegating—need to exist on the parent zone pointing to the servers that will be authoritative for the zones. The rest of the configuration must be done on the servers that are going to support the AD DNS zones. If that is one or more domain controllers, you will only need to add the DNS service and create the zone(s) on those servers.

Support and maintenance

Especially if you are using AD-integrated zones, ongoing support and maintenance of the AD DNS zones is very minimal. In fact, since the domain controllers can use DDNS to update each other, this is one of the primary benefits of using this method.

Integration issues

Unless you already run Windows DNS Server, it is unlikely you'll be able to manage the AD DNS zones in the same manner as your primary DNS. Figure 6-2 illustrates that by delegating the AD DNS zones, you can still have clients point to the same DNS servers they do today. A variation of this approach would be to point the clients at the AD DNS servers and configure forwarding as described in the next section.

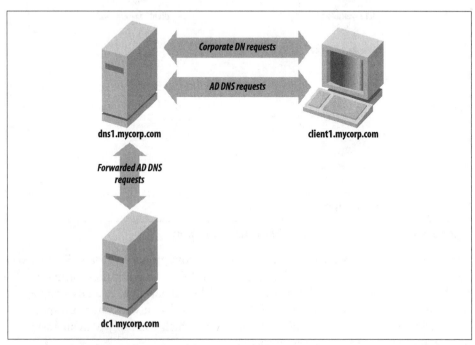

Figure 6-2. Client request flow when delegating the AD DNS zones

DNS for Standalone AD

Another scenario that is worth mentioning is creating a standalone Active Directory environment. By standalone, we mean an environment that can be set up without requiring your DNS admins to either create or delegate zones on the corporate DNS servers. This is often needed when setting up lab or test forests, which may be short-lived. Figure 6-3 shows that the resolver for the clients must be pointed to the AD DNS servers in this scenario or they will not be able to locate any domain controllers for the forest.

To set up a standalone environment, you simply need to install the DNS service on one or more domain controllers in the forest, add the DNS zones for the AD domains (for example *mycorp.local*), and then configure the DNS server to forward unresolved queries to one or more of your existing corporate DNS servers. Figures 6-4 and 6-5 show the screens from the DNS MMC snap-in for Windows 2000 and Win-

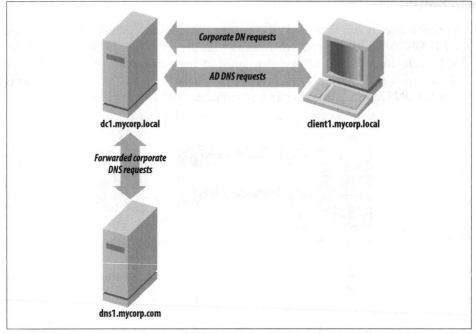

Figure 6-3. Client request flow in a standalone AD environment

dows Server 2003, respectively, that allow you to configure forwarders. Finally, you need to configure any clients of the mycorp.local forest to point their primary DNS resolver at the IP address of *dc1.mycorp.local*. When client1 makes a DNS request, it would first be sent to *dc1.mycorp.local*. If dc1 can resolve, it will return a response; if not, it will forward the query to *dns1.mycorp.com*, which will reply with an answer to dc1, who will then send the reply to client1.

The great thing about this configuration is that it requires nothing to be set up on the existing DNS servers. Since you will need to modify the DNS resolvers that clients point to, you may want to look at using a Group Policy Object (GPO). In Windows Server 2003, you can configure client DNS settings through GPOs for Windows Server 2003 servers and Windows XP workstations. The new settings allow you to control things such as client DNS suffix, DNS resolvers, and DDNS behavior.

> In this scenario, if the clients do not point at *dc1.mycorp.local* as their first resolver, they will never be able to contact the mycorp.local forest. The reason is that the corporate name servers do not know about the *mycorp.local* namespace since it was not delegated.

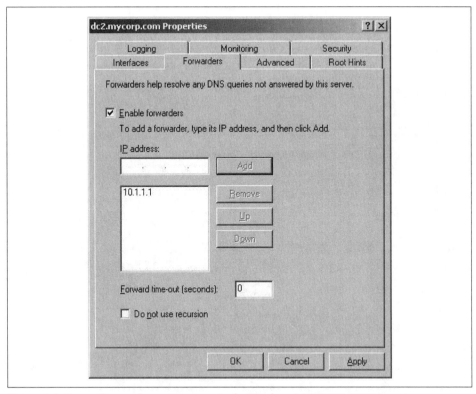

Figure 6-4. Forwarders configuration screen in the Windows 2000 DNS MMC snap-in

Active Directory Integrated DNS

If you've decided to host the AD DNS zones on your domain controllers, you should strongly consider using AD integrated zones. This section will explain some of the benefits of using AD integrated DNS versus standard primary zones.

In the normal world of DNS, you have two types of name servers: primary and secondary (a.k.a. slaves). The primary name server for a zone holds the data for the zone in a file on the host and reads the entries from there. Each zone typically has only one primary. A secondary gets the contents of its zone from the primary that is authoritative for the zone. Each primary name server can have multiple secondary name servers. When a secondary starts up, it contacts its primary and requests a copy of the relevant zone via zone transfer. The contents of the secondary file are then dynamically updated over time according to a set scheme. This is normally a periodic update or triggered automatically by a message from the primary stating that it has received an update. This is a very simplified picture, as each name server can host multiple zones, allowing each server to have a primary role for some zones and a secondary for others.

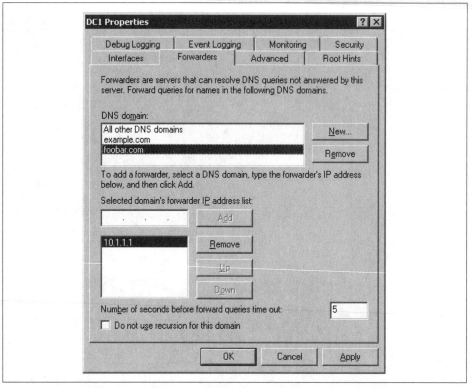

Figure 6-5. Forwarders configuration screen in the Windows Server 2003 DNS MMC snap-in

---

Conditional Forwarding

Conditional forwarding is a new feature available in Windows Server 2003; it gives administrators much more flexibility over how forwarding is handled than was available under Windows 2000. Figure 6-4 shows the forwarders configuration screen in the Windows 2000 MMC snap-in. It allows you to set up one or more IP addresses to forward all requests that cannot be handled by the local DNS server. Figure 6-5 shows the same configuration screen, but on Windows Server 2003. As you can see, we configured forwarding based on the domain name being queried.

- If query is for *foobar.com*, forward to 10.1.1.1.
- If the query is for *example.com*, forward to 10.1.2.1.
- If the query is for any other zone, forward to 10.1.3.1.

Conditional forwarding allows you to create a more efficient resolution topology by sending queries directly to servers responsible for the zones instead of using recursive queries to the Internet.

Each type of server can resolve name queries that come in. However, if a change must be made to the underlying contents of the DNS file, it has to be made on the primary name server for that zone. Secondary name servers cannot accept updates.*

Another option available with Active Directory and Windows DNS server is to integrate your DNS data into Active Directory. Effectively, this means that you can store the contents of the zone file in Active Directory as a hierarchical structure. Integrating DNS into Active Directory means that the DNS structure is replicated among all DCs of a domain. Each DC holds a writeable copy of the DNS data. The DNS objects stored in Active Directory could be updated on any DC via LDAP operations or through DDNS against DCs that are acting as DNS servers. This effectively makes the entire set of DCs act like primary name servers, where each DC can write to the zone and issue authoritative answers for the zone. This is a far cry from the standard model of one primary name server and one or more secondary name servers, which has the obvious downside of a single point of failure for updates to DNS.

Replication Impact

While AD Integrated DNS has many advantages, the one potential drawback is how DNS data gets replicated in Active Directory. Under Windows 2000, AD Integrated zones are stored in the System container for a domain. That means that every domain controller in that domain will replicate that zone data regardless of whether the domain controller is a DNS server. For domain controllers that are not DNS servers, there is no benefit to replicating the data. Fortunately, there is a better alternative in Windows Server 2003, using application partitions as described in the next section.

Using Application Partitions for DNS

Application partitions, as described in Chapter 3, are user-defined partitions that have customized replication scope. Domain controllers that are configured to contain replicas of an application partition will be the only servers that replicate the data contained within the partition. One of the benefits of application partitions is that they are not limited by domain boundaries. You can configure domain controllers in completely different domains to replicate an application partition. It is for these reasons that application partitions make a lot of sense for storing AD Integrated DNS zones. No longer do you have to store DNS data within the domain context and replicate to every domain controller in the domain, even if only a handful are DNS servers. With application partitions you can configure Active Directory to replicate only

---

* This isn't strictly true. While slaves cannot process updates, they can and do forward updates that they receive to the primary name server.

the DNS data between the domain controllers running the DNS service within a domain or forest.

When installing a new Windows Server 2003 Active Directory forest, the default DNS application partitions are created automatically. If you are upgrading from Windows 2000, you can manually create them by using the DNS MMC snap-in or the *dnscmd.exe* utility. There is one default application partition for each domain and forest. When configuring an AD Integrated zone in a Windows Server 2003 forest, you have several options for storing the DNS data. These options are listed in Table 6-2.

Table 6-2. Active Directory Integrated DNS zone storage options

Distinguished name	Replication scope
cn=System,*DomainDN* Example: cn=System,dc=amer,dc=mycorp,dc=com	To all domain controllers in the domain. This is the only storage method available under Windows 2000.
dc=domaindnszones,*DomainDN* Example: dc=domaindnszones,dc=amer, dc=mycorp,dc=com	To domain controllers in the domain that are also DNS servers.
dc=forestdnszones,*ForestDN* Example: dc=forestdnszones,dc=mycorp,dc=com	To domain controllers in the forest that are also DNS servers.
AppPartitionDN Example: dc=dnsdata,dc=mycorp,dc=com	To domain controllers that have been configured to replicate the application partition.

Summary

Active Directory relies heavily on DNS. In fact, Microsoft has shifted completely away from WINS for name resolution within the NOS in favor of standards-based DNS. The DC locator process is a core DNS-based function used within Active Directory to help domain controllers and clients locate domain controllers that have certain properties, such as residing in a particular site or being a Global Catalog server or PDC emulator. Deciding how to manage the AD DNS zones can be a difficult decision, with each option having its own advantages and disadvantages. If you delegate the zones to domain controllers, AD Integrated zones can save a lot of time in maintenance and upkeep. In Windows Server 2003, you can use application partitions to replicate AD Integrated zones to only the domain controllers that are acting as DNS servers. This can greatly reduce replication traffic in some situations compared to Windows 2000 Active Directory, which replicated DNS data to every domain controller in a domain regardless of whether it was a DNS server.

CHAPTER 7

Profiles and Group Policy Primer

Profiles and group policies are large topics, and they are worth treating properly so that you get the most from them in your environment. The goal of policy-based administration is for an administrator to define the environment for users and computers once, then rely on the system to enforce that state. Under Windows NT, this could be very challenging, but with Active Directory group policies, this capability is much more readily available. This chapter is the introduction to the subject, and Chapter 10 builds on it to show how policies work in Active Directory, how to design an OU structure to incorporate them effectively, and how to manage them with the Group Policy Management Console, a new MMC snap-in available for Windows Server 2003 Active Directory.

In Windows NT, system policies had a number of limitations. System policies:

- Were set at the domain level
- Were not secure
- Could only apply to users, groups of users, or computers
- Tended to set values until another policy specifically unset them
- Were limited to desktop lockdown

The scope and functionality of Active Directory group policies is much greater than system policies. Group policies:

- Can be applied to individual clients, sites, domains, and Organizational Units
- Are highly secure
- Can apply to users, computers, or groups of either
- Can set values and automatically unset them in specified situations
- Can do far more than just a desktop lockdown

With group policies, an administrator can define a large number of detailed settings to be enforced on users throughout the organization, and he can be confident that the system will take care of things. Let's take a simple example from Leicester University. Administrators wanted the Systems Administrator toolset, which normally is installed only on servers, to be available on workstations also. While they could install these tools on their own PCs, they actually wanted the tools to follow them around the network and be available from any PC that they chose to log on from. However, they didn't want to leave these tools installed on that PC when they logged off. Prior to Active Directory, the admins would have had to arrive at a client, log on, install the toolset, do whatever was required at a client, uninstall the toolset, and finally log off. This would be a considerable chore for a large number of machines. Active Directory group policies can be used to specify that the toolset is to be automatically installed on any client that an administrator logs on to. That way, an administrator could go straight to the Start menu and find the tools available. After logging off, the same group policy would uninstall the toolset from the machine.

Let's take another example. At Leicester University, a central logon script was used for every user. This is no different than under Windows NT. However, extra logon scripts for some sets of users were also applied based on which Organizational Unit the users were in. So some users get more than one logon script depending on where in Active Directory their accounts reside. That's a significant step forward from Windows NT, but the possibilities don't end there. A logoff script was also specified to run when a user logged off the system. Workstations also can have scripts, but instead of executing at logon and logoff, these scripts run at startup and shutdown. Want to install a new Dynamic Link Library (DLL) on all clients? You could use a startup script to do it. Have a desire to start a normally disabled service on a series of workstations? You could create a startup script that starts that service and apply it through group policy. Of course, as you've probably guessed, this startup script runs in addition to any other startup scripts, such as a central script for all workstations. So, rather than a single user logon script available for Windows NT, we now have multiple user logon/logoff scripts and multiple workstation startup/shutdown scripts, all of which can be customized using any of the data within Active Directory. And with Windows Server 2003 Active Directory, you can even use WMI filtering, which allows you to use any of the vast amount of data available in WMI to specify criteria for when group policies are applied.

Let's consider a final example. You are required to set the RunOnce registry key value for every client in your organization so that they can all receive an organization-wide company video broadcast from the chairman and CEO. You can set up a simple group policy with the customized registry changes configured and apply it to every computer in your organization. At present, this functionality may seem no different from what you could have achieved with Windows NT system policies. You apply these changes one evening, and the next morning, 20,000 workstations across your network can be rebooted so that they receive this policy on startup. The group policy applies and the settings are changed. However, if about an hour after you made the change you realize that one of the values in the registry needs to be changed again, you don't want to force 20,000 clients to reboot, as was necessary under Windows NT. And with Active Directory you don't have to. You can specify that this policy be reapplied every 15 minutes to all workstations after they have booted. You can make the change to the group policies and sit back, knowing that within 15–45 minutes,* every workstation will receive the policy again with the updated change.

With examples like these, it becomes quite easy to see the power of group policies. While some of the examples can be accomplished under Windows NT, it would require a lot more time and effort to achieve than with Active Directory's group policy.

Now that we've covered a few examples, lets dive into the details of profiles and group policies.

 Group policies are normally referred to simply as GPOs, corresponding to the term *group policy objects*.

A Profile Primer

Profiles and group policies are tightly related, but they serve completely different functions. To make things clear, we'll cover the essentials of profiles so that you can understand how to manipulate them using group policies.

Let's consider a Windows XP workstation with a newly created account for a user named Richard Lang with the username RLang. When Richard logs on to the client, the system creates a profile directory for him, corresponding to his username, in the *Documents and Settings* directory. If Richard were to log on to a Windows NT workstation or to a Windows 2000 workstation that was upgraded from a previous version of Windows NT, the profile would be created under the *%systemroot%\Profiles*† directory. On a fresh Windows 2000 install or Windows XP, the profiles are stored under *%systemdrive%\Document and Settings*.

Inside this directory, the system places a file called *NTUSER.DAT*, along with various other data files. Let's concentrate on the *NTUSER.DAT* file for a moment. This file contains what is known generally as the user portion of the registry. All Windows-based operating systems have a registry that consists of two parts: the so-called user portion represented by the file *NTUSER.DAT* (or *USER.DAT* on Windows *9x* systems) and the system or computer portion of the registry, which is stored in *%systemroot%\system32\config*. The user part of the registry holds information indi-

---

* A random time interval of 0–30 minutes is added so that all workstations do not attempt to download the policy at the same time.

† *%systemroot%* is the system environment variable that refers to the location of the Windows operating system files. If Windows NT were installed on drive C: in the normal way, *%systemroot%* would be *C:\WINNT*. The *%systemdrive%* variable contains the drive letter of the drive the operating system was installed on.

cating what screensaver should be used for that user; what colors, background, and event sounds are set; where the user's *My Documents* folder points to; and so on. The system portion of the registry holds hardware device settings, installed software information, and so on. When a user logs on to a client, the combined effects of the settings for the machine held in the system portion of the registry and the settings for the user held in the user portion of the registry take effect.

When you use a tool such as *REGEDIT.EXE* or *REGEDT32.EXE* to examine the registry on a machine, both portions of the registry are opened and displayed together for you to look at within one tool.

> The two registry tools were developed with different requirements in mind, but with Windows Server 2003 they have been merged. The REGEDIT tool was developed initially for Windows 9x clients and thus allows for management of the datatypes as well as for rapid searching for any key or value that contains a given word or phrase. REGEDT32, on the other hand, was designed to support the extra datatypes present in Windows NT and Windows 2000. However, REGEDT32 had an awful search mechanism that allowed searches only through keys. In Windows Server 2003, REGEDIT was updated to support many of the features present in REGEDT32. Now if you run REGEDT32, you will bring up the REGEDIT interface.

Figure 7-1 shows a view of the registry on a Windows 2000 client when viewed from REGEDIT. The screenshot also shows the five registry hives (as they are known) available to Windows 2000. The two important hives are HKEY_LOCAL_MACHINE, also known as HKLM, which corresponds to the system part of the registry, and HKEY_CURRENT_USER, also known as HKCU, which corresponds to the user portion of the registry.

When Richard logs on to the local client for the first time, the file is copied from the Default User profile directory that already exists on the machine under *Documents and Settings*. During Richard's first logon, the system also creates a series of directories under Richard's profile directory with names like *My Documents*, *Start Menu*, *Desktop*, and so on. If Richard ever places an icon on the desktop or saves a file from NotePad to the *My Documents* folder, the data is placed inside the relevant folders in Richard's profile. The *Start Menu* folder holds the Start menu structure that Richard sees when he clicks the Start button.

The Default User and All User Folders

The default contents placed inside all these folders in Richard's profile come directly from the same folders in the Default User profile. When Richard logs on, however, he may see icons or folders inside *My Documents*, *Start Menu*, and *Desktop* that do not appear in his own profile directories. These extra items are displayed as if they

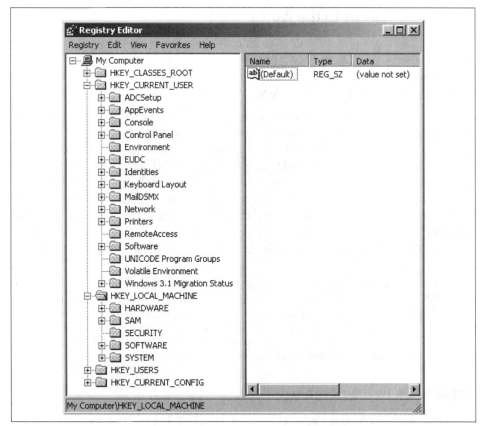

Figure 7-1. A REGEDIT view of the registry on a Windows 2000 Professional client

were part of Richard's profile, but they are part of the All Users profile that also resides on the computer. In fact, the settings from the *All Users\NTUSER.DAT* file also are available to Richard. The All Users profile is a great way of adding new items to every user's profile on the client without having to add each item manually. During installation, NT-aware software tends to ask whether the installation is just for the user installing the software or for all users of the client. If the software is told that it is for all users, it modifies the All Users profile.

To recap, when Richard logs on for the first time, a profile directory called *Documents and Settings\Rlang* is created for him, and everything from the *Documents and Settings\Default User* profile is copied into it. Richard's profile now contains an *NTUSER.DAT* file that contains all of his user settings, as well as a series of folders representing his Desktop, Start Menu, and My Documents folder, among others. In addition to any files or folders copied from the Default User profile, Richard also seamlessly sees all of the items corresponding to the *Documents and Settings\All Users* profile, although they will not exist in his own *Rlang* directory hierarchy. He also may not be able to remove or delete the files and shortcuts if he doesn't have the permission to do so.

Logging On Locally to the Workstation

Windows 2000 and later machines store much more data in Richard's profile than Windows NT or Windows 9x would. In addition, more registry keys have been added to both portions of the registry to enable much more fine-grained control over what happens in a profile. We'll have more to say about that later.

If Richard logs off and then on again, the system will detect that he already has a profile folder on the workstation and will continue to use that rather than create a new one. That is why when Richard creates a desktop file and logs off and on again, the file is still visible on Richard's desktop. If Richard logs off and an administrator logs on and installs software, the software is likely to install itself into the All Users profile, adding folders and files and changing the registry as required. When the administrator logs off and Richard logs back on, the new software in the All Users profile will be available to him as if it were part of his own profile; this includes providing any All Users *NTUSER.DAT* HKCU registry settings that he may need for the application.

 As the registry settings are held in the All Users profile, you might think that Richard cannot change them. This is not the case. As soon as he changes a setting, the system writes it out to his own registry, and this will override any future value for that setting from the All Users profile. Richard's profile will thus contain only the customizations that override the defaults passed in from the All Users profile.

Logging On to the Domain

Now let's say that Richard instead logs on to a Windows NT or Active Directory domain. If you set the system up in the standard manner, when Richard logs on to the domain for the first time, he is given a profile directory on the local workstation that he logs on to. In exactly the same manner as a logon to the workstation itself, this new profile is made from the Default User and All User profiles on the workstation. When Richard logs off, his profile stays at the workstation. If he then logs on to the domain from another workstation, he has a new profile created for him on that workstation. If Richard then logs off from this workstation and logs on at another, he gets a third profile created. Finally, if he logs back on to the first workstation, he will get the profile that he used there last. This default scenario is very limiting, and domain-based logins provide three key profile technologies for domain usage. You need to be aware of these technologies to manipulate profiles to work in a better manner for your organization:

- Roaming profiles
- Cached profile deletion
- Relocation of the Default User profile

Having profiles stored on each workstation makes little sense. It would make a lot more sense to store the profiles centrally and have them accessible from anywhere on the network. Roaming profiles make this possible. Under Windows NT, you simply filled in the relevant profile field for a user in the User Manager for Domains tool and pointed the new location at a share for that user. Under Active Directory, you use the Active Directory Users and Computers (ADUC) tool, but the concept is the same. If you did this for Richard, the system would detect at his first logon that he did not currently have a roaming profile, and his profile would be created on the workstation as before. However, when he logged out, his profile would be copied to the network location to become his roaming profile. Then when he logged back on again from anywhere on the network, including Terminal Service connections, his new profile on the network share would be downloaded to the workstation for him to use. This download on logon and upload on logout continues throughout the lifetime of the account, provided the account's profile property is not deleted.

Cached Profile Deletion

One problem can come up with this scenario. First, if Richard logs on at a hundred workstations throughout the life of the account, a hundred copies of his profile at various stages of development will exist, one on each of the hundred workstations. To combat this, administrators can set a registry key on the workstations that forces them to discard the profile after the roaming profile upload on logout. The key is held in the system part of the registry and is the same in Windows NT as in Windows 2000 and Windows XP. Setting it to a DWORDvalue of 1 turns it on:

> HKLM\SOFTWARE\Microsoft\WindowsNT\CurrentVersion\Winlogon\
> DeleteRoamingCache

This setting needs to be applied to all the computers from which you wish to delete cached profiles. The fastest way to implement such a change in an Active Directory environment is to use a GPO, unless you relish changing the registry manually on every client. You simply make this one change centrally and then have it roll out to all computers that you wish to affect. Under Active Directory, you do not even need to know that this is the key in the registry that is being modified, as this is one of the many default computer options that are available from the GUI, which hides the actual registry keys and values that you are changing.

A Server-Based Default User Profile

If you want to change a setting in the user portion of the registry or add a new icon to the desktop for all new users, you ordinarily need to modify the Default User profile on every client. In large environments, this is really an unacceptable solution. The simpler solution would be to store a centrally located copy of the Default User profile that the users automatically download on first logon. That way, if you need to make a change, you need to make it only on the centrally stored copy and not on every client. This can be achieved by placing the Default User profile in the *NETLOGON* share. Previously, we said that when the user logs on to the domain for the first time, the system copies the Default User profile from the client workstation. That is, in fact, true only when a Default User profile does not exist in the *NETLOGON* share; if a central Default User profile does reside in the *NETLOGON* share, that is used in creating the user's own profile.

 By default, the directory that NETLOGON actually refers to under Windows NT is *%systemroot%\system32\repl\import\scripts* and under Active Directory is *%systemroot%\SYSVOL\<ADDomainName>\ SCRIPTS*.

The basic point is that while Windows 2000 and Windows XP profiles may be stored under different locations, store more data, and be more customizable than Windows NT profiles, they work on the same principles as their direct predecessors.

This is not true when comparing Windows NT system policies and Active Directory group policies. We'll now cover some of the capabilities of group policies, which have not been available previously.

Capabilities of GPOs

GPOs can be edited using the Group Policy Object Editor (GPOE), formerly the-Group Policy Editor (GPE), which is an MMC snap-in. The GPOE is limited to managing a single GPO at a time and cannot be used to link a GPO. For this reason, Microsoft developed the Group Policy Management Console (GPMC) MMC snap-in, which was released around the same time as Windows Server 2003, as a web download from *http://download.microsoft.com*. The GPMC provides a single interface to manage all aspects of GPOs, including editing (through the GPOE), viewing the resultant set of policies (RSOP), and linking to domains, sites, and OUs. We will cover these tools in much more detail in Chapter 10.

Most settings in a GPO have three states: enabled, disabled, and unconfigured. By default, all settings in a GPO are unconfigured. Any unconfigured settings are ignored during application, so the GPO comes into play only when settings have actually been configured. Each setting needs to be configured as enabled or disabled before it can be used, and in some cases the option needs no other parameters. In other cases, a host of information must be entered to configure the option; it all depends on what the option itself does.

Enabling and disabling most options is fairly straightforward. However, due to Microsoft's choice for the names of certain settings for GPOs, you actually can have the choice of enabling or disabling options with names like "Disable Access to This Option". By default, this setting isn't in use, but you can disable the disable option (i.e., enable the option) or enable the disable option (i.e., disable the option). Be careful and make sure you know which way the setting is applied before you actually go through with the change.

GPOs can apply a very large number of changes to computers and users that are in Active Directory. These changes are grouped together within the GPOE under the three headings of Software Settings, Windows Settings, and Administrative Templates. There are two sets of these headings, one under Computer Configuration and one under User Configuration. The items under the three headings differ, as the settings that apply to users and to computers are not the same.

Some of the settings under Administrative Templates would look more sensible under the other two sections. However, the Administrative Templates section holds data that is entirely generated from the Administrative Template (ADM) files in the system volume; so it makes more sense to include all the ADM data together. ADM files contain the entire set of options available for each setting, including explanations that are shown on the various property pages in the GPOE.

 ADM files can be added and removed by right-clicking either Administrative Template location in the GPOE and choosing Add/Remove Templates. Very comprehensive information on customizing GPOs and adding in your own templates can be found in Microsoft's Windows 2000 Group Policy technical white paper. Check out the following URL for more information:

http://www.microsoft.com/windows2000/techinfo/howitworks/
management/grouppolwp.asp

In Windows Server 2003 Active Directory, Microsoft extended the capabilities of GPOs significantly. Over 160 new settings have been added, some of which cover new areas, such as the netlogon process, DNS configuration, networking QOS and wireless, and terminal services. We'll now give an overview of the main categories of settings available with GPOs and provide a brief explanation for some of the main capabilities of each.

Software Installation Settings (Computer and User)

GPOs provide the ability to deploy applications automatically to users or computers. These applications can now be installed, updated, repaired, and removed simply using GPOs and their interaction with a technology called the Microsoft Installer.

To comply with the Windows 2000 or Windows Server 2003 logo program, in which an application gets the ability to sport the "Designed for Windows 2000" logo or equivalent, each application must ship with an installation routine that uses the Microsoft Windows Installer (MSI) technology. During creation of a software application, the author can now create a new MSI file that is the descendant of the original *SETUP.EXE* files that used to be created. The MSI contains all the data required to fully install the application and then some. It knows about the files that are required by the application, including notes such as sizes and version numbers, and it maintains a host of other information, including language settings, where to install the application, what files are critical to the functional operation of the application, and so on. On any system that has the Microsoft Windows Installer service installed, the MSI file can be run as if it were an executable, and the application will install.

The administrator can customize the defaults for the MSI file to tailor the exact settings for the application, say installing it on drive Z: rather than C: or installing Spanish and Polish support in addition to English. The process of customizing the MSI file in this manner is known as creating a transform. The transform is used by the installer service to make sure that the MSI file installs the appropriate items in the correctly configured way.

That's not all, though: this technology has a lot more to it. First, it has the capability to self-repair applications. So let's say that a user accidentally deletes one or more of the core files required for the application to work. When the user attempts to run the application, the icon or application that the user tries to run first checks with the MSI and the transform to make sure that no critical data is missing. If it is, the data is copied to the appropriate locations, and the application is started. This effectively brings about fully functional, self-repairing applications.

Applications can also be deployed using GPOs so that users get them as soon as they log on or whenever they browse Active Directory to find the applications. You can even tell the MSI to auto-install on any client PC that attempts to open a file with an extension that an MSI-aware application can read.

While the Microsoft Windows Installer service is very useful, and its configuration will become second nature to administrators as time goes on, the actual technology itself is not really appropriate to this book. If you want to find out more on the Windows Installer service and how you can write your own MSI for both existing and new applications, check out the InstallShield web site *http://www.installshield.com* for the newer version of the InstallShield tool that compiles MSI files, or search the Microsoft web site *http://search.microsoft.com/us/dev/default.asp* for the phrase Windows Installer.

Microsoft Windows Installer files are inserted into a GPO from the Software Installation section. Figure 7-2 shows the GPOE with two GPOs snapped into it, one expanded in the scope pane to show the two Software Installation parts.

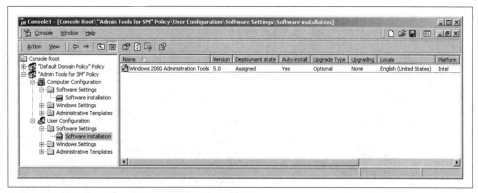

Figure 7-2. Software Installation settings for a GPO

Software Installation is listed under both the computer and user sections of the GPO, and thus you can deploy software installations to both computers and users through the two different parts of the GPO. In Figure 7-2, this GPO is deploying the Version 5.0 Systems Administration tools as an assigned application to all users that receive this GPO. If you remember the example from the start of this chapter, this GPO is used to auto-install the Systems Administration tools onto any client that certain systems administrators log on to. We know that it auto-installs, because that is one of the configured options enabled in the GPOE in Figure 7-2. More information on Microsoft Installer applications can be found in the next section.

Windows Settings (Computer)

This part of a GPO holds startup and shutdown scripts as well as security settings. In Figure 7-3, the GPO being edited is the Default Domain Policy installed by default on creation of a domain. This GPO applies to all computers in the domain, so any change that we make to this GPO will affect DCs, member servers, and ordinary workstations alike.

Startup and shutdown scripts can be made to execute asynchronously or synchronously. They can use VBScript, JScript, any other ActiveX scripting host language, or even plain old CMD/BAT files that you may already be familiar with. You can even pass parameters to the scripts by configuring the parameters into the GPO.

The Security Settings portion of the GPO is by far the larger of the two sections covered by the Windows Settings heading. The items displayed in Figure 7-3 cover the following areas:

Account Policies
   These policies allow you to apply settings that govern how accounts on the system work.

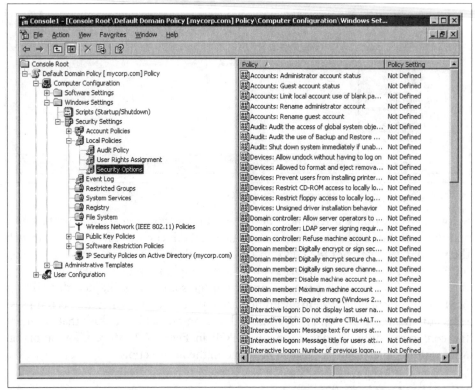

Figure 7-3. Computer Security Settings and scripts

 The settings for the following three policies can only be applied domainwide; they cannot have different values for different Organizational Units in a domain. This is why you need to consider multiple domains in the namespace design if you need to apply different settings to different sections of your organization.

Password Policy

These settings allow you to specify policy settings for passwords, such as how many days a password can exist before expiration.

Account Lockout Policy

These settings allow you to specify how many grace logons a user is allowed before she locks out her account due to bad logon attempts. You also specify how long the account should stay locked out.

Kerberos Policy

This setting is domain-wide only, so it exists only in the Default Domain Policy. It allows you to configure the various Kerberos security and ticketing policies that apply to the domain.

Local Policies

These policies directly affect the operation of a local machine, be it a workstation or a DC.

Audit Policy

These policies list items that, when turned on, will write audit entries for success and/or failure to the security event log of any machine that is affected. In other words, if you turn on Audit Logon Events (Failure) in the Default Domain Policy, any failed logon attempts on any machine within that domain are logged to the security event log on that same machine.

User Rights Assignment

While permissions are used to allow or deny access to an object in Active Directory or a part of a filesystem, user rights give special abilities to an account or the operating system, such as whether the machine can be accessed only locally or only across the network, whether an account can add workstations to a domain, and whether an account can act as part of the operating system and manipulate devices at a low level. These items used to be available from a menu in Windows NT's User Manager, but a few more items have been added to accommodate the changes to Windows 2000 and Windows Server 2003.

Security Options

These settings, which are displayed in the results pane of Figure 7-3, allow configuration of security on one or more computers throughout your organization.

Event Log

These settings allow you to set various properties of the three main event logs (security, application, and system)—such as the maximum size, how long to retain the logs, and so on—on any computer that receives this policy. Under Windows 2000 and later, these settings were contained in a subheading called "Settings for Event Logs."

Restricted Groups

This allows you to indicate specific groups on any computer that receives this policy and force them to be members of other groups or to have members themselves.

System Services

This setting allows you to manipulate services that may be running on any machine that receives this policy and set the permissions for access to those services. The permissions include who can start, stop, and change properties, as well as the default state (i.e., Automatic, Manual, or Disabled).

Registry

This setting allows you to add a registry key on any computer that receives this policy and automatically set its permissions and auditing properties. If you want to audit successful and unsuccessful accesses to the HKEY_USERS key for computers in one specific Organizational Unit only, you do so by adding an entry to a GPO that affects that Organizational Unit.

File System

This setting allows you to add a file or directory on any computer that receives this policy and automatically set its permissions and auditing properties. If you want to set read, write, and change access permissions to the *C:\WINNT* or *C:\WINNT\SYSTEM32* directory for every computer in one specific Organizational Unit only, you do so by adding an entry to a GPO that affects that Organizational Unit.

IP Security Policies on Active Directory

This allows you to configure whether a server requires use of Internet standards on IP security (IPSec) when clients attempt to communicate with the server or whether it just requests IPSec if the client is capable. From the client side this setting allows you to dictate whether a client will always use IPSec of a certain form or whether it will use IPSec only when a server requests it. All aspects of IPSec can be configured from here.

Public Key Policies

This location allows you to set all manner of Public Key Infrastructure (PKI) settings that are now natively supported in Active Directory. Administrators can specify that the system has a trusted certificate list that it considers reputable, that it will automatically pass certificates of a certain type out to users or computers without their intervention, and that key users (with the administrator as default) can be made Recovery Agents and thus gain the permission to use another user's public keys and certificates to decrypt that user's encrypted data. As these settings are specific to a GPO, and a GPO can be specific to a location in Active Directory, this allows you to set out a number of different policy settings that apply to different areas of the tree as required.

Software Restriction Policies (new in Windows Server 2003 Active Directory)

With these settings you can restrict which applications can run on client machines. You can restrict files from being executed by file type or even by user. Another interesting aspect of the software restriction policies is that if you have a virus outbreak, you can prevent clients from opening the file that is known to have a virus.

Wireless Network (new in Windows Server 2003 Active Directory)

This allows you to manage the wireless clients on your network by configuring the SSID, WEP, encryption, and numerous other 802.1x settings.

Administrative Templates (Computer)

The computer settings include:

Windows components

NetMeeting (new in Windows Server 2003 Active Directory)
> This contains one setting, which is to disable remote desktop sharing via NetMeeting.

Internet Explorer
> Several settings here allow an administrator to dictate whether IE can autodetect missing components and new versions as well as what its security zone settings are.

Task Scheduler
> Ordinary logged-on domain users normally can manipulate the task scheduler on a machine. As an administrator you may not want this, or you may want to set certain tasks and not allow users to delete them. These options allow you to disable creation and deletion of tasks, prevent the running or stopping of tasks on an ad hoc basis, prevent scheduling of any applications that do not appear anywhere other than the user's Start menu, and so on.

Terminal Services (new in Windows Server 2003 Active Directory)
> This section contains a bunch of setting that allow controlling and configuring of Terminal Services on clients.

Windows Installer
> These settings allow an administrator to configure a number of Microsoft Installer options that will apply to all applications installed on this computer. These include options such as whether to disable the use of MSI files on the client, whether to install all MSI files with elevated privileges (i.e., whether to install using the local SYSTEM account which has full rights to the files and folders on the machine's disks, which the user may have no rights to), how much logging is to be done, and so on.

Windows Messenger (new in Windows Server 2003 Active Directory)
> With this section you can enable Windows Messenger to run on system startup or disable it from running altogether.

Windows Update (new in Windows Server 2003 Active Directory)
> The two settings contained in this section allow you enable or disable the Windows Update service and to specify an internal server to use for updates instead of from Microsoft.

System
> The settings contained directly under this heading allow configuration of various system components that are not captured by the other headings.

User Profiles (new in Windows Server 2003 Active Directory)

This section contains settings related to local and roaming user profiles. It includes configuring deletion of roaming profiles, slow network detection, and whether roaming policies are allowed on systems.

Scripts (new in Windows Server 2003 Active Directory)

You can define various properties about login script execution. This includes settings to control whether to make scripts visible and whether to run scripts synchronously or asynchronously.

Logon

This section includes a number of items related to controlling the system during a user logon. You can set specific applications to run, disable the Run Once registry key, and disable the Getting Started screen.

Disk Quotas

This section contains settings that allow you to turn on disk quotas at any machines that receive this GPO, as well as manipulate a variety of settings.

NetLogon (new in Windows Server 2003 Active Directory)

These new settings give you a lot of control over how the netlogon process works. You can control which site a client thinks it is a member of and various DC discovery settings.

Group Policy

This is one of the most significant areas, as it contains settings that govern how computers this policy applies to are going to implement group policy. The contents are shown in Figure 7-4.

Remote Assistant (new in Windows Server 2003 Active Directory)

This setting allows you to configure whether technical support can take control of client machines for troubleshooting.

System Restore (new in Windows Server 2003 Active Directory)

System Restore is a new feature of Windows XP that lets clients restore their system to a known good previous state. This section contains settings for disabling system restore and its configuration.

Error Reporting (new in Windows Server 2003 Active Directory)

These settings control whether error reports about system or application failures are sent to Microsoft.

Windows File Protection (new in Windows Server 2003 Active Directory)

Controls the behavior of the Windows File Protection process that protects system files from being overwritten or corrupted.

Remote Procedure Call (new in Windows Server 2003 Active Directory)

These settings configure various properties of the Remote Procedure Call service.

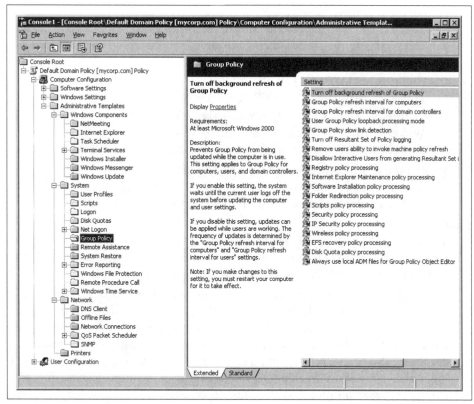

Figure 7-4. Computer administrative templates

Windows Time Service (new in Windows Server 2003 Active Directory)
> This section allows you to configure the NTP client, including time server, polling intervals, and verbosity of event logging.

Network
> These settings control various network-related properties, such as DNS client settings, QOS settings, and SNMP configuration, to mention a few.

DNS Client (new in Windows Server 2003 Active Directory)
> A much-needed addition to group policy, the DNS Client settings allow you to configure the primary DNS suffix, the DNS suffix search order, and dynamic DNS update settings.

Offline Files
> This section contains a large set of values that govern exactly how files and folders are to be made available on the local machine when it is offline. You can turn offline folders on and off, set the cache size to be used for such items, define how synchronization is to occur, and so on.

Network Connections

This location has one key that determines whether users can enable, disable, and configure the shared access feature of a network connection from any Windows-based computer that this policy applies to. Shared access lets users configure their system as an Internet gateway for a small network of machines, providing network services such as name resolution to that network.

QOS Packet Scheduler (new in Windows Server 2003 Active Directory)

Windows XP and Windows Server 2003 contain the ability to set QOS for network traffic. This section allows you to configure various QOS parameters.

SNMP (new in Windows Server 2003 Active Directory)

This contains SNMP configuration settings, including community strings, who can query SNMP on the client, and trap destinations.

Printers

This location has a series of keys that provide a number of new options for printers, dictating whether printers can be shared at all from a computer, whether they can be auto-published into Active Directory, and so on.

Printer objects in Active Directory have a large number of attributes that can and will be regularly searched. Take for example the attribute called Location: users can search for printers based on location from a simple pop-up box that appears when you choose Search...For Printers from the Start menu on a Windows client. Users also can search for "printers near me," making use of a location-tracking feature. Location tracking lets you design a location scheme for your enterprise, based on room number, floor number, building name, city, country, and so on, and assign computers and printers to locations in your scheme. Location tracking overrides the standard method of locating and associating users and printers, which uses the IP address and subnet mask of a computer to estimate its physical location and proximity to other computers. GPO settings allow you to force a workstation to search as if it were in a specific location (i.e., forcing your own value for location whenever that client searches for printers nearby), as well as turning on location tracking and its associated options.

Windows settings (user)

While this section contains only a few settings, the contents are likely to become very familiar to you. This area holds logon and logoff scripts, allows you to redirect core system folders to network areas from the normal hard disk locations, and allows you to specify IP security policies. Figure 7-5 shows a snapshot of the contents.

Folder Redirection

This is a very useful setting that is easy to understand and manage. It allows an administrator to redirect the *My Documents*, *My Pictures*, *Application Data*, *Desktop*, and *Start Menu* locations from their defaults. For example, roaming profiles were used at Leicester University, but they didn't want the *My Docu-*

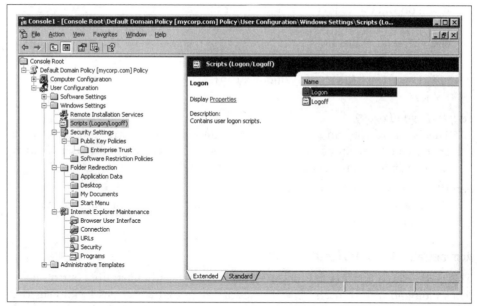

Figure 7-5. Windows Settings (user)

ments folder to roam with the user because of the large number of folders and files it can contain. In other words, downloading and uploading *My Documents* would slow down logon/logoff considerably. So instead we redirect the user's *My Documents* folder (and the *My Pictures* folder within it) to the network paths when he logs on. That way, whenever an application such as Microsoft's Office 2000 attempts to save a document to the *My Documents* folder, the folder that the user sees is the *My Documents* folder located in his home folder.

This part of the GPO is different from the others in that it doesn't contain settings as such. Instead, the folders listed should be right-clicked and the Properties item selected from the drop-down menu that appears. This brings up the main redirection settings window for that folder. This window allows you to redirect all users who receive this GPO to one folder or allow a finer-grained control so that users who are members of a certain group get Folder A, users who are members of another group get Folder B, and so on. You can then specify other settings, such as whether the existing folder is to be moved when this GPO takes effect and whether the folder is moved back when the policy stops being in effect.

 The main problem with these settings stems from the fact that you can't use environmental variables in the strings because the GPO will take effect before environmental variables are set. So if you have a set of users who are to have their *My Documents* redirected to folders that correspond to their usernames, there is no way of getting the usernames into the folder path using the *%USERNAME%* variable as there is for profiles.

If you do want to redirect but don't want the hassle of doing it this way, edit the relevant keys in the following two user registry locations to point the folders elsewhere. Note that both must be edited for the process to take effect:

HKCU\Software\Microsoft\Windows\CurrentVersion\Explorer\Shell Folders
HKCU\Software\Microsoft\Windows\CurrentVersion\Explorer\UserShell Folders

Scripts (Logon/Logoff)

This is where you can specify the user logon and logoff scripts. Whether these are executed synchronously or asynchronously is specified in the User Configuration Administrative Templates section of the GPO.

Security Settings → Public Key Policies

These settings correspond to those held under Windows Settings in the computer portion of the GPO.

Administrative templates (user)

This is the core of the settings that will govern how the administrator controls a system's look and feel for users. The settings are all geared to various lockdowns that you may wish to make to a user's account; if you do not wish to lock down a user's account, most of these settings will not be of much use. If roaming profiles are turned on, these settings roam with a user's profile on each client. Figure 7-6 shows the full branch expanded.

Start Menu & Taskbar

This location is used when the administrator wishes to customize how the Start menu and the taskbar appear to the users this policy applies to. Here you can disable various options on the Start menu, such as the control panel, printers, logoff, or the shutdown button, and can also remove various items, such as Run, Search, or Favorites, entirely if so desired.

Desktop

Like the last item, this section is used to lock down the desktop. Here you can remove the various icons, such as My Network Places, as well as configure whether the desktop settings themselves can be changed and whether they are even saved on logout. Active Desktop is configured (or disabled) from here.

Control Panel

> *Add/Remove Programs*
>
> This allows you to set how the control panel is customized for an individual user. You can disable the option entirely, hide some of the options, or even force the system to bypass the addition of other software but still add official components to the system by going straight to the Components menu.

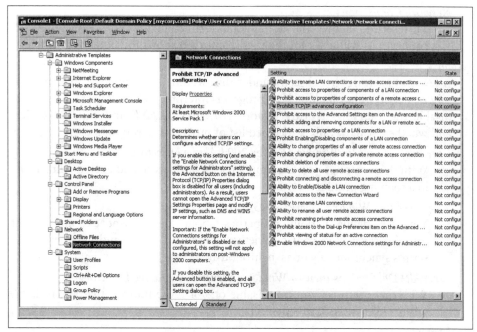

Figure 7-6. Administrative Templates (user)

Display
> This can be used to disable individual tabs on the Display control panel, so that users cannot change wallpaper, the screensaver, or the settings for their display (such as display drivers), which, as administrators well know, can cause immense problems.

Printers
> Here you can disable the adding or deleting of printers, as well as decide whether to hide various property pages on the Add Printer wizard.

Regional and Language Options (new to Windows Server 2003)
> This allows you to restrict users to a certain language.

Shared Folders (new in Windows Server 2003 Active Directory)
> This heading contains two settings that determine whether users can publish shared folders and DFS roots in Active Directory.

Network

Offline Files
> These settings allow the administrator to govern how cached files for offline access actually operate. For example, the settings control whether the files are automatically synchronized at logoff, how much event logging is done, how much space can be used up by the offline cache, and so on.

Network Connections

This section allows the administrator to configure how RAS and LAN connections will work for the user. Figure 7-6 shows the full list of options.

System

A few extra settings live directly under this heading, as they don't fit under any other category. They include how programs interpret two-digit years, whether to disable the Windows registry editors—*REGEDT32.EXE* and *REGEDIT.EXE*, and whether to allow only a specified list of programs to run for a user.

User Profiles (new in Windows Server 2003 Active Directory)

With these settings you can limit a user's profile size and exclude directories in a roaming profile.

Scripts (new in Windows Server 2003 Active Directory)

You can define various properties about login script execution. This includes settings to control whether scripts are visible and whether to run scripts synchronously or asynchronously.

Ctrl+Alt+Del Options (new in Windows Server 2003 Active Directory)

With these settings you can disable one or more buttons that are available when a user enters Ctrl+Alt+Del.

Logon

These settings allow an administrator to specify whether logon/logoff scripts run visibly and whether they run synchronously.* Administrators can also disable the Lock Workstation, Task Manager, Change Password, and Logoff buttons on the Windows Security screen that you get when you press Ctrl+Alt+Del while logged on.

Group Policy

As it was in the Computer section of Administrative Templates, this is one of the most significant areas. It contains configuration data that governs how group policies apply to users. For example, it allows you to configure when and how a slow link is detected, how often the user section of this GPO is refreshed, and whether GPOs are downloaded only from the PDC Emulator FSMO role owner (described in Chapter 2) or from any DC.

Power Management (new in Windows Server 2003 Active Directory)

This contains one setting that allows you to configure whether a user is prompted for their password when resuming from hibernate or suspend/ standby.

---

* You can't run a logon script synchronously if it needs to interact with the user's environment. Synchronous logon scripts will always finish prior to environment variables being set and prior to the user's profile being loaded. For example, it isn't possible to query the number of new mail messages a user has in a synchronous logon script by reading the user's name from the environment variables or profile, as the user is not yet fully logged on when the script runs. The solution is to run the script asynchronously.

Windows Components

NetMeeting

These settings can control virtually every aspect of NetMeeting to include what can be shared, whether audio or video can be used, whether the whiteboard can be used, whether directory services can be used, whether files can be sent and received, and many more.

Internet Explorer

Numerous settings are available to customize Internet Explorer, including look and feel, security zones, etc.

Help and Support Center (new to Windows Server 2003 Active Directory)

A single setting that controls if the "Did You Know" content will be shown by the Help and Support Center service.

Windows Explorer

These settings relate to how the shell and desktop look and feel. You can customize whether specific icons (such as drives in *My Computer* or Entire Network in *My Network Places*) are displayed, decide whether certain normal modes of operation (such as whether to disable workgroup contents in *My Network Places* or remove the Folder Options menu from the Tools menu) are blocked, or change the default settings (such as changing the maximum number of recent documents from 15 to a lower or higher value).

Windows Explorer → Common Open File Dialog

This setting allows administrators to tailor the dialog box that is displayed automatically by programs whenever users need to browse to and open a file. For example, you can specify whether the Back button or the Common Places bar—which contains icons representing History, Desktop, Favorites, *My Documents*, and *My Network Places*—are displayed.

Microsoft Management Console

While you may use the MMC to create your own consoles, you may wish users to be able to use only existing consoles and not create new ones. Alternatively, you may want to allow users to create consoles but limit them to only a few snap-ins. These settings allow you to do either.

Management Console → Restricted/Permitted Snap-ins

This section contains the entire set of snap-ins that are available standard. Administrators use this policy to prevent users from gaining access to individual snap-ins or explicitly permit them to use each one. As with all settings, by default these snap-ins are unconfigured, which means all users get all snap-ins.

Management Console → Restricted/Permitted → Extension snap-ins

Some snap-ins can come with what are termed extensions, extra sets of configurable options that you can add to give more functionality to the snap-in. This section contains a list of all permitted extensions and allows you to enable or disable them as you wish.

Management Console → Restricted/Permitted → Group Policy

These items correspond to the headings that we've been going through here. You can decide, for example, to allow a certain set of users access only to the Administrative Templates (User) section that we're discussing here. Another set of users may have access to manipulate GPOs, but the MMC allows them to see only the Software Installation (User) and Software Installation (Computer) parts. This effectively blocks their ability to manage parts of policies that you as the administrator don't give them rights to.

Task Scheduler

This contains settings to allow the administrator to configure the ability of users to use the task scheduler on clients. Administrators can disable the ability to create new tasks, prohibit viewing existing tasks, or limit certain functionality.

Terminal Services (new in Windows Server 2003 Active Directory)

These settings control user Terminal Services sessions, including time limits for active, idle, and disconnected sessions.

Windows Installer

This area contains configuration settings for users relating to the software packages in MSI form that have been deployed to the user. For example, the administrator can configure whether applications are always deployed with elevated privileges, in what order locations are searched for MSI packages (used when a user requests a list of packages or a user attempts to open a file with an unknown extension), and whether the ability to roll back a failed installation is enabled or disabled.

Windows Messenger (new in Windows Server 2003 Active Directory)

With this section you can enable Windows Messenger to run at login or disable it from running altogether.

Windows Update (new in Windows Server 2003 Active Directory)

This heading contains one setting that allows you to disable Windows Update from running.

Windows Media Player → User Interface (new in Windows Server 2003 Active Directory)

These two settings allow you to force a particular Windows Media Player skin to be used and hide the anchor window when the player is in skin mode.

Windows Media Player → Playback (new in Windows Server 2003 Active Directory)

This section contains a single setting that allows you to prevent downloading of new codecs.

Windows Media Player → Networking (new in Windows Server 2003 Active Directory)

These settings allow you to configure the networking options, including HTTP Proxy, MMS Proxy, and Network Buffering.

Summary

Whew! That's a lot of settings. Hopefully we've given you a good idea of just how powerful GPOs are in Active Directory. We've now covered the basics of what profiles can do and how modifications to a centralized profile make a lot of sense and are easy to manage. We've also taken a very in-depth look at the diverse sort of registry, user interface, file permission, and system changes that can be made using GPOs. In Chapter 10, we'll cover how to design and manage your GPOs.

This concludes our initial introduction to Active Directory. In Part 2, we will dive into some of the important issues around designing and maintaining an Active Directory environment.

PART II

Designing an Active Directory Infrastructure

You should start your Active Directory design with the namespace. However, you will not be able to complete the logical namespace design until you have the physical design sketched out. It's very much a chicken-and-egg situation. You should plan to go through and complete a rough draft of the namespace design, then make a rough draft of the physical design, then consider modifications to both.

Next you can consider the Group Policy Object (GPO) design. Group Policy Objects control such things as user-environment lockdown, forced registry changes, application availability, and so on, to sets of machines or users. Because these relate to sites, domains, Organizational Units, users, computers, and groups in your Active Directory, it makes sense in my experience to incorporate these changes into a namespace and site design that already exist.

You can then take a look at security and at tailoring Active Directory to your own requirements by modifications to the Schema. Finally, this section takes a brief look at the present and the future of integrating and interoperating Active Directory with other directories and operating systems and of migrating to Active Directory.

CHAPTER 8

Designing the Namespace

The basic emphasis of this chapter is on reducing the number of domains that you require for Active Directory while gaining administrative control over sections of the namespace using Organizational Units. This chapter aims to help you create a domain namespace design. That includes all the domains you will need, the forest and domain-tree hierarchies, and the contents of those domains in terms of Organizational Units and even groups.

There are a number of restrictions that you have to be aware of when beginning your Active Directory design. We will introduce you to them in context as we go along, but here are some important ones:

- Too many Group Policy Objects (GPOs) means a long logon time as the group policies are applied to sites, domains, and Organizational Units. This obviously has a bearing on your Organizational Unit structure, as a 10-deep Organizational Unit tree with GPOs applying at each branch will incur more GPO processing than a 5-deep Organizational Unit tree with GPOs at each branch.

- Under Windows 2000, you cannot rename a domain once it has been created. Fortunately, with Windows Server 2003, this limitation has been removed, although the rename process is tedious. You can even rename forest root domains once you've reached the Windows Server 2003 forest functional level.

- You can never remove the forest root domain without destroying the whole forest in the process. The forest root domain is the cornerstone of your forest.

- The Schema Admins and Enterprise Admins groups exist in the forest root domain only. So if you are migrating from a previous version of NT, be cognizant of the fact that the administrators of the first domain you migrate can have control over these groups and over Active Directory.

- Lack of a regional catalog is problematic. Imagine that you have 20 printers in your office in Sweden and 12 printers in your office in Brazil. The users in Sweden will never need to print to the printers in Brazil, and the users in Brazil will never need to print to the printers in Sweden. However, by default, details of all printers are published in the GC. Thus, whenever changes are made to printers in Sweden, all the changes get replicated to the GCs on the Brazil servers because the GC replicates all of its data everywhere. You have three options. You can decide not to replicate any printer data and force printer seraches to hit Active Directory each time, you can replicate all printer data everywhere, or you can create an application partition to host printer data and replicate it to designated domain controllers.

- Multiple domains cannot be hosted on a single DC. Imagine 3 domains off a root located in the United States, which correspond to 3 business units. Now imagine a small office of 15 people in Eastern Europe or Latin America with a slow link to the main site. The 15 users are made up of 3 sets of 5; each set of 5 users uses one of the 3 business units/domains. If you as an administrator decide that the slow link is too slow and you would like to put in a DC for the 3 domains at the local server and to ease replication, the small office will have to install 3 DCs.

The Complexities of a Design

Active Directory is a complex beast, and designing for it isn't easy. Take a look at a fictitious global company called PetroCorp, depicted in Figure 8-1.

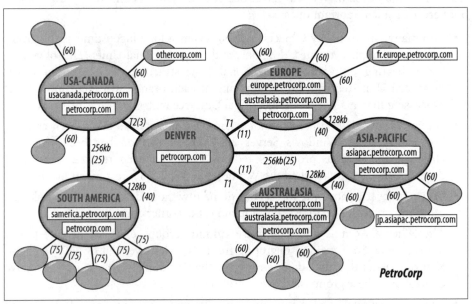

Figure 8-1. The sites and servers of a company called PetroCorp

Here you can see a huge network of sites linked with various network connections across wide area networks. A variety of domains seems to exist for *othercorp.com* and *petrocorp.com*, and as each one of those square boxes represents a single domain controller (the servers that host Active Directory in an organization), you can see that some of the servers will need to replicate data across those WAN links. *petrocorp.com*, for example, seems to need to replicate to all the major sites, since it has domain controllers (DCs) in each of those sites.

Take a look at Figure 8-2, which shows a much more complex hierarchy.

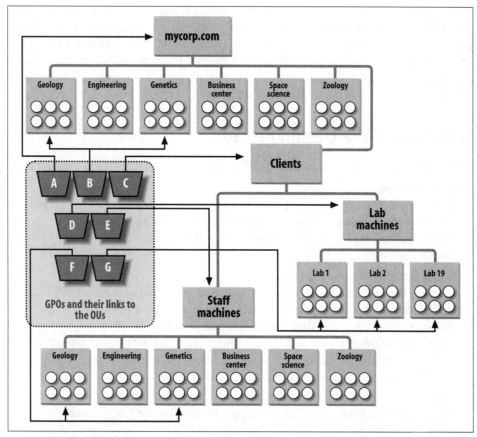

Figure 8-2. A complex domain tree showing GPOs

It's possible to see the users and computers in all the Organizational Units in this view, and the structure seems to be set up so that Group Policy Objects (GPOs, represented by trapezoids) can act on various portions of the tree. These GPOs could be anything from what menus appear on the screen to what applications can be run to what hardware is available for each user.

Following is a discussion of the principles and processes that will help you create complicated designs like these to mirror the complexities in your own organization.

Where to Start

Before you sit down to make your design, you will need to obtain some important pieces of information. You will need a copy of your organizational structure. This is effectively the document that explains how your organization's business units fit together in the hierarchy. Next you will need a copy of the geographical layout of your company. This includes the large-scale picture in continents and countries and also the individual states, counties, or areas in which you have business units. Third, you will need a copy of the network diagram, indicating the speeds of connection between the various sites. Finally, you need a copy of any diagrams and information on any systems that will need to interface to Active Directory, such as existing X.500 directories, so that you can take them into account. Once you've gathered the information, you can sit down and plan your design.

Overview of the Design Process

The namespace design process takes place in three stages:

Design of the domain namespace
> During the first stage, you deal with the namespace design itself. That means calculating the number of domains you need, designing the forest and tree structure, and defining the naming scheme for workstations, servers, and the network as a whole.

Design of the internal domain structure
> During the second stage, you need to concentrate on the internal structure of each domain that you have previously noted. Here you also need to use your business model as a template for the internal structure and then move on to consider how administration and other rights will be delegated. The internal structure can also be modified depending on how you intend to use Group Policy Objects; this will be covered in Chapter 10.

Global catalog design
> During the third stage, you work out your designs for the global catalog (GC).

 When you are finished with your design, you can implement the design by setting up a test forest in a lab environment. This will enable you to get a better feel for how the design actually works and whether there is anything you have failed to consider. We can't stress enough the use of a test environment.

Domain Namespace Design

The first stage in your design is to work out the domain, domain-tree, and forest configuration of your network. The best way to do this is to make a first pass at designing the domains and then structure them together into a series of trees. Before we start, however, let's take a look at our objectives for this part of the design.

Objectives

There are two objectives for the design of the domain namespace:

- Designing Active Directory to represent the structure of your business
- Minimizing the number of domains by making much more use of the more flexible Organizational Units

Represent the structure of your business

You need to make Active Directory look as much like your business structure, geographical or organizational, as possible. With geographical structure, your business runs itself as self-contained units within each geographical site. In this model, people at those sites handle administration for each site. Under the organizational or political model, the business is based on a series of departments that have members from a number of different geographical sites. Normally, with this structure, the organization has a head office for all departments at one location, but that is not always the case.

In the former model, finance units based in France and Australia would be separate finance departments. In the latter model, France and Australia would have geographical finance branches of a larger finance department controlled from a head office.

It doesn't matter to Active Directory which model you choose, except that the intention is to mirror the structure of your business in the Active Directory design. If your business crosses both of these boundaries, it becomes less clear-cut. To make your design simpler to understand, you should choose to go with one model or the other. We would not suggest a mix-and-match approach unless you can definitely rationalize it, adequately represent it on paper, and delegate administration effectively.

If you already have a large investment in a TCP/IP infrastructure with organization or geographic-centered DNS zones, or you if have a large existing Exchange organization, you can use this as the basis of your design. Simply stated, if your DNS or Exchange setup is based on one model, go with that model for your Active Directory design. It should be obvious that it will be easier for an administrator to think about both areas if the designs are based on the same model.

Minimize the number of domains

Remember that implementing Active Directory presents an opportunity to reduce the number of domains you support. Each forest can store tens of millions of objects, which is more than enough for all the users, groups, and computers in most organizations. So size isn't a consideration. Each domain can also be partitioned using Organizational Units, allowing you to delegate different administrators for each

Organizational Unit in a domain if you so desire. You do not have to create a new domain if you wish to delegate administration over a part of the system. These two aspects of Active Directory tend to eliminate a number of sizing and permission problems associated with traditional NT installations.

 If you're an experienced NT domain designer, start trying to push from your mind the tendency to create multiple domains. Think in terms of multiple Organizational Units instead.

Step 1—Decide on the Number of Domains

Start by imagining that every object is to be stored in one domain. This will give you a much simpler layout for administration. It doesn't matter what the domain is called for now; just label it as your organization's main/sole domain.

Now expand the number of domains that you have by adding other domains that you can give specific justification for. While the number of objects and delegation of administration are not good reasons for creating new domains, there are three main reasons that would require more domains:

- The need to isolate replication
- A requirement for a unique domain policy
- A requirement for keeping a Windows NT domain

If you can match any of these criteria, write down a new domain for that area.

Isolated replication

While replication is mainly discussed in the next chapter, it does have a bearing on domain design. If you have a headquarters and a branch office connected via a slow link, and you don't want to use up any bandwidth at all in replicating domain directory data from the main domain to the branch office, you need to consider creating a separate domain for the branch office. This will ensure that only limited traffic is replicated between both offices. In fact, this will be limited to the GC, configuration, and Schema information only.

So if you want to really minimize traffic down a link, create a new domain for the remote office. In most cases, this isn't necessary. Also, you can use Application Partitions to store application specific data and only replicate it to your regional sites.

 A slow link in an ideal case is defined as a 259 Kb link with 128 Kb spare capacity. However, each organization will need to make its own decision about what it will accept as a minimum for a slow link; the value could be 64 Kb or 1 Mb. As we are only drafting the namespace and physical site/replication designs and then coming back to revise both using the combined data, the exact figure for a slow link in your organization is not important right now.

Unique domain policy

In Chapters 7 and 10 we explain the basics of GPOs and how to properly design them. For now the important thing to understand is that policies are Active Directory objects that reference a number of settings that can be applied to users or computers. These settings are things like a fixed desktop, a certain core set of applications, the ability of users to perform a shutdown, and so on. If you're coming from a Windows NT background, these are Windows NT system policies on a much grander scale. GPOs can be applied to various parts of your Active Directory structure. If you create an Organizational Unit called Finance and then decide that OU=Finance needs special settings, you can create a GPO and assign it to OU=Finance. Then all the computer settings in the GPO will be applied to all computers in OU=Finance, and all the user settings in the GPO will be applied to the users in OU=Finance.

We now need to look at what settings have to be applied on a domain-by-domain basis. Here's a list of what types of settings can be set only on a domain-wide basis:

- Password policies, such as password length, password expiry interval, and so forth. This is effectively the same as for Windows NT 4.0.

- Account lockout policies, such as lockout threshold, lockout duration, and so forth. Again this is the same as for NT 4.0.

- Kerberos policies.

- Encrypted file system recovery policies.

- IP security policies.

- Public key encryption policies.

- Certificate authorities.

If you know that your organization already has three different password schemes that have to be maintained, you will need three domains. If a special department or geographical area needs special encryption, security safeguards, certificates, and so on, you may have another candidate for a domain.

In-place upgrade of current domain

Many organizations have large existing Windows NT infrastructures and will be planning to migrate at some point. During the design of your migration to Active Directory, you will need to consider the option of merging old Windows NT domain hierarchies into single domains. This is known as collapsing old domain structures. However, even though AD usually requires fewer domains than Windows NT, as it can accommodate more objects and allow delegation of administration without domains, organizations may wish to retain some of their current domains.

If your organization has a domain that you feel should not be removed for some reason, you need to indicate it on the list of domains. Then when it comes time to implement your Active Directory rollout, you can do an in-place upgrade on the existing domain rather than bringing it into an existing AD domain.

Final notes

You now should have your first draft of the list of domains that you think you will need. There is one more very important point on this subject. Domains are very inflexible and unforgiving, and due to the fact that you can host only a single domain on a domain controller, each domain means one more domain controller you have to support. Depending on how many domain controllers you would have to deploy for a domain, you can greatly decrease your total cost of ownership (TCO) for Active Directory by limiting the number of domains you support.

Step 2—Design and Name the Tree Structure

Now that you have the domains listed, you need to consider what sort of hierarchy to put them in. It is easiest to start with one domain, the one that will become the forest root.

Choose the forest root domain

The forest root domain is normally the largest domain left after you split off the smaller ones using the preceding domain design process, but it doesn't have to be. The empty forest root domain approach is also very common: you minimize the amount of data in that domain and put everything in subdomains. The key here is that this domain needs to be centrally managed by an IT group, capable of making solid policy and naming decisions. This domain has special properties. For example, the Schema Admins group exists only in the forest root domain. The administrators of this forest root domain have control over who is added to the Schema Admins group and thus allowed to modify the schema. While the administrators of the forest root domain can add any user from anywhere in the entire forest to the group (due to hierarchical and transitive trusts between all domains), it is the administrators of the forest root domain that call the shots. So this domain is special. Its administrators dictate how the network expands, who can and cannot add domains, and where domains should go. This group has the grand vision for the design and operation of the network.

Whichever domain corresponds to this is the one that should be the forest root domain. If you are having difficulty choosing, pick one of the likely candidates for now. If it becomes obvious later that it was the wrong choice, you can come back and readjust. Once you've chosen, grab a blank piece of paper and draw the forest root domain at the top of the sheet in a triangle. A triangle is the symbol used to represent an Active Directory domain.

Design the namespace naming scheme

As each domain has a DNS name to identify it, you need to consider what names you are going to choose. You can use any of the RFC 1123 standard characters:

- A–Z
- a–z
- 0–9
- – (dash character)

Microsoft's DNS supports a wider range of characters, such as the Unicode character set, but if you need compatibility with other DNS flavors, be very careful allowing these.

There are currently two schools of thought on how to pick the DNS names for your Active Directory network: root zone or subzone. The root zone method says that you name your root Active Directory domain based on the root zone for your organization. For the Mycorp Corporation, this would be *mycorp.com*. The subzone method suggests that you pick a new subdomain from your root zone and make that the base of your Active Directory namespace. For Mycorp, this could be *ad.mycorp.com*. If you choose the root zone method and wish to have a non-Windows DNS, you will need to either turn on dynamic update or manually register a number of records in the DNS as shown in Chapter 6. If you choose the root zone method and wish to have a Windows DNS at your root, you will need to migrate your existing entries, if you have any, to it. Both methods are fine, but they require configuration or migration at the root. A less invasive procedure would be to choose a new subzone for your Active Directory network and run your network from that. With this setup you still have two choices, but they are less disruptive to any existing structure and you won't have to affect the main root zone. Arguably, the easiest solution is to let two servers on your network run Windows DNS server and manage this DNS zone. This allows you to have a root that doesn't allow dynamic updates and a subdomain that does. The alternative would allow a non-Windows DNS to manage the zone.

Leicester University had a very large existing DNS infrastructure branching down from the root domain that we didn't want to affect with this new Active Directory infrastructure. The main DNS servers, while being dynamic update–capable, did not have dynamic update turned on for specific reasons. So we set up two domain controllers to run the Windows DNS service and gave them a subdomain to host. We then delegated that subdomain on the main DNS servers and told them which servers had authority for the new zone. We then modified DHCP to point all new client workstations at the two Windows DNS servers and configured the DNS servers to pass any queries that they could not resolve back to the main campus DNS servers. Clients could update the Windows DNS without affecting the main campus servers. However, external queries were still resolved by passing them to the main campus servers for resolution.

Start with the forest root and assign a DNS name to the domain, writing the name inside or beside the triangle on the paper. You should pick the name very, very carefully, for two reasons: first, renaming a domain is impossible in Windows 2000 Active Directory, and while it is possible under Windows Server 2003 Active Directory, the process is very invasive and requires all machines in the domain to be rebooted. Second, you can never remove the forest root domain from Active Directory. You would have to wipe your entire setup and start again.

Create additional trees

Having created and named your forest root, you need to consider your other domains. If you have two distinct business units that will require discontiguous names, you need two trees coming from a domain root. Draw all the other root domains that you think you will need as separate triangles at the same horizontal level on the paper and assign them valid DNS names. These domains are all root domains. A real-world example is the Microsoft brand name and the MSN brand name. Both *msn.com* and *microsoft.com* could be separate trees in the same forest. They couldn't be in the same tree without giving them a hierarchical link, i.e., *msn.microsoft.com*.

 If we think that Mycorp's finance department needs a separate domain, we will make a subdomain and call it *finance.mycorp.com*. Within Active Directory we could make *finance.mycorp.com* a separate tree in its own right, but as hierarchical and transitive trusts exist throughout a forest, we gain absolutely nothing by doing this. The only differences come in choosing finance to be a new domain (which we did) or a new forest in itself. Making it a new tree gains absolutely nothing.

Create additional forests

So far, we've been considering domains that will exist in the same forest. You may have business units that will require two entirely separate forests. How do you know if that is the case? If you have business units in an organization that are independent and in fact wish to be isolated from each other, then you must not combine them in a single forest. If you simply give each business unit its own domain, these business units can get the idea that they are autonomous and isolated from each other. However, in Active Directory, this level of autonomy and isolation can be achieved only through separate forests. This is also the case if you need to comply with regulatory or legal isolation requirements.

The first and most common reason may be political: certain business units may decide that they want to be as autonomous as possible. It may be that, politically, the finance department has to be completely separate, so you end up making a second forest with *finance.mycorp.com* as the second forest's forest root domain. In effect, you are treating this business unit as a separate, autonomous, and discontiguous part of the tree.

The second reason you may need two forests involves having two businesses that must be separately maintained.

The third reason is one born out of necessity. Remember from Chapter 2 that certain aspects of a namespace are forestwide in scope. If you want to isolate a separate schema, configuration, or GC, your only solution is to create a separate forest.

If any of these reasons is true, you need to create a second forest root domain and give it a unique DNS name, as you did for the first forest root domain. In effect, you need to separate your designs and do each forest individually. The best thing to do now is to figure out how many forests you need, which domains from your list are going to be the forest root domains, name these roots, and then use a separate piece of paper to draw each forest. Maintain separate lists of domains for each forest. You're now doing x designs, where x is the number of forests you have.

There is one other important point that you need to be aware of. While domains and trees in a forest maintain automatic trust relationships, it is possible to set up manual trust relationships with domains external to a forest. You can therefore set up manual trust relationships between forests. These relationships can be one-way trusts (A trusts B but B does not trust A) or two-way trusts (A trusts B and B trusts A).

If you require a limited trust situation (in the Windows NT/2000 sense), in which you wish to give access to your forest to vendors and partners, you can do this manually. If you have two forests that you wish to link, you have a few options: establish an explicit one-way trust, distribute a public Kerberos ticket, or create a transitive forest trust.

The first option allows other domains that are members of another domain tree in a different forest or that do not support Kerberos authentication to have limited access to a domain in the forest. Only resources in the domain will be visible; no other resources in the tree are available for access.

The second option allows a Kerberos negotiation to start with a client that is not already a trusted member of the domain. A public Kerberos ticket allows a user that is not a member of the domain at all to be authenticated by using an explicitly distributed and dated Kerberos ticket.

The last option is new to Windows Server 2003 Active Directory. Under Windows 2000, if you wanted all domains in one forest to trust all domains in a second forest, you had to create individual trusts to and from each domain. With the new forest trust, you can simply create a single transitive trust between two forests, and all domains in both forests will trust each other.

You can also allow access to Active Directory via a digital certificate. Effective use of digital certificates allows secure communication between two machines. A digital certificate is used for public-key encryption applications, mostly seen on the Internet where pages need a special certificate installed on the client to allow authentication over Secure Sockets Layer (SSL). A certificate server, such as the Microsoft Certificate Server that ships with Windows 2000 or Windows Server 2003, can be set up to issue, renew, and revoke digital certificates that allow access to Active Directory. The certificates are used to authenticate connections via specific computers and users. Active Directory has extensions that allow individual user and computer accounts to have digital certificates assigned to them, allowing authentication over this mechanism. While these concepts aren't difficult, they are outside the scope of this book.

Arrange subdomain hierarchy

You now have a forest root domain with a valid DNS name. You may have other domains that act as the roots of separate trees in the same forest; you may even have extra forest root domains representing separate forests entirely. Now you need to lay out the domain tree hierarchies. If you have a number of remaining domains listed on your sheet of paper from Step 1, these are the subdomains that will form your domain-tree hierarchy.

Start with the first forest. Representing each domain with a triangle on the paper, lay the forest out in a hierarchical fashion beneath one of the domain tree roots in the forest. Name the domain appropriately, according to its position in the hierarchy. Repeat this process for all domains in this forest, then move on to the next forest and repeat.

For example, if we have *mycorp.com* as a tree root, and finance, marketing, and sales all need separate domains, we call them *finance.mycorp.com*, *marketing.mycorp.com*, and *sales.mycorp.com*. If the sales domain needed separate domains for pre-sales and post-sales, we arrange these two domains beneath sales, as *pre.sales.mycorp.com* and *post.sales.mycorp.com*.

Each subdomain can manage its own accounts and data, or its parent in the hierarchy can manage them. That's the reason the hierarchy exists.

Step 3—Design the Workstation and Server Naming Scheme

You now have one or more forests of domain trees. Each tree is uniquely named in a hierarchical fashion. You can now consider the naming scheme for the servers and workstations.

> While we are considering the naming scheme here, the exact placement of machines in Active Directory is covered in Chapter 10 on designing GPOs. That is because GPOs can impact clients based on machine location.

Each client or server in an Active Directory network has to have a computer account somewhere in the forest to let users log on via that client. When a workstation is added to a domain in a forest, the computer account is created in Active Directory, and a trust relationship is set up between the client and the domain, so that the client is recognized as a valid member of the domain.

Where a client is placed in the forest determines part of the name. Standalone servers and DCs are placed in the individual domains that they host. Clients can be placed anywhere, but they are usually placed in the domain that the users of that client normally log on to.

Under Windows NT 4.0, if you had a single-master or multimaster domain model in which multiple resource domains had one-way trusts to one or more master user domains that held the accounts, the workstations normally were placed in the resource domains. This enabled the workstations to log on to both the resource domain and the user domain. Putting the clients only in the user domain would have meant that the clients could not be used to access the resources in the resource domains, as no trust existed in that direction.

 Cast this completely out of your mind in Active Directory. Each domain has a hierarchical and transitive trust between it and every other domain, so it no longer makes any difference where the clients are located.

All hosts are named *computer.domain*. For example, a server called *moose* in *mycorp.com* would be called *moose.mycorp.com*; a server called *moose* in the finance domain would be called *moose.finance.mycorp.com*.

While deploying Active Directory does not force you to change the names of any existing hosts that you have, if you are due to amalgamate a series of domains and have clients with identical names, you need to make modifications so that hostnames are unique throughout the entire forest. You can easily make use of ADSI (discussed in Part III) to script a query for a list of computers from every one of your domains and then check the lists via a second script for duplicate names.

If you don't already force a naming scheme, now is the time. Fully Qualified Domain Names must be unique across the entire forest. This is achieved by appending the domain component onto the computer name. That leaves you to worry about the prefix, meaning that computer names have to be unique only domain-wide.

To maintain backwards compatibility, names cannot be longer than 15 characters. This is because Active Directory still has some legacy support for NetBIOS names, and the hostname that you choose will be incorporated as the NetBIOS name on the client. NetBIOS names are limited to 15 characters.

You need to work out a forest-wide naming scheme, determining how you will name the clients within the 15-character limit using only the characters from the previous list. We can't help you much here; the choice of your naming scheme is up to you.

Remember that Windows 95 and Windows 98 devices do not require computer accounts in the domain. However, if you do deploy these clients and anticipate upgrading them later to Windows NT Workstation, Windows 2000 Professional, or Windows XP, the names of these clients will become an issue. It would be better to designate a name now to facilitate an easier upgrade later.

Design of the Internal Domain Structure

Having designed the domain namespace, you can now concentrate on the internals of each domain. The design process itself is the same for each domain, but the order is mostly up to you. The first domain that you should design is the forest root domain. After that, iterate through the tree, designing subdomains within that first tree. Once the tree is finished, go on to the next tree and start at the root as before.

In a tree with three subdomains called Finance, Sales, and Marketing under the root, you could either design the entire tree below Finance, then the entire tree below Sales, and so on, or you could design the three tier-two domains first, then do all the subdomains immediately below these three, and so on.

When designing the internals of a domain, you need to consider both the hierarchical structure of Organizational Units and the users and groups that will sit in those Organizational Units. Let's look at each of those in turn.

 When we refer to a hierarchy, a tree, or the directory tree, we mean the hierarchical Organizational Unit structure within a domain. We are not referring to the hierarchy of domain trees in a forest.

Step 4—Design the Hierarchy of Organizational Units

Earlier, when we discussed how to design domains, we spoke of how to minimize the number of domains you have. The idea is to represent most of your requirements for a hierarchical set of administrative permissions using Organizational Units instead.

Organizational Units are the best way to structure your data because of their flexibility. They can be renamed and easily moved around within and between domains and placed at any point in the hierarchy without affecting their contents. These two facts make them very easy for administrators to manage.

There are four main reasons to structure your data in an effective hierarchy:

To represent your business model to ease management
> Partitioning your data into an Organizational Unit structure that you will instantly recognize makes managing it much more comfortable than with every user and computer in one Organizational Unit.

To delegate administration

Active Directory allows you to set up a hierarchical administration structure that wasn't possible with Windows NT. If you have three branches, and the main administrator wants to make one branch completely autonomous with its own administrator but wants to continue to maintain control over the other two branches, it's easy to set up. In a way, most of the limitations that you come up against when structuring Active Directory are limits that you set: political necessities, organizational models, and so on. Active Directory really won't care how you structure your data.

To replace Windows NT resource domains

If you have a previous Windows NT installation with a master or multimaster domain model, you can replace your resource domains with Organizational Units in a single domain. This allows you to retain all the benefits of having resource domains (i.e., resource administration by local administrators who do not have account administration rights) without forcing you to have multiple domains that you don't really want or need.

To apply policies to subsets of your users and computers

As policies can be applied to each individual Organizational Unit in the hierarchy, you can specify that different computers and users get different policies depending on where you place them in the tree. For example, let's say that you want to place an interactive touch-screen client in the lobby of your headquarters and allow people to interact with whatever applications you specify, such as company reports, maps of the building, and so on. Locking this down in Windows NT (so that the client could not compromise your network in any way) required time and may have required that the client be in a separate domain or even standalone. With Active Directory, if you lock down a certain Organizational Unit hierarchy using policies, you can guarantee that any computer and user accounts that you create or move to that part of the tree will be so severely restricted that hacking the network from the client won't be possible.

Let's take Leicester University as an example. The university is a large single site with mostly 10/100 MB links around campus and 2 MB links to some outlying areas a couple of miles away. The domain model was multimaster under Windows NT, but under Active Directory it moved to a single domain, so it is much simpler than before. Administration is centrally managed, which means that delegation of administration was of little concern during design. We had a departmental organizational model for the Organizational Unit structure holding our accounts. We created a flat structure with more than a hundred Organizational Units directly off the root and almost no lower Organizational Units at all. Each Organizational Unit corresponded to one department, and it held all the users from that department. We also had an Organizational Unit hierarchy for the computer accounts separate from the department Organizational Units. This was due to our requirement for group policies; we'll come back and discuss this in more detail in Chapter 10.

When creating Organizational Units, you need to ask:

- How will the Organizational Units be used?
- Who are the administrators and what sets of administrator permissions should they have?
- What group policies will be applied?

The hierarchy should organize information in a manner pleasing to your administration and allowing you to delegate administration to various parts of the tree.

 You should not nest user or computer accounts in an Organizational Unit structure in such a way that the group polices that apply to the accounts incur a slowdown. Microsoft recommends nesting no more than 10 Organizational Units deep, but in fact, to a much greater extent, it's the actions of policies that impact how deep you go. This prevents slowdown on booting (policies applied to the computer account on boot up) or logon (policies applied to the user account on logon). If your users are in a 10-tier structure but only 4 policies were applied to the users, you shouldn't have a problem with logons. You can break this rule, but boot-up and/or logon will slow down as a result. By how much is a relative question and the easiest answer is to test it on your network to get your own feel for the delay if this becomes a problem. We cover this item in much more depth in Chapter 10 on GPOs. All you need to be aware of here is that this can be a problem.

Recreating the business model

The easiest way to start a design is to consider the business model that you sat down with when starting these designs. You now need to recreate that structure in Active Directory using Organizational Units as the building blocks. Create a complete Organizational Unit structure that exactly mirrors your business model as represented by that domain. In other words, if the domain you are designing is the Finance domain, implement the finance organizational structure within the Finance domain. You don't create the entire organization's business model within each Organizational Unit; you create only the part of the model that would actually apply to that Organizational Unit. Draw this structure out on a piece of paper. Figure 8-3 shows the Organizational Unit structure of *mycorp.com*'s domain. We've expanded only the Finance Organizational Unit here for the example.

Once you have drawn an Organizational Unit structure as a template for your Active Directory hierarchy within the domain, you can begin to tailor it to your specific requirements. The easiest way to tailor the initial Organizational Unit design is to consider the hierarchy that you wish to create for your delegation of administration.

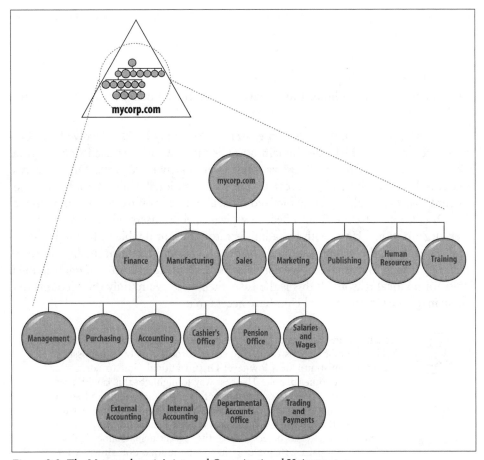

Figure 8-3. The Mycorp domain's internal Organizational Unit structure

Delegating full administration

First, identify any areas of your hierarchy where you need to grant administrators autonomous access over their branch of the tree. These Organizational Units need to have at least two administrators who will look after that Organizational Unit. These administrators will look after the structure below that Organizational Unit, creating whatever Organizational Units, users, groups, shares, and so on that they desire. They will not, however, have administrator access to any other part of the tree.

> You need two administrator accounts in case one of the accounts ever gets locked. That way, you can use the second account to unlock the first. Having the second account be the domain administrator is perfectly fine.

You need to note three pieces of information about each of the Organizational Units that you identify:

- Who will be the administrators?
- Which branch of the tree will they administer?
- Will the domain administrator have full or no administrative access to this branch?

The last is important. Let's take two examples. You may have a devolved administration scenario in which the domain administrator account is used only to grant administrator access to an Organizational Unit for two accounts. Once the two accounts have administrator access to the Organizational Unit, the administrator account's access is subsequently blocked by deliberate action from being inherited at that Organizational Unit. That effectively gives specific users administrative access over Organizational Units with the administrator account unable to be used to organize that data. In the second example, the domain administrator normally has access inherited throughout the tree, except at a number of key sensitive Organizational Units for political reasons. If this is the case, then once again, only the accounts that can manage the Organizational Unit have access to it.

You must ensure that delegated users take responsibility and can be held accountable. This cannot be stressed too strongly. It is possible for an administrator of a low-level Organizational Unit to corrupt a tree and affect other people. The best way to highlight this is with user accounts. Remember, user accounts are visible forestwide and so in some sense must be unique forestwide. In much the same way as with computers, the domain component normally is used here in an attribute of the user object called the userPrincipalName (UPN). While the normal username only has to be unique domainwide, the UPN attribute ensures forestwide uniqueness. Let's concentrate on the domainwide part.

If a low-level Organizational Unit administrator creates a user with a username that someone else wants to create in another Organizational Unit, that's tough. Only one account with a given username can exist. We deal with creating a naming scheme for administrators to follow later in Step 5.

If you do not have a company policy in this area, you need to create one and document it.

Delegating other rights

Having noted the three pieces of information for all Organizational Units that need full administrative access, you next need to identify those Organizational Units that require some users to have a more restricted set of permissions. You may want to set up account administrators that have the ability to create and delete user accounts, as well as setting passwords and account details. You may want accounts that can create and publish printers. We're interested in rights only in general terms at the moment, so just note the following:

- What the access rights are
- Which branch of the tree the access rights will be applied to
- Which users or groups (in general terms) will have these access rights

It is possible to set access rights of any sort down to the individual property level on a specific object if you require. That means you can allow a user named Richard Lang to change the password or telephone number of a user named Vicky Launders (and only that user) if you wish. Obviously the more minute the access, the more complex things can get, especially as permissions are inherited down a tree by default. To make things easier, Microsoft provides a simple Delegation Of Control wizard that allows you to set these access rights in a fairly easy manner. All this information on permissions to Active Directory is covered in much greater depth in Chapter 11. However, all we're concerned with at this stage in the design is delegation of control at the Organizational Unit level. From experience, we can tell you that assigning access rights at the Organizational Unit level is actually a lot simpler to manage than tracking permissions to individual objects and properties.

Step 5—Design of Users and Groups

Before starting this section, we must make clear the distinction between groups and Organizational Units. Organizational Units are containers for objects that allow the objects to be represented in a hierarchical structure within a domain. Placing objects in such a hierarchy allows delegation of administration to those Organizational Units on a selective basis. We've seen all this already. Groups, on the other hand, have only users or computers as members and can be used in assigning permissions or rights to the members collectively. Let's say that we have 50 users contained in an Organizational Unit called FinanceOU, and the users are also members of a group called FinanceGrp. When we want to grant these 50 users read permissions to a share or restricted access to certain parts of a domain's hierarchy, we assign the permissions to the FinanceGrp. The fact that they are in the Organizational Unit makes no difference when you wish to assign permissions to objects contained inside the Organizational Unit. However, if we wish to delegate someone to have permission to manage those 50 accounts, we place the administrative delegation onto the Organizational Unit. Here we'll be talking about how to effectively design user accounts and the groups those users belong to.

Naming and placing users

When you are designing users, the only thing you really have to worry about is the username or user identifier that the client logs on with. Each username (the sAM-AccountName property of a user object) must be unique throughout each domain.

Arguably, if you have decided to delegate administration within your organization, you need to create a naming scheme to which each administrator will adhere so that unique usernames are generated for all users throughout your forest. That way, if you ever collapse the existing domains, you never need to rename the users if there are any conflicts. Naming groups is important, too.

Another name that you must give to all Active Directory users is known as the user principal name (the userPrincipalName property of the user object). This property looks like an RFC 822 email address, i.e., *username@here.there.somewhere.com*. In fact, this property is not the email address but is a unique identifier for the user in the entire forest. It has to be unique as it is stored in the GC. So while the users AlistairGLN in *mycorp.com* and AlistairGLN in *finance.mycorp.com* are perfectly valid, their UPNs (as the attribute is more commonly called) must be different. The normal way to create a UPN is simply to append an @ symbol and the domain onto the end of the username. This ensures uniqueness because the username was unique in the domain, and appending the domain forces a unique forest-wide UPN. This makes *AlistairGLN@mycorp.com* and *AlistairGLN@finance.mycorp.com* the UPNs for the two users in the example.

However, while it is conventional to construct the UPNs in this way, you can in fact make the UPN of a user anything you wish. We could, for example, append the *domain@mycorp.com* to all our users, eliminating the need to rely on domains at all. If we do that though, we need to make sure that our usernames (sAMAccount-Name) in each domain are unique not only domain-wide but also forest-wide. In the previous example, we can't have two users with the username AlistairGLN. For such a scheme to work, a central database or allocating authority needs to be set up to uniquely generate and allocate names. Leicester University has maintained a separate database from the early 1980s for this purpose, as have many other universities and companies. If this database or authority can generate unique usernames via a reliable algorithm, you can make use of a much simpler UPN.

Just because we chose *@mycorp.com* as the suffix does not mean we are limited to a forest or domain name. We could just as easily have chosen *@moosebanana.com*, which has no relation to the domains or the forest. The UPN simply has to be unique for every user in the forest.

UPNs are very important. Imagine a user sitting down at a client anywhere in a forest and being presented with the logon dialog box. Here he can type in his username (sAMAccountName), password, and domain and be authenticated to the forest. However, it is perfectly valid to authenticate with the UPN. If the user, presented with the same logon dialog box, instead types a UPN in the first field, the domain box becomes grayed out and inaccessible. In other words, a UPN and a password are all that is needed to authenticate to the tree. This makes sense, since the UPN is unique forest-wide, so apart from a password, nothing else should be needed. You now should be able to see that even with a very large and complex set of domains in a forest, you can use a simplified UPN form that does not contain a domain component and simply instruct users to log on with a UPN and a password. This means that users never need to care about what domain they are in.

Your choice of where you place the user accounts in each domain's hierarchy really is affected only by who is to administer the accounts and what GPOs will be applied on the Organizational Unit the account is in. Other than that, it makes little difference.

Naming and placing groups

Groups (especially universal groups that get stored in the GC) need unique names, too. A naming scheme for groups should be laid out in the design. Where you put groups is less important. In effect, groups can go almost anywhere in the hierarchy. The GPOs that determine your placement of users, for example, do not apply to groups. However, as the groups available to you will differ based on the mode or functional level of your forest, the only way you can do a proper design is to know roughly how long you intend to stay in mixed or interim mode before upgrading. If you have no previous Windows NT infrastructure and do not require any applications that run on NT, you can go native and Windows 2003 forest functional level immediately.

If you are planning to wait a while on mixed/interim mode before upgrading, for whatever reason, you need to do two sets of group designs: what the groups will be prior to the upgrade and what you will convert them to after the upgrade. Of course, the two designs may be the same.

 Going native in one domain does not have to affect the mode of another domain. There is nothing wrong with *apac.ad.mycorp.com* going native while *ad.mycorp.com* is mixed mode or vice versa. Remember that mixed mode and native mode affect only the use of BDCs in a domain, not the use of Windows NT clients or member servers.

Creating proper security group designs

If your organization is based on a single site (in the sense of being a "fast interconnected set of subnets," which is detailed in the next chapter), you can use universal security groups entirely. You don't have to, but for the purposes of design, it will make very little difference in the long run which you choose.

Assuming, however, that your organization has multiple domains, you should make use of Domain Local Security and Domain Global Security groups as well as Universal Security groups. If you wish to use Universal Security groups, do not put individual users into them as members. Remember that the Universal Security group and its members are held in the GC, so if you only add other groups as members you are unlikely to create as many group memberships as you would using individual users. That will limit the size of the GC and thus the impact of replication.

Based on the tables in Chapter 2, for large complex organizations with many different sets of permissions to many individual resources, we would still suggest using two sets of security groups. One set of security groups has permissions to local resources on a particular server, and the other set of security groups contains the users. You then can add one set of security groups to another to control access. In this manner, you are maintaining a fine-grained control over the access permissions for groups while not having to add users many times over to multiple groups.

In mixed mode, we would use Domain Local Security groups for access to local resources and add users to Domain Global Security groups or even Universal Distribution groups. In native mode we would do one of three things:

- Continue as before, but now allow Universal Security groups to be members of Domain Local Security groups.
- Convert the Domain Local Security groups to Universal Security groups with the same membership as before, because this is now allowed under native mode.
- Convert the Domain Local Security groups and Domain Global Security groups to Universal Security groups, understanding the impact this will have on the GC and the potential for token explosion.

Step 6—Global Catalog Design

The GC is part friend, part enemy. When it comes to aiding searches, it is very useful, but the GC can be a real problem if it starts replicating data everywhere. If you properly design the GC and understand its limitations, you are unlikely to have problems.

The GC design is dependent partially on the namespace and partially on the replication design. On the namespace side, designing the GC's contents is important to properly respond to searches, and on the replication side, designing the GC to interact using a reasonable amount of your bandwidth is important. We'll consider only half the picture in this chapter and do a draft design, coming back and revising the draft design in the next chapter. You have the choice of adding multiple GC servers or of not even hosting the GC on a site at all if you wish.

With Windows Server 2003 Active Directory, the dependencies on the GC are not as great as with Windows 2000. With Windows 2000 Active Directory, a GC had to be available for clients to log in. This was necessary because a user's universal groups needed to be enumerated to ensure their token was complete and accurate. Universal group membership is stored in the GC, and since universal group objects can reside anywhere in a forest, the only way for a DC to determine what universal groups a user is a member of is by querying the GC. In Windows Server 2003, you can enable universal group caching and effectively eliminate the need for a GC to be present during login. This means you no longer have to deploy GC servers just to ensure users can log in.

 Universal group caching can be enabled on a per-site basis via the Active Directory Sites and Services MMC snap-in. The settings to enable universal group caching are available by editing the NTDS Site Settings object of the site you want to enable it for.

Each attribute in the Active Directory schema has a modifiable attribute that is used to indicate whether the attribute is to be contained in the GC. Most objects store at least one property in the GC, even if it is only their common name (cn) attribute. Examples of properties that are held in the GC include the password for all user objects (so that authentication is rapid) and the access permissions for each object (so that details on objects are not given out in responses if the requester does not have the relevant permissions).

 You can access the GC and look at its contents via an Active Directory viewer, such as ADSI Edit, by using the GC://Programmatic Identifier (ProgID).

If an attribute that you specifically do not want included is being placed in the GC, you can exclude it. You can do this either by unchecking the box in the Schema Manager MMC or programmatically via ADSI by setting isMemberOfPartialAttributeSet equal to FALSE. If you want an attribute included in the GC, the process is the reverse.

Obviously, the more data that you specify to be stored in the GC, the larger the GC will get. If the attribute that you include is for a class that contains only a handful of objects, the impact will be negligible. If you specify an attribute for a class of object that has tens of thousands of instances, you will impact the size of the GC.

 The larger the GC gets, the longer each search will take and the more bandwidth will be taken up as these extra attributes replicate every time they change.

This doesn't mean that you should not change anything. You just have to be aware of the potential impact. The time taken for searches is not immediately easy to measure. Every administrator knows that network bandwidth utilization is never the same twice and fluctuates every second with different numbers of users doing different tasks. This will affect your query times.

What you need to consider in this stage of namespace design is which attributes you wish to include and which default attributes you wish to exclude. This decision is affected by the fact that searches for properties that are contained in the GC are conducted forestwide, while searches for properties not contained in the GC are conducted only domainwide.

 Only members of the schema administrators group (Schema Admins) in the forest root domain can modify whether schema attributes are included in or excluded from the GC. This group can have members from any domain, but the group itself is contained in the forest root domain.

Including and Excluding Attributes

Microsoft has decided that a certain core set of attributes should go in the GC. If you wish to remove attributes from the GC, any searches on the attributes that you remove will be conducted only within the domain that generated the query.

You can add any attribute you want to the GC, but you have to be aware of the ramifications. When you add a new attribute to the GC, the value contained within that attribute for every object that uses that attribute must be replicated to every GC server. Depending on how you disperse your GC servers and the configuration of your network, this could be a major event. But if the attribute you are adding is not populated on many or any objects, the impact will be minimal.

 A script to write out a list of those attributes of a class that are included in the GC alongside a list of those that are excluded is contained in Chapter 24.

Finally, a word of caution: you must be careful when excluding attributes from the default set. It's fine to exclude attributes that seem to make little difference to the overall picture, but restricting attributes that other applications may be depending on can be problematic.

Step 7—Design the Application Partition Structure

Another significant namespace design issue to consider is the application partition structure for your forest. As described in Chapter 3, application partitions, new to Windows Server 2003 Active Directory, are user-defined partitions that have a customized replication scope. Application partitions can be especially helpful in branch office deployment scenarios where you have to deploy a lot of domain controllers. Often you'll have applications that want to store data in Active Directory, but that data is not pertinent or used frequently enough to warrant replicating to all domain controllers, especially in the branch offices. With application partitions, you can configure a new partition to hold application data that replicates data only among your hub domain controllers. The other great thing about application partitions is that you are not restricted by domain boundaries. If you want to replicate data globally and have domain controllers geographically located, you can create an application partition that replicates data between your geographically dispersed domain controllers regardless of which domain they reside in.

Application partitions have an impact on your namespace design because they are named very much like domains. For example, say you wanted to create an application partition in the *mycorp.com* forest; you could name it dc=apps,dc=mycorp,dc=com. In fact, application partitions have the same implications on the namespace and to DNS as do regular domains. So in the dc=apps,dc=mycorp,dc=com example, the *apps. mycorp.com* DNS domain will be populated with the standard SRV records, just like a domain.

You can also nest application partitions. For example, if you had a specific application you wanted to create a partition for, you could host it directly off the apps partition we just mentioned. We could name it dc=MyApp,dc=apps,dc=mycorp,dc=com.

Other Design Considerations

In many cases you may need to revise your namespace designs a number of times. Certainly GPOs will make a difference as to how you structure your users and computer objects, so we do not assume that one pass through a design process will be enough.

Once you have a basic design, there is nothing stopping you from putting that design to one side and working on identifying a perfect design for your Active Directory network, one that you would like to implement in your organization, ignoring all Active Directory–imposed design constraints. You then can work out how difficult it will be to move to that perfect design from the practical one that you worked out using the preceding steps. You can look at the feasibility of the move from one to the other and then rationalize and adjust your final design to take into account the factors you have listed. You can then use this as an iteration tool so that your final design is much closer to the perfection you are aiming for.

Apart from GPOs, which we cover in Chapters 7 and 10, there are other aspects of Active Directory design that we have not and will not be covering. For example, you are quite likely to want printers advertised in Active Directory so that they can be accessed easily using a simple search of Active Directory (which the Add Printer wizard now uses as the default option). You may want shares advertised in Active Directory, so that users can easily locate data partitions on a site nearest to them. The Distributed Filing System (DFS) that allows you to organize disjointed and distributed shares into a single contiguous hierarchy is a fine example of this in action. When you reference a share held by the DFS, the DFS uses Active Directory to automatically redirect your request to the closest share replica. There is also the matter of designing your own objects and attributes that you want to include. However, there are two points that you should consider:

- As a general rule, Active Directory should hold only static or relatively static data. At the very least, the lifetime of the data has to be greater than the time to replicate to all DCs throughout the organization. When considering which objects to add, don't consider adding objects with very short life spans.

- Any object that you include will have attributes that are held in the GC. For every type of object that you seek to store in Active Directory, check the schema class entry for that object to find out what attributes will be stored in the GC. Consider whether you need to add or remove items from that list by referring back to the design principles.

Design Examples

Having covered the design of the namespace, some real-world example designs are in order. We have created three fictitious companies that will serve as good models for demonstrations of the design process. We will also use these three companies in the following chapters. The companies themselves are not fully detailed here, although there is enough information to enable you to make a reasonable attempt at a namespace design. In the chapters that follow, we will expand the relevant information on each company as required for that part of the design.

We used a number of criteria to create these companies:

- The companies were set up to represent various organizations and structures.
- While each corporation has a large number of users and machines, the design principles will scale down to smaller organizations well.
- In these example corporations, we are not interested in how many servers each company has or where those servers are. These facts come into play in the next chapter on sites. We are interested in users, groups, machines, domains, and the business and administration models that are used.

TwoSiteCorp

TwoSiteCorp is an organization that employs 50,000 people using 50,000 machines. The organization spans 2 sites connected with a 128 Kb dedicated link. The London site has 40,000 clients and 40,000 employees, while the new expansion at the Leicester site has 10,000 clients and 10,000 employees. TwoSiteCorp's business model is based on a structure in which users are members of one of three divisions: U.K. Private Sector, U.K. Public Sector, and Foreign. No division is based entirely at one site. Various other minor divisions exist beneath these as required for the management structure. Administration is handled centrally from the major London site by a team of dedicated systems administrators.

Step 1—Set the number of domains

While TwoSiteCorp's 128 Kb link between its two physical locations is slow for site purposes, there is no need to split the two sites into two domains. No particular part of the organization has a unique policy requirement, because the administrators decided that they will implement one set of policies for all users. Finally, the sites already have two Windows NT domains installed. However, management has no desire to maintain either, so both will be rationalized into one domain. Thus, TwoSiteCorp will end up with one domain.

Step 2—Design and name the tree structure

TwoSiteCorp's single domain will be the forest root domain. The designers decide to name the domain *twositecorp.com* after their DNS domain name. With only one domain, they do not have to worry about any other trees or forests or the domain hierarchy.

Step 3—Design the workstation and server naming scheme

TwoSiteCorp decides that each machine name will be made up of four strings concatenated together. The first string is three characters representing the location of the machine (e.g., LEI or LON). The next three characters are used to indicate the operating system (e.g., WXP, W2K, NT4, or W98). The next string holds two or three letters indicating the type of machine (e.g., DC, SRV, or WKS). Finally, the last string is a six-digit numeric string that starts with 000001 and continues to 999999. The following are example machine names:

- LEIW2KDC000001
- LEIW2KDC000002
- LONNT4WKS000183

Step 4—Design the hierarchy of Organizational Units

TwoSiteCorp needs three major Organizational Units (U.K. Private Sector, U.K. Public Sector, and Foreign) based on its business model of divisions. The second and succeeding tiers of Organizational Units can then be created according to the lower-level management structure if required. There is no necessity to do so in this scenario, although it would make the structure easier to manage visually. In fact, this domain could be completely flat with all users and machines in one Organizational Unit, but then you aren't gaining much from Active Directory's ability to structure the data in a useful manner for administration. Speaking of administration, since it is handled centrally, there is no need to delegate administration for the three top-tier Organizational Units to any specific group of administrators, although there is room for expansion should that become necessary. Nor does TwoSiteCorp need to delegate any other permissions to the Organizational Unit structure. Now TwoSiteCorp has a fairly simple hierarchy that perfectly maps their domain.

Step 5—Design the users and groups

TwoSiteCorp has two Windows NT domains at present using a variety of global groups and local groups. During the migration, the company will have a mixed-mode domain. However, their ultimate aim is to move to native mode very quickly and reap the added benefits of universal groups. The design therefore needs to cover what universal groups the company would like for its resources. The existing global and local groups can be moved to Active Directory during migration, allowing the current setup to work with the new system. Once the switchover to native mode goes ahead, either the groups can be converted to universal groups and rationalized to fit into the new design, or they can be left as they are and new universal groups created according to the design to take the place of the old groups.

Step 6—Design the Global Catalog

TwoSite Corp has no specific GC requirements and therefore leaves the system to work out its own defaults.

Step 7—Design the application partition structure

Since TwoSiteCorp has only two sites to replicate, they do not need to create any application partitions.

Recap

This is a very simple system that maintains a good level of administration based on the structure of the organization while managing to maintain control over its expansion in the years to come.

RetailCorp

RetailCorp is a global, multibillion-dollar retail organization that has more than 600 stores spread throughout the world under 4 different store names. There are around 60,000 staff members in the company, with about 25,000 in the central office based in Leicester in the United Kingdom. Each store is connected to the central HQ via 64 Kb leased lines. Each store has a number of Windows NT point-of-sale workstations running database software and one or more large database servers in the back room. The database servers replicate the day's transactions down the links each evening to the central HQ.

RetailCorp is very centralized with almost no administrators at the stores themselves. The only really special requirement that the company has is that it would like the administrators to be able to easily hide the operating environment from staff on the tills at each branch. Changes to tills should be possible on an individual branch or global level.

Step 1—Identify the number of domains

RetailCorp has no need to isolate replication or do any in-place upgrades. The part about policies is a little tricky: do they need new domains for every branch in case policy changes need to be applied to one branch specifically? The answer is no. The administrators need to be able to apply policies to certain branches or all branches, but these policies have to do with the user interface and thus fall into the area of GPOs rather than individual domains. That effectively leaves them with one domain.

Step 2—Design and name the tree structure

RetailCorp, having only one domain, makes that the forest root domain. The namespace has the *retailcorp.com* global name that is already in use.

Step 3— Design the workstation and server naming scheme

RetailCorp uses a central database to register machines, which automatically produces a 15-character name based on a machine's location and purpose (i.e., client, database server, file and print server). Every time a machine is moved or its function changes, the name is updated in the central database, and the machine is renamed.

Step 4—Design the hierarchy of Organizational Units

It is decided to make each store an Organizational Unit, so that central administrators can delegate control over individual stores and their objects as required. However, to make things even easier to manage and delegate on a countrywide or regional basis, RetailCorp creates a series of country Organizational Units under the base. Each of these country Organizational Units contains either the shop Organizational Units directly (for countries with only a handful of stores) or a series of regional Organizational Units that themselves contain the store OUs.

Step 5— Design the users and groups

RetailCorp uses a central database to generate its own unique usernames and group names as needed. It has done this for many years, and the database produces a changes file on an hourly basis. A script picks up the changes file and applies it to Active Directory in the same manner that it does with all other systems.

Step 6—Design the Global Catalog

RetailCorp has had problems with printers before, with users printing to printers at the wrong site. To make sure that printer details are not replicated past boundaries, all printer attributes are removed from the GC. The rest of the defaults are accepted as standard, and the company intends to keep an eye on the situation to make sure that there are no problems with this in the future.

Step 7—Design the application partition structure

Since RetailCorp is using a centralized deployment model and has no special replication requirements, there is no need to create any application partitions.

Recap

This example shows how a geographically based company can do its own design. It's not particularly difficult, although this design does not take into account the slow links between the stores and the HQ. That is left until the next chapter, when we revisit RetailCorp from a physical-layer perspective.

PetroCorp

PetroCorp (see Figure 8-1) is a global multibillion dollar petrochemical organization that has more than 100,000 people and machines at about 100 sites around the world. The business has its global headquarters in Denver. There are 5 major sites that link to the HQ and to which the smaller 94 branch offices link. The major sites or hubs represent Asia-Pacific, Australasia, USA-Canada, South America, and Europe. The small sites link to the 5 hubs via 64 Kb links; the hubs connect to the HQ via T2, T1, 256 Kb, and 128 Kb links. Some of the hubs are also interconnected. Management structure is geographic, with each geographical unit running itself as an independent business as part of the global whole. The top level of the management structure is at HQ, which sits above the 5 hubs. Even though Denver could be considered within the USA-Canada area, the organization is not structured that way. In fact, Denver oversees the hubs in terms of selecting the administrators and how the network is to be structured. Corporate policy dictates that branches that have more than 500 people have their own administrator, backup support, and helpdesk staff locally. Branches with fewer than 500 people have to be managed by the administrators of the hub to which they connect (see Figure 8-4).

Other considerations include the following:

- Due to special company policies, public-key encryption and different language settings are used in each of the hubs (and their branches). So Europe and its branches have different settings from those in Australasia and its branches.
- Japan has a database system running on Windows NT 4.0 that must stay in its own domain.
- PetroCorp recently acquired OtherCorp, a Canadian company that has a strong brand name that PetroCorp would like to maintain. OtherCorp is solely based in a new branch in Canada.
- The links between the eight South American branches and the hub are very unreliable.

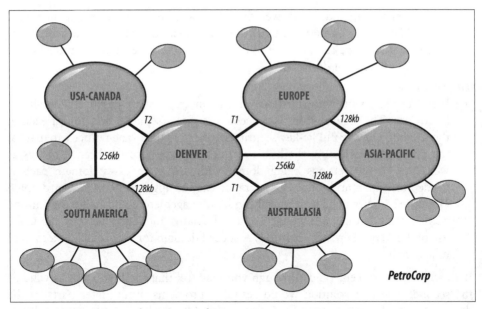

Figure 8-4. PetroCorp's wide area network

- The branch in France needs to maintain a number of Windows NT BDCs and member servers running legacy applications and services that will not run under Windows 2000. This requirement may exist for a few years.

- The Asia-Pacific 128 Kb link to Europe is severely congested at all times.

- Current U.S. laws explicitly state that information in a U.S. directory can be published anywhere except in countries that are subject to American export restrictions (currently including but not necessarily limited to Cuba, the Federal Republic of Yugoslavia (Serbia and Montenegro), Iran, Iraq, Libya, North Korea, and Syria). Since Active Directory is a directory that has the United States as its origin, it cannot be exported to those countries.

Step 1—Set the number of domains

There is a wrong way and a right way to look at PetroCorp:

The wrong way

PetroCorp starts off with five domains representing the hubs because each requires different public-key security settings.* As the branch offices are part of the domain at each hub, the hub's settings will apply to the branch offices as well because the settings are domainwide. So extra domains are not needed, although they are needed for each branch office for Japan and OtherCorp. As

---

* That they also require different language settings is a red herring: Windows 2000 can support different language settings on a per-client basis rather than a per-domain basis like Windows NT.

France cannot upgrade, whatever domain France is in must remain in mixed mode. Management could make the Europe domain mixed mode but would like it to be native mode to make use of the features. So a special domain for France makes a total of eight domains.

The right way

PetroCorp starts off with one domain: the one representing Denver, the HQ of PetroCorp. The organization then needs to create a separate domain for each of the five hubs for the public-key security settings. As the branch offices are part of the domain at each hub, the hub's settings will apply to the branch offices as well, due to the settings being domainwide. Now an extra domain each is needed for Japan and OtherCorp. France cannot upgrade, so whatever domain France is in must remain in mixed mode. Management could make the Europe domain mixed mode, but would like it to be native mode so that they can make use of the Active Directory features. A special domain for France makes a total of nine domains.

Both solutions can seem valid, although you may feel that the first is not as valid as the second. The first solution would result in problems during later parts of the design process. That there are different sites with different link speeds is not really an issue here. The issue revolves around the major HQ that is separate from but which oversees the five hubs in an administrative capacity. In the wrong design, one of these domains must become the forest root domain with the relevant authority that confers. USA-Canada is the natural choice. Then HQ administrators would effectively be running the USA-Canada domain, which conflicts with the initial company notes that each hub and the HQ has its own administrators. Consequently, the second design is better.

Step 2—Design and name the tree structure

PetroCorp chooses the Denver domain as the forest root domain. The forest root domain is to be called *petrocorp.com*.

When it comes to choosing a naming scheme for the domains corresponding to the hubs, the administrators choose a simple one. The domains will be called:

- *europe.petrocorp.com*
- *usacanada.petrocorp.com*
- *samerica.petrocorp.com*
- *asiapac.petrocorp.com*
- *australasia.petrocorp.com*

The domain representing OtherCorp will be called *othercorp.com*. They could have merged OtherCorp into PetroCorp's structure and just used multiple DNS names for the web servers and so on. However, the company may be sold for a profit in the future, and management wants to keep it politically separate.

There are obviously now two distinct trees. We'll put them in the same forest so that resources can be shared. The subdomain hierarchy is fairly easy to follow from now on. The domains for France and Japan will follow ISO 3166 country codes and be called *fr.europe.petrocorp.com* and *jp.asiapac.petrocorp.com*. Figure 8-5 shows the forest view of the domain trees.

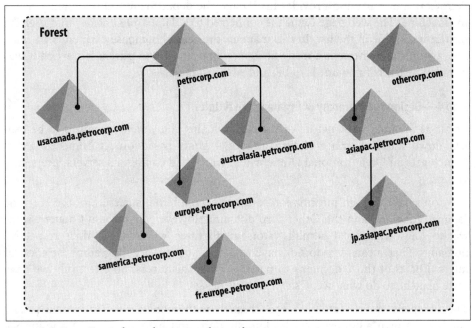

Figure 8-5. PetroCorp's forest domain tree hierarchies

Step 3—Design the workstation and server naming scheme

PetroCorp has decided that it specifically does not want to use any parts of its naming scheme to duplicate data that can be obtained elsewhere. For example, Petro-Corp does not want to use country, city, or building information, as this can be gathered from the exact Active Directory site that the client is in. For example, there's no point in including the data UK, London, Building 3 if the site that the computer resides in is called UK-London-Building3. They also do not want to include indications of the operating system or version, as they will be using Microsoft Systems Management Server (SMS) to inventory each device; the required information can be retrieved directly from SMS's own database. They do, however, want to include the department that the client is installed in.

They also decide to use this name as part of the worldwide asset-registering system under development, so that they can institute a worldwide rolling update program of older devices. Thus, they need to include the year the client was purchased and when the client was introduced to the network.

To do this, they decide to take a leaf from the FSMO RID Master's book and use a central pool of values at their HQ for the naming of machines. Names of machines will start with a department code of seven or fewer letters, followed by a two-digit year code and a number consisting of six or fewer digits, allocated from the central pool.

When a client is to be installed, the user doing the installation goes to a web page on PetroCorp's intranet and provides his ID and the department and two-digit year for the machine. The web page (which is connected to a database) allocates that user the next central value in the list. In this manner, the central database maintains an exact note of which department a machine is in, what year it was purchased, when it was installed, what its full name is to be, and who installed it.

Step 4—Design the hierarchy of Organizational Units

As far as the internal structure of the hub domains goes, each domain is to be broken down into a number of Organizational Units based on its branches. Every branch gets an Organizational Unit created, which will contain its servers, users, and groups.

We don't have enough information to specify the internal structure of the HQ, the Japanese domain, and the OtherCorp domain. However, that doesn't matter, since we do know that local administrators at all three will manage their respective domains. That means we do not have to worry about delegating administration of internal parts of those domains to particular administrators. So effectively we have carte blanche to do what we wish with those designs.

The company notes state that each branch with more than 500 people locally employs its own administrator, backup support, and helpdesk staff. Assuming we have identified the standard set of permissions that each of the 3 sets of staff require at each branch, we need to delegate administrative responsibility for the 3 functions to the relevant groups of staff in those branches. Branch staff members now have administrative responsibility for their branch Organizational Unit only, and branches without any staff will be centrally managed.

Step 5—Design the users and groups

In addition to whatever other groups the organization's designers decide it needs, three groups corresponding to the three delegated jobs need to be created in every branch that is to have autonomous control. These three groups will be used when delegating responsibility.

Any domains intending to stay on Windows NT (i.e., France) can run in mixed mode, with other domains going native as soon as is feasible. Domain Global Security and Domain Local Security will be mainly used, although a scattering of Domain Universal Security groups will be used in the native-mode domains as soon as conversion takes place.

Step 6—Design the Global Catalog

Current U.S. laws explicitly state that information in a U.S. directory can be published anywhere except in countries that are subject to American export restrictions. As PetroCorp's Active Directory is a directory that has the United States as its origin, Active Directory cannot be exported to those countries. That throws a monkey wrench into PetroCorp's design, as PetroCorp has offices in several of those countries.

PetroCorp has a number of solutions open to them. They could have Europe or Australia host the PetroCorp domain and make the Denver office a subdomain, with Denver managing both. That's not particularly appropriate here. There are many other variations along those lines as well as a number of solutions that are workable. Here are two examples:

- Create entirely separate domains in separate forests in those countries. These forests, being outside the central forest, will have no Global Catalog exporting issues.

- Create one entirely new forest called something like *export.petrocorp.com*, which is not in any way related to the existing *petrocorp.com* domain even though the name appears that way. The *export.petrocorp.com* forest could contain servers from all the companies that have export restrictions, holding them together under one manageable structure. This can be hosted (have the forest root domain in another country) and be remotely managed. Manual trusts between forests can now be considered as long as these don't also break the laws.

Step 7—Design the application partition structure

PetroCorp has several corporate applications that need to store data in Active Directory. Since everyone in the company uses these applications, placing the data in a single domain would not be sufficient. For this reason, an application partition should be created and replicated to a domain controller in each major geographic location.

Recap

This example shows how a global company can create its own design and maintain a large degree of control. It also shows how laws in the real world can wreak havoc with a good design!

Designing for the Real World

It's very easy to get bogged down in the early stages of the namespace design without actually progressing much further. The stumbling block seems to be that it feels conceptually wrong to have only one domain, yet administrators can't put their finger on what the problem is. Experienced Windows NT administrators who manage multiple domains seem to find this much more of a problem than those coming from another operating system.

If you follow the guidelines in the initial steps of the namespace design, you quite probably will end up with one domain to start with. That's the whole point of the design process: to reduce the number of domains you need. Yet NT administrators tend to feel that they have conceptually lost something very important; with only one domain, somehow this design doesn't "feel right."

This is partly a conceptual problem: a set of domains with individual objects managed by different teams can feel more secure and complete than a set of Organizational Units in a single domain containing individual objects managed by different teams. It's also partly an organizational problem and, possibly, a political problem. Putting in an Active Directory environment is a significant undertaking for an organization and shouldn't be taken lightly. This change is likely to impact everyone across the company, assuming you're deploying across the enterprise. Changes at that level are likely to require ratification by a person or group who may not be directly involved on a day-to-day basis with the team proposing the change. So you have to present a business case that explains the benefits of moving to Active Directory.

Identify the Number of Domains

Following our advice in this chapter and Microsoft's official guidelines from the white papers or Resource Kit will lead most companies to a single domain for their namespace design. It is your network, and you can do what you want. More domains give you better control over replication traffic but may mean more expense in terms of hardware. If you do decide to have multiple domains but have users in certain locations that need to log on to more than one domain, you need DCs for each domain that the users need in that location. This can be expensive. We'll come back to this again later, but let's start by considering the number of domains you need.

If the algorithm we use to help you determine the number of domains gives you too small a figure in your opinion, here's how you can raise it:

- Have one domain for every single-master and multimaster Windows NT domain that you have. If you are using the Windows NT multimaster domain model, consider the entire set of multimasters as one domain under Active Directory (use Organizational Units for your resource domains).

- Have one domain per geographical region, such as Asia-Pacific, Africa, Europe, and so on.

- Have extra domains whenever putting data into one domain would deny you the control over replication that you would like if you used Organizational Units instead. It's all very well for us to say that Organizational Units are better, but that isn't true in all situations. If you work through the algorithm and come up with a single domain holding five Organizational Units, but you don't want any of the replication traffic from any of those Organizational Units to go around to certain parts of your network, you need to consider separate domains.

Even Microsoft didn't end up with one domain. They did manage to collapse a lot of Windows NT domains, though, and that's what you should be aiming for if you have multiple Windows NT domains.

Design to Help Business Plans and Budget Proposals

There are two parts to this: how you construct a business case itself for such a wide-reaching change and how you can show that you're aiming to save money with this new plan.

Simply stated, your business case should answer two main questions:

- Why should you not stay where you are now?
- Why should you move to Active Directory?

If you can sensibly answer these two questions, you've probably solved half your business case; the other half is cost. Here we're talking about actual money. Will using Active Directory provide you with a tangible business cost reduction? Will it reduce your Total Cost of Ownership (TCO)? It sure will, but only if you design it correctly. Design it the wrong way, and you'll increase costs.

Imagine first that you have a company with two sites, Paris and Leicester, separated by a 64 Kb WAN link. Now imagine you have one domain run by Leicester. You do not have to place a DC in Paris if it is acceptable that when a user logs on, the WAN link uses bandwidth for items like these:

- Roaming user profiles
- Access to resources, such as server-based home directories
- GPOs
- Application deployment via Microsoft Installer (MSI) files

If authentication across the link from Paris would represent a reasonable amount of traffic, but you do not want profiles and resources coming across the slow link, you could combat that by putting a member server in Paris that could service those resources. You could even redirect application deployment mount points to the local member server in Paris (note that I'm saying member server and not DC here). However, if GPOs themselves won't go across the link, you need to consider a DC in Paris holding all the local resources. That gives you two sites, one domain, and two DCs.

Now let's expand this to imagine that you have a company with 50 WAN locations; they could be shops, banks, suppliers, or whatever. These are the Active Directory sites. Next, imagine that the same company has 10 major business units: Finance, Marketing, Sales, IS, and so on. You really have 3 choices when designing Active Directory for this environment:

- Assuming everything else is equal, create a single domain with a DC in whichever sites require faster access than they would get across any link. Now make the business units Organizational Units under the single domain.

Pro

Everything is in one domain.

Pro

You need as many DCs as you have sites with links that you consider too slow. If you want to count a rough minimum, make it 1 DC per site with more DCs for larger sites; that is a rough minimum of 50 DCs. This is a low-cost solution.

Pro

With one forest and one domain, any user can log on quickly anywhere because authentication is always to a local DC.

Con

Every part of the domain is replicated to every other part of the domain, so you have no granularity if you don't want objects from one business unit replicating to DCs everywhere.

- Create multiple domains representing the 10 major business units. Place DCs for each business unit in whichever sites require faster access than they would get across any link.

Pro

This means more domains than the previous solution, but replication can now be better controlled on a per-business unit basis between sites.

Con

Active Directory cannot host multiple domains on a single DC. This can make for an extremely high cost due to the large number of DCs that you may need. If you need to be able to log on to each of the 10 business unit domains from every site, you need 10 DCs per site, which makes 500 DCs. That's a much more costly solution.

Pro/Con

With one forest and multiple domains, any user can log on quickly at any site that has a local DC for her domain; otherwise, she would have to span a WAN link to authenticate her logon and send down her data.

- Create multiple domains representing geographical regions that encompass the 50 sites. Make these geographical regions the domains and have each domain hold Organizational Units representing business units that contain only the users from that region.

Pro

Even if you end up with 10 geographic regions, the DCs for each region are placed only in the sites belonging to that region. So if there were 5 sites per region (to make the math simple), each of the 5 needs only 1 DC. As the namespace model is a geographic model, you need to place a DC for Europe in the Asia-Pacific region only if the Asia-Pacific region ever has visiting users from Europe who need to authenticate faster than they would across the WAN link from Asia-Pacific to Europe. So the number of DCs that you need is going to be smaller.

Pro

Domain replication traffic occurs now only within a region and between regions that has DCs hosting the same domain.

Con

You end up duplicating the business units in all the domains... or maybe not, if some don't need all business units—you get the idea.

Pro/Con

With one forest and multiple domains, any user can log on quickly at any site that has a local DC for his domain; otherwise he would have to span a WAN link to authenticate his logon and send down his data.

We hope this illustrates that while it is easy to map a simple and elegant design on paper, there can be limitations on the feasibility of the design based on replication issues, DC placement, and cost.

Recognizing Nirvana's Problems

Arguably, there are a number of "best" ways to design depending on whom you talk to. We propose an iterative approach with Active Directory, and this is probably going to happen anyway due to the nature of the many competing factors that come into play. On your first pass through this chapter, you'll get a draft design in hand for the namespace. In Chapter 9, you'll get a draft site and replication design. Then you'll come up against the issue that your namespace design may need changing based on the new draft sites and replication design, specifically on the issues of domain replication and server placement that we have just covered. After you've revised the namespace design, you can sit down and look at the GPO design (using Chapters 7 and 10) in a broad sense, as this will have an impact on the Organizational Unit structure that you have previously drafted in your namespace design. And so it goes.

While this is the way to design, you will come up against parts of your organization that do not fit in with the design that you're making. The point is to realize that your job is to identify a very good solution for your organization and then decide how to adapt that solution to the real world that your company lives in. One domain may be ideal but may not be practicable in terms of cost or human resources. You have to go through stages of modifying the design to a compromise solution that you're happy with.

Summary

In this chapter, we presented a series of seven steps toward effective namespace design:

1. Decide on the number of domains.
2. Design and name the tree structure.
3. Design the workstation and server naming scheme.
4. Design the hierarchy of Organizational Units.
5. Design the users and groups.
6. Design the Global Catalog.
7. Design the application partition structure.

Following these seven steps allows you to solve the two main objectives of this chapter:

- Come up with an Active Directory namespace design to represent the structure of your business.
- Minimize the number of domains by making much more use of the more flexible Organizational Units.

While we've shown you how to start to design your Active Directory, there is still a long way to go. Designing the namespace of domains, trees, and forests and the internal Organizational Unit hierarchy according to the guidelines given here means that you should have a structural template that represents your business model within the preceding restrictions. Hopefully this design makes sense in terms of your organization and will be simpler to manage.

The rest of the design still needs to be completed. You need to look at the low-level network links between sites and how they will affect your replication decisions. You then need to tackle the subject of how to revise the initial namespace design based on Group Policy Objects, security delegation and auditing, schema changes, and so on. Next we'll move on to designing the physical site topology that the DCs use when communicating with one another.

CHAPTER 9

Creating a Site Topology

As we mentioned in Chapter 5, there are two aspects to replication:

- How data gets replicated around an existing network of links between DCs
- How the Knowledge Consistency Checker generates and maintains the replication links between servers, both intrasite and intersite

We covered the former in Chapter 5, and we'll cover the latter here, leading to an explanation of how to properly design a representation of your organization's network infrastructure within Active Directory.

Intrasite and Intersite Topologies

Two distinct types of replication links exist with Active Directory sites: intrasite (within sites) and intersite (between sites). An Active Directory service known as the Knowledge Consistency Checker (KCC) is responsible for automatically generating the replication links between intrasite DCs. The KCC will create intersite links automatically for you but only when an administrator has specified that two sites should be connected. Every aspect of the KCC and the links that are created is configurable, so you can manipulate what has been automatically created and what will be automatically created via manipulation of the various options. You can even disable the KCC if you wish and manually create all links.

Note that there is a large distinction between the KCC (the process that runs every 15 minutes and creates the replication topology) and the replication process itself. The KCC is not involved in the regular work of replicating the actual data in any way. Intrasite replication along the links created by the KCC uses a notification process to announce that changes have occurred. So each domain controller is responsible for notifying its replication partners of changes. If no changes occur at all within a 6-hour period, the replication process is kicked off automatically anyway just to make sure. Intersite replication, on the other hand, does not use a notification process. Instead it uses a replication schedule to transfer updates, using compression to reduce the total traffic size.

The KCC and the topologies it generates have been dramatically improved in Windows Server 2003 Active Directory. With Windows 2000 Active Directory, when there were more than 200 sites with domain controllers, it could take the KCC longer than 15 minutes to complete and also drive up CPU utilization. Since the KCC runs every 15 minutes, it could get backlogged or not finish. Typically when faced with this situation, administrators had to disable the KCC and manually create connection objects. With Windows Server 2003, Microsoft has stated that the new limit is closer to 5,000 sites when running a forest at the Windows Server 2003 forest functional level, which is a vast improvement. In fact, the KCC was largely rewritten in Windows Server 2003 and is much more scalable and efficient.

However, we don't think as an Active Directory administrator you should just accept the topologies it creates without examining them in detail. You should investigate and understand what has been done by the KCC. If you then look over the topology and are happy with it, you have actively, rather than passively, accepted what has been done. While letting the KCC do its own thing is fine, every organization is different, and you may have requirements for the site and link design that it is not aware of and cannot build automatically.

Other administrators will want to delve into the internals of Active Directory and turn off the KCC entirely, doing everything by hand. This approach is valid, as long as you know what you're doing, but we prefer to let the KCC do its work, helping it along with a guiding hand every now and then. We cover all these options in the design section later.

The KCC

DCs within sites have links created between them by the KCC. These links use the DC's GUID as the unique identifier. These links exist in Active Directory as connection objects and use only the Directory Service Remote Procedure Call (DS-RPC) transport to replicate with one another. No other replication transport mechanism is available. However, when you need to connect two sites, you manually create a site link via the Active Directory Sites and Services MMC snap-in and specify a replication transport to use. When you do this, the Intersite Topology Generator (ISTG) automatically creates connection objects in Active Directory between domain controllers in the two sites. Within each site, an ISTG is designated to generate the intersite topology for that particular site via the KCC process. There are two replication transports to choose from when creating a site link: standard DS-RPC or Inter-Site Mechanism Simple Mail Transport Protocol (ISM-SMTP). The latter means sending updates via the mail system using certificates and encryption for security.

There are two reasons that the ISTG cannot automatically create links between two sites. First, the ISTG has no idea which sites you will want to connect. Second, the ISTG does not know which replication transport protocol you will want to use.

The KCC runs locally every 15 minutes on each DC. The default time period can be changed, and it can be started manually on demand if required. If we create two servers called Server A and Server B in a new domain, the KCC will run on each server to create links. Each KCC is tasked with creating a link to define incoming replication only. The KCC on Server A will define an incoming link from Server B, and Server B's KCC will define an incoming link from Server A. The KCC creates only one incoming link per replication partner, so Server A will never have two incoming links from Server B, for example.

The KCC does not create one topology for all NCs, nor one topology per NC. The Configuration and Schema NCs share one replication topology, so the KCC creates a topology for these two together. The KCC also creates another topology on a per-domain basis. Because the Schema and Configuration are enterprisewide in scope, the KCC needs to replicate changes to these items across site links. The KCC needs to maintain a forestwide topology spanning all domains for these two NCs together. However, unless a domain is set up to span multiple sites, the topology for a particular domain will be made up of only intrasite connections. If the domain does span sites, the KCC needs to create a replication topology across those sites.

The GC is not a Naming Context in its own right, so it can't really have its own replication topology. As the GC is formed from a selection of attributes on those servers that host the GC in each domain, the GC replication becomes part of the replication for each domain. As two partners replicate a domain NC, the GC is replicated as well. There is no replication of the GC between different domains.

Automatic Intrasite Topology Generation by the KCC

For each NC, the KCC builds a bidirectional ring of links between the DCs in a site. However, while upstream and downstream links are created between partners around a ring, the KCC creates links across the ring as well. It does this to make sure that it stays within the following guidelines:

- Every DC must be within three hops of any other DC. This is known as the three-hop rule.
- The default latency (maximum time for replication between any two DCs) for replication is five minutes.
- The maximum convergence (maximum time for an update to reach all DCs) is 15 minutes.

Technically speaking, due to the three-hop rule, when you put in your eighth DC, the KCC will start adding branches across the circular ring.

Assuming you have five servers in a ring and you add a sixth, the other servers around the ring add and delete connection objects to accommodate the newcomer. So if Server C and Server D are linked, and Server F interposes itself between them, Server C and Server D delete their interconnections and create connections to Server F instead. Server F also creates connections to Server C and Server D. Let's take a look at this process in more detail.

Two servers

Mycorp starts off with one DC, Server A. When Server B is promoted as the second DC for the domain, the DCPROMO process uses Server A as its source for Active Directory information for the GC, Schema, and Configuration on Server B. During the promotion process, the Configuration Container is replicated from Server A to Server B, and Server B creates the relevant incoming connection object representing Server A. Server B then informs Server A that it exists, and Server A correspondingly creates the incoming connection object representing Server B. Replication now occurs for all NCs using the connection objects. While replication occurs separately for each NC, the same connection object is used for all three at this moment.

Three servers

The DCPROMO process is later started on Server C. Server C then uses a DNS lookup and picks one of the existing DCs to use as a promotion partner. For now we'll say that it picks Server B. During the promotion process, the Configuration container is replicated from Server B to Server C, and Server C creates the relevant incoming connection object representing Server B. Server C then informs Server B that it exists, and Server B correspondingly creates the incoming connection object representing Server C. Replication now occurs for all NCs using the connection objects.

At present, you have two-way links between Server A and Server B as well as between Server B and Server C. We have no links between Server A and Server C, but the KCC must create a ring topology for replication purposes. So as soon as Server B does a full replication to Server C, Server C knows about Server A from the Configuration NC. Server C's KCC then instantly creates an incoming connection object for Server A. Server A now finds out about Server C in one of two ways:

- Server A requests updates from Server B and identifies a new DC.
- Server C requests changes from Server A, and this allows Server A to identify the new DC.

Server A now creates an incoming connection object for Server C. This completes the Server A to Server B to Server C to Server A loop.

Four servers

Server D comes along, and the promotion process starts. It picks Server C to connect to. Server D ends up creating the incoming connection object for Server C. Server C also creates the incoming connection object for Server D. You now have the loop from the previous section plus a two-way link from Server C to Server D. See Figure 9-1 for this topology.

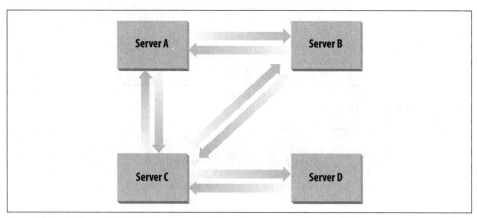

Figure 9-1. Adding a fourth DC to a site

Server D's KCC now uses the newly replicated data from Server C to go through the existing topology. It knows that it has to continue the ring topology, and as it is already linked to Server C, Server D has to create an incoming connection object for one of Server C's partners. It chooses Server B in this case. So Server D's KCC creates an incoming connection object for Server B. Server D then requests changes from Server B. The rest of the process can happen in a number of ways, so we'll just play out one scenario.

Server B now knows about Server D. Server B's KCC kicks into action and realizes that it doesn't need the link to Server C, so it deletes that connection and creates a new one directly to Server D itself. Finally, as replication takes place around the ring along the existing links, Server C notes that it has a now defunct incoming link from Server B and removes it. You now have a simple ring, as depicted in Figure 9-2.

Eight servers

Once you hit eight servers connected together, you need more links across the ring if you are to maintain the three-hop rule. If you look at Figure 9-3, you will see this demonstrated. If the cross-ring links did not exist, some servers would be four hops away from one another. The KCC figures out which servers it wishes to link by allowing the last server to enter the ring to make the initial choice. Thus, if Server H is the new server in the ring, it knows that Server D is four hops away and makes a connection to it. When Server D's KCC receives the new data that Server H has linked to it, it reciprocates and creates a link to Server H.

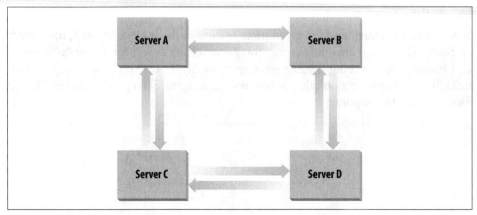

Figure 9-2. Ring of four DCs

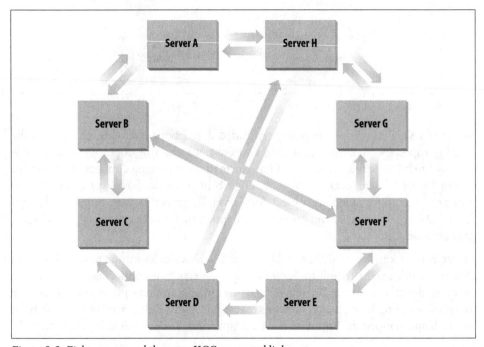

Figure 9-3. Eight servers and the extra KCC-generated links

However, this doesn't completely solve the problem. Consider Server B and Server F: they're still four hops away from each other. Now the KCC creates a link between these pairs to maintain the three-hop rule.

Now what?

We've now gone through the mechanism that the KCC uses for intrasite link generation between DCs. However, that's not the whole story. Remember that Active Directory can have multiple domains per site, so what happens if we add *othercorp.com* (a new domain in the same forest) to the same site or even *sales.mycorp.com* (a new child domain)? What happens then? The answer is the same for both, and it is based on NCs:

- The Schema and Configuration replicate across the enterprise, and they share a replication topology. Although they replicate separately, it is along the same links.

- Each domain replicates only domainwide, so the domain topologies for both domains stay in the same ring formation that they previously had.

Once the two domains integrate, the KCC-generated topologies for *mycorp.com* and the other domain stay the same. However, the KCC-generated Configuration/Schema replication topology that exists separately on both domains will form itself into its own ring, encompassing both domains according to standard KCC rules.

To summarize, when you have multiple domains in a site, each domain its own KCC-generated topology connecting its DCs, but all the DCs in the site, no matter what domain they come from, linked in a separate topology representing Schema/Configuration replication.

Site Links—The Basic Building Blocks of Intersite Topologies

Having sites is all well and good, but you need to be able to connect them if you are ever going to replicate any data. An intersite connection of this type is known as a *site link*. Site links are created manually by the administrator and are used to indicate that it is possible for two or more sites to replicate with each other. Site links connect more than two sites if the underlying physical network already connects multiple sites together using ATM, Frame Relay, MANs with T1 connections, or similar connections. For example, if a 64 Kbps Frame Relay network exists and is shared by multiple sites, all those sites can share a single site link.

Sites do not have to be physically connected by a network for replication to occur. Replication can occur via multiple links between any two hosts from separate sites. However, for Active Directory to be able to understand that replication should be occurring between these two sites, you have to create a site link between them.

Figure 9-4 shows part of a network that has two site links connecting three sites.

The site links correspond to the underlying physical network of two dedicated leased-line connections, with one network having a slightly higher cost than the other (not a monetary cost, but a value set by the administrator indicating the speed of the link). The Sales domain has two domain controllers that need to replicate, one in London and one in Brasilia. However, in this figure replication is broken, as the two DCs cannot directly replicate with each other over a single site link. This may

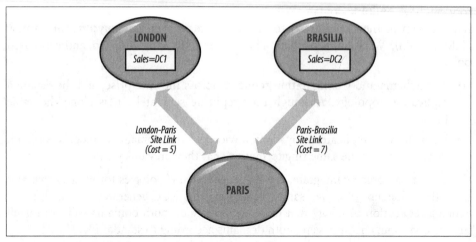

Figure 9-4. Broken Sales domain replication over site links

seem confusing as both servers are more than likely able to see each other across the network, but you must nevertheless create a site link between sites that have DCs that need to replicate.

Consider it another way. There are three ways to fix the problem. First, you could add a new Sales DC, say Sales=DC3, to Paris. This allows Sales=DC1 to replicate with Sales=DC3 and Sales=DC3 to replicate with Sales=DC2. Second, you could use a site link bridge, discussed in the next section. Third, you could create a third site link (with the combined cost of the two physical networks that will be used for the replication traffic) that indicates to the two servers that they can replicate with each other. Figure 9-5 shows that new site link in place.

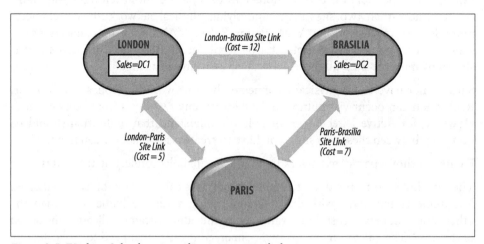

Figure 9-5. Working Sales domain replication over site links

Replication of the Sales domain is now possible between Sales=DC1 and Sales=DC2. Replication traffic will go over the existing physical links, for a total cost of 12 to use those links.

We've mentioned that site links have a cost, but that's not their only property. In fact, site links have four important properties:

Name
An identifying name for the site link.

Cost
An integer weighting for the site link that indicates the speed of the link relative to the other links that exist. Lower costs are faster; higher costs are slower.

Schedule
The times that are available for replication to occur. Replication does not occur on the site link outside of the scheduled times.

Transports
The protocols that are used for replication along this link.

Cost

As each link has a cost, it is possible to calculate the total cost of traveling over any one route by adding up all the costs of the individual routes. If multiple routes exist between two disparate sites, the KCC will automatically identify the lowest-cost route and use that for replication.

Schedule

The schedule on a link represents the time period that replication is allowed across that link. Servers also maintain times that they are allowed to replicate. Obviously, if two servers and a link do not have times that coincide, no replication will ever be possible.

Between the scheduled start and stop times for replication on a site link, the server is available to open so-called windows for replication to occur. As soon as any server that replicates through that link becomes available for replication, a replication window is opened between the site link and that server. As soon as two servers that need to replicate with each other have two windows that coincide, replication can occur. Once a server becomes unavailable for replication, the window is removed for that server. Once the site link becomes unavailable, all windows close.

 If two servers that need to replicate never have two replication windows that coincide, their connection is deemed to be unavailable

Transport

Site links can currently replicate using two transport mechanisms:

- Directory Service Remote Procedure Call (DS-RPC)
- Inter-Site Mechanism Simple Mail Transport Protocol (ISM-SMTP)

A site link using DS-RPC means that servers wishing to replicate using that site link can make direct synchronous connections using TCP/IP across the link. As the transport protocol is synchronous, the replication across the connection is conducted and negotiated in real time between two partners. This is the normal sort of connection for a real-time link. However, some sites may not be connected all the time. In fact, they may dial up only every half hour to send and receive email or be connected across the Internet, or they may even have a very unreliable link. This sort of link is where ISM-SMTP comes into play.

The SMTP connector, as a site link using the ISM-SMTP transport is called, allows partner DCs to encrypt and email their updates to each other. In this scenario, Active Directory assumes that you already have an underlying SMTP-based connection mechanism between these two sites. If you don't, you'll have to set one up for this to work. If a connection is in place, the SMTP Connector assumes that the existing underlying mail routing structure will sort out how mail is transferred. To that end, a site link using the SMTP Connector ignores the scheduling tab, as it will send and receive updates automatically via the underlying system whenever the email system sends and receives them itself.

SMTP Connector messages are encrypted using digital signatures, so to encrypt the messages, you need to install the optional Certificate Server service and obtain your own digital signature for your organization.

 The SMTP Connector cannot be used for domain NC replication. It can, however, be used to replicate GC, Schema, and configuration information. This means that multisite domains with slow links will be required to use DS-RPC for domain replication. Of course, this doesn't mean that the physical connection between sites has to be up all the time, only that it must be up when the DCs in each site communicate.

When the KCC becomes involved

When you have two sites that you want to connect, you have two options. You can manually create a site link between them, at which point the KCC will automatically connect together one DC from each site. The KCC will automatically select the DCs and create the relevant incoming connection objects for both servers. Alternatively, you can create the incoming connection objects manually in Active Directory using the Sites and Services snap-in. The two DCs that link two sites, no matter how the connection objects are created, are known as bridgehead servers.

The KCC actively uses site link costs to identify which routes it should be using for replication purposes. If a stable series of site links exists in an organization, and a new route is added with a lower cost, the KCC will switch over to use the new link where appropriate and delete the old link. The network of connections that the KCC creates is known as a minimum-cost-spanning tree.

Having the KCC compound your mistakes

If you make a mistake with site link costs, you can cause network problems very quickly. For this reason, you need to be aware of what the KCC is doing. If you bring up a new site link with a very high cost, say 50, and you accidentally leave off the zero, the route cost of 5 for the new site link may cause the KCCs on all DCs to suddenly reorganize the links to route through your new slow link. Your link becomes saturated, and your servers replicate much more slowly, if at all, over the slow link.

In fact, the KCC didn't make the mistake, but it has compounded it by following its algorithm. If a real cost-5 link were introduced that represented a real cost saving over many other routes, it is the KCC's job to switch over and use that link. That's why you always need to check your data for the intersite replication topology carefully.

While it's difficult to guard against occassionally making a mistake like this, no matter how careful an administrator you are, if you understand how the KCC works, you can use this information to debug potential problems much more rapidly.

Site Link Bridges—The Second Building Blocks of Intersite Topologies

While site links are used to indicate that replication can take place between two sites, site link bridges indicate that replication is possible between two sites that don't have a direct site link. Site link bridges can be created automatically by the KCC, or they can be created manually. When a bridge is created, certain specified site links become members of that bridge and are designated as being interconnected (or bridged) for replication purposes. The bridge knows how these sites are connected, so you could specify, for example, that this site link bridge bridged the London–Paris link and the Paris–Brasilia link. Then servers in Brasilia or London will see that a replication connection is now possible via the site link bridge, and the site link bridge will know that for traffic to get from London to Brasilia, it must use the London–Paris and then Paris–Brasilia links, in that order. Figure 9-6 demonstrates this in action.

The point here is that a site link bridge knows how the site links in its care are interconnected and thus how to route requests from one site through to another along its network of site links.

For a more complex example, consider the network of site links corresponding to physical networks in Figure 9-7.

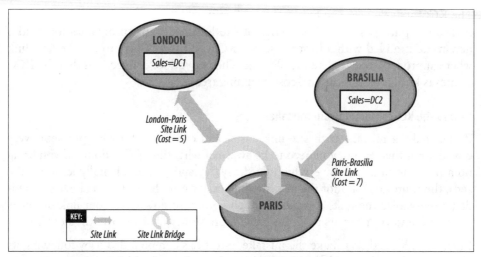

Figure 9-6. Working Sales domain replication using a site link bridge

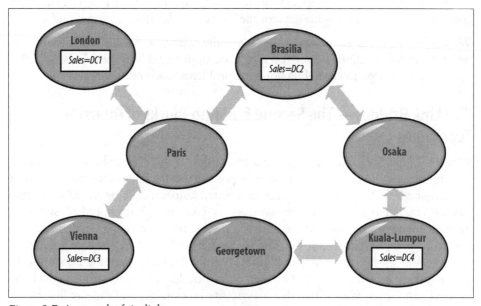

Figure 9-7. A network of site links

If you had to connect all four DCs using only site links, you would have to manually connect London and Vienna to Brasilia using something like Vienna–London and London–Brasilia (although that isn't the only solution) and then connect Brasilia–Kuala Lumpur. However, with a site link bridge, you could bridge every site link except Kuala Lumpur to Georgetown (capital of the Pulau–Pinang province in Malaysia, by the way). Bridging all the links except this one tells the servers in those sites that are bridged that they can replicate to any sites that are bridged over the existing site links. So when Vienna wishes to replicate to Kuala Lumpur, the site link bridge knows that the traffic should go from Vienna to Paris to Brasilia to Osaka and finally to Kuala Lumpur.

Bridging the Kuala Lumpur–Georgetown site link would probably make sense, but in this example there is no need, as no Sales domain servers currently exist in that site.

There are a number of reasons why site link bridges make great sense:

- The ability to bridge multiple site links saves you creating multiple site links that do not mirror your physical network solely for Active Directory replication purposes.

- If you do not have a fully routed IP network throughout your organization, using a site link bridge enables you to connect nonrouted IP networks for replication purposes.

- The KCC determines what route to use across all site links within a bridge, based on the costs of all possible links. Thus, if you have more than one link between sites, bridging all links will make sure the KCC picks the best one when creating a replication connection.

- The KCC can be configured to automatically bridge all site links that use a common transport.

- Site link bridges can be used to force replication to go through certain hub sites. Look at Figure 9-7 again. Imagine you had networks directly between London and Brasilia, London and Vienna, and Vienna and Brasilia, but you did not want to use them for replication traffic under any circumstances. That means you should not create site links between these three sites, since the KCC will detect the link as available for replication purposes and create connection objects across it. Instead, use a site link bridge and force replication traffic between these three sites to be replicated across the existing site links in Figure 9-7 by routing it all through Paris.

Now that you've seen the site links and site link bridges, let's look at how to design your sites and their replication links.

Designing Sites and Links for Replication

There is only one really important point, which is the overriding factor when designing a replication strategy for your network: how much traffic and over what period will you be replicating across the network? However, replication isn't the only reason for creating sites. Sites also need to exist to group sets of machines together for ease of locating data, finding the nearest DC to authenticate with, or finding the nearest DFS share mount point.

Step 1—Gather Background Data for Your Network

Before you sit down to design your site and WAN topology, you need to obtain the map of your existing network infrastructure. This map should contain all physical locations where your company has computers, along with every link between those locations. The speed and reliability of each link should be noted.

If you have an existing IP infrastructure, write down all the subnets that correspond to the sites you have noted.

Step 2—Design the Sites

From the network diagram, you need to draw your site structure and name each site, using a one-to-one mapping from the network diagram as your starting point. If you have 50 physical WAN locations, you have 50 sites. If only 30 of these will be used for Active Directory, you may not see a need to include the entire set of sites in Active Directory. If you do include the entire set, however, it is much easier to visualize your entire network and add clients or servers to those locations later.

 When drawing Active Directory networks, sites normally are represented by ovals.

Remember that a site is a well-connected set of subnets (well-connected tends to mean about 10 Mbps LAN speed). A site does not have to have a server in it; it can be composed entirely of clients. If you have two buildings—or an entire campus—that is connected over 10/100 Mbps links, your entire location is a single site.

This is not a hard and fast rule. By the normal rules, two locations connected over a 2 Mbps link represent two distinct sites. You can, however, group networks together into single sites if you want to. You have to appreciate that there will be more replication than if you had created two sites and a site link, because DCs in both physical locations will maintain the intrasite replication ring topology. If you had created two sites and a site link, only two bridgehead servers would replicate with each other.

We've also successfully used a single site to represent two networks, one with clients and one with servers, separated by a 2 Mbps link. The clients at the end of the 2 Mbps link successfully authenticated quickly and downloaded profiles from a server at the other end of the other link. If we'd used two sites, we would have had to create a site link between them, but the clients still would have had to authenticate across the link anyway.

To summarize, we would suggest that, by default, you create one site per 10 Mbps or higher location, unless you have an overriding reason not to do so.

Step 3—Design the Domain Controller Locations

Placing of DCs is fairly easy, but the number of DCs to use is a different matter entirely.

Where to put DCs

Each workstation in a domain exists in a single site that it knows about. When a user tries to log on to the domain at that workstation, the workstation authenticates to a DC from the local site, which it originally locates via a DNS query. If no DC is available in the local site, the workstation finds a remote site, and by a process of negotiation with a DC in that site, either authenticates with that DC or is redirected to a more local DC.

This consideration governs the placement of DCs. You should place one DC for authentication purposes per domain in all sites that meet any of the following criteria:

- The site has links that are not fast enough for logon purposes to a particular domain.

- The site has links that may be fast enough for logon, but you do not wish to authenticate across them for a particular domain.

- Under Windows 2000, if you made heavy use of universal groups, you needed to place a server at a site if you did not want to impact logons due to a network failure. But with Windows Server 2003 Active Directory, you can enable universal group membership caching (with the Sites and Services snap-in) so that this is no longer a requirement.

The first and second points also need to be considered in light of the number of users and workstations at the sites. If a branch office has a 64 Kbps link, would you want users to log on using a centrally located DC at the other end of that link? If you had 10 users in that office, it may be no problem. If you had 20 users, you may not be so sure. If you had 50 it would be impossible, so you should put in a DC at that site.

How many DCs to have

Deciding how many DCs to create is never easy, as Windows NT administrators well know. The problem is that it depends on the power of the individual server and what else the server is doing at the time as much as it depends on the operating system's ability to authenticate users. If you have an Intel server that's already serving 500 heavy users and is close to its load limit, could it authenticate 100 additional users quickly enough at the same time? Powerful servers can authenticate hundreds of users simultaneously, but even these servers will balk if they are already heavily loaded.

We can't answer this question for you. The only way to decide is to consider how many users will need to use DCs for authentication purposes and what pattern of logons occur throughout the day at your organization. That way, you should be able to judge for yourself how many DCs you may need for authentication purposes.

Reasons for putting a server in more than one site

By default, any server that you install or bring into a domain will belong to one site only. However, there can be instances in which you may want to configure a server to belong to multiple sites. For example, you might want to make sure that workstations from a number of sites all authenticate using one DC.

Here's an example: imagine five sites (Cairo, Delhi, Bangkok, Sydney, and Rio de Janeiro), each representing a 20-user branch office of a large centralized company. Each site has a 64 Kbps link back to the main office in London. You've decided that each site can authenticate down the slow link to a central server, even though all 20 users will log on at 9:00 each morning, because time zone differences effectively stagger the load. In addition, to make sure that these clients do not authenticate with any other servers, you have to provide them with their own central server that is also a member of all the remote sites. That way, when the clients attempt to log on, they will do so down the slow link, but only to that one server.

While sites are used for replication, for clients to find resources, and to cut down on traffic on intersite connections, modifying the site membership can cause performance problems. However, in this case we understand the consequences, and this looks like a good decision.

 Configuring a server to have multiple site membership is fairly straightforward. First, manually create the sites that the server is to be a member of if they do not already exist. Then edit the registry on the server that is to have multiple site membership and add a REG_MULTI_SZ value called SiteCoverage to the HKLM\SYSTEM\CurrentControlSet\ServicesNetlogon\Parameters subkey. Add the names of the sites to this value. If you're using RegEdit or RegEdt32, use Shift-Enter to add the data for multiple lines.

Step 4—Plan Intrasite Replication

This is a short step. Your only requirement is to set the schedules that the replication cycles use. As for the connection objects themselves, if you don't specifically need to change the intrasite replication topologies that the KCC sets up, don't. Leave the KCC to do its stuff by itself; it takes care of things pretty well. You could remove the default links and make a long linked list of replication partners—A to B to C to D to E—rather than a ring if you wanted to, but you have to have a very good reason to do so.

If you do want to manipulate the existing setup of replication between DCs, you'll have to stop the KCC service generating the intrasite topology for that site.

You can turn off intrasite or intersite topology generation by the KCC by using the Sites and Services snap-in to look at the properties of the specific NTDS Site Settings object that you are interested in.

Step 5—Decide How You Will Use the KCC to Your Advantage

There are really three ways to use the KCC to your advantage over intersite links:

- Manually create all the connection objects and turn off the KCC for intersite replication. This isn't something we recommend unless you know exactly what you're doing.

- Let the KCC generate your entire topology for you automatically. This is the default and what Microsoft recommends as standard. You still need to create all site links manually, but if you leave site link transitiveness on by default, the KCC will not need you to create extra site links to replicate data via sites that do not have the relevant DCs. Site link bridges are not used in this scenario.

You can define multiple site links between two distinct sets of bridge-head servers at separate sites if you wish, i.e., DC1 in Site A connects to DC3 in Site B and DC2 in Site A connects to DC4 in Site B. This will help in case one of the servers at one end of a single site link goes down, as this means that you will lose only one site link and not the intersite connectivity.

- A mixture of the two can be had by forcing the KCC to make decisions based on certain key information that you provide. For example, if you make sure that you leave site links nontransitive, the KCC will be able to replicate only across site links that do exist. You then can make use of site link bridges to force the KCC to use certain routes for replication.

If you have many connections that need to be created but don't want to use the KCC, you can use the KCC to start with, allow it to create its default objects, turn it off, and modify the objects to whatever you choose. If you have 500 links, for example, but want to manipulate only one, this is the best way of doing things.

You can leave this step until after you have designed the site links (Steps 6, 7, and 8) if you are not sure what to do. The example design for PetroCorp shows later why this is useful.

Step 6—Create Site Links for Low-Cost, Well-Connected Links

Now that you have all the sites down on paper, you need to think about the links. In this step we identify those sites that are interconnected with what can be considered very fast links or backbones.

Site links should be created along 2 Mbps or faster connections between distinct sites. For each link, you need to choose an appropriate name, cost, and transport. The name should be distinct and immediately conjure up what the link represents. The transport for low-cost links is normally DS-RPC; such a high-capacity network can cope with traffic of this nature. However, if you only want to use email across a link, make the transport ISM-SMTP. If you set up both for some reason, you normally would set a slightly higher cost for the SMTP connectors than you would for standard DS-RPC-based replication.

When choosing costs, the values you choose depend entirely on the different inter-site link speeds that you have in your organization. If you have only 64 Kbps and 1 Mbps[*] links between sites, you really need only 2 values. If you use both transport types, you'll need 4. However, if your sites have many different types of connection, such as 10 Mbps, T3, T2, T1, 256 Kbps, and 64 Kbps, you'll need many more. The values you use should represent in your own mind the difference in cost for using a route. The key to using costs is to realize that everything is relative. After all, if you have two routes to a site and they have costs of 1 and 2, respectively, 2 seems twice as slow as 1. That isn't true; it is just a slower link—not twice as slow. Because the numbers are so close together, there is almost nothing between these values. However, the difference between 10 and 20 is more significant. When determining values, we suggest that as a starting point, use 1 through 10 for low-cost fast links, 11 through 20 for medium-cost links, and 21 and above for higher-cost routes.

Create all the site links along fast-interconnected links between sites.

Step 7—Create Site Links for Medium-Cost Links

Having identified the fastest links and created site links for them, you now need to create any links that are interconnected with a similar transport at medium cost. These are sites such as those connected via MANs with T1 connections, interconnected via frame relay clouds, or entirely connected together. Create these sites now, and remember to use a slightly slower value for any SMTP connectors.

---

[*] In the U.K., 64 Kbps links are known as *kilostream links* and 1 Mbps links are known as *megastream links*.

Step 8—Create Site Links for High-Cost Links

Finally, you have the WAN connections that are high cost due to their slow speed or unreliability. You now need to create those site links and allocate a name, transport, and cost as before. For unreliable links, consider using an SMTP connector with a certificate to encrypt the data. This will ensure that as soon as a link is available for email, your updates will propagate backward and forward as required. For more reliable links, use the standard DS-RPC connector; later in Step 10 you can configure the replication times to be suitable to that link.

Step 9—Create Site Link Bridges

If you chose the third option in Step 5 and turned off site link transitiveness, you now need to create site link bridges or more site links to satisfy your desire to force the KCC to create its topology along certain paths.

Step 10—Design the Replication Schedule

Now sit down with your entire map and identify in which time windows you will allow replication along the various links. Low-cost links may allow traffic all day. Medium-cost links may allow traffic from late afternoon until early morning, and high-cost links may allow replication windows only at very specific times. It all depends on you. In my mind, there is certainly a split between the high-, medium-, and low-cost link replication schedules that you create. Remember that you must have a common window for replication across all routes.

Examples

Having considered the 10 steps, let's take another brief look at the 3 examples from the previous chapter and see what they will need in terms of sites.

TwoSiteCorp

TwoSiteCorp has two locations split by a 128 Kbps link. This means creation of two sites separated by a single site link, with DCs for domain authentication in each site. The site link cost is not an issue, as only one route exists between the two sites. Here the only issue is scheduling the replication, which depends on the existing traffic levels of the link. Schedule replication during the least busy times for a slow link like this. If replication has to take place all the time, as changes need to be propagated rapidly, it is time to consider increasing the capacity of the link.

RetailCorp

RetailCorp has a large centralized retail organization with 600 shops connected via 64 Kbps links to a large centralized 10/100 Mbps interconnected headquarters in London. In this situation, you have one site for HQ and 600 sites for the stores. RetailCorp also uses a DC in each store. They then have to create 600 high-cost site links, each with the same cost. RetailCorp decides this is one very good reason to use ADSI (discussed in Part III) and writes a script to automate the creation of the site link objects in the configuration. The only aspect of the site links that is important here is the schedule. Can central HQ cope with all of the servers replicating intersite at the same time? Does the replication have to be staggered? The decision is made that all data has to be replicated during the times that the stores are closed; for stores that do not close, data is replicated during the least busy times. There is no need to worry about site link bridges or site link transitiveness as all links go through the central hub, and no stores need to intercommunicate. The administrators decide to let the KCC pick the bridgehead servers automatically.

PetroCorp

PetroCorp has 94 outlying branch offices. These branch offices are connected via 64 Kbps links to 5 central hub sites. These 5 hubs are connected to the central organization's HQ in Denver via T2, T1, 256 Kbps, and 128 Kbps links. Some of the hubs also are interconnected. To make it easier to understand, look at PetroCorp's network again (Figure 9-8).

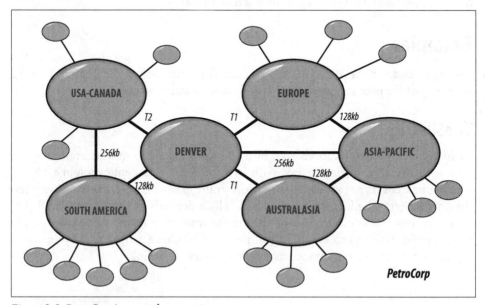

Figure 9-8. PetroCorp's network connections

Initially, you need to create 100 sites representing HQ, the hubs, and the branch offices. How many servers do you need per site? From the design we made in Chapter 8, we decided on 9 domains in the forest. Each of those distinct domains must obviously have a server within it that forms part of the single forest. However, although the description doesn't say so, there is very little cross-pollination of clients from one hub needing to log on to servers from another hub. As this is the case, there is no need to put a server for every domain in every hub. If a user from Denver travels to the *asiapac.petrocorp.com* domain, the user can still log on to *petrocorp.com* from the Asia-Pacific hub, albeit much more slowly. PetroCorp sees that what little cross-pollination traffic it has is made up of two types of user:

- Senior *petrocorp.com* IT and business managers traveling to all hubs.

- Groups of Europe and Australasia users regularly staying at the alternate hub for periods during joint research. This means that *europe.petrocorp.com* users need to log on in the Australasia hub and *australasia.petrocorp.com* users need to log on in the Europe hub.

While the senior managers' use is infrequent, these key decision makers need to log on as rapidly as possible to access email and their data. Money is found to ultimately place *petrocorp.com* servers for authentication purposes in each of the five hubs. The second requirement means that servers for each domain need to be added to the alternate hub. Due to this limitation, only enough money is found to support *petrocorp.com* from outside its own Denver location and the Europe/Australasia hubs hosting each other's domains (see Figure 9-9).

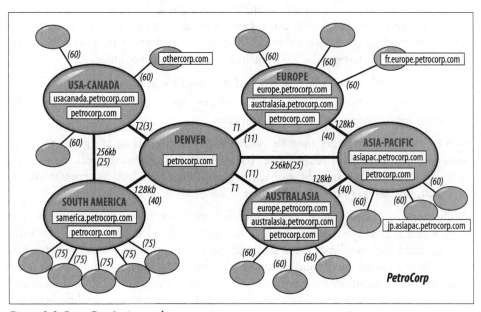

Figure 9-9. PetroCorp's sites and servers

While domains normally are represented by triangles in diagrams, here the rectangular borders around a domain name represent servers that host that domain. Each domain is hosted by multiple servers represented by a single rectangle, although you could run this structure using only one server per rectangle. You can see that *petrocorp.com* is hosted in Denver, as well as in all other hubs.

Regarding intrasite KCC topology generation: PetroCorp has decided to let the KCC automatically generate intradomain server links. If this causes a problem, local administrators should be able to handle it.

The site links are depicted in Figure 9-9 with parentheses to indicate the costs. They can also be described as follows:

- Create one low-cost (3) DS-RPC site link for the T2 connection.
- Create two medium-cost (11) DS-RPC site links representing the T1 connections.
- Create high-cost DS-RPC site links for the five remaining interhub connections of 256 Kbps (25) and 128 Kbps (40).

What about the branches? All links are stable except the links between the eight South America branches and the hub, which are very unreliable. In this case, you have two choices: you can either let the clients in those eight sites authenticate across the less-than-reliable links, or you can place servers in those branches so that authentication is always possible, even when the link is down. PetroCorp opts for the latter and places servers in each of the eight branches. However, DS-RPC is not the best replication mechanism for asynchronous links like these, so PetroCorp instead creates digital certificates and rolls out a certificate server to those sites to enable the replication mechanism to use the underlying mail transport via an SMTP connector for each link. That changes the list to include the following site links:

- Create 86 high-cost DS-RPC site links for each of the stable 64 Kbps (60) links.
- Create eight high-cost ISM-SMTP site links for each of the unstable 64 Kbps (75) links representing South America branches.

PetroCorp's administrators then sit back and decide that they are going to create some redundant site links of the same cost so that if a single bridgehead server is lost in any of the major hubs, replication can still continue. Each hub has enough DCs to cope with this, so they add the redundant links.

While Steps 6, 7, and 8 have been completed, we have, however, appeared to skip Steps 4 and 5. Step 5 was left until now on purpose, since the administrators wanted to wait until the site links were designed to see whether site link transitiveness should be turned on or off and whether bridging routes might help. Now you can easily see that transitivity is important between the Europe and Australasia hubs. If you don't turn transitiveness on by default, you need to create a site link bridge in Denver that allows the *europe.petrocorp.com* and *australasia.petrocorp.com* domains to replicate across the two T1 links even though they have no direct links.

Now look at the diagram again, and consider that transitiveness is turned on. This means any site can use any connection to any other site based on the lowest cost. So if you leave site link transitiveness on and let the KCC create the intersite connection objects and bridgehead servers, replication traffic between Denver and South America is likely to route through USA-Canada, as the total cost across those two links (28) is lower than the direct link (40). This also is true for Asia-Pacific to either Europe (40) or Australasia (40). All traffic is likely to route through Denver (36) because of that. All this means is that the slow 128 Kbps links will not have their bandwidth used up by replication; instead, the 256 Kbps links will absorb the overflow. In the eastern link you have potentially added two lots of bidirectional replication traffic across the 256 Kbps link. Whether this is a problem is up to PetroCorp to decide. They have four main choices:

- Turn off transitiveness throughout the network. This forces the KCC to use only directly connected routes to replicate. This forces the use of the 128 Kbps links by default. Now add the site link bridge at Denver as mentioned previously, then add any other site link bridges to enforce using certain routes when the directly connected routes are not to be used for replication.

- Turn off transitiveness throughout the network. This forces the KCC to use only directly connected routes to replicate, which forces the use of the 128 Kbps links by default. Add the site link bridge at Denver as mentioned previously, and add any other site link bridges to enforce use of certain routes when the directly connected routes are not to be used for replication. Finally, turn off the KCC intersite topology generation in key sites where the bridgehead servers need to be handpicked from the available DCs, creating the connection objects manually.

- Leave transitiveness turned on throughout the network, automatically bridge all site links of the same DS-RPC transport, allow the KCC to choose the lowest cost routes, and accept the routes it chooses, controlling it with schedules.

- Leave transitiveness turned on throughout the network, automatically bridge all site links of the same DS-RPC transport, and turn off the KCC intersite topology generation in key sites where the bridgehead servers need to be handpicked from the available DCs, creating the connection objects manually.

Which of these is chosen depends entirely on the traffic use of the links, the requirements on those links, and how much use the administrators wish to make of the KCC. PetroCorp decides that it wants the KCC to make most of the connections but still wants to retain the greatest control and the potential to force the KCC to use certain routes. To that end, they select the second option.

In the end, the company chooses to bridge South America to Denver via USA-Canada to free up the 128 Kbps link for other traffic. They also choose to bridge Europe to Asia-Pacific via Denver to free up what is currently a congested link. The KCC automatically routes all traffic via Denver, as this bridge cost is lower than the single site link. Finally, the administrators allow the KCC in the Denver site to generate the eight intersite site links (four connections, each with two site links for redundancy) and then turn off intersite generation for that site. They then modify the connection objects created (deleting some and creating others), because they have a number of DCs that they do not want to use for replication purposes within Denver that the KCC picked up and used.

This is a fairly complicated site problem, but one that wasn't difficult to solve. There are many other viable solutions. We could easily have made all the redundant links that we created use the SMTP connector with a higher cost to make sure that they were used only in an emergency. Many options are available to you as well. That's why a design is so important.

Summary

After this chapter, you should have more of an insight into creating the site and replication infrastructure for your own Active Directory network. Having a basic understanding of the replication process (from Chapter 5) and how the KCC operates should allow you to make much more informed judgments on how much control you want to exert over the KCC in your designs. We feel that it is always better to give free reign to the KCC if possible, while maintaining a firm grip over what it has authority to do. While this can seem contradictory, we hope that our explanations on using site link bridges and restricting transitiveness when appropriate show how this is possible in practice.

The next chapter deals with how to update your designs to reflect your requirements for Group Policy Objects in your organization.

CHAPTER 10

Designing Organization-Wide Group Policies

This chapter takes an in-depth look at Group Policy Objects (GPOs), focusing on three areas:

- How GPOs work in Active Directory
- How to manage GPOs with the Group Policy Object Editor and Group Policy Management Console
- How to structure your Active Directory effectively using Organizational Units and groups so that you can make the best use of the GPOs required in your organization.

How GPOs Work

Group policies are very simple to understand, but their uses can be quite complex. Each GPO can consist of two parts: one that applies to a computer (such as a startup script or a change to the system portion of the registry) and one that applies to a user (such as a logoff script or a change to the user portion of the registry). You can use GPOs that contain only computer policies, only user policies, or a mixture of the two.

How GPOs Are Stored in Active Directory

GPOs themselves are stored in two places: Group Policy Configuration (GPC) data is stored in Active Directory, and certain key Group Policy Template (GPT) data is stored as files and directories in the system volume. They are split because while there is definitely a need to store GPOs in Active Directory if the system is to associate them with locations in the tree, you do not want to store all the registry changes, logon scripts, and so on in Active Directory itself. To do so could greatly increase the size of your DIT file. To that end, each GPO consists of the object holding GPC data, which itself is linked to a companion directory in the system volume that may or may not have GPTs stored within. The GPT data is essentially a folder structure that stores Administrative Template–based policies, security settings, applications available for software installation, and script files. GPT data is stored in the System Volume folder of DCs in the *Policies* subfolder.

 Third-party developers can extend GPOs by incorporating options that do not reside in the normal GPT location.

The GPO objects themselves are held as instances of the groupPolicyContainer class within a single container in Active Directory at this location:

    CN=Policies,CN=System,dc=mycorp,dc=com

Through a process known as linking, the GPOs are associated with the locations in the tree that are to receive the group policy.* In other words, one object can be linked to multiple locations in the tree, which explains how one GPO can be applied to many Organizational Units, sites, or domains as required.

Let's consider the groupPolicyContainer class objects themselves. Take a look at Figure 10-1; we are using one of the Windows Support Tools utilities, ADSI Edit, to show the view of the Policies container and its children.

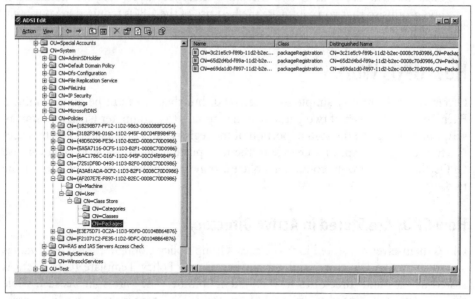

Figure 10-1. GPOs in the Policies container

---

* The GPC data part of a GPO is an object in Active Directory. This object, like all others, has attributes. One of the attributes of a GPO is a multivalued attribute called gPLink that stores the DN of the containers that the GPO is linked to.

Here you can see 10 groupPolicyContainer objects shown with their GUID as the cn field. The displayName attribute of these objects holds the name that administrators of Active Directory would see when using one of the normal tools to view these objects. Each GPO also has a gPCFileSysPath that holds the full path to the corresponding directory in the system volume.

If you were to look under the Policies container on a default installation, you would find only two children. These children would correspond to the Default Domain Policy* and the Default Domain Controllers Policy, the only GPOs created automatically by the system on installation. The Default Domain Policy is also associated with a special system container created on installation and located at:

```
LDAP://CN=Default Domain Policy, CN=System, dc=mycorp, dc=com
```

Looking at Figure 10-1, you see that the eighth GPO down the list has more children within the User container than all the other GPOs. That's because it is a policy to deploy an MSI application to users. In fact, this GPO also has under the Classes container 80 entries that we haven't displayed. This particular policy is the one described in the introduction to a previous chapter. It applies the Administrator tools MSI file during an administrator-equivalent logon to install the tools on whatever workstation the administrator happens to log onto. When the administrator logs off, it completely uninstalls the tools so that no subsequent users have access to them at that client computer.

How GPOs Are Used in Active Directory

Any GPO is initially created as a standalone object in Active Directory. Each object can then be linked one or more times to three different container types: Sites, Domains, and Organizational Units. GPOs for domains and Organizational Units are held in the domain relating to their application, but creating a GPO for a site stores that GPO in the forest root domain by default; administrators can change this if they wish.

In the normal state of affairs, what you as an administrator would do is open up the properties of the Site, Domain, or Organizational Unit, then create a GPO and link it to that location. For all intents and purposes, it appears that you have created a GPO at that location in the tree, rather than what really happened, which was that the system created the GPO as a standalone object in the Policies container and then linked it to that container.

To apply a GPO to a set of users or computers, you simply create a GPO in Active Directory and then link it to a Site, Domain, or Organizational Unit. Then by default, the user portion of the GPO will apply to all users in the container and its children,

---

* The default settings for these two policies can be found in Microsoft's Windows 2000 Group Policy white paper located at *http://www.microsoft.com/windows2000/techinfo/howitworks/management/grouppolwp.asp*.

and the computer portion of the GPO will apply to all computers in the container and its children.

Thus, if we were to create a policy and link it to a site or domain, all computers and users of that site or domain, respectively, would get the policy. If we were to create a policy and link it to an Organizational Unit, all users and computers in that Organizational Unit and all the users and computers within Organizational Units beneath that Organizational Unit and so on down the tree would get the policy.

To identify the links on a GPO, you simply look at the Links tab of the GPO's properties in the Group Policy Object Editor (GPOE). Figure 10-2 shows the results of a scan for the locations in the domain where the Default Domain Policy GPO has been linked. It seems that Mycorp has chosen to link the Default Domain Policy to a location farther down the tree as well, the Users Organizational Unit within the finance Organizational Unit, within the *mycorp.com* domain.

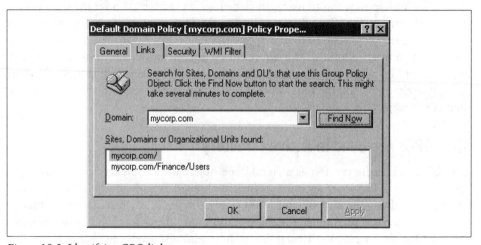

Figure 10-2. Identifying GPO links

We want to make three major points here:

- GPOs apply only to sites, domains, and Organizational Units.
- A single GPO can be linked to multiple locations in the tree.
- GPOs by default affect all of the users and computers in a container.

This generates further questions. If multiple policies apply to different locations in a tree, can multiple GPOs apply to the same container, and if so, what takes precedence? Why would you want to apply one GPO to different parts of the tree? In addition, how can we stop the GPO from applying to the entire set of users and computers in the container? Let's consider each of these questions to understand policies better.

Prioritizing the Application of Multiple Policies

Let's say that we set a GPO for all users in a site to run a logon script that executes a news system local to that site. Let's also say that we set a domain GPO to set a series of Kerberos security settings for each user. Finally, we have two user logon scripts that we need to run in a specific order for specific Organizational Units in that domain. GPOs for larger containers get applied before GPOs for smaller containers. That means that any GPOs on the site get applied first, followed by any GPOs on the domain, followed by any GPOs on the Organizational Units that a user or computer resides in. This process is known as SDOU. If multiple GPOs are linked to a single site, domain, or Organizational Unit, the administrator can prioritize the order in which the GPOs are applied to that container. So in this scenario, the site news system runs first, then the Kerberos settings are applied, and finally the two logon scripts are applied in the order determined by the administrator. We know that each computer and user will exist in one site and one domain. However, while each object will exist in only one Organizational Unit as well, there is an Organizational Unit hierarchy to be considered. And there is the domain tree hierarchy, too.

To account for this, the GPOs for the site that the object resides in are applied first in prioritized order. No other sites have any influence over this. Then, the GPOs for the domain that the object resides in are applied in prioritized order. GPOs applied to parent domains in the domain tree have no influence on objects in domains lower down the tree. Domain trees do not impact GPO application at all. The Organizational Unit structure, however, has a significant bearing on what happens with GPOs. GPO links are inherited down the tree. So while a child Organizational Unit can have its own GPOs linked to it, it also will inherit all of its parent's GPO links. These Organizational Unit GPOs are applied in order according to the Organizational Unit hierarchy once the site and domain GPOs have been applied.

 There are exceptions. You can block inheritance, force an override, and even define ACLs on objects. We'll cover all these later in this section.

For example, Paul Burke has the following DN to his account (see Figure 10-3):

```
cn=PaulBurke,ou=Databases,ou=Gurus,ou=Financial Sector,dc=mycorp,dc=com
```

The site GPOs are applied first, and the *mycorp.com* domain GPOs are applied next. Then come the GPOs on the Financial Sector Organizational Unit, the GPOs on the Gurus Organizational Unit, and the GPOs on the Databases Organizational Unit. From this, it's fairly easy to see how Organizational Unit hierarchy design has a significant effect on GPO precedence.

Remember that GPOs have a computer part as well as a user part. When a computer boots, any site GPOs that have computer settings are applied in prioritized order. This is followed by any domain GPOs with computer settings, and so on down the Organizational Unit hierarchy until any GPOs on the Organizational Unit that the

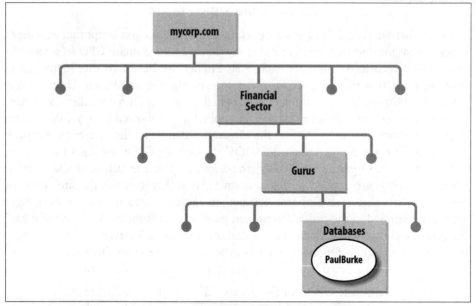

Figure 10-3. Graphical representation of the location of the Paul Burke user

computer resides in are applied. During boot up, the user portions of these GPOs are ignored. Later, when a user logs on, the same process applies, this time with the user settings. The computer settings are ignored during user logon.*

Standard GPO Inheritance Rules in Organizational Units

Any unconfigured settings anywhere in a GPO can be ignored since they are not inherited down the tree; only configured settings are inherited. There are three possible scenarios:

- A parent has a value for a setting, and a child does not.
- A parent has a value for a setting, and a child has a nonconflicting value for the same setting.
- A parent has a value for a setting, and a child has a conflicting value for the same setting.

If a GPO has settings configured for a parent Organizational Unit, and the same policy settings are unconfigured for a child Organizational Unit, the child inherits the parent's GPO settings. That makes sense.

---

* This is the default case. There is a setting that you can use to force a different mode of operation. We'll explain this later when we cover loopback mode.

If a GPO has settings configured for a parent Organizational Unit that do not conflict with a GPO on a child Organizational Unit, the child Organizational Unit inherits the parent GPO settings and applies its own GPOs as well. A good example of this is two logon scripts; these scripts don't conflict, so both are run.

If a GPO has settings configured for a parent Organizational Unit that conflict with the same settings in another GPO configured for a child Organizational Unit, the child Organizational Unit does not inherit that specific GPO setting from the parent Organizational Unit. The setting in the GPO child policy takes priority, although there is one case in which this is not true. If the parent disables a setting and the child makes a change to that setting, the child's change is ignored. In other words, the disabling of a setting is always inherited down the hierarchy.

Blocking Inheritance and Overriding the Block in Organizational Unit GPOs

It is possible to force the settings of a GPO to be applied as the final settings for a child.

Blocking inheritance is a fairly simple concept. If you block inheritance to a specific Organizational Unit, GPOs linked to parent Organizational Units up the tree are not applied to objects in this specific Organizational Unit or its children.

 LGPOs (Local GPOs, discussed shortly) are processed even when Block Policy Inheritance is checked.

Refer back to Figure 10-3. If we decide to block inheritance at the Databases Organizational Unit, Paul Burke will receive only GPOs directly defined on the Databases Organizational Unit. If we decide to block inheritance at the Gurus Organizational Unit, Paul Burke will receive only GPOs on the Databases Organizational Unit and those inherited from the Gurus Organizational Unit. The Organizational Unit that you block inheritance at stops any higher-level GPOs from applying to the branch starting at the blocked Organizational Unit. In fact, we can block inheritance on any of the Organizational Units within the *mycorp.com* domain. For example, blocking inheritance on the Financial Sector Organizational Unit makes sense if we want to block site-level GPOs from applying.

This can cause problems. For example, let's say that you have delegated control over an Organizational Unit branch to a group of administrators and allowed them access to manipulate GPOs on that branch. You may be applying GPOs to Organizational Units farther up the hierarchy that you wish this delegated branch to receive. However, your branch admins have the ability to block inheritance of these parent Organizational Unit policies of yours. The branch administrators also have the ability to configure a setting that conflicts with one you set in a parent GPO; the branch administrator's child setting will take precedence in conflicts.

To prevent this, you can check the No Override box on an individual GPO. This allows administrators to force GPOs to be inherited by all children of an Organizational Unit. However, it has one further effect: it prevents GPO settings in child Organizational Units from overriding conflicting settings in a parent OU.

Let's say that we change a registry setting using a GPO on the Financial Sector Organizational Unit. Unfortunately, another administrator then sets the same registry setting (among many others) to a conflicting value on the Gurus Organizational Unit and also blocks inheritance at the Databases Organizational Unit. By default, the registry setting will be correctly applied only to the Financial Sector Organizational Unit, as the Gurus Organizational Unit receives the different setting (child overrides parent on conflicts due to inheritance rules), and the Databases Organizational Unit doesn't inherit either policy. To fix both problems, we could set the original Financial Sector Organizational Unit policy to No Override. It then prevents the specific setting on the GPO on the Gurus Organizational Unit from modifying it without affecting any of the other GPO settings. Our GPO also is forced down past the Block Inheritance set up at the Databases Organizational Unit.

 If you are making use of No Override on a policy, we suggest that you consider setting up an ACL on that policy to restrict the abilities of others to edit that GPO, leaving just a core group of administrators with the relevant permissions. This will ensure that the GPO is not changed without the knowledge of the core group.

Summary

- If Block Inheritance has been checked for a child-level GPO, and No Override has not been checked for any parent GPOs, the child GPO will not inherit any policies from any parent GPOs farther up the hierarchy.

- If No Override has been checked for a parent-level GPO, the child-level GPO will inherit all of the parent's configured policies, even if those policies conflict with the child's policies, and even if Block Inheritance has been set for the child.

When Policies Apply

We've already said that the computer portion of a GPO applies during boot up and the user portion of a GPO applies during logon. However, that isn't the only time that a policy can apply. The policies also can be set to refresh periodically after a certain time interval. How often this occurs and what conditions are attached to this refreshing are specified under the System\Group Policy key under the Administrative Templates section of the computer and user sections of a GPO.

Set the refresh value to 0 to have the policy continually apply every seven seconds. This is very useful for a test environment but obviously not for a live service.*

 For Windows 2000 or earlier clients, you also can manually refresh policies on a client using the *SECEDIT.EXE* tool with the command `SECEDIT /refreshpolicy`. Windows Server 2003 has a utility called *GPUPDATE* that can accomplish the same thing.

Refreshing is very useful for users who do not shut down their computers or log off from the system for days. In that case, GPOs apply in the normal way, but at very irregular intervals over long periods. Consequently, setting up policy refresh means that you can manage to apply those settings to such users at whatever interval you decide.

You may think that refreshing should be fairly straightforward—a policy refreshes or doesn't refresh—but there is quite a bit more to it. The problems come when you attempt to refresh settings that could potentially affect a currently logged-on user and cause her machine to behave in an unusual or unstable manner. Let's consider a few examples:

- We decide to use a GPO to deploy Office 2003, which comes with its own MSI files for use with the Application Deployment GPOs. The deployment goes well, but we later decide that we need to change a few registry keys governing the way Office operates. We add these into the appropriate parts of the GPO so that new users receive them and so that rolling out these new registry keys to users currently running Office will not cause the running application to fail. We have to be careful as to whether we want the registry keys to apply during a refresh or during the next logon or boot up of the machine (depending on whether the keys are user or computer registry settings).

- We have deployed an application using an MSI file that has insinuated itself into all users' registries. Unfortunately, there is a serious problem with the application and we want to remove it, so we remove it from the list of deployable applications. Users who are not logged on now will have the application auto-uninstalled when they next log on, but what about currently logged-on users? If the policy is set to auto-refresh, the application will attempt to uninstall itself while users are logged on, even if some of them are using the application at the time.

- We decide to add a new logon script to a GPO so that users are alerted about the number of new mail messages. If this policy is set to auto-refresh, the system may detect that this logon script is new and automatically run it against any logged-on clients. Users who logged on at 9:00 A.M. and receive a logon script

---

* There is a chance that this will be taken out of the final version of the product.

message at 3:00 P.M. welcoming them to the system and telling them they have new mail could be confused.

These examples show the problems with refresh. What if you do want refresh to occur? Consider the following example.

We decide that we want a script that alerts users about system changes. This script fires up a dialog box that explains various changes to the system during a critical upgrade, for example. It could even auto-open a browser window to an intranet web page holding important changes. We need this script to run once during logon and then every time the page changes. Every time we make a system change, we remove and re-add the logon script for the specific GPO that we wish to apply to all affected users. We then specify that the GPO should refresh periodically. The script is then run whenever we require it to do so, and all users who are logged on at the time will have an alert message pop up on their screens, generated by the script running again on their client.

All of these items and more are configurable in the GPO. The point is that if you do turn on refresh, make sure you go through both areas of the GPO thoroughly to make sure that the specific items being refreshed will not cause problems for logged-on users.

Local Group Policy Objects

Windows 2000 and later machines have their own Local Group Policy Objects, known as LGPOs or Local Security Policies. LGPOs are applied prior to any GPOs on the site, but they have restrictions in that they can contain only security settings, software policies, and scripts. File deployment and application deployment are not available in LGPOs.

 LGPOs are applied before site GPOs. This is normally represented by the string LSDOU.

While GPOs consist of two parts, the Active Directory object and the templates in the system volume (SYSVOL), LGPOs consist of only the template portion. These templates cannot be stored in the system volume because the concept does not exist on the local machine. Instead, the LGPO templates are stored in *%systemroot%\ System32\GroupPolicy*. These ADM files can be added to and extended in the same way as standard GPOs.

While LGPOs are very useful in environments in which no DCs exist and Windows NT system policies failed to deliver, their use in enterprise organizations is likely to be quite limited. In some cases, LGPOs will be useful if an administrator requires a machine-specific policy to execute before all others or if a domain client is not to execute any domain GPOs, but mostly their use is confined to standalone environments.

 LGPOs are processed even when Block Policy Inheritance is checked.

If conflicts occur on a domain client with an LGPO and subsequently applied Active Directory GPOs, the Active Directory GPO prevails over the original LGPO.

 If you have a requirement for a domain client not to execute domain GPOs, you need to change a setting in the LGPO that will make a registry change on that local client when it is next booted. This key is checked both when the client boots and when a user logs onto the domain. If the key is properly set, the user and computer will have only the LGPO applied, and any domain GPOs will be ignored.

How Existing Windows NT 4.0 System Policies Affect GPO Processing

Windows NT 4.0 system policies were useful in making sure that a setting was applied with a specific value somewhere in the registry. These policies dotted the registry with settings throughout its structure and were known as tattooing the registry. Once these settings were applied, to unset them the administrator had to either edit the registry or create another policy to force the different settings to the system. By default, ordinary users also had the ability to change registry settings in the user portion (HKCU) held in their profile, so they could easily unset values that the administrator wished to be firmly set.

To counteract this and bring all the policy settings under one roof, so to speak, Windows 2000 and later were designed so that the GPOs exist as registry keys and values in locations that are restricted to administrator access. These locations are:

- HKEY_CURRENT_USER\Software\Policies
- HKEY_LOCAL_MACHINE\Software\Policies
- HKEY_CURRENT_USER\Software\Microsoft\Windows\CurrentVersion\ Policies
- HKEY_LOCAL_MACHINE\Software\Microsoft\Windows\CurrentVersion\ Policies

The first two keys are the preferred locations for all new policies. An administrator can specify that a value be set in a user's registry and then reset on a regular basis. Any settings that users have set themselves will be overwritten by the proper administrator-set values. However, administrators can still import any ADM files and modify keys throughout the registry as they wish. It is up to administrators to make sure that the policy is reapplied regularly or is in a part of the registry to which the user has no access, unless they wish the user to be able to change the registry permanently.

When to Use Windows NT System Policies

During an upgrade, Windows NT system policies that reside in the *NETLOGON* share will be transferred to domain controller's *NETLOGON* share (now known as the *SYSVOL*). However, only Windows NT and Windows *9x* downlevel clients will use these policies; Active Directory clients will not use them. Active Directory GPOs do not affect downlevel clients at all.

Windows NT System Policies

Windows NT provided a tool called System Policy Editor (*POLEDIT.EXE*) that was installed with the resource kit. This was a very basic graphical tool that allowed you to manage three types of policies: computer, user, and group. By default, the only two policies were Default User and Default Computer.

Do not confuse the Default User policy with the Default User profile; they are not the same thing at all.

If you decided that your entire organization would have only one set of policies for everyone, you would simply modify the Default User and Default Computer policies. Whenever a client booted in your organization, it would retrieve the Default Computer policy and lock itself down (or unlock itself) according to that policy. Whenever a user logged on to that client, the Default User policy would apply and lock or unlock the settings for that account.

The default policies basically allowed you to lock down the desktop settings of the machine based on a series of template files, also known as ADM files. It was always possible to create your own ADM files or modify the existing ones with settings that corresponded to registry changes you wanted to make. If you created a new file, you just imported it into the tool and could then start applying the policy.

If you did not want just one policy for every computer and user in your organization, you could create policies for individual users, computers, or groups. When a client booted or a user logged on, the system would determine, according to a set of rules, which of the policies would apply to that computer or user. Only one policy was ever applied to a user or computer.

If you have downlevel clients that need policies applied to them, whether these policies already exist or need to be created from scratch, you need to fall back on the old system policies that were provided for use on these systems. You cannot use the Group Policy Object Editor to administer these older policies, so you will need to use the old System Policy Editor (*poledit.exe*) tool that has been reissued with Windows 2000 and later clients to manipulate such policies. The POL files generated by the

System Policy Editor will still need to be placed in the *NETLOGON* share as they were under previous versions of Windows NT.

There is one benefit to administrators who have been using system policies to administer downlevel clients for some time; while the system policies themselves are not transferable, GPOs can be extended using ADM files of the exact format. This means that administrators can migrate their old template files over from system policies to GPOs as required.

 If you have any system policy functionality that you wish to apply to your Windows 2000 or later clients, you will have to reimplement your system policies as GPOs because system policies are not upgraded when migrating to Active Directory.

We don't intend to cover system policies any more here since there are a number of white papers and other documents within Microsoft's Knowledge Base at *http://support.microsoft.com* that do the job very well. The best way to find them is to search for the string "System Policies."

How Policies Apply to Clients with Different Operating Systems

If you have a Windows NT 4.0 client in a workgroup or a domain, the only policies that can apply are downlevel Windows NT 4.0 policy (POL) file policies.

If you have a standalone Windows 2000, Windows XP, or Windows Server 2003 client or member server, policies are evaluated in the following order:

- Downlevel Windows NT 4.0 policy (POL) file
- Local GPO

If you have a Windows 2000 or later client or member server in a mixed-mode or Windows Server 2003 Interim domain, policies are evaluated in the following order:

- Downlevel Windows NT 4.0 policy (POL) file
- Local GPO
- Site GPOs in priority order
- Domain GPOs in priority order
- Organizational Unit GPOs in priority order, applied in a hierarchical fashion down the tree ending with the Organizational Unit that the computer or user resides in

As this extends the LSDOU process to include Windows NT 4.0 system policies, this process is commonly written as 4LSDOU.

If you have a Windows 2000 or later client or member server in a Windows 2000 native-mode or Windows Windows Server 2003 domain, policies are evaluated in LSDOU order.

Combating Slowdown Due to GPOs

If you apply too many policies, there will be slowdowns. But there are no good guidelines for how many policies to apply. We can tell you that in a lab environment, we saw a slowdown when we started applying more than 12 policies. Unfortunately, that data is of absolutely no use to you. Read on to see why.

Limiting the number of GPOs that apply

The problem with trying to test the impact of GPOs on speed of the client during boot up and logon is possible only by direct testing. We would not advocate taking our value as a hard and fast rule. Each policy has to be identified, opened, read to see if it applies, actually applied, and finally closed before moving on to the next policy. This process, which is done automatically by the system, will take time. So executing 3 policies of 20 changes each will be slower than implementing 1 change of 60. We arrived at the value of 12 by using a series of tests with large and small policies in the test domain in our lab environment. Without knowing what settings were in the policies, the layout of the network, the specification and bandwidth capabilities of our clients and servers, and so on, that data is of little use to you. Even if we provided it, there is little chance that it would be similar to your layout, so you'll need to do your own testing to work out what's acceptable. Lab test simulation is really the best way to get a feel for how much the policies that you want will impact your clients.

Microsoft has its own take on designing your Active Directory for GPOs. They recommend that you should not have Organizational Unit structures more than 10 deep so that policies do not take too much time during logon. This advice is still only half helpful, and we'll come back to it in the design section later.

Block Inheritance and No Override

If you use either Block Inheritance or No Override, you incur extra processing. For this reason you should be cautious in their use.

Disabling parts of GPOs

There is another way to speed up policies. Let's say that you have an Organizational Unit that has three policies on it: a computer startup script, a computer shutdown script, and a user logon script. Let's also say that you have a need for three policies rather than one, perhaps because they are applied elsewhere in the Organizational Unit hierarchy as well. When a user in your Organizational Unit logs on, the system will attempt to apply any user settings from all three GPOs. We know that two of the policies have no relevance whatsoever to a user. Wouldn't it be a nice touch to have some way to tell the system not to bother processing the user portion for GPOs that deal only with computer data and vice versa. In fact, this is a very simple process. Just look at the properties of a GPO and check one box or the other in the General tab, as shown in Figure 10-4.

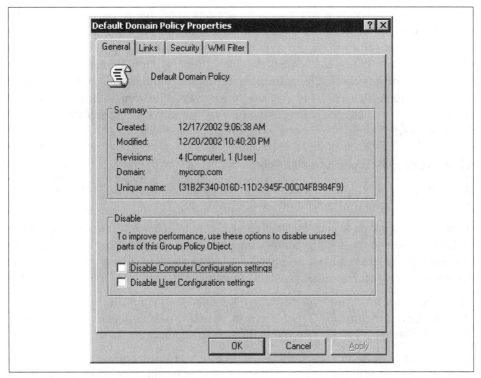

Figure 10-4. Disabling part of a GPO

With all the settings in a GPO, browsing both user and computer parts of the tree to see if each part was empty and whether any changes had been made would normally be a lengthy process. However, Microsoft has thought of this, and as Figure 10-4 shows, the revisions indicate exactly how many changes have been made to the GPO. This guides you in whether to disable or enable parts of a GPO.

GPOs with no revisions in a section are skipped; disabling part of the policy stops the need to check the revision level and thus can partially speed up the process.

Limiting cross-domain linking

It is possible for an administrator of one domain to create a GPO and for it to be applied to an SDOU in another domain. For example, if the administrator of *other-corp.com* is given access to centralized setup GPOs within *mycorp.com*, he can link the *mycorp.com* GPOs to SDOUs in the *othercorp.com* domain.

Cross-domain linking is possible only because GPO links are held in the GC.

While this is feasible, it is not normally recommended due to network bandwidth considerations, since the objects in Active Directory and the templates in the system volume need to be read on the remote domain. Normally it's better to consider duplicating the GPO in the second domain instead of cross-domain linking to it. However, if the links between the domains are as fast and reliable as the links within the second domain that is to receive the policy, and if the domain holding the GPO can apply it to the user or computer fast enough to make the administrator happy, there is nothing stopping you from doing this.

Limiting GPO application across WAN links

This shouldn't be a problem if you set up your sites' configuration correctly, but you need to be aware of the implications, nonetheless.

Data on GPOs linked to site objects is copied to all DCs in a forest because site information is part of the Configuration container that is replicated to all DCs in all domains in the entire forest. So any GPO linked to a site object is applied to all machines in that site regardless of which domain in the forest they are in.

However, while multiple domains receive the link information, those same domains do not receive the entire GPO itself. Instead, the GPO resides in one domain, and clients in the site read the GPO from that domain as required.

In the normal course of events, this shouldn't be a problem since a site is supposed to be an area of well-connected subnets. A site hosts three domains—Domain A, Domain B, and Domain C; Domain A holds the site GPO itself, and clients of all three domains will access the GPO from Domain A. However, if Domain B was mistakenly down a slow WAN link of some kind, the machines in Domain B would be accessing the GPO across that slow link. If you use site GPOs and the site spans slow WAN links (which it shouldn't do), you will cause GPOs to be accessed across those links.

Use simple queries in WMI filters

If you have a WMI filter applied to a GPO, a WMI query will be run before the GPO is applied to a user or computer. If the WMI query is very complex, it could significantly impact the time it takes to process the GPO. If you have multiple GPOs that contain a WMI filter, you need to pay special attention to the impact those queries will have.

The Power of Access Control Lists on Group Policy Objects

The real problem with all the information we've given you so far is that a policy appears to apply to all users and/or computers in whatever container it is linked to. There is a way of changing that, which is why they're now called group policies rather than just policies.

As each GPO is an object in Active Directory, and all objects have Access Control Lists (ACL) associated with them, it follows that it must be possible to allow and deny access to a GPO using that ACL. With ACLs it is possible to allow and deny access to GPOs based on security group membership. It is also possible to go to an even finer-grained detail and set access control for an individual computer or user. Figure 10-5 shows us that the system security group called Authenticated Users will be able to read and apply the Group Policy. If we unchecked the Apply Group Policy checkbox, the Authenticated Users group would not receive this policy.

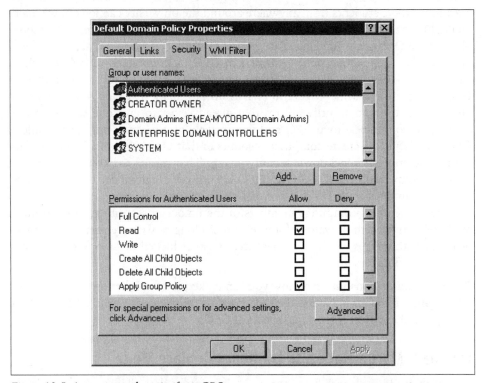

Figure 10-5. Access control entries for a GPO

This is a significant feature of GPOs and one that you can use heavily to your advantage. Let's take a simple example, in which we create a single GPO to roll out an internal application and link it to the Finance and Marketing Organizational Units in one domain. Now all users in the Finance and Marketing Organizational Units will receive that application via the GPO on logon. Let's also say that a certain subset of users from both Organizational Units are not to receive this application. All we need to do is create a security group to hold that user subset and set up an Access Control Entry (ACE) to the Application Deployment GPO and check the Deny Apply Group Policy checkbox. Now, every user that we make a member of that new security group will not receive the policy.

Deny always overrides Allow. Let's say a user or computer is a member of four security groups. If a GPO has an ACL that contains an ACE for the individual user or computer with Read and Apply rights, an ACE for three of the security groups that have Read and Apply rights, and an ACE for the fourth security group that has Apply rights denied, the GPO will not be applied.

This has practical applications, too. At Leicester University we maintain a separate Organizational Unit structure for our computer objects. On our open-area lab machines, where students from anywhere around the university can log on, we maintain tight security. Each computer in that lab has a corresponding computer account object in an Organizational Unit that represents that lab. Two GPOs are created and linked to that single Organizational Unit; one GPO locks down that machine tightly, and the other GPO unlocks it. In other words, we set two completely conflicting GPOs to act on the same Organizational Unit. Normally that would be plain silly, but we then use two security groups that already exist to give one security group access only to the lockdown GPO and one security group access only to the unlock GPO. Whenever we create computer accounts in that Organizational Unit, we place the computers in the lockdown security group. That means the computers in that security group automatically receive the lockdown policy. If we decide that we need to do work in that lab and wish a particular client, or all clients, unlocked, all we do is make the relevant computers members of the unlocked security group and finish off by rebooting them or waiting for a refresh. As long as we never place a computer object in both groups, we have a client that is either locked or unlocked depending on its group memberships.

This is a good demonstration of how you can make use of conflicting GPOs on a single Organizational Unit based solely on permission granted by the ACLs to those GPOs, one of the most important aspects of GPOs.

Loopback Merge Mode and Loopback Replace Mode

Loopback mode is a specially configured GPO option that allows you to apply the user portion of a GPO to a user based on the computer he is logging on from. For example, imagine we have a suite of public kiosks in the foyer of our organization to give outsiders information about the company. Company employees can also use these devices if they want to check email quickly on their way in or out. Since literally anyone in the building can use the kiosks, we need a lot of security. We don't want those kiosks to allow company employees to have all the privileges and permissions that they normally would at their desktop devices; we want them to be able to use only email. What we can do is tie a set of user restrictions into the user portion of a GPO that sits on the Organizational Unit that holds the computer objects. Then employees are locked down at the kiosks and nowhere else. This effectively allows us to restrict what employees can do to their own settings on a per-machine basis.

Many administrators can see the use of this setting in certain environments and for certain situations. Take a lab of machines in a university where staff accounts are to be locked down like student accounts while the staff members are in the lab, but not when they are at their private machines. As a final example, consider that the Finance Organizational Unit users have a lot of deployed applications specific to Finance. These applications are to work only when accessed from the finance computers and not from anywhere else. So you would put them as deployed applications into the computer section of GPOs that apply to the Finance Organizational Unit. However, if you also deployed to finance users (via the user portion of a GPO) applications that were supposed to roam with the users everywhere except in sales and marketing, you could use loopback mode to stop the applications from being advertised specifically in those two Organizational Units.

Loopback mode can be found in the Group Policy settings of the computer portion of any GPO (i.e., Computer Configuration → Administrative Templates → System → Group Policy → User Group Policy loopback processing mode). If you open that item, you get the dialog box shown in Figure 10-6, which allows you to switch between the two modes of loopback operation: merge mode and replace mode.

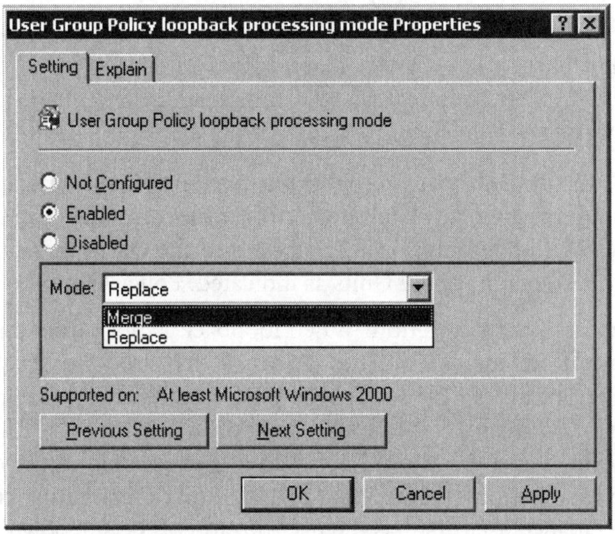

Figure 10-6. Setting loopback mode

When a user logs on to a machine that uses loopback merge mode, the user policies are applied first as normal; the user portion of any GPOs that apply to the computer are applied in sequence, overriding any of the previous user policies as appropriate. Replace mode, by contrast, ignores the GPOs that would apply to the user and instead applies only the user portions of the GPOs that apply to the computers. Figure 10-7 illustrates this.

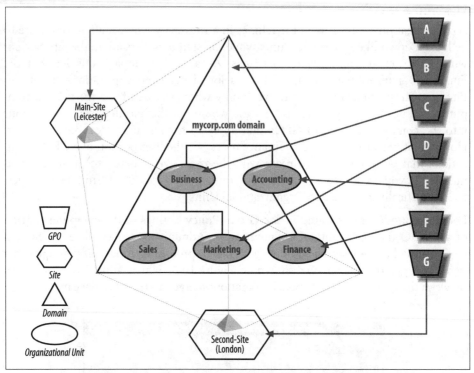

Figure 10-7. Loopback mode processing

In Figure 10-7, the domain *mycorp.com* spans two sites, Main-Site and Second-Site. Marketing computers exist in Main-Site, and finance computers in Second-Site. Policy A applies to Main-Site only, Policy B applies to the entire domain, and C, D, E, and F apply to the Organizational Units as indicated. Policy G applies to Second-Site.

Table 10-1 summarizes the position. When loopback is not turned on, the only real difference comes from the site policies (A or G) that are applied. When you turn replace mode on for all the GPOs, it becomes more obvious what will happen. In each case, the policy relating to the user is applied first in order, followed by the entire set of policy items that would apply to a user residing in the computer location. Take the example of a finance user logging on at a marketing computer in the main site. The Finance user first has the user portion of the site policy that she is logging on from applied (A), followed by the user portion of the domain policy (B), the user portion of the Accounting Organizational Unit (E), and the user portion of the Finance Organizational Unit (F). After this, the user portion of the site (A) is applied again, followed by the user portion of the domain policy (B), the user portion of the Business Organizational Unit (C), and finally the user portion of the Marketing Organizational Unit (D).

Table 10-1. Resultant set of policies for Figure 10-7

Loopback mode in use	Organizational unit that user resides in	Where computer resides	Resultant set of policies
No	Marketing	OU=marketing (main site)	ABCD
No	Finance	OU=finance (second site)	GBEF
No	Marketing	OU=finance (second site)	GBCD
No	Finance	OU=marketing (main site)	ABEF
Merge	Marketing	OU=marketing (main site)	ABCDABCD
Merge	Finance	OU=finance (second site)	GBEFGBEF
Merge	Marketing	OU=finance (second site)	GBCDGBEF
Merge	Finance	OU=marketing (main site)	ABEFABCD
Replace	Marketing	OU=marketing (main site)	ABCD
Replace	Finance	OU=finance (second site)	GBEF
Replace	Marketing	OU=finance (second site)	GBEF
Replace	Finance	OU=marketing (main site)	ABCD

Remember that later policies can override earlier policies, so the user portion of the policies applying to the location of the computer will always override previous policies if there is a conflict. With policy order ABEFABCD, D can override C, which can override B, which can override A, which can override F, and so on. Also, in all these cases, if any of the computer GPOs do not have any defined settings in the user portion, the policy is ignored.

Loopback replace mode is used when the user portion of the GPOs that apply to a computer are to be the only ones set. For the finance user logging on to a computer in marketing in the main site, the only policies that get applied to that user are ABCD, the user portions of the GPOs that apply to the marketing computer.

 Administrators must be aware that loopback mode can impose a significant amount of extra load on the processing at the client, especially when using loopback in its merge mode.

WMI Filtering in Windows Server 2003

Microsoft has added a powerful new GPO filtering option in Windows Server 2003 Active Directory called Windows Management Interface (WMI) filtering. With WMI filtering you can associate a WMI query with a GPO, which will run for each user and computer that the GPO applies to. A WMI filter can utilize any WMI-based information that is accessible from the client's machine, including computer hardware and configuration, user profile, and environment settings. This presents a lot of options for targeting GPOs to clients that have certain properties. For example, lets say you want to apply a certain GPO if a client is accessing your network over VPN.

Depending on which VPN software the client is running, your WMI query could check for the existence of a process or service or even an IP address range. If the query returns true, the GPO will be applied; if it returns false, it will not be applied. Figure 10-8 shows the screen in the Group Policy Object Editor that allows you to configure a WMI filter.

Figure 10-8. WMI filter setting

 Windows 2000 clients ignore WMI filtering. It only applies to Windows XP and later systems.

How GPOs Work Across RAS and Slow Links

GPOs and even user profiles can still work across slow links, and a lot of the configuration is left in the hands of the administrator. Administrators can specify what speed is used in the definition of a slow link. For computers and users, the following policy areas need looking at:

Computer Configuration → Administrative Templates → System → Group Policy → Group Policy Slow Link Detection

User Configuration → Administrative Templates → System → Group Policy → Group Policy Slow Link Detection

In both cases, the default setting is 500 KBps, but administrators can set any KBps connection speed time that they wish. This speed is used against a slow-link-detection algorithm; if the speed is above the value, the link is fast; a speed below the value indicates a slow link.

This is the algorithm in pseudocode:

```
Ping server with 0KB of data : Receive response#1 as a time in
  milliseconds (ms)
If response#1 < 10ms Then
   Else
        milliseconds
   End If
Ping server with 0KB of data : Receive response#1 as a time in
  milliseconds
If response#1 < 10ms Then
   Else
          milliseconds
   End If
Ping server with 0KB of data : Receive response#1 as a time in
  milliseconds
If response#1 < 10ms Then
   Else
          milliseconds
   End If

'Average the total speed of (response#2-response#1)
Difference-in-milliseconds = Total-Speed/3
'If we know 4KB (32,768 bits) was moved in a certain number of
  milliseconds,
'then we need to calculate the number of bits moved per second
  (not per ms)
Bits-per-second-value = (32768 * 1000/Difference-in-milliseconds)
'Eight bits is a byte, so calculate bytes/second
bps-value = (Bits-per-second-value * 8)
'Calculate kilobytes/second to compare against GPO value
Kbps-value = bps-value / 1024
```

User profiles work in a similar manner. The following setting supports both checking the performance of the filesystem and checking the speed of the user profile server in both kilobytes per second and milliseconds. This was included by Microsoft to get past problems where the user profile server was not IP capable; in this case, it checks the filesystem performance instead:

Computer Configuration→Administrative Templates→System→Group Policy→
Slow network connection timeout for user profiles

The following GPOs are applied across slow links:

- When a user dials in from a RAS connection, both computer and user GPOs are applied.
- When a user logs in using the "Logon using dial-up connection" checkbox on the logon screen, user policies are applied.
- When the computer is a member of the same domain as the RAS server or is in a domain with a trust relationship to the one the RAS server is in, both are applied.

GPOs are not applied:

- When the logon is done using cached credentials which then include a RAS connection.
- To computers that are members of a different domain or workgroup.

By default in all these cases, security settings (i.e., IP security, EFS recovery, etc.) and Administrative Template settings are the only ones to be applied by default; folder redirection, disk quotas, scripts, and software installation policies are not applied. You can't turn off registry settings you have to apply. You can, however, alter the default state of any of the others, including the security settings, using the relevant sections of those GPOs.

Summary of Policy Options

That's a lot of information on GPOs. Let's summarize what we've covered about the workings of GPOs so far:

- GPOs exist in a split state. The configuration data for the GPO, known in shorthand form as GPC data, is held in the AD object itself. The template files and settings that tell the GPO what its capabilities are, known in shorthand form as GPT data, are stored in the SYSVOL.
- Individual GPOs can be linked to multiple sites, domains, and Organizational Units in Active Directory as required.
- GPOs can contain policies that apply to both computers and users in a container. The default operation of a GPO on a container is to apply the computer portion of the GPO to every computer in that container during boot up and to apply the user portion of the GPO to every user in that container during logon. GPOs also can be set to refresh periodically.
- Multiple GPOs linked to a particular container in Active Directory will be applied in a strict order according to a series of priorities. The default-prioritized order corresponds to the exact order in which the GPOs were linked to the container. Administrators can adjust the priorities as required.
- While GPOs exist only in a domain environment due to their dependence on Active Directory, individual domain or workgroup computers can have local GPOs, known as LGPOs, defined for them.
- Windows NT 4.0 system policies also can apply to standalone Windows NT or later clients or to mixed-mode or Windows Server 2003 Interim domain clients.
- GPOs are inherited down the Organizational Unit hierarchy by default. This can be blocked using the properties of an OU, domain, or site. Administrators can also set a checkbox that allows a policy to override all lower settings and bypass any blocks.

- Loopback mode allows the administrator to specify that user settings can be overridden on a per-machine basis. Effectively, this means that the user parts of policies that normally apply only to computers are applied to the users as well as (merge mode) or instead of (replace mode) the existing user policies.

- A new feature in Windows Server 2003 Active Directory called WMI filtering allows you to configure a WMI query that can be used as additional criteria to determine whether a GPO should be applied. If the filter evaluates to true, the GPO will continue to be processed; if it evaluates to false, the GPO will not be processed. This is a powerful feature because you have the vast amount of WMI data available to determine whether GPOs should be applied.

- A number of things can slow down processing on a client, including attempting to process many policies one after the other. Use of loopback, especially in merge mode, can significantly impact this. Attempting to apply GPOs across domains can also lead to slowdowns depending on the network speed between the domains. Finally, complex queries in WMI filters can also have a negative impact on GPO processing.

- Policies are applied in a strict order known as 4LSDOU. This notation indicates that Windows NT 4.0 system policies are applied first, followed by any LGPO policies, followed by site GPOs, domain GPOs, and finally any Organizational Unit GPOs hierarchically down the tree. At each point, the policies are applied in prioritized order if multiple policies exist at a location.

- When policies are to be applied to a client, the system identifies the entire list of policies to be applied before actually applying them in order. This is to determine whether any blocking, overriding, or loopback has been put in place that could alter the order or application of the policies.

- ACLs can be used to limit the application of GPOs to certain individual users or computers or groups of users or computers. Specifically setting up the ACLs on a GPO to deny or allow access means that you can tailor the impact of a policy from the normal method of applying the GPO to all users or computers in a container.

- If you use the GPOE MMC interface and look at the properties of an individual GPO, four tabs are displayed on the property page. The General tab shows you summary details on the policy and allows you to disable the computer or user part of the policy if you require. The Links tab allows you to find all locations in Active Directory that have links to that GPO. The Security tab allows you to limit the scope of the GPO on a container via ACLs. Finally, the WMI Filter tab allows you to configure a WMI filter to be used for GPO processing.

- Finally, both user profiles and policies can be applied across a slow link, but the speed that the system uses to determine whether a link is slow is configurable by the administrator within an individual GPO. In addition, while security settings and administrative templates normally are applied by default, the exact settings that will apply across a slow link when one is detected are configurable by the administrator as well. The only exception is that administrative templates will always be applied; the administrator has no control over this.

Managing Group Policies

The Microsoft tools available to manage GPOs under Windows 2000 were pretty limited, consisting of the Group Policy Object Editor (formerly Group Policy Editor) and built-in support in the Active Directory Users and Computers and Active Directory Sites and Services snap-ins. While these tools could get the job done, they did not provide any support for viewing the Resultant Set of Policy (RSoP), viewing how GPOs had been applied throughout a domain, or backing up or restoring GPOs. Luckily these tools weren't the only option: third-party vendor Full Armor produced Fazam 2000, which has comprehensive group policy management functionality.

Directly after the release of Windows Server 2003, Microsoft released the Group Policy Management Console (GPMC) as a separate web download. The GPMC is a much-needed addition to Microsoft's GPO management tools and provides nearly every GPO management function that an organization might need, including scripting support.

The other new feature available in the Windows Server 2003 Active Directory administrative tools and in GPMC is support for viewing the RSoP for a given domain, site or Organizational Unit based on certain criteria. RSoP allows administrators to determine what settings will be applied to a user and can aid in troubleshooting GPO problems. RSoP will be described in more detail in the section on debugging group policies.

Using the Group Policy Object Editor

When you add a GPOE snap-in to a console, you can only focus on a particular GPO/LGPO. Each GPO/LGPO that you wish to change has to be loaded in as a separate GPOE snap-in to the MMC; unfortunately, you can't tell the GPOE to show you all policies in the tree, but you can use the GPMC for that.

Managing LGPOs is done using the same GPOE tool that you would use to manage GPOs. If you use the GPOE from a workstation or server in a domain, you can focus the snap-in to look at an LGPO on a local client. If you use the GPOE on a standalone server or a workstation, the GPOE will automatically focus on the LGPO for that machine. No matter how the focus is shifted to look at an LGPO, the GPOE will load only the extensions that are appropriate to the templates in use locally on that client. Domain-specific extensions are not loaded for LGPOs.

Starting an MMC and adding the GPOE snap-in is not the normal method of accessing GPOs. In fact, there is a whole extended interface available from the Active

Directory Sites and Services snap-in, Active Directory Users and Computers (ADUC) tool, or the group Policy Management Console. If you open up the Sites and Services snap-in, you can right-click any site and from the drop-down list select Properties, finally clicking the Group Policy tab on the resulting property page. If you open the ADUC, right-click any domain or Organizational Unit container and follow the same steps. Ultimately, the Group Policy property page from any of these tools produces a window like Figure 10-9 with a number of options. Figure 10-9 shows the policies linked to the root of the *mycorp.com* domain. The following buttons are found on the *Mycorp.com* Properties menu:

New

> This button allows you to create new GPOs and automatically link them to the container for this property page. Since Figure 10-9 is the property page for the domain, any policies that are created and linked in here would be applied to the entire domain.

Add

> This button allows you to link an existing GPO to the container for this property page.

Edit

> This button allows you to manipulate the selected policy in the display pane.

Delete

> This button allows you to remove a policy. If you do this, a dialog box will appear and ask if you wish to remove just the GPO's link to the container for this property page or to permanently delete the GPO.

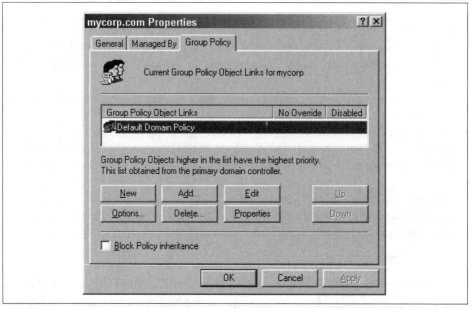

Figure 10-9. Looking at the domain policies

Properties

This button allows you to bring up the properties of the GPO itself, i.e., the General, Links, Security, and WMI Filter tabs in Figures 10-4, 10-2, 10-5, and 10-8, respectively.

Options

This button allows you to set two specific options relating to the application of this GPO by bringing up a dialog box similar to that shown in Figure 10-10.

No Override

This option allows you to force the settings of this GPO to apply no matter what other GPOs later attempt to block inheritance.

Disabled

This option allows you to completely disable the GPO's application to the current container. If you choose this option, any ACLs that you have set on this GPO to explicitly allow or deny application of this policy to individual users, computers, or groups will be ignored. This policy will not be applied under any circumstances.

 Disabling the GPO is not the same as setting an ACE with the Apply Group Policy checkbox cleared for the group Authenticated Users. Denying the ability to apply group policy for a GPO to a group via an ACE is much more restrictive, as the restriction will apply to the GPO across all containers and not just for the one container, which is what the Options button allows you to do.

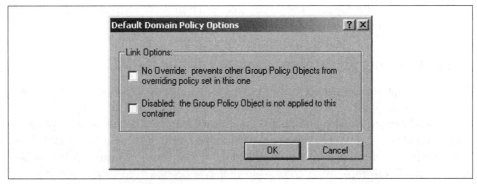

Figure 10-10. Domain policy options

Block policy inheritance

This checkbox is used to indicate that policies from further up the 4LSDOU inheritance chain are not to be inherited by objects at this point and below. This is used when you want a particular level in the tree to define its own policies without inheriting previously defined ones above it. For example, a block at the site level blocks Windows NT system policies and LGPOs (i.e., 4L) from applying; a block at the domain level blocks 4LS; a block at an Organizational Unit level blocks 4LSD in addition to any other Organizational Unit parents above this level in the tree.

Up/down arrows

These buttons allow you to prioritize multiple GPOs in the display pane. In Figure 10-9 only one GPO is displayed, so these buttons are displayed

GPOE GUI Shortcuts

Some useful shortcuts supported by Explorer have been copied over to the GPOE . For example, you can highlight a branch in the GPOE and press * on the numeric keypad to automatically expand the entire tree at that point. You can press + and – on the numeric keypad to expand and collapse individual highlighted branches. You can also use the cursor keys to navigate up and down the list. The Tab key switches back and forth between the scope pane and the results pane.

One last point that is very useful: if you open up the GPOE and double-click on any item, it brings up a floating property page window. There is nothing to stop you from going back to the GPOE and highlighting any other location in the tree, navigating using the cursor keys, and using the keys in the previous paragraph. Each item that you select, however, correspondingly modifies the floating property page. You can see each item's description and options in the floating property page while navigating through the GPOE as before.

If you've installed the GPMC, the Group Policy tab in those snap-ins is not available and you need to use GPMC, which provides a lot more functionality.

Using the Group Policy Management Console (GPMC)

The GPMC is a one-stop shop for all your GPO management needs. You can browse a forest and see where GPOs are applied; you can create and link GPOs; you can import and export, backup and restore, delegate control, and view RSoP reports, all from the GPMC. Not only does the GPMC have a bunch of new functionality not available in any of the previous standard tools, it also integrates the existing tools—such as the GPOE for editing GPOs—so that you do not need to go outside of the GPMC to perform those tasks.

Figure 10-11 shows what the GPMC looks like when viewing a GPO. As you can see in the left pane, you can browse through the domains in a forest down to specific Organizational Units. If you right-click on a domain, you'll get the following options:

- Create and Link a GPO
- Link an Existing GPO
- Block Inheritance
- Search for GPOs
- Create a New Organizational Unit

If you right-click on an Organizational Unit, you'll get many of the same options, except for Search.

In Figure 10-11, the Domain Controllers Organizational Unit has been expanded to show that the Default Domain Controllers Policy has been linked to it (i.e., icon with a shortcut/arrow symbol). A virtual Group Policy Objects container is expanded, which shows all of the GPOs that have been created in the domain (currently just the two default GPOs exist). There is also a virtual WMI Filters container that holds any WMI filter objects that have been created. Note that the Group Policy Objects and WMI Filters container are virtual. This was done so that instead of requiring drilling down into the System container to locate GPOs, they would be readily available directly under a domain.

 You can also browse the GPOs that have been linked to a site by right clicking on the Sites container and selecting Show Sites. You have an option of which sites to display.

If we take a look at Figure 10-11 again, we can see that the Default Domain Controllers Policy was selected in the left pane, and several options and settings are displayed in the right pane. The following list is a summary of each tab:

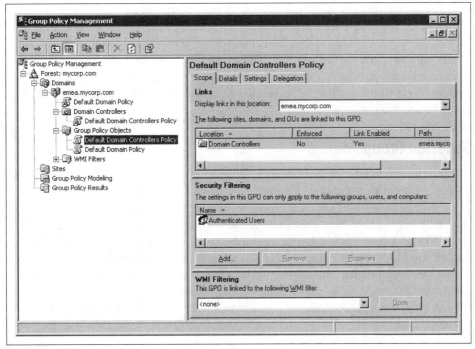

Figure 10-11. GPO properties in the GPMC

Scope

Under the Scope tab you can view the domains, sites, or Organizational Units that have been linked to the GPO and delete them if necessary. You can also view what security groups the GPO applies to, and add and remove groups from the list. Finally, you can set the WMI filter that should be associated with the GPO.

Details

The Details tab contains information about who created the GPO, the date it was created and last modified, and the current user version and computer version. The only thing that can be set on this page is beside GPO Status, which defines whether the user and/or computer settings are enabled.

Settings

The Settings tab provides a nice shortcut to view which settings have been configured in a GPO. Unlike the GPOE, in which you have to drill down through each folder to determine which settings have been configured, you can view the Settings tab for a GPO in the GPMC to see only the options that have been set.

Delegation

The Delegation tab is similar to the Delegation of Control wizard, but it's specifically for GPOs. We'll cover this screen in more detail later in the chapter.

One last feature that is worth mentioning is the Group Policy Modeling and Group Policy Results. Group Policy Modeling is very similar to the RSoP option that is available in the ADUC, which is described at the end of the chapter. Group Policy Results is very similar to the Group Policy Modeling/RSoP, except that it is not a simulation. The results are returned from the client, not simulated on a domain controller. Group Policy Results will only work on a computer running Windows XP or Windows Server 2003.

Scripting Group Policies

Another hurdle to efficiently managing GPOs with the initial release of Active Directory was the lack of scripting support. Not having the ability to automate the creation or maintenance of GPOs meant that administrators had to spend a lot of time manually managing GPOs. Fortunately, the GPMC also provides scripting capabilities. Whenever you install the GPMC, it registers several COM-based objects that can be used to automate most of the tasks you'd need to do with GPOs. The word "most" is used because the GPMC COM objects do not allow you configure any GPO settings; you still have to do that manually. On the other hand, you can copy or import a GPO and its settings, so if you have a template GPO or a GPO you want to create in multiple domains, you can conceivably create it once, then use the COM objects to copy it to other domains.

The following is a list of some of the tasks you can perform via scripts with the GPMC objects. For more information on the objects and interfaces, check out the *GPMC. chm* help file available with the GPMC installation in the Scripts sub-directory.

- Create a GPO with the default settings.
- Copy a GPO.
- Import GPO settings.
- Set GPO permissions.
- Delete a GPO.
- Search for GPOs.
- List GPOs.
- Retrieve GPO information.
- Back up GPOs.
- Restore GPOs.
- Generate a RSoP report for GPOs.

Using GPOs to Help Design the Organizational Unit Structure

In Chapter 8, we described the design of the Active Directory Organizational Unit hierarchy. We also explained that other items have a bearing on that design. You see, there are two key design issues that affect the structure of your Organizational Units: permissions delegation and GPO placement. If you decide that your Active Directory is to be managed centrally rather than in a distributed fashion and that you will employ only a few GPOs that will be implemented mostly domainwide (rather than many GPOs on many Organizational Units), your Organizational Unit structure can be almost any way that you want it to be. It shouldn't make much difference whether you have 400 branches coming off the root or one container with every item inside it. However, if permissions over specific objects do need to be delegated to specific sets of administrators, it will make more sense to structure your domain Organizational Units in a manner that facilitates that administration. This doesn't have to be the case, but it makes it much easier to use Organizational Units.

For example, if we have 1,000 users and 10 managers who each manage 100 users, we could put the 1,000 users in one Organizational Unit and give the 10 admins permission to modify only their 100 users. This is a slow and daft way to run systems administration. It would be better to create 10 Organizational Units and put 100 users in each, giving each administrator permission over his particular Organizational Unit. This makes much more sense, as the administrator can be changed very easily, it is easier to report on access, and so on. Sense and reducing management overhead are the overriding keys here. Either solution is feasible; one is just easier to implement and maintain.

 Permissions delegation is covered in more detail in Chapter 11.

The same fundamental facts apply to GPOs. If you are going to need to apply multiple policies to multiple sets of users, it makes more sense and will be easier to manage if you set up multiple Organizational Units. However, this isn't always possible, for example, if the Organizational Unit structure that you have as an ideal conflicts with the one that you will need for permissions delegation, which again conflicts with the one you would like for GPO structuring.

Identifying Areas of Policy

We will assume that within your organization, you will be writing a document that describes your plan for the security features you wish to use in your Active Directory environment and exactly how those features will be implemented. Part of this document will relate to other security features of AD, such as Kerberos, firewalls, permissions, and so on, but here we're concerned with GPOs.

First you need to identify the general policy goals that you wish to achieve with GPOs. There's no need to go into the exact details of each GPO setting and its value at this moment. Instead, you're looking at items like "Deploy financial applications" and "Restrict desktop settings." As you identify each general policy area, you need to note whether it is to apply to all computers or users in a site, to all computers or users in a single domain, or to a subsection of the user and computer accounts. If you aren't sure for some items, put the items in more than one category. You end up with items like "Deploy financial applications to accountants in France" and "Restrict desktop settings in southern Europe."

Once you have the general policy areas constructed, you need to construct an Organizational Unit structure that facilitates implementation of this policy design. At this point, you start placing computers and users in various Organizational Units, deciding if all objects in each container are to receive the policy or whether you will restrict application to the policy via ACLs. There are a number of questions you can ask yourself during this stage. To help with this, a loose set of guidelines follows the example in the next section.

Ultimately the document will need to specify exactly which GPO settings are to be applied, which groups you will set up for ACL permission restrictions, and what the Organizational Unit structure is going to be. It helps to explain justifications for any decisions you make.

To make the guidelines more meaningful, we'll show how you can structure a tree in different ways using a real-world example.

How GPOs Influenced a Real Organizational Unit Design

Leicester University needed an Organizational Unit structure that represented its user and computer population. The system needed to allow users from every department to roam anywhere on campus and log on to the system. User accounts were fairly generic across the system, with the main differences resulting only from membership in certain groups indicating the type of account the user had (staff, undergraduate, and so on). The main distinction came in the two sorts of machines that we maintain on campus: staff devices that exist in a number of staff member's offices, and open devices that exist in areas known as open-area labs, which anyone could use. While staff machines always exist within a department, labs exist in certain locations and buildings throughout the university campus.

Having full Internet and drop-in access, we needed to make sure that these open area client devices were as secure as they could possibly be. This security had to extend to all users who logged on at the machines, whether they were staff or student. However, we also wanted to make sure that staff accounts were not locked down in their own departments. In other words, we wanted the user profiles of the staff users to be much more locked down only in the open-area labs and nowhere else.

In terms of policies, we needed to apply quite a few. While the specifics aren't important here, we needed a number of policies to apply to different areas:

Area	Policies to apply to
A	All computers and users in the domain
B	Users in specific departments
C	All clients (not servers)
D	All open-area clients
E	All staff clients
F	Staff clients in specific departments
G	Open-area clients in specific labs

With these requirements, we came up with a design. This was a lengthy process, but we'll try to break it down so that it makes sense. Let's take a look at the users themselves to start with.

Users were always members of a specific department, and this was how the university was structured in terms of its business, so it seemed logical to name the Organizational Units after the university departments. We should add, by the way, that Leicester University needed only one domain, the forest root domain in a single forest, for its organization; the Organizational Unit structure was much more important than the domain structure in this case. The overall Organizational Unit structure came out something like that shown in Figure 10-12. Each department is joined directly to the root of the domain, with the users (represented by the circles) being children of the departmental containers.

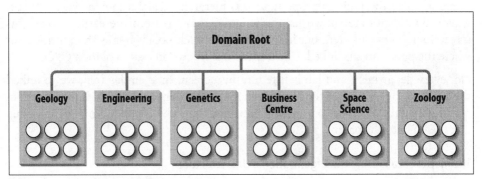

Figure 10-12. OU structure to hold user objects

Next, we needed an Organizational Unit structure that represented the distinct divisions of computers that existed throughout the university. There's no necessity to presume that your computers should go in the same Organizational Unit structure as your users, and that's how we approached the concept at Leicester. Initially, based on the policy areas, it seemed sensible to us to create an entirely new client tree that held only the machine accounts. This hierarchy ended up looking like the one in Figure 10-13.

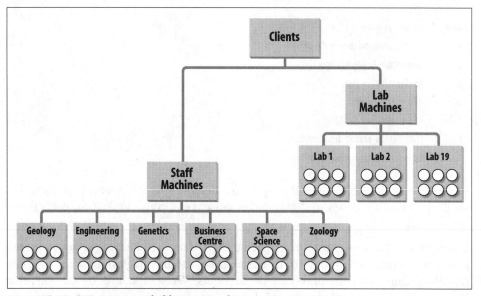

Figure 10-13. OU structure to hold computer objects

Here you can see the branch solely for the computer accounts, with two children that each hold lab locations or departments themselves. Notice how the staff machine branch of the tree looks remarkably like the user structure diagram from Figure 10-12. We'll come back to that in a minute. For now, let's see if we can successfully apply the policies properly to this hierarchy. Take a look at Figure 10-14; where the policies are shown using the letter notation from the earlier table. This screen looks very cluttered, but it simply depicts each policy area with indications of where the policy area is linked. The trapezoid is Microsoft's symbol for a GPO.

Not every department and lab is listed in this screen. In a similar vein, we've linked the GPOs to only some of the Organizational Units, since that would be the case in reality. After all, if every department or lab were to receive a policy, you might as well link the GPO to the parent.

The merits of collapsing the Organizational Unit structure

We've created a structure that is understandable and perfectly represents the business that we operate. That's a good achievement from this design. The next step is to consider whether the domain would be easier to manage if we merged the duplicated staff organizational units.

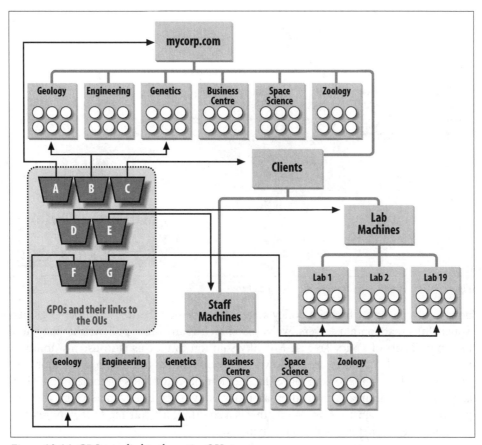

Figure 10-14. GPOs applied to the entire OU structure

Take a look at Figure 10-15. This is the hierarchy if we do away with all the staff machine Organizational Units and put the staff computers directly into the departmental Organizational Units. Policy areas A and B stay the same. Policy area C has to apply to all clients, so we can't use the Clients Organizational Unit any more. We have two choices: link the policy to the domain and have it apply to all Organizational Units containing computers beneath the root, or link the policy to each Organizational Unit under the root by hand. The latter solution also requires us to link the GPO to any new Organizational Units that we create under the root, if they are to receive the policy.

The former is the easier solution to manage, so let's run with it and link policy area C to the domain root. Unfortunately, this means that the GPO is going to apply to any computer objects in the domain, including Organizational Units that we store servers in, such as the Domain Controllers Organizational Unit that exists under the root of the domain. We don't want this, so the only way forward here is to block policy inheritance at these server Organizational Units. You may see where this is going

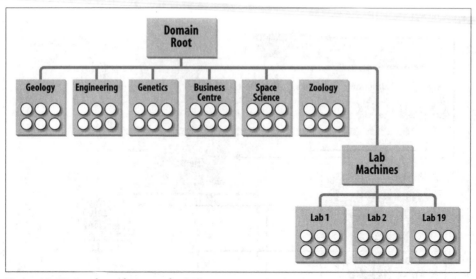

Figure 10-15. Another solution to the OU structure

now. We've not only blocked policy area C from being inherited by these Organizational Units that contain servers, we've also blocked any other policies that may need to apply as part of policy area A. My only solution to fix this is to use my ability to force an override of policy area A down the tree. So much for a simpler solution. We now have at least one block in place (for the domain controllers Organizational Unit) and policies from area A overriding all blocks down the tree to make sure they get past the blocks we just set up. While this is a solution, it's starting to feel more complex than the one before. Isn't there a better way?

Yes, by making use of security groups. Forget about the blocks and inheritance for now and consider that instead we put all the computers that are not to get policy area C in a security group. We can then deny the Apply Group Policy permission to this particular security group, so that no members of the group ever have that policy applied to them. This is a much easier solution. However, it does mean that the administrators must remember that if a new computer is created and is not to receive the policy, it must be added to the group.

Policy areas D and G can still apply as they did before. Policy area F applies only to certain Organizational Units, so we just link F to the various departments under the root and carry on as before. However, we have more problems with E. Again, the choices are similar to the previous predicament: we could apply E to the department Organizational Units individually (remembering to do this for each new department we create), we could apply the policy to the domain root and use block inheritance-force override as before, or we could use groups again. The use of groups seems simpler, so let's go with that option. If we create a group for all the staff machines, we can just give the group permission to apply group policy to policy E in addition to removing the default permission for authenticated users to apply group policy. Now all users won't run the policy by default, but members of the staff machines group will.

This is a different solution that now achieves the same goal. The solution that Leicester chose (the first design) required fewer groups and allowed a computer's or user's location in the hierarchy to dictate which policies were applied. The new solution that we've just worked through collapses the tree structure but instead makes more use of groups to indicate which policies are to be applied.

In fact, this tends to be a rule: as you collapse a structure where a number of GPOs apply, you need greater control via groups or the use of block inheritance and overrides.

A bridge too far

We could go one stage further and remove the lab machines' Organizational Unit entirely. That would cause the same problems with policy area D that we had with E. The simpler solution is to add all lab machines into a group and allow only members of that group to access the policy.

You can continue on in this manner, removing Organizational Units and creating more groups until you actually end up with all objects in a single Organizational Unit under the domain. At that point, all the GPOs are applied to that Organizational Unit, and you control access to the Organizational Units via groups. Prioritization of the order that the multiple GPOs would be applied might be more of a nightmare in this situation.

We hope you can see that there are a number of options open to you when designing your Organizational Unit structure for GPOs. It doesn't really matter which method you choose, as long as you're happy with it. The Organizational Unit structure that Leicester adopted requires less maintenance, because you don't have to put an object in a group after creation; you just create it in the place in the tree that it is to receive policies from. That's less of an issue with the capabilities of ADSI, since the code to bind to the parent group and add the newly created object to that group is just two extra lines.

We also created some other Organizational Units for specific functions. For example, one Organizational Unit holds all the groups that we ever created. That way, when we want to find a group, we know where it is. We also created a test Organizational Unit so that we could roll out policies and do testing with users and computers within the domain without affecting the existing user setup.

It may appear that Leicester doesn't make much use of groups to control access to GPOs, but that's not the case. Just because we set up the Organizational Unit structure in a way that made sense to us doesn't mean that we shouldn't make good use of groups as well. Let me give you some examples. Look back at Figure 10-14. Policy areas D and G actually consist of a number of completely different and opposing GPOs that can affect all lab machines (D) or machines in specific labs (G). One group of settings entirely locks down the workstations in those labs from access to the hard disk and various control panels and places other security measures. Another raft of settings serves to unlock the machines entirely; in other words, this GPO is the complete opposite of the first. Further sets of GPOs allow us to put the lab into a mixture of the two states with some areas locked down and others remaining unlocked. These policies are applied as required to the specific lab Organizational Units, so that if all were to apply at the same time, it would be a complete fiasco. Instead, we use global security groups, one for access to each GPO, and make the computers from that lab members of each group.

To gain access to the policies, we move the computers from one group into another. If a client needs to be unlocked entirely, we move it to the unlocked group and reboot or wait until the policy refreshes. Similarly, if a user from zoology decides that he wants his machine locked down, we can apply the relevant GPOs to the zoology Organizational Unit, then place that machine in the global group that allows access to the GPO.

If we had a situation in which the client was either locked down or not locked down, we could have used just one group and had a lockdown state by default, with membership in the group implying an unlocked state or vice versa.

Loopback mode

We've held one important aspect of Leicester's GPO design until now, that of loopback mode. Leicester needs to use loopback mode to lock down both staff and students while they are in a lab environment. To do this successfully requires that the computer policies be separate from the user policies. When you add this requirement to the equation, it makes more sense to keep the lab part of the tree separate in some way from the other part of the tree. This ensures that the user sections of the computer policies do not apply to any user accounts except during loopback mode. Both Figures 10-12 and 10-13 have structures that will happily accommodate the requirement.

Guidelines for Designing GPOs

In this section, we provide guidelines that help you toward two critical design goals:

- All policies should be applied quickly, so that users do not feel a significant impact due to policy processing.
- All policies should be as easy as possible to administer and maintain.

With these two concepts in mind, let's take a look at the guidelines:

Design in a way that you feel comfortable with
  As shown in the example in the last section, it can be easier to do large designs by considering the user Organizational Unit and computer Organizational Unit

structures separately. If you want to do them together and have a small enough network that you can do so easily, that's fine. If not, try it the way we first did.

Restrict as best you can the number of policies that apply

In a perfect world, this wouldn't be important. But in the real world, the more policies you have, the more processing the client has to do in addition to its normal logon/boot up, and the longer it takes to complete the process.

If you have multiple policies applying to an object from the same location in a tree, consider collapsing them into a single object, since this will process faster than multiple policies will. If the number of policies you are applying during a logon/boot up is larger than you can effectively get out to the client across the network or, more importantly, larger than you can get the client to process, you need to consider reducing or collapsing the policies. If you need to apply a significantly large set of policies with many settings that extends logon to five minutes, but you feel that is acceptable to achieve this level of policy, that's fine.

When it comes down to it, only you know what you can accept, and you will need to do your own testing in this area to satisfy your constraints. If you have to have a client logged on in less than 4 seconds, you have to work within that constraint. Microsoft likes to recommend no more than 10 Organizational Units deep to make sure that you don't use too many GPOs. As we know, this isn't very helpful. Having one GPO applying at a site, one at the domain, and one at each of 5 Organizational Units means only 7 GPOs. Applying 10 at each level is 70. So it's not only how deep you nest your Organizational Unit structure that matters, it's how many policies you can apply. The unfortunate part, of course, is that it always comes back to how many settings you are applying in each policy.

The simple answer is that a faster machine with more RAM can apply more policies in less time than a slower PC with less RAM; consequently, for a network of heterogeneous clients, you need to do testing on your own network to see how fast application of policies is and how much bandwidth they take up. Sorry, but that's the way it is for now.

Use security groups to tailor access

While you can set up ACLs to allow or deny application of policy to an individual user or computer, it makes more sense to use groups to do this whenever you can. If you use groups, it lets you keep all policy access in one object, and it can make complex systems much more manageable.

Limit the use of block/force inheritance

You should be very cautious of blocking inheritance at locations in the tree unless you are quite sure that this is the right way to solve your problem. The repercussions from a simple blocking of inheritance can spiral quickly as you encounter areas of policy that need to override the block. Your well-designed system can become quite difficult to maintain if you block and override regularly. This is not to say that you should never use them; just exercise caution in their use.

Collapse the Organizational Unit design

If you wish, you can collapse your Organizational Unit design and make more use of groups (or even block inheritance/force override) to govern access to specific policies. These are both perfectly valid solutions, and you should use whichever you are more comfortable with. Remember the axiom that the more you collapse the Organizational Unit structure while maintaining or increasing the number of GPOs, the greater need for control via groups or block inheritance/force override.

Avoid using cross-domain GPO links

If you link GPOs across domains, the entire set of *SYSVOL* data as well as the object information itself needs to transfer over from the source domain whenever a user or computer needs to access it. So unless you have very fast links between the two domains with enough available bandwidth, you should duplicate the functionality of the GPO in the target domain instead of cross-domain linking unless the domain controllers for each domain are co-located on the same network.

Prioritize GPOs

Remember that it is possible to prioritize applications of multiple GPOs at the site, domain, or Organizational Unit level. This ordering of the application of policies allows you to add useful options to the administrator's toolkit. For example, if you need a group of users to reverse specific settings that are being applied by default as part of a larger set, create a new GPO with ACLs for this group that apply in the priority list to unset all the previous settings. This solution allows you to override a selection of previous settings without creating two GPOs, one with settings for everyone and one for just this group. The former solution allows you to add in settings to the main GPO and still have them apply to everyone, without needing to add them to the second GPO of the latter solution. Prioritizing GPOs can be very useful.

Increase processing speed

The main ways to increase processing speed are to reduce the number of GPOs that you apply, disable the computer or user portion of a GPO if it is not needed, or limit the use of block inheritance, force override, cross-domain linking, and loopback mode. All of these place an extra processing load on the client to some degree. A really bad mistake would be to use combinations of them.

Be cautious with loopback mode

Loopback mode is a very useful tool but is another technology that you need to approach with caution. As a completely different set of policies (replace mode) or a very large number of policies (merge mode) will be applied to your users, and since there are no Resultant Set of Policy (RSoP) tools in existence as we write this, you need to take great care to ensure that the policy received by a user is the one you expect.

In most cases, loopback merge mode will incur significant extra processing load on the client PC and extra bandwidth on the network. That's not to say it isn't useful, but you have to be very aware of the delays that could occur after its introduction. Loopback replace mode imposes less of a processing load, but it can still be a problem. If you are contemplating loopback mode, ensure adequate stress testing of user impact.

Limit how often GPOs are updated

This relates to two specific times. You should limit your modifications to GPOs that could immediately cause a policy refresh on all clients or users, as this could impose a slowdown across the network and on the client. It would be better to make the updates during scheduled systems maintenance times. You should also carefully control the policy refresh interval. You have to ask yourself if you really need to refresh policy every 10 minutes when every 24 hours might be sufficient.

Thoroughly test WMI filters

If you are using WMI filters, be sure to test the queries thoroughly before releasing in production. If you use an unoptimized query or one that is very resource-intensive, it could cause significant delays during GPO processing. Creating a simple script or even using the new WMI tool called WMIC can help facilitate the testing.

Restrict blocking of domain GPOs

You should not block domain GPOs to specifically use LGPOs on a domain client without very good reasons. If you do choose to apply LGPOs only to a client, you need to be aware of the management overhead because each client needs to be managed individually. If you have 20 orphaned clients using LGPOs and you need to make a change, you need to make it 20 times, once per client. The whole concept behind GPOs was to aid centralized management and administration of distributed resources, not distributed management of distributed resources. Think carefully before going down this path.

Use test GPOs

We always recommend creating test GPOs and linking them to a branch of test Organizational Units set up for this purpose. No GPO should ever be applied to users or computers unless it has been fully tested. And with the new tools, such as GPMC or the Resultant Set of Policies (described in more detail shortly), it is much easier to assess the impact GPOs will have on your client base.

Choose monolithic or segmented GPOs

While we would recommend keeping similar settings—or all settings relating to a particular item—in the same GPO, there is nothing stopping you from having only a few huge GPOs as opposed to a number of smaller GPOs. If you go for the monolithic approach, you process fewer GPOs, which is obviously faster;

however, delegation is not as easy due to the fact that the policy contains so many settings. Segmented GPOs allow easier delegation but can impact performance. Mix and match the two to a level that you are comfortable with and that works for your network.

Designing Delegation and Change Control

Now that you've designed a policy-based implementation for your organization, you have to work out how you will maintain firm control over GPOs once you start deploying them. Specifically, you need to consider who will be managing your GPOs and how you will keep control over the wide-ranging changes they can make.

The importance of change-control procedures

The best way to keep track of GPOs in your organization is through a series of change-control procedures. These work well whether your GPO administrators are domain administrators or not. We suggest a file such as a Word document with tables, a spreadsheet, or even a database in a central location to hold data on each GPO, the settings that it applies, whether it applies to computers and users or both, the containers in Active Directory that it applies to, and so on. You also should add extra columns/fields to the data for the proposer of the original GPO and those people who ratified the change. If you add those fields/columns, every time a new change is made, it is added by the proposer to the existing data set. Then the proposer or the system automatically contacts the rest of the GPO administrators and asks them to review and ratify the change in the data set. Discussions could continue via email if there were problems preventing ratification or if items needed clarification. Finally, when the GPO data is ratified by all, it can be regression-tested on test systems if that hasn't already been done and then implemented within Active Directory.

Designing the delegation of GPO administration

There are three types of permission that can be considered here:

- The permission to allow sets of users to link policies to a domain or an Organizational Unit branch
- The permission to allow sets of users to create GPOs
- The permission to allow sets of users to change the GPOs themselves

Link delegation can be easily accomplished using the Delegation of Control Wizard* that you get by right-clicking an Organizational Unit, domain, or site in Active Directory and choosing Delegate Control. You'll want to use the "Manage Group Policy

---

* This wizard is discussed more fully in Chapter 11.

Links" task. Here you are actually delegating read and write access to the gPLink* attribute of the GPO.

The other GPO attribute that can be delegated in this way is called gPOptions. As discussed earlier and shown in Figure 10-10, this deals with the area of blocking inheritance. If you're interested in how these attributes work, set up a few GPOs in your Active Directory. Then use ADSI Edit from the Windows Support Tools to examine the attributes of the newly created GPOs in this location:

```
LDAP://CN=Policies,CN=System,dc=windows,dc=mycorp,dc=com
```

Creation of GPOs is limited to those indicated in the sidebar by default. However, you can add users to the Group Policy Creator Owners security group, which allows members to create new GPOs. If a member of Group Policy Creator Owners creates a GPO, that user is set as the Creator Owner† of the GPO and can continue to manage it. The Creator Owner of a GPO can manage the GPO even if the user is removed from all groups that give GPO management privileges.

---

* The GPC data part of a GPO is an object in Active Directory. This object, like all others, has attributes. One of the attributes of a GPO is a multivalued one called gPLink that stores Active Directory ADsPaths of the containers that the GPO is linked to.

† When administrators create GPOs, the Domain Admins group becomes the Creator Owner.

GPC data in Active Directory (i.e., the actual Active Directory object itself) will never inherit security permissions from parents up the tree. There is a special block in place that prevents this in Active Directory, so that all GPO ACLs have to be modified from within the Group Policy tools.

You can delegate edit access to new GPOs, as long as the people creating those GPOs are the ones who will be editing them, by placing those users into the Group Policy Creator Owners group. If you also want to delegate edit access to more people or to GPOs that a user is not the Creator Owner of, use the GPMC. Navigate to the Group Policy Object folder under the domain in which the GPO you want edit is contained. Click on the GPO you want to delegate and select the Delegation tab in the right pane as shown in Figure 10-16. Click the Add button, which will bring up the object picker, which allows you to select which users or groups you want to have access. Next you'll need to pick the permission you want to grant. You have three options:

- Read
- Edit settings
- Edit settings, delete, modify security

Finally, click OK and the delegation will be applied.

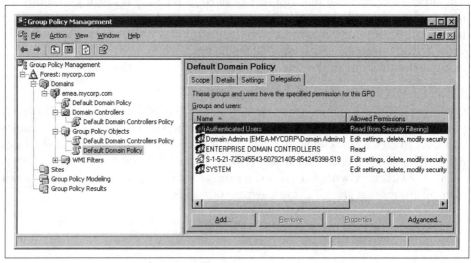

Figure 10-16. GPO delegation in the GPMC

A word of warning before we finish up here. Correctly applied, GPOs are fundamental to the wellbeing of your Active Directory. Policies incorrectly applied to the root of the domain could lock down the Administrator account or disallow logons at domain controllers. This is obviously a worst-case scenario, but there are some mistakes that are much more likely to occur: a mistyped registry value that forces users to an invalid proxy server and thus stops Internet Explorer from working, forgetting to clear a checkbox and thus applying a policy down an entire branch of the tree (the default) when it was only to apply to the root of the branch, and so on. These changes have the potential to affect all users or computers throughout the tree, so we would caution you to keep GPO administrators to a very select subset. If you allow nonadministrators the ability to create, change, and delete GPOs, they have to be able to take responsibility for and be accountable for their actions. Users who are already administrator-equivalent will automatically be able to administer GPOs and should already be held accountable.

Creating customized GPOEs for administrators

The GPOE comes with a series of permitted snap-ins that normal administrators will get by default. These snap-ins allow administrators to manage all parts of a GPO. However, it is possible to ship customized GPOEs that focus on only one GPO and load only certain permitted snap-ins. This allows you to state that Group 1 can manage this part of a policy and Group 2 that part of the same policy. This is a very useful tool that we encourage you to use when delegating administration, but you must be aware that just giving a restricted tool to certain users will not stop them from being able to manipulate other aspects of a GPO if they open up their own GPOE and point it at the same policy.

To solve this problem, cast your mind back to the section when we was discussing the Administrative Templates (User) section, specifically the Windows Components → Microsoft Management Console → Restricted → Permitted snap-ins → Group Policy section. The best solution is to use the Restricted → Permitted snap-ins → Group Policy section of a GPO in order to allow and deny users or groups access to certain extensions. This covers you completely, since your users or groups can now run up only their own GPOE with the extensions that you have explicitly permitted them to use.

Debugging Group Policies

If at any point you need to debug group policies, there are couple of options you can use. The first is new to Windows Server 2003 and is called the Resultant Set of Policy, which some people may be familiar with if you've used tools like Full Armor's Fazam 2000. The Resultant Set of Policy (RSoP) allows you to specify certain user, computer, group, and GPO criteria to determine what will be applied. Another option is to enable some extra logging that can help point out GPO processing problems.

Using the RSoP

The RSoP is a very powerful tool to help identify what GPO settings will be applied to a user or computer. Before RSoP, administrators were left to do their own estimates as to what GPOs took precedence and what settings were actually applied to users and computers. RSoP removes much of the guesswork with an easy-to-use wizard interface.

To start the RSoP wizard, open Active Directory Users and Computers and browse to the domain or Organizational Unit that contains the users you want to simulate. Right click on the container and select All Tasks → Resultant Set Of Policy (Planning). Figure 10-17 shows the initial screen.

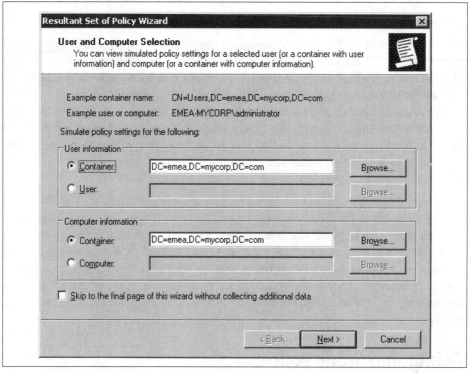

Figure 10-17. User and Computer Selection Options

You must first select a specific object DN of a user or computer, an Organizational Unit that contains users or computers, or a domain. After clicking Next, you will come to the Advanced Simulation Options screen where you can select whether to pretend you are over a slow network, whether to use loopback mode, and whether a specific site should be used. Figure 10-18 shows what this screen looks like with the MySite1 site selected.

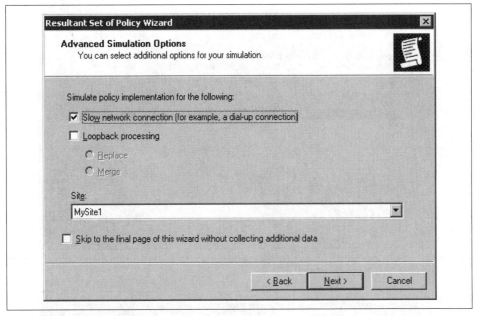

Figure 10-18. Advanced Simulation Options

The next screen, as shown in Figure 10-19, allows you to configure any additional security groups that should be considered while processing GPOs. You will actually see two screens like the one seen in Figure 10-18; the first will allow you to select user security groups and the second will allow you to select any computer security groups.

In the next screen, you will be able to select one or more WMI filters or use the ones that have been linked to existing GPOs. Just as with the security groups, you can select WMI filters for users and computers independently. The WMI filter screen for users is shown in Figure 10-20.

After you finish the wizard, a console that looks very similar to the GPOE will be opened that contains the settings that would apply to the user and computer. Figure 10-21 shows that the password policy will be applied based on the simulation criteria we entered.

One of the nice features of the RSoP console is that you can save it and refer to it later. You can also change or refresh the query by right-clicking the title and selecting Change Query or Refresh Query.

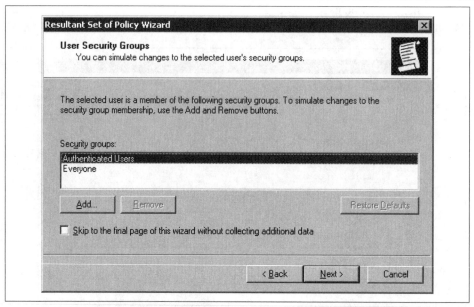

Figure 10-19. Security group simulation

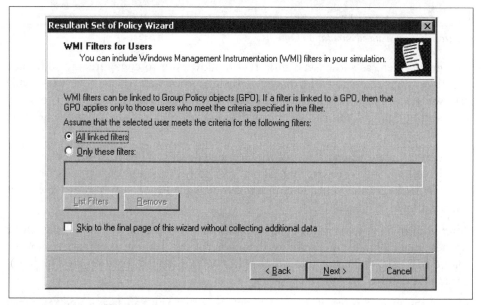

Figure 10-20. WMI filters simulation

Enabling Extra Logging

You can turn on verbose logging in the event log for group policy–related events simply by setting a registry key. Once the key exists with the correct value, logging is

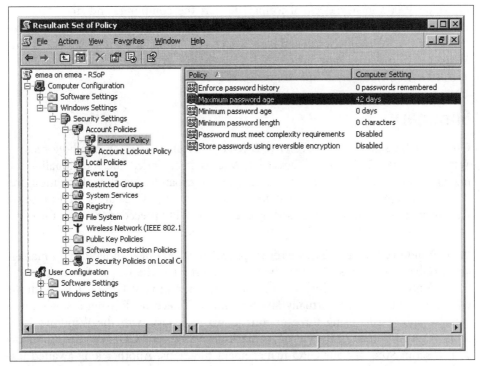

Figure 10-21. RSoP results

done automatically. The value, a REG_DWORD, is called RunDiagnosticLogging-GroupPolicy and needs to be created with a value of 1 in the HKLM\Software\Microsoft\WindowsNT\CurrentVersion\Diagnostics key.

The value of 1 sets the logging to verbose mode; setting the value to 0 is the same as having the key absent and is known as normal logging. In other words, the key makes a difference only when set to a value of 1. It's really as simple as that.

> This key is actually one of four currently supported keys that you can use at this location. You also can create RunDiagnosticLoggingIntel-limirror, RunDiagnosticLoggingAppDeploy, and RunDiagnostic-LoggingGlobal. The last turns Application Deployment, Intellimirror, and Group Policy logging on without needing to set all three individually. For more information, check out Microsoft Knowledge Base article 186454, which can be found at *http://support.microsoft.com/default.aspx?scid=kb;en-us;186454*.

If the verbose logging in the event log is not providing enough information, another option is to enable debug logging for policy and profile processing. To do so, create a value called UserEnvDebugLevel as a REG_DWORD in the HKLM\Software\Microsoft\WindowsNT\CurrentVersion\Winlogon key. Assign UserEnvDebugLevel the value 10002 in hexadecimal format. Restart the computer, and from then on, extensive logging information will be recorded on the machine in the file *%SystemRoot%\Debug\UserMode\Userenv.log*. For more information, check out Microsoft Knowledge Base article 221833, which can be found at *http://support. microsoft.com/default.aspx?scid=kb;en-us;221833*.

Summary

One of the big selling points of Active Directory has always been group policy and in Windows Server 2003 Active Directory, Microsoft extended the functionality and management of GPOs greatly. In this chapter we expanded on the information presented in Chapter 7, to cover the details of how group policies are stored in Active Directory, how GPOs are processed by clients, the GPO precedence order, the effect of inheritance, and the role ACLs play.

With Windows Server 2003, Microsoft provided several new tools to help manage and troubleshoot GPOs. Perhaps the most important is the Group Policy Management Console (GPMC), which is a one-stop shop for all your GPO needs. With the GPMC you can perform virtually any function you need to do from a single interface, as opposed to using three or four as wa necessary with the Windows 2000 tools. Another benefit of the GPMC is that is installs several COM objects that allow you to script 90% of your GPO management functions. Another long-awaited feature that is available now is the Resultant Set of Policy (RSoP) that allows for modeling and testing of GPOs. With RSoP you can configure several different settings including the container to process, any security groups to include, whether to use a specific site, whether to use loopback mode, whether to use a specific WMI filter, and more. The end result is a GPOE view of the settings that would be applied.

CHAPTER 11

Active Directory Security: Permissions and Auditing

Permissions can be set in Active Directory in the same way they are set for files. While you may not care that everyone in the tree can read all your users' phone numbers, you may want to store more sensitive information and restrict that access. Reading is not the only problem, of course. You also have create, modify, and delete privileges to worry about, and the last thing you need is a disgruntled or clever employee finding a way to delete all the users in an Organizational Unit. And inheritance increases the complexity in the typical way.

None of this should be new to system managers who already deal with Windows NT Access Control Lists and Access Masks, IntraNetWare's Trustee Lists and Inherited Rights Masks, and Unix's access permissions in file masks. In fact, Microsoft has carried the NT terminology from file permissions forward to Active Directory, so if you already know these terms, you're well ahead. If you are not familiar with them, don't worry. Microsoft has a great tradition of calling a shovel a ground-insertion-earth-management device. Terminology in permissions can seem confusing at first, so we'll go through it all in detail.

Managing the permissions in Active Directory doesn't have to be a headache. You can design sensible permissions schemes using guidelines on inheritance and complexity that will allow you to have a much easier time as a systems administrator. The GUI that Microsoft provides is fairly good for simple tasks but more cumbersome for complex multiple permissions. In Windows Server 2003, the GUI has been enhanced to provide an "effective permissions" option that lets you determine the effective permissions a user group has on the container or object. Also, Active Directory permissions are supported by ADSI, which opens up a whole raft of opportunities for you to use scripts to track problems and manipulate access simply and effectively. Finally, the DSACLS utility allows administrators to manage permissions from a command line if you prefer an alternative to the GUI

Yet permissions are only half the story. If you allow a user to modify details of every user in a specific branch below a certain Organizational Unit, you can monitor the creations, deletions, and changes to objects and properties within that branch using auditing entries. In fact, you can monitor any aspect of modification to Active Directory using auditing. The system keeps track of logging the auditing events and you can then periodically check them or use a script or third-party tool to alert you quickly to any problems.

Figure 11-1 shows the basics. Each object stores a value called a Security Descriptor, or SD, that holds all the information describing the security for that object. Included with the information are two important collections called Access Control Lists, or ACLs, which hold the relevant permissions. The first ACL, called the System-Audit ACL or SACL, defines the permission events that will trigger both success and failure audit messages. The second, called the Discretionary ACL or DACL, defines the permissions that users have to the object, its properties, and its children. Each of the two ACLs holds a collection of Access Control Entries, or ACEs, that correspond to individual audit or permission entries.

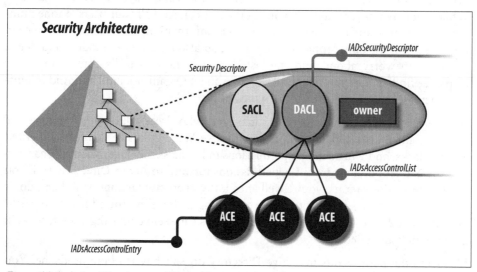

Figure 11-1. Active Directory security architecture

ACEs can apply to the object as a whole or to the individual properties of the object. This allows an administrator to control not just which users can see an object, but what properties those users can see. An object is never revealed to users who do not have the permission to see the object. For example, all users might be granted read access to the telephone number and email properties for all other users, but Security Descriptors of users might be denied to all but members of a specially created security administrators group. Individual users might be granted write access to personal properties such as the telephone numbers and mailing addresses on their own user objects. The possibilities are limited only by the objects and their corresponding properties in the tree. The Active Directory schema is extensible, so organization-specific permissions can be allowed and denied for all the objects and properties your organization creates.

Deny permissions always override allow permissions.

Auditing takes place when the system logs an event in the security event log on a particular DC to indicate that an Active Directory event has taken place. You can monitor the creation, modification, or deletion of any object in Active Directory. This can, of course, be useful for maintaining records of security problems, as well as in dealing with unusual behavior by the system.

Using the GUI to Examine Permissions

To access the default permissions for any object, select the Active Directory Users and Computers MMC and right-click on it. Choose Properties from the drop-down menu and select the Security tab of the properties window that is displayed.

 To make the Security tab visible, you need to right-click in the display pane of the Active Directory Users and Computers MMC, choosing View Advanced Features from the pop-up menu. If you reopen the properties window of the object to which you wish to assign permissions, you should see a Security tab.

The window in Figure 11-2 is your first point of contact for permissions. The top area contains a complete list of all groups and users who have permissions to the object whose properties we are looking at. The Permissions section below this list displays which general permissions are allowed and denied for the highlighted user or group. The general permissions listed are only those deemed to be the most likely to be set on a regular basis. Each general permission is only an umbrella term representing a complex set of actual implemented permissions hidden underneath the item. Consequently, the general permission called Read translates to specific permissions like Read All Properties and List Contents, as we will show later. Below the Permissions section are three important parts of this window:

Advanced button
> The Advanced button allows you to delve further into the object, so that permissions can be set using a more fine-grained approach.

Text display area
> The second part of this area of the window is used to display a message, such as that shown in Figure 11-2. The text shows that the permissions for the current object are more complex than can be displayed here. Consequently, we would have to press the Advanced button to see them.

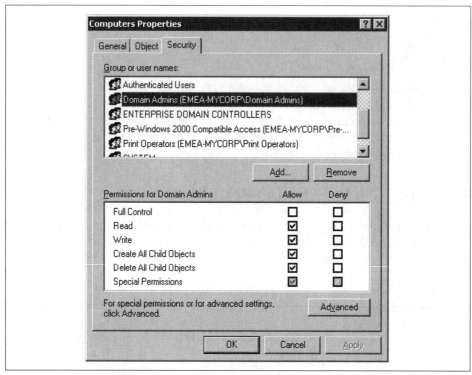

Figure 11-2. Security properties of an object

Inheritance checkbox (Windows 2000 only; not shown in Figure 11-2)

The "Allow inheritable permissions from parent to propagate to this object" checkbox allows you to orphan (my term) this object from the tree. When you clear the checkbox on the security properties or Access Control Settings windows mentioned later, the system pops up a Yes/No/Cancel dialog box that asks if you want to convert your inherited entries to normal entries. If you click Cancel, the operation aborts. Clicking No removes all inherited entries and orphans the object or branch. Clicking Yes converts the inherited entries to standard entries, as if you had manually applied the old inherited permissions to this object manually. All normal permission entries for the object are unchanged by whatever choice you make. We will cover this in more detail later in the book. For Windows Server 2003, this checkbox is available from the Advanced screen. Clicking the Advanced button actually displays the same users and groups again, but in slightly more detail. Figure 11-3 shows this window, known as the Advanced Security Settings for the object.

While the Advanced Security Settings window gives only slightly more information than the previous window, it serves an important purpose: it is a gateway to the lowest, most atomic level of permissions. The Advanced window allows you to view the

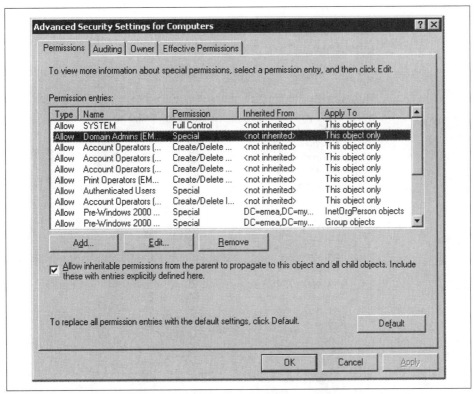

Figure 11-3. Advanced Security Settings for an object

globally set permissions from Figure 11-2, as well as a brief summary of the advanced permissions that may be set for each object. While the Name and Permission columns effectively duplicate information from Figure 11-2, the Type field shows whether the permissions to the object for this user or group are Allow or Deny. If a group has some allow and some deny permissions, two entries are recorded in this window. The Inherited From field is a new addition in Windows Server 2003 that allows you to see what object, if any, the permission was inherited from. The Apply To column usefully indicates what the permission applies to. This could be to this object only, the object and all subobjects, or just to an individual property, say telephoneNumber, of a user object. Again this window allows you to indicate whether to orphan the object.

You now have two choices to view the atomic permissions. You can click Add, which pops up a window allowing you to add a new user or group to those with permissions set on this object. Alternatively, you can highlight an existing user or group and click the Edit button (or View/Edit on Windows 2000). If you highlight a user or group or add one from the pop-up window, the next screens you see are the PE windows, shown in Figures 11-4 and 11-5.

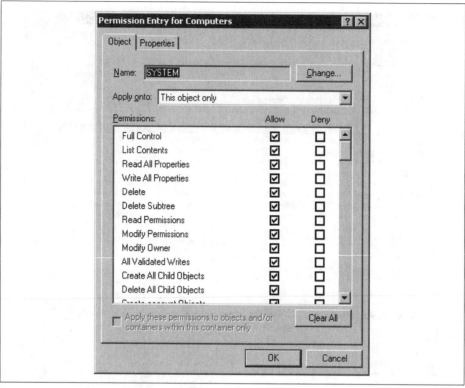

Figure 11-4. Permission Entry for an object

Until you know exactly what you are doing with permissions, we suggest that you create a few test users and groups to play with permissions settings. The last thing you want to do is make a simple mistake with a built-in group or user and deny yourself access to the tree. If you create two test users and three test groups, put each user in a separate group, and then put both users in the third group, you will have the basis of a test system.

The PE windows are two sides of the same coin, one representing permissions to the object and the other representing permissions to the properties of that object. This is the lowest, most atomic level you can get to when setting permissions. Here is where you can really tailor a system to do exactly what you want.

The object name is displayed in the title of the PE window, with the name of the user or group that has permissions prominently displayed in the field at the top. The user or group then has permissions allowed and denied from the column entries. The entries in the window are relative and vary depending on the entry in the drop-down list under the heading of Apply Onto. What is not immediately obvious from this window is how large the drop-down box can actually get. Figure 11-6 shows this

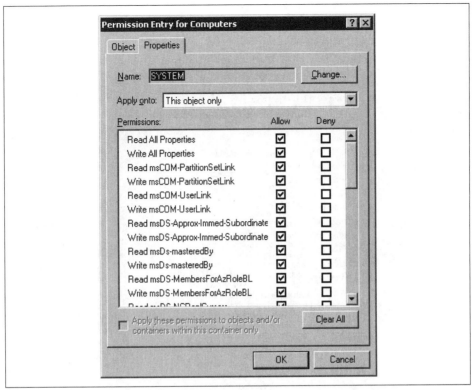

Figure 11-5. Permission Entry for an object's properties

nicely. If you look at the scroll bar, you will get an idea of how many items are currently not displayed.

To set a permission from the PE window, pick where you want to apply the permission and then click the relevant Allow and Deny boxes, selecting OK when done. Since Microsoft has not provided an Apply button, you cannot specify a set of permissions applied onto one area, click Apply, and then repeat the cycle until you are done with this user and group. You have to click OK, which means the window closes, whereupon you then have to click Add again, and so on. This is a tiresome problem if you are implementing multiple changes from a set of prepared designs, but one you have to live with.

Reverting to the Default Permissions

In Figure 11-3 you may have noticed the Default button at the bottom. This is a new feature in Windows Server 2003 that allows you to revert the current permission set to the default security as defined in the schema for the objectclass of the object. If you click Default for an object you have not modified the permissions on, you may notice that the list still changes. If you look closer, you'll see that the inherited per-

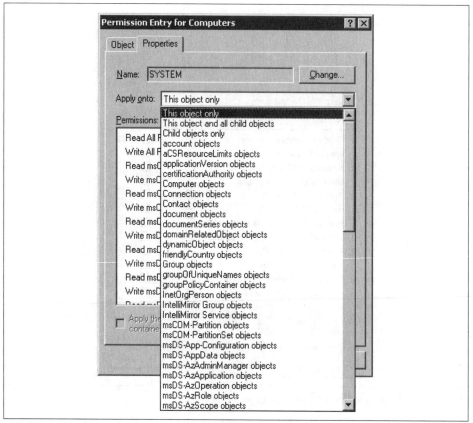

Figure 11-6. Permission Entry window showing the large number of targets to which permissions can be applied

missions were the ones removed. That is because inherited permissions are not defined as part of the default security of an object and will be removed. Even if you then click OK to apply the permissions, as long as the Allow Inheritable Permissions box is checked, the inherited permissions will still apply. Having the ability to apply the default permissions is a useful feature, especially for administrators who are trying to determine what changes have been made from the default installation.

Viewing the Effective Permissions for a User or Group

Another new feature in Windows Server 2003 is Effective Permissions, which is available from the Advanced button when viewing the security for an object. The Effective Permissions screen allows you to select a user or group and determine its effective (or actual) permissions to the object taking into account group membership and permission inheritance. Figure 11-7 shows the results of the effective permissions for Authenticated Users on the EMEA domain object. As you can see, Authenticated Users have List Contents, Read All Properties, and Read Permissions. All objects in the forest will inherit these permissions unless inheritance has been blocked. As you might guess, this is a significant feature that allows for much easier troubleshooting of permission problems. There are some limitations to be aware of, however.

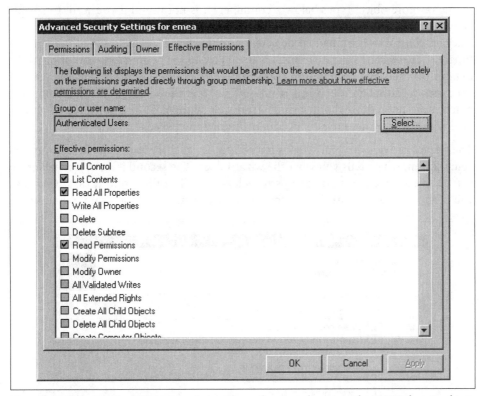

Figure 11-7. Viewing the effective permissions for authenticated users on the EMEA domain object

The Effective Permissions tool is only an approximation of the actual permissions a user or group has and does not take into account many of the well-known security principals such as Anonymous Logon and Network. Another potential issue to be mindful of is that the user running the Effective Permissions tool must have the rights to read the group membership of the target user or group. By default, Authenticated Users has this right.

Using the Delegation of Control Wizard

To help with delegating permissions for objects in Active Directory, Windows 2000 and Windows Server 2003 come with a wizard called the Delegation of Control wizard. It is intended to allow administrators to delegate management of certain types of objects to key individuals or groups in the organization. It is activated by right-clicking almost any container in the DIT and selecting the wizard from the pop-up menu. Builtin and LostAndFound are the two containers for which it does not work by default.

The wizard is useful only when you need to clearly apply general allow permissions to one or more object types below a container. It is not useful if you want to specify deny permissions (which it doesn't support), remove previously delegated control, delegate control over individual objects, or apply special permissions to branches of the tree. The wizard's great strength is its ability to set permissions and apply them to multiple users and groups at the same time. We use the wizard to set these sorts of permissions, although much less regularly than we do the standard GUI, since it is much more limited in what it can do. Scripting with ADSI also provides a solution here which is more adaptive to an administrator's own needs.

The wizard provides several screens for you to navigate through. The first is the welcome screen, which tells you what the wizard does. The second is an object picker for you to select which users or groups to delegate to. The third screen asks what task you wish to delegate control for in that container. Figure 11-8 shows this window.

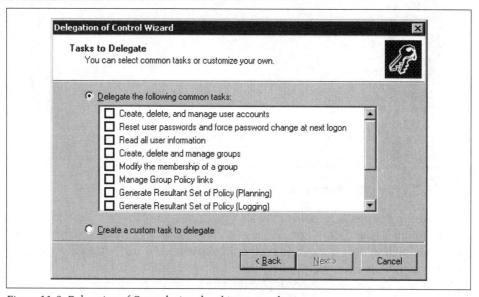

Figure 11-8. Delegation of Control wizard—object type selection

The default is to delegate control for a specific task, and there are several to choose from. In fact, several new tasks have been added in Windows Server 2003. Since the list scrolled off the screen in Figure 11-8, we'll list them here:

- Create, delete, and manage user accounts
- Reset user passwords and force user change password at next logon

- Read all user information
- Create, delete, and manage groups
- Modify the membership of a group
- Manage Group Policy links
- Generate Resultant Set of Policy (Planning)
- Generate Resultant Set of Policy (Logging)
- Create, delete, and manage inetOrgPerson accounts
- Reset inetOrgPerson passwords and force password change at next logon
- Read all inetOrgPerson information

If you choose the Custom radio button and click Next, an extra page opens, allowing you to specify individual objects. Figure 11-9 shows this.

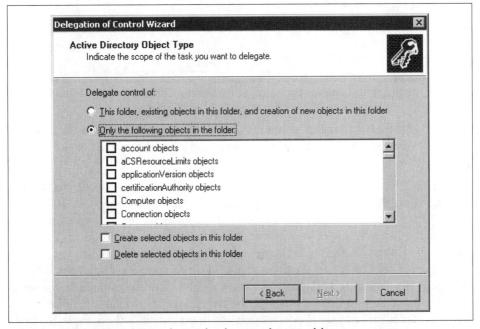

Figure 11-9. Delegation of Control wizard—choosing objects to delegate

If you want to delegate certain permissions to computer or user objects in a specific container or branch, you can do it from here. The next screen of the wizard allows you to specify what permissions you wish to assign for the selected users/ groups. Figure 11-10 shows this screen.

When the window opens initially, only the first checkbox is checked. As you click each of the other boxes, the list of specific permissions that you can delegate becomes very large as it encompasses all of the permissions that you could poten-

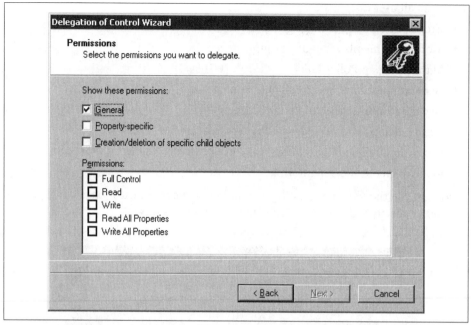

Figure 11-10. Delegation of Control wizard—access rights selection

tially delegate. Finally, the last screen of the wizard summarizes the previous answers and allows the user to go back, cancel, or finish and grant the permissions.

However, just as the permissions listed in the security properties for an object (Figure 11-2) can change, so can the permissions listed in the access rights box, depending on the object(s) to which permissions are being applied. A good demonstration of this is to open up the security permissions for any user and scroll through the displayed list of permissions. Next open up the wizard on any container and specify Custom Task (see the screen shown in Figure 11-8) and only user objects (see Figure 11-9). The screen shown in Figure 11-10 should then display the same list that the screen in Figure 11-2 does. This makes sense since they should be the same; available permissions for one user should be the same as the available permissions for all users. It is still nice to see the correlation and appreciate it in the flesh, so to speak.

Using the GUI to Examine Auditing

Examining auditing entries is almost identical to viewing permissions entries. If you go back to the screen shown in Figure 11-3 and click on the Auditing tab, a screen similar to that in Figure 11-11 is displayed.

This window shows the list of Auditing Entries (AEs) that have been defined on the object. This object has one AE, and it's not very helpful viewing it from here since the detail is too limited. So just as you would do with permissions, you can click the Edit button (or View/Edit with Windows 2000), drill down, view the individual AE itself.

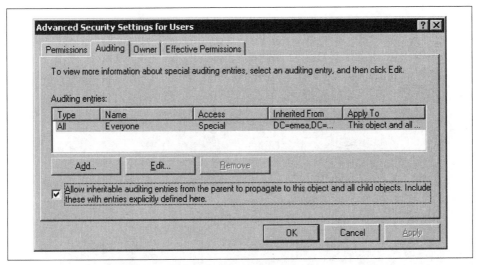

Figure 11-11. Advanced Settings window showing auditing entries

Figure 11-12 shows the successful and failed items that are being awaited. The items are grayed out because this entry is inherited from further up the tree, i.e., it is not defined directly on this object but instead further up the hierarchy.

Figure 11-13 shows an example AE window for successful and failed auditing of properties. Here you are auditing only property writes.

Designing Permission Schemes

Having worked through many designs for different domain structures, we have come up with a series of rules or guidelines you can follow to structure the design process effectively. The idea is that if you design your permissions schemes using these rules, you will be more likely to create a design with global scope and minimum effort.

The Five Golden Rules of Permissions Design

This list is not exhaustive. We are sure you will be able to think of others beyond these. If, however, these rules spark your creative juices and help you design more effectively, they will have done their job.

The rules are:

1. Whenever possible, assign object permissions to groups of users rather than individual users.
2. Design group permissions so that you have a minimum of duplication.
3. Manage permissions globally from the ACL window.
4. Allow inheritance: do not orphan sections of the tree.

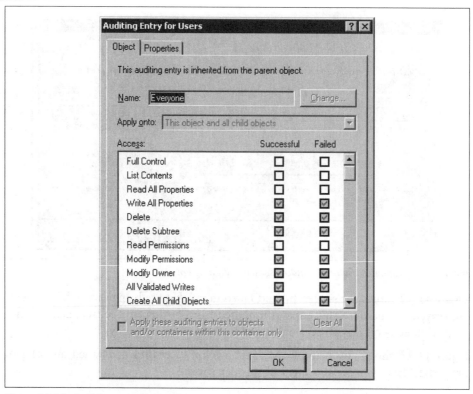

Figure 11-12. Auditing entry for an object

5. Keep a log of every unusual change that you have made to the tree, especially when you have orphaned sections of it or applied special rights to certain users.

Let's look at these rules in more detail.

Rule 1—Apply permissions to groups whenever possible

By default, you should use groups to manage your user permissions. At its simplest, this rule makes sense whenever you have more than one user for whom you wish to set certain permissions.

Some things need to be made very clear about how groups are different between Windows NT and Active Directory:

• Active Directory supports the concept of two types of group: security and distribution. A distribution group is one that contains users for mailing purposes and cannot have security rights assigned to it. Consequently, we are only dealing with security groups here.

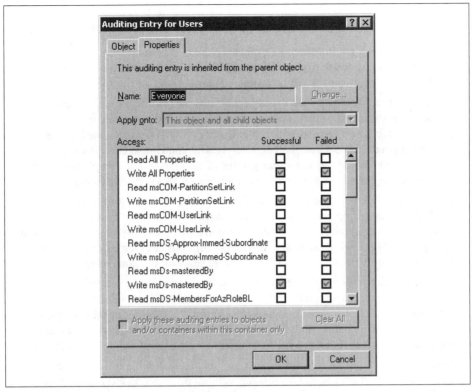

Figure 11-13. Auditing entry for an object's properties

- Windows 2000 mixed-mode and Windows Server 2003 Interim domains natively support Security groups that have two types of scope: Global or Local. These correspond to the Windows NT 4.0 Domain Global and Local groups.

- Windows 2000 native-mode or Windows Server 2003 domains have access to a third scope, universal. Universal groups contain other groups and have permissions assigned to them.

 More detailed information on the differences between Windows NT groups and Active Directory groups and how Active Directory groups differ in the various modes and functional levels can be found in Chapter 2.

Under Windows 2000 mixed-mode and Windows Server 2003 Interim functional level, the paths you can choose are clear. You either follow the method outlined in the sidebar, or you choose to assign permissions in some other manner of your own choosing.

When you convert your domain to native mode, you have a more difficult decision: do you choose "Domain users go into universal groups, universal groups go into uni-

Global Group and Local Group Permissions Under Windows NT 4.0

Under Windows NT 4.0, Microsoft's preferred method of applying file and directory permissions was to create two sets of groups: Local Groups, which had permissions, and Domain Global Groups, which contained users.

The Local Group would exist on the server that had the resource, and the relevant permissions were assigned to that. Local groups were allowed to contain both users and groups. Domain Users were then placed in Domain Global Groups, which themselves were placed in the Local Groups on each server. Domain Global Groups were allowed to contain only users and not other groups. This may sound complicated, but it worked well in practice. A good way of demonstrating this is through an example.

Consider an NT 4.0 domain called Mycorp containing a Global Domain Group called Marketing. This group has four members. Within Mycorp are two servers, called Server1 and Server2, each of which has published a share. Each server also has a Local Group SH_USERS, which contains the Global Group Marketing as a member. Each SH_USERS group has read access to the relevant share on the same server.

You use global groups in this scenario because it is faster to deal with a large number of users as one group than it is to deal with them individually. In a similar vein, it makes sense to keep control over permissions to resources by creating Local Groups, each with a relevant set of permissions. That way, if you ever need to modify the permissions for a particular set of users, you need to modify only the Local Group's permissions.

So if we decide that Keith and Sue should have full permissions to the share on Server1, we could create a Local Group on Server1 with full permissions and add a newly created Global Group, say MKTG_ADMIN, to it with Keith and Sue as members. Future users who need full permissions are added to this Global Group.

versal groups, universal groups are assigned resources"? Or do you move to "Domain users go into universal groups, universal groups are assigned resources"? Or do you assign permissions in a manner of your own choosing?

We're not advocating the use of one group or two, as we'll explain in more detail in the next section on how to plan permissions. We are advocating that whichever way you choose to implement group permissions, you should add users to groups and apply permissions to groups, even if the group initially contains only one user. This removes organizational dependence on one particular account. Time after time, we have seen organizations in which individual users with a whole raft of permissions to various objects suddenly leave or change roles. The new administrator then has to go in and unravel differing permissions settings from this account. We have even seen one administrator, who looked in anguish at the tangled mess of a recently departed administrator's account, delete his own account and rename the departed user's account just so that he could get the correct permission set without having to figure out the mess! If the old administrator had been a member of, say, five different groups, each with the relevant permissions, the new administrator could simply have replaced the group memberships of the old account with his new account. This is a much simpler approach, and we are sure that none of the preceding common sense is very new to systems administrators.

Rule 2—Design group permissions so that you have minimum duplication

It makes much more sense to create groups with simple permission sets than it does to create multiple groups with overlapping permissions. If you decide that some of your users need, say, create and modify, while others need modify and delete, and a third set needs just modify, it makes much more sense to create three separate groups with create, delete, and modify, than it does to make three groups with the permissions sets described. Let's consider an example. We will call the three groups CRE_MOD, MOD_DEL, and MOD. Let's now say we add 10 users to each group. If the only modifications ever to happen to these groups are occasional membership changes, this solution fits adequately. However, let's say that as with every large organization, the permissions requirements change over time. If Dave Peace, a member of CRE_MOD, now needs delete, what do we do? Do we make a special case of Dave's account and add the delete permission to his account only? Arguably, that is the simple solution, but according to Rule 1, we really should create a group to manage the permission. Do we create a DEL group and add Dave's account or create a CRE_MOD_DEL group and move his membership from CRE_MOD to the new group? Both are valid solutions.

Let's say we go with the former and create a DEL group, adding Dave as a member of that group. Things change again, and Mark Newell joins. Mark needs to be a member of groups giving him both MOD and DEL, so do we add him to MOD_DEL or MOD and DEL? Either way, we now have potential confusion. Whenever we have to check for members who can modify and delete, we have to check three groups, not one.

If we'd taken the second approach and chosen to create CRE_MOD_DEL rather than the DEL group, Mark is added to MOD_DEL when he joins, and things seem to be working fine. Paul Burke now moves from another team and requires create only, so a CRE group is created and his account added to that. Later, three others join the CRE group, but Paul now needs create and delete, so CRE_DEL is created, and he is moved to this group. Now we have six groups: CRE, MOD, CRE_DEL, CRE_MOD, MOD_DEL, and CRE_MOD_DEL. Unfortunately, if we ever have to check who has create and modify permission, we have to check the three groups: CRE, MOD, and CRE_MOD.

This example has been heavily contrived. However, we hope it serves to show that duplication will occur whenever you have users requiring separate permissions to an object or property and users requiring combinations of those permissions. It is for this very reason that we suggest creating separate groups for the lowest-common-denominator permissions that you need to set.

For example, if you have users who always need read, list, and create but require different combinations of delete and modify, it makes no sense to have three groups—one each for read, list, and create. You would instead create one group with the read, list, and create permissions assigned to it, one group for delete, and one for modify. Then you would use multiple group memberships to assemble the group permissions as you require them.

The most important point to note is that we are talking about minimizing and simplifying the number of groups. If you need only CRE_MOD_DEL to an object, you do not create three groups; you create one.

If after you have created a group with multiple permissions, you find that you now need groups with individual permissions, create the smaller groups and migrate the users. Then you can remove the larger group. This simplifies your workload, meaning not only do you manage fewer groups, but you also are revising and extending your permissions design to cope with changes. In fact, following this rule allows you to create a permissions scheme that you can be confident is fully flexible and enables you to cope with any changes in the future.

Rule 3—Manage Advanced permissions only when absolutely necessary

(Please note that this says "permissions" and not "auditing." Auditing entries can be accessed only from the Advanced tab, so this rule makes less sense for auditing entries.)

Whenever you right-click an object to view its properties, the Security Properties window that appears has an Advanced button on it. This was shown in Figure 11-2 in the previous section. The Security Properties window itself typically has the following allow and deny options as General Permissions:

- Full control
- Read
- Write
- Create all child objects
- Delete all child objects

The screen also allows you to specify whether the object inherits permissions from its parent. In other words, it allows you to orphan the object from its parents.

The general permissions are not limited to those five in the previous list, and indeed they change depending on the object you are looking at. For example, the security properties for any user object display additional general permissions, such as Reset Password, Modify Web Information, and Send As. While these general permissions make sense for the user object, they are not all appropriate for other objects. This rule suggests that you manage permissions for objects from the Security Properties window as often as you can. You should choose the Advanced button only when you wish to allow or deny a permission to one aspect of an object rather than the whole object. An example would be manipulating the permission to a user object's telephone number rather than the whole account details.

While there is nothing wrong with managing atomic permissions to objects and properties, permissions are much easier to manage from a higher level. The main permissions that administrators might want to set were put here for this express purpose, so that users and groups can easily manage the tree without having to worry about the large amount of individual properties.

Rule 4—Allow inheritance; do not orphan branches of the domain tree unless you have to

If you allow or deny permission for a group or user to all objects of a certain type in a container, by default the permissions are applied recursively to all objects of that type in all the child containers down the tree. It is possible to block inheritance, but we recommend leaving inheritance in place (the default) and orphaning other branches on an individual basis only when there are good justifications for doing so. The reason is simple: if you specify that children do not inherit certain permissions from their parents, you are setting your Active Directory up to be more complex to manage. Here is a very contrived example of when it could be appropriate to orphan a branch. Let's say you have a domain tree called *mycorp.com* with a policy that all members of Mycorp should be able to print to all printers in the organization. Consequently, everyone has print rights to every printer down the tree by default. Now mycorp.com has, among others, two Organizational Units called Finance and Sales off the root. The Finance Organizational Unit has two printers that the Finance people specifically do not want Sales staff using. Consequently, having obtained a special dispensation from management to override the policy, they specify that a domain group containing all sales staff, called SALES_GRP and contained in the Sales Organizational Unit, has no access to view or list the printers in the Finance Organizational Unit and all its children. This is effectively using a PE window on the Finance Organizational Unit and setting a Deny on Full Control to apply this to Print-Queue Objects only.

Now the Finance Organizational Unit has three child Organizational Units called Loans, Borrowing, and Markets. The Sales team regularly uses a legacy application, which has to print results to a printer in the Borrowing Organizational Unit. Unfortunately, as SALES_GRP has no access to printers in the Borrowing Organizational Unit because of the permissions restriction, they are initially out of luck. Here are three of the many solutions to the problem:

- Create a second printer, which resides in Sales, to the same device, and allow SALES_GRP to print to that.

- Remove the SALES_GRP restriction from the Finance Organizational Unit and its children down the tree; that brings you back to the starting point where you allow everyone to print to every printer. Now manually apply the same restrictions for SALES_GRP to the Finance, Loans, and Markets Organizational Units, but do not apply them down the tree. Of course this means that everyone in Sales can print to all printers in Borrowing, but we could further restrict this by applying restrictions on all printers to which Sales should have no access.

- Orphan the Borrowing Organizational Unit so that it does not inherit the printer permissions for SALES_GRP from its parent. This should allow print permission for the SALES_GRP to the printers in the Borrowing Organizational Unit.

Both the second and third items should allow print permission for the SALES_GRP to the printers in the Borrowing Organizational Unit. At first glance, the second and third items may appear to be identical. However, if the number of Organizational Units under Finance were 20 or 30, we would much rather choose the third method than the second. We have better things to do than to manually assign 20 or 30 sets of permissions.

There are two other important differences between the second and the third items. First, if we add a new Organizational Unit called Payments under Finance, in the third example Payments automatically inherits the permissions from Finance as they are applied down the tree on creation. Consequently, all the printers in Payments are restricted from SALES_GRP as per the dispensation. In the second example, the permissions are not applied down the tree and the administrator has to remember to apply restrictions to SALES_GRP for Payments if the dispensation is to be consistently applied.

The second point is that the Borrowing Organizational Unit in the third example loses all inherited permissions that would be applied by inheritance from its parent. This is significant if Borrowing had multiple inherited entries and every other inherited entry should stay put. When you orphan the Organizational Unit, you could specify that the inherited permissions for the Organizational Unit be converted to normal permission entries specific to this Organizational Unit. This saves you the trouble of manually applying inherited permission entries now. However, these manual changes will have to be remembered for the day when the permissions are changed on the parent, so that the administrator can come back and manually change them on Borrowing.

Ultimately, the preceding example shows that there is nothing wrong with orphaning sections of the tree or choosing not to apply permissions down the branch of a tree. It is just important to remember that every time you do it, you are creating slightly more work for yourself. As an administrator of a tree, you should keep track of these changes in a log, so that you can easily reference your special cases when required.

Rule 5—Keep a log of unusual changes

This may sound like an obvious statement, but it is surprising how many administrators overlook such a simple requirement. Simply put, it is always wise to keep a log of custom changes that you make to a default installation so that you and others have something to refer back to. There will be times when you may not be available and this sort of information is required. The following list shows the relevant fields of a basic Active Directory ACL log:

- Unique name of object or LDAP location of object in tree
- Object class being modified
- Object or property being modified
- User or group to whom permissions are being assigned
- Permissions being assigned
- Notes on reasons why this change is being made

Let's now look at how you can put these rules into practice in your own designs.

How to Plan Permissions

There are a number of Active Directory Users and Computers permission sets that administrators may need to implement in their organizations. Some examples are:

- A set of centralized teams, each with responsibility for certain areas. Users can be members of more than one area: account modifiers, printer managers, computer account managers, publishing managers, and so on.
- A manager for each individual major Organizational Unit under a domain.
- Again, a manager for each individual major Organizational Unit under a domain, but this time each manager is also able to delegate responsibility for lower Organizational Units.
- An administrator of the top-level domain is given permission to every subdomain by each subdomain's administrators.

While we could go through each of the preceding settings and show how to design permissions in each case, every organization is different. For that reason, it seems better to try to show what we consider to be the best way to design Active Directory permissions for all types of organizations.

First, create two documents, one called Allow and the other called Deny. On each document, label two sections, one called Global Tree Permissions and the other Specific Tree Permissions. Place two subheadings under each of the two sections, calling one General Permissions and the other Special Permissions. You should end up with three columns for each general and special heading: LDAP path, What to set, and To whom.

The first six columns relate to permissions that will apply throughout the whole tree; the last six relate to permissions that will apply to specific locations in the tree. The latter is likely to be the much larger of the two. The General columns relate to permissions that can be set without recourse to the use of the Advanced button, such as read access to all objects below an Organizational Unit. The Special columns relate to those permissions that you have to manually bring up a PE window for, such as allowing read access to all telephone numbers of user objects below a particular Organizational Unit. The last three columns relate to the LDAP path to the object that is to have properties set, the permissions that are being set, and the group or user to whom the permissions are being assigned.

The LDAP path under Global Tree Permissions is, strictly speaking, unnecessary, since these columns relate to permissions applied to the domain as a whole. If, however, you have a special need to apply permissions to a large number of Organizational Units directly below the root, you could use this column for this purpose.

Now you should go through your Active Directory design and begin to populate both the Allow and Deny tables. For a first pass, you should concentrate on a thorough design, listing all the permissions that you think you will need. Print out a number of copies of the table. Once you have a list in front of you, you can start amalgamating identical permissions into groups. It is likely that you will need to go through many iterations of these designs until you get a pared-down list that you are happy with. As you go through the design, you will start identifying groups of users to which you need to apply permissions. When designing the groups, you have two choices, as previously discussed under Rule 2. You can either create a single group to which permissions are set and which contains users, or you can create two groups, one to hold permissions and one to hold users.

The decision on whether to go for single or dual groups is not necessarily an easy one. My preference is to use single groups as often as possible, unless we need extra flexibility or have a lot of permissions to assign to many groups. In order to help you to make a bit more sense of the decision, a few reasons why you would want to consider one or the other are shown in Table 11-1.

Table 11-1. When to consider user groups and permission groups or combined groups

You should consider one group if	You should consider two groups if
You want to keep the number of groups to a minimum.	You want greater flexibility. Having one group for permissions and one for users means that you are always able to manage the system with a minimum of fuss.
You have only a small or simple tree, where it would be fairly easy to track down problems.	You have a large or complex tree, in which you need to be able to identify any problems quickly.
You need to assign only a few simple permissions.	You need to assign a large number of permissions.

Table 11-1. When to consider user groups and permission groups or combined groups (continued)

You should consider one group if	You should consider two groups if
You have very little change in the membership of groups and very few changes to permissions.	You have regular changes in your group membership or permissions.
You have little cross-membership of groups.	You have major cross-membership of groups, where a user could exist in more than one group with conflicting permissions. (Two groups make it easier to debug problems in a large environment.)
You very rarely need new groups.	You regularly need new groups with subsets of your existing users who have been assigned to some task.
You very rarely have to split user groups so that each user group subset has different permissions than the original group had.	You regularly have to split an existing group into more than one group, because each requires a different set of permissions than the old group used to have.

One last point: if you are creating permission groups and user groups, remember to name them sensibly from the outset, using something like pg_Finance and ug_Finance, for example. It makes it easier when managing and scripting if you can easily identify which type of groups are which.

Bringing Order Out of Chaos

We've had people ask what we would recommend to someone arriving at a new company where the previous directory services administrator had left a tree with no proper permissions design or consistency. In this situation, start by analyzing what the organization requires and work from there. You also should analyze what permissions Active Directory currently has assigned, although concentrating solely on this could be detrimental. After all, if the last administrator was not competent or knowledgeable enough to set up a sensible permissions scheme from the start, he may not have accurately implemented the permissions required by the organization.

When analyzing Active Directory, you need to start by identifying the members of the built-in groups on the server, such as Domain Administrators, Backup Operators, and so on. Now do the same for the other groups that are specific to the organization. Once this is done, using the previously described tables, you need to list the permissions on the root of the first domain in the tree you are responsible for. From there you should look at the permissions for the first container or Organizational Unit in that list. Then navigate the branch represented by that container, looking sequentially at the child containers, continually recursing the tree. Once this first branch of the root is mapped out for the container permissions, you may be getting an idea of what permissions are required. Now go through all the objects in that branch, including printers, users, shares, and so on. This is time-consuming and annoying, but after a while you may start getting an idea of what is going on. All of this is just a sensible approach to going through Active Directory, not a quick-fix solution. You still have to continue throughout the domains you are responsible for to complete the process. It is also legitimate to use a script to iterate through Active Directory and print all the ACLs out to a file. For help on this, consult Chapter 23.

Your first main goal should be to move the individual user permissions to groups with users assigned to them as often as possible, thus making Active Directory simpler to manage and comprehend. These groups should be sensibly named for what they do rather than whom they contain (after all, you are looking to understand Active Directory first). Ideally, you can start consolidating users with identical permissions into the same group.

Your second goal is to remove permissions that users or your newly created groups should not have. This may of course mean that your new groups need to have their members split into two or more separate extra groups. For example, a group that has Read All Properties and Write All Properties to an object may actually need three groups with permissions instead: one to have Read All Properties, one to have both Read and Write All Properties, and one to have Read and selected Write rather than complete Write access. This may be evident from your Active Directory analysis, or it may come out of discussions with users or their managers, with whom you should at least confirm the changes before implementing them just to make sure your analysis is correct.

Ultimately, your third goal, having rationalized the array of Active Directory permissions, is to try to limit the orphaning of objects and branches and to try to move as many advanced permissions to general permissions as you can. You might think that it makes more sense to do this earlier, and in some cases this is true, especially when the whole tree is almost a complete set of orphaned objects. However, if you complete the first two goals, you will have an Active Directory tree that you understand and that has been brought back into line with sensible rules. It is much easier to attempt to fix problems with orphaning and advanced permissions once you have a manageable and rationalized tree. You may end up going back and changing groups or permissions that you already sorted out in attaining the first two goals, but consider how much more difficult it would be to attempt to do these concurrently. After all, you are trying to make the best of an already annoying task. There is no sense in trying to do everything at once. As you go through the tree checking for orphaning, you should document the orphans, as specified in Rule 5, just as if you had set up the orphans from scratch yourself. That way, you can use the tables to analyze and keep track, crossing off those that are of no use as you rationalize the tree.

Designing Auditing Schemes

Designing auditing schemes, in contrast to permissions, is a relatively easy process. Imagine the circumstances in which you may need to check what is happening in Active Directory, and then set things up accordingly.

You must remember that every Active Directory event that is audited causes the system to incur extra processing. Having auditing turned on all the time at the root for every modification by anyone is a great way to get all DCs to really slow down if a lot of Active Directory access occurs on those DCs.

That point bears repeating. Auditing changes to anywhere in the domain Naming Context (NC) will propagate domainwide and cause logging to the security event log on every DC that services the Domain NC. Auditing changes to the Configuration NC or Schema NC will cause all DCs in a forest to begin auditing to their security event logs. You must have tools in place to retrieve logs from multiple DCs if you wish to see every security event that occurs. After all, if you have 100 DCs and are logging Configuration NC changes, then because changes can occur on any DC, you need to amalgamate 100 security event logs to gather a complete picture.[*]

Here are a few examples where designing auditing schemes could come in handy:

- Someone complains that user details are being set to silly values by someone else as a joke.
- You notice that new objects you weren't expecting have been created or deleted in a container.
- The Active Directory hierarchy has changed and you weren't informed.
- You suspect a security problem.

In all these scenarios, you will need to set auditing options on a container or a leaf object. These auditing entries do not have to exist all the time, so you could write them up and then code them into a script that you run at the first sign of trouble. That way, the system is immediately updated and ready to monitor the situation. This can happen only if you are prepared.

You need to analyze the scenarios that you envisage cropping up and then translate them into exact sets of auditing entry specifications. After you have written up each scenario and an emergency occurs, you will be able to follow the exact instructions that you previously laid down and set up a proper rapid response, which is what auditing is all about.

Step one in a real emergency may be to turn all auditing on at the root to make sure that you capture everything to the security log. Step two may be to turn on auditing for the specific items that you need to audit, so that with step three you can finally remove the Audit-All at the root that normally would cause a severe slowdown. That way, you slow Active Directory briefly while setting up the auditing you actually

---

[*] Applications for consolidation of event logs are SeNTry by Mission Critical, Event Admin by Aelita, and AppManager by NetIQ. Also, note that Microsoft's WMI technology has excellent event logging, reporting, and notification capabilities if you wish to script such items yourself.

require, but you don't lose any audit entries during that time. The point is that having a properly prepared set of scripts will save you trouble in the long run as you can quickly use your "Audit all object creations and deletions below a container" or "Audit this object only for any changes" scripts to take the object or container DN as a parameter and so make the scripts generic. Creating scripts is covered later in the book in Chapter 23.

Real-World Examples

It now seems appropriate to put what we have laid out earlier into practice. We will use a series of tasks that could crop up during your everyday work as an administrator. The solutions we propose probably are not the only solutions to the problems. That is often the case with Active Directory; there are many ways of solving the same problem.

Hiding Specific Personal Details for All Users in an Organizational Unit from a Group

In this example, an Organizational Unit called Hardware Support Staff contains the user accounts of an in-house team of people whose job is to repair and fix broken computers within your organization. Whenever a user has a fault, he rings the central faults hotline to request a support engineer. An engineer is assigned the job, which is added to the end of her existing list of faults to deal with. The user is informed about which engineer will be calling and approximately when she will arrive. As with all jobs of this sort, some take longer than others, and users have discovered how to find the mobile or pager number of the engineer they have been assigned and have taken to calling her to get an arrival time update rather than ringing the central desk. Management has decided that they want to restrict who can ring the pager or mobile, but they do not want to stop giving out the engineer's name as they feel it is part of the friendly service. Consequently, they have asked you to find a way of hiding the pager and mobile numbers in Active Directory from all users who should not have access.

The solution that we will use is to remove the default ability of every user to see the property of the Engineer objects by default. We can do this either from the parent OU or manually for each engineer. This ensures that only users or groups that we allow to see the properties will do so. Since this is a simple problem with a simple solution, it is easier to use the GUI than to write a script.

We start by creating a group for users who are allowed to see these properties, calling it Support Phone or something similar. Now we have to make the decision: do we select the parent Organizational Unit itself and assign permissions to hide the property for objects within the container and down the tree, or do we manually apply permissions to every support engineer's account? The latter is likely to take much longer with any reasonable number of support staff, and it comes with the added problem that we will have to do the same tasks every time a new support staff member joins the team. In this instance, we will choose the former; however, it should be noted that this will hide all the mobile and pager numbers of all users under the Hardware Support Staff Organizational Unit, even if some of them are not engineers. This is covered in the next example.

We open the ACS window for the Hardware Support Staff Organizational Unit and click Add. We then locate the Support Phone group and click OK. This opens the PE window for Support Phone relating to the Organizational Unit. Now we click the Properties tab, specify to apply to this object and all subobjects, and then click Allow for both the properties Read Phone-Pager-Primary and Read Phone-Mobile- Primary. These two items may already be allowed by default. If we now click OK, the permissions are applied down the tree, so that everyone in the Support Phone group can now read the mobile and pager properties of all user objects below that Organizational Unit.

We need to restrict the rest of the tree from viewing these two properties. From the ACS window for the Organizational Unit, we add a group in the same manner as before, this time specifying Everyone as the group. We select the Properties tab, find the Read Phone-Pager-Primary and Read Phone-Mobile-Primary properties, and remove the check marks which occur in the two allow fields. We click OK, and all members of the group Everyone have no rights to the two properties below this Organizational Unit. This differs from specifically denying all members access.

If we had denied the Everyone group from reading the two properties as our first step, then when we opened up the PE window for the Support Phone group, it would not have had the existing check marks inside it for the two fields. This is because Active Directory would already have realized that the members of Support Phone were obviously members of Everyone, the group containing every user on the system, and consequently would have removed the two settings.

Hiding Specific Personal Details for Some Users in an Organizational Unit from a Group

Let's extend the previous example. We now have 100 engineers and 30 admin staff members directly under this Hardware Support Staff Organizational Unit. There are no child containers splitting up the users. The support staff would like others to be able to find their pager and mobile details and not have them restricted like the engineers. Having completed the previous task, we have successfully restricted both the admins' and engineers' details.

The less elegant restricting inheritance solution

To allow admins' numbers to be visible, we can orphan the admin staff. This is a slow process, since we have to individually select each admin user and, from the Security tab of the Properties window, clear the inherit permissions from their parents' checkbox. Obviously, we could script this to speed up the process. Having done this for all 30 users, it means that the user objects do not inherit:

- The Everyone group's inability to read the Read Phone-Pager-Primary and Read Phone-Mobile-Primary properties by default
- The Support Phone group's ability to read the two properties

Consequently, the default permissions apply, which means that these two properties are visible by default.

The other important aspect to note about this solution is that any other permissions applied to the parent Organizational Unit will not be applied to these children. This may conflict with your other permissions requirements and is covered in the example after next.

The more elegant rearrange-the-tree solution

We will solve this by creating two Organizational Units under Hardware Support Staff called Admin and Engineers. We then move all of the 30 admin users into the Admin Organizational Unit and the 100 engineers into the Engineers Organizational Unit.

We also should remove all previously applied permissions and restrictions to bring back a default set of permissions for the Hardware Support Staff Organizational Unit.

We open a PE window on the Engineers Organizational Unit for the group Everyone, then clear the check marks from the Read Phone-Pager-Primary and Read Phone-Mobile-Primary property checkboxes and click OK. We then assign the Support Phone group permissions to the Engineers Organizational Unit in a similar manner to the previous example. That effectively solves the problem in a much neater and less time-consuming way.

A More Complex Hiding Problem

Now we will modify the previous problem again. The engineers' pager and mobile numbers are still to be restricted from everyone, but this time the admin staff wishes to have their pager numbers restricted while having their mobile numbers visible. Let's look at adapting both of the previous solutions to this problem.

The less elegant restricting inheritance solution

Here we have orphaned the admin staff from the tree, so they cannot inherit the pager restriction. The only solution is to manually apply the Everyone group's pager restriction to each of the 30 admin accounts.

The more elegant rearrange-the-tree solution

With users in both the child Organizational Units, this is a simple problem to solve. We just specify that the group Everyone has no permissions to access the pager property of the parent Organizational Unit for this object and all subobjects. We then apply the same sort of restriction for the Read Phone-Mobile-Primary for Everyone to the Engineers Organizational Unit only.

This elegantly solves the problem. There was originally no reason to move the admin users to their own Organizational Unit, other than conventions of balance and form with all users under the parent residing under their own child Organizational Unit according to their type. We also could have left the engineers in the parent Organizational Unit and manually applied 100 sets of identical restrictions, but why waste that sort of time, when Active Directory was designed to have containers to solve this sort of problem.

Allowing Only a Specific Group of Users to Access a New Published Resource

The Finance department has created a new share called *Budget_Details* and had it published in the tree. The permissions to the share itself allow only the correctly authorized staff to read and view the contents, but everyone by default can see the share in the tree. The Finance department does not want the share visible to anyone who is not a member of the Finance group.

This is a simple example due to the fact that we have recognized, existing groups, Everyone and Finance, to which permissions are to be applied. This in fact is very similar to the telephone restrictions of the previous examples. All we do is open up the PE window for the share object relevant to the Everyone group and remove the allow permissions. We then open up the PE window for the share object relevant to the Finance group and assign Read and List permissions. A simple solution to a simple problem.

Restricting Users in an Organizational Unit from Viewing Properties of Users Outside That Organizational Unit

Let's say the administrator wishes to restrict the ability of users to search and view personal details of users outside their Organizational Unit. It seems like a simple request: with such a powerful Active Directory, we should be able to restrict browse rights on user object permissions up the tree for users in each Organizational Unit. This example serves to show how a request can appear to be simple on the surface, while in fact being one of the worst management nightmares. Hopefully this example will show you that you need to be very careful about what can and cannot be done with Active Directory at present.

Ultimately this may seem like a strange request, even foolish, given that Active Directory is supposed to be set up as a global information store for searching. This problem is made more difficult because it is actually many problems, all of the same type. If you have 100 Organizational Units off the root in your Active Directory, you are looking at 100 identical problems, not one. In addition, the problem is global-deny/selective-allow, not global-allow/selective-deny. As deny overrides allow, you cannot just deny globally and open up an allow when you need it as you could if the situation were reversed; you have to create denials everywhere except certain locations, which is not a simple task.

Again, at first glance, you appear to be helped toward a solution because each set of users is contained in individual Organizational Units. In fact, that will not directly help in any way. Users in ou=Finance will have to be grouped together to apply permissions for them to ou=Accounts, ou=Marketing, and so on. It appears that the users in Finance will benefit from being in Finance because it seems you should be able to say "All these users in ou=Finance have no rights to ou=Marketing," and so on. However, permissions can only be set for users and groups that apply to containers. First you add all the users in each Organizational Unit to a group that represents their location in their particular Organizational Unit. For example, the Finance Organizational Unit would contain users who would be members of the USER_Finance group and so on. For 100 Organizational Units, that is 100 groups. We will call these groups user groups for now.

Now we create 100 groups representing the deny permissions that need to be applied. For example, we would create a DRUP_Finance (Deny Read User Permissions) or similar; the name will make sense later. Each of the 100 groups would be created and assigned a deny permission entry for user object attributes of the relevant Organizational Unit and below. We will call these groups "permission groups" for now.

Now we add the user groups, rather than the individual members, as members of the permission groups. This means that we will be adding 99 user group entries to each permission group entry. That is 9,900 operations, a horrific amount. We can use a script because, while setting permissions is not possible within ADSI, here all we are doing is adding groups as members of other groups, something that can be done with ADSI.

This solution implies 100 user groups to manage and 100 permission groups with one permission each and 99 members to manage. This is the best and easiest solution to the problem. Chapter 21 includes the code for this task.

What about orphaning as a solution instead? Surely we could specify that each user group have no permissions to read personal details of anyone in the root domain and below. Then we could just orphan each Organizational Unit. Unfortunately, that would work for one Organizational Unit but not for many. With each Organizational Unit orphaned, none of the Organizational Units actually inherit any of the deny restrictions. Consequently, all we end up with is a management nightmare without a solution.

You may be thinking at this point that we could apply all 100 deny restrictions at the root and then orphan each Organizational Unit, specifying that the system convert inherited entries to normal entries. Then we could remove each individual restriction relating to the members of that particular Organizational Unit. This would help in implementing a lot of individual entries.

Let's assess the results of this solution. First, we apply 100 separate ACS deny entries to the root. We then perform 100 orphan operations. With each orphan operation, we convert inherited to normal and remove the offending ACS entry, implying each orphaned entry has 99 separate permission-denial normal entries. This means at the end that we are looking at managing 9,900 separate permission entries on 100 Organizational Units.

These are the most important things to remember:

- Do not assume that simply stated problems are easy to solve in Active Directory. Always consider how many users, groups, and permissions you are likely to need to implement.

- If you are looking at a global-deny/selective-allow throughout the tree, you are looking at a complex problem.

- When it comes to a job that looks as if you have thousands of permission operations to accomplish, create permission groups and user groups and use a script to automate the creation. We would hate to have to implement such a system because of the ongoing management nightmare that would accompany such a decision after the initial setup. However, there may be a time when you or your boss or organization decides for security reasons that you have to restrict objects in this way.

Summary

Security is always important, and when access to your organization's network is concerned, it's paramount. We hope this chapter has given you an understanding of how permission to access can be allowed or denied to entire domains or individual properties of a single object. Auditing is also part of security, and having mechanisms already designed—so that they can be constantly working or dropped in when required—is the best way to keep track of such a system.

Assigning permission and auditing entries to an object appears to be a simple subject on the surface. However, once you start delving into the art of setting permissions and auditing entries, it quickly becomes obvious how much there is to consider. Global design is the necessary first step.

While expanding your tree later by adding extra containers is rarely a problem, in a large tree it makes sense to have some overall guidelines or rules that allow you to impose a sense of structure on the whole process of design and redesign. Ideally, the golden rules and tables that we created should allow you to plan and implement sensible permissions schemes, which was the goal of the chapter.

CHAPTER 12

Designing and Implementing Schema Extensions

For Active Directory to hold any object, such as a user, it needs to know what the attributes and characteristics of that object are. In other words, it needs a blueprint for that object. The Active Directory schema is the blueprint for all classes, attributes, and syntaxes that potentially can be stored in Active Directory.

The default schema definition is defined in the *%systemroot%\ntds\schema.ini* file that also contains the initial structure for the *ntds.dit* (Active Directory database). This file contains plain ASCII file and can be viewed using Notepad or any text editor.

The following considerations should be kept in mind when you contemplate extending your schema:

- Microsoft designed Active Directory to hold the most common objects and attributes you would require. Because they could never anticipate every class of object or every specific attribute (languages spoken, professional qualifications) that a company would need, Active Directory was designed to be extensible. After all, if these objects and properties are going to be in everyday use, the design shouldn't be taken lightly. Administrators need to be aware of the importance of the schema and how to extend it. Extending the schema is a useful and simple solution to a variety of problems. Not being aware of the potential means that you will have a hard time identifying it as a solution to problems you might encounter.

- Designing schema extensions is very important, in part because any new class or attribute that you create in the schema is a permanent addition. While unused objects can be disabled if you no longer require them, they cannot be removed. In Windows 2003 Active Directory, you can redefine schema extensions, but you cannot totally remove them.

- While it is easy to extend Active Directory, it's surprising how many companies are reluctant to implement schema extensions due to concerns over the impact to Active Directory. One of the biggest impediments in Windows 2000 was that anytime the partial attribute set was extended (i.e., an attribute added to the Global Catalog) a full resync had to be done for all Global Catalog servers. Fortunately, Microsoft resolved this in Windows 2003, and a full resync is no longer performed.

This chapter takes you through the process of extending the schema, from the initial design of the changes through the implementation, and discusses how to avoid the pitfalls that can crop up. We then talk about analyzing the choices available and seeing if you can obtain the required design result some other way, because schema changes are not to be undertaken lightly. We obviously cover how to implement schema changes from first principles, but before that we identify the steps in designing or modifying a class or attribute. Finally, we cover some pitfalls to be aware of when administering the schema.

We don't spend much time introducing a large number of specific examples. This is mainly because there's no way we can conceive of every sort of class that you will require. Consequently, for examples we use only one new generic class as well as a few attribute extensions to the default user object. When giving examples of modifying a class, we extend the user object class.

Let's look at how you would design the changes you may wish to make in an enterprise environment.

Nominating Responsible People in Your Organization

If you don't already have a central person or group of people responsible for the OID namespace for your organization, you need to form such a group. This OID Managers group is responsible for obtaining an OID namespace, designing a structure for the namespace that makes sense to your organization, managing that namespace by maintaining a diagram of the structure and a list of the allocated OIDs, and issuing appropriate OIDs for new classes from that structure as required. Whenever a new class of attribute or object is to be created in your organization's forest, the OID Managers provide a unique OID for that new class, which is then logged by the OID Managers with a set of details about the reason for the request and the type of class that it is to be used for. All these details need to be defined by the OID Managers group.

The Schema Managers, by comparison, are responsible for designing and creating proper classes in the schema for a forest. They are responsible for actually making changes to the schema via requests from within the organization, for ensuring that redundant objects doing the same thing are not created, that inheritance is used to best effect, that the appropriate objects are indexed, and that the GC contains the right attributes.

The Schema Managers need to decide on the membership of the Schema Admins universal group that resides in the Forest Root Domain of a particular forest. One possibility is that the Schema Managers wish to keep a set of user accounts as members of Schema Admins by default all the time. Instead, they may decide to remove every member of the Schema Admins group so that no unintentional changes can be made to the schema. In this case, the Schema Managers need to be given permissions to add and remove members of the Schema Admins group to enable any of the Schema Managers to add themselves to the Schema Admins group whenever changes are to be made to the schema.

> If you are designing code that will modify some other organization's schema, the documentation accompanying that code should make it explicitly clear exactly what classes are being created and why. The documentation also should explain that the code needs to be run with the privilege of a member of the Schema Admins group, since some organizations may have an Active Directory in which the Schema Admins group is empty most of the time, as mentioned earlier.

Note that the membership of OID Managers does not necessarily coincide with that of Schema Managers, although it is a possibility.

Thinking of Changing the Schema

Before you start thinking of changing the schema, you need to consider not just the namespace, but also the data your Active Directory will hold. After all, if you know your data, you can decide what changes you want to make and whom those changes might impact.

Designing the Data

No matter how you migrated to Active Directory, at some point you'll need to determine exactly what data you will add or migrate for the objects you create. Will you use the physicalDeliveryOfficeName attribute of the user object? What about the telephonePager attribute? Do you want to merge the internal staff office location list and telephone database during the migration? What if you really need also to know what languages each of your staff speaks or qualifications they hold? What about their shoe size, their shirt size, number of children, and whether they like animals? The point is that some of these already exist in the Active Directory schema and some don't. At some point you need to design the actual data that you want to include.

Let's consider MyUnixCorp, a large fictional organization that for many years has run perfectly well on a large mainframe system. The system is unusual in that the login process has been completely replaced in-house with a two-tier password system. A file called *additional-passwd* maintains a list of usernames and their second Unix password in an encrypted format. Your design for the migration for MyUnix-Corp's system has to take account of the extra login check. In this scenario, either MyUnixCorp accepts that the new Active Directory Kerberos security mechanism is secure enough for its site, or it has to add entries to the schema for the second password attribute and write a new Active Directory logon interface that incorporates both checks.

This example serves to outline that the data that is to be stored in Active Directory has a bearing on the schema structure and consequently has to be incorporated into the design phase.

To Change or Not to Change

When you identify a deficiency in the schema for your own Active Directory, you have to look hard into whether modifying the schema is the correct way forward. Finding that the schema lacks a complete series of objects along with multiple attributes is a far cry from identifying that the Person-who-needs-to-refill-the-printer-with-toner attribute of the printer object is missing from the schema. There's no rule, either, that says that once you wish to create three extra attributes on an existing object, you should modify the schema. It all comes down to choice.

 There is one useful guideline: you should identify all the data you wish to hold in Active Directory prior to considering your design. If you consider how to implement each change in Active Directory one at a time, you may simply lose sight of the overall picture.

To help you make that choice, you should ask yourself whether there are any other objects or attributes that you could use to solve your problem.

Let's say you were looking for an attribute of a user object that would hold a staff identification number for your users. You need to ask whether there is an existing attribute of the user object that could hold the staff ID number and that you are not going to use. This saves you from modifying the schema if you don't have to. Take Leicester University as an example. We had a large user base that we were going to register, and we needed to hold a special ID number for our students. In Great Britain, every university student has a so-called University and Colleges Administration System number, more commonly known as the UCAS number, a unique alphanumeric string that UCAS assigns independent of a student's particular university affiliation. Students receive their UCAS numbers when they first begin looking into universities. The numbers identify students to their prospective universities, stay with students throughout their undergraduate careers, and are good identifiers for checking the validity of students' details. By default, there is no schema attribute called UCAS-Number, so we had two choices. We could find an appropriately named attribute that we were not going to use and make use of that, or we could modify the schema.

Since we were initially only looking to store this piece of information in addition to the default user information, we were not talking about a huge change in any case. We simply looked to see whether we could use any other schema attributes to contain the data. We soon found the employeeID user attribute that we were not ever intending to use, and which seemed to fit the bill, so we decided to use that. While it isn't as appropriately named as an attribute called UCAS-Number would be, it did mean that we didn't have to modify the base schema in this instance.

The important point here is that we chose not to modify the schema, having found a spare attribute that we were satisfied with. We could just as easily have found no appropriate attributes and decided to go through making the schema changes using our own customized attributes.

If you've installed Exchange 2000 into the forest, there is also a set of attributes available to use for whatever you need. These are known as the extension or custom attributes and have names like extensionAttribute1, extensionAttribute2, and so on. These are never used by the operating system and have been left in for you to use as you wish. There are 20 created by default, thus giving you spare attribute capacity already in Active Directory. So if we wanted to store the number of languages spoken by a user, we could just store that value inside extensionAttribute1 if we chose. You can see how these attributes have been designed by using the Schema Manager.

Extension attributes and making use of unused attributes works well for a small number of cases. However, if there were 20, 30, or more complex attributes each with a specific syntax, or if we needed to store 20 objects with 30 attributes each, we would have more difficulty. When you have data like that, you need to consider the bigger picture.

The Global Picture

So you have a list of all your data and suspect either that the schema will not hold your data or that it will not do so to your satisfaction. You now need to consider the future of your organization's schema and design it accordingly. The following questions should help you decide how to design for each new classSchema or attributeSchema object.

1. Is this classSchema or attributeSchema object already held in the schema in some form? In other words, does the attribute already exist by default or has someone already created it? If it doesn't exist, you can create it. If it does already exist in some form, can you make use of that existing attribute? If you can, you need to consider doing so. If you can't, you need to consider modifying the existing attribute to cope with your needs or creating a second attribute that essentially holds similar or identical data, which is wasteful. If the existing attribute is

of no use, can you create a new one and migrate the values for the existing attribute to the new one and disable the old one? These are the sorts of questions you need to be thinking of.

2. Is this a classSchema or attributeSchema object that is to be used only for a very specific purpose, or could this object potentially be made of use (i.e., created, changed, and modified) by others in the organization? If the object is for only a specific purpose, the person suggesting the change should know what is required. If the object may impact others, care should be taken to ensure it is designed to cope with the requirements of all potential users, for example, that it can later be extended if necessary, without affecting the existing object instances at the moment the schema object is updated. For an attribute, for example, you should ask whether the attribute's syntax and maximum/minimum values (for strings or integers) are valid or whether they should be made more applicable to the needs of the many. Specifically, if you created a CASE_INSENSITIVE_STRING of between 5 and 20 characters now and later you require that attribute to be a CASE_SENSITIVE_STRING of between 5 and 20 characters, you may or may not have a problem depending on whether you care that the values for the case-insensitive strings are now case-sensitive. You obviously could write a script that goes through Active Directory and modifies each string appropriately, but what if you had changed the schema attribute to a CASE_SENSITIVE_STRING of between 8 and 20 characters? Then you have another problem if there are any strings of between 5 and 7 letters. These attributes would be invalid, since their contents are wrong. We think you can see the sort of problems that can occur.

3. Are you modifying an existing object with an attribute? If so, would this attribute be better if it were not applied directly to the object, but instead added to a set of attributes within an auxiliary class classSchema object?

4. Are you adding a mandatory attribute to an existing object that will suddenly make all existing instances invalid? Say you added a new mandatory attribute called languages-spoken to the User class. Since none of the existing users have this attribute set initially, you instantly make all the users invalid. You have to make sure, though, in this specific case, that you will never create users via Active Directory Users and Computers MMC, because this tool will not be aware of your new mandatory requirement and so cannot create valid users any more. You must be aware of the impact that your changes may have on existing tools and ones that you design yourself.

Basically, these questions boil down to four much simpler ones:

- Is the change that needs to be made valid and sensible for all potential uses and users of this object?

- Will my change impact any other changes that may need to be made to this and other objects in the future?

- Will my change impact anyone else now or in the future?
- Will my change impact any applications that people inside or outside the company are developing?

 In a similar fashion to getting a valid OID namespace, make sure that the classSchema and attributeSchema objects are created with sensible names. These names should have a unique company prefix for easy identification and be capitalized words separated by hyphens. For specific examples, see Chapter 24.

The Schema Managers group needs to sit down with all groups of people who potentially would like to make changes to the schema, brief them on how the schema operates, and attempt to identify the sorts of changes that need to be made by these groups. If a series of meetings is not your style, consider creating a briefing paper, followed by a form to request schema updates, issued to all relevant department heads. If you allow enough time, you will be able to collate responses received and make a good stab at an initial design. You can find attributes that may conflict, ways of making auxiliary classes rather than modifications to individual attributes, and so on. This gives the Schema Managers a good chance to come up with a valid initial design for the schema changes prior to or during a rollout.

An important rule of thumb is never to modify default system attributes. It makes sure that we never conflict with anything considered as default by the operating system, which might eventually cause problems during upgrades or with other applications such as Exchange. Adding extra attributes to objects is fine, but avoid modifying existing ones.

 If we need a longer string for an existing attribute, or if it needs to be of a slightly different type, we just create a new one with a similar name and the class we want.

Creating Schema Extensions

There are three ways to modify the schema: through the Schema Manager MMC, using LDIF files, or programmatically using ADSI. We will not cover the use of the Schema Manager MMC very heavily here since it is fairly straightforward to use, although we will cover its use in managing the Schema FSMO role. Typically you should not use the Schema Manager MMC to extend the schema and instead use LDIF files or ADSI. Most vendors provide LDIF files, which contain the schema extensions that you can run at your leisure. We cover extending the schema with ADSI in Chapter 24.

Running the Schema Manager MMC for the First Time

The Schema Manager MMC is not available from the Administrative Tools menu like the other Active Directory snap-ins. To use it, you need to first register the Dynamic Link Library (DLL) file for the MMC snap-in by typing the following command at the command prompt:

```
regsvr32.exe schmmgmt.dll
```

You can then start the Schema Manager console by creating a custom MMC and adding the Active Directory Schema snap-in to it. To create a console, go to the Run menu from the Start button, type mmc.exe, and click OK. Then in the empty MMC, choose the Console menu and select Add/Remove Snap-in. From here, you can click the Add button and select Active Directory Schema as the item. If you then click the Add button, followed by Close, and then the OK button, that will give you an MMC hosting the Schema Manager snap-in for you to use and later save as required.

The Schema Cache

Each domain controller maintains a copy of the entire schema in memory. This is known as the schema cache. It is used to provide a very rapid response when requesting a schema object OID from a name.

The schema cache is actually a set of hash tables of all the classSchema and attribute-Schema objects known to the system, along with specific indices (attributeID and lDAPDisplayName for attributeSchema objects and governsID, lDAPDisplayName, and mapiID for classSchema objects) for fast searching.

The hash table sizes are dynamic in terms of the amount of memory that is allocated for the stored objects. Initially, the tables are set to a size capable of holding 2,048 attributes and 1,024 classes. The system keeps count of the number of attributes and classes in the schema and is responsible for making sure that the table sizes are kept greater than twice the number of attributes (for the attribute hash tables) or twice the number of classes (for the class hash tables). If at any time the number of attributes or classes increases enough that the table sizes are not at least twice as big, as required, the cache table sizes are incremented in blocks of 2,048 or 1,024, as appropriate.

The objects are loaded into the schema cache when the DC is booted and then five minutes after an update. However, if you need the schema cache to be updated immediately for some reason, say after the creation of a new object or attribute class, you can force an immediate reload of the cache.

As we said, the system holds a copy in memory solely to aid in searches that require quick and regular access to the schema. If the system were to keep both the cache and the actual Active Directory schema in parity, it could be costly in terms of performance; making changes to the schema is an intensive process due to the significant checking and setting of object defaults by the system upon creation of new

Allowing the Schema to be modified on Windows 2000

Under Windows 2000, there was a safeguard you had to bypass for the Schema FSMO to allow you to modify the schema. With Windows 2003 Active Directory, this is no longer required. First, the user who is to make the changes has to be a member of the Schema Admins group, which exists in the forest root domain. Second, you need to make a change to the registry on the DC that you wish to make the changes on.

The fastest and probably best solution is to use the checkbox from the Schema Master MMC, shown later in the chapter.

Alternatively, on the DC itself, open up the registry using *regedit32.exe* or *regedit.exe* and locate the following key:

> HKEY_LOCAL_MACHINE\SYSTEM\CurrentControlSet\Services\NTDS\ Parameters

Now, create a new REG_DWORD value called "Schema Update Allowed" (no quotes) and set the value to 1. That's all you need to do. You now can edit the Schema on that DC.

Another alternative method for making the change is to copy the following three lines to a text file with a REG extension and open it (i.e., execute it) on the DC where you wish to enable schema updates. This will automatically modify the registry for you without the need to open the registry by hand:

```
REGEDIT4
[HKEY_LOCAL_MACHINE\SYSTEM\CurrentControlSet\Services\NTDS\Parameters]
"Schema Update Allowed"=dword:00000001
```

Once you've modified the registry on a particular DC and placed the user account that is to make the changes into the Schema Admins group, any changes you make to the schema on that DC will be accepted. If you wish changes to be accepted on any DC, you need to modify the registry correspondingly on every DC.

objects. Consequently, there is a time delay between changes made to the underlying schema and the cached copy. Typically the schema tends to be updated in bunches. This is likely to be due to applications creating multiple classes for their own purposes during an installation or even normal operation. If classes are still being created after five minutes, the system updates the cache in five-minute increments after the first five-minute update has completed. This continues for as long as schema class updates continue.

During the intervening five-minute period, when the underlying schema has been modified but the cache has yet to be updated, instances of objects or attributes of the new classes cannot be created. If you try to create an object, the system will return an error. This is due to the fact that object creations refer to the cache and not the underlying schema. To get around this problem, you can force an immediate reload of the cache by adding a special operational attribute to the Root DSE. We'll cover this later when we consider how to use the Schema Manager interface to create and delete classes. In a similar vein, if you mark an object as defunct, this will not take effect until the cache is reloaded.

While you cannot create new instances, since this would reference the schema cache, you can add new attributes or classes that you have created to other classes that you are creating. For example, if you create a new attribute, you can immediately add it to a new class. Why? Because the attribute or class is added using an OID, and the system thus doesn't need to do any lookups in the schema cache. While all system checks by Active Directory confirming that the data is valid (covered in detail a couple of sections later) will still be performed, the checks are performed on the schema in Active Directory, not in the cache. If this weren't the case, you would have to wait for at least five minutes before any new attributes that you created could be added to new classes, and that would be unacceptable.

The Schema FSMO

The Schema FSMO is the server where changes to the schema take place so that multiple users or applications cannot modify the schema on two or more different domain controllers at the same time. When Active Directory is installed in an enterprise, the first server in the first domain in the forest (the forest root domain) becomes the nominated Schema FSMO. Later, if changes need to be made to the schema, they can be made at the current master.

Let's take two servers, Server A and Server B. Server A is the current Schema FSMO. When the role is to be transferred, Server A modifies the fSMORoleOwner attribute to represent Server B and then passes that attribute to Server B along with any other schema changes that Server B may not yet have seen. Server B then applies any schema changes it hasn't seen, including the fSMORoleOwner attribute, and thus becomes the new Schema FSMO. This new role is replicated out when the Schema NC data is next replicated.

You can transfer the role from an existing Schema Master in three ways: via the Schema Manager MMC, via the NTDSUTIL tool, or via code that makes use of ADSI.

Using the Schema Manager MMC to make the changes is easy. First you need to connect to the server that is to be the new master (*dc2.mycorp.com*), then you need to force the role to change to the server to which you are now connected. To start the process, simply run the MMC and right-click Active Directory Schema in the left-hand scope pane. From the context menu that drops down, select Change Domain Controller. A dialog box similar to Figure 12-1 then appears.

You can now select a new server to connect to. You should transfer any FSMO roles (not just the Schema Master) to a new server before shutting a server down for an extended period, such as for maintenance. You may wish just to transfer the role to

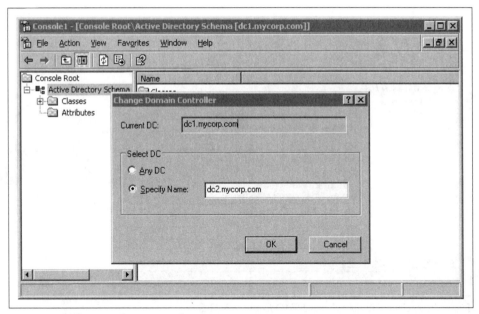

Figure 12-1. Changing the connected server

any other server, rather than to a specific one, which is why there is an option to connect to any other server. Once that has been done, right-click on Active Directory Domains Schema in the scope pane and select Operations Master from the context menu. A dialog box will appear showing the current DC holding the Schema FSMO role, as well as an option to change the role to the currently connected server. Figure 12-2 shows this dialog box.

Click the Change button and change the schema role. There is also an option to modify the registry on the DC you are currently connected to so that schema changes will be allowed on this new Schema FSMO.

If a server corruption or crash takes the Schema FSMO out of the enterprise, no server will automatically assume the role. In this situation, you can use similar methods to force the Schema FSMO role on a server. It is possible to force a server to assume the role, but this can cause data corruption if the old server comes back online. This is covered later under the section entitled "Wreaking Havoc with Your Schema."

If you are writing ADSI scripts to manipulate the schema, just connect to the Schema FSMO directly and make the changes there, rather than worrying about checking to see if the server you wish to make the changes on is the Schema FSMO. We'll show you how to do that later in the book.

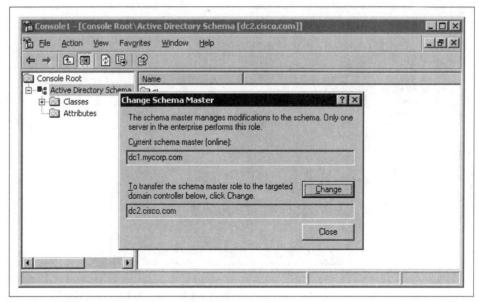

Figure 12-2. Changing the Schema FSMO from the MMC

Using LDIF to Extend the Schema

One of the most commonly used ways to extend the schema is with LDIF. The LDAP Data Interchange Format was defined in RFC 2849 (*http://www.ietf.org/rfc/rfc2849.txt*) and provides a way to represent directory data via a human-readable text file. You can export data from Active Directory in LDIF format, and you can also add, modify and delete data with LDIF. The LDIFDE program comes installed as part of any Windows 2000 or Windows 2003 Server and can be used to import and export LDIF data. To import the contents of an LDIF file, run the following command:

```
c:> ldifde -v -i -f import.ldf
```

Replace import.ldf with the name of the LDIF file you want to import.

LDIF files contain one or more entries, with each entry containing one or more attributes that should be added, replaced or removed. The format is straightforward but very strict. The following is an LDIF that would add a group object to the Users container:

```
dn: cn=mygroup,cn=users,dc=mycorp,dc=com
changetype: add
objectclass: group
description: My Group
member: cn=administrator,cn=users,dc=mycorp,dc=com
member: cn=guest,cn=users,dc=mycorp,dc=com
```

The first line must be the DN of the object. The second line is changetype:, which is one of add, modify, or delete. When using add as in this case, we must specify all the mandatory attributes for the object. For group objects, we need to specify only objectClass. The cn attribute is not required because it is already specified as part of the DN.

It is easy to create portable schema extensions using LDIF files. Simply create an LDIF file with all the necessary classSchema or attributeSchema object additions or modifications, and administrators using any LDIF-based client can easily import it into Active Directory. The following LDIF shows how to create an attribute and auxiliary class that contains the new attribute.

```
dn: cn=myCorp-ITUserBuilding,cn=schema,cn=configuration,dc=mycorp,dc=com
changetype: add
attributeID: 1.2.3.4.111.1
attributeSyntax: 2.5.5.1
oMSyntax: 127
isSingleValued: TRUE
lDAPDisplayName: myCorp-ITUserBuilding
objectClass: attributeSchema
dn:
changetype: modify
add: schemaUpdateNow
schemaUpdateNow: 1
-
dn: cn=myCorp-ITUser,cn=schema,cn=configuration,dc=mycorp,dc=com
changetype: add
objectclass: classSchema
description: Class for MyCorp Employees
lDAPDisplayName: myCorp-ITUser
governsID: 1.2.3.4.111.2
objectClassCategory: 3
subClassOf: top
mayContain: myCorp-ITUserBuilding
dn:
changetype: modify
add: schemaUpdateNow
schemaUpdateNow: 1
-
```

As we mentioned before, all mandatory attributes for attributeSchema and classSchema objects must be specified. The order of the additions is also important. Since we wanted to add the new attribute to the class, we needed to create it first. We also needed to reload the schema cache before attempting to reference the new attribute or a failure would have occurred. When each entry is added or modified, it is only committed to memory, not disk. When we reference the attribute as part of the mayContain for the new class, the attribute must also have been written to the disk. To accomplish that, we perform a modify operation against the Root DSE (i.e., blank DN) and write to the schemaUpdateNow attribute.

The benefits of using LDIF to implement schema extensions are two-fold. First, since LDIF is human-readable with a well-defined syntax, it is easy for those that need to implement the extensions to see what is going to be done. If you use a program that the administrator cannot see the source for, they will not have as much visibility into what changes are made. Along the same lines, LDIF files provide a crude documentation mechanism for schema extensions. Since LDIF files are just text-based files, schema administrators can archive the files on a server and have instant access to exactly what changes were made for certain applications.

Checks the System Makes When You Modify the Schema

When you create a new class or attribute, the system performs some basic checks within Active Directory to see if the data is valid, in addition to any checks you provide. The checks for attributes are shown in Table 12-1, and those for new classes are in Table 12-2.

Table 12-1. System checks made when creating new attributes

Attribute	System check performed
lDAPDisplayName	Must be unique in Active Directory.
attributeId	Must be unique in Active Directory.
mapiId	If present, must be unique in Active Directory.
schemaIDGUID	Must be unique in Active Directory.
attributeSyntax	Must correlate with oMSyntax.
oMSyntax	Must correlate with attributeSyntax.
rangeLower	If rangeUpper is present as well, the following should be true: rangeUpper > rangeLower.
rangeUpper	If Range-Lower is present as well, thefollowing should be true: rangeUpper > rangeLower.

Table 12-2. System checks made when creating new classes

Attribute	System check performed
lDAPDisplayName	Must be unique in Active Directory.
governsId	Must be unique in Active Directory.
schemaIDGUID	Must be unique in Active Directory.
subClassOf	Checks to make sure that the X.500 specifications are not contravened, (i.e., that an auxiliary class cannot inherit from a structural class, and an abstract class can only inherit from another abstract class). All classes defined in this attribute must already exist.
rDNAttID	Must have a Unicode string as its syntax.
mayContain	All classes defined in this attribute must already exist.
systemMayContain	All classes defined in this attribute must already exist.
mustContain	All classes defined in this attribute must already exist.
systemMustContain	All classes defined in this attribute must already exist.
auxiliaryClass	All classes defined in this attribute must already exist and must have an objectClassCategory indicating either 88-Class or Auxiliary.

Table 12-2. System checks made when creating new classes (continued)

Attribute	System check performed
systemAuxiliaryClass	All classes defined in this attribute must already exist and must have an objectClassCategory indicating either 88-Class or Auxiliary.
possSuperiors	All classes defined in this attribute must already exist and must have an objectClassCategory indicating either 88-Class or Auxiliary.
systemPossSuperiors	All classes defined in this attribute must already exist and must have an objectClassCategory indicating either 88-Class or Auxiliary.

Making Classes and Attributes Defunct

It is not possible to delete objects from the schema, because to delete a class or attribute, the system would have to perform a forestwide cleanup operation to make sure that no instances of the object existed. Due to the distributed nature of Active Directory, this is virtually impossible. If your forest is running at Windows 2003 functional level, you can redefine classes and attributes. This is a new feature in Windows 2003, which allows you to correct potential mistakes you may have made or to repurpose classes or attributes you are no longer using.

If you create a class or attribute of some sort and decide that you don't want it any more, you can simply make it defunct. This is achieved by setting the isDefunct attribute on the schema object to True. For this to succeed for an attribute, the system makes sure that the attribute is not a mandatory or optional attribute of any nondefunct class. For this to succeed for a class, the system makes sure that the class is not a parent of any other nondefunct class, is not an auxiliary class to any other nondefunct class, and is not a possible superior of any other non-defunct class. While an object is defunct, no changes can be made to it. If you then decide that you want to use the schema object again, set the value of isDefunct to False. The checks that occur when doing this are the same as for creating a new schema object of the appropriate type in the first place.

When a schema object is defunct, attempts to create instances of it fail as if it doesn't exist. The same applies to modifying existing instances, whether an attribute on an object or an object itself, as they will appear not to exist. You can, however, delete instances of defunct classes. Searches for defunct classes will happily succeed, as will searches on nondefunct classes that contain defunct attributes. All attributes, defunct or not, can be read. This is all required to enable the administrator or application author to clean up and remove the now defunct object instances and all values from now defunct attributes.

 Even though a schema object is defunct, it still exists in terms of its distinguishedName, OID, and lDAPDisplayName. You cannot create a second schema object that has these values, but you can change them when running Windows 2003 forest functional level.

Wreaking Havoc with Your Schema

There are a number of ways to cause problems in your Active Directory schema. We include a few examples here so that you can be fully aware of the problems.

Let's start by considering the main base classes of attributeSchema, classSchema, and top. Imagine we decide to add a new mandatory attribute to top. As all classes derive from top, the mandatory attribute requirement is suddenly added to every class and attribute throughout the schema in one go. Since none of the existing classes and attributes have this value, they all suddenly become marked as invalid. They still exist and can be used, but they cannot be modified at all. New timestamps cannot be added, USNs cannot be changed, replication stops, and effectively your Active Directory grinds to a halt. The reason that the objects cannot be modified is that Active Directory does a special check when existing instances of objects are modified to make sure that all mandatory attributes have been set. If they have not all been set, which they won't have been in this case, Active Directory will not allow any attribute changes from now on. The only solution is to remove the new mandatory attribute or set a value for the attribute on every single object in every NC in the entire forest.

There are also concurrency problems. Having a Schema FSMO is perfectly fine, but that doesn't necessarily stop members of Schema Admins from attempting to run two schema-modifying applications at the same time. Every time an application or piece of code attempts to write to the schema, it automatically writes a special system attribute at the same time. Two system-attribute writes anywhere in Active Directory cannot occur simultaneously, so one will fail if this is the case. In the scenario of simultaneous applications executing, the changes to the schema may all be handled sequentially and the requests from both applications may be interleaved, but the two applications at some point may attempt to write together. At that point, one of them will fail. If the failed application is rerun, it must be coded to detect the existence of each object (i.e., the previous creation succeeded) prior to creating the object, or else the object-creation process will continually fail.

You can also make instances of objects invalid quite easily. For example, let's say that we define that new class we mentioned earlier called Finance-User, and create an instance of it called cn=SimonWilliams. If we then remove Languages-Spoken from Finance-User's mandatory attributes, the SimonWilliams user becomes invalid because the SimonWilliams instance has an attribute that is not now allowed in the schema definition for Finance-User. Again, it is up to the person or code that makes the Languages-Spoken attribute defunct to go through Active Directory and find all instances of Finance-User and modify them to remove the value in this now-defunct attribute. If this isn't done, any instances of Finance-User with the Languages-Spoken attribute defined (all, in this case, as it was mandatory) remain invalid.

You cannot cause invalid instances by modifying existing attributeSchema objects, as all the key attributes are defined in system attributes. However, you can cause havoc with existing classSchema objects. Ways of doing this are:

- Removing classes as possible superiors; this can leave instances under invalid parent containers.
- Adding classes to the list of auxiliary classes; this can change what attributes are now considered mandatory.
- Removing classes from the list of auxiliary classes; this can change what attributes are now considered mandatory and optional and can thus leave instances with now nonexistent attributes.
- Directly removing mandatory or optional attributes; this can leave instances with now nonexistent attributes.

If the DC holding the Schema FSMO role unexpectedly disappears, you can force another server to assume the role. But if the original DC ever comes back, you have two Schema FSMOs, and you will need to rectify that by making sure only one server has the role. However, if the original server had some updates applied prior to its crash, and you allow updates to be made on the new Schema Master, the updates from the old DC will eventually propagate around the network. Your problems to be aware of in this scenario are twofold:

- If the new Schema FSMO created objects that conflict with some created on the original master prior to its departure, some objects will be removed from Active Directory during the conflict-resolution process.
- If the two DCs are online and both believe they are the Schema FSMO, both will accept schema updates equally.

A simple solution, if you can live with it, is either not to force a FSMO until the old DC returns and assumes its role or to force a FSMO temporarily and remove everyone from the Schema Admins group to prevent changes in the meantime. In the latter case, when the original DC comes back, force the FSMO role onto it.

Finally, the system itself will protect you from some forms of stupidity using the system-only attribute and Access Control Lists (ACLs). These work together to prevent you from deleting the user or group object from Active Directory or removing the securityPrincipal as an auxiliary class of both. While you may be aware of this already from our many examples of the use of the four system attributes, it bears mentioning one final time. For attributeSchema object classes, the attributeId, attributeSyntax, and oMSyntax are marked as system-only attributes and so cannot be changed or deleted. For classSchema objects, the subClassOf, governsId, system-MayContain, systemMustContain, systemAuxiliaryClass, and systemPossSuperiors are marked as system-only attributes and so cannot be changed or deleted. Other very important classes and attributes cannot be deleted as their ACLs are locked to prevent this.

Summary

Carefully designing the changes that you make to the Active Directory schema cannot be stressed highly enough for large corporations or application developers. Selecting a team of Schema Managers and OID Managers and creating documentation to accompany and justify changes will smooth that process. Whether you are a small company or a large multinational, creating sensible structures should mean that you rarely make mistakes and almost never have to make objects defunct.

Hopefully we have shown you not only the perils and pitfalls of modifying the schema but also why the schema is necessary and how it underpins the entire Active Directory. While you should be cautious when modifying Active Directory, a sensible administrator should have as little to fear from the Active Directory schema as he does from the Windows Registry.

CHAPTER 13

Backup, Recovery, and Maintenance

A very important though often overlooked aspect of maintaining Active Directory is having a solid disaster recovery plan in place. While the reported incidents of corruption of Active Directory have been minimal, it has happened and is something you should be prepared for regardless of how unlikely it is to occur. Restoring accidentally deleted objects is much more likely to happen than complete corruption, and thus you should be equally prepared. Do you have a plan in place for what to do if a domain controller that has a FSMO role suddenly goes offline, and you are unable to bring it back? All the scenarios we've just described typically happen under times of duress. That is, clients are complaining or an application is no longer working correctly and people aren't happy. It is during times like this that you don't want to have to scramble to find a solution. Having well-documented procedures to handle these issues is critical.

In this chapter, we will look at how to prepare for failures by backing up Active Directory. We will then describe how you can recover all or portions of your Active Directory from backup. We will then cover how to recover from FSMO failures. Finally, we will look at other preventive maintenance operations you can do to ensure the health of Active Directory.

Backing Up Active Directory

Backing up Active Directory is a straightforward operation. It can be done using the NT Backup utility provided with the Windows operating system or with a third-party backup package such as Veritas NetBackup. Fortunately, you can backup Active Directory while it is online, so you do not have to worry about taking outages just to perform backups like you do with other systems, such as Exchange 2000.

To back up Active Directory, you have to back up the System State of one or more domain controllers within each domain in the forest. If you want to be able to restore any domain controller in the forest, you'll need to back up every domain controller. On a domain controller, the System State contains the following:

Active Directory
> This includes the files in the NTDS folder that contains the Active Directory database (*ntds.dit*), the checkpoint file (*edb.chk*), transaction log files (*edb*.log*), and reserved transaction logs (*res1.log* and *res2.log*).

Boot Files
> The files necessary for the machine to boot up.

COM+ Class Registration Database
> The database for registered COM components.

Registry
> The contents of the registry.

SYSVOL
> This includes the files contained in the *NETLOGON* share, which typically contain user logon and logoff scripts and system startup and shutdown scripts. It also includes the file-based portion of GPOs, which are stored in *SYSVOL*.

Certificate Services
> This applies only to DCs that are running Certificate Services.

 While most backup packages allow you to perform incremental backups, with Active Directory you can only perform full backups of the system state.

The user that performs the backup must be a member of the Backup Operators group or have Domain Admins equivalent privileges.

Due to the way Active Directory handles deleted objects, your backups are only good for a certain period of time. When objects are deleted in Active Directory, initially they are not removed completely. A copy of the object still resides in Active Directory for the duration of the tombstone lifetime. The tombstone lifetime value dictates how long Active Directory keeps deleted objects before completely removing them. The tombstone lifetime is configurable and is defined in the tombStoneLifetime attribute on the following object:

```
cn=Directory Services, cn=WindowsNT, cn=Services, cn=Configuration, <ForestDN>
```

The default value for tombStoneLifetime is 60 days. That means deleted objects are purged from Active Directory 2 months after they are initially deleted. As far as backups go, you should not restore a backup that is older than the tombstone lifetime because deleted objects will be reintroduced. If for whatever reason you are not able to get successful backups at least every 60 days, consider increasing the value of tombStoneLifetime.

Another issue to be mindful of in regard to how long you keep copies of your backup has to do with passwords. Computer accounts change their passwords every 30 days. They keep their previous passwords and attempt to use them if their current passwords do not work. So if you restore computer objects from a backup that is older than 60 days, those computers will more than likely not be able to participate in the domain and will have to be reset. Trust relationships can also be affected. Like computer accounts, the current and previous passwords are stored with the trust objects, but unlike computer accounts, trust passwords are changed every 7 days. That means if you restore trust objects from a backup that is older than 14 days, then you will need to reset the trust.

Using the NT Backup Utility

The NT Backup utility is installed on all Windows 2000 and Windows Server 2003 machines. It is available by going to Start → All Programs → Accessories → System Tools → Backup. You can also start it up by going to Start → Run, entering ntbackup, and clicking OK. Figure 13-1 shows the first screen of the NT Backup utility under Windows Server 2003.

Figure 13-1. NT Backup Wizard

The NT Backup utility can be used to back up the system and also to perform a restore. We will cover restores in the next section. If you click on the "Advanced Mode" link in the first screen, you'll then see a screen such as that in Figure 13-2.

In this case, we clicked on the Backup tab and then selected the box beside System State. We could also back up any of the other drives if we wanted, but the System State is all that is required when doing a basic restore of Active Directory.

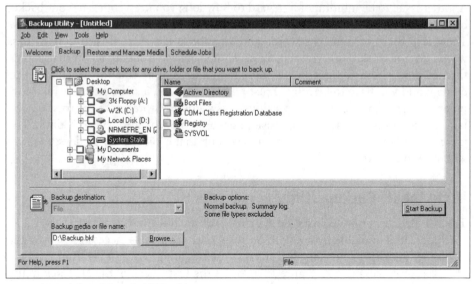

Figure 13-2. Advanced mode NT backup

By clicking the "Start Backup" button, we can kick off the backup. In Figure 13-2, we configured the *D:* drive to be where the backup file gets stored. This could have been to a remote file server or other backup media if we wanted.

We can also schedule a backup to run at an interval of our choosing by clicking the "Start Backup" button and then the "Schedule" button. After that, we click the "Properties" button and the screen shown in Figure 13-3 pops up.

In this case we've configured the backup to run once a day at 7:30 A.M. The screen in Figure 13-3 is actually part of Scheduled Tasks, which is the job scheduling system available in Windows 2000 and Windows Server 2003.

Restoring a Domain Controller

One of the benefits of Active Directory is built-in redundancy. When you lose a single domain controller, the impact can be insignificant. With many services, such as DHCP, the architecture dictates a dependency on a specific server. When that server becomes unavailable, clients are impacted. Over the years, failover or redundancy has been built into most of these services, including DHCP. With Active Directory, the architecture is built around redundancy. Clients are not dependent on a single DC; they can failover to another DC seamlessly if a failure occurs.

When a failure does occur, you should ask yourself several questions to assess the impact:

Is the domain controller the only one for the domain?
This is the worst-case scenario. The redundancy in Active Directory applies only if you have more than one domain controller in a domain. If there is only one,

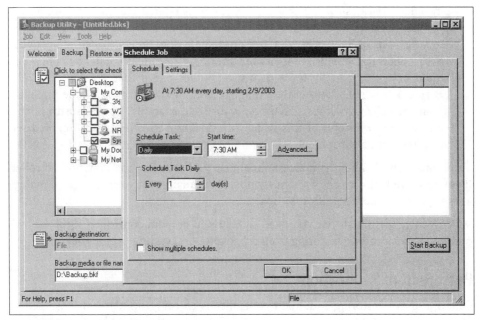

Figure 13-3. Scheduling NT backup

you have a single point of failure. You could irrevocably lose the domain unless you can get that domain controller back online or restore it from backup.

Does the domain controller have a FSMO role?

The five FSMO roles outlined in Chapter 2 play an important part in Active Directory. FSMO roles are not redundant, so if a FSMO role owner becomes unavailable, you'll need to seize the FSMO role on another domain controller. Check out the FSMO recovery section later in this chapter for more information.

Is the domain controller a Global Catalog server?

The Global Catalog is a function that any domain controller can perform if enabled. But if you have only one Global Catalog server in a site and it becomes unavailable, it can impact user's ability to login. As long as clients can access a Global Catalog, even if it isn't in the most optimal location, they will be able to login. If a site without a Global Catalog for some reason loses connectivity with the rest of the network, it would impact user's ability to login. With Windows Server 2003, you can enable universal group caching on a per-site basis to limit this potential issue.

Is the domain controller necessary from a capacity perspective?

If your domain controllers are running near capacity and one fails, it could overwhelm the remaining servers. At this point, clients could start to experience login failures or extreme slowness when authenticating.

Are any other services, such as Exchange 2000, relying on that specific domain controller?

Early versions of Exchange 2000 did not handle domain controller failures well. In fact, once an Exchange 2000 server targeted a specific domain controller, you would have to manually force it to use another one if that domain controller became unavailable. During the outage period, mail delivery could be impacted along with client lookups. Exchange is just one example, but it illustrates that you have to be careful of this when introducing Active Directory–enabled services into your environment.

These questions can help you assess the urgency of restoring the domain controller. If you answered "no" to all of the questions, the domain controller can stay down for a short period without significant impact.

When you've identified that you need to restore a domain controller, there are two options to choose from: restoring from replication or restoring from a backup.

Restore from Replication

One option for restoring a domain controller is to bring up a freshly installed or repaired machine and promote it into Active Directory. You would use this option if you had a single domain controller failure due to hardware and did not have a recent backup of the machine. This method allows you to replace the server in AD by promoting a newly installed machine and allowing replication to copy all of the data to the DC. Here are the steps to perform this type of restore:

1. Rebuild OS. Reinstall the operating system and any other applications you support on your domain controllers.

2. Remove DC from AD. The old remnants of the domain controller must be removed from Active Directory before you promote the freshly installed server. We describe the exact steps to do this shortly.

3. Promote server. After you've allowed time for the DC removal process to replicate throughout the forest, you can then promote the new server into AD.

4. Configure any necessary roles. If the failed server had any FSMO roles or was a GC, you can configure the new server to have these roles.

 A best practice we have found valuable is to keep a spare server that already has the OS and any other software installed ready to ship or onsite at all locations. That way, if you have a major failure with one of your domain controllers, you can use the spare server without needing to stress over getting the hardware replaced immediately in the failed machine.

The biggest potential drawback with this method is the restore time. Depending on the size of your DIT file and how fast your network connections are between the new

DC and the server it will replicate with, the restore time could be several hours or even days. If this is problematic for you, you'll want to look at the restore from backup option that we describe next.

Manually removing a domain controller from Active Directory

One of the key steps with the restore from replication method is removing the objects that are associated with the domain controller before it gets added to AD again. This is a three-step process. The first step is to remove the associated metadata. That can be accomplished with the *ntdsutil* utility. The following example shows the commands necessary to remove the DC3 domain controller, which is in the RTP site, from the *emea.mycorp.com* domain.

```
C:\>ntdsutil
ntdsutil: metadata cleanup
metadata cleanup: connections
```

Next, we need to connect to an existing domain controller in the domain the domain controller you want to remove is in. In this case, we connect to DC2.

```
server connections: connect to server dc2
Binding to dc2 ...
Connected to dc2 using credentials of locally logged on user.
server connections: quit
metadata cleanup: select operation target
```

Now we need to select the domain the domain controller is in. In this case, it is *emea. mycorp.com*.

```
select operation target: list domains
Found 2 domain(s)
0 - DC=mycorp,DC=com
1 - DC=emea,DC=mycorp,DC=com
select operation target: select domain 1
No current site
Domain - DC=emea,DC=mycorp,DC=com
No current server
No current Naming Context
```

Next we must select the site the domain controller is in. In this case, it is the RTP site.

```
select operation target: list sites
Found 4 site(s)
0 - CN=Default-First-Site-Name,CN=Sites,CN=Configuration,DC=mycorp,DC=com
1 - CN=RTP,CN=Sites,CN=Configuration,DC=mycorp,DC=com
2 - CN=SJC,CN=Sites,CN=Configuration,DC=mycorp,DC=com
3 - CN=NYC,CN=Sites,CN=Configuration,DC=mycorp,DC=com
select operation target: select site 1
Site - CN=RTP,CN=Sites,CN=Configuration,DC=mycorp,DC=com
Domain - DC=emea,DC=mycorp,DC=com
No current server
No current Naming Context
```

After listing the servers in the site, we must select the server we want to remove. In this case, it is DC3.

```
select operation target: list servers in site
Found 3 server(s)
0 - CN=DC1,CN=Servers,CN=RTP,CN=Sites,CN=Configuration,DC=mycorp,DC=com
1 - CN=DC2,CN=Servers,CN=RTP,CN=Sites,CN=Configuration,DC=mycorp,DC=com
2 - CN=DC3,CN=Servers,CN=RTP,CN=Sites,CN=Configuration,DC=mycorp,DC=com
select operation target: select server 2
Site - CN=RTP,CN=Sites,CN=Configuration, DC=mycorp,DC=com
Domain - DC=emea,DC=mycorp,DC=com
Server - CN=DC3,CN=Servers,CN=RTP,CN=Sites,CN=Configuration,DC=mycorp,DC=com
    DSA object - CN=NTDS Settings,CN=DC3,CN=Servers,CN=RTP,CN=Sites,
CN=Configuration,DC=mycorp,DC=com
    Computer object - CN=DC3,OU=Domain Controllers,DC=emea,DC=mycorp,DC=com
No current Naming Context
select operation target: quit
```

The last step removes the metadata for the selected domain controller.

```
metadata cleanup: remove selected server
```

At this point, you should receive confirmation that the DC was removed success-fully. If you receive an error that the object could not be found, it might have already been removed if you tried to demote the server with *dcpromo*.

You will then need to manually remove a couple more objects from Active Directory. Via the Active Directory Users and Computers tool, you should remove the computer object in the Domain Controllers OU for the DC. Finally, bring up the Active Directory Sites and Services tool and delete the server object for the DC, which is contained under the site the DC was located in.

Restore from Backup

Another option to reestablish a failed domain controller is to restore the machine using a backup. This approach is cleaner than the restore from replication method we just described because you do not have to remove any objects from Active Directory. When you restore a DC from a backup, the latest changes will replicate to make it current. If time is of the essence, this will be the quicker approach, because only the latest changes since the last backup, instead of the whole directory tree, will be replicated over the network.

Here are the steps to restore from backup:

1. Rebuild OS. Reinstall the operating system and any other applications you sup-port on your domain controllers. Leave the server as a standalone or member server.

2. Restore from backup. Use your backup package, e.g., NT Backup, to restore at least the System State onto the machine. In the next section, we will walk through the NT Backup utility to show how this is done.

3. Reboot server and allow replication to complete. If the failed server had any FSMO roles or was a GC, you can configure the new server to have these roles.

It is also possible to restore the backup of a machine onto a machine that has different hardware. Here are some issues to be aware of when doing so:

- The number of drives and drive letters should be the same.
- The disk drive controller and configuration should be the same.
- The attached cards, such as network cards, video adapter, and processors, should be the same. After the restore you can install the new cards, which should be recognized by Plug and Play.
- The *boot.ini* from the failed machine will be restored, which may not be compatible with the new hardware, so you'll need to make any necessary changes.
- If the HAL is different between machines, you can run into problems. For example, if the failed machine was single processor and the new machine is multiprocessor, you will have a compatibility problem. The only workaround is to copy the *Hal.dll*, which is not included as part of System State, from the old machine and put it on the new machine. The obvious drawback to this is it will make the new multiprocessor machine act like a single processor machine.

Since there are numerous things that can go wrong with restoring to different hardware, we highly suggest you test and document the process thoroughly. The last thing you want to do is troubleshoot hardware compatibility issues when you are trying to restore a crucial domain controller.

Restoring Active Directory

No one ever wants to be in a position where you have to restore Active Directory, but nevertheless you should prepare for it. Restoring Active Directory comes in a few different flavors, which we'll cover now.

Nonauthoritative Restore

A nonauthoritative restore is a restore where you simply bring a domain controller back to a known good state using a backup. You then let replication resync the contents of the latest changes in Active Directory since the backup. The restore from backup method we described earlier to handle DC failures is an example of a nonauthoritative restore. The only difference between that scenario and the one we'll describe here is that previously we assumed that the failed server you rebuilt or replaced was not a domain controller yet. There may be some circumstances when you want to perform a similar restore, but the server is a domain controller. One example might be if some changes were made on a particular domain controller that you wanted to take back. If you were able to disconnect the domain controller from the network in time before it replicated, you could perform a nonauthoritative restore to get it back to a known state before the changes were made. This would effectively nullify the changes as long as they didn't replicate to another server.

A nonauthoritative restore simply restores Active Directory without marking any of the data as authoritative. Since the data will be "nonauthoritative," any changes that have happened since the backup will replicate to the restored server. Also, any changes that were made on the server that had not replicated will be lost.

To perform a non-authoritative restore of a domain controller, you need to boot the DC into "Directory Services Restore Mode." The reason you have to do this is that when a domain controller is live, it locks the Active Directory database (*ntds.dit*) in exclusive mode. That means that no other processes can modify its contents. To restore over the DIT file, you must boot into DS Restore Mode, which is a version of Safe Mode for domain controllers. If you try to restore a live domain controller, you'll get an error like the one shown in Figure 13-4.

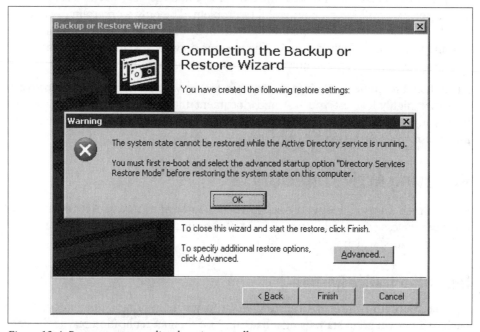

Figure 13-4. Restore error on a live domain controller

You can get into DS Restore Mode by hitting the F8 key during the initial system startup. After doing so you'll see the screen shown in Figure 13-5.

Once you receive a logon prompt, you have to login with the DS Restore Administrator account and password. You set the password for this account when you initially dcpromo the machine into Active Directory. Since Active Directory is offline in DS Restore Mode, you have to log in with the local Administrator account that is stored in the local SAM and that can only be used in this mode.

```
Windows Advanced Options Menu
Please select an option:

    Safe Mode
    Safe Mode with Networking
    Safe Mode with Command Prompt

    Enable Boot Logging
    Enable VGA Mode
    Last Known Good Configuration (your most recent settings that worked)
    Directory Services Restore Mode (Windows domain controllers only)
    Debugging Mode

    Start Windows Normally
    Reboot

Use the up and down arrow keys to move the highlight to your choice.
```

Figure 13-5. Directory Services Restore Mode

After logging into the system, you'll need to bring up the NT Backup utility or other backup software. We will walk through how to do the restore using NT Backup. After clicking Next at the initial wizard screen, you'll see the screen shown in Figure 13-6.

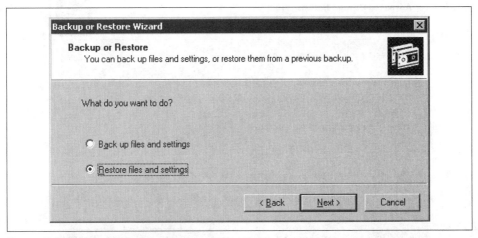

Figure 13-6. Backup or restore options

Select "Restore Files and Settings" and click Next. You'll now be brought to a screen to select what to restore. You should restore at least the System State, but you can also restore the System Drive and other drives if necessary. Figure 13-7 shows the selection screen.

After you've made your selection and clicked Next, the summary screen will be displayed showing what will be restored. Before finishing, you need to click the Advanced button and walk through the advanced screens to ensure that junction points will be restored, as shown in Figure 13-8.

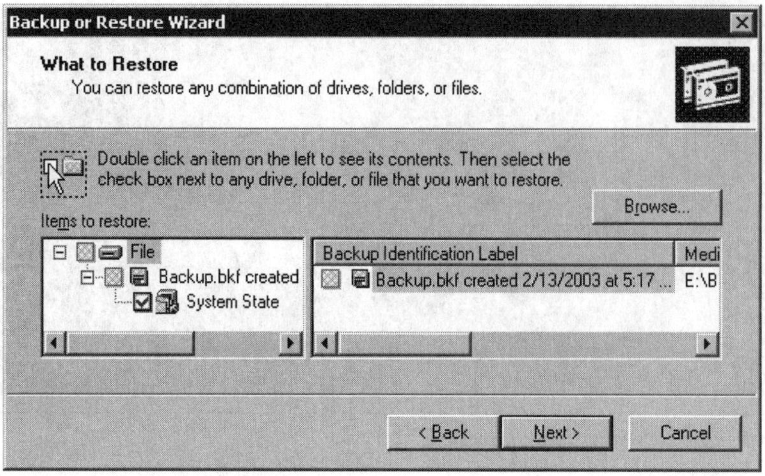

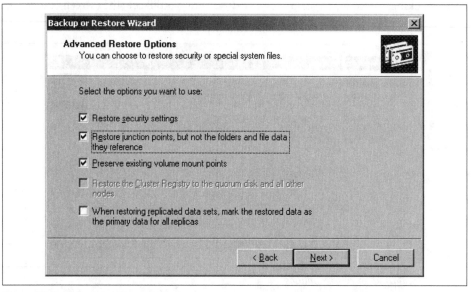

Figure 13-7. Restore selection

Figure 13-8. Restore junction points

Click Finish to kick off the restore. After the restore is complete, you'll need to reboot into normal mode. At this point, the domain controller will replicate the latest changes with its replication partners. Give time for the replication to complete and then monitor the server and check the event logs to make sure it is functioning correctly.

Partial Authoritative Restore

In some situations, you may need to restore data in Active Directory. In the examples we've shown so far of restoring a domain controller and performing a non-authoritative restore, we simply wanted to get the domain controller back up and running. There are certain situations, though, in which you may need to do an authoritative restore. Here are a few examples:

- Accidental deletion of important objects
- Accidental deletion of a subtree
- Corruption of objects or the entire directory
- Reversing certain object additions or modifications

In all of these scenarios, you can do a partial authoritative restore to reverse the changes. If the entire directory gets corrupted, you'll need to do a complete authoritative restore, which we will touch on shortly.

You have two options for doing an authoritative restore. You can either find a domain controller that has the data it is supposed to, perhaps because the changes haven't replicated to it yet, or you can restore the data from a backup. In either case, you need to boot into DS Restore Mode as described in the previous section. Again, this is necessary due to the fact that the Active Directory database is locked when the DC is live, and no modifications can be made. Once you are in DS Restore Mode, you can restore from backup if necessary, as described earlier.

At this point we need to mark the data we want restored as authoritative in our offline Active Directory database. This is done with the *ntdsutil* utility. There are several options to choose from under the authoritative restore menu shown here:

```
ntdsutil: authoritative restore
authoritative restore: ?
 ?                              - Show this help information
 Help                           - Show this help information
 List NC CRs                    - Lists Partitions and cross-refs.  You need
                                  the cross-ref of a Application Directory
                                  Partition to restore it.
 Quit                           - Return to the prior menu

 Restore database               - Authoritatively restore entire database
 Restore database verinc %d     - ... and override version increase
 Restore object %s              - Authoritatively restore an object
 Restore object %s verinc %d    - ... and override version increase
 Restore subtree %s             - Authoritatively restore a subtree
 Restore subtree %s verinc %d   - ... and override version increase
authoritative restore:
```

When doing a partial restore, you can use either the restore object %s subcommand to restore a single object or the restore subtree %s subcommand to restore an entire subtree of objects. In the following example, we will restore the jsmith user object:

```
authoritative restore: restore object cn=jsmith,ou=sales,dc=mycorp,dc=com
Opening DIT database... Done.
The current time is 02-16-03 10:15.54.
Most recent database update occured at 02-14-03 12:29.37.
Increasing attribute version numbers by 200000.
Counting records that need updating...
Records found: 0000000004
Done.
Found 4 records to update.
Updating records...
Records remaining: 0000000000
Done.
Successfully updated 4 records.
Authoritative Restore completed successfully.
authoritative restore: quit
```

As you can see, *ntdsutil* increases the object's version number (USN) by 200,000. This is how it is marked as authoritative in the database. After you reboot into normal mode, the domain controller will check with its replication partners and determine that the jsmith user object has a higher USN than the version its partners have. It will then replicate this out to them. And likewise, all other objects that have been updated on the partner will be replicated to this server.

 If for whatever reason the auto-increment of 200,000 is not enough for the object(s), you can use the alternate subcommand of `restore object %s verinc %d` where %d is the version increase to increment.

Complete Authoritative Restore

Restoring the entire Active Directory database is similar in concept to restoring individual objects or subtrees, except you are restoring all of the objects. This should be done with caution and only under the most extreme situations. We highly recommend that you test this out in a lab environment to ensure you have the process correctly documented and you actually have experience with doing restores.

Again, to run the restore command, you have to be in DS Restore Mode, and you need to have restored the system from backup as described in the "Nonauthoritative Restore" section. The following is example output from the `restore database` subcommand.

```
authoritative restore: restore database
Opening DIT database... Done.
The current time is 02-16-03 10:29.21.
Most recent database update occured at 02-16-03 10:15.54.
Increasing attribute version numbers by 100000.
Counting records that need updating...
Records found: 0000005126
```

```
Done.
Found 5126 records to update.
Updating records...
Records remaining: 0000000000
Done.
Successfully updated 5126 records.
Authoritative Restore completed successfully.
authoritative restore: quit
```

If you have to perform a complete authoritative restore, the assumption is that something catastrophic happened on a domain controller that caused some form of Active Directory corruption. The safest thing may in fact be to restore one domain controller per domain and rebuild the rest. You would need to manually remove each of the rebuilt domain controllers from Active Directory—see the "Manually removing a domain controller from Active Directory" section earlier in the chapter—and then repromote each. Again, this is only a suggestion, and each situation must be thoroughly thought out before taking such drastic measures.

FSMO Recovery

The FSMO roles were described in Chapter 2. These roles are considered special in Active Directory because they are hosted on a single domain controller within a forest or domain. The architecture of Active Directory is highly redundant, except for FSMO roles. It is for this reason that you need to have a plan on how to handle FSMO failures.

It would be a really nice feature if domain controllers could detect that they are being shut down and gracefully transfer any FSMO roles to other domain controllers. In fact, the Active Directory development team is considering this feature for the next major release of Active Directory after Windows Server 2003, but that is a ways out.

Without having the graceful FSMO role transfer, you have to do manual transfers. Manually transferring a role is pretty straightforward. You bring up the appropriate Active Directory snap-in, bring up the FSMO property page, select a new role owner, and perform the transfer. Here is a list of the FSMO roles and the corresponding snap-in that can be used to transfer it to another domain controller:

- Schema Master: Active Directory Schema
- Domain Naming Master: Active Directory Domains and Trusts
- RID Master: Active Directory Users and Computers
- PDC Emulator: Active Directory Users and Computers
- Infrastructure Master: Active Directory Users and Computers

Figure 13-9 shows the Active Directory Domains and Trusts screen for changing the Domain Naming FSMO.

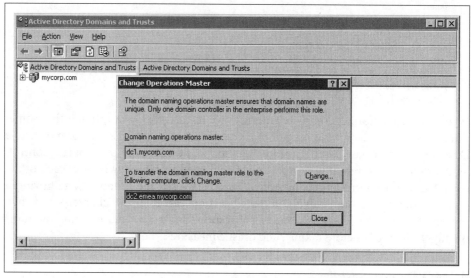

Figure 13-9. Changing the Domain Naming FSMO role owner

When a FSMO role owner goes down and cannot be brought back online, you no longer can transfer the role; you instead have to "seize" it. And unfortunately you cannot seize FSMO roles using the Active Directory snap-ins as you can to transfer them. To seize a FSMO role you need to use the *ntdsutil* utility that we used earlier to do restores. We will now walk through the *ntdsutil* commands that are used to seize a FSMO role. Note that due to the width of the output, some of the text wraps to the following line.

We first start off by getting into the *ntdsutil* interactive mode and looking at the options for the roles command.

```
C:\> ntdsutil
ntdsutil: roles
fsmo maintenance: ?
 ?                              - Show this help information
 Connections                    - Connect to a specific domain controller
 Help                           - Show this help information
 Quit                           - Return to the prior menu
 Seize domain naming master     - Overwrite domain role on connected server
 Seize infrastructure master    - Overwrite infrastructure role on connected server
 Seize PDC                      - Overwrite PDC role on connected server
 Seize RID master               - Overwrite RID role on connected server
 Seize schema master            - Overwrite schema role on connected server
 Select operation target        - Select sites, servers, domains, roles and
                                  naming contexts
 Transfer domain naming master - Make connected server the domain naming master
 Transfer infrastructure master - Make connected server the infrastructure master
 Transfer PDC                   - Make connected server the PDC
 Transfer RID master            - Make connected server the RID master
 Transfer schema master         - Make connected server the schema master
```

We must now connect to the domain controller to which we want to seize the role. In this case, we will connect to DC1.

```
fsmo maintenance: connections
server connections: connect to server dc1
Binding to dc1 ...
Connected to dc1 using credentials of locally logged on user.
server connections: quit
```

At this point we can transfer and seize any available FSMO role to the DC1 domain controller. In the next example, we will attempt to seize the Schema Master. The current Schema Master is DC2. If we tried to perform a seizure and DC2 was operational, we would effectively do a graceful transfer of the role to DC1. If DC2 is not available then, a seizure will take place, as shown in the following output (note that some lines may wrap due to their length):

```
fsmo maintenance: seize schema master
Attempting safe transfer of schema FSMO before seizure.
ldap_modify_sW error 0x34(52 (Unavailable).
Ldap extended error message is 000020AF: SvcErr: DSID-03210300, problem 5002
(UNAVAILABLE), data 1753
Win32 error returned is 0x20af(The requested FSMO operation failed. The currentFSMO
holder could not be contacted.)
)
Depending on the error code this may indicate a connection,
ldap, or role transfer error.
Transfer of schema FSMO failed, proceeding with seizure ...
Server "dc1" knows about 5 roles
Schema - CN=NTDS
Settings,CN=DC1,CN=Servers,CN=RTP,CN=Sites,CN=Configuration,DC=mycorp,DC=com
Domain - CN=NTDS Settings,CN=DC1,CN=Servers,CN=RTP,CN=Configuration, DC=mycorp,DC=com
PDC - CN=NTDS Settings,CN=DC1,CN=Servers,CN=RTP,CN=Sites,CN=Configuration,
DC=mycorp,DC=com
RID - CN=NTDS Settings,CN=DC1,CN=Servers,CN=RTP,CN=Sites,CN=Configuration,
DC=mycorp,DC=com
Infrastructure - CN=NTDS Settings,CN=DC1,CN=Servers,CN=RTP,CN=Sites,CN=Configuration,
DC=mycorp,DC=com
```

Note that a connection is first attempted to the current role owner, and if it cannot be reached, *ntdsutil* does the seizure.

One of the nice features of the quirky *ntdsutil* command is that it can be run in interactive mode as we just showed, or it can be run from a single command line. To accomplish the same seizure using a single command line, the command would look as follows:

```
C:\> ntdsutil roles conn "co to ser dc1" q "seize schema master" q q
```

Depending on your needs, you could write a batch script pretty easily to prompt for the role you want to seize and the DC to transfer or seize the role to. This could help when it gets down to crunch time, you need to seize the role quickly, and you do not want to thumb through this book trying to find all of the commands.

DIT Maintenance

On a periodic basis, such as a couple of times a year, you should check the health of the DIT file (*ntds.dit*) on your domain controllers. Using the *ntdsutil* utility, you can check the integrity and semantics of the Active Directory database and reclaim whitespace, which can dramatically reduce the size of the DIT. Also, just as you should rotate the password for the Administrator accounts in the forest, you should also change the DS Restore Mode Administrator password as well. You may even need to do this more frequently depending on whether you have people leave your team that should no longer know the password.

Unfortunately, to accomplish all these tasks—except changing the DS Restore Mode Administrator password—you have to boot the domain controller into DS Restore Mode. That means you will have to have schedule downtime for the machine. Also, to use DS Restore Mode, you need console access either through being physically at the machine or with out-of-band access, such as with Compaq's Remote Insight Lights Out Board (RILOE). There is one other option using Terminal Services. You can modify the *boot.ini* file on the domain controller to automatically start up in DS Restore Mode. You can then use a Terminal Services connection to log in to the machine. For more information, check out MS Knowledge Base article 256588 from *http://support.microsoft.com*.

Checking the Integrity of the DIT

There are several checks you can perform against the DIT file to determine whether it is healthy. The first we'll show checks the integrity of the DIT file. The integrity check inspects the database at a low level to determine whether there is any binary corruption. It scans the entire file, so depending on the size of your DIT file, it can take a while to complete. We've seen some estimates that state it can check around 2 gigabytes per hour, so allocate your change notification accordingly.

 Before running any integrity checks, be sure you have at least two successful backups of the system.

To start the integrity check, run the *ntdsutil* command from within DS Restore Mode. The `integrity` subcommand can be found within the `files` menu.

```
C:\> ntdsutil
ntdsutil: files
file maintenance: integrity
Opening database [Current].
Executing Command: C:\WINDOWS\system32\esentutl.exe /g"C:\WINDOWS\NTDS\ntds.dit" /o
Initiating INTEGRITY mode...
        Database: C:\WINDOWS\NTDS\ntds.dit
   Temp. Database: TEMPINTEG1752.EDB
```

```
Checking database integrity.
                    Scanning Status (% complete)
         0    10   20   30   40   50   60   70   80   90  100
         |----|----|----|----|----|----|----|----|----|----|
         ..................................................
Integrity check successful.
Operation completed successfully in 11.766 seconds.
Spawned Process Exit code 0x0(0)
If integrity was successful, it is recommended
 you run semantic database analysis to ensure
 semantic database consistency as well.
file maintenance: quit
```

The integrity check looks at the database headers to make sure they are correct and also checks all database tables to make sure they are working correctly. If the database integrity check fails or encounters errors, you may then want to run a repair command to try to fix the problem. Running an integrity check won't damage your Active Directory, but running a repair can, and that's why it is imperative you have a good backup before proceeding.

If the integrity check succeeds, you should then run a semantics check. Whereas the integrity check examines the database as a whole, the semantics check will examine the database to determine whether it is healthy as it pertains to Active Directory semantics. Some of the things the semantics check looks at include security descriptors, reference counts, distinguished name tag (DNT) consistency, and deleted objects.

To start a semantics check, run the go subcommand from the semantic database analysis menu.

```
ntdsutil: semantic database analysis
semantic checker: ?
 ?                              - Show this help information
 Get %d                         - Get record info with given DNT
 Go                             - Start Semantic Checker With No Fixup
 Go Fixup                       - Start Semantic Checker with Fixup
 Help                           - Show this help information
 Quit                           - Return to the prior menu
 Verbose %s                     - Turn verbose mode on/off
semantic checker: go
Fixup mode is turned off
Opening database [Current].......Done.
Getting record count...3019 records
Getting security descriptor count...85 security descriptors
Writing summary into log file dsdit.dmp.0
SDs scanned:            85
Records scanned:      3019
Processing records..Done.
semantic checker: quit
```

If any errors are reported, you can then run go fixup, which will attempt to repair any problems.

If you have to run the repair or go fixup commands, after you boot back into normal mode, you should perform a backup as soon as possible and be sure to indicate on the backup that a repair was performed. If for some reason you need to restore the domain controller at a later point, and if you restore from a backup prior to the repair, you'll need to perform the same commands to fix the database again. Alternatively, if you start experiencing problems immediately after the repair, you want to know where the last backup was before the repair occurred and restore that copy.

Reclaiming Space

If your domain controllers are running low on disk space, or if you have deleted a lot of objects since you promoted your domain controllers, you may want to perform an offline defragmentation of the DIT file. You've probably seen the online defragmentation events that get logged to the Directory Service Event Log. This includes event 700, which states that an online defrag is about to begin, and event 701, which states that the online defrag completed. The online defrag process by default runs twice a day and reclaims space within the DIT file so it can be used for new objects. The online defrag process does not reclaim any disk space used by the DIT file. To do that, you must perform an offline defragmentation.

An offline defragmentation must be done while the domain controller is in Directory Service Restore Mode. You can then use the *ntdsutil* command to compact, that is defrag, the *ntds.dit* file. This process actually creates a copy of the *ntds.dit* file in an alternate location. You can then decide to overwrite the existing DIT file with the new compacted version.

The following shows how to perform an offline defragmentation using *ntdsutil*. After you enter the files menu, you'll need to issue the compact to *directorypath* command. The *directorypath* should be the directory the new compacted *ntds.dit* file would be created in. If the directory does not exist, it will be created automatically.

```
ntdsutil: files
file maintenance: compact to c:\windows\ntds\compact
Opening database [Current].
Creating dir: c:\windows\ntds\compact
Executing Command: C:\WINDOWS\system32\esentutl.exe /d"C:\WINDOWS\NTDS\ntds.dit"
 /t"c:\windows\ntds\compact\ntds.dit" /p /o
Initiating DEFRAGMENTATION mode...
            Database: C:\WINDOWS\NTDS\ntds.dit
      Temp. Database: c:\windows\ntds\compact\ntds.dit
            Defragmentation Status (% complete)
       0    10   20   30   40   50   60   70   80   90  100
       |----|----|----|----|----|----|----|----|----|----|
       ..................................................
Note:
   It is recommended that you immediately perform a full backup
   of this database. If you restore a backup made before the
   defragmentation, the database will be rolled back to the state
   it was in at the time of that backup.
```

```
Operation completed successfully in 20.961 seconds.
Spawned Process Exit code 0x0(0)
If compaction was successful you need to:
    copy "c:\windows\ntds\compact\ntds.dit" "C:\WINDOWS\NTDS\ntds.dit"
and delete the old log files:
    del C:\WINDOWS\NTDS\*.log
file maintenance: quit
```

After you've completed the compaction, you can then decide whether you want to overwrite your current *ntds.dit* file.

Performing an offline defrag of a machine affects only that machine. To reclaim space on your other domain controllers, you'll need to follow the same procedures for all other servers.

After you do an offline defrag, you should also make sure a backup is taken soon after. If for some reason you have to do a restore, and you have not done a backup since you did the offline defrag, the *ntds.dit* file on the domain controller will go right back to the size it was prior to the defrag.

Changing the DS Restore Mode Admin Password

It is a good practice to periodically change the password for your domain Administrator accounts. This should be done so that the password does not find its way to more people than it should, and so that you don't have former administrators trying to perform tasks they shouldn't if they are no longer in the AD group.

The domain Administrator account should not be the only one you are concerned about. The DS Restore Mode Administrator account is just as important and can be used to do very damaging things, such as directly modifying the contents of the Active Directory database. For this reason, you should also periodically rotate the DS Restore Mode Administrator password.

Unfortunately, with Windows 2000 the only way to change the DS Restore Mode Administrator password was by booting into DS Restore Mode. This was very problematic because there was no easy way to automate the process. With Windows Server 2003, a command was added to the *ntdsutil* utility to allow changing the password even when a domain controller is live. The set reset password on server %s subcommand can be used from the set dsrm password menu, where %s is the name of the server to target. Leave %s blank if you want to change the password on the local machine. In the following example, we set the password for the DC1 domain controller.

```
ntdsutil: set dsrm password
Reset DSRM Administrator Password: reset password on server dc1
Please type password for DS Restore Mode Administrator Account: **********
Please confirm new password: **********
Password has been set successfully.
Reset DSRM Administrator Password: quit
```

You cannot use *ntdsutil* to set the DS Restore Mode administrator password if the target machine is currently in DS Restore Mode.

Summary

In this chapter we reviewed all the elements necessary to develop a disaster recovery plan. We covered how to back up Active Directory and some of the gotchas related to the tombstone lifetime and password change cycles. We then discussed the various options for restoring Active Directory, including restore by replication, authoritative restores, and nonauthoritative restores. We discussed the FSMO transfer process and what is needed to seize FSMO roles. Finally, we delved into some of the maintenance tasks that can be done with the Active Directory DIT files.

CHAPTER 14

Upgrading to Windows Server 2003

The first version of Active Directory with Windows 2000 was surprisingly stable and robust. Microsoft does not have the best track record for initial releases of products, but they must be commended for Windows 2000 Active Directory in terms of its feature rich-ness and reliability. That said, since Active Directory is such a complex and broad technology, there was still much room for improvement. There were some issues with scalability, such as the infamous 5,000-member limit with groups or the 300-site limit, which may have imposed artificial limitations on how you implemented Active Directory. Both of these issues have been resolved in Windows Server 2003. The default security setup with Windows 2000 Active Directory out-of-the-box was not as secure as it should have been. Signed LDAP traffic and other security enhancements have since been added into service packs, but they are provided by default with Windows Server 2003. Finally, manageability was another area that needed work in Active Directory, and in Windows Server 2003 numerous command-line utilities have been added along with some significant improvements to the AD Administrative snap-ins.

We have highlighted a few key areas where Active Directory has been improved in Windows Server 2003, and we'll describe more new features in the next section. If you already have a Windows 2000 Active Directory infrastructure deployed, your next big decision will be whether and when to upgrade to Windows Server 2003. Fortunately, the transition to Windows Server 2003 is evolutionary, not revolutionary, as with the migration from Windows NT to Active Directory. In fact, Microsoft's goal was to make the move to Windows Server 2003 as seamless as possible, and for the most part they have accomplished this. You can introduce Windows Server 2003 domain controllers at any rate you wish into your existing Active Directory environment; they are fully compatible with Windows 2000 domain controllers.

Before you can introduce Windows Server 2003 domain controllers, you must prepare the forest and domains with the ADPrep utility, which primes the forest for new features that will be available once you raise the functional level of the domain or forest. Functional levels are similar in nature to domain modes in Windows 2000 Active

Directory. They allow you to configure different levels of functionality that will be available in the domain or forest based on which operating systems are running on the domain controllers.

Before we cover the upgrade process to Windows Server 2003, we'll first discuss some of the major new features in Windows Server 2003 and some of the functionality differences with Windows 2000. Based on this information, you should be able to prioritize the importance of how quickly you should start migrating.

New Features in Windows Server 2003

While the release of Windows Server 2003 is viewed as evolutionary, there are quite a few new features that make the upgrade attractive.

 By "feature" we mean new functionality that is not just a modification of the way it worked in Windows 2000. In this sense, a feature is something you have to use or implement explicitly. Functionality differences with Windows 2000 are covered in the next section.

We suggest you carefully review each of these features and rate them according to the following categories:

1. You would use the feature immediately.
2. You would use the feature eventually.
3. You would never use the feature or it is not important.

Rating each feature will help you determine how much you could benefit from the upgrade. The following is the list of new features, in no particular order:

Application partitions
> You can create partitions that can replicate to any domain controller in the forest.

Concurrent LDAP binds
> Concurrent LDAP binds do not generate a Kerberos ticket and security token and are therefore much faster than a simple LDAP bind.

Cross-forest trust
> This is a transitive trust that allows all the domains in two different forests to trust each other via a single trust defined between two forest root domains.

Domain controller rename
> The rename procedure for domain controllers requires a single reboot.

Domain rename
> Domains can now be renamed, but not without significant impact to the user base (e.g. all member computers must be rebooted twice). For more

information, check out the following whitepaper: *http://www.microsoft.com/ windowsserver2003/downloads/domainrename.mspx*.

Dynamic auxiliary classes

There is now support for the standards-based implementation of dynamic auxiliary classes. Under Windows 2000, auxiliary classes are considered "static" because they are statically defined in the schema. With dynamic auxiliary classes, you can link one when creating an object without it being defined in the schema as an auxiliary class for the object's objectClass.

Dynamic objects

Traditionally, objects are stored in Active Directory until they are explicitly deleted. With dynamic objects, you can create objects that have a time to live (TTL) value that dictates when they will be automatically deleted unless refreshed.

Install from media

A much-needed feature allows replica domain controllers to be promoted into a forest using a backup from another domain controller. This can greatly decrease the amount of time it takes to promote domain controllers in large domains.

MMC and CLI enhancements

The Active Directory Users and Computers (ADUC) tool has been enhanced to allow multiselect of objects; other tools such as *repadmin* and *netdom* have new options.

New DS CLI tools

A new set of CLI tools provides greater flexibility with managing Active Directory from a commandline. These tools include *dsadd*, *dsmod*, *dsrm*, *dsget* and *dsquery*.

New GPO settings

Over 100 new GPO settings have been added, providing greater flexibility in managing Active Directory clients.

GPO RSoP

Resultant Set of Policy (RSoP) has been built into ADUC and can be fully utilized with the Group Policy Management Console (GPMC). RSoP allows administrators to determine what settings of GPOs will be applied to end users and computers.

TLS support

With Windows 2000, only SSL was supported to encrypt traffic over the wire. TLS, the latest standards-based approach for encrypting LDAP traffic, is now also supported.

Quotas

In Windows 2000, if users had access to create objects, they could create as many as they wanted, and there was no way to limit it. Quotas allow you to define how many objects a user or group of users can create. Quotas can also dictate how many objects of a certain objectClass can be created.

Query based groups
> Used for role-based authorization, the new Authorization Manager allows you to create flexible groups based on information stored with users (e.g., department).

Redirect users and computers
> You can redirect the default location to store new users and computers with the *redirusr* and *redircmp* commands, respectively.

Schema redefine
> You can defunct and then redefine attributes and classes in the schema.

Universal Group Caching
> You can eliminate the requirement to have a global catalog server present during login by enabling Universal Group Caching. This is enabled at the site level and applies to any clients that log on to domain controllers in the site.

Last logon timestamp attribute
> A classic problem in a NOS environment is trying to determine the last time a user or computer logged in. The new lastLogonTimestamp attribute is replicated, which means you can use a single query to find all users or computers that have not logged in within a certain period of time.

WMI filtering of GPOs
> In addition to the OU, site, domain, and security group criteria that can be used to filter GPOs, you can now use WMI information on a client's machine to determine if a GPO should be applied.

WMI providers for trust and replication monitoring
> These new WMI providers provide the ability to query and monitor the health of trusts and replication programmatically.

If you find that you would immediately use more than four or five features or eventually use four or five of them, the benefit may be great enough to warrant a near-term move to Windows Server 2003. If you don't find that you'll take advantage of many of these new features, take a look at the next section to see if you would benefit from any of the functionality differences with Windows 2000.

Differences With Windows 2000

Even though Active Directory was scalable enough to meet the needs of most organizations, there were some improvements to be made after several years of real-world deployment experience. Many of the functionality differences with Windows 2000 are the direct result of feedback from AD administrators.

As with the new features, we suggest you carefully review each of the differences and rate them according to the following categories:

1. It would positively affect my environment to a large degree.
2. It would positively affect my environment to a small degree.
3. It would negatively affect my environment.

The vast majority of differences are actually improvements that translate into something positive for you, but in some situations, such as with the security-related changes, the impact may cause you additional work initially.

Single instance store
> Unique security descriptors are stored once no matter how many times they are used as opposed to being stored separately for each instance. This alone can save upwards of 20%–40% of the space in your DIT after upgrading. Note that an offline defragmentation will have to be performed to reclaim the disk space.

Account Lockout enhancements
> Several bugs have been fixed which erroneously caused user lockouts in Windows 2000. A new Active Directory Users and Computers property page called Additional Account Info and the *lockoutstatus.exe* utility are great troubleshooting tools for diagnosing lockout problems.

Improved event log messages
> There are several new event log messages that will aid in troubleshooting replication, DNS, FRS, etc.

Link value replication (LVR)
> Replication in Active Directory is done at the attribute level. That is, when an attribute is modified, the whole attribute is replicated. This was problematic for some attributes, such as the member attribute on group objects, which could only store roughly 5,000 members. LVR replication means that certain attributes, such as member, will only replicate the changes within the attribute and not the contents of the whole attribute whenever it is updated.

Intrasite replication frequency changed to 15 seconds
> The previous default was 5 minutes, which has now been changed to 15 seconds.

No global catalog sync for PAS addition
> With Windows Server 2003, whenever an attribute is added to the Partial Attribute Set (PAS), a global catalog sync is no longer performed as it was with Windows 2000. This was especially painful to administrators of large, globally dispersed Windows 2000 domains.

Signed LDAP traffic
> Instead of sending LDAP traffic, including usernames and passwords, over the wire in plain text with tools such as ADUC and ADSI Edit, the traffic is signed and therefore encrypted.

ISTG and KCC scalability improvements
> The algorithms used to generate the intersite connections have been greatly improved to the point where the previous limit of 300 to 400 sites has been raised to support roughly 3,000–5,000 sites.

Faster global catalog removal
> With Windows 2000, whenever you disabled the global catalog on a DC, the global catalog removal process could only remove 500 objects every 15 minutes. This has been changed so that the process is much quicker.

Distributed Link Tracking (DLT) service stopped by default
> The DLT service can be the source of thousands if not millions of linkTrackO-MTEntry objects that are nestled within the System container of a domain. By default, the DLT service is disabled on Windows Server 2003 domain controllers.

Changes with Pre-Windows 2000 Compatible Access
> To enhance security, the Everyone security principal no longer means all unauthenticated and authenticated users. It instead represents only authenticated users. To grant the equivalent of anonymous access in Windows Server 2003, the Anonymous Logon account should be added to the Pre-Windows 2000 Compatible Access group.

If you find that more than two or three of these would benefit your environment significantly, and fewer than one or two would have a negative affect, that is another good indication that an upgrade to Windows Server 2003 would benefit you enough to start in the near-term. This is by no means a hard-and-fast rule, since some features or differences may be more important than others. For example, if you have over 300 or 400 sites with domain controllers, the improvements in the KCC could potentially help you out significantly. Likewise, if you see the need to add attributes to the partial attribute set in the future, and you have large geographically disperse global catalog servers, then the no global catalog sync behavior could save you some long weekends babysitting replication. You may view other features, such as the MMC enhancements, as benefit, but not to the same degree as the other two just described. You'll have to weigh the priorities of each when you are considering them.

Functional Levels Explained

Now that you are sufficiently excited about the new features with Active Directory and improvements since Windows 2000, we will now cover how you can actually enable these features in Windows Server 2003. If you've already deployed Windows 2000 Active Directory, you are most certainly familiar with the domain mode concept. With Windows 2000 Active Directory, you had mixed- and native-mode domains. Domain mode simply dictated what operating systems were allowed to run on the domain controllers and nothing more. New features were enabled with the move to native mode, including universal groups and group nesting to name a couple. Think of functional levels like domain modes, but taken a step further.

Windows Server 2003 functional levels are very similar to Windows 2000 domain modes from the standpoint that they dictate what operating systems can run on domain controllers, and they can only be increased or raised and never reversed. One common misunderstanding with domain modes, which hopefully will not be carried over to functional levels, is that they have virtually no impact on clients and what operating systems your clients run. For example, you can have Windows 9x clients in mixed- or native-mode Windows 2000 domains and also in domains that are at the Windows 2000 or Windows Server 2003 domain functional level.

 For information about which operating systems are allowed at the various functional levels, check out the "Windows Server 2003 Functional Levels" section in Chapter 2.

An important difference with functional levels is that they apply both to domains and at the forest level. The reason for this is that some features of Windows Server 2003 Active Directory require either that all the domain controllers in a domain are running Windows Server 2003 or that all the domain controllers in the entire forest are running Windows Server 2003.

To illustrate why this is necessary, let's look at two examples. First, let's look at the new "Last logon timestamp attribute" feature. With this feature, a new attribute called lastLogonTimestamp is populated when a user or computer logs on to a domain, and it is replicated to all the domain controllers in a domain. This attribute provides an easier way to identify whether a user or computer has logged on recently than using the lastLogon attribute, which is not replicated and therefore must be queried on every domain controller in the domain. For lastLogonTimestamp to be of use, all domain controllers in the domain need to know to update it when they receive a logon request from a user or computer. Domain controllers from other domains only need to worry about the objects within their domain, so for this reason this feature has a domain scope. Windows 2000 domain controllers do not know about lastLogonTimestamp and do not update it. Therefore, for that attribute to be truly useful, all domain controllers in the domain should be running Windows Server 2003. All the domain controllers must know that all the other domain controllers are running Windows Server 2003, and they can do this by querying the functional level for the domain. Once they discover the domain is at a certain functional level, they start utilizing features specific to that function level.

Likewise, there are times when all domain controllers in the forest must be running Windows Server 2003 before a certain feature can be used. A good example is with the replication improvements. If some of the ISTGs were using the old site topology algorithms and others were using the new ones, you could have replication chaos. All domain controllers in the forest need to be running Windows Server 2003 before the new algorithms are enabled. Until then, they will revert to the Windows 2000 algorithms.

How to Raise the Functional Level

To raise the functional level of a domain or forest, you can use the Active Directory Domains and Trusts MMC snap-in. To raise the functional level of a domain, open the snap-in, browse to the domain you want to raise, right-click on it in the left pane, and select "Raise Domain Functional Level...". You will then see a screen similar to that in Figure 14-1.

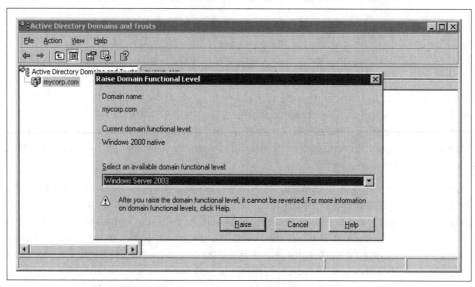

Figure 14-1. Raising the domain functional level

Select the new functional level and click the Raise button. You will then get a confirmation that it was successful or an error stating why it couldn't be raised. Figure 14-2 shows the message returned after successfully raising the functional level. Follow the same procedure to raise the functional level of a forest, but right-click on "Active Directory Domains and Trusts" in the left pane and select "Raise Forest Functional Level...".

You can determine the functional level of a domain or forest two other ways. First, you can look at the msDS-Behavior-Version attribute on the Domain Naming Context (e.g., dc=mycorp,dc=com) for domains or the Partitions container in the Configuration Naming Context (e.g., cn=partitions,cn=configuration,dc=mycorp,dc=com) for the forest. A value of 0 indicates Windows 2000 functional level, 1 indicates Windows Interim functional level, and 2 indicates Windows Server 2003 functional level.

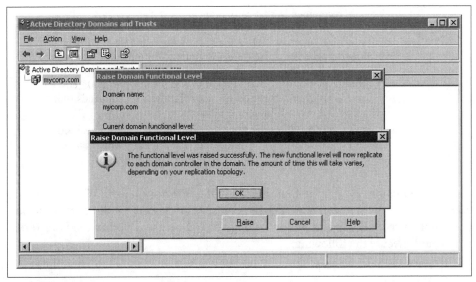

Figure 14-2. Result raising the domain functional level

Alternatively, you can view this information by simply looking at the RootDSE for a domain controller. On Windows Server 2003 domain controllers, the RootDSE contains two new attributes that describe the current functional level:

domainFunctionality
> This value mirrors the msDS-Behavior-Version value on the Domain Naming Context.

forestFunctionality
> This value mirrors the msDS-Behavior-Version value on the Partitions container.

Preparing for ADPrep

Before you can start enabling functional levels, you have to go through the process of upgrading your existing infrastructure to Windows Server 2003. The first step before you can promote your first Windows Server 2003 domain controller is to prepare the forest with the ADPrep utility.

If you've installed Exchange 2000 into your Active Directory forest, you are undoubtedly familiar with the Exchange *setup.exe* /forestprep and /domainprep switches. These switches are run independently from the Exchange server install to allow Active Directory administrators to take care of the AD-related tasks necessary to support Exchange. The Exchange /forestprep command extends the schema and adds some objects in the Configuration Naming Context. The Exchange /domainprep command adds objects within the Domain Naming Context of the domain it is being run on and sets some ACLs. The ADPrep command follows the same logic and performs similar tasks to prepare for the upgrade to Windows Server 2003.

Microsoft recommends that you have at least Service Pack (SP) 2 installed on your domain controllers before running ADPrep. SP 2 fixed a critical internal AD bug, which can manifest itself when extending the schema. There were also some fixes to improve the replication delay that can be seen when indexing attributes. If you plan on supporting a mixed Windows 2000 and Windows Server 2003 environment for an extended period of time, Microsoft recommends that you have SP 3 on your Windows 2000 domain controllers.

For more information on the Microsoft recommendations, check out Microsoft Knowledge Base Article 331161 from *http://support. microsoft.com*.

The ADPrep command can be found in the \i386 directory on the Windows Server 2003 CD. The ADPrep command depends on several files in that directory so it cannot simply be copied out and put on a floppy or CD by itself. To run the ForestPrep, you would execute the following:

```
X:\i386\adprep /forestprep
```

where *X*: is a CD drive or mapped drive to a network share containing the Windows Server 2003 CD. Similarly, to run DomainPrep you would execute the following:

```
X:\i386\adprep /domainprep
```

You can view detailed output of the ADPrep command by looking at the log files in the *%SystemRoot%\system32\debug\adprep\logs* directory. Each time ADPrep is executed, a new log file is generated that contains the actions taken during that particular invocation. The log files are named based on the time and date ADPrep was run.

Now we will review what ForestPrep and DomainPrep do.

ForestPrep

The ADPrep /forestprep command extends the schema with quite a few new classes and attributes. These new schema objects are necessary for the new features supported by Windows Server 2003. You can view the schema extensions by looking at the *.ldf* files in the \i386 directory on the Windows Server 2003 CD. These files contain LDIF entries for adding and modifying new and existing classes and attributes.

Microsoft warns against manually extending the schema with the ADPrep LDIF files. You should instead let ADPrep do it for you.

ForestPrep hardens some default security descriptors and modifies some of the ACLs on the containers in the Configuration NC. New displaySpecifier objects are added and some existing ones modified to support new features within the Active Directory Administrative snap-ins. A NTDS Quotas container is added at the root of the

Configuration container. This is a new container that hosts the quota objects that dictate how many objects a user or group of users can add within a container or OU.

One of the clever aspects of ADPrep is that it stores its progress in Active Directory. This is very neat because it can gracefully recover from failures halfway through execution. It also provides a quick way to determine whether all of the necessary operations have completed and whether ADPrep was successful. Another benefit of storing the operations in Active Directory is in case you encounter problems and need to call Microsoft Product Support Services (PSS). You can look at this container and list out all of the operations that have been successful. PSS would then be able to look up which operation is failing.

A ForestUpdates container is created directly under the Configuration container. Within the ForestUpdates container are two other containers, one called Operations and the other called Windows2003Update. The Operations container contains additional containers, each one representing a certain task that ADPrep completed. For example, one operation might be to create new displaySpecifier objects. The operation container names are GUIDs, and the objects themselves do not contain any information that would be of interest. There should be a total of 36 of these operation containers after ForestPrep completes.

The other object within the ForestUpdates container is called Windows2003Update. This object is created after ADPrep finishes. If that object exists, it signifies that ADPrep completed ForestPrep successfully. If you are interested to find out when ForestPrep completed in a forest, simply look at the whenCreated attribute on the Windows2003Update object. Figure 14-3 shows what these containers look like with the ADSI Edit snap-in from the Windows Support Tools.

You only need to execute ForestPrep once. You can run it multiple times, but due to the fact that it keeps track of its progress in Active Directory under the ForestUpdates container, it will only do something if it determines that an operation did not complete previously.

Since the schema is extended and objects are added in several places in the Configuration NC, the user running ForestPrep must be a member of both the Schema Admins and Enterprise Admins groups. In addition, you should run the command directly on the Schema Master for the forest. Importing the schema extensions is fairly resource-intensive, which is why it is necessary to run it from the Schema Master. Also, if you have large domains containing a lot of objects, ForestPrep may take a while to complete. ForestPrep indexes several attributes, which requires a lot of processing while it updates the AD database.

DomainPrep

Before you can run ADPrep /domainprep, you must be sure that the updates from ForestPrep have replicated to all domain controllers in the forest. DomainPrep must

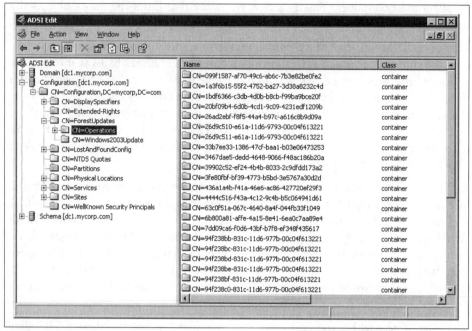

Figure 14-3. ADPrep forest update operations

be run on the Infrastructure Master of a domain and under the credentials of someone in the Domain Admins group. If you try to run DomainPrep before ForestPrep has been run or before it has replicated all its changes out, you will get an error message. Again, if you are unsure about the error, check the ADPrep logs in the *%SystemRoot%\system32\debug\adprep\logs* directory for more information.

DomainPrep creates new containers and objects, modifies ACLs on some objects, and changes the meaning of the Everyone security principal.

Unlike the ForestPrep command, which was fairly resource-intensive, DomainPrep completes quickly. The changes in comparison to ForestPrep are relatively minor. Two new top-level containers are created, one called NTDS Quotas, just like what ForestPrep added in the Configuration container, and another container called Program Data. This is intended to be a starting point for applications to store their data instead of each vendor coming up with their own top-level OU structure.

Just like with ForestPrep, DomainPrep stores the status of its completion in Active Directory. Under the System container, a DomainUpdates container is created. Within that container, two other containers are created, called DomainUpdates and Windows2003Update. The same principles apply here as did for ForestPrep. Each of the operations that DomainPrep performs is stored as an individual object within the Operations container. For DomainPrep there are 52 operations. After all the operations complete, the Windows2003Update object is written, which indicates Domain-

Prep has completed. Figure 14-4 shows an example of what this container structure looks like using ADSI Edit.

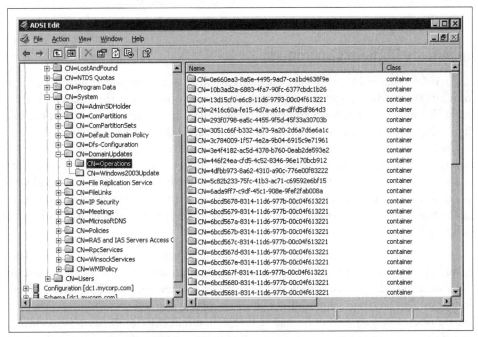

Figure 14-4. ADPrep domain update operations

Once you've run both ForestPrep and DomainPrep and allowed time for the changes to replicate to all domain controllers, you can then start upgrading your domain controllers to Windows Server 2003 or installing new Windows Server 2003 domain controllers.

Upgrade Process

The upgrade process to Windows Server 2003 should be straightforward for most deployments. No forest restructuring is required, no user profile or workstation changes are necessary assuming you are running the latest service pack and hotfixes, and there should be no need for political turf battles over namespace usage and ownership like there might have been with Windows 2000.

We are going to outline five high-level steps that you should follow to upgrade to Windows Server 2003. They include performing an inventory of your domain controllers and clients to determine if there will be any compatibility showstoppers. You are then ready to do a trial run and perform extensive testing to see what impact the upgrade may have on functionality. Next, you have to prepare your forest and domains with ADPrep, which we've already discussed in some depth. Finally, you'll upgrade your domain controllers to Windows Server 2003. In the "Post Upgrade Tasks" section, we will describe what to do after you've upgraded your domain controllers as far as monitoring, raising functional levels, and taking advantage of new features goes.

Inventory Domain Controllers

A good first step before you start the upgrade process is to do a complete inventory of all of the hardware and software that is on your domain controllers. You'll then want to contact your vendors to determine whether they've already done compatibility testing and can verify support for Windows Server 2003. The last thing you want to do is start the upgrade process and find out halfway through that a critical monitoring application or backup software that runs on your domain controllers does not work correctly. Much of this testing can be done in your own labs, but it is always good to check with the vendors and get their seal of approval. After all, if a problem does arise, you'll want to make sure they are supporting the new platform and won't push back on you.

Next you'll want to ensure you have all the necessary hotfixes and service packs installed. A good overview of Microsoft's recommendations is documented in Microsoft Knowledge Base Article 331161. What you need to install depends on how long you plan on having your Windows 2000 domain controllers around. If you plan on a quick upgrade, you'll only need to do the minimal amount of patching required. But if you are going to have a prolonged migration, you should consider applying all the current fixes and service packs.

After you are sure that your hardware and software is fully up to date and will work under Windows Server 2003, you'll then want to do a very thorough check of your current domain controllers and make sure they are running without error. Go through the event logs and resolve any errors and warnings that may be occurring. The *dcdiag* and *netdiag* commands are useful for identifying potential issues. Also, if you don't already trend CPU and memory statistics, you'll need to start. The reason for collecting all this data is that if problems occur after the upgrade to Windows Server 2003, you'll want to narrow it down to whether it was previously a problem or if it is new, most likely as a result of the upgrade. If you don't collect this data, you are setting yourself up for trouble.

A good compatibility test is to run the /checkupgradeonly switch with the Windows Server 2003 installer (*winnt32.exe*).

```
X:\> i386\winnt32.exe /checkupgradeonly
```

This command will go through the steps as if you were upgrading, but it will check only the applications you have installed and the status of the forest. If you have not run ADPrep yet, it will return an error about that.

At this point you'll also want to check the status of your backups. Before you run ADPrep you should have successful backups for at least two domain controllers in every forest and every FSMO role owner. You should also ensure that your disaster-recovery procedures are well documented and have been tested.

Inventory Clients

The good news as far as clients go is that there aren't a lot of requirements for them to work in a Windows Server 2003 forest. In fact, there are no changes required for Windows XP and Windows 2000 machines. For NT 4.0 clients, you should have at least Service Pack 3, and Microsoft recommends Service Pack 6a. For Windows 98 and Windows 95 clients, they will need the DS Client installed as described in Microsoft Knowledge Base Article 323466 or to have their OS upgraded to Windows 2000 or later (not a bad idea anyway if you can get away with it).

Other than that, your clients are fine as is. That said, any wise AD administrator would make sure the clients are thoroughly tested before starting the upgrade. Especially with a new version of Active Directory, there are undoubtedly issues that have yet to be discovered, and you don't want to be the first to find them after you've already upgraded!

Trial Run

While we can go on all day about how easy the upgrade process is, the proof is in the proverbial pudding. We consider it a mandatory step that before you upgrade your first production domain controller to Windows Server 2003, you go through extensive testing in a "production-like" Active Directory forest. So what do we mean by "production-like"? That depends on how much time and resources you have. Perhaps the best way to simulate your production environment is to actually take a production domain controller from each domain in the forest off of the network and put it on a private network. You can then build up the forest on the private network, and all the data that is in production is now in the test environment you just set up. Before we go any further, we want to make it clear that this is the most painstaking option for building a test network, because Active Directory does not self-heal after you put the domain controller on the private network. In fact, you may encounter problems getting the DC to work at all since it cannot initially contact any of the FSMO masters. Microsoft has stated that they'd like to make this process easier and even suggested they may document how to do it, but at the time of publication of this book, nothing of the sort was available. Your other alternative is to populate the test forest with as much of the data from production as possible. If you already have provisioning scripts or a metadirectory that feeds your production Active Directory environment, you may be able to utilize a similar process to populate the test forest.

Once you have a test forest that simulates production up and running, you should add as many clients as possible that represent your users and the various operating systems you support. If you are running Exchange 2000, you should also install it, along with any other directory-enabled applications. Sounds tedious? It is necessary to cover your bases no matter how trivial Microsoft says the upgrade will be. The last thing you want to happen is a major blow-up and then having to explain to your CIO that you didn't do very extensive testing because Microsoft said the upgrade was easy.

The key with the trial run is to document everything thoroughly. If you see anomalies, be sure to document them and follow up to determine whether it is going to be a problem. By the time you are done with the trial-run period, you should have an end-to-end document that describes how you are going to upgrade, how long you plan to wait before you raise functional levels, and in what priority you are going to enable new features.

Prepare the Forest and Domains

As we outlined earlier, before you can promote the first Windows Server 2003 domain controller into your forest, you have to run the ADPrep command. After you've done the DC and client inventories and determined there are no showstoppers to moving forward, you should run ADPrep.

First, you must run ADPrep /forestprep, and after the changes have replicated throughout the forest, you need to run ADPrep /domainprep in every domain. Pretty easy, right? There are a couple of gotchas to be aware of with the schema.

Exchange 2000

If you've installed Exchange 2000 into the forest before running ADPrep, you have to correct some mistakes that were made in the Exchange 2000 schema extensions. Specifically, both ADPrep and Exchange 2000 define labledURI, houseIdentifier and secretary attributes, but Exchange 2000 does not use the correct LDAP display names (lDAPDisplayName) as defined in RFC 2798. If you run ADPrep after Exchange 2000 has been installed without fixing these attributes, you can end up with duplicate schema objects with different lDAPDisplayName attributes. To solve the problem, you must run the *inetorgpersonfix.ldf* file that is located in *\support\ tools\support.cab*. This LDIF file fixes the lDAPDisplayName attributes of the three attributes.

First save the *inetorgpersonfix.ldf* file, then import it using the *ldifde* utility. Here is an example where we will be importing into the *mycorp.com* forest:

```
ldifde.exe /i /f inetOrgPersonFix.ldf /c "DC=X" "DC=mycorp,DC=com"
```

Note that *inetorgpersonfix.ldf* uses DC=X as the forest path, which is why we needed to use the /c switch to replace it with our own forest path.

SFU 2.0

If you've installed Microsoft Services For UNIX (SFU) 2.0 in your Windows 2000 forest, you can run across a similar to issue as the one just described with Exchange 2000. The problem again comes back to an incorrectly defined attribute. In this case it is the uid attribute. Microsoft has developed a hotfix for this issue, which is described in Microsoft Knowledge Base Article 293783.

 This applies only to SFU 2.0. If you are running SFU 3.0, you will not encounter this problem.

Upgrade Domain Controllers

Now comes the easy part. You may be wondering how we could possibly say that doing the upgrade is the easy part. Perhaps we should preface it with this: if you've done all your homework, this will be the easy part. All of the hard work comes from doing the DC and client inventory, checking for compatibility issues, monitoring, checking event logs, getting a representative baseline, performing mock upgrades, etc. By the time you get the point of actually doing the upgrades in production, it should be second nature to you.

You can proceed with the upgrade process as slowly or as quickly as you want. Windows Server 2003 domain controllers are fully compatible with Windows 2000 domain controllers. They can also serve any role in a forest, including acting as a global catalog server, any FSMO master, ISTG or Bridgehead server.

Post-Upgrade Tasks

After you've upgraded one or more of your domain controllers to Windows Server 2003, you need to do some additional tasks to fully complete the migration. First and foremost, you need to monitor the domain controllers every step of the way and especially after they have been upgraded. You are setting yourself up for failure if you are not adequately monitoring Active Directory.

Monitor

The criticality of monitoring cannot be overstated. If you are not monitoring, how can you determine whether something broke during the upgrade? Here are several things you should check after you upgrade your first domain controller in a domain, any FSMO role owner, and after all DCs have been upgraded:

Responds to all services
> Query LDAP, Kerberos, GC (if applicable), and DNS (if applicable) and be sure authentication and login requests are being processed. The *dcdiag* command can run many of these tests.

Processor and Memory utilization

Trend processor and memory utilization for some period before you do the upgrade so you can compare to the numbers after the upgrade.

DIT growth

The growth of the DIT should not be significant. You may in fact want to do an offline defrag after the upgrade to reclaim any space due to single- instance store of ACLs.

Event logs

This is a no-brainer, but you should always check the event logs to see whether any errors are being logged.

DC resource records registered

Ensure that all of the SRV, CNAME, and A records for the domain controllers are registered. The *dcdiag* command can perform these checks.

Replication is working

Run repadmin /showreps and repadmin /replsum and watch for anything out of the ordinary.

Group Policies are being applied

You may want to add a new setting to an existing GPO or create a new GPO and see if the settings apply on a client that should be receiving it.

NETLOGON and SYSVOL shares exist

This can consist of opening an Explorer window and browsing the available shares on the domain controller.

FRS is replicating correctly

You can test this out by placing a test file in the SYSVOL share on a domain controller and waiting for it to replicate to the other domain controllers.

This is not a comprehensive list of everything you should possibly monitor, but it is a good start. If everything checks out over a period of a week, you can feel pretty comfortable that the upgrade was successful. If nothing else, as long as you keep a close eye on the event logs, you should be able to catch the majority of problems.

Raise Functional Levels

After you feel comfortable that the upgrades have completed successfully, your next step should be to start raising the functional levels. If you've only upgraded the domain controllers in a single domain, you can raise the functional level for only that domain to Windows Server 2003. If you've upgraded all the domain controllers in the forest, you can also proceed to upgrade the forest functional level to Windows Server 2003.

If youwant to err on the side of caution, and you support multiple domains, you may want to raise the functional level of a single domain and repeat the monitoring steps over a week before raising the forest functional level.

After you raise the functional level of a domain or forest, you should add some additional steps to what you monitor to include testing out new features in Windows Server 2003. For example, to test the Windows Server 2003 domain functional level, you should log on to a domain controller and view the lastLogonTimestamp attribute of your user object that we discussed earlier in the chapter. This is a new replicated attribute that will contain your logon time. If after a period of time, you don't see that attribute getting populated, you'll need to dig deeper to determine what is going on.

Perhaps the easiest test to determine whether a functional level has been set for a domain or forest is to query the Root DSE and look at the domainFunctionality and forestFunctionality attributes. A value of 2 indicates the domain or forest is at the Windows Server 2003 functional level.

Tweak Settings

Once the functional levels have been defined, you'll want to tweak any settings that you discovered during your testing that are set differently than what you want or what you have configured previously. Of special interest should be the settings related to security and account lockout. If you need to disable SMB Signing, you can do so via Group Policy in the Domain Controller Policy → Windows Settings → Security Settings → Local Policies → Security Options → Digitally Sign Communications.

A common pain point for Windows 2000 Active Directory administrators was account lockouts. All of the bug fixes that were incorporated into Service Packs 2 and 3 are included in Windows Server 2003. You may want to revisit your account lockout and password expiration settings. Microsoft's recommendations are included in their Security Template file located at *%SystemRoot%\security\templates\ SECUREDC.INF* on a Windows Server 2003 domain controller.

If you had to hardcode any settings on domain controllers in the Registry, you should reevaluate those settings to see whether you still need them. For example, many people increased the intrasite replication frequency from 5 minutes to 15–60 seconds. With Windows Server 2003, the default frequency has changed to 15 seconds.

Start Implementing New Features

After you've upgraded your domain controllers and raised the functional level of a domain or forest, you are ready to start taking advantage of the new features. Some of them, such as the MMC and CLI enhancements, you can start utilizing immediately. With others, such as quotas, you'll want to think out exactly how to implement them and have them properly documented and communicated before you start using them. If you are using AD-Integrated DNS zones, you should look at converting to application partitions to store DNS data. This is a fairly easy conversion that can be done with the DNS MMC snap-in. In some cases, you may need to completely rethink your current processes. For example, if you start using the "Install from media" feature, you may change how you build and deploy domain controllers.

Summary

In this chapter, we covered the new features in Windows Server 2003 and some of the differences with Windows 2000, most of which were instigated by real-world deployment issues. We then went over how you can enable new features with the use of functional levels and why they are necessary. Next we discussed the ADPrep process and how that must be done before the first Windows Server 2003 domain controller can be promoted. Once you have your forest and domains prepared, you can start the upgrade process. We described some of the important issues to be aware of when upgrading, and finally what to do after you've completed the upgrade.

While this chapter focused mainly on upgrading from an existing Windows 2000 Active Directory infrastructure, in the next chapter we discuss some of the key issues with migrating from Windows NT straight to Windows Server 2003 Active Directory.

CHAPTER 15

Migrating from Windows NT

Knowing how to design Active Directory is very useful, but it's not the end of the story. You may already have an existing NetWare or Windows NT infrastructure and want to consider migrating to Active Directory. Alternatively, you may have existing directories and networks that you would like Active Directory to complement rather than replace. One of the most important features of Active Directory is its ability to integrate with other directory services.

In this chapter we will cover some of the issues to consider when migrating from a Windows NT environment to Active Directory. Migrating to Active Directory from an existing NOS infrastructure is analogous to jumping from one moving car to another. This is due to the fact that organizations rarely get the opportunity to take extended downtime from both the client and server perspective to move everyone to Active Directory. In fact, limiting downtime for users is typically one of the top priorities, so having a well-thought-out migration and fallback plan is critical to reduce the impact to your user base.

The Principles of Upgrading Windows NT Domains

There are many reasons that you will want to upgrade your Windows NT domains to Active Directory, not least of which is to make use of Active Directory and other features. It's possible to have significantly fewer domains in Active Directory because each domain can now store millions of objects. While fewer domains means less administration, the added benefit of using organizational units to segregate objects makes the Active Directory represent a business more accurately, both geographically and organizationally, and is a significant step forward. Couple this with the ability to set ACLs on objects and their properties in Active Directory, and you get much more fine-grained control for administrative delegation than before. You also can start phasing out old services, such as Windows Internet Naming Service (WINS) and extraneous Windows NT Backup Domain Controller (BDC) servers, since the clients now make more efficient use of DCs via TCP/IP and DNS. With all these improvements, the goals of upgrading a domain are easy to state:

- Reduce the number of domains in use since it is easier to administer fewer domains.
- Gain an extensible schema that allows much more corporate information to be stored than was previously possible.
- Create a hierarchical namespace that as closely as possible mirrors the organizational structure of the business.
- Gain much more fine-grained control over delegation of administration without needing to resort to the use of multiple domains.
- Reduce network bandwidth use by DCs through both multimaster replication and a significantly more efficient set of replication algorithms.
- Reduce the number of PDCs/BDCs to a smaller number of DCs through a more efficient use of DCs by clients.
- Eliminate the need for reliance on WINS servers and move to the Internet-standard DNS for name resolution.

 To get the maximum benefit from the new technologies, you really need to upgrade both clients and servers.

Preparing for a Domain Upgrade

There are three important steps in preparing for a domain upgrade:

1. Test the upgrade on an isolated network segment set aside for testing.
2. Do a full backup of the SAM and all core data prior to the actual upgrade.
3. Set up a fallback position in case of problems.

We cannot stress strongly enough how enlightening doing initial testing on a separate network segment can be. It can show a wide variety of upgrade problems, show you areas that you never considered, and in cases in which you have considered everything, give you the confidence that your trial run did exactly what you expected. In the world of today's complex systems, some organizations still try to roll out operating system upgrades and patches without full testing; this is just plain daft. The first part of your plan should be for a test of your upgrade plans.

When you do the domain upgrade itself, it goes without saying that you should have full backups of the Windows NT SAM and the data on the servers. You would think this is obvious, but again we have seen a number of organizations attempt this without doing backups first.

The best fallback position is to have an ace up your sleeve, and in Windows NT upgrade terms, that means you need a copy of the SAM somewhere safe. While backup tapes are good for this, there are better solutions for rapid recovery of a domain. These recipes for success require keeping a PDC or a BDC of your domain safely somewhere. In this context, by safely we mean off the main network. Your first option is to take the PDC off the network. This effectively stores it safely in case anything serious goes wrong. Next, as your domain now has no PDC, you need to promote a BDC to be the PDC for the domain. Once that has been done successfully, and you've manipulated any other services that statically pointed at the old PDC, you can upgrade that new PDC with the knowledge that your old PDC is safe in case of problems. The second option is to make sure that an existing BDC is fully replicated, then take it offline and store it. Both solutions give you a fallback PDC in case of problems.

Forests and the Forest Root Domain

Remember that the first domain in a forest is a significant domain and cannot be deleted. That means you cannot create a test domain tree called *testdom.mycorp.com*, add a completely different noncontiguous tree called *mycorp.com* to the same forest, and subsequently remove *testdom.mycorp.com*. You have to make sure that the first domain that you ever upgrade is the major or root domain for the company. In Windows NT domain model terms, that means upgrading the master domains prior to the resource domains. The resource domains may end up being Organizational Units instead anyway now, unless political, cultural, or bandwidth reasons force you to want to keep them as domains.

Windows NT Domain Upgrades

Single Windows NT domains and complete trust domains can be upgraded with few problems. With a single domain, you have just one to convert, and with complete trust domains, every domain that you convert will still maintain a complete trust with all the others. However, when you upgrade master domains or multimaster domains, there are account and resource domains that need to be considered. No matter how many master domains you have, the upgrade of these domains has to be done in a certain manner to preserve the trust relationships and functionality of the organization as a whole. We'll now explain the three broad ways to upgrade your master domain structure.

Let's assume that you have one or more single-master or multimaster domains that you wish to convert. Your first task will be to create the forest root domain. This domain will act as your placeholder and allow you to join the rest of the domains to it. The forest root domain can be an entirely new domain that you set up, or you can make the first domain that you migrate the forest root domain.

Take a look at Figure 15-1, which shows a Windows NT multimaster domain. Each domain that holds resources trusts the domains that hold user accounts, allowing the users to log on to any of the resource domains and use the respective resources.

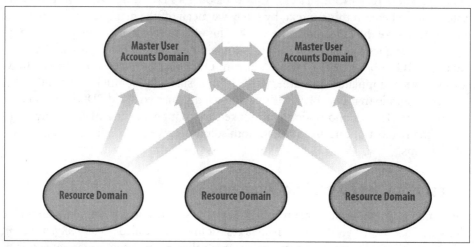

Figure 15-1. Windows NT multimaster domain prior to migration

There are three main ways to upgrade this domain. None of them is necessarily any better than the other, as each design would be based on choices that you made in your namespace design notes from Chapter 8.

Solution 1—Migration to a new forest root domain

First, the domains could all be joined as one tree under an entirely new root. Each master domain would represent a branch under the root with each resource domain joined to one of the masters. This is shown in Figure 15-2.

 While it is conventional to think of the resource domains under the master domains, there is nothing to stop you from joining resource domains under resource domains if you like; it will make no difference for access to the resource domain's data.

Solution 2—Migration with one domain as the domain-tree root

The second option is to aim toward making one of the master domains the root of the new tree. All resource domains could then join to the root, one of the other master domains, or one of the resource domains. Figure 15-3 shows this in more detail. Two resource domains have been joined to one of the master domains, but the third resource domain can still go to one of three parents, as indicated by the dashed lines.

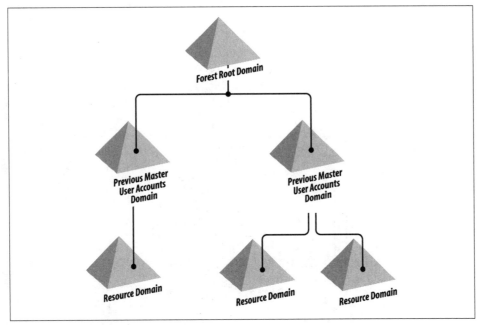

Figure 15-2. Migration to a new forest root domain

Solution 3—Migration to separate domain trees in a forest

Finally, you could make each domain a separate tree. While the first master domain that you migrate will be the forest root domain, the rest of the master domains will simply be tree roots in their own right.

A Solution-Independent Migration Process

Let's now consider the process for migrating these domains. We must migrate the master account domains first, since they are the ones that the resource domains depend on. To start the process, convert any one of the master account domains over to Active Directory by upgrading the PDC of that master domain. If any of the trust relationships have been broken between this domain and the other master and resource domains during migration, reestablish them. Once the PDC is upgraded, proceed to upgrade the other BDCs of that domain (or you can leave the domain running with Windows NT BDCs; it doesn't really matter to the rest of the migration).

The next step is to migrate the other master domains. You continue in the same manner as you did with the first domain until all master domains have been converted. Once each domain is converted, you need to reestablish only trust relationships with the existing Windows NT domains; the Active Directory domains in the forest will each have hierarchical and transitive trusts automatically anyway. So

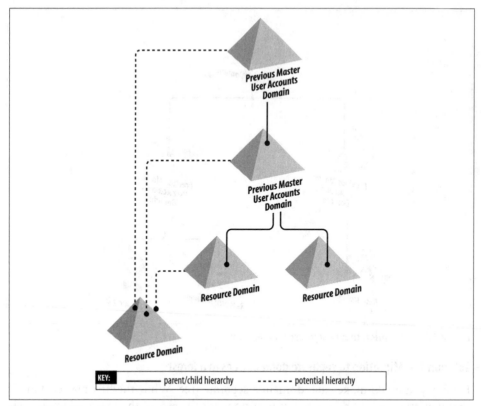

Figure 15-3. Migration with one domain as tree root

now you end up with a series of Active Directory master domains in a tree/forest and a series of Windows NT resource domains with manual trusts in place.

Once all the master domains are converted, you can start consolidating them (as discussed in the next section), or you can immediately convert the resource domains. Either way, once all domains are converted, you are likely to start a consolidation process to reduce the number of domains that you have in existence. Part of that consolidation will be to convert existing resource domains to Organizational Units. This is because resource domains by their very nature tend to fit in well as Organizational Units.* For that to happen, these future Organizational Units will need to be children of one of the migrated master or resource domains. It doesn't matter which master or resource domain acts as the parent, since there are consolidation tools available that allow you to move entire branches of the tree between domains. The

---

* Resource domains were created because of Windows NT's inability to allow delegation of authority within a domain. Now Organizational Units provide that functionality, so separate resource domains are no longer required. Thus, old resource domains can become Organizational Units under Windows 2000 and still maintain all their functionality.

process is simple: you take each resource domain in turn and convert it to a child domain of one of the existing Active Directory master or resource domains. Once they are all converted, you can really begin consolidation.

Consolidating Domains After the Move

Upgrading your domains is not the end of the story. Many administrators implemented multiple Windows NT domains to cope with the size constraints inherent in Windows NT domains. With Active Directory, those constraints are lifted, and each domain in a forest can easily share resources with any other domain. This allows administrators to begin removing from the directory information that has become unnecessary in an Active Directory environment.

Windows 2003 Interim and Windows 2003 functional levels and groups

When your final Windows NT 4.0 BDC for a domain has been taken out of service or upgraded, you are ready to convert the domain to Windows 2003 functional level. After the conversion, you have some decisions to make about the groups you have in this domain. You can leave all groups as they are or start converting some or all groups to universal groups. With multiple domains in a single forest, you can consolidate groups from more than one domain together into one universal group. This allows you to combine resources and accounts from many domains into single groups.

There are two methods for bringing these groups online:

- Setting up parallel groups
- Moving existing groups

In a parallel group setup, the idea is that the administrator sets up groups that hold the same members as existing groups. In this way, users become members of both groups at the same time, and the old group and a user's membership can be removed in a calculated manner over time. The arguably easier solution is to move existing groups, but to do that you need to follow a series of steps. Take the following example, which leads you through what's involved.

Three global groups—part_time_staff in *finance.mycorp.com*, part_time_staff in *mktg.mycorp.com*, and part_time_staff in *sales.mycorp. com*—need merging into one universal group, to be called part_time_staff in *mycorp.com*. The following is the step-by-step procedure:

1. All part_time_staff global groups are converted to universal groups in their current domains.
2. To make the part_time_staff universal group names unique so that they can all exist in one domain, the group needs to be renamed with the domain element. That means finance\part_time_staff, mktg\part_time_staff, and sales\part_time_

staff become finance\finance_part_time_staff, mktg\mktg_part_time_staff, and sales\sales_part_time_staff.

3. Make use of the Windows 2003 functional level ability to move groups, and move the three groups to the *mycorp.com* domain. This leaves you with mycorp\finance_part_time_staff, mycorp\mktg_part_time_staff, and mycorp\sales_part_time_staff.

4. Create a new universal group called part_time_staff in the *mycorp. com* domain.

5. Make the mycorp\finance_part_time_staff, mycorp\mktg_part_time_ staff, and mycorp\sales_part_time_staff groups members of the new mycorp\part_time_staff universal group.

You can then remove the three old groups as soon as it is convenient. Remember that, while this is an easy series of steps, there may be an entire infrastructure of scripts, servers, and applications relying on these groups. If that is the case, you will need either to perform the steps completely, modifying the infrastructure to look at the new single universal group after Step 5, or modify the groups immediately after you complete Step 2 and then again after you complete Steps 3 to 5 in quick succession. We favor the former, since it requires that the work be done once, not twice.

 You should not underestimate the amount of work in analyzing what parts of the infrastructure make use of each group, planning the changes to that infrastructure, and ultimately implementing the changes. The preceding example was for one set of groups. If you have a significant number of groups, this is no small undertaking, and managers should be made aware of this fact.

Computers

When it comes to considering computer accounts, things are relatively straightforward. Under Windows NT, a computer could exist in only one domain at a time, since that computer and domain required a trust relationship to be established to allow domain users to log on to the domain at that client. You could set up bidirectional trust relationships manually between domains, allowing a client in Domain A to authenticate Domain B users to Domain B, but this was not common. With Active Directory, all domains in a forest implicitly trust one another automatically. As long as the computer has a trust relationship with one domain, users from any other domain can log on to their domain via the client by default. The following is a rough list of items to consider:

- Moving computer accounts between domains to gain better control over delegation
- Joining computers to the domain
- Creating computer groups
- Defining system policies

In all of these, it is important to understand that the source domain does not have to be at the Windows 2003 functional level to move computers to a new domain. In addition, administrators can use the NETDOM utility in the Windows Support Tools to add and remove domain computer objects/accounts; join a client to a domain, move a client between domains; verify, reset, and manage the trust relationship between domains; and so on.

While you may have had computer accounts in a series of domains before, you now can move these accounts anywhere you wish in the forest to aid your delegation of control. Group Policy Object processing also has a significant impact on where your computer accounts should reside. However, you now can work out what sort of Organizational Unit hierarchy you would ideally wish for your computer accounts and attempt to bring this about. Moving computers between domains is as simple as the following NETDOM command.

Here we want to move a workstation or member server, called *mycomputerorserver*, from the domain *sales.mycorp.com* to the location LDAP://ou=computers,ou=finance,dc=mycorp,dc=com. We specifically want to use the *myDC* domain controller and the MYCORP\JOINTODOMAIN account to do the move. Connection to the client will be done with the SALES\Administrator account, which uses an asterisk (*) in the password field to indicate to prompt for the password. We could just as easily have used an account on the client itself. We also include a 60-second grace period before the client is automatically rebooted:

```
NETDOM MOVE mycomputerorserver /DOMAIN:mycorp.com /OU:Finance/Computers
    /UserD:jointodomain /PasswordD:thepassword
    /Server:myDC
    /UserO:SALES\Administrator /PasswordO:*
    /REBOOT:60
```

This is actually the long-winded version, split up onto multiple lines for visibility; here's the short form:

```
NETDOM MOVE /D:mycorp.com /OU:Finance/Computers /UD:jointodomain
    /PD:thepassword /S:myDC /UO:SALES\Administrator /PO:* /REB:60
```

Note that moving a Windows NT computer doesn't delete the original account, and moving a Windows 2000 computer just disables it in the source domain.

You also need to consider who will be able to add workstations to the domain. You can set up an account with join-domain privileges only, i.e., an account with the ability to make and break trust relationships for clients. We've used this approach with a lot of success, and it means that an administrator-equivalent user is no longer required for joining clients to a domain. Let's take the previous example, but this time we wish to both create an account and join a new computer to the domain with that account. This is the code to do that using NETDOM:

```
NETDOM JOIN mycomputerorserver /D:mycorp.com /OU:Finance/Computers
    /UD:jointodomain /PD:thepassword /S:myDC /UO:SALES\Administrator /PO:* /REB:60
```

In all these NETDOM examples, we're using a specially constructed account that only has privileges to add computer objects to this specific Organizational Unit. At Leicester we precreated all the computer accounts, and the jointodomain account was used only to establish trusts between existing accounts; it had no privilege to create accounts in any way.

You also need to be aware that workstation accounts under Windows NT could not go into groups. Under Active Directory, that has all changed, and you can now add computers to groups. So when moving computers between domains for whatever purposes, you now can use hierarchical Organizational Unit structures to delegate administrative/join-domain control, as well as using groups to facilitate Group Policy Object (GPO) upgrades from system policies.

System policies themselves are not upgradeable. However, as explained in Chapters 7 and 10, you can use system policies with Active Directory clients and bring GPOs online slowly. In other words, you can keep your system policies going and then incrementally introduce the same functionality into GPOs. Since each part of each system policy is included in the GPO, you can remove that functionality from the system policy while still maintaining the policies application. Ultimately, you will end up replacing all the functionality incrementally, and the system policies will have no more policies left so can be deleted.

Users

When consolidating domains, you'll need at some point to move users around to better represent the organization's structure, to gain better control over delegation of administration, or for group policy reasons. Whichever of these it is, there are useful tools to help you move users between domains.

To be able to transfer users between domains, you need to have gone to Windows 2000 functional level, and this will have ditched all your Windows NT BDCs. This allows a seamless transfer of the user object, including the password. A good method for transferring users and groups so that no problems occur is as follows:

1. The first stage is to transfer all the required domain global groups to the destination domain. This maintains the links to all users within the source domain, even though the groups themselves have moved.

2. Now the users themselves are transferred to the destination domain. The domain global group memberships are now updated with the fact that the users have now joined the same domain.

3. You then can consolidate the domain global groups or move the domain global groups back out to the original domain again. This latter option is similar to Step 1, where you move the groups and preserve the existing links during the move.

4. Clean up the user's Access Control Lists to resources on local computers and servers, since they will need to be modified after the change.

If you do it this way, you may have fewer problems with group memberships during the transition. As for moving users, while you can use the Active Directory Users and Computers MMC to move containers of objects from one domain to another, there are also two utilities—called MOVETREE and SIDWALK—in the Resource Kit that can come in very handy.

MOVETREE allows you to move containers from one part of a tree in one domain to a tree in a completely different domain. For example, suppose we wish to move the branch of the tree under an Organizational Unit called Managers from the *sales. mycorp.com* domain to the Organizational Unit called Sales-Managers on the *mycorp.com* domain. The command we would use to start the move is something like the following, preceded by a full check:

```
MOVETREE /start /s sales.mycorp.com /d mycorp.com
   /sdn OU=Managers,DC=sales /ddn OU=Sales-Managers
   /u SALES\Administrator /p thepassword
```

The SIDWALK utility is designed to support a three-stage approach to modifying ACLs. Each stage of changing ACLs can take a while to complete and verify, sometimes a day or more. It thus requires some amount of system resources and administrator time. The stages are:

Planning
> The administrator needs to determine what users have been granted access to resources (file shares, print shares, NTFS files, registry keys, and local group membership) on a particular computer.

Account mapping
> Based on who has access to what resources on the system, the administrator can chose to delete old, unused security identities or replace them with corresponding new identities, such as new security groups.

Converting ACLs
> Using the information from the planning and mapping phases, the third stage is the conversion of security identities found anywhere on a system to corresponding new identities.

 At the time of going to press, these utilities were not finalized, and still others were coming onto the scene.

Specifically, MOVETREE has been updated to make modifications to the SIDhistory attribute of security principals. A new set of "cloning" tools (e.g., ClonePrincipal) is to be made available to allow a user or group to be cloned from a Windows NT or Active Directory domain to a Windows 2000 functional level or higher domain without removing the source account.

Member servers and removing domains

After you've migrated, you may want to get rid of some old domains entirely, move member servers between domains, consolidate multiple servers together, or possibly even convert a member server to become a DC. Whatever you're considering, moving member servers and their data while maintaining group memberships and ACLs to resources can be done. Again, as with users and computers, taking the process in stages helps ensure that there is less chance of a problem.

If you're considering moving member servers between domains or removing domains in general, these are the steps that you need to consider:

1. Make sure that the source domain and the destination domain are at the Windows 2000 or higher functional level.

2. Move all groups from the source domain to the target domain to preserve memberships.

3. Move the member servers to the destination domain.

4. Demote the DCs to member servers, removing the domain in the process.

5. Clean up the Access Control Lists to resources on local computers and servers, since they will need to be modified after the change.

Summary

This chapter focused on the principles behind the migration of existing Windows NT domains to Active Directory. Microsoft has taken the time to properly think through a very scalable and stable directory service in its Active Directory implementation. It has, in its own words, "bet the barn on Active Directory."

The next chapter takes a look at the potential for integrating Microsoft Exchange into Active Directory.

CHAPTER 16

Integrating Microsoft Exchange

Exchange 2000 has been the driving reason behind many companies' move to Active Directory. Exchange 2000 requires an Active Directory infrastructure, and the dependencies it places on AD are not small. In fact, the Exchange 2000 schema extensions roughly double the size of the default Active Directory schema. There are also restrictions on the location of your domain controllers relative to the Exchange servers. For these reasons and the critical nature of email, calendar, and collaboration services, all of which Exchange can provide, it is clear that Exchange 2000 can be the most significant application you integrate into Active Directory.

In this chapter, we will briefly touch on some of the important issues regarding the integration of Exchange with Active Directory. We'll cover how to prepare the forest for Exchange and describe some of the changes this causes. Finally, we will review the Active Directory Connector (ADC), which aids in the transition from Exchange 5.5 to Exchange 2000.

Quick Word about Exchange Server 2003

Exchange Server 2003, the next major release of Exchange, is currently due out in the summer of 2003. While there are many new features planned for that release, the way it integrates with Active Directory largely remains the same. This chapter focuses on Exchange 2000, but the concepts and procedures we describe map very closely to Exchange Server 2003 as well.

Here are a few key points to note about Exchange Server 2003 and Windows Server 2003:

- Exchange 2000 can only run on Windows 2000.
- Exchange Server 2003 can run on Windows 2000 and Windows Server 2003.
- Exchange 2000 can run in a Windows Server 2003 or Windows 2000 Active Directory forest.

- Exchange Server 2003 can run in a Windows Server 2003 or Windows 2000 Active Directory forest.

- Exchange 5.5 can interoperate with Exchange Server 2003 and Windows Server 2003 just as it could with Exchange 2000 and Windows 2000.

- The Outlook 2003 mail client allows cross-forest authentication with Windows Server 2003 forests.

Preparing Active Directory for Exchange 2000

Before you can install the first Exchange 2000 server in Active Directory, you have to prepare your forest. The Exchange setup program provides two options called /forestprep and /domainprep, which perform various tasks such as extending the schema, creating groups, creating containers for Exchange, and setting permissions on those containers. Due to the extent of changes caused by running these commands and the elevated privileges required to do so, it is imperative that AD administrators have a thorough understanding of what they do.

Forestprep

The Forestprep option of the Exchange 2000 setup extends the schema and makes some changes to the Configuration container. Forestprep must be run before Domainprep can be executed and subsequently before you can install your first Exchange 2000 server. The user that runs Forestprep must be a member of both the Enterprise Admins and Schema Admins groups. Here is a list of some of the tasks Forestprep takes care of:

- Extends the schema with close to 2000 schema additions and modifications. Forestprep effectively doubles the number of classes and attributes in the default Active Directory schema. Several attributes are also added to the Global Catalog, which will cause a GC resync with Windows 2000 Active Directory.

- Creates the Exchange organization with the following distinguished name:

    cn=<ExchangeOrgName>,cn=MicrosoftExchange,cn=Services,cn=Configuration,<ForestDN>.

- This container is where Exchange stores most of its data in Active Directory, including the address lists, administrative groups, recipient policies, and other global settings.

- Grants full control rights to the designated user or group over the Exchange organization. The rights granted are equivalent to the Exchange Full Administrator rights when using the Exchange Delegation of Control wizard.

Due to the massive number of schema extensions, you should consider running Forestprep on the Schema FSMO role owner. This can speed up the time it takes for complete Forestprep. Before moving forward to Domainprep, you must ensure that the schema extensions and objects injected by Forestprep have replicated across the forest.

Domainprep

After you've successfully run Forestprep, you need to run Domainprep in any domain in which you plan to install an Exchange 2000 server or have mail-enabled users. The user that runs Domainprep must be a member of the Domain Admins group for the target domain. Some of the tasks performed during Domainprep include the following:

- Creates a container for the System mailboxes under cn=Microsoft Exchange System Objects,<DomainDN>
- Creates the Exchange Domain Servers global group, which is the default location for new Exchange 2000 servers in the domain.
- Creates the Exchange Enterprise Servers domain local group. The Recipient Update Service eventually adds all the Exchange Domain Servers groups from each domain to this group.
- The Exchange admin account specified during Forestprep is granted administrative control over the Exchange Domain Servers and Exchange Enterprise Servers groups.
- Grants the "Manage audit and security log" privilege to the Exchange Enterprise Servers group on the Domain Controller Security Policy.

Note that after Domainprep completes, the Exchange administrators will only have the rights to add Exchange servers to the domain. They will not have the privileges to create mailboxes for users. To do that, you will need to grant them Account Operators or equivalent rights.

Running Forestprep and Domainprep

To run Forestprep or Domainprep, insert an Exchange 2000 Server CD into a computer where you are logged in with the appropriate credentials as described earlier. To run Forestprep, run the following command (replace *E*: with your CD drive letter):

```
> E:\setup\i386\setup /forestprep
```

To complete the Forestprep wizard, you will need to know the name of the Exchange organization you want to create and the user or group account that should be given Exchange Full Administrator rights. If you are joining an existing Exchange 5.5 organization, you'll need to know the name of that organization and the Exchange 5.5 service account and password.

After Forestprep completes, you should wait until the schema extensions have replicated across your forest. Domainprep will fail to complete if the targeted server has not received the Forestprep changes. If you are still running Windows 2000, the replication delay may be significant due to the Global Catalog sync that is caused by Forestprep adding to the partial attribute set. You may even want to run Domainprep several days after Forestprep to ensure that everything has replicated. Because of replication improvements and the fact that a Global Catalog sync is no longer required in Windows Server 2003 Active Directory, you can expect a shorter replication period if you've upgraded your forest to the Windows Server 2003 forest functional level.

To run Domainprep, run the following command (replace *E:* with your CD drive letter):

```
> E:\setup\i386\setup /domainprep
```

After Domainprep has run and replicated throughout the domain, your Exchange administrators should then be able to install Exchange 2000 servers. One other caveat to be aware of when installing Exchange servers is that the subnet the Exchange servers are on must be in the Active Directory site topology or else the setup process will fail.

Other Considerations

Microsoft went the route of splitting up the install process for Exchange, but you have the option of doing it all at the same time. If the user you install Exchange with for the first time is a member of the Enterprise Admins and Schema Admins group, the setup process perform both the Forestprep and Domainprep functions. While it is generally a good practice to split up the install, you do have the option of doing it all at once.

When you implement Exchange 2000, keeping the Active Directory site topology up to date becomes even more important. The Exchange installation process will abort if the server does not have a subnet that maps to a site in the topology. Exchange uses the site topology to determine which domain controller clients should be querying. If a client doesn't map to a site, they could be performing email-based lookups against a remote domain controller.

Perhaps the most significant impact of Exchange 2000 on Active Directory is the dependencies it places in regard to domain controller location. The general best practice recommendation is to have domain controllers on the same subnet as your Exchange servers. This isn't feasible in all situations, so as long as the domain controllers are relatively close from a network perspective, you should be OK. The latency between the Exchange servers and domain controllers should be less than 100 ms.

Exchange 5.5 and the Active Directory Connector

A lot of companies that are migrating to Exchange 2000 had Exchange 5.5 deployed previously. To help with the transition process, Microsoft created the Active Directory Connector (ADC), which allows you to migrate at your own pace while maintaining both environments.

The ADC is comprised of a service that does the work and an MMC console to manage the service. While the console can be installed on any client or server, the ADC service has to be installed on a DC for it to work.

 To support connection to the ADC, you will need Microsoft Exchange 5.5 Service Pack 1 or above.

When you install the ADC for the first time in a forest, it extends the schema to include new Exchange objects and attributes, as well as modifying existing Active Directory objects to include new Exchange-relevant attributes. The Exchange Schema is also modified if you intend to replicate Active Directory data to Exchange. For example, the User class object in the Active Directory Schema is directly modified to include three Exchange-relevant auxiliary classes in the auxiliary class attribute: msExchMailStorage, msExchCustomAttributes, and msExchCertificateInformation. Auxiliary classes and schema are discussed more fully in Chapter 4.

Once the Active Directory schema is extended, Active Directory then can hold mail attributes for groups, users, and contacts just as the Exchange directory can. This means that the ADC now can replicate data bidirectionally, knowing that either end can store the same data. This allows you to run the ADC in one of three ways:

From Active Directory to Exchange
> Every new creation of a user, distribution group, security group, or contact object that is mail-enabled in a designated Organizational Unit will be copied over to a designated Recipients container on Exchange. Every change to the attributes of an existing mail-enabled object will also be passed. Deletions also can be synchronized.

From Exchange to Active Directory
> Every new creation of a user, mailing list, or contact object in Exchange automatically creates a corresponding user account in a specified Organizational Unit in Active Directory. Attribute changes also get passed, as do deletions.

Bidirectional replication
> Changes at either end get replicated over to the other system.

If you choose to manage one-way replication, you must appreciate that you can update the details only for those objects on the one-way source directory from that time on. If you were to update the target directory, the changes you made could potentially be erased during the next update as the system realizes that the target is no longer in synchronization with the source. To fully appreciate this and see why bidirectional replication does not necessarily help you here, see the later sections on "Mail-Enabling Objects via the GUI" and "Why Bidirectional Replication May Not Solve Your Problems."

There are other implications that need to be understood for these scenarios. When passing information from Active Directory to Exchange, for example, you must designate a set of specific Organizational Units that will contain the objects to be replicated. Any Organizational Units that you do not list will never have objects replicated, even if they are mail-enabled objects.

Once the ADC is installed, the Active Directory Users and Computers MMC has three extra property pages available to it. Two of these pages are visible only if you choose the Advanced option from the View menu. One word of warning: to see the extra pages in the Active Directory Users and Computers MMC on any server or workstation, you must have the ADC MMC installed onto that client first. Installing the MMC part of the ADC onto a client configures the Active Directory User and Computers MMC with the extra snap-in options for these pages.

We'll now take a look at how to configure the ADC for your use and follow on with how to mail-enable a user using the GUI and ADSI.

Configuring the ADC

Once you've installed the ADC, you need to designate a DC to hold what's known as a connection agreement. This agreement is an Active Directory msExch-ConnectionAgreement object that will hold all the information relating to the replication of the data you require. Specifically, when you set up an agreement, it adds an item to a part of the Configuration Naming Context with a path similar to this:

```
cn=My Connection Agreement, cn=Active Directory Connections, cn=Microsoft Exchange,
cn=Services, cn=Configuration, dc=windows, dc=mycorp, dc=com.
```

The agreement stores all the data as attributes of the agreement object itself. Attributes hold information such as which direction replication will take place, when it will take place, what parts of Active Directory or Exchange actually hold the objects that you wish to replicate, and so on. For example, the attribute that holds Active Directory Organizational Units to replicate to Exchange is known as the msExchServer1ExportContainers attribute. Figure 16-1 shows a sample connection agreement running on a DC called *Mint* and connecting to an Exchange server called *Sumac*.

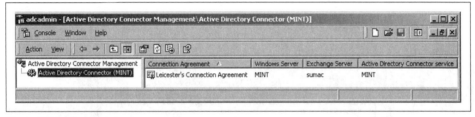

Figure 16-1. A connection agreement

 If you right-click the agreement in the display pane, you can replicate the agreement immediately. You also can create new agreements from here as well.

If you have more than one Exchange site or multiple Windows 2000 domains that you wish to replicate to or from, you need more than one connection agreement. Similarly, if you have only one Exchange server, but you need to replicate differently for various parts of the service (e.g., the Finance Organizational Unit replicates once nightly to an Exchange container, the Sales Organizational Unit replicates hourly to an Exchange container, but the Marketing Exchange container replicates every 15 minutes back to Active Directory), you will need more than one agreement (in this case three).

When you set a connector up and try to replicate objects and attributes back and forth, it's not surprising that there might be a few problems at first while you begin to understand how things work. To help with this, you can open up the properties of any connection agreement and specify a set of logging levels for various aspects of the agreement. Figure 16-2 shows these.

When you select a logging level, events are logged to the event log. The highest level produces copious amounts of information and thus is very useful when debugging. When we go to create a new connection agreement from the ADC MMC, seven property pages are available. We've had a lot of personal experience with these pages, so we'll try to help you understand them better. The first page that appears is shown in Figure 16-3.

The agreement needs a name, which is what the screen is prompting for. The agreement is currently unidirectional from Exchange to Active Directory, and the ADC service is running on the DC called *Mint* at present. Depending on the replication direction that you choose, the From Windows and From Exchange tabs will be modified. Having typed in the name, we then need to tell the ADC what server is hosting the Exchange services and what server is hosting the ADC service. We do that from Figure 16-4 which is the Connections property page.

Here *Mint*, a DC in the domain CFS, is using Windows Challenge/Response authentication and connecting to the Exchange server *Sumac*, also in the CFS domain, as

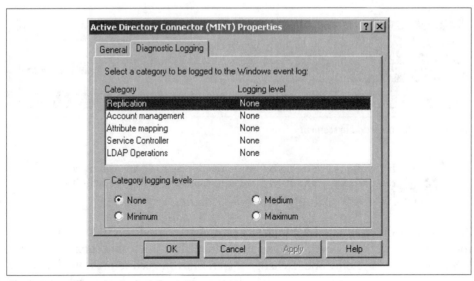

Figure 16-2. Diagnostic logging for the connector

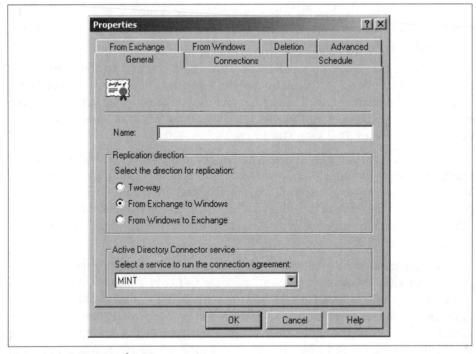

Figure 16-3. Properties of a new connection agreement

the Administrator user from the CFS domain. Any account can be used for connection; we've just chosen the standard account here for the test domain. The only

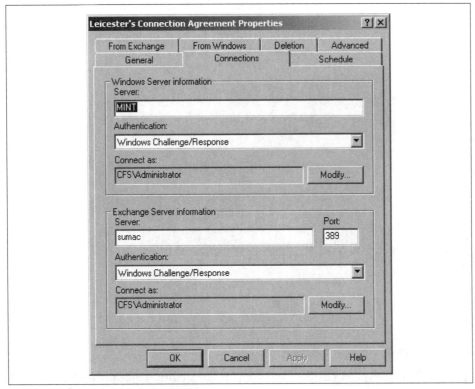

Figure 16-4. Connections property page

requirement is that the account has full privilege in both directions to be able to replicate and update the required databases. Once this page is completed, we need to consider when we want the agreement to run. We do this from the Schedule property page shown in Figure 16-5.

Figure 16-5 appears to show that we can specify the replication interval in 15-minute or hourly cycles. In fact, this isn't the case. While this screen allows you to see a weekly replication cycle in 15-minute or hourly slots, replication will occur once during every 15-minute slot. Figure 16-5 shows a replication schedule from 8 A.M. to 10 P.M. This means that replication will occur every 15 minutes between 8 A.M. and 10 P.M., i.e., 56 times. If we want the replication to occur once an hour, the only recourse is to switch to a 15-minute view and highlight the 15-minute time period when we want replication to take place. For example, we could switch to the 15 minute view and choose 08:45-09:00, 09:45-10:00, 10:45-11:00, and so on, making sure that no other 15-minute slots were enabled.

While we have chosen to replicate at the selected times on this screen, there are two other options available. The first is never to replicate the agreement. If you ever need to stop replicating this agreement, this is where you come to disable replication. The

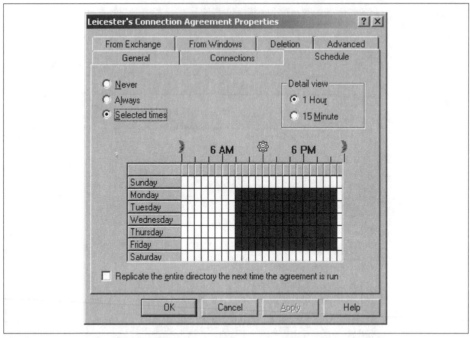

Figure 16-5. Schedule property page

option called Always forces the agreement to constantly replicate with almost no breathing space. Almost as soon as the agreement has finished replicating, it starts the replication cycle again. It is unlikely to be replicating a significant amount of data each time the agreement replicates, as there will have been so little time since the previous cycle. However, one or both databases will still be scanned to see whether any updates have occurred since last time, so it is important to realize that turning this on will produce a performance hit, however small. Only you will know how much traffic is likely to be replicated between the two databases for your organization, so testing is the only way to see if there is a problem with turning this setting to Always.

The last checkbox is very useful in fully updating one database or another, and we used it most during testing of the ADC. If you choose to replicate the entire directory, every object in the target is fully updated by every object in the source. But hang on, you may be thinking, if all the items are replicated, what's the point in replicating the whole lot again? Consider that you're setting up the ADC on a new site, replicating from Exchange to Active Directory, and want to make sure that everything works correctly when the data is replicated to Active Directory. To that end, you decide to test-replicate a number of the Exchange Recipients containers to one Active Directory test Organizational Unit. Replication goes well the first time, but you want to do some more tests. You empty the test Organizational Unit of users in Active Directory and then open up the agreement to replicate the entire directory the next time replication takes place. You then can go back to the main agreement,

Figure 16-1, and right-click the agreement to select Replicate Now. Every object is immediately replicated again, just as if this were the first time that the agreement had ever been replicated.

Figure 16-6 shows the property page detailing the settings for replication from Exchange as the source to Active Directory as the target. You can specify for this agreement that mailboxes, custom recipients, and distribution lists will be copied from a series of Recipients containers to a single Organizational Unit in Active Directory.

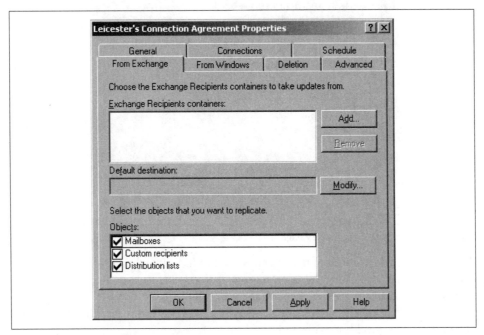

Figure 16-6. From Exchange property page

 Remember that you can have only one target for either direction of a connection agreement. If you want to replicate distribution lists from the Recipients container(s) to a specific Organizational Unit, custom recipients from the Recipients container(s) to another Organizational Unit, and mailboxes to a third Organizational Unit, you need three agreements. Each agreement would replicate one type of source object from multiple recipient containers to a single target Organizational Unit.

The property page relating to replication in the direction from Active Directory to Exchange is very similar, as shown in Figure 16-7. Here, instead, you specify multiple Organizational Units going to a single Recipients container. Again, users, contacts, and groups can be specified as being copied during replication. In Figure 16-7, only users are being copied.

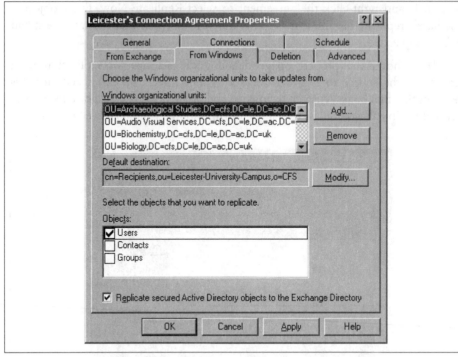

Figure 16-7. From Windows property page

The checkbox at the bottom of the screen is used to indicate whether you wish to use or ignore the Access Control Lists that are defined on user, contact, and group objects to filter the items that get replicated. While items that are not mailbox-enabled are never copied, neither are items whose ACL indicates that they should be filtered out if this checkbox is cleared.

Figure 16-8 indicates what should happen when you replicate through a deletion in either direction. When an Active Directory user is deleted, her mailbox can be removed immediately. Alternatively, the information can be stored in a Comma-Separated-Value (CSV) file for later action using the Bulk Import command in the Exchange Administrator or via a script. If you choose the CSV option, the system sets the Hide Mailbox flag on the object and writes information to a file in this location: *ADC Path\Connection Agreement Name\LocalToRemote\ra.csv*.

The converse also is true. When an Exchange mailbox is deleted, Active Directory users can also be immediately deleted or the information kept in a CSV for later action. In the latter case, the system sets the Mail-Enabled attribute to False and records the deletion information into the file: *ADC Path\Connection Agreement Name\RemoteToLocal\ra.csv*. If you want to use this CSV file to delete the users later, the file first has to be converted to an LDAP Data Interchange File Format (LDF), using the LDIF Directory Synchronization Bulk Import/Export tool found on a DC: *%systemroot%\system32\ldifde.exe*. The option that you choose depends on

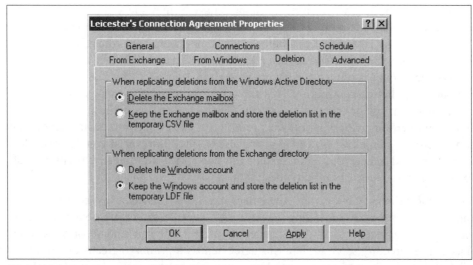

Figure 16-8. Deletion property page

your own environment and whether you wish to keep users that have no mailbox or mailboxes that have no corresponding user for a time period to comply with internal regulations.

The last property page, Advanced, shown in Figure 16-9, is a selection of items that don't fit anywhere else.

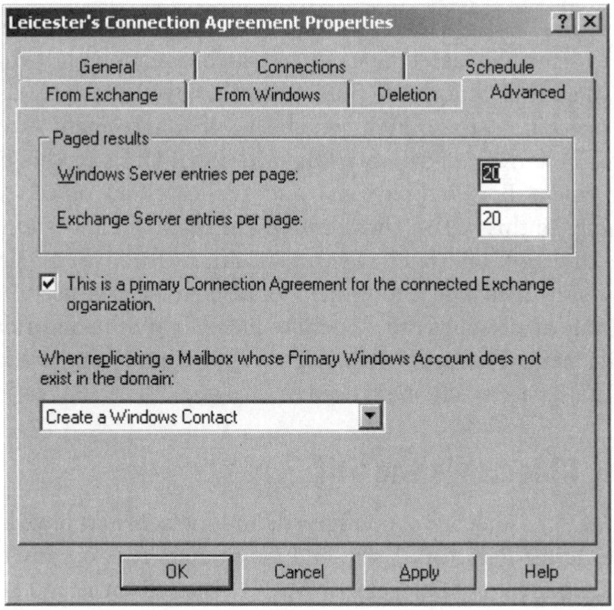

Figure 16-9. Advanced property page

There are certain times when so many changes have been made and need replicating in a single run that the memory needed to store and send them is too large for the DC to cope with. To combat this before it becomes a problem, the ADC can page results, so that the updates are placed on pages, each holding a certain set of updates. Each page is sent to Exchange, then the system waits for the page to complete updating before continuing. This slows down the process slightly but is much less likely to impede or cripple any systems. The Advanced page allows you to specify the number of entries that you wish to hold for each direction. In normal operations, there shouldn't be any need to alter these values. However, if you do have a lot of memory and believe that your system can cope with hundreds or thousands of updates in one go, you can modify these values.

The simple Primary Connection Agreement checkbox tucked away here belies its importance. A primary connection agreement is one that can create objects in a target directory service; a secondary connection agreement can update only existing objects in a directory service. Here this agreement is a primary agreement, so it has full authority. We can create a number of secondary agreements on other DCs if we wish to enable fault tolerance and load balancing.

Finally, when a mailbox is replicated without an associated user, the system allows one of three options. A windows contact can be created, a disabled user can be created, or a fully specified user can be created and enabled. This covers the fact that certain mailboxes may be placeholders for external contacts that do not have associated user accounts, and the ADC needs to know what you want to do with these sorts of replicated items.

The limitations of the ADC are that it is not possible from looking at the set of multiple agreements to see which agreements go in which direction and which containers are copied over in each direction. We think it would have been more useful to have a second tool that acts almost as a map, which says that agreement A replicates mailboxes only from these Active Directory Organizational Units to this Exchange container, and agreement B is bidirectional and replicates all objects in this single Exchange container to this Active Directory Organizational Unit, and vice versa. For complex Active Directory and Exchange organizations that will be slowly adopting Active Directory and Exchange 2000, this would have been a useful addition. The only way to do this at present is to somehow incorporate this information into the name of the agreement. That's the only gripe we have, and compared to the usefulness of the tool, it's a very small one indeed.

Mail-Enabling Objects via the GUI

Now that the ADC is installed and configured, and the schemas have been modified, you can run the Active Directory Users and Computers tool on any client that has Active Directory Connector Management MMC installed on it and see extra property pages relating to the Exchange attributes of users. You will need to enable Advanced view from the View menu of the MMC to see all three pages.

The extra property pages are not visible from a client that does not have Active Directory Connector Management MMC installed on it.

Figure 16-10 shows the Exchange General tab, the first of the three new property pages available to you. It allows you to configure various options that you used to need the Exchange Administrator program to do directly. The property page shown in Figure 16-11 allows you to set new email addresses in any of the available types that Exchange supports.

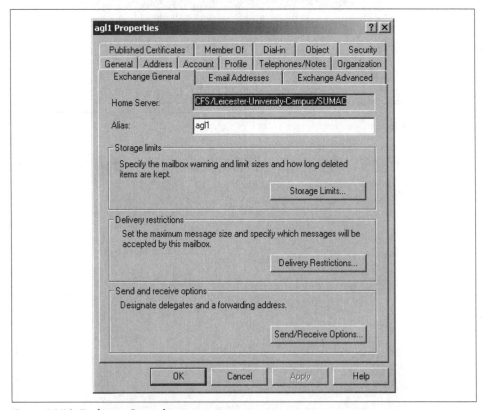

Figure 16-10. Exchange General property page

The page shown in Figure 16-12 allows you to configure the less used and more advanced settings.

If we now go back to the Exchange General property page and click on the Storage Limits button, the screen shown in Figure 16-13 appears. We are not going to go through every option in this manner, but Figure 16-13 serves to highlight an example of when you can get into problems.

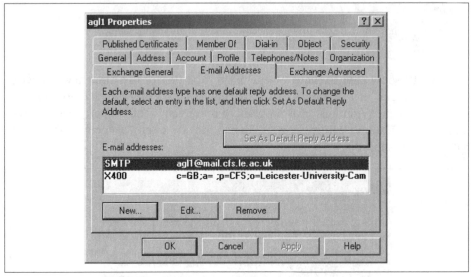

Figure 16-11. Exchange E-mail Addresses property page

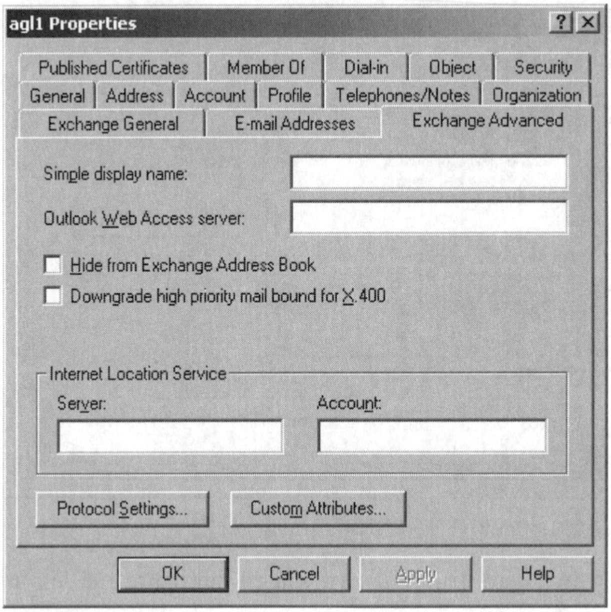

Figure 16-12. Exchange Advanced property page

Any Exchange mailbox can have a set of three custom limits for the private information store, the user's own mailbox. The Exchange service as a whole can also have default limits defined; any users who have no custom limits defined get the defaults. These limits cause warnings to be issued to transgressors on a daily basis by default

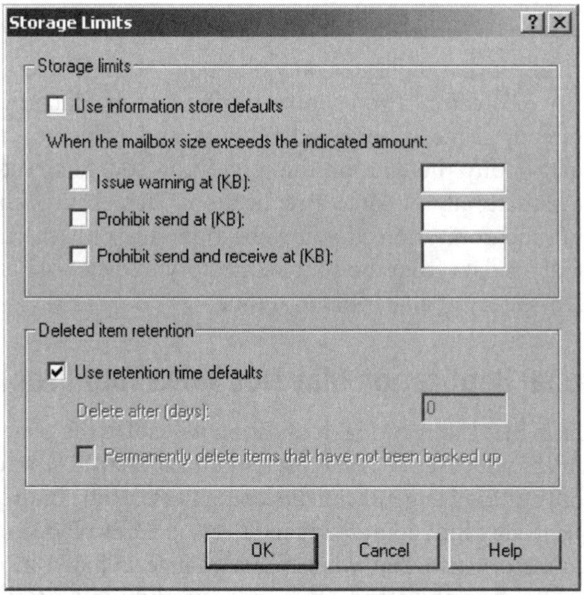

Figure 16-13. Storage Limits options

based on whether certain conditions have been met. In addition, as soon as the user exceeds the Prohibit Send limit, he can send mail no more. When he reaches the Prohibit Receive limit, he cannot receive mail any more, and all further mail to that mailbox is returned to the sender. Figure 16-13 shows that for this particular Active Directory user, the "Use information store defaults" checkbox is not checked but cleared. This means that this user is not using the Exchange information store default limits and instead will use the values indicated on the form. But hang on; there are no values on the form. None of the next three checkboxes been set. This means that you've told the Exchange system not to use its default limits and not to set any custom limits for this user either. In other words, the user has no limits defined for his mailbox. On the second part of the form, you can see that the Deleted Item Retention time, how long the system keeps messages after they have been deleted by the user, is set to the defaults.

It is now possible to manage a lot of the Exchange user functionality from these property pages. If you are used to managing this data on Exchange, and your ADC connection agreement(s) state that data is being transferred one way from Active Directory to Exchange, you need to get into a new mindset of managing the data on Active Directory now. Otherwise, any data that you change on the Exchange server has the potential to be wiped out during two specific replication cycles:

- When any change is made to the same options for the user in Active Directory
- When the connection agreement is told to replicate all data during the next replication cycle

Of course, this also applies to data being replicated one way from Exchange to Active Directory.

If you have an agreement that replicates only one way (Active Directory to Exchange or Exchange to Active Directory), you should not modify the data on the replication target directory directly. This is very bad practice and liable to cause problems. Instead, you should modify the data on the replication source directory and let the data replicate across naturally or force a replication. This ensures the data in both directories stays in synchronization. If you were to modify only the target directory, there is the potential for data from the source directory to overwrite any changes you made to the target directory at a later point in time.

Why Bidirectional Replication May Not Solve Your Problems

While you may think that bidirectional replication will solve the problems, in fact, it probably won't unless your Active Directory Organizational Unit structure tends to mirror the setup of your Exchange Recipients containers. While bidirectional replication appears to specifically link up individual objects in Active Directory with objects in the Exchange directory—so that whenever a change is made in one, the corresponding change is made in the other—this isn't exactly true. In fact, as shown earlier, to replicate from Active Directory to Exchange, you have to designate one or more Organizational Units in Active Directory as the source and only one Recipient container in Exchange as the target. Then the data can be replicated from Active Directory objects in the source Organizational Units to the target container in Exchange. If you wish to have data going from Exchange to Active Directory, you have to specify one or more Recipient containers in the Exchange directory as the source and one Organizational Unit in Active Directory as the target. The point is that you do not have a one-to-one mapping of the containers; you have a many-to-one mapping.

So no matter which direction one-way replication takes place, with only one target in either connection agreement we have the following problem, best shown as an example. Let's say that we have Test as the only Organizational Unit as the source in the one-way connection agreement and a Recipients container as the target. If we want Exchange modifications to replicate back to Active Directory, then with a one-to-one mapping existing between containers in the agreement, we can simply set the agreement up bidirectionally. But what would happen if we add a second Organizational Unit to the one-way agreement, called Finance? Now a Test user's data gets replicated over to Exchange as before. But when you want any changes to that user's Exchange mailbox replicated back and set the agreement up bidirectionally, you have to tell the system that the single Recipients container that receives updates from Test and Finance now has to replicate its data back to one and only one Organizational Unit. This is a severe problem.

The only solution is to mirror the Organizational Unit structure that you use in your connection agreement with the same structure of Recipients folders in Exchange. To get proper bidirectional replication, we would need to set up two Exchange recipients containers that represented Test users and Finance users and then set up multiple one-to-one connection agreements.

Obviously, when Exchange 2000 comes along and uses Active Directory as its directory service rather than its own Exchange directory service, there will no longer be any need to worry about the ADC and replication of data.

Summary

The importance of Exchange 2000 in the enterprise is ever increasing. Exchange has steadily eaten away at the messaging market to the point where it is currently the market leader. In fact, the initial driving force behind the move to Active Directory for many organizations is the need to deploy Exchange 2000. Integrating Exchange into Active Directory is no small feat due to its heavy reliance on AD. For companies migrating from Exchange 5.5, the Active Directory Connector (ADC) can help in the transition, but it introduces additional support overhead.

While Exchange 2000 can be the most significant application you'll integrate with Active Directory, it is by no means the only one you can or should integrate. In the next chapter, we will dive into more details around the future of Microsoft's Directory Services strategy and how that impacts integration of applications with Active Directory.

CHAPTER 17

Interoperability, Integration, and Future Direction

Microsoft's Directory Services strategy has come a long way in the past few years. Even before Active Directory, several Microsoft products utilized a directory, although most used one that was built in. Some examples include the NetMeeting ILS server and Exchange 5.5, which was the precursor to Active Directory. With the introduction of Active Directory in 1999, Microsoft finally had the first signs of a coherent Directory Services strategy. With the release of Windows Server 2003, plus a major overhaul of Microsoft Metadirectory Server and the introduction of Active Directory Application Mode, Microsoft has one of the most diverse and robust directory offerings of any of the major directory vendors in the market today. In this chapter, we will discuss Microsoft's future plans for Directory Services and cover how that plan fits in with interoperating with other directories and integrating with applications and services.

Microsoft's Directory Strategy

After the initial release of Active Directory, Microsoft thought, like many in the industry, that the direction most companies were headed was deployment of a single enterprise directory that would be all things to all clients. Microsoft's intent was for Active Directory to serve the NOS directory role, replacing NT 4.0, and also the application directory role, which had typically been dominated by SunOne (formerly iPlanet) and OpenLDAP. But after three years of implementations, it became evident that although most companies would like to implement a single directory, in practice it did not work out that way. A lot of applications are developed with a particular directory in mind and in some cases, like Exchange 2000, an application can work only with a specific directory. After Microsoft realized that multiple directories would be a reality in most organizations of any size, they decided to rework their strategy. This happened to coincide with their plans to release a major update of the Windows Server operating system, Windows Server 2003.

There are three main components to Microsoft's current Directory Services roadmap: Active Directory Application Mode (AD/AM) as the application directory, Microsoft Metadirectory Services (MMS) as the central provisioning source, and Active Directory as the NOS or Infrastructure directory. We'll now examine each of these products.

Active Directory Application Mode

When Microsoft announced plans in July 2002 to release a "lightweight" version of Active Directory sometime after the release of Windows Server 2003, many AD administrators breathed a sigh of relief. The reason for the relief is that when Active Directory serves as a NOS directory, as it does in the vast majority of implementations, it does not lend itself well to being a flexible application directory. We describe some of the challenges of using Active Directory in both roles in the section "Integrating Applications and Services," later in the chapter.

Active Directory Application Mode, or AD/AM for short, will help reduce the need for Active Directory to serve dual purposes. AD/AM is closer to what most consider a traditional LDAP directory, such as that offered by SunONE and OpenLDAP. It has many AD-specific features stripped out, such as KDC support and DNS SRV requirements, which are necessary for the DC Locator process. AD/AM actually uses the same code base as Active Directory, but the unwanted features are disabled. Some of the similarities with Active Directory include:

- Support for many of the same tools (e.g., ADSI Edit and LDP)
- Support for ADSI and LDAP
- Support for multimaster replication
- Support for a fully extensible schema, although a very minimal schema is provided out of the box
- Inclusion of Configuration, Schema, and Application Partitions (but no Domain Partitions)

Some of the differences from Active Directory include:

- Easy setup process (not *dcpromo*) with no reboot required
- Support for installing multiple instances on a single computer
- Capability to run each instance as a service and to stop and start services without a reboot
- Support on Windows XP Professional
- Capability to have any root naming (e.g. o= or c=)
- No DNS SRV requirements
- No KDC capabilities

- No MAPI protocol support
- No FRS dependencies

One of the big benefits of AD/AM is that you can use Windows Integrated Authentication to control access to data in AD/AM. That means you can utilize Active Directory as an authentication directory, while at the same time compartmentalizing AD/AM instances to serve specific functions without impacting the NOS environment.

Microsoft Metadirectory Services

Metadirectories are used to centralize the provisioning of data across disparate systems. They allow you to define rules for how data should flow based on customized business logic. That is, you can set a rule stating that if system Y has attribute A updated, attribute B in system Z should be updated. Metadirectories become increasingly important as the number of directories and databases you have to support in your environment increase. As we mentioned, supporting multiple directories is a necessary evil that most organizations have to cope with, and metadirectories can help reduce the amount of time you have to spend provisioning data in each.

Microsoft's previous metadirectory offering, Microsoft Metadirectory Services (MMS) Version 2.2, was difficult to setup and maintain. In fact, to purchase MMS 2.2 you had to purchase a support contract from Microsoft as well, which included the installation and setup of the product. With the release of MMS 2003, Microsoft has completely revamped the application to make it easier to configure and manage. Microsoft is positioning MMS 2003 as the glue between Active Directory, AD/AM, and any other information repositories you may need to provision or extract data from.

The challenge with MMS 2003 is the fundamental issue behind metadirectories: they can be difficult to set up and configure. Other options exist to solve the provisioning problem. If you have in-house programming expertise or can hire contractors, you can write automation scripts that can provision data and accounts between systems. Programming with LDAP is not very complicated, and using ADSI is even easier. Going this route has its own challenges, such as the need for solid expertise and a good idea of exactly what you want to build, so in the long run a metadirectory may be more appealing.

MMS 2003 comes in two flavors, both requiring Windows Server 2003 Enterprise Edition: MMS 2003 Standard Edition and MMS 2003 Enterprise Edition.

The Standard Edition was made available as a free download from Microsoft's web site soon after Windows Server 2003's launch. It requires MSDE, SQL Server 2000 Standard Edition, or SQL Server 2000 Enterprise Edition as its database store, and supports AD, AD/AM, and Exchange Server 2000/2003 only. This version is meant to help you with compatibility between these core directories only. Standard edition enables easy and secure, synchronization and provisioning of identity information across multiple Active Directory forests, Exchange 2000/2003 implementations for GAL synchronization or with Active Directory/Application Mode installations.

The Enterprise Edition is a paid-for product from Microsoft, and requires SQL Server 2000 Enterprise Edition as its database store. This edition supports AD, AD/AM, DSML 2.0, XML, CSV files, text files, Exchange, LDIF, Lotus Notes/Domino v4.6/ v5.0, Sun/iPlanet/Netscape directory 4.x/5.x, SQL Server 7.0, SQL Server 2000, Oracle, IBM DB2, Windows NT4, Novell NDS/DirXML, SunOne, Critical Path Meta-Connect/X.500, and more. A significant number of partners also provide connectivity for other corporate repositories and directories like SAP.

The major changes since MMS 2.2 are as follows:

- MMS 2.2 Zstore replaced by SQL Server 2000 for the database store to aid performance, scalability, failover clustering, and the like.
- MMS 2.2 Zscript replaced by any .NET language for scripting purposes.
- MMS 2003 now supports unicode and double-byte character sets.
- MMS 2003 now supports self-service and helpdesk password management and resetting to enable those operations to be performed much more easily.
- MMS 2003 now is integrated with WMI for the first time.

There is a lot inside MMS that administrators have not been aware of simply due to the restricted nature of MMS 2.2's distribution. We encourage you to go and take a look in detail at MMS for your organization to see where it might be useful. More details can be found on Microsoft's web site by searching for MMS or Microsoft Metadirectory Services, or try here: *http://www.microsoft.com/mms/*.

Active Directory's Role

Under Microsoft's current direction, the role of Active Directory has been reduced, but its importance has by no means been lessened. Active Directory's primary purpose is that of a NOS directory, as which its main function is to authenticate and authorize clients so they can access directory and network resources. In some cases, applications may still want to integrate directly with Active Directory as opposed to using an application directory such as AD/AM. Since Exchange 2000 is so dependent on the directory store and ties heavily into AD resources such as users, groups, and contacts, it may make sense to keep it integrated directly with Active Directory as opposed to AD/AM. Thus, while the general trend will be to move to AD/AM in the application space, some applications will still need tight integration with Active Directory. Regardless, AD/AM will alleviate a lot of the pressure to integrate all applications with Active Directory and therefore allow you to maintain tight control in your NOS environment.

Interoperating with Other Directories

Now that we've covered what Microsoft is doing with their directory products, let's review some of the issues around integrating a mixed directory environment. As we mentioned earlier, supporting multiple directories within a large organization is a necessary practice. You may already have several directories deployed, some of which are not Microsoft-based. A common question in this scenario is how to get your directories to work together.

Getting Data from One Directory to Another

Perhaps the most common use of a directory is to access employee, customer, or student information. One of the problems of supporting multiple directories is that for each directory to be useful, it needs to store similar data. It would be very helpful if there were a standard RFC that defined a replication scheme for LDAP directories, but unfortunately there is not. As a result, each directory vendor has implemented their own way to replicate data between servers. This is where metadirectories come into play. The primary purpose of a metadirectory is to facilitate data flow and provisioning across systems. If you have several directories, and writing your own scripts to replicate data is not a possibility, implementing a metadirectory is a valid option.

Using Common Tools Across Directories

One of the biggest reasons for not wanting to implement multiple directories is that they have to be managed differently. Fortunately, both Active Directory and AD/AM are based on LDAP, so any of the standard LDAP SDK tools such as *ldapsearch* and *ldapadd* will work. Also, the Microsoft LDP tool, a graphical user interface for querying and managing content in Active Directory, has become very popular. LDP is an LDAP-based tool and works against any LDAP directory. The same cannot be said for tools such as ADSI Edit and the Active Directory administrative snap-ins, which works only with Active Directory.

One popular approach for managing content in SunONE and OpenLDAP directories is to use the LDAP Data Interchange Format (LDIF). LDIF has a strict format that is both human- and machine-readable, but it is easy to work with. Microsoft provides the LDIFDE program on the Windows Server platforms, which allows for importing and exporting LDIF files. You can also use an LDIF-based tool on a non-Windows platform to manage content in Active Directory.

Porting Scripts to Work Across Directories

The story for porting scripts is much the same as the one for using similar tools for managing different directories. Most directories today are LDAP-based, so if your scripts are using an LDAP API, they should work regardless of what directory is being used. That said, there are some fairly significant differences with how Active Directory was implemented that may cause problems in your scripts. Most LDAP directories, including AD/AM, have a flat namespace. That means you can make a single query to a server and retrieve all objects the server knows about. With Active Directory, it is a little different in multidomain environments. When you implement multiple domains, you are essentially segregating your LDAP namespace. A domain controller knows about only the objects in its domain. For this reason, Microsoft designed the Global Catalog so that you can perform a single query to search against all objects in a forest, but the GC contains only a subset of information for all objects. The impact to scripts may be less than obvious, but to perform a query such as retrieving all attributes for any user in the forest that has a department equal to "Sales", you first must query the GC. To then retrieve all defined attributes for each user, you have to run separate queries against the domains the users are in. The other option is to skip the GC and query the domains individually, but regardless this simple task can require several queries.

Making Searches Across Directories Seamless

If you foresee supporting multiple directories, you might have the notion of trying to unify the namespace used by each. So perhaps your Active Directory root is dc=mycorp,dc=com and you have an OpenLDAP server that has a root at dc=apps,dc=mycorp,dc=com. You can create referral objects using the crossRef objectclass so that a query for dc=apps,dc=mycorp,dc=com against an Active Directory domain controller will refer the client to an OpenLDAP server. The LDIF representation of the referral object looks like the following, where nCName is the name of the partition and dNSRoot is the hostname to refer clients too:

```
dn: cn=OpenLDAP,cn=Partitions,cn=Configuration,dc=mycorp,dc=com
objectclass: crossRef
nCName: dc=apps,dc=mycorp,dc=com
dNSRoot: openldap.mycorp.com
```

An issue with using referrals to access data in different directories is that clients from each directory typically can't authenticate in each. Unless you are synchronizing user accounts and passwords between directories or you allow anonymous binds, when the referral passes to the OpenLDAP server, the query will fail due to a logon failure.

Integrating Applications and Services

Many applications rely on a directory to access user information and store application data. Since Active Directory was Microsoft's first true directory offering, many application vendors attempted to integrate their products into it, only to find there were a lot of issues from both technology and political perspectives. We'll now discuss some of these challenges.

The Application Integration Challenge

While trying to use Active Directory as both a NOS and application directory can initially reap significant rewards from reduced total cost of ownership, it also presents several challenges as well. In fact, many of the features that make Active Directory a great NOS directory (a repository of user, group, and computer accounts) also make integrating applications much more difficult.

Challenges for application vendors

Many of the challenges for application vendors are related more to incompatibilities with integrating with the NOS than directly to insufficiencies with Active Directory. In fact, Active Directory could be used as a pure application directory with few differences from what you would see using a SunONE or OpenLDAP directory server. But that is not how Active Directory is typically being used in the enterprise. In fact, most organizations are still trying to balance the effects of maintaining a stable NOS environment that has consistent reliability and response times with an application directory that could impact the end-user experience with increased server load and directory bloat.

We have seen numerous vendors struggle with trying to integrate products with Active Directory, especially on their first attempt. Most companies do not have a lot of Active Directory or even LDAP expertise, so they make do with what they have, which often results in poorly integrated applications. In fact, it is not sufficient for vendors to have just LDAP expertise, because Active Directory has many features, such as the Global Catalog, never seen in any other directory server product. Often vendors gain the expertise they need only after they have struggled through the painful experiences of several customers that have deployed their product. Some of the major issues application vendors face are described in the following list.

Hierarchical structure
> One of the biggest roadblocks for applications using Active Directory is accessing data in a multidomain model. Most medium- to largescale Active Directory implementations use multiple domains to segregate data, regulate administrative access, limit exposure during disaster recovery situations, and reduce the amount of data that replicates between domain controllers. Typically, the domains are spread across geographic and sometimes organizational boundaries. Figure 17-1 illustrates an example of a simple geographic domain structure that is commonly used.

> Before Active Directory, most directory-enabled applications could rely on a flat namespace. A single query could search against all objects in the directory. In a multidomain model, it is not that easy. To help combat this problem, Microsoft introduced the Global Catalog. In a lot of situations, the data available in the Global Catalog may be sufficient for applications, but often it is not. If more data is needed for an object than what is provided by the Global Catalog, a sec-

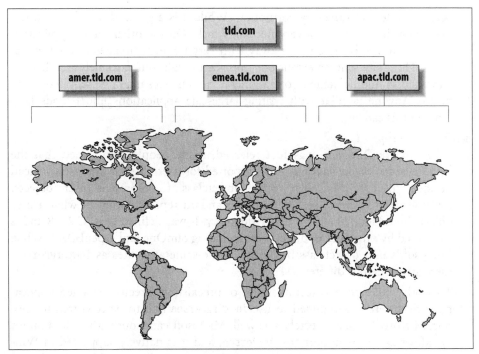

Figure 17-1. Typical geographic domain model

ond search must be done against a domain controller that is authoritative for the domain the object is in. This can result in many more queries than are needed when searching a flat namespace.

Multimaster replication

A common problem faced by nearly all distributed applications using Active Directory is how to handle multimaster replication. Active Directory is loosely consistent, which means that at no point can you assume that all updates have replicated to all domain controllers. As a rule of thumb, the best thing a directory-enabled application can do is to not assume that updates made to the directory are immediately available unless the same server being queried was used for the updates. In some environments it can take several hours or even days for updates to replicate to all domain controllers.

Schema extensions

Applications that want to publish data in Active Directory generally need to make schema extensions. The base schema provided by Active Directory contains a lot of classes and attributes, but for anything other than the most trivial application, customized extensions will need to be developed. Updating the Active Directory schema is a very sensitive operation, and Microsoft has done a good job of communicating the need to have a strict schema update policy. In some cases, we've even heard of administrators refusing to extend the schema because of fear of directory corruption. While it is a good idea to be cautious, extending the schema is a very necessary task. On the other hand, application vendors will not be able to get away with very frequent updates of their extensions. Thus, any schema extensions must be thought out extremely well beforehand and should be flexible so that only minor changes might be required in the future. Anyone familiar with writing largescale applications understands how difficult this can be.

inetOrgPerson support

When Active Directory was first released, many people complained that the inetOrgPerson objectclass was not supported for user objects. Microsoft instead decided to use their own user objectclass to represent user objects. inetOrgPerson is the closest thing to a standard representation of what a user object should look like in an LDAP directory. It was defined in RFC 2798 and is supported by other LDAP directories, including SunOne and OpenLDAP. While Microsoft's user objectclass has many of the same attributes as inetOrgPerson, there are numerous differences.

To work with Active Directory, a lot of preexisting directory-enabled applications that were programmed to use inetOrgPerson had to be rewritten to support Microsoft's user objectclass as well. Microsoft came out with an add-on for Windows 2000 to support inetOrgPerson, and it is natively supported in Windows 2003 Active Directory. Unfortunately, many applications have already had to be reworked to use Microsoft's user class, and it is unlikely that most administrators will want to switch to inetOrgPerson.

Service location

Typically, directory-enabled applications are developed to work against multiple directories, such as Active Directory, OpenLDAP, iPlanet, Novell, etc. For these types of applications, there is generally a configuration process to hardcode the directory server(s) to query. In an Active Directory environment that may be distributed to several locations globally, the application should use the closest server possible. It is possible to use Microsoft APIs to locate domain controllers dynamically, but this may not be acceptable if you are trying to write directory-neutral applications.

Challenges for Active Directory administrators

While application vendors have many challenges in writing well-behaved Active Directory–enabled products, administrators have a different set of challenges facing them. Most of the issues administrators face can be addressed by developing well-defined and documented processes for how applications will be used in Active Directory. Many of the problems become increasingly difficult as the number of applications being supported grows. Some of the major issues administrators face are described in the following list:

Application engagement and testing

All enterprise Active Directory environments should use a development or test forest for testing applications before moving them into production. As stated earlier, many of the Active Directory–enabled products on the market have serious flaws with how they are integrated with Active Directory. It is extremely important to put an application through its paces in a development forest not only to identify issues that may cause problems in your production environment, but also to understand how the application uses Active Directory.

The other important aspect of testing is having a well-defined application engagement process. Groups that want to integrate their applications with Active Directory need a starting place for engaging your Active Directory team. However you choose for users to start the engagement process, you should document information about each application, including name, contacts, description, directory usage, etc. It is also beneficial to publish guidelines for how to request application account(s), perform load testing, and request consulting services if needed.

If not already apparent, having an application engagement process requires significant resources to support. Someone has to interact with the application groups and support them as they move their application from the test forest to production. The support burden is even more significant for applications that write data to Active Directory since the schema will need to be extended. Those types of applications typically are more complex and thus require a greater understanding of the interaction with Active Directory.

Application accounts

Most Active Directory implementations will not have anonymous access enabled. It is generally not a good idea to allow anonymous access, especially when Active Directory is assuming both the NOS and application directory roles. That means applications need to bind or authenticate to access directory data. Each application needs to have a user account in which to bind. Using a separate account perapplication is typically a good idea because it is much easier to track down problems if only a single application is using an account. Some of these problems may include account lockout because of failed bind attempts or directory spamming due to unoptimized or buggy LDAP queries.

Another issue that must be stressed regarding application accounts is password expiration. Requiring passwords to be changed on a periodic basis is a good practice for user accounts, but it can be difficult to implement for application accounts. This is a significant issue when dealing with accounts that run as a service, which are constantly logged on. It can be extremely difficult to ensure that each logged-on instance of the account is using the correct password when the password has been changed.

One possible workaround to this problem is to use dual accounts. Instead of using one account per application, you could use two. When a password needs to be rotated, instead of changing the account password and making sure all instances of the application are using the new password, you instead change the application to use a different account. At that point, the original account's password can be changed and used during the next iteration. As long as the second account has all the same privileges as the first, using dual accounts can be much easier to implement and lacks the synchronization problem with changing passwords of a single account.

Directory bloat

Any application that needs the schema extended will be storing data in Active Directory. Over time, as more and more applications store data in Active Directory, the AD DIT (Directory Information Tree) file will grow. Although Active Directory is orders of magnitude more scalable than Windows NT when it comes to the amount of data that can be stored, it is crucial to put processes in place to clean out unused data from existing and decommissioned applications. If provisions are not put in place to do this, you may run into issues with storage on your domain controllers or even performance degradation in queries to the directory.

Application conflicts

As you support more applications in Active Directory, the chance for applications to conflict with one another increases. In some cases, applications have had conflicting schema extensions, which could result in serious incompatibilities. It could also be a problem if a particular application is not well behaved and overloads a domain controller, effectively causing a denial of service for other applications that are trying to use it as well.

AD/AM to the rescue

Fortunately, there is a solution to most of these issues. AD/AM allows you to segregate your NOS and application directory needs across different servers. We'll quickly review each of the challenges discussed previously to see whether AD/AM will help:

Hierarchal structure

AD/AM does not have the concept of a domain, so this isn't inherently a problem. You can set up a hierarchal structure across several AD/AM servers, but it is not required.

Multimaster replication

AD/AM supports multimaster replication, so this will continue to be an issue that application vendors will need to be cognizant of.

Schema extensions

Since AD/AM has its own schema, you can make extensions without impacting Active Directory.

inetOrgPerson support

AD/AM fully supports the inetOrgPerson class.

Service location
> This continues to be an issue, and, due to the fact that AD/AM doesn't support SRV records, administrators will have to use other means for distributing load across servers.

Application engagement and testing
> If you are using AD/AM, you do not have to be as concerned about the impact it will have on Active Directory, and you will not require testing to be as strenuous.

Application accounts
> If you have a business need to allow anonymous access to your directory, you can set that up with AD/AM and have much less risk than you would with Active Directory.

Directory bloat
> By using AD/AM, you can reduce the amount of data stored in Active Directory and the eventual bloat that results.

Application conflicts
> With AD/AM, application conflicts occur only if you are allowing multiple applications to use the same instance. While an errant application can affect the availability of an AD/AM instance, it will not necessarily hurt your NOS performance.

While AD/AM may not solve all the problems, it does provide a lot more flexibility and options for setting up a Microsoft-based directory environment.

Integrating Unix

Most people consider integrating a directory service with applications that need to query employee or customer data to be a no-brainer, but what about your Unix infrastructure? The term "single sign-on" has been buzzing around the industry for many years, but few have to come to realize it. Most have not been able to achieve even reduced sign-on. If reduced sign-on is your goal, and your Active Directory contains a username and password for everyone in your organization, it makes sense to collapse as many authentication repositories as possible. This may include attempting to eliminate the authentication services provided by your Unix infrastructure, such as NIS. There are several aspects of integrating Unix with Active Directory, and we'll review them now.

Kerberos and LDAP support

Long before Active Directory supported Kerberos, it was a mainstay in the Unix environment. While many were initially perturbed by Microsoft's extension of Kerberos, primarily because of the lack of documentation, you can use a standard MIT Kerberos client to get a ticket from an Active Directory KDC.

Another benefit of Active Directory supporting standards such as LDAP is that you can use the traditional LDAP tools, such as *ldapsearch*, to query and update Active Directory from a Unix platform. You can also use LDIF for query and update purposes along with any LDAPv3-compliant API, such as the C-style API or Java Naming and Directory Interface (JNDI).

Migrating from NIS

You have a couple of options for migrating away from Sun's Network Information System (NIS). First, there are two NIS gateways available that can act as NIS servers that backend to Active Directory. Microsoft Services For Unix 3.0 includes a NIS Server that can do just that and runs on a Windows server. PADL Software (*http://www.padl.com*) also has a NIS/LDAP gateway that can work with different directories, including Active Directory. The PADL gateway can run on a variety of Unix platforms.

Another option is to switch your Unix-based clients to support LDAP natively instead of continuing to use NIS. Luckily, most of the major Unix and Linux vendors provide support for LDAP, although each varies slightly. For more information on how to make Unix clients work with LDAP, check out *LDAP System Administration* by Gerald Carter (O'Reilly).

Integrating with NFS

With the NFS Server provided in Services for Unix 3.0, you can have a Windows server act as an NFS server. This means you can consolidate file servers in your environment by allowing both Unix and PC-based clients to use the same file server.

Synchronizing passwords

Microsoft's Services For Unix 3.0 provides password synchronization that allows you to sync passwords from Unix to Active Directory and viceversa. This means that if all you to do is ensure that your Unix users are using the same password as that in Active Directory, you can sync from AD to your Unix hosts. And if you use a Unix-based LDAP directory, such as SunONE, you can use Microsoft Metadirectory (MMS) to synchronize accounts and passwords.

Admittedly, we just barely touched on the subject of integrating Unix. It is a very broad topic and would take several chapters to adequately cover everything. Again, we highly recommend the *LDAP System Administration* book for more information on the topic.

Summary

Integrating applications into Active Directory is not an easy task. There are several potential pitfalls not only for Active Directory administrators but for application developers as well. Active Directory Application Mode (AD/AM), which is a light-weight version of Active Directory, should help relieve some of the burden from Active Directory as an application directory. Integrating Unix with Active Directory also has its challenges, but it is possible.

While integrating applications can be a challenge, getting competing directory services to interoperate is downright difficult. Even though most directory servers are based on standards-based RFCs, such as LDAP, there are no standards that define how they can replicate or authorize seamlessly with each other. The two best options for integrating multiple directories is either through a metadirectory, such as MMS, or a programming interface, such as ADSI or LDAP.

This concludes Part II. In Part III, we will cover many of the programmatic concepts and interfaces that can be used to automate and manage your Active Directory environment.

PART III

Scripting Active Directory with ADSI, ADO, and WMI

In the networks of today, companies can have tens of thousands of users on hundreds of servers in an organization that spans many sites. Managing complex systems can take a lot of time, and setting up the mechanisms to effect sensible management can be cumbersome.

Windows Server 2003 and Windows 2000 provide the administrator with a variety of tools to manage Active Directory. Unfortunately, these tools are no help for a variety of tasks that you may need to do en masse. No one in his right mind creates thousands of user accounts using the Active Directory Users and Computers snap-in. You can also manage and manipulate the Active Directory objects using scripts—and very powerful scripts at that. You can write scripts to manipulate any object and its properties, and you can port these scripts to the web, allowing administration through a browser interface.

Before we start, we want to state categorically that scripting Active Directory is easy. You don't have to know complex code algorithms, pointer structures, object class inheritance, or any of the weird world of complex program languages. Here we use Microsoft's VBScript language, a very simple language both to use and to understand. You should have no problem coming to this section with zero knowledge and being able to understand and implement the concepts behind the chapters in the section.

CHAPTER 18

Scripting with ADSI

This chapter covers the basics of ADSI and VBScript so that even inexperienced programmers and system administrators can understand how to write useful scripts. If you're used to another language, such as VB, you'll find that it is very easy to convert the ADSI examples from VBScript, which is covered in detail in Chapter 25. In Chapter 25 we also cover how to add VBScript code to HTML web pages so that you can write web applications that utilize ADSI. In Chapter 20, we show you how to use ADO to search Active Directory and retrieve sets of records according to the powerful search conditions that you impose. Other chapters take this knowledge and extend it so that you can manipulate other aspects of Active Directory, such as permissions and auditing (Chapter 23) and modifying the schema (Chapter 24). Several additional references to web pages containing further information and documentation are included at the end of this chapter, so that you can find more information.

What Are All These Buzzwords?

First, let's take a look at some of the underlying technologies that you'll use when developing scripts.

ActiveX

ActiveX, the base component of a number of these technologies, enables software components to interact with one another in a networked environment, regardless of the language in which they were created. Think of ActiveX as the method developers use to specify objects that the rest of us then create and access with our scripts in whatever language we choose. Microsoft currently provides three hosts that run scripts to manipulate ActiveX objects: the Internet Information Server (IIS) web server, the Internet Explorer (IE) web browser, and the Windows Scripting Host (WSH). IIS allows scripts called from HTML pages to run on the host server, and IE runs scripts called from HTML pages on the client. WSH allows scripts to run directly or remotely on a host from a command-line or GUI interface. WSH is an integral part of the Windows operating system.

Windows Scripting Host (WSH)

WSH is an important technology for a number of reasons:

- You need no other software to start scripting.
- The development environment for WSH has no special requirements to build or compile programs; your favorite text editor will do.
- You can execute any WSH script with a VBS, JS, or WSF extension just by double-clicking it.
- You can actually execute scripts from the command line, directing window output to that command line. This is possible because WSH has two interpreters, one called *wscript.exe*, which interprets scripts in the GUI Windows environment, and one called *cscript.exe*, which interprets scripts in the command-line environment of a *cmd.exe* session. By default, if you double-click a script called *myscript.vbs*, the system passes that script to *wscript.exe*, just as if you had manually typed `wscript.exe myscript.vbs`. The default interpreter can be changed generally or on a per-script basis along with other settings.
- WSH comes with a series of procedures that allow you to script interactions with the target machine. There are procedures for running programs, reading from and writing to the registry, creating and deleting files and shortcuts, manipulating the contents of files, reading and writing environment variables, mapping and removing drives, and adding, removing, and setting default printers. These procedures are native to WSH, meaning that only scripts executing under WSH can access them. Being able to access these settings is very useful when configuring users' environments, since you can now write logon scripts using VBScript or JScript if you wish.

 WSH comes bundled with Windows Server 2003, Windows XP, Windows 2000, and Windows 98, and it can be downloaded from *http:// www.microsoft.com/msdownload/vbscript/scripting.asp* and installed on Windows 95 and Windows NT 4.0 servers and workstations.

Active Server Pages (ASPs)

When a VBScript is wrapped inside an HTML page, it is called an Active Server Page (ASP) because it can contain dynamic (or active) content. This means that the web page displayed to the user differs depending on the results of a script incorporated as part of that web page. Imagine a web server connected to a database. You can write ASPs to contain server-side scripts that query the database and return the results to the user. You can also include client-side scripts to gather information from the user to pass with the query.

Active Directory Service Interfaces (ADSI)

In February 1997, Microsoft released a set of generic interfaces, called the Active Directory Service Interfaces (ADSI), to access and manipulate different directory services. ADSI is a collection of classes and methods that allow developers using any language that supports COM to access and manipulate objects on a server or in a directory service. Contrary to its name, it was written to be generic and extensible rather than specific to Active Directory. This means that developers can write code to access objects on various directory servers without the need to know vendor-specific library routines. ADSI is also extensible, so developers of other directory services can write the underlying Dynamic Link Library (DLL) code that will allow ADSI to interact with their systems. This is possible because Microsoft publishes the specifications that a directory service provider (code that implements the ADSI spec for a particular directory service) must meet to work correctly with ADSI. This means that whenever you call an ADSI procedure or reference any object via ADSI against a valid provider, you can guarantee that the procedure performs according to ADSI's formal documentation no matter who the provider is. While there are several directory service provider–specific extensions, ADSI also supports Lightweight Directory Access Protocol (LDAP), which provides the majority of functionality that most directory vendors need.

LDAP is a network protocol that is the primary mechanism for accessing directory services over TCP/IP, and it has become the de facto standard for directory service access on the Internet. A directory server simply has to support LDAP 2.0 or later, and ADSI can instantly access the directory service without a provider-specific DLL.

Natively supporting LDAP in ADSI means that the list of directory services that can be accessed is very large. For the older directories such as NT4, several vendors have written providers to support ADSI. The list of supported directory services includes the following:

- Active Directory
- Microsoft Exchange Server
- Windows NT 4.0 and NT 3.51 systems
- NetWare 3.x's bindery-based system
- NetWare and IntraNetware 4.x's and 5.x's Novell Directory Service (NDS)
- Netscape Commerce Server
- Netscape iPlanet/Sun ONE
- OpenLDAP
- IBM's Lotus Notes
- Microsoft's Internet Information Server (IIS) objects
- Microsoft Commercial Internet System's (MCIS's) Address Book Server
- Microsoft Site Server

ActiveX Data Objects (ADO)

In the same way that ADSI is a general set of interfaces to access and manipulate data in any directory service, ActiveX Data Objects (ADO) is a generic interface that allows developers to write scripts and applications to query and manipulate data held in a database server. For a database server to work with ADO, the database server vendor must develop an OLE DB provider. This is relevant to Active Directory because Microsoft wrote an OLE DB provider for ADSI. This allows developers to access Active Directory, or indeed any other directory service, via ADO. This provider effectively considers Active Directory a database and provides extremely fast and powerful searching capabilities. For example, using ADO, you can search Active Directory for all computers whose names begin with CF or all users whose accounts are disabled and get back the ADsPath of each one using a SQL-based query language. While it is possible to search and retrieve sets of records using standard ADSI calls, you would have to write your own set of routines to iterate through a directory service. When the developers of ADSI came to this requirement, they developed a provider so that the database searching algorithms that already existed in ADO could be leveraged for use by ADSI.

There is, however, one important caveat for ADO use with ADSI: the ADSI OLE DB provider is read-only even as of Windows Server 2003, so many of the useful ADO methods for updating data aren't available. Until this changes, you can use ADO only for searching and retrieving data.

Windows Management Instrumentation (WMI)

The Windows Management Instrumentation (WMI) API was developed by Microsoft in 1998 in response to the ever-growing need for developers and system administrators to have a common, scriptable API to manage the components of the Windows operating system. Before WMI, if you wanted to manage some component of the operating system, you had to resort to using one of the component-specific Win32 API's, such as the Registry API or Event Log API. Each API typically had its own implementation quirks and required way too much work to do simple tasks. The other big problem with the Win32 API's is that scripting languages such as VBScript could not use them. This really limited how much an inexperienced programmer or system administrator could do to programmatically manage systems. WMI changes all this by providing a single API that can be used to query and manage the Event Log, the Registry, processes, the filesystem, or any other operating system component. For more information on WMI, check out Chapter 26.

.NET and .NET Framework

Unless you've been hiding in a cave in recent years, you've undoubtedly heard of Microsoft's latest initiative, called .NET. At a high level, .NET is a move to embrace web technologies such as XML Web Services in an effort to better integrate Microsoft products and other third-party applications. At a low level, .NET is the basis for a new programming platform, including a completely new set of APIs, called the .NET Framework, to manage Microsoft-based products and develop Windows applications. Microsoft even released a new programming language in conjunction with .NET called C# (C-sharp). The .NET Framework is a new set of interfaces intended to replace the old Win32 and COM APIs. A couple of the major design goals for the .NET Framework were to make programming in a Windows environment much simpler and more consistent. The .NET Framework has two major components: the common language runtime (CLR) and the .NET Framework class library. For information on these technologies, check out Chapter 28.

Writing and Running Scripts

The third part of this book is dedicated to showing you techniques to access and manipulate Active Directory programmatically. It not only contains a plethora of useful scripts that you will be able to adapt for use in your organization, but it also contains a lot of information on how you can write your own scripts to access Active Directory to do whatever you need. Let's take a quick look at how to get started writing and running scripts.

A Brief Primer on COM and WSH

Since the release of Windows 2000, each operating system Microsoft has produced comes with a technology called the Windows Scripting Host, more commonly known as WSH, which allows scripts to execute directly on the client. WSH-based scripts can open and read files, attach to network resources, automate Word and Excel to create reports and graphs, automate Outlook to manipulate email and news, change values in the registry, and so on. The reason these scripts can be so versatile is that WSH supports scripting access to all Component Object Model (COM) objects installed on the client.

COM is a Microsoft technology that allows programmers to automate and manipulate virtually anything you require on a host by defining each host component as a set of objects. When someone needs to create or manage a new component on a Windows-based host, she creates a COM interface, which can be thought of as the definition of the object and the entire set of operations that can be performed on that object. Interfaces normally are stored in DLL files.*

---

* There are other file types, such as OCX controls that define graphical forms and windows you can use in your scripts, but they are beyond the scope of this book.

For example, if you want to manipulate a file, you actually need to manipulate a file COM object. The file COM object definition is stored in an interface held in a DLL. The interface also holds all of the operations, such as creating the file, deleting the file, writing to the file, and so on. The interface also defines a series of properties of the object, such as the filename and owner, which can be accessed and modified. Procedures that operate on an object are known as methods, whereas the properties of an object are known simply as properties.

In addition to methods and properties provided by interfaces, each scripting language that you use has a series of defined functions, such as writing to the screen or adding two numbers together.

You can write scripts that execute using WSH and access any COM objects available to you using the methods and properties defined in the interface for that object and any functions in your chosen scripting language. By default, you can use Microsoft VBScript or Microsoft JScript (Microsoft's version of JavaScript). WSH is fully extensible, so other language vendors can provide installation routines that update WSH on a client to allow support for other languages. A good example is PerlScript, the WSH scripting language that provides support for the Perl language.

How to Write Scripts

WSH scripts are simple to write. The following example is a very simple script written in VBScript and called *simple.vbs*:

```
MsgBox "Hi World!"
```

All you have to do is open up your favorite text editor type in the command, then save the file with a specific filename extension (VBS for VBScript or JS for JScript). Then you can double-click the script and it will run using WSH. Figure 18-1 shows the output of the script, which is a simple dialog box with a text string in it. The script uses the VBScript MsgBox function.

Figure 18-1. Output from a very simple script

Now let's take a look at a slightly more complex script called *simple adsi.vbs*. This script makes use of ADSI to display the description of a user.

```
Dim objUser 'A variable representing my user

Set objUser = _
```

```
GetObject("LDAP://cn=Richard Lang,ou=Pre-Sales,ou=Sales,dc=mycorp,dc=com")

MsgBox objUser.Description

Set objUser = Nothing
```

The first line is a variable declaration. We are declaring that objUser is the name for an object we are going to retrieve from Active Directory. The Dim keyword is used to declare a variable, and the apostrophe (') indicates that everything following it is a comment that will not be executed.

The second line is too long to print on the page, so we have broken it into two with an underscore (_) continuation character at the end of the line. It tells the interpreter that it should read the next line as if it were joined to the end of the first. The entire line, ignoring the underscore, uses the objUser variable to hold a reference to a user object via a call to VBScript's GetObject function, passing the ADsPath of the user.

The third line simply uses the VBScript MsgBox function again to print out the description of the Richard Lang user object. The dot signifies that we are accessing a property method available for the specific type of object we are accessing, which in this case is a user.

The last line simply discards the reference to Richard Lang, and objUser becomes empty again. Strictly speaking, at the end of a script, the system discards all references anyway, but we are including it for completeness.

As you can see, printing out properties of objects in Active Directory isn't very hard at all.

WSH 2.0 Versus 5.6

WSH 2.0 comes bundled with Windows 2000 and Windows 98, while WSH 5.6 comes bundled with Windows Server 2003 and Windows XP. WSH is also available for download for Windows 95 and Windows NT. Do not be alarmed by the dramatic increase in version numbers; 5.6 was the next major version after 2.0. In fact, for most people writing scripts, the differences between 2.0 and 5.6 are not significant enough to worry about. Version 5.6 offers a new security model and, perhaps most importantly, the ability to execute scripts remotely, but neither of these affects our ADSI-based scripts to a large extent.

As of WSH 2.0, two types of file formats are supported. The first is traditional script files, which contain pure VBScript or JScript and have a language-specific file extension (e.g., *.vbs*), and the second is Windows Script File (WSF), which has a *.wsf* extension.

WSF is actually an Extensible Markup Language (XML) file, with the scripting code embedded inside <script>...</script> tags which is then embedded in <job>...</job>

tags. The following example shows how the *simple.vbs* example would look using the WSF format:

```
<job>
<script language="VBScript">

MsgBox "Hello World"

</script>
</job>
```

The XML defines that the file contains a single script (a job) and that the script to be run is written in VBScript. At its simplest, to write WSF scripts instead the traditional script files, all you have to do is prefix your code with the first two lines and end your code with the last two lines, as shown here:

```
<job>
<script language="VBScript">

Dim objUser 'A variable representing my user

Set objUser = _
   GetObject("LDAP://cn=Richard Lang,ou=Pre-Sales,ou=Sales,dc=mycorp,dc=com")

MsgBox objUser.Description

Set objUser = Nothing

</script>
</job>
```

To keep the examples straightforward and the focus on scripting Active Directory, only the code will be shown and not the tags necessary to make a WSF file. You can then decide whether you want to utilize the WSF format or just use the traditional script file.

We also encourage you to find out more about WSH to fully utilize its capabilities. For more information on WSH, including advanced functionality and running scripts using WSF, check out *Windows Script Host Programmer's Reference* by Dino Esposito (Wrox Press) or Bob Wells' WSH articles in *Windows Scripting Solutions* (*http://www.win32scripting.com*). Finally, the WSH help file can be a very useful reference. It is available for download at *http://msdn.microsoft.com/scripting/*.

ADSI

Before you can start writing scripts that use ADSI, you first need to understand the basic COM concept of interfaces and ADSI's concepts of namespaces, programmatic identifiers (ProgIDs), and ADsPaths.

Objects and Interfaces

A COM interface defines the properties associated with an item, how to access those properties, and how to access specific functionality of the item, more commonly referred to as an object. For example, WSH has a number of objects that represent files, shortcuts, network access, and so on. ADSI provides a specification for interfaces that each directory service provider must implement to maintain uniformity. Each ADSI interface normally supports methods that can be called to perform a specific action, and properties (or property methods) to retrieve information about the object.

A method is a procedure or function that is defined on an object and interacts with the object. So an interface to access Active Directory group objects would have Add and Remove methods, so that members could be added or removed from a group. Methods are normally represented as Interface::MethodName when referenced, and this is the form we adopt in this book. Objects also have properties that are retrieved using the IADs::Get or IADs::GetEx methods and set or replaced using the IADs::Put or IADs::PutEx methods.

Each ADSI object supports an IADs interface that provides six basic pieces of information about that object:

Name
> Relative name for the object (RDN in the case of Active Directory)

ADsPath
> Unique identifier for object

GUID
> 128-bit Globally Unique Identifier of object

Class
> Objectclass of the object

Schema
> ADsPath to the objectclass of the object

Parent
> ADsPath to the parent object

If you wanted to retrieve the GUID property of an object, you would use the following:

```
strGUID = objX.Get("GUID")
```

You can see that we are calling the IADs::Get method on the object called objX; the dot (.) indicates the invocation of a property or method. The IADs::Get method takes as its one parameter the property to retrieve, which in this case is the GUID, and passes it out to a variable that we have called strGUID. So that you do not have to use the IADs::Get method for the most common properties, certain interfaces define these common properties with property methods. In these specific cases, you use the dotted method notation to retrieve the property by using the property method of the same name. In the previous GUID example, the GUID property has a property method of the same name (i.e., IADs::GUID). We could therefore retrieve the GUID with:

```
strGUID = objX.GUID
```

We won't go into the interfaces in any more depth here; we just want to give you a feel for the fact that methods and properties can be accessed on an object via ADSI interfaces. Although an object can support more than one interface without a problem, each object supports only the interfaces that are relevant to it. For example, the user object does not support the interface that works for groups. The other interfaces, of which there are around 40, begin with the prefix IADs. Interfaces can relate to many different types of objects, including objects that reside in directory services (e.g., IADsUser and IADsGroup), transient objects that don't exist in a directory service (e.g., IADsPrintJob), and security-related objects (e.g., IADsOpenDSObject and IADsAccessControlList). Note that not all objects have a specific IADs interface that applies its objectclass (e.g., IADsUser), so in those cases you have to use the more generic IADs or IADsContainer interfaces.

Because each directory service is slightly different, not every ADSI interface method and property works in every directory service. If you make a method call to a directory service that doesn't support that method, you'll receive an error message specifying that the provider doesn't support that method. According to the ADSI specification, each service provider must reject inappropriate calls with the correct ADSI error message.

Namespaces, ProgIDs, and ADsPaths

To reference different types of servers (e.g., Windows NT 4.0, NetWare, etc.) with ADSI, you must use the namespaces that correspond to the ADSI providers used by that directory service. ADSI uses a unique prefix called a ProgID to distinguish between these namespaces. Each ProgID is synonymous with a particular namespace and directory provider.

In a script, you specify the ProgID, which is used behind the scenes to correctly connect and bind to the corresponding directory service. For example, you specify WinNT:// to access individual Windows NT 3.51, 4.0, Windows 2000, and Windows Server 2003 systems; you use LDAP:// to access Active Directory and other LDAP directories. When ADSI encounters the ProgID, ADSI loads an appropriate ADSI-provider DLL to correctly process the bind request and method invocations.

 ProgIDs are case-sensitive. WinNT:// will work, whereas WINNT:// will not.

Since each ProgID is synonymous with a particular namespace, the term ProgID usually is dropped. For example, individual systems are accessed using the PRogID WinNT:. However, conventionally, this namespace is referred to as the *WinNT namespace* rather than the *WinNT ProgID*. This is the convention adopted in the book.

This references JoeB, a user on computer MOOSE in WORKGROUP:

    WinNT://WORKGROUP/MOOSE/JoeB

This references JoeB, a user on computer MOOSE:

    WinNT://MOOSE/JoeB

As these examples show, you can reference each object by using only its name or, more properly, by using its name and type, if two or three identically named objects with different types exist.

Each namespace has a unique format for the ADsPath string, so you need to make sure that you're using the correct ADsPath notation. For example, each of these ADsPaths references a unique object.

This ADsPath references JoeB, a user in DOMAIN:

    WinNT://DOMAIN/JoeB, User

This next one references JoeB, a user in the Finance Organizational Unit (OU) within the Mycorp organization of the IntraNetWare tree called MyNetWareTree:

    NDS://MyNetWareTree/O=MYCORP/OU=FINANCE/CN=JoeB

This one references JoeB, a NetWare 3.x or 4.x (bindery services) user that exists on server *MYSERVER:*

    NWCOMPAT://MYSERVER/JoeB

Finally, this one references the WWW service component of IIS running on the local host:

    IIS://localhost/w3svc/1

In the preceding examples, NDS: refers to IntraNetWare 5.x and 4.x. (Because IntraNetWare 5.x is LDAP-compliant, you also can use LDAP paths with it.) NWCOMPAT: refers to NetWare 4.x, 3.2, 3.12, and 3.11 servers in bindery-emulation mode. IIS: refers to metabase paths on a host running IIS 3.0 or later.

One of the most commonly used namespaces is the LDAP namespace. You can use LDAP with ADSI to access a variety of directory services, including Active Directory. Although you can use the WinNT namespace to access Active Directory, you need to use the LDAP namespace to fully utilize all of ADSI's methods and properties. For this reason, our primary focus will be on the LDAP namespace.

You can use several formats to refer to LDAP directories. For example, all the following ADsPaths reference the Administrator object within the Users container of the *moose* directory server in the *mycorp.com* zone:

```
LDAP://cn=administrator,cn=users,dc=mycorp,dc=com
LDAP://moose.mycorp.com/cn=administrator,cn=users,dc=mycorp,dc=com
LDAP://moose/cn=administrator,cn=users,dc=mycorp,dc=com
LDAP://DC=com/DC=mycorp/CN=Users/CN=Administrator
LDAP://moose.mycorp.com/DC=com/DC=mycorp/CN=Users/CN=Administrator
```

In these examples, CN stands for common name, and DC stands for domain component. These examples show that you can specify the LDAP namespace ADsPath going down or up the hierarchical Directory Information Tree (DIT). Most people have adopted the naming style used in the first three examples, where the most specific element of an object is used first. Also note that you can specify a fully qualified Domain Name System (DNS) server name after LDAP://, using a forward slash character (/) to separate the DNS server name from the rest of the path.

If a name includes some unusual characters, such as a forward slash or a comma, you can use double quotation marks ("/") or a single backslash (\) to specify that the character should be interpreted as part of the ADsPath itself. For example, if you have a user called AC/DC on the server, this is wrong:

```
LDAP://cn=ac/dc,cn=users,dc=amer,dc=mycorp,dc=com
```

This will interpret the path using cn=ac followed by dc followed by cn=users and so on. As dc on its own is not a valid part of the path, the ADsPath is invalid. Here are the correct paths:

```
LDAP://cn=ac\/dc,cn=users,dc=amer,dc=mycorp,dc=com
LDAP://"cn=ac/dc",cn=users,dc=amer,dc=mycorp,dc=com
```

Obviously, as the backslash is a special character, you would need to do the following for an object called cn=hot\cold:

```
LDAP://cn=hot\\cold,cn=users,dc=amer,dc=mycorp,dc=com
LDAP://"cn=hot\cold",cn=users,dc=amer,dc=mycorp,dc=com
```

The first specifies that the character following the first backslash is to be interpreted as part of the name, and the latter says to specify that the whole first name is a valid string.[*]

Retrieving Objects

Now that you know how to use ADsPaths to distinguish between different namespaces, we'll demonstrate how to establish a connection and authenticate to the server containing the directory service you want to access. Authenticating a connec-

---

[*] Unfortunately, the latter, while valid, will not work with VBScript's GetObject function due to the extra quotation marks ("/").

When to Use the LDAP and WinNT Namespaces

Contrary to popular belief, the fact that WinNT namespace is used to access Windows NT servers does not mean it is of little use to Windows 2000 and Windows Server 2003. Actually, while the LDAP namespace is used to access Active Directory, the WinNT namespace is used to access users, groups, and other objects on individual computers. Active Directory only exists on DCs in your forest. If you have a server or client that is a member of a workgroup or domain, that machine also has objects on it. These could be local users, such as Administrator or Guest, printers, shares, and so on. Obviously, these objects are not part of Active Directory if they are unique to the machine. As individual machines do not support direct access via LDAP, you have to use the WinNT namespace.

tion isn't always necessary; some directories, such as Active Directory, can allow anonymous read-only access to certain parts of the directory tree if you configure it that way. In general, allowing anonymous access is not a good practice. It can make things much more difficult to troubleshoot if you discover that one of your domain controllers is being impacted by an overzealous client. When using ADSI, if authentication is not done explicitly, the credentials of the account the script is running under will be used. If the account running the script is not part of the Active Directory you want to query or in a trusted domain, you will not be able to do very much. That's why performing explicit authentication in ADSI scripts is generally the best way to go.

If you just want to use the current account's credentials to bind to a directory server to get a reference to an object, use the GetObject function:[*]

```
Dim strPath       'path to the directory server
Dim objMyObject   'root object of the directory

strPath = "LDAP://dc=amer,dc=mycorp,dc=com"

Set objMyDomain = GetObject(strPath)
```

The code begins by declaring two variables with VBScript Dim statements. The first variable, strPath, is an ADsPath. The prefix str specifies that this ADsPath is a text string; see the sidebar about typical VBScript naming conventions. The second variable, objMyDomain, is a pointer to the object in the directory that the ADsPath represents. The prefix obj specifies that the variable is an object.

---

[*] Visual Basic and JScript also have the GetObject function.

Next, we assign the strPath variable to the path of the directory server we want to bind to, in this case, LDAP://dc=amer,dc=mycorp,dc=com. You need to enclose this path in quotation marks, because it's a text string.

Finally, we use VBScript's Set statement with the GetObject method to create a reference between the variable we declared and the existing object we want to interact with. In this case, we're creating a reference between objMyObject and the existing object that the ADsPath LDAP://dc=amer,dc=mycorp,dc=com represents (i.e., the domain object of the *amer.mycorp.com* domain). After we've established this reference, we can use other IADs-based interfaces to interact with that object.

Variable Prefix Conventions

You can use whatever name you like for a variable. However, the consensus is to use a prefix with a descriptive name. The prefix, which represents the type of data, typically contains one lowercase character or three lowercase characters. Commonly used three-character prefixes include:

- str = string
- int = integer
- bol = boolean
- obj = object
- arr = array
- lgn = long integer
- sgl = single precision value
- dbl = double precision value

In the descriptive name, you capitalize the first letter of each word but don't put hyphens between words, for example: strMyPassword.

To explicitly authenticate to a directory server, use the IADsOpenDSObject interface, which contains only one method: OpenDSObject, which takes four arguments:

- ADsPath to authenticate to
- User DN or UPN to bind as
- User's password
- Additional security setting(s)

The following listing shows how to use IADsOpenDSObject::OpenDSObject to authenticate to a directory server. We begin by declaring three string variables (strPath, strUsername, and strPassword) and two object variables (objNamespaceLDAP and objMyObject):

```
Dim strPath              'path to authenticate to in the                directory
service
Dim strUsername          'DN of the username
Dim strPassword          'plain text password
Dim objNamespaceLDAP     'ADSI namespace object
Dim objMyObject          'root object of the directory

strPath = "LDAP://dc=amer,dc=mycorp,dc=com"
strUsername = "cn=Administrator,cn=Users,dc=amer,dc=mycorp,dc=com"
strPassword = "the password goes here in plain text"

Set objNamespaceLDAP = GetObject("LDAP:")
Set objMyObject = objNamespaceLDAP.OpenDSObject(strPath,strUsername,strPassword,0)
```

We then assign the strPath, strUsername, and strPassword variables the appropriate ADsPath, username, and password strings. The username string, which is also called the Distinguished Name (DN), references the username's exact location in the directory. A User Principal Name (UPN) can also be used in place of a DN. A UPN typically has the format of *username@ForestDnsName* (e.g., *administrator@mycorp.com*).

The strPath is used to authenticate to a specific point in Active Directory if you wish. This can be used if the user authenticating does not have permission to work at the root and has to authenticate further down the tree.

Next, we use a Set statement with GetObject to create a reference for the variable called objNamespaceLDAP. Notice that we're using "LDAP:" rather than strPath as an argument to GetObject. Using the LDAP namespace might seem unusual, but it is necessary so that in the next line, you can call the IADsOpenDSObject::OpenDSObject method on the LDAP namespace that ADSI returns. The last IADsOpenDSObject:: OpenDSObject argument is to specify any security settings that should be applied to the connection. When set to 0 or left blank, no security is enabled for the connection. That is typically not the optimal choice, considering that all traffic between client and server will be sent in plain text over the network.

The following two constants are important to use if at all possible:

ADS_SECURE_AUTHENTICATION (0x1)
> Negotiates with the server to use the most secure authentication possible. For the WinNT provider, NT LAN Manager (NTLM) will be used. For Active Directory, Kerberos is the first option with NTLM being used if Kerberos isn't available.

ADS_USE_ENCRYPTION/ADS_USE_SSL (0x2)
> Encrypts the data between client and server. SSL must be available on the target domain controller.

You use multiple constants by adding them together—i.e., (ADS_SECURE_ AUTHENTICATION + ADS_USE_ENCRYPTION) as they represent integer values. While these are defined constants, they cannot be used by name from VBScript. The entire set of values from the ADS_AUTHENTICATION_ENUM enumerated type can be found under the MSDN Library (*http://msdn.microsoft.com/library/*), by following this path: Networking and Directory Services → Active Directory, ADSI and Directory Services → SDK Documentation → Directory Services → Active Directory Service Interfaces → Active Directory Service Interfaces Reference → ADSI Enumerations → ADS_AUTHENTICATION_ENUM.

 We want to emphasize the importance of using encryption. If encryption is not used, anyone using a network sniffer such as NetMon on the network might be able to see the information being passed, including the username and password specified in the IADsOpenDSObject:: OpenDSObject call.

The following code is slightly modified from the previous example to show how to enable ADS_SECURE_AUTHENTICATION and ADS_USE_ENCRYPTION for a connection:

```
Const ADS_SECURE_AUTHENTICATION = 1
Const ADS_USE_ENCRYPTION        = 2

Dim strPath             'path to authenticate to in the directory service
Dim strUsername         'DN of the username
Dim strPassword         'plain text password
Dim objNamespaceLDAP    'ADSI namespace object
Dim objMyObject         'root object of the directory

strPath = "LDAP://dc=amer,dc=mycorp,dc=com"
strUsername = "cn=Administrator,cn=Users,dc=amer,dc=mycorp,dc=com"
strPassword = "the password goes here in plain text"

Set objNamespaceLDAP = GetObject("LDAP:")
Set objMyObject = objNamespaceLDAP.OpenDSObject(strPath, _
                             strUsername, strPassword, _
             ADS_USE_ENCRYPTION + ADS_SECURE_AUTHENTICATION)
```

While securing the connection to the domain controller is an important precaution to take, including an administrator's password in a script can obviously be pretty insecure. If you don't want to include plain-text passwords, you have several options. The first option is to assign a value to strPassword from the VBScript Input-Box function. The following listing shows this:

```
Const ADS_SECURE_AUTHENTICATION = 1
Const ADS_USE_ENCRYPTION        = 2

Dim strPath             'path to authenticate to in the directory service
Dim strUsername         'DN of the username
Dim strPassword         'plain-text password
Dim objNamespaceLDAP    'ADSI namespace object
Dim objMyObject         'root object of the directory

strPath = "LDAP://dc=amer,dc=mycorp,dc=com"
strUsername = "cn=Administrator,cn=Users,dc=amer,dc=mycorp,dc=com"
```

```
strPassword = InputBox("Enter the Administrator password","Password entry box")

Set objNamespaceLDAP = GetObject("LDAP:")
Set objMyObject = objNamespaceLDAP.OpenDSObject(strPath, _
                              strUsername, strPassword, _
              ADS_USE_ENCRYPTION + ADS_SECURE_AUTHENTICATION)
```

When you run the script, the InputBox prompts you to enter the administrator's password. However, the InputBox echoes the password in plain text while you type it into the password entry box, so this approach isn't terribly secure itself.

Three other options are secure. However, because VBScript doesn't natively support password retrieval boxes, you can't use these solutions without some work:

- One solution requires that you obtain a custom ActiveX component for VBScript to extend WSH's functionality to natively support password dialog boxes. One such control is available for by downloading the code from the *Windows Script Host Programmer's Reference* by Dino Esposito, which can be found at *http://www.wrox.com*.

- The second solution is to write a script in a language other than VBScript that supports password boxes natively. For example, you can use the Perl Tk modules to create an Entry widget with the -show parameter as an asterisk. For Perl aficionados, this Entry widget would look like this:

```
$dlg->Entry(qw/-show * -width 35/)->pack(); # arbitrary width
```

- The third solution requires that you write the script from within Active Server Pages (ASP). You use the password field in an ASP form to retrieve the password.

If you want to authenticate a connection but have already logged on to the directory, you can use the default credentials for your existing connection. You simply use the VBScript vbNullString constant in both the username and password fields, as the following listing shows:

```
Dim strPath             'path to authenticate to in the directory service
Dim objNamespaceLDAP    'ADSI namespace object
Dim objMyObject         'root object of the directory

strPath = "LDAP://dc=amer,dc=mycorp,dc=com"

Set objNamespaceLDAP = GetObject("LDAP:")
Set objMyObject = objNamespaceLDAP.OpenDSObject(strPath, vbNullString, _
  vbNullString,0)
```

Note the use of the underscore (_) character on the second to last line. This tells VBScript that we have split this line from the next, but it should treat them as one long line. You can use multiple underscores to concatenate multiple lines together in this manner.

From now on, most of the scripts will use GetObject for simplicity, but if you need to, you can just as easily use IADsOpenDSObject::OpenDSObject without modifying any of the other code.

Simple Manipulation of ADSI Objects

Let's now take a look at simple manipulation of Active Directory objects using ADSI. We are using Active Directory as the primary target for these scripts, but the underlying concepts are the same for any supported ADSI namespace and automation language. All the scripts use GetObject to instantiate objects, assuming you are logged in already with an account that has administrator privileges; if you aren't, you need to use IADsOpenDSObject::OpenDSObject as shown earlier in the chapter.

The easiest way to show how to manipulate objects with ADSI is through a series of real-world examples, the sort of simple tasks that form the building blocks of everyday scripting. To that end, imagine that you want to perform the following tasks on the *mycorp.com* Active Directory forest:

1. Create an Organizational Unit called Sales.

2. Create two users in the Sales OU.

3. Iterate through the Sales OU and delete each user.

4. Delete the Organizational Unit.

This list of tasks is a great introduction to how ADSI works because we will reference some of the major interfaces using these examples.

Creating the OU

The creation process for the Sales Organizational Unit is the same as for any object. First you need to get a pointer to the container in which you want to create the object. You do that using the following code:

```
Set objContainer = GetObject("LDAP://dc=mycorp,dc=com")
```

 While VBScript and VB have the GetObject function, VC++ has no such built-in function. ADSI provides the ADsGetObject function for use by those languages that need it.

Since we are creating a container of other objects, rather than a leaf object, you can use the IADsContainer interface methods and properties. The IADsContainer::Create method is used to create a container object, as shown in the following code:

```
Set objSalesOU = objContainer.Create("organizationalUnit","ou=Sales")
```

Here we pass two arguments to IADsContainer::Create: the objectclass of the class of object you wish to create and the Relative Distinguished Name (RDN) of the object itself. We use the ou= prefix because the type of object is an Organizational Unit. Most other objects use the cn= prefix for the RDN.

The IADsContainer interface enables you to create, delete, and manage other Active Directory objects directly from a container. Think of it as the interface that allows you to manage the directory hierarchy. A second interface called IADs goes hand in hand with IADsContainer, but while IADsContainer works only on containers, IADs will work on any object.

To commit the object creation to Active Directory, we now have to call IADs:: SetInfo:

```
objSalesOU.SetInfo
```

ADSI implements a caching mechanism in which object creation and modification are first written to an area of memory called the property cache on the client executing the script. Each object has its own property cache, and each cache has to be explicitly written out to Active Directory using IADs::SetInfo for any creations or modifications to be physically written to Active Directory. This may sound counterintuitive but in fact makes sense for a number of reasons, mostly involved with reducing network traffic. The property cache is discussed in more detail in Chapter 19.

Each object has a number of properties, some mandatory and some optional. Mandatory properties have to be defined during the creation of an object. They serve to uniquely identify the object from its other class members and are necessary to make the object usable in Active Directory. If you need to create an object with a large number of mandatory properties, it makes sense to write them all into a cache first and then commit them to Active Directory in one operation, rather than perform a sequence of SetInfo operations.

While the Organizational Unit example has no other mandatory properties, other objects do. User objects, for example, require sAMAccountName to be set before they can be written out successfully. In addition, you can also choose to set any of the optional properties before you use IADs::SetInfo.

Putting it all together, we have our first simple script that creates an OU:

```
Set objContainer = GetObject("LDAP://dc=mycorp,dc=com")
Set objSalesOU = objContainer.Create("organizationalUnit", "ou=Sales")
objSalesOU.SetInfo
```

Creating the Users

We now will move to the second task of creating a couple user objects. Creating user objects is not much different from creating an OU in the previous task. We use the same IADsContainer::Create method again as in the following:

```
Set objUser1 = objSalesOU.Create("user", "cn=Sue Peace")
objUser1.Put "sAMAccountName", "SueP"
```

```
objUser1.SetInfo

Set objUser2 = objSalesOU.Create("user", "cn=Keith Cooper")
objUser2.Put "sAMAccountName", "KeithC"
objUser2.SetInfo
```

The IADs::Put method is used here to set the SAM Account Name, a mandatory attribute that has no default value. The SAM Account Name is the name of the user as it would have appeared in previous versions of NT and is used to communicate with down-level NT domains and clients. It is still required because Active Directory supports accessing resources in down-level Windows NT domains, which use the SAM Account Name.

It is also worth pointing out that the IADs::SetInfo calls can be put at the end of the script if you want to. As long as they go in the right order (i.e., the OU must exist before the user objects within that OU exist), the following works:

```
Set objContainer = GetObject("LDAP://dc=mycorp,dc=com")
Set objSalesOU = objContainer.Create("organizationalUnit", "ou=Sales")

Set objUser1 = objSalesOU.Create("user", "cn=Sue Peace")
objUser1.Put "sAMAccountName", "SueP"

Set objUser2 = objSalesOU.Create("user", "cn=Keith Cooper")
objUser2.Put "sAMAccountName", "KeithC"

objSalesOU.SetInfo
objUser1.SetInfo
objUser2.SetInfo
```

This works because the property cache is the only thing being updated until the SetInfo call is issued. Since ADSI works against the property cache and not Active Directory directly, you could put off the SetInfo calls until the end of your scripts. There is no special benefit to doing scripts this way, and it can lead to confusion if you believe incorrectly that properties exist in the underlying service during later portions of the script. In addition, if you bunch up cache writes, and the server crashes, none of your writes will have gone through, which I suppose you could see as a good thing. However, we will not be using this method; we prefer to flush the cache as soon as feasible. Bunching caches to write at the end of a script encourages developers to neglect proper error checking and progress logging to a file from within scripts.

Tearing Down What Was Created

As you've seen, creating objects is a breeze with ADSI. Deleting objects is also very straightforward. Let's iterate through the Sales OU and deleting the two users we just created:

```
for each objUser in objSalesOU
  objUser.DeleteObject(0)
Next
```

We used a For Each loop to enumerate over the objects in objSalesOU. The objUser variable will get set to a reference of each child object in the Sales OU. We then use IADsDeleteOps::DeleteObject method to delete the object. The value 0 must be passed in to DeleteObject, but it does not hold any special significance (it is reserved for later use).

The final step is to delete the Sales OU using the same method (IADsDeleteOps::DeleteObject) that we used to delete users:

```
objSalesOU.DeleteObject(0)
Set objSalesOU = Nothing
```

The IADsDeleteOps::DeleteObject method can delete all the objects within a container, so it wasn't really necessary for us to delete each user object individually. We could have instead used DeleteObject on the Sales OU to delete the OU and all child objects within the OU. This method should be used with care since a lot of objects can be wiped out by using DeleteObject on the wrong container.

The Nothing keyword in VBScript is used to disassociate an object variable from any object. This prevents you from being able to use the variable later in your code. Setting the value of each object to Nothing may seem less than worthwhile when the script is due to end soon. However, you must get into this habit, and we can't stress its importance enough. After you have deleted an object from the underlying directory service, the property cache for that object still exists. If you do not remove the reference to it, and you use it again later, it refers to data that no longer exists. Trying to do a SetInfo (or a GetInfo, which is covered in the next chapter) on a deleted object's property cache generates a failure.

Further Information

This is by no means an in-depth discussion on ADSI. For more information, you should look at the Microsoft Developer Network (MSDN) library documentation, which contains all of the documentation on the specifics of VBScript, JScript, ADO, ADSI, and WSH. There are a few ways to get hold of the MSDN library: you can purchase an MSDN library subscription from Microsoft and get quarterly CDs with all of the documentation, or you can access the documentation directly via the Internet. MSDN online can be found at *http://msdn.microsoft.com/library/*. Once you enter the MSDN library from the CD-ROM or the Web, you will see a list of contents on the left-hand menu, which you can browse.

Table 18-1 lists some useful Internet sites to find additional information on the topics covered in this chapter.

Table 18-1. Useful Internet sites

Description	URL
Microsoft's main scripting web site	*http://msdn.microsoft.com/scripting/*
MSDN Library root	*http://msdn.microsoft.com/library/*
WSH docs	*http://msdn.microsoft.com/library/default.asp?url=/nhp/Default.asp?contentid=28001169*
Microsoft's universal data access components site (including the official pages for ADO)	*http://www.microsoft.com/data/*
A fantastic site for developers of ASP, ADSI, and ADO pages and scripts (including a superb ADSI mailing list)	*http://www.15seconds.com*
O'Reilly's Windows and VB sites detailing its resources and books	*http://windows.oreilly.com*
	http://vb.oreilly.com
Clarence Washington's repository for scripting solutions on the Internet	*http://cwashington.netreach.net*
Wrox publishes books on ADSI, ADO, VB, and WSH	*http://www.wrox.com*
Windows and .NET Magazine (formerly *Windows 2000 Magazine*) is published monthly, as is the Windows Scripting Solutions (formerly Win32 Scripting Journal), both of which provide a lot of good information on Active Directory and scripting	*http://www.winnetmag.com* *http://www.win32scripting.com*

Summary

Hopefully you now understand the basics of ADSI enough to be useful. It's a very robust API that allows you to interface to all aspects of both Active Directory and Windows NT, Windows 2000, and Windows Server 2003 servers. Even though the majority of this chapter covers Microsoft operating systems, the code does use the LDAP namespace and is portable to many other directory services. One of ADSI's biggest strengths is its ability to communicate with a variety of directory services using either LDAP or a provider-specific namespace.

In the next chapter, we will cover the IADs interface in more depth along with a discussion of the Property Cache. A chapter covering ADO will follow that, which should give you all the necessary tools to query and manipulate Active Directory.

CHAPTER 19

IADs and the Property Cache

Each object in a directory has a series of attributes, or properties, that uniquely define it. Although properties can vary from object to object, ADSI supports the manipulation of a core set of six properties common to all objects using the IADs interface. These properties are common to all objects because IADs is the most basic interface in ADSI.

The IADs Properties

The IADs properties are as follows:

Class
> The object's schema class

GUID
> The object's Globally Unique ID (GUID)

Name
> The object's name

ADsPath
> The ADsPath to the object in the current namespace

Parent
> The ADsPath to the object's parent

Schema
> The ADsPath to the object's schema class

Each of these properties has a corresponding property method in the IADs interface. You can use the property method, which has the same name as the property, to access that property's value. Example 19-1 contains code to display the six IADs properties for a user object.

Example 19-1. Using the explicit property methods to display the six IADs properties

```
Dim objUser 'An ADSI User object
Dim str     'A text string

` User object using the WinNT namespace
Set objUser=GetObject("WinNT://MYCORP/Administrator,User")
str = "Name: " & objUser.Name & vbCrLf
str = str & "GUID: " & objUser.GUID & vbCrLf
str = str & "Class: " & objUser.Class & vbCrLf
str = str & "ADsPath: " & objUser.ADsPath & vbCrLf
str = str & "Parent: " & objUser.Parent & vbCrLf
str = str & "Schema: " & objUser.Schema & vbCrLf & vbCrLf
Set objUser = Nothing

` User object using the LDAP namespace
Set objUser=GetObject("LDAP://cn=Administrator,cn=Users,dc=mycorp,dc=com")
Str = str & "Name: " & objUser.Name & vbCrLf
Str = str & "GUID: " & objUser.GUID & vbCrLf
Str = str & "Class: " & objUser.Class & vbCrLf
Str = str & "ADsPath: " & objUser.ADsPath & vbCrLf
Str = str & "Parent: " & objUser.Parent & vbCrLf
str = str & "Schema: " & objUser.Schema & vbCrLf & vbCrLf

WScript.Echo str

Set objUser = Nothing
```

To begin, we declare two variables (i.e., str and objUser), invoke the GetObject method to create a reference to the user object, and assign it to objUser. We then set the str variable to the string "Name:" and apply the IADs::Name property method (i.e., objUser.Name) to retrieve the Name property's value (i.e., Administrator). The carriage-return line-feed constant (vbCrLf) specifies to move to the start of a new line. At this point, str represents the string "Name: Administrator."

In the next line, we use the IADs::GUID property method (objUser.GUID) to retrieve the GUID property's value (i.e., {D83F1060-1E71-11CF-B1F3-02608C9E7553}). We are appending the GUID to previous value set in str so the new str represents the Name property value and the GUID property value. This was repeated until all six core properties in both the WinNT and the LDAP namespaces were retrieved.

You might be surprised to find out that enumerating properties in different namespaces produces different output, as Figure 19-1 shows. For example, the Name property under the LDAP namespace has "cn=" included, whereas the Name property under the WinNT namespace doesn't.

Both the code and the figure demonstrate another important point: The type of directory can affect the results. For example, using the IADs::Parent property makes sense when you're using the LDAP namespace to access a hierarchical directory such as Active Directory, because you can see parent-child relationships (e.g., you can see that the Users container is the parent for the Administrator User object). However,

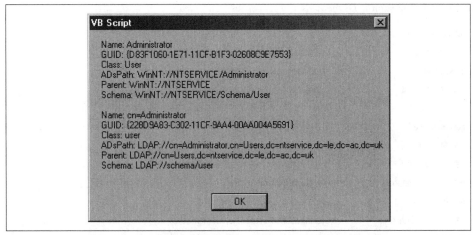

Figure 19-1. The IADs properties from the WinNT and LDAP namespaces

using the IADs::Parent property to look at NT's Security Accounts Manager (SAM) doesn't make sense where domains are concerned because the contents are all in one flat namespace.

Using IADs::Get and IADs::Put

While you can use property methods to access an object's properties, you can also use the IADs interface's IADs::Get and IADs::Put methods to retrieve any attribute on the object.

In other words, the following two sets of statements are equivalent:

```
strName = objUser.description
objUser.description = strName

strName = objUser.Get("description")
objUser.Put "description", strName
```

However, using the IADs::Get and IADs::Put methods is more of a performance hit as it involves internally doing a search for the property specified. Compared to this, the direct use of a property is what is known as a direct vtable binding per the COM documentation and is the faster of the two. IADs::Get and IADs::Put should be used only when a generic browser or program is written to work with any ADSI object. See Table 19-1 for the full set of methods and property methods for the IADs interface.

Table 19-1. The main IADs methods and properties

IADs methods and properties	Action
Get method	Retrieves a single item from the property cache
Put method	Sets a single item in the property cache
GetEx method	Retrieves a multivalued item from the property cache

Table 19-1. The main IADs methods and properties (continued)

IADs methods and properties	Action
PutEx method	Sets a multivalued item in the property cache
GetInfo method	Retrieves all of an object's properties into the property cache
GetInfoEx method	Retrieves one or more of an object's properties into the cache
SetInfo method	Writes out all the items in the property cache to the directory
get_Name method	Gets the name of the object[a]
get_GUID method	Gets the GUID of the object
get_Class method	Gets the schema class name of the object
get_ADsPath method	Gets the ADsPath of the object
get_Parent method	Gets the parent ADsPath of the object
get_Schema method	Gets the ADsPath of the object's schema class
Class property	Represents the Schema class of the object
GUID property	Represents the GUID of the object
Name property	Represents the name of the object
AdsPath property	Represents the ADsPath of the object
Parent property	Represents the ADsPath to the parent of this object
Schema property	Represents the ADsPath of the object's schema class

[a] A VC++ method. We won't include these in the future interface definitions, but they do serve as an example that VC++ does not support setting properties in a similar way to VBScript.

 Why Microsoft couldn't have named IADs::SetInfo PutInfo, or renamed IADs::Put and IADs::PutEx Set and SetEx for consistency is beyond us.

For example, the next script shows how you use IADs::Get and IADs::Put to retrieve, change, and return the mail property. After we set the objGroup variable to the pointer to the Managers group, we use the IADs::Get method (objGroup.Get) with the "mail" argument to retrieve the mail property's value. The WScript.Echo method displays the results in a window.

Changing the value and returning it to the property cache is just as simple. You use the IADs::Put method with the argument "mail". You don't put the argument in parentheses when you use the IADs::Put method: the method in a subprocedure, not a function, and it doesn't return a value. The string that follows the IADs::Put function contains the Managers group's new mail contact address. To write the new mail property to Active Directory, you use IADs::SetInfo:

```
Set objGroup = GetObject("LDAP://cn=Managers,ou=Sales,dc=mycorp,dc=com")
WScript.Echo objGroup.Get("mail")

objGroup.Put "mail", "agl1@mycorp.com"
objGroup.SetInfo
```

The Property Cache

Having looked at properties and property methods, let's take a look at the property cache, a location in memory on the local machine running the script that stores properties for objects. Each object that you bind to has a personal property cache; the OS creates this cache the instant the bind succeeds. However, the OS doesn't immediately populate the cache with values.

Accessing the Property Cache with Microsoft Visual C++

VC++ cannot use the same property method mechanism that automation languages like VBScript can use to get and set values in the property cache. Instead, Microsoft designed a variety of nonautomation interfaces, methods, and properties VC++ can make use of.

For example, when setting properties for a group, VC++ has access to the IADs::Get and IADs::Put methods in the same way that VBScript does. In addition, it also has access to the IADsGroup::get_Description and IADs::put_Description methods. This is because VC++ cannot use the IADs::Description property method. Code in VC++ would look like this using IADs::Put:

```
// Declare the variables
IADsGroup  *pGroup;
IADs       *pObject;
ADsGetObject(
  TEXT("LDAP://cn=Managers,ou=Sales,dc=mycorp,dc=com"),
  IID_IADsGroup,
  (void**) &pGroup);
// Set using IADs::Put method
pGroup->QueryInterface(IID_IADs,(void **) &pObject);
pObject->Put("Description",TEXT("My new group description goes here"))
pGroup->SetInfo;
```

Code in VC++ would look like this when using the IADsGroup::put_Description method:

```
// Declare the variables
IADsGroup  *pGroup;
IADs       *pObject;
ADsGetObject(
  TEXT("LDAP://cn=Managers,ou=Sales,dc=mycorp,dc=com"),
  IID_IADsGroup,
  (void**) &pGroup);
// Set using IADsGroup::put_Description property method
pGroup->put_Description(TEXT("My new group description goes here"));
pGroup->SetInfo;
```

When you use the IADs::Get method to retrieve an object's property, ADSI doesn't go to Active Directory to retrieve the value. Instead, ADSI reads the value from the property cache on the client executing the script. If ADSI doesn't find the property in the property cache when the call comes in, the system implicitly executes an IADs::GetInfo call to read all the properties for the current object into the cache. (You also can explicitly use the IADs::GetInfo method to populate the property cache with an object's properties.) The IADs::Get method then reads the appropriate value from the newly created cache.

Microsoft designed the property cache with efficiency in mind. The property cache lets you access an object's properties with a minimum number of calls, thereby minimizing network traffic. Retrieving all of an object's properties with one IADs::GetInfo call is more efficient than individually retrieving each property. Similarly, the process of writing all of an object's properties first to the cache and then to Active Directory with one IADs::SetInfo call is more efficient than writing each property individually to Active Directory.

Be Careful

The IADs::GetInfo and IADs::SetInfo methods are two of the most important methods you'll use. However, you need to be aware of two possible problems.

The first problem can arise if you try to access a property that doesn't have a value. For example, when you create a group object, the mail property doesn't automatically receive a value; you must provide a value, such as *agl1@mycorp.com*. When you use the IADs::GetInfo method, only those properties that have values appear in the property cache. Thus, if you don't give the mail property a value and you use IADs::GetInfo, the mail property value won't be in the property cache. If you try to access a property that doesn't exist in the cache, the script will give an empty value as the result.

 Later on we talk about navigating the property cache. If you want to see a good example of how this actually works, try this: create a new object of type group, which has around 21 properties set by the system by default. You then use IADs::GetInfo in a script and display the number of properties, and possibly their names, in a dialog box. Then set the description. Now, when you rerun the script, you will find that you have one more property in the cache than you did before the description. In other words, the description does not appear in the cache until you do an IADs::GetInfo after it has been set.

Another problem can arise if you forget to use IADs::SetInfo after modifying a property. For example, suppose you want to change the Managers group's mail property value and you create the script shown in Example 19-2.

Example 19-2. Making the mistake of forgetting the SetInfo call

```
Dim objGroup   'An ADSI group object

Set objGroup = GetObject("LDAP://cn=Managers,ou=Sales,dc=mycorp,dc=com")
```

Example 19-2. Making the mistake of forgetting the SetInfo call (continued)

```
'**********************************************************************
'Get and write the mail property value, which forces an
'implicit GetInfo call
'**********************************************************************
WScript.Echo objGroup.Get("mail")


'**********************************************************************
'Set the new mail address in the cache
'**********************************************************************
objGroup.Put "mail", "new-address@mycorp.com"


'**********************************************************************
'Use an explicit GetInfo call to again retrieve all items into the cache
'**********************************************************************
objGroup.GetInfo

WScript.Echo objGroup.mail
```

In Example 19-2, we set the objGroup variable to the pointer to the Managers group. To display the current mail property value in a window, we use the WScript::Echo method with the IADs::Get method, which forces an implicit IADs::GetInfo call. We then set the new value for the objGroup's mail property, after which we use an explicit IADs::GetInfo call to again retrieve all the object's properties into the cache. Finally, we use the WScript.Echo method to display the results in a window.

When you run the script, two windows pop up. To your dismay, both windows state the original value of the mail property, which means that the system didn't write the new mail address to Active Directory. This cache write didn't occur because you need to explicitly call the IADs::SetInfo method to write out data from the cache to Active Directory. To fix the script, you need to insert the line:

```
objGroup.SetInfo
```

between the line setting the new mail address and the line making the explicit IADs::GetInfo call.

More Complexities of Property Access: IADs::GetEx and IADs::PutEx

Using the IADs interface's IADs::Get method works well for properties with one value. However, some properties have multiple values, such as a user with several telephone numbers. If a property stores multiple values, you need to use the IADs interface's IADs::GetEx* and IADs::PutEx methods to retrieve and return the values.

---

* You also can use IADs::GetEx for single-value properties.

Using IADs::GetEx

The following script shows how to use IADs::GetEx. In this script, we pass the multiple-value property as an argument to the IADs::GetEx method. We then use a For Each...Next loop on the resulting list.

```
Dim objUser        'An ADSI user object
Dim arrPhoneList   'An array of phone numbers
Dim strPhoneNumber 'An individual phone number
Set objUser=GetObject("LDAP://cn=administrator,cn=Users,dc=mycorp,dc=com")
arrPhoneList = objUser.GetEx("telephoneNumber")
For Each strPhoneNumber In arrPhoneList
  WScript.Echo strPhoneNumber
Next
```

When we make the IADs::GetEx call, the system makes an implicit IADs::GetInfoEx call rather than an implicit IADs::GetInfo call to Active Directory. You can use an explicit IADs::GetInfoEx call to get one or more properties if you don't want to use IADs::GetInfo to get all the property values. However, few scriptwriters use IADs::GetInfoEx for this purpose, because they typically use implicit calls or use IADs::GetInfo to read all values into the property cache. In addition, if you use IADs::GetEx for every property retrieval rather than using IADs::GetInfo, your underlying network traffic will increase. Instead of sending one request to the server for all the information, you'll be sending several requests for smaller amounts of information.

Although IADs::GetInfoEx isn't a good substitute for IADs::GetInfo, it works well for selectively reading properties into the property cache. Example 19-3 shows how to selectively retrieve only two properties.

Example 19-3. Selectively reading properties into the property cache using the GetInfo method

```
Dim objUser  'An ADSI user object
Dim arrProps 'An array of properties to return

Set objUser=GetObject("LDAP://cn=administrator,cn=Users,dc=mycorp,dc=com")

'********************************************************************
'Set the list of properties to return
'********************************************************************
ArrProps = Array("cn","ADsPath")

'********************************************************************
'Get the specified properties
'********************************************************************
objUser.GetInfoEx arrProps, 0

WScript.Echo objUser.cn & vbTab & objUser.ADsPath
```

After we set the objUser variable, we create an array containing the properties we want (i.e., cn and ADsPath). Next, we pass that array to the IADs::GetInfoEx method as the first parameter. (The second parameter must be 0 for all actions; however, it is reserved and could be used in a later version of ADSI.) Then, the last line uses the WScript.Echo method to print the cn and ADsPath attributes, separating them with a tab.

Using IADs::PutEx

To set multivalue properties, you use the IADs::PutEx method. This is slightly more complicated than using IADs::GetEx. Suppose a property already has three values (e.g., pager numbers), and you want to put in two more. You must let IADs::PutEx know whether it needs to overwrite, update, or add to the existing values. You use the constants in Table 19-2 to tell IADs::PutEx what to do.

Table 19-2. The constants for updating the property cache with the PutEx method

Constant name	Value	Action
ADS_PROPERTY_CLEAR	1	Use when clearing all values
ADS_PROPERTY_UPDATE	2	Use when replacing all existing values
ADS_PROPERTY_APPEND	3	Use when adding to existing values
ADS_PROPERTY_DELETE	4	Use when deleting specific values

Use the constant name only if you're using VB. If you use VBScript with the WSH, you must either define the constants, as we've done in Example 19-4, or use the values directly. The four values are fairly straightforward to use, as the example script shows.

Example 19-4. Using constants with the PutEx method to update the property cache

```
Const ADS_PROPERTY_CLEAR = 1
Const ADS_PROPERTY_UPDATE = 2
Const ADS_PROPERTY_APPEND = 3
Const ADS_PROPERTY_DELETE = 4

Dim objUser  'An ADSI User object
Dim strPager 'A text string holding a phone number

Set objUser=GetObject("LDAP://cn=Administrator,cn=Users,dc=mycorp,dc=com")

'*********************************************************************
'Set three telephone numbers for the Administrator account
'*********************************************************************
objUser.PutEx ADS_PROPERTY_UPDATE, "pager", _
  Array("123-1234", "234-2345", "345-3456")
objUser.SetInfo
objUser.GetInfo
For Each strPager in objUser.telephoneNumber
  WScript.Echo strPager
Next

'*********************************************************************
```

```
'Delete the first and last number
'**********************************************************************
objUser.PutEx ADS_PROPERTY_DELETE, "pager", Array("123-1234", "345-3456")
objUser.SetInfo
objUser.GetInfo
For Each strPager in objUser.telephoneNumber
  WScript.Echo strPager
Next


'**********************************************************************
'Add a new telephone number without deleting the remaining number
'**********************************************************************
objUser.PutEx ADS_PROPERTY_APPEND, "pager", Array("456-4567")
objUser.SetInfo
objUser.GetInfo
For Each strPager in objUser.telephoneNumber
  WScript.Echo strPager
Next


'**********************************************************************
'Delete all values
'**********************************************************************
objUser.PutEx ADS_PROPERTY_CLEAR, "pager", vbNull
objUser.SetInfo
objUser.GetInfo
For Each strPager in objUser.telephoneNumber
  WScript.Echo strPager
Next
```

After binding to the user object, three pager numbers are set for the Administrator account, wiping out any existing values. The property cache is then reloaded explicitly to make sure it contains the new values that were just set. Now, a For Each loop is used to go through the newly set property to show the individual pager numbers. The first and last pager numbers of the new property are deleted in the cache and written to Active Directory with SetInfo.

At this point, Active Directory should contain only one pager number, which is displayed by looping through the values again. Next we append a number to the value held for that property in the cache and subsequently write it out to Active Directory, leaving two numbers in Active Directory for that property. Looping through the values again shows there are two numbers. Finally, all values in the property cache for that property are deleted, and the changes are updated in Active Directory. Using the For Each loop one last time should show no values.

Knowing now that you can access all of an object's properties from the cache individually, it would make sense if there were a way to count the number of items, display their names as well as their values, and so on. For this purpose, Microsoft provided three interfaces: IADsPropertyList, IADsPropertyEntry, and IADsPropertyValue.

Manipulating the Property Cache

There will be times when you need to write a script that queries all the values that have been set in the underlying directory for a particular object. For example, suppose you're one of several systems administrators who work with your company's Active Directory implementation. You need to write a script that queries all the property values that the administrators have set for a particular user.

Discovering the set property values for an object can be a long, tedious job. Fortunately, ADSI provides a quick method. If someone has set a value for a property, it must be in that object's property cache. So all you need to do is walk through the property cache, displaying and optionally modifying each item as you go.

In this section, we'll describe the property cache mechanics and show you how to write scripts that use several ADSI methods and properties to add individual values, add a set of values, walk through the property cache, and write modifications to the cache and to the directory. Although these examples access the Lightweight Directory Access Protocol (LDAP) namespace, you can just as easily substitute the WinNT namespace in any of the scripts and run them against Windows NT servers.

Details of the property cache interfaces can be found at the MSDN Library (*http://msdn.microsoft.com/library/*) by clicking through the following links: Networking and Directory Services → Active Directory, ADSI, Directory Services → SDK Documentation → Directory Services → Active Directory Service Interfaces → Active Directory Service Interfaces Reference → ADSI Interfaces → Property Cache Interfaces.

Property Cache Mechanics

Every object has properties. When you perform an explicit IADs::GetInfo call (or an implicit IADs::GetInfo call using IADs::Get) on an object that you previously bound to, the OS loads all the properties for that specific object into that object's property cache. Consider the property cache a simple list of properties. The PropertyList object represents this list. You can use several IADsPropertyList methods to navigate through the list and access items. For example, you can navigate the list and access each item, every *n*th item, or one particular item based on its name.

Each item in the property list is a property entry represented by the PropertyEntry object. You use the IADsPropertyEntry interface to access property entries. A property entry can have one or more property values. To access values in a property entry, you use the IADsPropertyValue interface.

To summarize, use IADsPropertyList to navigate through and access property entries in the property list. When you want to manipulate a property, use IADsPropertyEntry. To access the values of that property entry, use IADsPropertyValue.

Adding Individual Values

To show you how to add an individual value, we'll expand on one of the examples from the previous section: the pager property of the User object. The pager property is an array of text strings representing multiple pager numbers.

Consider that any property represents data. Data can take several forms, including a string, an integer, or a Boolean value. In the cache, each property has two attributes: one attribute specifies the type of data the property represents, and the other attribute specifies the value of that data type. For example, each pager property has two attributes: a Unicode string (the type of data) and the pager number (the value of that Unicode string). The User object's lastLogon property, which specifies the time the user last logged on, has the two attributes, a LargeInteger (type of data) and a date/time stamp (the value of that LargeInteger).

The pager and lastLogon properties are instances of the PropertyValue object, so you manipulate them with the method and property methods of the IADsPropertyValue interface. For example, you use the IADsPropertyValue::ADsType property method to set the PropertyValue's type of data. Table 19-3 shows some of the corresponding constant names and values that you can set for the IADsPropertyValue::ADsType property.

Table 19-3. Constants for the IADsPropertyValue::ADsType property

Constant name	IADsPropertyValue property method (if appropriate)	Value
ADSTYPE_INVALID	None	0
ADSTYPE_DN_STRING	IADsPropertyValue::DNString	1
ADSTYPE_CASE_EXACT_STRING	IADsPropertyValue::CaseExactString	2
ADSTYPE_CASE_IGNORE_STRING	IADsPropertyValue::CaseIgnoreString	3
ADSTYPE_PRINTABLE_STRING	IADsPropertyValue::PrintableString	4
ADSTYPE_NUMERIC_STRING	IADsPropertyValue::NumericString	5
ADSTYPE_BOOLEAN	IADsPropertyValue::Boolean	6
ADSTYPE_INTEGER	IADsPropertyValue::Integer	7
ADSTYPE_OCTET_STRING	IADsPropertyValue::OctetString	8
ADSTYPE_UTC_TIME	IADsPropertyValue::UTCTime	9
ADSTYPE_LARGE_INTEGER	IADsPropertyValue::LargeInteger	10
ADSTYPE_PROV_SPECIFIC	None	11
ADSTYPE_OBJECT_CLASS	None	12
ADSTYPE_CASEIGNORE_LIST	None	13
ADSTYPE_OCTET_LIST	None	14
ADSTYPE_PATH	None	15
ADSTYPE_POSTALADDRESS	None	16
ADSTYPE_TIMESTAMP	None	17

Table 19-3. Constants for the IADsPropertyValue::ADsType property (continued)

Constant name	IADsPropertyValue property method (if appropriate)	Value
ADSTYPE_BACKLINK	None	18
ADSTYPE_TYPEDNAME	None	19
ADSTYPE_HOLD	None	20
ADSTYPE_NETADDRESS	None	21
ADSTYPE_REPLICAPOINTER	None	22
ADSTYPE_FAXNUMBER	None	23
ADSTYPE_EMAIL	None	24
ADSTYPE_NT_SECURITY_DESCRIPTOR	IADsPropertyValue::SecurityDescriptor	25
ADSTYPE_UNKNOWN	None	26

Suppose you want to add a `PropertyValue` object with the value of "Hi There!" The two attributes are a case-sensitive string (i.e., the type of data, or `IADsPropertyValue::ADsType` property) and "Hi There!" (i.e., the value of that case-sensitive string or the `IADsPropertyValue::CaseExactString` property). The constant for the `IADsPropertyValue::ADsType` of a case-sensitive string is ADSTYPE_CASE_EXACT_STRING, which has a numeric value of 2. As shown in Table 19-3, `IADsPropertyValue::CaseExactString` is one of a number of `IADsPropertyValue` property methods that exist, each relating to a specific data type. It is the value in `IADsPropertyValue::ADsType` that determines which of the many property methods are actually used to get and set the data.

The following script shows how to create this new `PropertyValue` object. We begin by setting the ADSTYPE_CASE_EXACT_STRING constant to its numeric value (i.e., 2) and declaring the `objPropValue` variable. As we mentioned earlier, if you use VBScript with WSH, you must either define the constants, as the script does, or use the values directly:

```
Const ADSTYPE_CASE_EXACT_STRING = 2

Dim objPropValue    'An ADSI PropertyValue object

Set objPropValue = CreateObject("PropertyValue")
objPropValue.ADsType = ADSTYPE_CASE_EXACT_STRING
objPropValue.CaseExactString = "Hi There!"
```

We use VBScript's `CreateObject` method to create an instance of the `PropertyValue` object and set it to the `objPropValue` variable. Then two attributes are assigned to the `PropertyValue` object. The `objPropValue`'s `IADsPropertyValue::ADsType` property method is used to assign the property's data type to the ADSTYPE_CASE_EXACT_STRING constant. Finally, we use `objPropValue`'s `IADsPropertyValue::CaseExactString` property method to assign the property's value to "Hi There!"

Adding Sets of Values

As we mentioned previously, some properties hold one value (e.g., the lastLogon property); others hold multiple values in an array (e.g., the pager property). The PropertyEntry object holds the entire set of values for a property, be it one value or many values.

However, the PropertyEntry object does more than store values. This object's properties dictate how you can manipulate those values. The PropertyEntry object supports the IADsPropertyEntry interface that has four property methods:

IADsPropertyEntry::Name

The IADsPropertyEntry::Name property method sets the name of the property that you want to manipulate (e.g., pager).

IADsPropertyEntry::Values

The IADsPropertyEntry::Values property method sets an array containing those values you want to manipulate (e.g., the pager numbers).

IADsPropertyEntry::ADsType

The IADsPropertyEntry::ADsType property method determines the data type of those values (e.g., Unicode string).

IADsPropertyEntry::ControlCode

The IADsPropertyEntry::ControlCode property method tells the cache whether to overwrite, update, or add to the property's existing values. You use the constants in Table 19-4 with the IADsPropertyEntry::ControlCode property. These constants are the same as the constants for the IADs::PutEx method described earlier. Because IADsPropertyEntry::ControlCode constants work the same way as the IADs::PutEx method constants, we won't go through them again here.

Table 19-4. The constants for the IADsPropertyEntry::ControlCode property method

Constant name	Value	Action
ADS_PROPERTY_CLEAR	1	Use when clearing all values
ADS_PROPERTY_UPDATE	2	Use when replacing all existing values
ADS_PROPERTY_APPEND	3	Use when adding to existing values
ADS_PROPERTY_DELETE	4	Use when deleting specific values

The next script shows how to create a PropertyEntry object from one property value:

```
Const ADSTYPE_CASE_IGNORE_STRING = 3
Const ADS_PROPERTY_UPDATE = 2

Dim objPropValue 'An ADSI PropertyValue object
Dim objPropEntry 'An ADSI PropertyEntry object

Set objPropValue = CreateObject("PropertyValue")
objPropValue.ADsType = ADSTYPE_CASE_IGNORE_STRING
```

```
objPropValue.CaseIgnoreString = "0123-456-7890"

Set objPropEntry = CreateObject("PropertyEntry")
objPropEntry.Name = "pager"
objPropEntry.Values = Array(objPropValue)
objPropEntry.ADsType = ADSTYPE_CASE_IGNORE_STRING
objPropEntry.ControlCode = ADS_PROPERTY_UPDATE
```

The first part of the script is similar to the previous one. We begin by setting the constants to their numeric values and declaring the variables. Next, we create an instance of the PropertyValue object and set it to the objPropValue variable. We then use the IADsPropertyValue::ADsType property method to assign the property's data type to the ADSTYPE_CASE_IGNORE_STRING constant and the IADsPropertyValue::CaseIgnoreString property method to assign the property's value to 0123-456-7890.

The second part of the script begins by creating an instance of the PropertyEntry object and setting it to the objPropEntry variable. Then all four PropertyEntry properties are set. For the IADsPropertyEntry::Values property, you must use the VBScript Array( ) function to force the values into an array, even if you set only one value. For the IADsPropertyEntry::ControlCode property, you're replacing the existing values with the ones you're passing in.

Walking Through the Property Cache

For any object, the property cache consists of PropertyEntry objects that correspond to each property. When you use the IADs::Get method, it reads the cache's PropertyEntry for that particular property.

As we've previously mentioned, whenever you call GetObject or IADsOpenDSObject:: OpenDSObject, as explained later, the object that is returned can use the IADs interface in addition to any interface designed for that object. The IADsPropertyList interface also is directly available for any object. It is of no real use without a call to GetInfo first, without which the property cache will be empty. Once the cache is populated, however, the methods and properties come into their own. Table 19-5 lists the IADsPropertyList methods and properties.

Table 19-5. IADsPropertyList methods and properties

IADsPropertyList methods and properties	Action
Next method	Retrieves the value of the next item in the property list
Skip method	Skips a number of items in the property list
Reset method	Puts the pointer back to the beginning of the list
Add method	Adds a new property to the list
Remove method	Removes a property from the list
Item method	Gets an item from the property list

Table 19-5. IADsPropertyList methods and properties (continued)

IADsPropertyList methods and properties	Action
GetPropertyItem method	Gets an item in the property list
PutPropertyItem method	Puts an item in the property list
ResetPropertyItem method	Resets an item in the property list back to its original value
PurgePropertyList method	Deletes all items in the property list
PropertyCount property	The number of properties in the property list

The PropertyList object represents the entire set of properties for an object. The methods and property methods of the IADsPropertyList interface can be used to manipulate the PropertyList object. Example 19-5 uses several of those methods and property methods to demonstrate three ways of walking through the property cache.

Example 19-5. Walking through the property cache with the IADsPropertyList interface

```
Option Explicit

'*********************************************************************
'Force error checking within the code using the Err.Number property
'method in approaches 2 and 3
'*********************************************************************
On Error Resume Next

'*********************************************************************
'Declare the variables
'*********************************************************************
Dim objGroup       'The group whose property list you want to investigate
Dim strText        'A text string that displays results in one message box
Dim intPropCount   'The number of properties
Dim intIndex       'The index used while looping through the property list
Dim objPropEntry   'An individual property entry used in a loop

Set objGroup = GetObject("LDAP://cn=Managers,ou=Sales,dc=mycorp,dc=com")
objGroup.GetInfo

intPropCount = objGroup.PropertyCount
WScript.Echo "There are " & intPropCount & " values in the property cache."

'*********************************************************************
'Approach 1: PropertyCount property method
'*********************************************************************
strText = ""
For intIndex = 0 To (intPropCount-1)
  strText = strText & objGroup.Item(intIndex).Name & vbTab _
  & objGroup.Item(intIndex).ADsType & vbCrLf
Next
WScript.Echo strText

'*********************************************************************
'Approach 2: Next method
```

Example 19-5. Walking through the property cache with the IADsPropertyList interface (continued)

```
'***********************************************************************
strText = ""
Set objPropEntry = objGroup.Next
While (Not (IsNull(objPropEntry))) And Err.Number = 0)
  strText = strText & objPropEntry.Name & vbTab & objPropEntry.ADsType
          & vbCrLf
  Set objPropEntry = objGroup.Next
Wend
WScript.Echo strText
Set objPropEntry = Nothing


'***********************************************************************
'Approach 3: Next and Skip methods
'***********************************************************************
strText = ""
objGroup.Reset
Set objPropEntry = objGroup.Next
While (Not (IsNull(objPropEntry))) And Err.Number = 0)
  strText = strText & objPropEntry.Name & vbTab & objPropEntry.ADsType
          & vbCrLf
  objGroup.Skip(2)
  Set objPropEntry = objGroup.Next
Wend
WScript.Echo strText
Set objPropEntry = Nothing
```

The script begins by using VBScript's `Option Explicit` statement (which requires you to declare all variables before using them) and the `On Error Resume Next` statement (which allows you to do error handling). Then, after declaring the variables, the `GetObject` method is used to bind to the group whose property cache we want to look at. In this case, we want to view the properties for the Manager group object. Next, the `IADs::GetInfo` method is called to load the property cache for this group. Since we won't be using the `IADs::Get` method in the script, the system won't implicitly use the `IADs::GetInfo` method to load the cache, so we have to explicitly load it in.

Each object in `objGroup` has a `PropertyList` object, so we use the `IADsPropertyList::PropertyCount` property method to count each `PropertyList` object. We store the count for later use by setting it to the `intPropCount` variable, and we print it out in a message box using WSH's `Echo` method.

We now know how many properties `objGroup` has, but we need to find out the values of those properties. We can use one of three approaches to walk through the property cache to get this information.

Approach 1—Using the IADsPropertyList::PropertyCount property method

We begin by walking through the property list by counting the items in the index 0 through `intPropCount-1`. We need to specify this index, because the property list index starts at 0 rather than 1. For example, a property list with 15 items has an index ranging from 0 to 14.

For each item in the index, you concatenate (&) two property methods to retrieve the property's IADs::Name and IADsPropertyValue::ADsType. The script processes concatenated statements from left to right, so it first uses the IADsPropertyList::Item method with the intIndex value as the item number to retrieve a property entry, to which it applies the IADs::Name property method to get the property's name. The script then uses the same process to retrieve the same property entry, to which it applies the IADsPropertyValue::ADsType property method to get the property's datatype. Forcing the script to process IADsPropertyList::Item twice is inefficient. We processed it twice only to illustrate how to walk through the property list. The concatenated code includes more than just the two property methods. The code also concatenates a tab (vbTab) between the two property methods and a carriage-return line-feed (vbCrLf), or new line, after the second property method. But even more important, the code first concatenates the existing strText variable onto the front (i.e., strText = strText & property method 1 & property method 2), which means that, in the output, these property values are appended to the existing strText string. As a result, the WSH displays all the property values in one message box if you use WSH's *wscript.exe* scripting engine to run the script. If you're using WSH's *cscript.exe* scripting engine, using this append technique makes no difference. If you don't concatenate the strText variable (i.e., strText = property method 1 & property method 2), WSH displays a separate message box for each property.

When the script finishes looping through the property list index, it prints the appended strText string in the message box. Approaches 2 and 3 also use the append technique to display all their output in one message box.

Approach 2—Using the IADsPropertyList::Next method

We start this approach by resetting the strText variable to a zero-length string to ensure that no values from the previous approach are left in the string. Then the IADsPropertyList::Next method is called to retrieve a copy of the first property entry and set the result to the objPropEntry variable. Because we called the IADsPropertyList::Next method, we can use a while loop to iterate through the cache until we encounter a null value, which specifies that we're at the end of the list.

Providing that the first property entry isn't a null entry, we enter the while loop. The And Err.Number = 0 code designates a test to see whether an error has occurred. A value of 0 indicates no error; any other value specifies an error. If a valid entry (i.e., not a null entry) is retrieved and an error hasn't occurred (i.e., the error number is equal to 0), we enter the loop. Within the loop, the property name and data type are appended to the strText string in a similar manner as before. To move to the next property entry in the property cache, we again call the IADsPropertyList::Next method. As long as this value isn't null and isn't generating an error code, the process continues until it hits a null entry, which means we're at the end of the list. The wend keyword signifies the end of the while loop. Finally, the results are printed.

Approach 3—Using the IADsPropertyList::Next and IADsPropertyList::Skip methods

The code in this approach is identical to the code used in Approach 2, except for the addition of two lines. The `IADsPropertyList::Reset` property method sets the property list pointer to the first property entry in the cache. If we don't use the `IADsPropertyList::Reset` property method, the pointer will be at the end of the cache, which would generate a null entry. The `IADsPropertyList::Skip` code tells the `IADsPropertyList::Next` property method to skip the next two property entries. In other words, the `IADsPropertyList::Next` property method is retrieving every third property, so this approach returns only property entries 1, 4, 7, 10, and so on.

Writing the Modifications

Now that we've shown how to walk through the cache, next we will review how to write modifications to the cache and back to the directory. Example 19-6 illustrates these procedures. This script is an amalgam of the code in the earlier examples. As such, it shows how to assemble the pieces of code into a usable script.

Example 19-6. Writing modifications to the cache and back to the directory

```
Option Explicit

'*******************************************************************
'Force error checking within the code using the Err.Number property
'method in approaches 2 and 3
'*******************************************************************
On Error Resume Next

'*******************************************************************
'Declare the constants and variables
'*******************************************************************
Const ADSTYPE_CASE_IGNORE_STRING = 3
Const ADS_PROPERTY_UPDATE = 2

Dim objPropValue   'An ADSI PropertyValue object
Dim objPropEntry   'An ADSI PropertyEntry object
Dim objUser        'The user whose property list you want to investigate
Dim strText        'A text string that displays results in one message box
Dim intPropCount   'The number of properties
Dim intIndex       'The index used while looping through the property list

Set objUser = GetObject("LDAP://cn=AlistairGLN,ou=Sales,dc=mycorp,dc=com")
objUser.GetInfo

'*******************************************************************
'Section A: Calculate the property count, and enumerate each
'property's name and datatype
'*******************************************************************
intPropCount = objUser.PropertyCount
```

Example 19-6. Writing modifications to the cache and back to the directory (continued)

```
WScript.Echo "There are " & intPropCount _
  & " values in the property cache before adding the new one."

strText = ""
For intIndex = 0 To (intPropCount-1)
  strText = strText & objUser.Item(intIndex).Name & vbTab _
    & objUser.Item(intIndex).ADsType & vbCrLf
Next
WScript.Echo strText

'**********************************************************************
'Section B: Create a property entry, and write it to the cache
'**********************************************************************
Set objPropValue = CreateObject("PropertyValue")
objPropValue.ADsType = ADSTYPE_CASE_IGNORE_STRING
objPropValue.CaseExactString = "0123-456-7890"

Set objPropEntry = CreateObject("PropertyEntry")
objPropEntry.Name = "pager"
objPropEntry.Values = Array(objPropValue)
objPropEntry.ADsType = ADSTYPE_CASE_IGNORE_STRING
objPropEntry.ControlCode = ADS_PROPERTY_UPDATE

objUser.PutPropertyItem(objPropEntry)

'**********************************************************************
'Section C: Write out the cache to Active Directory and read the new
'cache explicitly back in from the object
'**********************************************************************
objUser.SetInfo
objUser.GetInfo

'**********************************************************************
'Section D: Recalculate the property count, and re-enumerate each
'property's name and datatype to see the changes
'**********************************************************************
intPropCount = objUser.PropertyCount

WScript.Echo "There are " & intPropCount _
  & " values in the property cache before adding the new one."

strText = ""
For intIndex = 0 To (intPropCount-1)
  strText = strText & objUser.Item(intIndex).Name _
    & vbTab & objUser.Item(intIndex).ADsType & vbCrLf
Next
WScript.Echo strText
```

The script begins with Option Explicit and On Error Resume Next, after which it sets the constants, declares the variables, and sets the objUser variable to the Alistair-GLN user object. The script then divides into four sections:

Section A

Determines the User object's property count and lists each property's name and data type.

Section B

Creates a property entry and writes it to the cache. The last line uses the IADs-PropertyList::PutPropertyItem method to write the new property entry for objUser to the cache. However, the IADs::SetInfo method must be used to write this entry to the directory.

Section C

Contains new code. The first line uses the IADs::SetInfo method to write the cache to the directory. The second line uses the explicit IADs::GetInfo method to read it back into the cache. Although the second line might not seem necessary, it is. If we don't use an explicit IADs::GetInfo call, we'll be accessing the same cache that we accessed before we added the new property entry. The explicit IADs::GetInfo call retrieves any new properties that anyone else has updated since the last implicit or explicit IADs::GetInfo call.

Section D

Recalculates the property count and reenumerates each property's name and data type so that we can see the modifications. If we see the property count increase by one after we write the cache to the directory, the script has successfully executed.

Walking the Property Cache—The Solution

Example 19-7 is quite long. It walks through the property cache for an object and prints the name, data type, and values of each entry. Some of the properties are not printable strings, so printing them in a text format makes little sense. Thus, this script prints only the text strings. We used a VBScript dictionary object to map the data type integers (ADsType) to descriptive names. A dictionary is similar in nature to an associative array or hash, which are common in other programming languages. After instantiating a dictionary object, you can use the Add method to add new key value pairs to it.

The script also illustrates how you can just as easily use the WinNT namespace rather than the LDAP namespace to display properties of objects, and how you can run the script against Windows NT domains and Windows NT or later member servers rather than Active Directory.

Example 19-7. Walking through the property cache of an object

```
Option Explicit
On Error Resume Next


'***********************************************************************
'Declare the hash (dictionary), constants and variables
```

Example 19-7. Walking through the property cache of an object (continued)

```
'***********************************************************************
Dim dicADsType
Set dicADsType = CreateObject("Scripting.Dictionary")
dicADsType.Add 0, "INVALID"
dicADsType.Add 1, "DN_STRING"
dicADsType.Add 2, "CASE_EXACT_STRING"
dicADsType.Add 3, "CASE_IGNORE_STRING"
dicADsType.Add 4, "PRINTABLE_STRING"
dicADsType.Add 5, "NUMERIC_STRING"
dicADsType.Add 6, "BOOLEAN"
dicADsType.Add 7, "INTEGER"
dicADsType.Add 8, "OCTET_STRING"
dicADsType.Add 9, "UTC_TIME"
dicADsType.Add 10, "LARGE_INTEGER"
dicADsType.Add 11, "PROV_SPECIFIC"
dicADsType.Add 12, "OBJECT_CLASS"
dicADsType.Add 13, "CASEIGNORE_LIST"
dicADsType.Add 14, "OCTET_LIST"
dicADsType.Add 15, "PATH"
dicADsType.Add 16, "POSTALADDRESS"
dicADsType.Add 17, "TIMESTAMP"
dicADsType.Add 18, "BACKLINK"
dicADsType.Add 19, "TYPEDNAME"
dicADsType.Add 20, "HOLD"
dicADsType.Add 21, "NETADDRESS"
dicADsType.Add 22, "REPLICAPOINTER"
dicADsType.Add 23, "FAXNUMBER"
dicADsType.Add 24, "EMAIL"
dicADsType.Add 25, "NT_SECURITY_DESCRIPTOR"
dicADsType.Add 26, "UNKNOWN"

Const ADS_PROPERTY_CLEAR = 1
Const ADS_PROPERTY_UPDATE = 2
Const ADS_PROPERTY_APPEND = 3
Const ADS_PROPERTY_DELETE = 4

Dim objPropValue    'An individual property value within a loop
Dim objPropEntry    'An ADSI PropertyEntry object
Dim objObject       'The object whose property list we wish to investigate
Dim strText         'A text string used to display results in one go
Dim intPropCount    'The number of properties in
Dim intIndex        'The index used while looping through the property list
Dim intCount        'Used to display property values in a numbered sequence

'***********************************************************************
'Uncomment one of these lines and modify it to your own environment.
'The first uses the LDAP namespace; the second uses the WinNT namespace.
'***********************************************************************
' Set objObject = GetObject("LDAP://cn=administrator,cn=users,dc=mycorp,dc=com")
' Set objObject = GetObject("WinNT://WINDOWS/Managers,Group")
objObject.GetInfo
if (Err.Number > 0) Then
```

Example 19-7. Walking through the property cache of an object (continued)

```
    Wscript.Echo "Object not found, returning..."
    Wscript.Quit
End if

'**********************************************************************
'Write out the current property cache total to the string that is
'storing output
'**********************************************************************
intPropCount = objObject.PropertyCount
strText = "There are " & intPropCount & _
          " values in the property cache." & vbCrLf

'**********************************************************************
'The extra vbTabs used in the first loop are to space the results so
'that they are nicely formatted with the list of values in the second loop
'**********************************************************************
For intIndex = 0 To (intPropCount-1)

  Set objPropEntry = objObject.Item(intIndex)
  strText = strText & objPropEntry.Name & vbCrLf

  strText = strText & vbTab & "Type:" & vbTab & vbTab & _
            dicADsType.Item(objPropEntry.ADsType) & vbCrLf

  '**********************************************************************
  'Go through each property value in the property entry and use the AdsType
  'to print out the appropriate value, prefixed by a count (intCount), i.e.:
  '
  '   Value #1: Vicky Launders
  '   Value #2: Alistair Lowe-Norris
  '   Value #3: Robbie Allen
  '**********************************************************************
  intCount = 1

  For Each objPropValue In objPropEntry.Values

    If (dicADsType(objPropValue.ADsType) = "STRING") Then
      strText = strText & vbTab & "Value #" & intCount & ":" _
        & vbTab & objPropValue.DNString & vbCrLf

    ElseIf (dicADsType(objPropValue.ADsType) = "CASE_EXACT_STRING") Then
      strText = strText & vbTab & "Value #" & intCount & ":" _
        & vbTab & objPropValue.CaseExactString & vbCrLf

    ElseIf (dicADsType(objPropValue.ADsType) = "CASE_IGNORE_STRING") Then
      strText = strText & vbTab & "Value #" & intCount & ":" _
        & vbTab & objPropValue.CaseIgnoreString & vbCrLf

    ElseIf (dicADsType(objPropValue.ADsType) = "PRINTABLE_STRING") Then
      strText = strText & vbTab & "Value #" & intCount & ":" _
        & vbTab & objPropValue.PrintableString & vbCrLf
```

Example 19-7. Walking through the property cache of an object (continued)

```
    ElseIf (dicADsType(objPropValue.ADsType) = "NUMERIC_STRING") Then
        strText = strText & vbTab & "Value #" & intCount & ":" _
          & vbTab & objPropValue.NumericString & vbCrLf

    ElseIf (dicADsType(objPropValue.ADsType) = "BOOLEAN") Then
        strText = strText & vbTab & "Value #" & intCount & ":" _
          & vbTab & CStr(objPropValue.Boolean) & vbCrLf

    ElseIf (dicADsType(objPropValue.ADsType) = "INTEGER") Then
        strText = strText & vbTab & "Value #" & intCount & ":" _
          & vbTab & objPropValue.Integer & vbCrLf

    End If

    intCount=intCount+1

  Next
Next

WScript.Echo strText
```

This script displays every value in the property cache for an object. However, there may come a time when you wish to see the entire potential property cache for an object and list which of all possible values have been set. To do that, you need to query the formal schema class definition for the object. This leads us to the final section on the property cache.

Walking the Property Cache Using the Formal Schema Class Definition

There is one other way to walk the property list for a particular object: using its schema class details. Chapter 4 explained how the schema is the blueprint for objects in Active Directory. As each schema class actually is stored in Active Directory, you can navigate the object's properties by using the IADsClass interface to display each individual item according to its formal name in the schema class. To do this, we first obtain a reference to the object in the normal manner. We then obtain a reference to the schema class for that object. We can do this using the IADs::Schema property method, which returns the full ADsPath of the schema class. For example, the user objectclass in the *mycorp.com* domain has the following schema ADsPath:

```
LDAP://cn=User,cn=Schema,cn=Configuration,dc=mycorp,dc=com
```

Then we can use the IADsClass::MandatoryProperties and IADsClass:: OptionalProperties methods to retrieve the appropriate properties. The following example nicely brings together IADs::GetEx for retrieving multiple properties and writing to a file, which is required due to the large number of properties.

Example 19-8 uses `On Error Resume Next` because all properties may not display, and the program will fail if any do not. The script also differs from the previous script in that it lists all possible properties and whether they've been set. The previous example listed only those that had been set. The script is also generic; it will print out the property cache for any object class. Just change the ADsPath passed to `GetObject`.

Example 19-8. Walking the property cache using the formal schema class definition

```
Option Explicit
'**********************************************************************
'Force error checking within the code using the Err.Number property
'method in approaches 2 and 3
'**********************************************************************
On Error Resume Next

'**********************************************************************
'Declare the constants and variables
'**********************************************************************
Dim objObject      'Active Directory object
Dim objClass       'ADSI Class object
Dim objProp        'An individual property
Dim intCount       'Incremental counter for display
Dim fileadsect     'A FileSystemObject
Dim outTextFile    'A TextStream Object

'**********************************************************************
'Create a VBScript file object and use it to open a text file. The
'second parameter specifies to overwrite any existing file that exists.
'**********************************************************************
Set fileadsect = CreateObject("Scripting.FileSystemObject")
Set outTextFile = fileadsect.CreateTextFile("c:\out.txt", TRUE)

'**********************************************************************
'Bind to the object and get a pointer to the appropriate schema class,
'i.e., User in this case
'**********************************************************************
Set objObject =
        GetObject("LDAP://cn=administrator,cn=Users,dc=mycorp,dc=com")
Set objClass = GetObject(objObject.Schema)

intCount = 1

'**********************************************************************
'Iterate through all the mandatory properties
'**********************************************************************
For Each objProp in objClass.MandatoryProperties
  EnumerateProperties objProp, outTextFile, objObject
  intCount=intCount+1
Next

'**********************************************************************
'Iterate through all the optional properties
'**********************************************************************
```

Example 19-8. Walking the property cache using the formal schema class definition (continued)

```
For Each objProp in objClass.OptionalProperties
  EnumerateProperties objProp
  intCount=intCount+1
Next

outTextFile.Close

'**********************************************************************
'Subroutine EnumerateProperties
'**********************************************************************
Sub EnumerateProperties(ByVal objProp, ByVal tsFile, ByVal objObj)

  Dim objProperty  'ADSI Property object
  Dim arrElement   'Array of elements

  '**********************************************************************
  'Get pointer to the schema property object
  '**********************************************************************
  Set objProperty = GetObject("LDAP://Schema/" & objProp)

  '**********************************************************************
  'Check whether property requires GetEx using IADsProperty::MultiValued
  '**********************************************************************
  If objProperty.MultiValued Then
    tsFile.WriteLine intCount & ") " & objProp & _
      " (" & objProperty.Syntax & ") (MULTI-VALUED)"

    '**********************************************************************
    'Check whether array returned from GetEx is empty using VBScript
    ' function
    '**********************************************************************
    If (IsEmpty(objObj.GetEx(objProp))) Then
      tsFile.WriteLine vbTab & "= " & "NO VALUES SET!"
    Else
      For Each arrElement in objObj.GetEx(objProp)
        tsFile.WriteLine vbTab & "= " & arrElement
      Next
    End If

  Else
    tsFile.WriteLine intCount & ") " & objProp _
      & " (" & objProperty.Syntax & ")"

    Err.Clear
    If Err=0 Then
      tsFile.WriteLine vbTab & "= " & objObj.Get(objProp)
    Else
      tsFile.WriteLine vbTab & "= " & "Not Set!"
    End If

  End If
End Sub
```

Checking for Errors in VBScript

It is worthwhile to look at error handling in a little more detail now. Normally errors that occur in a script are termed fatal errors. This means that execution of the script terminates whenever an error occurs. When this happens, a dialog box opens and gives you the unique number and description of the error. While this is useful, sometimes you may like to set errors to be nonfatal, so that execution continues after the error. To do this, you include the following line in your code:

```
On Error Resume Next
```

Once you have done this, any line with an error is ignored. This can cause confusion, as can be seen from the following code. Note the missing P in LDAP:

```
On Error Resume Next

Set objGroup = GetObject("LDA://cn=Managers,ou=Sales,dc=mycorp,dc=com")

objGroup.GetInfo
WScript.Echo objGroup.Description
objGroup.Description = "My new group description goes here"
objGroup.GetInfo
WScript.Echo objGroup.Description
```

This script fails to execute any of the lines after the On Error Resume Next statement, as the first LDAP call into the objGroup variable failed. However, it will not terminate as usual with an error after the GetObject line, due to the On Error statement. To get around this, you should add a couple lines to do error checking. Example 19-9 is a good example of error checking in a different script.

Example 19-9. Error checking in VBScript

```
On Error Resume Next

'*********************************************************************
'Clear errors
'*********************************************************************
Err.Clear

'*********************************************************************
'Get a pointer to the Administrator account
'*********************************************************************
Set objUser = GetObject ("LDAP://cn=Administrator,cn=Users,dc=mycorp,dc=com")
If Hex(Err.Number)="&H80005000" Then
  WScript.Echo "Bad ADSI path!" & vbCrLf & "Err. Number: " _
    & vbTab & CStr(Hex(Err.Number)) & vbCrLf & "Err. Descr.: " _
    & vbTab & Err.Description
  WScript.Quit
End If

'*********************************************************************
'Explicitly call GetInfo for completeness
```

Example 19-9. Error checking in VBScript (continued)

```
'**********************************************************************
objUser.GetInfo

'**********************************************************************
'Clear any previous errors
'**********************************************************************
Err.Clear

'**********************************************************************
'Try and get a pointer to the "moose" attribute of the user (which
'doesn't exist)
'**********************************************************************
x = objUser.Get("moose")

'**********************************************************************
'Check for property does not exist error
'**********************************************************************
If Hex(Err.Number)="&H8000500D" Then
  WScript.Echo "No such property!" & vbCrLf & "Err. Number: " _
    & vbTab & CStr(Hex(Err.Number)) & vbCrLf & "Err. Descr.: " _
    & vbTab & Err.Description
End If
```

This is a simple example; the path does exist and the moose property does not exist for the user. ADSI errors start at 80005 in hexadecimal, and 8000500D is the error indicating that there is no such property. The &H prefix indicates that the following string is a hexadecimal number. You must use the Err::Clear method from the Err interface to clear any existing error information, prior to making a call that could generate an error. If an error has occurred, the value of Err.Number is nonzero; if Err. Number is 0, no error occurred. If an error has occurred, Err.Description contains any description that has been set for that error.

We use the functions Hex and CStr in the example one after the other to print out the hexadecimal string of the error number. We choose to do this because Microsoft specifies error numbers in hexadecimal, and if you are to look them up easily in Microsoft's documentation, you need to see the hexadecimal rather than getting out a calculator. The CStr function converts the newly converted hexadecimal value to a text string that can be printed out.

Since most calls to the Err interface will be to retrieve the Err::Number property, the Err::Number property is set as the default property method, meaning that you don't have to state it explicitly. For example, these two statements are equivalent:

```
If Hex(Err)="&H8000500D" Then
If Hex(Err.Number)="&H8000500D" Then
```

In addition, as Hex(0) is the same as 0, most sample code that you will see using VBScript looks like this:

```
On Error Resume Next

'Some_code_goes_here

Err.Clear
Set x = GetObject(something_goes_here)
If Err=0 Then
  'No error occurred
  Some_success_code_goes_here
Else
  'Error occurred
  Some_failure_code_goes_here
End If
```

Finally, to reset error checking back to the default as if the On Error Resume Next statement had not been included, we use the following code:

```
'The last character is a zero, not a capital "o"
On Error Goto 0
```

A full list of ADSI errors can be found in the MSDN library (*http://msdn.microsoft. com/library/*) under Networking and Directory Services → Active Directory, Active Directory Service Interfaces and Directory Services → SDK Documentation → Directory Services → Active Directory Service Interfaces → Active Directory Service Interfaces Reference → ADSI Error Codes.

Summary

Over the last two chapters, we've covered the interfaces, methods, and property methods that allow you to use access and manipulate generic objects in Active Directory. These interfaces include:

- IADs
- IADsContainer (covered more fully later)
- IADsPropertyList
- IADsPropertyEntry
- IADsPropertyValue

We've also looked at how to supply credentials to authenticate with alternate credentials using the ADsOpenDSObject interface.

In the next chapter, we cover how to search Active Directory using a database query interface called ADO.

CHAPTER 20
Using ADO for Searching

Microsoft's ADO technology lets you conduct database searches and retrieve the results through a flexible interface called resultsets. ADO also lets you update information in a database directly or with stored procedures. Because Microsoft created an ADO database provider for ADSI (the ADSI OLE DB provider), you can also use ADO's database query technology to query Active Directory. However, the ADSI OLE DB provider is currently read-only, so many of the useful ADO methods for updating data aren't available yet. You can use ADO only for searching and retrieving objects. Despite the read-only limitation, using ADO is still a boon. It is significantly faster to search Active Directory using ADO than it is to use ADSI to bind to each object recursively down a branch. Even using IADsContainer::Filter is slow in comparison. So if you need to search Active Directory rapidly for attributes matching criteria, ADO is exactly what you should use. The ADO object model consists of nine objects (Command, Connection, Error, Field, Parameter, Property, Record, Recordset, and Streams) and four collection objects (Errors, Fields, Parameters, and Properties). However, some of these objects aren't useful if you're using the ADSI OLE DB provider, as they are more often used for accessing full-fledged database services. For example, the Parameter object lets you pass parameters to stored procedures, but this object is of little use because the ADSI provider doesn't support stored procedures.

The objects that are appropriate to ADSI in a read-only environment are the Command, Connection, Error, Field, Property, and Recordset objects. We use them to show you how to perform complex searches. For a full description of the ADO object model and the available functions, check out the following on the MSDN Library (*http://msdn.microsoft.com/library/*): Data Access → Microsoft Data Access Components (MDAC) → SDK Documentation → Microsoft ActiveX Data Objects (ADO).

 If you wish to make use of the tools in this chapter in a VB project rather than a VBScript script, you need to include the Microsoft ActiveX Data Objects 2.x library from the Reference item on the Project menu of the Visual Basic Environment.

One point to note: ADO is written to work with all types of databases, so there are a numerous ways of doing exactly the same thing. We will attempt to cover examples of each different way as they crop up so that you will be able to choose the method that suits you best or that you are familiar with.

The First Search

The easiest way to explain basic searching using ADO is with an example. Here we'll build an ADO query to search and display the ADsPaths of all users in Active Directory. You can create a simple script to do this search in six steps.

Step 1—Define the Constants and Variables

For this script, you need to define one constant and three variables. The constant is adStateOpen, which we set to 1. If you're using VBScript, you use this constant later to determine whether you made a successful connection to the database. If you're using Visual Basic (VB), you don't have to include this constant because VB has already defined it. The two main variables are objConn (an ADO Connection object that lets you connect to the AD database) and objRS (an ADO Recordset object that holds the retrieved resultset). The third variable holds the output of the resultset, as shown in the following example:

```
Option Explicit

Const adStateOpen = 1

Dim objConn      'ADO Connection object
Dim objRS        'ADO Recordset object
Dim strOutput    'The output of the search
```

The Option Explicit statement at the beginning of the script is optional, but we recommend that you include it. This statement forces the script to declare variables, so you can quickly spot errors.

Step 2—Establish an ADO Database Connection

To perform an ADO query, you need to establish an ADO connection, which is completely separate from any ADSI connections you may have opened with IADsOpen-DSObject::OpenDSObject. Before you can establish this connection, you must create an ADO Connection object to use. This object can be created the same way you create a file system object: use the CreateObject method, with "ADODB.Connection" as a parameter. You use the ADODB prefix to create all ADO objects, and Connection is the top-level object in the ADO object model:

```
Set objConn = CreateObject("ADODB.Connection")
```

Just as you use different programmatic identifiers (ProgIDs) (e.g., WinNT:, LDAP:) to tell ADSI which directory to access, you use different OLE DB providers to tell ADO which query syntax to use. An OLE DB provider implements OLE DB interfaces so that different applications can use the same uniform process to access data. The ADSI OLE DB connector supports two forms of syntax: the SQL dialect and the LDAP dialect. Although you can use the SQL dialect to query the ADSI namespace, most scriptwriters use the LDAP dialect because Microsoft defined it specifically for ADO queries to directory services. However, the default for the Connection object's read/write property, objConn.Provider, is MSDASQL, which specifies the use of SQL syntax. Because you want to use the ADSI provider, you need to set objConn.Provider to "ADsDSOObject", which specifies the use of the LDAP syntax. By setting this specific provider, you force the script to use not only a specific syntax but also a specific set of arguments in the calls to the Connection object's methods.

```
objConn.Provider = "ADSDSOObject"
```

Step 3—Open the ADO Connection

You can open a connection to the directory by calling the Connection::Open method. When describing the methods and property methods of COM interfaces in text, the established notation is to use a double colon (::) separator. For example, Connection:: Open specifies the Open method of the Connection object, as shown in the following example:

```
objConn.Open _
    "", "CN=Administrator,CN=Users,dc=mycorp,dc=com", ""
```

As the code shows, the Open method takes three parameters. The first parameter is the Connection::ConnectionString parameter, which contains information that the script needs to establish a connection to the data source. In this case, it is blank. The second parameter contains the user DN to bind with, and the third is the user's password.

In this code, you're authenticating with a username DN or UPN (the second parameter) and that user's password (the third parameter). You can leave the first parameter blank. Here's why: in ADO, you can perform the same task many ways because the Command, Connection, and Recordset objects heavily interrelate. If you set the properties of one object, you can use those same properties to open the connection of another object as long as you're not setting any new options. Such is the case in the preceding section of code; you're opening the connection without setting any new options. You then use an If...Then...Else statement to see whether the Open call worked. If the call succeeded (i.e., the connection state has a value of 1), the script prints the message "Authentication Successful" and proceeds to the query. If the call didn't work (i.e., the connection state has a value of 0), the script prints the message "Authentication Failed" and quits, setting the returned error code to 1:

```
If objConn.State = 1 Then
    WScript.Echo "Authentication Successful!"
```

```
Else
  WScript.Echo "Authentication Failed."
  WScript.Quit(1)
End If
```

Step 4—Execute the Query

The Connection::Execute method is used to perform a query. Connection::Execute accepts a string containing four arguments separated by semicolons:

```
Set objRS = objConn.Execute _
  ("<LDAP://dc=mycorp,dc=com>;(objectclass=user);" _
  & "Name,ADsPath;SubTree")
```

If the string contains spaces before or after the semicolons, the code will fail. It's easy to forget this, and it's very annoying to try to debug, as the error just states that a parameter is invalid. You must also remember to enclose the parameter in parentheses because you're passing the Execute method's result to a variable.

The four arguments for any LDAP query you want to execute are:

Search base

The search base specifies the point in the directory from which the search will start. You must use a full ADsPath to specify the search base and enclose the ADsPath in angle brackets (< >). In this script, we are starting from the directory's root (i.e., LDAP://dc=mycorp,dc=com).

Filter

The filter defines criteria to match objects with. You must enclose this argument in parentheses. You also must use the format defined in RFC 2254. Filters are covered in greater detail later in the "Understanding Search Filters" section. The previous script used the search filter (objectclass=user) which means that only user objects will be returned.

Attributes

The attributes argument is a comma-delimited list of attributes to return. You must specify each attribute individually. Unlike the IADs::Get method, which executes an implicit GetInfo call to obtain all attributes, this ADO search returns only the specified attributes in the resultset. In this case, the ADO search will return the Name and ADsPath attributes. The ADsPath is a useful attribute to retrieve because it lets you use ADSI to bind to that object. You then can perform an explicit GetInfo to obtain all the attributes for that object.

Scope

The scope specifies how far down from the query's starting point (i.e., search base) to search. You can specify one of three string constants: Base, OneLevel, or Subtree. If you set the scope to Base, the ADO search will only match the object specified by the search base only if the search filter matches as well. If you set the scope to OneLevel, the ADO search checks any object directly under the search base, one level down. If you set the scope to Subtree, as this script does, the ADO search checks every container under the search base but does not include the search base.

Step 5—Navigate Through the Resultset

The objRS variable holds the resultset, also known as the recordset. Recordset objects have a table-like structure. The structure's columns are fields, and the rows are records. Fields correspond to the attributes you want to return and assume the titles of those attributes (e.g., Name or ADsPath). ADO also numbers the fields from left to right, starting with 0. Thus, you can access fields using attribute names or index numbers. Records correspond to the values of those attributes.

To manage the members of objRS, the simplest approach is to use the Recordset::MoveNext method (which navigates to the next record in the resultset) while checking the Recordset::EOF (end-of-file) method. The RecordSet::EOF method returns true if you're at the end of the resultset. The following code sample uses both of these methods:

```
While Not objRS.EOF
  Wscript.Echo objRS.Fields.Item("Name").Value _
    & vbCrLf & objRS.Fields.Item("ADsPath").Value
  objRS.MoveNext
Wend
```

As this section of code shows, we're using these two methods in a simple while loop to move through each record. If Recordset::EOF returns a value of false (i.e., you're not at the end of the resultset), the script stores the contents of the record for each field into the output variable and moves on to the next record. If Recordset::EOF returns a value of true (i.e., end of the resultset), the script exits the while loop.

To access the values of each matching object, we are using objRS.Fields, which is a Fields collection object. As with all collections, Fields has a method called Item. The Fields::Item method takes an argument that equates to either the name of the field or its index number. The Fields::Item method returns a Field object, which has a Value property method that allows us to get the value for that specific property of the object. In other words, the code:

```
objRS.Fields.Item("Name").Value
```

returns the value of the individual field called Name from the collection of all possible fields in the recordset. We'll come back to this more in the later examples on navigating resultsets.

Step 6—Close the ADO Connection

The `Connection::Close` method is used to close the ADO connection to the directory. To be complete, you may also want to set the `Recordset` object to `Nothing` to make sure it doesn't mistakenly get reused. That isn't mandatory if your script is done at that point, because it will automatically get cleaned up, but it is good practice nonetheless. That way, if you later add code to the end of the script, you can't mistakenly reuse the now-defunct `objRS` variable without reinitializing it first. Here is example code illustrating how to properly close down an ADO session:

```
objConn.Close
Set objRS = Nothing
```

The Entire Script for a Simple Search

The following is the entire script:

```
Option Explicit

Const adStateOpen = 1

Dim objConn   'ADO Connection object
Dim objRS     'ADO Recordset object

Set objConn = CreateObject("ADODB.Connection")
objConn.Provider = "ADSDSOObject"
objConn.Open "","CN=Administrator,CN=Users,dc=mycorp,dc=com", ""
If objConn.State = adStateOpen Then
  WScript.Echo "Authentication Successful!"
Else
  WScript.Echo "Authentication Failed."
  WScript.Quit(1)
End If

Set objRS = objConn.Execute _
  ("<LDAP://dc=mycorp,dc=com>;(objectclass=User);" _
  & "Name,ADsPath;SubTree")

While Not objRS.EOF
  Wscript.Echo objRS.Fields.Item("Name").Value _
    & vbCrLf & objRS.Fields.Item("ADsPath").Value
  objRS.MoveNext
Wend

objConn.Close
Set objRS = Nothing
```

 While we open and close the connection within the short script, we could keep the connection open for every query if we had many queries to execute. This is how ADO normally is used.

Other Ways of Connecting and Retrieving Results

As mentioned earlier, there are a number of ways of authenticating an ADO connection to Active Directory. The simplest is the way outlined earlier using the `Connection::Provider` set with the username and password as second and third arguments:

```
Set objConn = CreateObject("ADODB.Connection")
objConn.Provider = "ADSDSOObject"
objConn.Open "", _
            "CN=Administrator,CN=Users,dc=mycorp,dc=com", _
            "mypass"
```

Because ADO is designed for databases, it is often necessary to specify a number of other requirements when opening a connection. These include a different provider, a different server, or a specific database. All of these items can be set prior to opening the connection. However, none of these make a difference to the AD provider. If you wish to open a connection by setting these values in the `ConnectionString` property, then do so as shown in the following code:

```
Set objConn = CreateObject("ADODB.Connection")
objConn.Provider = "ADSDSOObject":objConn.ConnectionString = _
   "DSN=;UID=CN=Administrator,CN=Users,dc=mycorp,dc=com;PWD=mypass"
objConn.Open
```

Semicolons separate the arguments, with the expected DataSourceName (DSN) specified as empty at the start of the string.

One important point: do not authenticate using both methods with the same connection—use one or the other. The following code uses both methods to illustrate what not to do:

```
Set objConn = CreateObject("ADODB.Connection")
objConn.Provider = "ADSDSOObject"
objConn.Open _
   "DSN=;UID=CN=Administrator,CN=Users,dc=mycorp,dc=com;PWD=mypass", _
   "CN=Administrator,CN=Users,dc=mycorp,dc=com", "mypass"
```

This is a slightly different version, but still wrong:

```
Set objConn = CreateObject("ADODB.Connection")
objConn.Provider = "ADSDSOObject"
objConn.ConnectionString = _
   "DSN=;UID=CN=Administrator,CN=Users,dc=mycorp,dc=com;PWD=mypass"
objConn.Open "", "CN=Administrator,CN=Users,dc=mycorp,dc=com", _
   "mypass"
```

Searching With SQL

You can retrieve resultsets in a variety of ways and get exactly the same values. We will now discuss how to use the Command object and the Recordset::Open method, using SQL-formatted queries to retrieve resultsets. SQL is a powerful query language that is the de facto standard to query database tables. We do not propose to go through the details of SQL here, but we will cover some examples for those who may already be familiar with SQL and would find using it to be a more comfortable way of querying Active Directory than using LDAP search filters.

Using the Connection::Execute method

You can pass a SQL select statement to a connection using the Execute method as we've done previously with LDAP-based queries:

```
Set objConn = CreateObject("ADODB.Connection")
objConn.Provider = "ADSDSOObject"
objConn.Open "", "CN=Administrator,CN=Users,dc=mycorp,dc=com", ""

Set objRS = objConn.Execute "Select Name, ADsPath" _
  & " FROM 'LDAP://dc=mycorp,dc=com' where objectclass = 'user'"
```

Using the Recordset::Open method

Next we will set the Recordset::ActiveConnection and Recordset::Source properties before the Recordset::Open method is called; the second passes values directly to the Recordset::Open method.

Setting the properties first:

```
Set objConn = CreateObject("ADODB.Connection")
objConn.Provider = "ADSDSOObject"
objConn.Open "", "CN=Administrator,CN=Users,dc=mycorp,dc=com", ""

'Open a recordset based on a SQL string by presetting the properties

Set objRS = CreateObject("ADODB.Recordset")
objRS.ActiveConnection = objConn
objRS.Source = "Select Name, ADsPath FROM " _
  & "'LDAP://dc=mycorp,dc=com' where objectclass = 'user'"
objRS.Open
```

Passing values directly:

```
Set objConn = CreateObject("ADODB.Connection")
objConn.Provider = "ADSDSOObject"
objConn.Open "", "CN=Administrator,CN=Users,dc=mycorp,dc=com", ""

'Open a recordset based on a SQL string

'Set the SQL search string
strSource = "Select Name, ADsPath FROM 'LDAP://dc=mycorp,dc=com' " _
  & "where objectclass = 'user'"
```

```
'Pass what will become the Source and ActiveConnection properties to
'the Recordset::Open call
objRS.Open strSource, objConn
```

Executing a specific command

You can use the Command object's methods and properties to pass a complete command to an already open connection:

```
Set objConn = CreateObject("ADODB.Connection")
objConn.Provider = "ADSDSOObject"
objConn.Open "", "CN=Administrator,CN=Users,dc=mycorp,dc=com", ""

'Opening a recordset based on a command object

Set objComm = CreateObject("ADODB.Command")
Set objComm.ActiveConnection = objConn
objComm.CommandText = "Select Name, ADsPath FROM" _
  & " 'LDAP://dc=mycorp,dc=com' where objectclass = 'user'"

Set objRS = objComm.Execute()
```

Or you can do this:

```
Set objConn = CreateObject("ADODB.Connection")
objConn.Provider = "ADSDSOObject"
objConn.Open "", "CN=Administrator,CN=Users,dc=mycorp,dc=com", ""

'Opening a recordset based on a Command object

Set objComm = CreateObject("ADODB.Command")
Set objComm.ActiveConnection = objConn

Set objRS = objComm.Execute "Select Name, ADsPath FROM" _
  & " 'LDAP://dc=mycorp,dc=com' where objectclass = 'user'"
```

Controlling How a Search Is Conducted

When conducting a search, the Command object can take a number of extra parameters. For example, a parameter can dictate how many results are returned (Page Size), how long in seconds the command can take before it fails (Timeout), how far to search in the database (Searchscope), and whether the resultset is cached in memory for faster access at a later date (Cache Results). These four values are shown in the following code section:

```
Const ADS_SCOPE_SUBTREE = 2
Set objComm = CreateObject("ADODB.Command")
objComm.Properties("Page Size") = 10000
objComm.Properties("Timeout") = 60
objComm.Properties("Searchscope") = ADS_SCOPE_SUBTREE
objComm.Properties("Cache Results") = False
```

For more information, consult the ADO Command object in MSDN.

The Command object and Recordset::Open

You can even combine the Command object and Recordset::Open, like this:

```
Set objConn = CreateObject("ADODB.Connection")
objConn.Provider = "ADSDSOObject"
objConn.Open "", "CN=Administrator,CN=Users,dc=mycorp,dc=com", ""

Set objComm = CreateObject("ADODB.Command")
Set objComm.ActiveConnection = objConn
objComm.CommandText = "Select Name, ADsPath FROM" _
  & " 'LDAP://dc=mycorp,dc=com' where objectclass = 'user'"

'Pass what will become the Source and ActiveConnection properties to
'the Recordset::Open call
objRS.Open objComm, objConn
```

Understanding Search Filters

When you use the LDAP dialect with the ADSI OLE DB provider to conduct a search, you must use an LDAP search filter to specify your search criteria. In a simple case, (objectclass=user) would be used to select every object with the user objectclass under the search base. You can in fact use a filter to match the presence of a value (or not) for any attribute of an object. This enables you to create powerful searches with complex criteria. For example, you can search for any group object that has a certain user as a member and that has a description matching a certain substring.

> Filters must follow the format specified in RFC 2254. You can download RFC 2254 from *http://www.ietf.org/rfc/rfc2254.txt*.

Although filters let you conduct powerful searches, working with them can seem complex because of the format used, known as prefix notation. To make it easier to understand, we have divided the discussion of filters into two parts: items within a filter and items connecting filters.

Items Within a Filter

Within a filter, you can have three types of items:

Operators
> A filter can include one of three operators. The equal-to (=) operator checks for exact equivalence. An example is (name=janet). The greater-than-or-equal-to (>=) and less-than-or-equal-to (<=) operators check for compliance with a range. Examples are (size>=5) and (size<=20).

Attributes

> You can include attributes in filters when you want to determine whether an attribute exists. You simply specify the attribute, followed by the = operator and an asterisk (*). For example, the (mooseHerderProperty=*) filter searches for objects that have the mooseHerderProperty attribute populated.

Substrings

> You can include substrings in filters when you want to search for objects with specific strings. Test for substrings by placing the attribute type (e.g., cn for common name, sn for surname) to the left of the = operator and the substring you're searching for to the right. Use the * character to specify where that substring occurs in the string. The (cn=Keith*) filter searches for common name (CN) attributes that begin with the substring "Keith"; the (cn=*Cooper) filter searches for CN strings that end with the substring "Cooper". Depending on the search, the latter form of substring searches can take a long time to return. Under Windows Server 2003, the substring searches perform much better than previously.

You can place several substrings together by using an asterisk character several times. For example, the (cn=Kei*Coo*) filter searches for two substrings in the string: the first substring begins with "Kei", followed by the second substring that begins with "Coo". Similarly, the (cn=*ith*per) filter searches for strings that have two substrings: the first substring ends in "ith" followed by the second substring that ends in "per".

The resultset of a substring search might contain objects that you don't want. For example, if you use the filter (cn=Kei*Coo*) to search for the object representing "Keith Cooper", your resultset might contain two objects: one representing "Keith Cooper" and another representing "Keith Coolidge". To address that issue, you can connect multiple filter strings together to refine your search even more.

Connecting Filters

Compound filters can be created by using the ampersand (&), the vertical bar (|), and the exclamation mark (!). Let's start by creating a filter to find all groups whose common name begins with the letter a. The following is the filter for this search:

```
(&(objectclass=group)(cn=a*))
```

This filter actually consists of two filters: (objectclass=group) and (cn=a*), but because you're enclosing the filters in parentheses, you're treating them as one filter. The & prefix specifies the use of the logical AND operator. In other words, you're searching for objects that are in the group objectclass and have a CN that begins with the letter a.

You can continue to add additional filters to narrow the search even more. Suppose that in groups whose CN begins with the letter a, you want to find only those users whose surnames begins with the letter d. To perform this search, you use the following filter:

```
(&(objectclass=group)(cn=a*)(sn=d*))
```

You also can widen a search. Instead of using the & operator, you use the | prefix, which specifies the logical OR operator. For example, if you want to find all group or user objects, you use the following filter:

```
(|(objectclass=group)(objectclass=user))
```

You can nest sets of filters, as long as each filter conforms to the correct notation. For example, if you want to find all groups whose CN begins with the letter a or whose description begins with the substring "Special groups", you use the following filter:

```
(&(objectclass=group)(|(cn=a*)(description=Special groups*)))
```

So far, we've been searching for objects that have a certain characteristic. You can also search for objects that don't have a certain characteristic. Use the ! prefix, which specifies the NOT, or negation, operator. For example, you can search for all objects that do not have an objectclass equal to User with the following filter:

```
(!(objectclass=User))
```

By combining the &, |, and ! operators, you can perform powerful searches. For example, consider the following query:

```
(&
  (|(objectclass=container)(objectclass=organizationalUnit))
  (!(MyCorpSpecial=*))
  (|(cn=*cor*)(cn=J*))
)
```

This query is searching for any container or organizational unit (OU) that doesn't contain the MyCorpSpecial property and whose CN contains the letters "cor" or starts with the letter J. Here's how to include this filter in a script:

```
filterStr = _
  "(&(|(objectclass=container)(objectclass=organizationalUnit))" & _
    "(!(MyCorpSpecial=*))" & _
    "(|(cn=*cor*)(cn=J*))" & _
  ")"
```

There are no spaces in the string, yet the quotation marks do not overly detract from the formatting.

As you can see, this is a very powerful specification.

 If a value you are trying to match contains an asterisk or parenthesis, which are special characters used in filters, those characters must be preceded by a backslash (\)

Optimizing Searches

Whether you are searching Active Directory using filters or with SQL, there are some important guidelines to follow that can help reduce load on the domain controllers, increase performance of your scripts and applications, and reduce the amount of traffic generated on the network. It is also important to socialize these concepts with others as much as possible. It takes only a couple of badly written search filters in a heavily used application to severely impact the performance of your domain controllers!

Efficient Searching

Understanding how to write efficient search criteria is the first important step to optimizing searches. By understanding a few key points, you can greatly improve the performance of your searches. It is also important to reuse data retrieved from searches or connections to Active Directory as much as possible. The following list describes several key points to remember about searching:

- Use at least one indexed attribute per search. Certain attributes are marked as "indexed" in Active Directory, which allows for fast pattern matching. They are typically single-valued and unique, which means searches using indexed attributes can determine which objects match them very quickly. If you don't use indexed attributes, the database equivalent of a full table scan must be done to determine the matches.

- Use a combination of objectclass and objectcategory in every search. While most of the queries used so far in this chapter have used only objectclass, you should make it a practice always to use a combination of objectclass and objectcategory. The problem with using only objectclass is that it is not indexed because it is multivalued and not unique, while objectcategory is single-valued and indexed. See the next section on "Objectclass Versus Objectcategory" for more information.

- Try to limit the use of trailing (name=*llen) or middle match (name=*lle*) searches. Unlike other directories, Active Directory is not optimized to handle these types of searches, and they should be avoided if possible. In some cases these types of searches can take upwards of 10–15 seconds to complete under Windows 2000!

- Use the appropriate search scope. Avoid using subtree searches unless you truly want to search more than one level down. If you only want to search directly below the search base, use the OneLevel scope.

- Use paged searching for queries that can potentially return thousands of entries. Most subtree searches should have paging enabled unless you are positive the search will not return more than 1,000 entries or do not want it to return more than 1,000 entries.

- Reuse ADO `Connection` and `Command` objects as much as possible. ADO `Connection` and `Command` objects can be used for multiple searches so there is no need to create additional ones.

Objectclass Versus Objectcategory

It is very important to understand the differences between `objectclass` and `objectcategory` and how they should be used during searches. `Objectclass` is a multivalued attribute that contains the `objectclass` hierarchy for an instantiated object. For example, a user object has the following values as part of its `objectclass` attribute:

- `top`
- `person`
- `organizationalPerson`
- `user`

That is because the `user` class inherits from the `organizationalPerson` class, which inherits from the `person` class, which inherits from the `top` class. When a class inherits from another, the attributes of the inherited class (also known as the parent class) are available for the inheriting class to use. A class can inherit attributes from abstract and structural classes, which would show up in the `objectclass` attribute for an instantiated object, but auxiliary classes that get associated with a particular class do not. That's because classes do not inherit attributes from auxiliary classes the way they do from structural and abstract classes. Auxiliary classes allow for a grouping of attributes to be associated with one or more classes in a similar manner to just adding attributes directly to a class's definition.

`Objectcategory`, on the other hand, is a single-value *indexed* attribute, which specifies a classification for a type of object. `Objectcategory` is intended to be an easy way to query for a certain "category" of objects, such as "Person". As an example, both user and contact objects have an `objectcategory` of Person, so by simply searching for (`objectcategory=Person`), you could possibly retrieve user or contact objects.

In practice, it is pretty unlikely that you would want to use `objectcategory` as a means to query a certain category of objects. Also, the majority of objects in Active Directory have an `objectcategory` that is the same as the `objectclass` in which they were instantiated, making classification applicable only in a few cases.

Nevertheless, most queries should in fact use a combination of `objectclass` and `objectcategory` as part of the search filter or SQL. One of the primary reasons for not using just `objectclass` is that it is not indexed and is multivalued, which does not make for an efficient query. The other classic problem with using only `objectclass` is that you can end up with more object types than you were expecting. This is a common problem with using (`objectclass=user`). You would think you'd only get user objects back using that filter, but you can also potentially get computer objects as well, since the computer objectclass is inherited from the user class (therefore causing it to be one of the values for the objectclass attribute for every computer object). And even though it would be efficient to use only objectcategory because it is indexed, it falls into the same trap as objectclass, because additional objects other than the one you are targeting may get returned (e.g., user objects and contact objects). It is for these reasons that you should try always to use a combination of objectclass and objectcategory in your searches.

Several examples are included next to illustrate what using various combinations of objectclass and objectcategory can return:

People (i.e., Users and Contacts)
    (objectcategory=person)

Contacts
    (&(objectclass=contact)(objectcategory=person))

Users
    (&(objectclass=user)(objectcategory=person))

Users and computers (not optimized)
    (objectclass=user)

Users and computers (optimized)
    (&(|(objectcategory=person)(objectcategory=computer))(objectclass=user))

Groups
    (&(objectclass=group)(objectcategory=group))

Containers
    (&(objectclass=container)(objectcategory=container))

Organizational Units
    (&(objectclass=organizationalunit)(objectcategory=OrganizationalUnit))

Filtering an Existing Resultset

An optimization technique that can be used when you need to perform a lot of queries is to instead perform one large query and repeatedly filter the resultset to get the subset of entries you want. It is possible to select particular items from a resultset by using the Recordset::Filter property method. Once the Recordset::Filter property has been set, you can access only the items in the resultset that match the filter. Properties such as the Recordset::RecordCount return only the number of items that match the filter. If you then set the filter back to an empty string, the whole resultset is available again. Since filtering a resultset relies on data that is present in the resultset, you can only filter using the Fields object and its values. For example, if you only specify to return the givenName and sn attributes in a query, you can use only those attributes to filter the resultset later. If you do not return cn as a field, there is no way to filter on it later.

Being able to filter an existing resultset is a useful tool but only in certain situations. In our experience, it is especially useful in three situations:

- You want to use filtered resultsets to access entries instead of multiple queries.
- You want to refine a large resultset without looping through every value.
- You want to reduce the load on Active Directory by performing one large query as opposed to several separate queries.

Let's consider a contrived example where use of the Recordset::Filter makes some sense. Let's say we want to count how many usernames begin with each of the 26 letters of the alphabet. The most intuitive method is probably to execute 26 ADO searches and record the Recordset::RecordCount property for each. However, this will hit Active Directory with 26 separate searches. Now let's expand the requirement and say we need these totals recorded continually in a file every minute or so. By now, you may be unwilling to keep hitting Active Directory with this sort of traffic every minute. The other alternative is to execute a single search for all users and loop through the resultset using Recordset::MoveNext, updating an array of 26 counts as we go. This hits Active Directory only once, but it iterates through every item. This process is fast for a moderate number of users, but for a really large number of users, it is much slower. If your resultset returns, say, 20,000 users in a single search, you need to use Recordset::Filter.

To solve the problem, we can write a piece of code that executes one search and then sets 26 separate filters, recording the Recordset::RecordCount value at each stage. Example 20-1 contains the sample code, from which the values are written to the *C:\ out.txt* file.

Example 20-1. Using recordset filters to reduce the load on Active Directory

```
Option Explicit

Const adStateOpen = 1

Dim objFileSystem  'A FileSystemObject
Dim objOutput      'A TextStream Object
Dim objConn        'An ADO Connection object
Dim objRS          'An ADO Recordset object
Dim intCount       'An integer

'**************************************************************************
'Create the file if it doesn't exist or truncate it if it does exist
'**************************************************************************
Set objFileSystem = CreateObject("Scripting.FileSystemObject")
Set objOutput = objFileSystem.CreateTextFile("c:\out.txt", TRUE)

'**************************************************************************
'Write out the current time and date using the VBScript 'Now' function
'**************************************************************************
objOutput.WriteLine "Starting..." & Now
```

```
Set objConn = CreateObject("ADODB.Connection")
objConn.Provider = "ADSDSOObject"
objConn.Open "", "CN=Administrator,CN=Users,dc=mycorp,dc=com", ""
If objConn.State = adStateOpen Then
  objOutput.WriteLine "Authentication Successful!"
Else
  objOutput.WriteLine "Authentication Failed."
  WScript.Quit(1)
End If

Set objRS = objConn.Execute _
  ("<LDAP://dc=mycorp,dc=com>;(&(objectclass=user)(objectcategory=Person));cn;SubTree")

'*****************************************************************************
'Loop through the ASCII characters letters Asc("a") to Asc("z")
'where Asc("a") = 97 and Chr(97) = "a"
'*****************************************************************************
For intCount = 97 To 122
  objRS.Filter = "cn LIKE '" & Chr(intCount) & "*'"
  objOutput.WriteLine(Chr(intCount) & " = " & objRS.RecordCount)
Next

objConn.Close
Set objRS = Nothing

objOutput.Close
```

The filter property must be set using a SQL-like query string, not an LDAP search filter. The recordset filter notation is fairly simple to use. The string can b an empty string (""), which removes the current filter; a criteria string; or an array of bookmarks. Bookmarks will be explained in more detail shortly.

Using a criteria string

The criteria string can take a number of different forms, which basically can be broken down to:

```
Field-name  operator  value-to-check
```

Here are some simple examples:

```
Name = vicky      'Checks for exact equivalence (=)
size < 10         'Checks for less-than (<)
size > 10         'Checks for greater-than (>)
size >= 5         'Checks greater-than-or-equal-to (>=)
size <= 20        'Checks less-than-or-equal-to (<=)
size <> 10        'Checks for not-equal-to (<>)
```

Dates are simple to check if you surround them with pound signs (#):

```
Date = #12/12/99#
```

You also can use the keyword LIKE:

```
cn LIKE 'a*'           'Checks for all cn's beginning with "a"
cn LIKE 'ca%'          'Checks for all three-letter cn's beginning with "ca"
cn LIKE '*eithCoo*'
```

You can also use AND and OR:

```
size > 10 AND size < 20
cn LIKE 'a*' OR cn LIKE 'b*'
```

However, there is a strict rule to follow if you want to group a criteria string containing OR with another string using AND. Again, this is sloppy, and Microsoft should look to fixing it in a later release:

```
(cn LIKE 'a*' OR cn LIKE 'b*') AND (size <> 10)           'This is WRONG!
(cn LIKE 'a*' AND size <> 10) OR (cn LIKE 'b*' AND size <> 10) 'This is CORRECT!
```

That should be enough to get you started.

Using bookmarks

Each object in a resultset has a bookmark associated with it. You can always obtain the bookmark for the current record and store it for later use by retrieving the value of ResultSet::Bookmark. After recording the bookmark, you can instantly jump to that record in the resultset at any time by writing the recorded value back to the bookmark property. For example:

```
'Record the bookmark for the current record
objBookMark = objRS.Bookmark

'Do something

'Now return the current record to the record indicated by the bookmark
objRS.Bookmark = objBookMark
```

If you read up about the ADO object model on the MSDN site, you will come across the Recordset::Clone method for cloning a resultset. Cloning a resultset will clone bookmarks. However, each recordset's bookmarks can be used only with its own resultset.

Advanced Search Function—SearchAD

We will now take many of the concepts from this chapter and apply them in a useful example called SearchAD. SearchAD can be included in any VBScript and used immediately as is.

SearchAD takes five parameters and returns a Boolean indicating whether it succeeded or failed in the search. You should recognize most of these parameters.

- The base ADsPath to start the search from
- A valid ADO criteria string

- The depth that you wish to search, represented by one of the exact strings Base, OneLevel, or SubTree

- The comma-separated list of attributes that is to be returned

- A variable that will hold the returned results of the search in an array

The last parameter does not have any values when passed in, but if SearchAD is successful, the array contains the resultset.

Here is an example use of SearchAD:

```
bolIsSuccess = SearchAD("LDAP://ou=Finance,dc=mycorp,dc=com", _
  "(cn=a*)", "Base", "cn,description", arrSearchResults)
```

You can also use it as part of an If...Then condition:

```
If SearchAD("LDAP://dc=mycorp,dc=com", "(description=moose)", "SubTree", _
  "ADsPath,cn,description", arrSearchResults) Then
  'success code using arrSearchResults
Else
  'failure code
End If
```

The array that is returned is a two-dimensional array of attributes that match the criteria. If there were 12 results returned for the preceding query, this is how you access the results:

```
arrSearchResults(0,0) 'ADsPath of first result
arrSearchResults(0,1) 'CN of first result
arrSearchResults(0,2) 'Description of first result
arrSearchResults(1,0) 'ADsPath of second result
arrSearchResults(1,1) 'CN of second result
arrSearchResults(1,2) 'Description of second result
arrSearchResults(2,0) 'ADsPath of third result
arrSearchResults(2,1) 'CN of third result
arrSearchResults(2,2) 'Description of third result
arrSearchResults(3,0) 'ADsPath of fourth result
arrSearchResults(3,1) 'CN of fourth result
arrSearchResults(3,2) 'Description of fourth result
  .
  .
  .
arrSearchResults(11,0) 'ADsPath of 11th result
arrSearchResults(11,1) 'CN of 11th result
arrSearchResults(11,2) 'Description of 11th result
```

You can loop through these values in your own code using VBScript's built-in function UBound to find the maximum upper bound of an array:

```
UBound(arrSearchResults,1) 'This results in a value of 11

UBound(arrSearchResults,2) 'This results in a value of 2
```

The first UBound gives the upper bound of the array's first dimension, and the second gives the upper bound of the second dimension. Thus you can loop through an index from 0 to these values to iterate through the array. For example:

```
'Iterate through the entire set of records
For i=0 To UBound(arrSearchResults,1)
  'Now for each record iterate through the list of that record's values
  For j=0 To UBound(arrSearchResults,2)
    'Do something with arrSearchResults(i,j), e.g., the next line
    MsgBox arrSearchResults(i,j)
  Next
Next
```

So, without further ado, here is Example 20-2, which contains the SearchAD function.

Example 20-2. SearchAD, an advanced search function

```
'*************************************************************************
'SearchAD Function (returns Boolean success or failure)
'*************************************************************************
Function SearchAD(ByVal strLDAPBase, ByVal strCriteria, ByVal strDepth, _
  ByVal strAttributeList, ByRef arrResults())

  Dim objConn, objComm, objRS, intArrayIndex, arrAttributes
  Dim intAttributeArrayIndex

  On Error Resume Next

  '*********************************************************************
  'Used to specify an unsuccessful ADO connection
  '*********************************************************************
  Const adStateClosed = 0

  '*********************************************************************
  'Defined in ADS_SCOPEENUM (in the ADSI documentation) for a full
  'subtree search starting at the defined root
  '*********************************************************************
  Const ADS_SCOPE_SUBTREE = 2

  Set objConn = CreateObject("ADODB.Connection")
  Set objComm = CreateObject("ADODB.Command")
  Set objRS = CreateObject("ADODB.Recordset")

  objConn.Provider = "ADSDSOObject"
  objConn.Open "", vbNullString, vbNullString

  '*********************************************************************
  'If connection failed, then return FALSE
  '*********************************************************************
  If objConn.State = adStateClosed Then
    SearchAD = False
    Exit Function
  End If
```

Example 20-2. SearchAD, an advanced search function (continued)

```
'**********************************************************************
'Link the now-open connection with the empty command object
'**********************************************************************
Set objComm.ActiveConnection = objConn


'**********************************************************************
'Populate the command object in order to execute a query through the
'linked connection. Set the text of the query command (i.e., the search),
'the max number of results to return, the timeout in seconds to wait
'for the query, and whether the results are to be cached.
'**********************************************************************
objComm.CommandText = "<" & strLDAPBase & ">;" & strCriteria & ";" _
  & strAttributeList & ";" & strDepth
objComm.Properties("Page Size") = 10000
objComm.Properties("Timeout") = 60
objComm.Properties("searchscope") = ADS_SCOPE_SUBTREE
objComm.Properties("Cache Results") = False


'**********************************************************************
'Execute the command through the linked connection
'**********************************************************************
Err.Clear
Set objRS = objComm.Execute
'**********************************************************************
'If there was an error, then return FALSE
'**********************************************************************
If Err Then
  objConn.Close
  Set objRS = Nothing
  SearchAD = False
Else
  '**********************************************************************
  'If we're pointing at the end of the resultset already (EOF) then there
  'were no records returned (although the query did search the AD), so
  'return FALSE
  '**********************************************************************
  If objRS.EOF Then
    objConn.Close
    Set objRS = Nothing
    SearchAD = False
  Else
    '**********************************************************************
    'Count number of attributes passed in by splitting the attributes up
    'using commas as separators into an array of elements. Then we can use
    'that array to find the upper bound (i.e., number of attributes).
    '**********************************************************************
    arrAttributes = Split(strAttributeList,",")


    '**********************************************************************
    'Now in order to place all the resulting attributes into the array that
    'we'll pass back out, we need to redimension the array so that it is
    'large enough to hold the records. The array is multidimensional in
    'order to hold all the attribute fields.
```

Example 20-2. SearchAD, an advanced search function (continued)

```
'**********************************************************************
ReDim arrResults((objRS.RecordCount - 1),UBound(arrAttributes))

'**********************************************************************
'Loop through the newly redimensioned array, starting at zero, and add
'each field to the array
'**********************************************************************
intArrayIndex = 0
While Not objRS.EOF
  For intAttributeArrayIndex = 0 To UBound(arrAttributes)
    arrResults(intArrayIndex,intAttributeArrayIndex) = _
      objRS.Fields.Item(arrAttributes(intAttributeArrayIndex)).Value
  Next
  intArrayIndex = intArrayIndex + 1
  objRS.MoveNext
Wend

'**********************************************************************
'Close the connection and return TRUE
'**********************************************************************
objConn.Close
Set objRS = Nothing
SearchAD = True
    End If
  End If
End Function
```

Summary

In this chapter, we reviewed the basics of ADO, which provides a robust search interface for Active Directory. While originally intended for databases, ADO was adapted to Active Directory to allow queries based on LDAP search filters or SQL. Several techniques for optimizing searches in Active Directory were reviewed, including a discussion of using objectclass versus objectcategory. We ended the chapter by covering a fully functional SearchAD procedure that can be used as is in any VBScript to easily search Active Directory based on specified criteria. SearchAD hides all the underlying ADO logic, including connection setup, query execution, and recordset manipulation.

After providing a good background for ADSI and ADO in Chapters 18 through 20, we are now ready to move to more practical applications. The next several chapters show some of the capabilities these interfaces provide and a lot of sample code to get you started.

CHAPTER 21

Users and Groups

In this chapter, we will show you how to automate the creation and manipulation of user and group accounts. Although tools to create user and group accounts already exist (e.g., the Resource Kit's Addusers utility), ADSI's versatility lets you quickly write a script that creates 1,000 fully featured user or group accounts based on whatever business logic you require. You can also create command-line utilities or web-based interfaces using the techniques shown in this chapter to perform such functions as unlocking locked-out user accounts or adding users to groups.

Creating a Simple User Account

You can quickly create a user account with minimal attributes with ADSI. The following code shows how to create a user in an NT domain, a local computer, and an Active Directory domain.

```
Option Explicit
Dim objDomain, objUser
'Creating a user in a Windows NT domain

Set objDomain = GetObject("WinNT://MYDOMAIN")
Set objUser = objDomain.Create("user","vlaunders")
objUser.SetInfo

'Creating a local user on a computer or member server
'Valid for Windows NT/2000/2003
Set objComputer = GetObject("WinNT://MYCOMPUTER,Computer")
Set objUser = objComputer.Create("user","vlaunders")
objUser.SetInfo

'Creating a user in Active Directory
Set objDomain = GetObject("LDAP://cn=Users,dc=mycorp,dc=com")
Set objUser = objDomain.Create("user","cn=vlaunders")
objUser.Put "sAMAccountName", "vlaunders"
objUser.Put "userPrincipalName", "vlaunders@mycorp.com"
objUser.SetInfo
```

The code is composed of three sections. The first two sections use the WinNT provider to create a user account in an NT 4.0 domain, and in a computer that could be a member server or part of a workgroup. The third section uses the LDAP provider to create a user account in an Active Directory domain.

When you create users in an Active Directory domain, you need to be aware of two important User object attributes: sAMAccountName and userPrincipalName. The User object has several mandatory attributes. The system sets many of these mandatory attributes, except for one, sAMAccountName, which allows Active Directory–based clients to interact with older clients and NT domains. You must set the sAMAccountName attribute before you call IADs::SetInfo or the creation will fail. The userPrincipalName attribute isn't mandatory, but it is recommend so users can log on using an email-style address as defined in RFC 822 (*http://www.ietf.org/rfc/rfc822.txt*).

Creating a Full-Featured User Account

Creating user accounts as we've done previously is fine for an introduction, but typically you'll need to set many more attributes to make them usable in your environment. The approaches you use to create fully featured users in the NT and Active Directory environments differ slightly; Active Directory offers considerably more properties than NT, such as the office and home addresses of users, as well as lists of email addresses and pager, fax, and phone numbers.

You can manipulate User objects with a special interface called IADsUser. IADsUser's methods and property methods let you directly set many of the User object's property values. Tables 21-1 through 21-3 contain the methods, read-write property methods, and read-only property methods, respectively, for the IADsUser interface. The corresponding Active Directory attribute is included in parentheses for the property methods that can be set with the LDAP provider.

Table 21-1. IADsUser methods

Method	Description
IADsUser::ChangePassword	Changes the existing password.
IADsUser::SetPassword	Sets a new password without needing the old one.
IADsUser::Groups	Gets a list of groups of which the user is a member. You can use the IADsMembers interface to iterate through the list.

Table 21-2. IADsUser read-write property methods

Property method	Available with WinNT or LDAP?
IADsUser::AccountDisabled	WinNT, LDAP (userAccountControl mask)
IADsUser::AccountExpirationDate	WinNT, LDAP (accountExpires)
IADsUser::Department	LDAP (department)
IADsUser::Description	WinNT, LDAP (description)

Table 21-2. IADsUser read-write property methods (continued)

Property method	Available with WinNT or LDAP?
IADsUser::Division	LDAP (division)
IADsUser::EmailAddress	LDAP (mail)
IADsUser::EmployeeID	LDAP (employeeID)
IADsUser::FaxNumber	LDAP (facsimileTelephoneNumber)
IADsUser::FirstName	LDAP (givenName)
IADsUser::FullName	WinNT, LDAP (displayName)
IADsUser::GraceLoginsAllowed	Neither
IADsUser::GraceLoginsRemaining	Neither
IADsUser::HomeDirectory	WinNT, LDAP (homeDirectory)
IADsUser::HomePage	LDAP (wWWHomePage)
IADsUser::IsAccountLocked	WinNT, LDAP (userAccountControl)
IADsUser::Languages	LDAP (languages)
IADsUser::LastName	LDAP (sn)
IADsUser::LoginHours	WinNT, LDAP (logonHours)
IADsUser::LoginScript	WinNT, LDAP (scriptPath)
IADsUser::LoginWorkstations	WinNT, LDAP (userWorkstations)
IADsUser::Manager	LDAP (manager)
IADsUser::MaxLogins	WinNT
IADsUser::MaxStorage	WinNT, LDAP (maxStorage)
IADsUser::NamePrefix	LDAP (personalTitle)
IADsUser::NameSuffix	LDAP (generationQualifier)
IADsUser::OfficeLocations	LDAP (physicalDeliveryOfficeName)
IADsUser::OtherName	LDAP (middleName)
IADsUser::PasswordExpirationDate	WinNT
IADsUser::PasswordMinimumLength	WinNT
IADsUser::PasswordRequired	WinNT, LDAP (userAccountControl mask)
IADsUser::Picture	LDAP (thumbNailPhoto)
IADsUser::PostalAddresses	LDAP (postalAddress)
IADsUser::PostalCodes	LDAP (postalCode)
IADsUser::Profile	WinNT, LDAP (profilePath)
IADsUser::RequireUniquePassword	WinNT
IADsUser::SeeAlso	LDAP (seeAlso)
IADsUser::TelephoneHome	LDAP (homePhone)
IADsUser::TelephoneMobile	LDAP (mobile)
IADsUser::TelephoneNumber	LDAP (telephoneNumber)
IADsUser::TelephonePager	LDAP (pager)
IADsUser::Title	LDAP (title)

Table 21-3. IADsUser read-only property methods

Property method	Available with WinNT or LDAP?
IADsUser::BadLoginAddress	Neither
IADsUser::BadLoginCount	WinNT, LDAP (badPwdCount)
IADsUser::LastFailedLogin	LDAP (badPasswordTime)
IADsUser::LastLogin	WinNT, LDAP (lastLogin)
IADsUser::LastLogoff	WinNT, LDAP (lastLogoff)
IADsUser::PasswordLastChanged	LDAP (pwdLastSet)

For more information on IADsUser, check out the following location in the MSDN Library (*http://msdn.microsoft.com/library/*): Networking and Directory Services → Active Directory, ADSI and Directory Services → SDK Documentation → Directory Services → Active Directory Service Interfaces → Active Directory Service Interfaces Reference → ADSI Interfaces → Persistent Object Interfaces → IADsUser.

Now let's apply some of this knowledge to two examples. The first shows how to create a fully featured user in Windows NT, and the second shows how to create a fully featured user in Active Directory.

WinNT Provider

Example 21-1 uses several IADsUser property methods and several constant values to create a fully featured user in NT.

Example 21-1. Creating a full-featured user account in Windows NT

```
Option Explicit

'**********************************************************************
'Flag constants. See the later sidebar on "Boolean Arithmetic with
'Hexadecimal Values."
'**********************************************************************
Const UF_SCRIPT = &H1
Const UF_ACCOUNTDISABLE = &H2
Const UF_LOCKOUT = &H10
Const UF_PASSWD_NOTREQD = &H20
Const UF_PASSWORD_CANT_CHANGE = &H40
Const UF_ENCRYPTED_TEXT_PASSWORD_ALLOWED = &H80
Const UF_DONT_EXPIRE_PASSWD = &H10000

Dim objDomain, objUser, fso, intUserFlags, intNewUserFlags
Dim fldUserHomedir, wshShell

Set objDomain = GetObject("WinNT://MYDOMAIN")
Set objUser = objDomain.Create("user","vlaunders")

'**********************************************************************
'Write the newly created object out from the property cache and read
'all the properties for the object, including the ones set by the
```

Example 21-1. Creating a full-featured user account in Windows NT (continued)

```
'system on creation
'**********************************************************************
objUser.SetInfo
objUser.GetInfo


'**********************************************************************
'Set the properties
'**********************************************************************
objUser.AccountDisabled = False
objUser.AccountExpirationDate = "02/05/04"
objUser.Description = "My description goes here!"
objUser.FullName = "Victoria Launders"
objUser.IsAccountLocked = False
objUser.LoginScript = "login.vbs"
objUser.PasswordRequired = True


'**********************************************************************
'Set all the properties for the user and read back the data, including
'any default so that you can set the flags
'**********************************************************************
objUser.SetInfo
objUser.GetInfo


'**********************************************************************
'Make sure the password never expires and the user can't change it
'**********************************************************************
intUserFlags = objUser.Get("userFlags")
intNewUserFlags = intUserFlags Or UF_DONT_EXPIRE_PASSWD
intNewUserFlags = intNewUserFlags Or UF_PASSWORD_CANT_CHANGE
objUser.Put "userFlags", intNewUserFlags
objUser.SetInfo


'**********************************************************************
'Set the password
'**********************************************************************
objUser.SetPassword "thepassword"
```

Most of the code in the script is self-explanatory, except for making sure the password never expires. We used two hexadecimal constants to explicitly force the new user account to have a password that never expires and that the user can't change. The code to set these password requirements might seem complicated, but it involves simple arithmetic; the sidebar "Boolean Arithmetic with Hexadecimal Values" explains this arithmetic. If you prefer not to use hex constants, you might be able to use a User object property method. For example, you can use the IADsUser:: AccountDisabled property method instead of the UF_ACCOUNTDISABLE constant to disable an account. Similarly, you can use the IADsUser::IsAccountLocked property method instead of the UF_LOCKOUT constant to lock an account. These IADs property methods hide the arithmetic within a simple Boolean value.

Boolean Arithmetic with Hexadecimal Values

Assume that you want an attribute of an object (e.g., userFlags of the User object) to set 8 values. You use an 8-bit binary number to represent those 8 values. If you want the attribute to hold 11 values, you use an 11-bit binary number.

The binary system is a base-2 system in which 0 typically represents a false condition and 1 typically represents a true condition. In this example, 0 means the value isn't set, and 1 means the value is set. If you want to set only the third and eighth values of an 8-value attribute, you set the third and eighth bits of an 8-bit binary number to 1, or &B10000100. (You read binary numbers from right to left.) The prefix &B specifies that the number is binary.

However, attributes store data as decimal values. Thus, you need to convert the binary number into a decimal value, which is base-10. For example, the binary number &B10000100 translates into:

$$2^7 + 2^2 = 128 + 4 = 132$$

You use the Boolean AND operator to check whether a bit is set and the OR operator to set a bit. For example, suppose you want to see whether the fourth bit is set in an 8-bit binary number that has a decimal value of 132. You can check for the existence of this bit using the AND operator to compare the number to a binary mask indicating that the fourth bit is set. The equation to do this is:

&B10000100 AND &B00001000 = &B00000000

You solve this equation by resolving the AND operation for each bit individually. For example, the first bit in &B10000100 is 0, and the first bit in &B00001000 is 0: 0 AND 0 is 0. The second bit in &B10000100 is 0, and the second bit in &B00001000 is 0: 0 AND 0 is 0. The third bit in &B10000100 is 1, and the third bit in &B00001000 is 0; 1 AND 0 is 0. When you calculate all eight bits, the result is &B00000000. In other words, the fourth bit isn't set.

Suppose you want to test whether the third bit is set:

&B10000100 AND &B0000100 = &B00000100

Because the third bit in &B10000100 is 1, and the third bit in &B0000100 is 1, the resulting bit is 1 (1 AND 1 is 1), which specifies that the value for the third bit is set.

Let's translate this binary equation into decimal and hex equations:

&B10000100 AND &B0000100 = &B00000100
132 AND 4 = 4
&H84 AND &H4 = &H4

If the return value is 0 or &H0, the bit isn't set. If the return value is the bit's actual value (in this case, 4 or &H4), the bit is set.

132 OR 8 = 140
&H84 OR &H8 = &H8C

—continued—

Just like the AND operator, the OR operator works with binary, decimal, and hex systems. Taking the example just given, let's try to set the third bit, which happens to be already set:

&B10000100 OR &B0000100 = &B10000100
132 OR 4 = 132
&H84 OR &H4 = &H84

In other words, the result is the new value with that bit set. Because that bit was already set, nothing changes. Let's try setting the fourth bit, which isn't already set:

&B10000100 OR &B00001000 = &B10001100

The result includes a newly set fourth bit. You can even set two bits at once. For example, here's how you set the fourth and fifth bits:

&B10000100 OR &B00011000 = &B10011100
132 OR 24 = 156
&H84 OR &H18 = &H9C

Although the Boolean mathematics is straightforward, luckily you don't have to include this code in a script. Instead, you typically use constants. For example, if you declare the constant:

```
Const UF_DONT_EXPIRE_PASSWD = &H10000
```

you just need to specify that constant in the script. To determine this bit's existence, use the code:

```
If intUserFlags And UF_DONT_EXPIRE_PASSWD = 0 Then

'UF_DONT_EXPIRE_PASSWD is not set

Else

'UF_DONT_EXPIRE_PASSWD is set

End If
```

You set bits in a similar fashion. For example, to set the &H10000 bit, use the code:

```
intUserFlags = intUserFlags Or UF_DONT_EXPIRE_PASSWD
```

LDAP Provider

Example 21-2 shows how to create a fully featured user in Active Directory. This script is similar to the last one, with a couple of major differences. The property name userFlags changes to userAccountControl for the extended settings. Home directory attributes are set along with creation of the home directory folder if it doesn't exist. Other minor differences exist, such as the use of more constants and property methods. Active Directory lets you set many property values for users, including multivalue properties that you set via an array. For example, you can list several telephone numbers for the TelephoneNumber, TelephoneMobile, and TelephoneHome properties. Through the use of constants, you can even set up Active Directory to let users log on with smart cards.

Example 21-2. Creating a full-featured user account in Active Directory

```
Option Explicit

'**********************************************************************
'WshShell::Run constants
'**********************************************************************
Const vbMinimizedNoFocus = 6

'**********************************************************************
'Flag constants. See the later sidebar on "Boolean Arithmetic with
'Hexadecimal Values."
'**********************************************************************
Const UF_SCRIPT = &H1
Const UF_ACCOUNTDISABLE = &H2
Const UF_HOMEDIR_REQUIRED = &H8
Const UF_LOCKOUT = &H10
Const UF_PASSWD_NOTREQD = &H20
Const UF_PASSWORD_CANT_CHANGE = &H40
Const UF_ENCRYPTED_TEXT_PASSWORD_ALLOWED = &H80
Const UF_DONT_EXPIRE_PASSWD = &H10000
Const UF_MNS_LOGON_ACCOUNT = &H20000
Const UF_SMARTCARD_REQUIRED = &H40000
Const UF_TRUSTED_FOR_DELEGATION = &H80000
Const UF_NOT_DELEGATED = &H100000

Const ADS_PROPERTY_UPDATE = 2

Dim objDomain, objUser, fso, intUserFlags, intNewUserFlags
Dim fldUserHomedir, wshShell

Set objDomain = GetObject("LDAP://cn=Users,dc=mycorp,dc=com")
Set objUser = objDomain.Create("user","cn=vlaunders")
objUser.Put "sAMAccountName", "vlaunders"
objUser.Put "userPrincipalName", "vlaunders@mycorp.com"

'**********************************************************************
'Write the newly created object out from the property cache and read
'all the properties for the object, including the ones set by the
'system on creation
'**********************************************************************
objUser.SetInfo
objUser.GetInfo

'**********************************************************************
'Set the properties
'**********************************************************************
objUser.AccountDisabled = False
objUser.AccountExpirationDate = "02/05/01"
```

```
objUser.Description = "My description goes here!"
objUser.IsAccountLocked = False
objUser.LoginScript = "login.vbs"
objUser.Profile = "\\MYDOMAIN\DFS\Users\vlaunders\profile"
objUser.PasswordRequired = True
objUser.TelephoneHome = Array("0123-555-7890")
objUser.PutEx ADS_PROPERTY_UPDATE, "otherHomePhone", _
  Array("0123 555 7891", "0123 555 7892")
objUser.TelephoneNumber = Array("0123 555 7890")
objUser.PutEx ADS_PROPERTY_UPDATE, "otherTelephone", _
  Array("0123 555 7891", "0123 555 7892")
objUser.TelephoneMobile = Array("0123 555 7890")
objUser.PutEx ADS_PROPERTY_UPDATE, "otherMobile", _
  Array("0123 555 7891", "0123 555 7892")
objUser.NamePrefix = "Ms."
objUser.FirstName = "Victoria"
objUser.LastName = "Launders"
objUser.DisplayName = "Victoria Launders"


'*********************************************************************
'Set the drive that you'll map to
'*********************************************************************
objUser.HomeDirectory = "\\MYDOMAIN\DFS\Users\vlaunders"
objUser.Put "homeDrive", "Z:"


'*********************************************************************
'Set all the properties for the user and read back the data, including
'any defaults, so that you can set the flags
'*********************************************************************
objUser.SetInfo
objUser.GetInfo


'*********************************************************************
'Make sure the password never expires and the user can't change it
'*********************************************************************
intUserFlags = objUser.Get("userAccountControl")
intNewUserFlags = intUserFlags Or UF_DONT_EXPIRE_PASSWD
intNewUserFlags = intNewUserFlags Or UF_PASSWORD_CANT_CHANGE
objUser.Put "userAccountControl", intNewUserFlags
objUser.SetInfo


'*********************************************************************
'Create the home directory
'*********************************************************************
Set fso = CreateObject("Scripting.FileSystemObject")
If Not fso.FolderExists("\\MYDOMAIN\DFS\Users\vlaunders") Then
Set fldUserHomedir = fso.CreateFolder("\\MYDOMAIN\DFS\Users\vlaunders")
End If


'*********************************************************************
'Set full rights for the user to the home directory
'*********************************************************************
```

Example 21-2. Creating a full-featured user account in Active Directory (continued)

```
Set wshShell = WScript.CreateObject("Wscript.Shell")
wshShell.Run "cacls.exe \\MYDOMAIN\DFS\Users\vlaunders /e /g vlaunders:F",
vbMinimizedNoFocus, True

'**********************************************************************
'Set the password
'**********************************************************************
objUser.SetPassword "thepassword"
```

We created the home directory by obtaining a reference to a FileSystemObject object and calling the `FileSystemObject::CreateFolder` method if the directory doesn't already exist. The permissions were set by running the *cacls.exe* command available from the Resource Kit using the `WshShell::Run` method. When calling `WshShell::Run`, you need to include three parameters. The first parameter is the command you want to execute; the second parameter can be any of the following constant values that describe how you want to treat the new window produced by executing the command:

```
Const vbHide = 0              ` hides the window
Const vbNormalFocus = 1       ` displays the window
Const vbMinimizedFocus = 2    ` minimizes the window with focus
Const vbMaximizedFocus = 3    ` maximizes the window with focus
Const vbNormalNoFocus = 4     ` displays the window w/o focus
Const vbMinimizedNoFocus = 6  ` minimizes the window w/o focus
```

The last parameter to the `WshShell::Run` method should be to set to true if you want the script to wait until CACLS finishes before continuing to the next line.

 As an alternative to using CACLS to set permissions, you could write a script that makes use of the interfaces described in Chapter 23, or you could use the *ADsSecurity.dll* provided available in the Platform SDK.

Creating Many User Accounts

User-specific scripts work well if you have to create only a few user accounts. If you need to create many user accounts at one time, or if you create new accounts often, using a script with an input file is more efficient. The input file includes the user data so that you can use the script to create any user account. For example, the output shown below represents the *users-to-create.txt* input file that provides the user data for the universal script in Example 21-3. Although this input file includes only four data sets, you can include as many data sets as you want. You include a data set for each user account that you want to create.

```
vlaunders:12/09/01:The description:Victoria Launders:onebanana
aglowenorris:08/07/00:Another user:Alistair Lowe-Norris:twobanana
kbemowski:03/03/03:A third user:Karen Bemowski:threebanana
jkellett:08/09/99:A fourth user:Jenneth Kellett:four
```

As the output shows, each data set goes on a separate line. A data set can contain as many values as you want. The data sets in the *users-to-create.txt* file have five values: username, expiration date, description, full name, and password. You use colons to separate the values.*

Example 21-3. Creating many user accounts using a script with an input file

```
Option Explicit

Const ForReading = 1

Dim objDomain, objUser, fso, tsInputFile, strLine, arrInput
Dim fldUserHomedir, wshShell

Set objDomain = GetObject("LDAP://cn=Users,dc=mycorp,dc=com")
Set fso = CreateObject("Scripting.FileSystemObject")

'*********************************************************************
'Open the text file as a text stream for reading.
'Don't create a file if users-to-create.txt doesn't exist
'*********************************************************************
Set tsInputFile = fso.OpenTextFile("c:\users-to-create.txt", ForReading, False)

'*********************************************************************
'Execute the lines inside the loop, even though you're not at the end
'of the file
'*********************************************************************
While Not tsInputFile.AtEndOfStream

    '*********************************************************************
    'Read a line, and use the Split function to split the data set into
    'its separate parts
    '*********************************************************************
    strLine = tsInputFile.ReadLine
    arrInput = Split(strLine, ":")

    Set objUser = objDomain.Create("user","cn=" & arrInput(0))
    objUser.Put "sAMAccountName", & arrInput(0)
    objUser.Put "userPrincipalName", arrInput(0) & "@mycorp.com"

    '*********************************************************************
    'Write the newly created object out from the property cache
    'Read all the properties for the object, including
    'the ones set by the system on creation
    '*********************************************************************
    objUser.SetInfo
    objUser.GetInfo
```

---

* While comma-separate-value (CSV) files are the norm for this sort of thing, the comma is more often used in properties that will be added for users, so I use the colon here instead.

Example 21-3. Creating many user accounts using a script with an input file (continued)

```
'********************************************************************
'Set the properties
'********************************************************************
objUser.AccountDisabled = False
objUser.AccountExpirationDate = arrInput(1)
objUser.Description = arrInput(2)
objUser.IsAccountLocked = False
objUser.LoginScript = "\\MYDOMAIN\DFS\Loginscripts\" & arrInput(0) & ".vbs"
objUser.Profile = "\\MYDOMAIN\DFS\Users\" & arrInput(0) & "\profile"
objUser.PasswordRequired = True
objUser.DisplayName = arrInput(3)

'********************************************************************
'Set the drive that you'll map to
'********************************************************************
objUser.HomeDirectory = "\\MYDOMAIN\DFS\Users\" & arrInput(0)
objUser.Put "homeDrive", "Z:"
objUser.SetInfo

'********************************************************************
'Create the home directory
'********************************************************************
If Not fso.FolderExists("\\MYDOMAIN\DFS\Users\" & arrInput(0)) Then
   Set fldUserHomedir = fso.CreateFolder("\\MYDOMAIN\DFS\Users\" & arrInput(0))
End If

'********************************************************************
'Set full rights for the user to the home directory
'********************************************************************
Set wshShell = WScript.CreateObject("Wscript.Shell")
wshShell.Run "cacls \\MYDOMAIN\DFS\Users\" & arrInput(0) _
   & " /e /g " & arrInput(0) & ":F", 1, True

'********************************************************************
'Set the password
'********************************************************************
objUser.SetPassword arrInput(4)

'********************************************************************
'Stop referencing this user
'********************************************************************
   Set objUser = Nothing
Wend

'Close the file
tsInputFile.Close
```

The script reads in the user data to create the user accounts. As the script shows, you use FileSystemObject (FSO) and TextStream (TS) objects to manipulate the user data. For information about FSO and TS objects, see *http://msdn.microsoft.com/library/default.asp?url=/nhp/Default.asp?contentid=28001169*. After you create a reference to an FSO object and assign that reference to the `fso` variable, apply the `FileSystemObject::OpenTextFile` method to open the *users-to-create.txt* file, setting the user data to the `tsInputFile` TS variable. Then use a while loop with the `Text-Stream::AtEndOfStream` method to loop through each line in `tsInputFile` until the end of the file. Once you reach the end of the file, use the `TextStream::Close` method to end the script.

The while loop is the heart of the script. Begin the while loop by applying the `TextStream::ReadLine` method to read in one line of `tsInputFile` at a time. The `strLine` string variable holds the retrieved data from that line, which you pass to VBScript's `Split` function. Using the colon as the separator, this function splits the data set into its five parts, assigning the data to the `arrInput` array variable. This array has index values that correspond to the five parts: 0 represents the username, 1 represents the expiration date, 2 represents the description, 3 represents the full name, and 4 represents the password.

The code in the middle of the while loop is similar to the code used earlier. After we create a reference to an ADSI User object and assign that reference to the `objUser` variable, we set that user's property values (including the home drive). We then use `IADs::SetInfo`, create the home directory, set the directory permissions, and set the password. However, instead of specifying each user's username, expiration date, description, full name, and password in the code, we specify the appropriate array index value. For example, for those property values in which you need to specify the username, you specify `arrInput(0)` instead of vlaunders, aglowenorris, kbemowski, or jkellett.

The while loop ends with setting `objUser` to `Nothing`. We need to clear `objUser` because we use this variable again when the `TextStream::ReadLine` method reads in the next line from `tsInputFile` to create the next user account.

Instead of reading in user data from a text file, you can read in data from other sources, such as a web-based form, a Microsoft Word document, a Excel spreadsheet, a database, or even a specially formatted Microsoft Outlook email message. You also can use command-line arguments to pass in user data, as we will show in a later example.

Modifying Many User Accounts

Once you have created the user accounts in a domain, you will more than likely need to modify them at some point. The modifications may consist only of changing individual properties of a user, such as the description or name fields. In these cases, you can perform the change manually or write a command-line script as shown in the next section. In some situations, you will need to make a large number of changes to your user accounts, as would be the case if you changed the name of your login script and wanted to point all users at the new script.

For Windows NT and even Active Directory domains, you can use the `IADsContainer::Filter` method to iterate through all the objects of a particular type. Thus, changing all users' login script is a pretty easy to do:

```
Option Explicit
On Error Resume Next
Dim objDomain, objUser
Set objDomain = GetObject("WinNT://MYCORP")
objDomain.Filter = Array("User")
'********************************************************************
' Iterate over each user and set the LoginScript
' Print an error if one occurs
'********************************************************************
for each objUser in objDomain
   objUser.LoginScript = "login-new.vbs"
   objUser.SetInfo

   if Err.Number <> 0 Then
      Wscript.Echo objUser.Name & " error occurred"
      Err.Clear
   Else
      Wscript.Echo objUser.Name & " modified"
   End if
next
```

While the previous code is straightforward, it is also limiting. The only filter option you have is object type, such as all users, and no additional criteria are allowed. That is why in most cases with Active Directory domains, you will want to use ADO to find objects, as explained in Chapter 20. So for our next example, let's say that we want to change the login script for all users in the domain that have a department attribute equal to "Sales". Example 21-4 shows how this can be done using ADO.

Example 21-4. Modifying the login script for all users in Sales

```
Option Explicit
On Error Resume Next
Dim objConn, objComm, objRS, objUser
Dim strBase, strFilter, strAttrs, strScope
'********************************************************************
'Set the ADO search criteria
'********************************************************************
strBase   = "<LDAP://dc=mycorp,dc=com>;"
strFilter = "(&(objectclass=user)(objectcategory=Person)(department=Sales));"
strAttrs  = "ADsPath;"
strScope  = "Subtree"

set objConn = CreateObject("ADODB.Connection")
objConn.Provider = "ADsDSOObject"
objConn.Open
'********************************************************************
'Need to enable Paging in case there are more than 1000 objects returned
'********************************************************************
Set objComm = CreateObject("ADODB.Command")
```

Example 21-4. Modifying the login script for all users in Sales (continued)

```
Set objComm.ActiveConnection = objConn
objComm.CommandText = strBase & strFilter & strAttrs & strScope
objComm.Properties("Page Size") = 1000
Set objRS = objComm.Execute( )
While not objRS.EOF
  Set objUser = GetObject( objRS.Fields.Item("ADsPath").Value )
  objUser.LoginScript = "login-sales.vbs"
  objUser.SetInfo
  if Err.Number <> 0 Then
     Wscript.Echo objUser.Name & " error occurred"
     Err.Clear
  Else
     Wscript.Echo objUser.Name & " modified"
  End if
  objRS.MoveNext
Wend
```

Note that we enabled Paging by setting up an ADO Command option and set the "Page Size" property to 1,000. This will ensure that we get all matching records. If we did not set "Page Size", the maximum number of records returned would be whatever the administrative limit is for your Active Directory (the default is 1,000).

Account Unlocker Utility

Imagine that you need a utility that quickly enables and unlocks an NT or Active Directory user account. The account was locked because the password was entered incorrectly too many times in succession or because the account exceeded its expiration date. Writing a user-specific script is inefficient if you have many users. Using an input file to pass in the needed user data to a script also is inefficient. You'd have to create the input file just before running the script, because you can't predict whose account you need to unlock. The best approach is to use command-line arguments to pass in the user data as you need it.

Examples 21-5 and 21-6 use this approach to enable and unlock NT and Active Directory user accounts, respectively. If you have a mixed NT and Active Directory network, you can even combine these two utilities into one script.

Example 21-5 implements the unlocker with the WinNT provider.

Example 21-5. Account unlocker utility for Windows NT

```
'*********************************************************************
'How to unlock and enable a Windows NT user via arguments to this script
'
'Parameters should be <domain> <username>
'*********************************************************************
Option Explicit
```

Example 21-5. Account unlocker utility for Windows NT (continued)

```
Dim wshArgs, objUser, strOutput

On Error Resume Next

'************************************************************************
'Get the arguments
'************************************************************************
Set wshArgs = Wscript.Arguments

'************************************************************************
'If no arguments passed in, then quit
'************************************************************************
If wshArgs.Count = 0 Then
  WScript.Echo "ERROR: No arguments passed in." & vbCrLf & vbCrLf _
    & "Please use NTUNLOCK <domain> <username>" & vbCrLf & vbCrLf
  WScript.Quit
End If

'************************************************************************
'Error checking of the arguments could go here if we were bothered
'************************************************************************

'************************************************************************
'Attempt to bind to the user
'************************************************************************
Set objUser = GetObject("WinNT://" & wshArgs(0) & "/" & wshArgs(1) & ",user")
If Err Then
  Wscript.Echo "Error: Could not bind to the following user: " & vbCrLf _
    & vbCrLf & "WinNT://" & wshArgs(0) & "/" & wshArgs(1) & vbCrLf & vbCrLf
  WScript.Quit
Else
  strOutput = "Connected to user WinNT://" & wshArgs(0) & "/" & wshArgs(1) _
    & vbCrLf
End If

'************************************************************************
'Attempt to enable the user (but don't quit if you fail)
'************************************************************************
Err.Clear
objUser.AccountDisabled = False
objUser.SetInfo
If Err Then
  strOutput = strOutput & vbTab & "Error: Could not enable the user account." _
    & vbCrLf
Else
  strOutput = strOutput & vbTab & "User account enabled." & vbCrLf
End If

'************************************************************************
'Attempt to unlock the user
'************************************************************************
Err.Clear
```

Example 21-5. Account unlocker utility for Windows NT (continued)

```
objUser.IsAccountLocked = False
objUser.SetInfo
If Err Then
  strOutput = strOutput & vbTab & "Error: Could not unlock the user account." _
    & vbCrLf
Else
  strOutput = strOutput & vbTab & "User account unlocked." & vbCrLf
End If

WScript.Echo strOutput
```

You pass in two arguments, domain and username, to the script. We use the `Wscript::Arguments` property method to retrieve the arguments. The `Wscript::Arguments` property method stores the arguments as a collection, indexing them from 0 to the number of arguments minus 1. The `wshArgs` collection in the script includes the argument `wshArgs(0)`, which represents the domain, and `wshArgs(1)`, which represents the username.

We use the `WshArguments::Count` method to count the number of arguments. If the count is 0, the script sends an error message and then quits. Use the `Wscript.Echo` method to display the error message so that you can use *cscript.exe* or *wscript.exe* to run the script. If you use the VBScript `MsgBox` function (which displays messages as dialog boxes) in a script that you run from *cscript.exe*, the error messages will be illegible in the command window.

Next, we use the `GetObject` method to try to connect to the user account. Instead of specifying the actual ADsPath to the User object (which would make the script user-specific), we concatenated (`&`) the following elements in this order: `"WinNT://"` (i.e., the provider), `wshArgs(0)` (i.e., the domain name), `"/"` (i.e., the slash that separates the domain name and username), `wshArgs(1)` (i.e., the username), and `",user"` (i.e., a comma and the object class).

If the connection attempt fails, the script writes an error message and then quits. If the attempt succeeds, the script puts the output from that attempt into the `strOutput` text string variable. That way, if you're running *wscript.exe* rather than *cscript.exe*, the results appear in one dialog box.

The next two sections attempt to enable and unlock the user account. However, the script doesn't quit if an attempt fails. The `Err::Clear` method, which works only if you enable `On Error Resume Next`, clears the error object so that you can detect the next error.

Whether an attempt succeeds or fails, the output goes to the `strOutput` string variable, where it's appended to any existing text. The `vbTab` constant and the `vbCrLf` constant ensure that any new text that we concatenate appears in separate indented lines underneath the user's ADsPath. Finally, we use the `WScript::Echo` method to print the results in `strOutput`.

This script is simple but powerful. You can easily add to the script to perform other tasks, such as changing passwords and account expiration dates.

Because Active Directory supports the WinNT namespace, you can use the previous listing to enable and unlock Active Directory user accounts. However, we recommend that you instead use the script in Example 21-6, because accessing Active Directory via the LDAP provider is a more elegant and efficient approach.

Example 21-6. Account unlocker utility for Active Directory using the LDAP provider

```
'**********************************************************************
'How to unlock and enable a Active Directory user via arguments to this script
'
' Parameters should be <domain> <username>, where domain specifies
' a fully qualified AD domain like dc=mycorp,dc=com
'**********************************************************************
Option Explicit

Const adStateOpen = 0' Used to specify an unsuccessful ADO connection

Dim adoConnection, adoRecordset, wshArgs, objUser, strOutput

On Error Resume Next

'**********************************************************************
'Get the arguments
'**********************************************************************
Set wshArgs = Wscript.Arguments

'**********************************************************************
'If no arguments passed in, then quit
'**********************************************************************
If wshArgs.Count = 0 Then
  WScript.Echo "ERROR: No arguments passed in." & vbCrLf & vbCrLf _
    & "Please use AD-UNLOCK <domain> <username>" & vbCrLf & vbCrLf
  WScript.Quit
End If

'**********************************************************************
'Error checking of the arguments could go here if we were bothered
'**********************************************************************

'**********************************************************************
'Use SearchAD function from the end of Chapter 20 to scan the entire
'Active Directory for this user and return the ADsPath. If the search
'failed for whatever reason, then quit
'**********************************************************************
If Not SearchAD("LDAP://" & wshArgs(0), _
  "((objectClass=User)(cn=" & wshArgs(1) & "))", _
  "SubTree", "ADsPath", arrSearchResults) Then

  WScript.Echo "ERROR: No users found." & vbCrLf & vbCrLf
  WScript.Quit
```

Example 21-6. Account unlocker utility for Active Directory using the LDAP provider (continued)

```
Else
  '**********************************************************************
  'Attempt to bind to the first ADsPath specified in the array
  '(as there should be only one)
  '**********************************************************************
  Set objUser = GetObject(arrSearchResults(0,0))
  If Err Then
    Wscript.Echo "Error: Could not bind to the following user: " & vbCrLf _
      & vbCrLf & arrSearchResults(0,0) & vbCrLf & vbCrLf
    WScript.Quit
  Else
    strOutput = "Connected to user " & arrSearchResults(0,0) & vbCrLf
  End If


  '**********************************************************************
  'Attempt to enable the user (but don't quit if you fail)
  '**********************************************************************
  Err.Clear
  objUser.AccountDisabled = False
  objUser.SetInfo
  If Err Then
    strOutput = strOutput & vbTab & "Error: Could not enable the user." & vbCrLf
  Else
    strOutput = strOutput & vbTab & "User enabled." & vbCrLf
  End If


  '**********************************************************************
  'Attempt to unlock the user
  '**********************************************************************
  Err.Clear
  objUser.IsAccountLocked = False
  objUser.SetInfo
  If Err Then
    strOutput = strOutput & vbTab & "Error: Could not unlock the user." & vbCrLf
  Else
    strOutput = strOutput & vbTab & "User unlocked." & vbCrLf
  End If

  WScript.Echo strOutput
End If
```

Although more elegant and efficient, using the LDAP provider is a little tricky because users can exist in any container anywhere in a domain tree. Thus, you can't immediately attempt to bind to the user account because you don't know the ADs-Path. You first must conduct an ADO search to obtain the ADsPath.

At the end of Chapter 20, we showed how to use ADO to construct the Active Directory search routine SearchAD. We use the routine here to search Active Directory for the user's ADsPath and store it in arrSearchResults(0,0). The search is executed using a set of arguments, including wshArgs(0) and wshArgs(1). If you put the individual filters on separate lines and substitute the domain and username for wshArgs(0) and wshArgs(1), the set of arguments looks something like this:

```
LDAP://dc=mycorp,dc=com
((objectClass=User)(cn=vlaunders))
ADsPath
SubTree
arrSearchResults
```

If the search fails, the script displays an error message and then quits. If the search succeeds, the script attempts to bind to the ADsPath. The rest of the script proceeds similarly to the one for Windows NT.

Creating a Group

Now we will move on to creating groups. Creating a group is very similar to creating a user. You use the same IADsContainer::Create method:

```
Set objGroup = objSalesOU.Create("group", "cn=Managers")
objGroup.Put "sAMAccountName", "Managers"
objGroup.SetInfo
```

This code assumes we already have a pointer to an OU in the objSalesOU variable. The IADs::Put method is used to set the sAMAccountName, a mandatory attribute with no default value, just like with users.

The IADsGroup interface that operates on group objects supports four methods and one property that is specific to the group object, as listed in Table 21-4.

Table 21-4. The IADsGroup interface

IADsGroup methods and properties	Action
Add	Adds users to the group as members
Remove	Removes user members from the group
IsMember	Tests to see if a user is a member of a group
Members	Returns a list of all the members of the group
Description	Returns the text describing the group

In Example 21-7, we show how to create a group with both the WinNT and LDAP providers.

Example 21-7. Creating a group with both the WinNT and LDAP providers

```
Option Explicit

Dim objDomain, objGroup

'Creating a group in a Windows NT domain
Set objDomain = GetObject("WinNT://MYDOMAIN")
Set objGroup = objDomain.Create("group","My Group")
```

Example 21-7. Creating a group with both the WinNT and LDAP providers (continued)

```
ObjGroup.SetInfo

'Creating a local group on a computer or member server

'Valid for Windows NT, Windows 2000 and Windows Server 2003
Set objComputer = GetObject("WinNT://MYCOMPUTER,Computer")
Set objGroup = objComputer.Create("group","My Group")
ObjGroup.SetInfo

'Creating a group in Active Directory
Set objDomain = GetObject("LDAP://cn=Users,dc=mycorp,dc=com")
Set objGroup = objDomain.Create("user","cn=My Group")
ObjGroup.Put "sAMAccountName", "MyGroup"
ObjGroup.SetInfo
```

Adding Members to a Group

Adding objects as members of a group can be done with IADsGroup::Add, a simple method that takes the DN of the object to be added:

```
objGroup.Add("LDAP://cn=Sue Peace,cn=Users,dc=mycorp,dc=com")
objGroup.Add("LDAP://cn=Keith Cooper,cn=Users,dc=mycorp,dc=com")
```

Groups can contain virtually any other type of object as a member, including users, computers, and other groups.

Adding Many USER Groups to DRUP Groups

In the section on "Restricting Users in an Organizational Unit from Viewing Properties of Users Outside That Organizational Unit" in Chapter 11, we described the need to add many user groups as members of several permission groups. Example 21-8 contains the code necessary to implement this functionality. It scans for all groups prefixed with USER_ and DRUP_. It then adds all the USER groups to each DRUP group, except for the group where the suffix matches. In other words, all USER_ groups except USER_Finance are added to DRUP_Finance. This was why the names were set up this way.

 These searches make use of the ADO search function called SearchAD from Chapter 20.

Example 21-8. Adding many user groups as members of several permission groups

```
'***************************************************************************
'Search the entire AD for all groups starting USER_ and return the cn
'and AdsPath variables in the following structure
'
```

```
'    arrUSERGroup(0,index) = cn attributes
'    arrUSERGroup(1,index) = ADsPath attribute
'
'where index goes from 0 to (the maximum number of results returned -1)
'**************************************************************************
If SearchAD( _
    "LDAP://dc=mycorp,dc=com", "(&(objectClass=group)(cn=USER_*))", _
    "SubTree", "cn,ADsPath", arrUSERGroup) Then

    '**********************************************************************
    'As above but for DRUP_ groups
    '**********************************************************************
    If SearchAD( _
        "LDAP://dc=mycorp,dc=com", "(&(objectClass=group)(cn=DRUP_*))", _
        "SubTree", "cn,ADsPath", arrDRUPGroup) Then

        '******************************************************************
        'Set up an index to allow us to iterate through the USER_ groups. The
        'Ubound function here counts the maximum number of elements in the
        'array's second dimension of values (the first dimension has only two
        'values, "cn" and "ADsPath")
        '******************************************************************
        For intUSERGroupIndex = 0 To Ubound(arrUSERGroups,2)
            '**************************************************************
            'As above but for DRUP_ groups
            '**************************************************************
            For intDRUPGroupIndex = 0 To Ubound(arrDRUPGroups,2)
                '**********************************************************
                'Extract the portion of the name that corresponds to all letters after
                'the "cn=USER_" or "cn=DRUP_" parts (i.e., eight  letters)
                '**********************************************************
                txtUSERGroupSuffixName = Right(arrUSERGroup(0,intUSERGroupIndex), _
                    Len(arrUSERGroup(0,intUSERGroupIndex))-8)
                txtDRUPGroupSuffixName = Right(arrDRUPGroup(0,intDRUPGroupIndex), _
                    Len(arrDRUPGroup(0,intDRUPGroupIndex))-8)
                '**********************************************************
                'If the two extracted strings are not the same, then add the USER group
                'to the DRUP group
                '**********************************************************
                If Not txtUSERGroupSuffix = txtDRUPGroupSuffix Then
                    Set objDRUPGroup = GetObject(arrDRUPGroup(1,intDRUPGroupIndex))
                    objDRUPGroup.Add(arrUSERGroup(1,intUSERGroupIndex))
                End If
            Next
        Next
    End If
End If
```

You should note, by the way, that the For loop evaluates the UBound condition every time it completes a loop. To speed up the code, you really should put the result of the UBound in a variable and use the For loop with that directly.

Evaluating Group Membership

The `IADsGroup::IsMember` method takes one argument, the DN of the object to check, just as `Add` and `Remove` do. It returns a Boolean, i.e., true or false. That allows you to use it in an `If...Then` statement like this:

```
Set objGroup = GetObject("LDAP://cn=Managers,ou=Sales," _
  & "dc=mycorp,dc=com")
If objGroup.IsMember("LDAP://cn=Vicky Launders,ou=Sales," _
  & "dc=mycorp,dc=com") Then
    WScript.Echo "Is a Member!"
Else
    WScript.Echo "Is NOT a Member!"
End If
```

This should seem fairly straightforward after the examples we've already gone through. Two of the lines in the previous code snippet are too long to fit on the page, so the VBScript underscore (_) character was used again to tell VBScript that it should treat the current line as continuous with the next line. However, when you use the underscore to separate long strings, you must enclose both strings in quotation marks and then use the ampersand character (&) to concatenate two strings together.

To get a list of members in a group, the `IADsGroup::Members` method can be used. The `IADsGroup::Members` function is different from the other `IADsGroup` methods we have shown so far, since it returns a pointer to an `IADsMembers` object. Table 21-5 shows the two methods `IADsMembers` support.

Table 21-5. The IADsMembers interface

IADsMembers methods	Action
Count	The number of items in the container. If there is a filter set, only the number of items that match the filter are returned.
Filter	A filter, consisting of an array of object class strings, which can restrict the number of objects returned during enumeration of the container.

There are a number of ways of enumerating the members of a group. The `For Each...In...Next` loop is the most common. This is how it works:

```
Set objGroup = GetObject("LDAP://cn=Managers,ou=Sales," _
  & "dc=mycorp,dc=com")
WScript.Echo "Number of members of the group: " & objGroup.Members.Count
For Each objMember In objGroup.Members
  WScript.Echo objMember.Name
Next
```

This script displays the number of members and then prints each member's name. As the `For` loop executes, `objMember` ends up holding an IADs object representing each member of the group.

Another useful feature of IADsMembers is the Filter method. It can be used to filter certain object classes during enumeration just like you can with containers. To view only the members of a group that are users, you would modify the previous example to do the following:

```
objMembers = objGroup.Members
objMembers.Filter = Array("User")
For Each objMember In objMembers
   WScript.Echo objMember.Name
Next
```

Summary

In this chapter, we looked at how to create and manipulate properties of user and group objects in Active Directory and the Windows NT SAM. We used this knowledge to show how to write a script to create thousands of users easily from a set of data in a file or from a database. We then showed how to create simple tools, such as an account unlocker, that you can use in your day-to-day management of Active Directory. Next we showed how to create groups and modify group members. Finally, we reviewed how to determine group membership and iterate through all the members of a group.

CHAPTER 22

Manipulating Persistent and Dynamic Objects

ADSI can be used for much more than just user, group, or generic directory manipulation. ADSI provides many interfaces that you can use to manipulate persistent and dynamic objects for a computer. Persistent objects are permanent parts of a directory or computer, such as shares, services, users, and groups. Dynamic objects aren't permanent but instead are things such as sessions (i.e., connections to a machine) and print jobs that a user initiates. In other words, ADSI lets you do the following:

- Dynamically start, stop, and manage services and manipulate the permanent attributes of those services
- Dynamically manipulate shares, creating and deleting them as required
- Dynamically manipulate computers' open resources and users' active sessions and manipulate the permanent objects representing those computers and users
- Dynamically manipulate print jobs and manipulate the permanent queues

Many of you may already be familiar with the Windows Management Instrumentation (WMI) interface, which overlaps with several of these functions. Depending on your preference, you can use ADSI or WMI for many of these tasks. We describe WMI in more detail in Chapter 26.

The Interface Methods and Properties

Rather than describe the various methods and properties as we've done with the earlier interfaces, we'll concentrate on how to use those methods and properties in scripts. You can find complete descriptions of the interface methods and properties we cover in the MSDN Library or Platform SDK. To access the descriptions on the MSDN web site (*http://msdn.microsoft.com/library/*), navigate to Networking and Directory Services → Active Directory, ADSI and Directory Services → SDK Documentation → Directory Services → Active Directory Service Interfaces → Active Directory Service Interfaces Reference → ADSI Interfaces. From this point, you can navigate to:

Core Interfaces

IADs, IADsContainer, IADsNamespaces, and IADsOpenDSObject

Persistent Object Interfaces

IADsCollection, IADsFileShare, IADsService, IADsPrintJob, and IADsPrintQueue

Dynamic Object Interfaces

IADsServiceOperations, IADsComputerOperations, IADsFileServiceOperations, IADsResource, IADsSession, IADsPrintJobOperations, and IADsPrintQueue-Operations

Utility Interfaces

IADsADSystemInfo, IADsDeleteOps, IADsNameTranslate, IADsObjectOptions, IADsPathname, and IADsWinNTSystemInfo

 The ADSI documentation, however, leaves out three important quirks of the IADsSession and IADsResource interfaces. First, the WinNT provider doesn't currently support the IADsSession::UserPath, IADsSession::ComputerPath, and IADsResource::UserPath property methods. Second, although the documentation states that the IADsSession::ConnectTime and IADsSession::IdleTime property methods return results in minutes, they actually return results in seconds. Finally, the IADsSession::Computer property method returns NetBIOS names for Windows NT and Windows 9x clients but returns TCP/IP addresses for Windows 2000 and later clients.

Creating and Manipulating Shares with ADSI

The following code shows how easily you can create shares with ADSI:

```
Dim objComputer, objFileShare

Set objComputer = GetObject("WinNT://mydomainorworkgroup/mycomputer/LanmanServer")

Set objFileShare = objComputer.Create("FileShare", "MyNewShare")
objFileShare.Path = "c:\mydirectory"
objFileShare.Description = "My new Share"
objFileShare.MaxUserCount = 8
objFileShare.SetInfo
```

After we declare the objComputer and objFileShare variables, we bind to the LanmanServer object on the computer on which we want to create the shares. LanmanServer is the object name of the server service that runs on all Windows NT and later computers. We bind to this object because NT's predecessor was LAN Manager and is still present to a large extent in the Windows OS.

Next, we use the IADsContainer::Create method to create an object of class FileShare and apply the IADsFileShare property methods to set the path, description, and maximum number of users. On an NT, Windows 2000, or Windows Server 2003 server, you can grant all users access to a share or limit access to as many users as you want. On a workstation, you can grant all users access to a share or limit access to between 1 and 10 users at a time. The latter restriction is due to the 10-connection limit that the OS imposes. The values that the IADsFileShare::MaxUserCount method accepts are –1 (which grants all users access), any numerical value between 1 and 10 on workstations, and, within reason, any numerical value on the server family of OSs.

Finally, we end the script with IADs::SetInfo, which writes the information from the property cache to the directory.

Enumerating existing shares is just as easy as creating them. The next piece of code shows how to enumerate normal shares.*

```
Dim objService, objFileShare, strOutput

strOutput = ""

Set objService = GetObject("WinNT://workgroup/vicky/LanmanServer")

For Each objFileShare In objService
  strOutput = strOutput & "Name of share : " & objFileShare.Name & vbCrLf
  strOutput = strOutput & "Path to share : " & objFileShare.Path & vbCrLf
  strOutput = strOutput & "Description : " & objFileShare.Description & vbCrLf

  If objFileShare.MaxUserCount = -1 Then
    strOutput = strOutput & "Max users : No limit" & vbCrLf
  Else
    strOutput = strOutput & "Max users : " & objFileShare.MaxUserCount & vbCrLf
  End If

  strOutput = strOutput & "Host Computer : " _
    & objFileShare.HostComputer & vbCrLf & vbCrLf
Next


WScript.Echo strOutput
```

This code is similar to that in the previous script for creating a share. This is a sample of the output:

```
Name of share : NETLOGON
Path to share : C:\WINNT35\system32\Repl\Import\Scripts
Description   : Logon server share
Max users     : No limit
Host Computer : WinNT://WORKGROUP/VICKY

Name of share : Add-ins
Path to share : C:\exchsrvr\ADD-INS
Description   : "Access to EDK objects"
Max users     : No limit
Host Computer : WinNT://WORKGROUP/VICKY
```

---

* Hidden shares aren't shown due to their very nature.

```
Name of share : Logs
Path to share : C:\exchsrvr\tracking.log
Description   : "Exchange message tracking logs"
Max users     : No limit
Host Computer : WinNT://WORKGROUP/VICKY

Name of share : Resources
Path to share : C:\exchsrvr\RES
Description   : "Event logging files"
Max users     : No limit
Host Computer : WinNT://WORKGROUP/VICKY

Name of share : Drivers
Path to share : C:\WINNT\system32\spool\drivers
Description   : Printer Drivers
Max users     : No limit
Host Computer : WinNT://WORKGROUP/VICKY

Name of share : Clients
Path to share : C:\clients
Description   : Network Client Distribution Share
Max users     : No limit
Host Computer : WinNT://WORKGROUP/VICKY
```

Enumerating Sessions and Resources

We now want to show you how to use ADSI to do the following:

- Enumerate a client's sessions and resources
- Show which users are currently logged on to a server and count all the logged-on users across a domain's PDCs, BDCs, and other servers

Windows NT, Windows 2000, and Windows Server 2003 machines host two kinds of dynamic objects that you can access with ADSI: sessions (i.e., instances of users connected to a computer) and resources (i.e., instances of file or queue access on a computer). When users connect to a file or a share on a computer, that creates both a session and a resource object. When the user disconnects, these dynamic objects cease to exist.

You can access dynamic objects by connecting directly to the Server service on the machine. Although each Server service has a user-friendly display name that appears in the Computer Management console in Windows 2000 and Windows Server 2003 or the Services applet in Control Panel in NT, each Server service also has an ordinary name that you use when connecting to it with ADSI. For example, Server is the display name of the service that has the short name LanManServer. If you enumerate all the services on a machine, you can use IADsService::DisplayName to print the display name and IADs::Name to print the short name.

LanManServer is an object of type `FileService`. `FileService` objects are responsible for maintaining the sessions and resources in their jurisdictions. You can use the `IADsFileServiceOperations` interface to access information about these sessions and resources. This simple interface has two methods: `IADsFileServiceOperations::Sessions` and `IADsFileServiceOperations::Resources`. Both methods return collections of objects that you can iterate through with a `For Each...Next` loop. When you're iterating through a collection in this manner, the system is using `IADsCollection::GetObject` to retrieve each item from the collection. As a result, you can use the same `IADsCollection::GetObject` method to retrieve a specific session or resource object. You then can use the `IADsSession` or `IADsResource` interface to manipulate that session or resource object's properties to access information. For example, if you retrieve a session object, you can access such information as the username of the user who is logged on and how long that user has been logged on.

Identifying a Machine's Sessions

The following script uses `IADsSession` to iterate through all the sessions on a particular machine:

```
On Error Resume Next

Dim objComputer, objSession, strOutput

strOutput = ""

Set objComputer = GetObject("WinNT://mydomainorworkgroup/mycomputer/LanManServer")

For Each objSession In objComputer.Sessions
    strOutput = strOutput & "Session Object Name : " & objSession.Name & vbCrLf
    strOutput = strOutput & "Client Computer Name: " & objSession.Computer & vbCrLf
    strOutput = strOutput & "Seconds connected   : " _
        & objSession.ConnectTime & vbCrLf
    strOutput = strOutput & "Seconds idle        : " & objSession.IdleTime & vbCrLf
    strOutput = strOutput & "Connected User      : " & objSession.User & vbCrLf
    strOutput = strOutput & vbCrLf
Next

WScript.Echo strOutput
```

This is straightforward. It uses the `IADs::Name` property method and `IADsSession` property methods to retrieve data about the session. The `IADs::Name` property method displays the object name, which is the name that you would use with `IADsCollection::GetObject` to retrieve the specific session individually. As Figure 22-1 shows, the object name always follows the format *user\COMPUTER*. In some sessions, the underlying system rather than a person is connecting to the computer. Here, the object name follows the format *\COMPUTER*.

You can use `IADsSession` property methods to retrieve the individual components of the object name. The `IADsSession::Computer` property method retrieves the com-

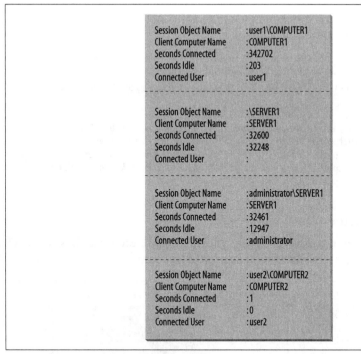

Figure 22-1. The sessions on a computer

puter component (e.g., COMPUTER1). The Connected User and Client Computer Name fields in Figure 22-1 contain the results of these property methods. The IADsSession::User property method retrieves the user component of the object name (e.g., user1).

The next line highlights an important consideration when you're specifying WinNT provider paths in a script:

```
Set objComputer = GetObject("WinNT://mydomainorworkgroup/mycomputer/LanManServer")
```

If you use only the computer name in the path with code such as the following, your script will execute slowly because the system must locate the machine and its workgroup:

```
WinNT://MYCOMPUTER,computer
```

However, if you include the workgroup in the path, your script will execute significantly faster because the system can immediately access the machine:

```
WinNT://MYDOMAIN/MYCOMPUTER,computer
```

Identifying a Machine's Resources

The following script enumerates the resources in use on a machine:

```
On Error Resume Next

Dim objComputer, objSession, strOutput

strOutput = ""

Set objComputer = GetObject("WinNT://mydomainorworkgroup/mycomputer/LanManServer")

For Each objResource In objComputer.Resources
    strOutput = strOutput & "Resource Name: " & objResource.Name & vbCrLf
    strOutput = strOutput & "User          : " & objResource.User & vbCrLf
    strOutput = strOutput & "Path          : " & objResource.Path & vbCrLf
    strOutput = strOutput & "Lock count    : " & objResource.LockCount & vbCrLf
    strOutput = strOutput & vbCrLf
Next

Wscript.Echo strOutput
```

Figure 22-2 shows the output, which lists those files that each user has open. The Microsoft Excel spreadsheet that user3 has open is locked.

```
Resource Name    :11237
User             :USER1
Path             :H:\dir1\folder1\Internet Explorer\Temporary Internet Files\Content.IE5\index.dat
Lock Count       :0
- - - - - - - - - - - - - - - - - - - - - - - - - - - - - - - - - - - - - - - - - - -
Resource Name    :11239
User             :USER1
Path             :H:\dir1\folder1\Internet Explorer\History\History.IE5\index.dat
Lock Count       :0
- - - - - - - - - - - - - - - - - - - - - - - - - - - - - - - - - - - - - - - - - - -
Resource Name    :59403
User             :USER2
Path             :K:\dir1\folder1\My Documents
Lock Count       :0
- - - - - - - - - - - - - - - - - - - - - - - - - - - - - - - - - - - - - - - - - - -
Resource Name    :11765
User             :USER3
Path             :E:\dir2\folder1\default.xls
Lock Count       :3
```

Figure 22-2. The resources on a computer

If you want to see locks in action, have one user open a shared document and have another user then try to open it.

A Utility to Show User Sessions

You can use ADSI to write a script that displays which users are currently logged on to a server and counts all the logged-on users across a domain. For simplicity, suppose that you have only two servers in your domain. You want to determine and display the maximum number of simultaneous sessions on each server, the total number of sessions across the domain, the total number of unique connected users on the domain, and an alphabetized list of usernames. Users can simultaneously connect to both servers from their computers. However, you want to count these users only once.

You can use the session object to construct *ShowUsers.vbs*, a useful utility that runs from your desktop and displays this user session information. What follows is an overview of how the *ShowUsers.vbs* utility obtains, manipulates, and displays the data. We heavily commented this script to show how it works line by line. The script follows the discussion of how it works.

Obtaining the data

ShowUsers.vbs begins by iterating through all your servers. To specify the servers you want to scan, you can either hardcode the server information in the script or have the script dynamically retrieve this information.* We've hardcoded the server information in *ShowUsers.vbs*.

When the utility iterates through all the servers, it ignores any empty usernames (which specify interserver connections) and usernames with a trailing dollar sign (which denote users that are actually computers connecting to one another). For each valid session, the script records the username and increments the session count by one.

The script uses a dynamic array (arrResults) to store the username data because the number of usernames in the array will change each time you run the utility.

The script uses a multidimensional array (arrServerResults) to store the servers' names and maximum number of connected sessions:

```
'********************************************************************
'Sets up multidimensional array to hold server names and user counts
'********************************************************************
arrServerResults(0,0) = "server1"
arrServerResults(1,0) = "server2"
arrServerResults(0,1) = 0
arrServerResults(1,1) = 0
```

---

* For Active Directory, a domain's DCs are always in the Domain Controllers Organizational Unit off the root of the domain. Member servers will be in the Computers container by default.

The arrServerResults array stores this information in a simple table, putting the server names in the first column, the counts in the second column, and the data in the rows. To access data in arrServerResults, we include the indexes of first and second dimensions, respectively, in parentheses. For example, arrServerResults(0,1) accesses the data in the first row (0), second column (1). Thus, the server names are in arrServerResults(0,0) and arrServerResults(1,0). The corresponding session counts are in arrServerResults(0,1) and arrServerResults(1,1).

The script can iterate through the servers by using a For loop to go from 0 to UBound(arrServerResults). The VBScript UBound function retrieves the upper array bound for an array and takes two parameters: the array to check and the dimension to count the upper bound of.

 Note that UBound's second parameter specifying the dimension starts from 1, not 0 as the actual array does.

If the second parameter is left off, the first dimension is used; these are equivalent:

```
UBound(arrServerResults,1)
UBound(arrServerResults)
```

Manipulating the data

After the script iterates through every server, you have a list of server session counts and a list of the usernames of those users who were connected to the servers at that time. This section of code achieves this:

```
For Each objSession In objFSO.Sessions
  If (Not objSession.User = "") And (Not Right(objSession.User,1) = "$") Then
    arrResults(UBound(arrResults)) = objSession.User & vbCrLf
    ReDim Preserve arrResults(UBound(arrResults) + 1)
    arrServerResults(intIndex,1) = arrServerResults(intIndex,1) + 1
  End If
Next
```

Note the use of ReDim to preserve the existing contents of the array, while expanding the array's upper bound by one. If the upper bound is 12, you can increase the array to 13 elements with the following code:

```
ReDim Preserve arrResults(13)
```

Using the upper bound of the existing array as the parameter makes the code generic. The following line is used to increase the count of the users by one in the second dimension of the array:

```
arrServerResults(intIndex,1) = arrServerResults(intIndex,1) + 1
```

Because some users might have been connected to both servers and hence might appear in the username list twice, the script uses two subprocedures to manipulate the data. One subprocedure sorts the usernames; the other subprocedure removes duplicate usernames.

The sort subprocedure

You likely remember from your college days having to perform bubble sorts and shell sorts. Although including in VBScript a general-purpose quick sort like the bubble or shell sort would've made sense, Microsoft failed to do so.

The Quicksort subprocedure we use in the next example takes in an array indexed from 0 to UBound(array) and sorts the values in the array between the two indexes you pass in as arguments. For example, if you specify the following code, Quicksort sorts elements 7 through 19 in arrMyArray:

```
Quicksort(arrMyArray, 7, 19)
```

Quicksort's own subprocedure has the ability to sort between two indexes in case we ever want to reuse the procedure in another script that needs that functionality. However, in *ShowUsers.vbs*, we need to sort the whole array of usernames between indexes 0 and UBound(array).

The duplicate-removal subprocedure

After Quicksort sorts the username list, the RemoveDuplicates subprocedure removes any duplicate usernames. Like Quicksort, RemoveDuplicates takes an array and two indexes as arguments.* When RemoveDuplicates enumerates through a sorted list, it ignores items with the same name as the next item in the list and then passes the remaining elements to a new array. For example, let's say that a sorted list reads:

```
bill, bill, bill, sandy, sandy, steve
```

RemoveDuplicates reads the list as:

```
<ignore>, <ignore>, bill, <ignore>, sandy, steve
```

This enumerates to:

```
bill, sandy, steve
```

RemoveDuplicates then passes the remaining elements to a new array because placing the results into a second array is faster than manipulating the existing array.

Displaying the data

Here are the constants we use for setting the location of the temporary file and opening it for write:

```
Const TEMPFILE = "C:\SHOWUSERS-TEMP.TXT"
Const ForWriting = 2
```

---

* When we created this subprocedure, we gave it the ability to work between two indexes so that Remove-Duplicates and Quicksort are comparable.

We then open the temporary text file for writing by creating a `FileSystemObject` and using the `FileSystemObject::OpenTextFile` method to open it. The third parameter states that if the text file already exists, it should be overwritten:

```
Set fso = CreateObject("Scripting.FileSystemObject")
Set ts = fso.OpenTextFile(TEMPFILE, ForWriting, True)
```

We then use the `TextStream::WriteLine` and `TextStream::Write` functions to write the data to the file and ultimately use the `TextStream::Close` method to close it.

Having the file written is only half the battle. We now want to display the file automatically using Notepad, maximize the window, display the results, and delete the file, again automatically, when we close Notepad. This is actually accomplished simply, as follows:

```
Set objShell = CreateObject("WScript.Shell")
intRC = objShell.Run ("notepad.exe " & TEMPFILE, vbMaximizedFocus, TRUE)
fso.DeleteFile(TEMPFILE)
```

The `Shell::Run` method allows you to open and use an application such as Notepad synchronously or asynchronously with a script. The first parameter uses the temporary file as a parameter to Notepad, so that Notepad opens the file. The second parameter is one of the VBScript constants that came up before while setting rights to home directories for newly created users. The third parameter indicates whether to run the command synchronously (true) or asynchronously (false). In this case, the script pauses execution when Notepad is open and doesn't start up again until you close Notepad. The script effectively stops executing until you close Notepad. When that happens, a return code is placed into the variable `intRC`. This is to accommodate applications and commands that return a value that you may require. In this case, you don't care about a value being returned, so when Notepad is closed, the script deletes the file.

The full code for ShowUsers is listed in Example 22-1.

Example 22-1. The ShowUsers.vbs utility

```
'**********************************************************************
'The ShowUsers.vbs Utility
'**********************************************************************
Option Explicit

On Error Resume Next

'**********************************************************************
'Maximizes the Notepad screen when started
'**********************************************************************
Const vbMaximizedFocus   = 3

'**********************************************************************
'The domain or workgroup in which the servers or workstations reside
'**********************************************************************
```

Example 22-1. The ShowUsers.vbs utility (continued)

```
Const strDomainOrWorkGroupName = "MYDOMAIN"

'***********************************************************************
'Sets the location of the temporary file
'***********************************************************************
Const TEMPFILE = "C:\SHOWUSERS-TEMP.TXT"

'***********************************************************************
'Opens a file and lets you start writing from the beginning of the
'file
'***********************************************************************
Const ForWriting = 2

'***********************************************************************
'Declare all variables. As arrResults will be continually increased
'in size as more results are fed in, you have to initially declare it
'as an unbounded array
'***********************************************************************
Dim objShell, objFSO, objSession, arrServerResults(1,1), arrResults()
Dim arrResults2(), fso, ts, intRC, intMaxSessions, intIndex, strItem

'***********************************************************************
'Sets up multidimensional array to hold server names and user counts
'***********************************************************************
arrServerResults(0,0) = "server1"
arrServerResults(1,0) = "server2"
arrServerResults(0,1) = 0
arrServerResults(1,1) = 0

'***********************************************************************
'Redimensions arrResults to one element to start with
'***********************************************************************
ReDim arrResults(0)

'***********************************************************************
'Iterates through the array, connecting to the server service of
'each server and looks at each session on that server
'
'If the session has an empty user (is an interserver connection) or
'the user is a computer (the trailing character is a dollar sign), the
'script ignores that session and proceeds to the next session
'
'If the session is valid, the script adds the username to the last
'element of the arrResults array and expands the array by one element
'to cope with the next result when it arrives. The script also
'increments the session count for the corresponding server by one
'***********************************************************************
For intIndex = 0 To UBound(arrServerResults)
  Set objFSO = GetObject("WinNT://" & strDomainOrWorkGroupName & "/" _
    & arrServerResults(intIndex,0) & "/LanmanServer")

  For Each objSession In objFSO.Sessions
```

Example 22-1. The ShowUsers.vbs utility (continued)

```
    If (Not objSession.User = "") And (Not Right(objSession.User,1) = "$") Then
      arrResults(UBound(arrResults)) = objSession.User & vbCrLf
      ReDim Preserve arrResults(UBound(arrResults) + 1)
      ArrServerResults(intIndex,1) = arrServerResults(intIndex,1) + 1
    End If
  Next


  Set objFSO = Nothing
Next

'***********************************************************************
'Sorts the entire arrResults array and then removes duplicates from
'it, placing the results in arrResults2
'***********************************************************************
Quicksort arrResults, 0, UBound(arrResults)
RemoveDuplicates arrResults, 0, UBound(arrResults), arrResults2


'***********************************************************************
'Opens the temporary text file for writing. If the text file already
'exists, overwrite it.
'***********************************************************************
Set fso = CreateObject("Scripting.FileSystemObject")
Set ts = fso.OpenTextFile(TEMPFILE, ForWriting, True)


'***********************************************************************
'Counts the max sessions by iterating through each server and adding
'up the sessions count in the second column of each row of the
'multidimensional array
'
'Writes out the user sessions for each server to the temporary file
'as the script iterates through the list. When the script finishes
'counting, it writes out the max sessions to the file as well.
'***********************************************************************
intMaxSessions = 0
For intIndex = 0 To UBound(arrServerResults)
  ts.WriteLine "Total User Sessions on " & arrServerResults(intIndex,0) _
    & ": " & arrServerResults(intIndex,1)
  intMaxSessions = intMaxSessions + arrServerResults(intIndex,1)
Next
ts.WriteLine "Total User sessions on CFS: " & intMaxSessions
ts.WriteLine


'***********************************************************************
'Writes out the total number of unique users connected to the domain,
'followed by each username in alphabetic order
'***********************************************************************
ts.WriteLine "Total Users on CFS: " & UBound(arrResults2)
ts.WriteLine
For Each strItem in arrResults2
  ts.Write strItem
Next
ts.Close
```

Example 22-1. The ShowUsers.vbs utility (continued)

```
'***********************************************************************
'Sets the third parameter of the Shell::Run method to TRUE, which
'allows the script to open up the file in Notepad and maximize the
'screen. The script stops executing until you close Notepad, which
'places a return code into intRC. When Notepad is closed, the script
'deletes the file.
'***********************************************************************
Set objShell = CreateObject("WScript.Shell")
intRC = objShell.Run ("notepad.exe " & TEMPFILE, vbMaximizedFocus, TRUE)
fso.DeleteFile(TEMPFILE)


'***********************************************************************
'Subroutine Quicksort
'
'Sorts the items in the array (between the two values you pass in)
'***********************************************************************
Sub Quicksort(strValues( ), ByVal min, ByVal max)

  Dim strMediumValue, high, low, i

  '***********************************************************************
  'If the list has only 1 item, it's sorted
  '***********************************************************************
  If min >= max Then Exit Sub

  '***********************************************************************
  'Pick a dividing item randomly
  '***********************************************************************
  we = min + Int(Rnd(max - min + 1))
  strMediumValue = strValues(i)

  '***********************************************************************
  'Swap the dividing item to the front of the list
  '***********************************************************************
  strValues(i) = strValues(min)

  '***********************************************************************
  'Separate the list into sublists
  '***********************************************************************
  low = min
  high = max
  Do
     '***********************************************************************
     'Look down from high for a value < strMediumValue
     '***********************************************************************
     Do While strValues(high) >= strMediumValue
       high = high - 1
       If high <= low Then Exit Do
     Loop

     If high <= low Then
       '***********************************************************************
```

Example 22-1. The ShowUsers.vbs utility (continued)

```
      'The list is separated
      '*******************************************************************
      strValues(low) = strMediumValue
      Exit Do
   End If


   '*******************************************************************
   'Swap the low and high strValues
   '*******************************************************************
   strValues(low) = strValues(high)


   '*******************************************************************
   'Look up from low for a value >= strMediumValue
   '*******************************************************************
   low = low + 1
   Do While strValues(low) < strMediumValue
     low = low + 1
     If low >= high Then Exit Do
   Loop


   If low >= high Then
      '*******************************************************************
      'The list is separated
      '*******************************************************************
      low = high
      strValues(high) = strMediumValue
      Exit Do
   End If


   '*******************************************************************
   'Swap the low and high strValues
   '*******************************************************************
   strValues(high) = strValues(low)
  Loop 'Loop until the list is separated.


  '*******************************************************************
  'Recursively sort the sublists
  '*******************************************************************
  Quicksort strValues, min, low - 1
  Quicksort strValues, low + 1, max

End Sub

'*******************************************************************
'Subroutine RemoveDuplicates
'
'Removes duplicate items in the strValues array (between the two
'values you pass in) and writes the results to strNewValues()
'*******************************************************************
Sub RemoveDuplicates(ByVal strValues(), ByVal min, ByVal max, strNewValues() )

  Dim strValuesIndex, strNewValuesIndex
```

Example 22-1. The ShowUsers.vbs utility (continued)

```
ReDim strNewValues(0)
strNewValuesIndex = 0

For strValuesIndex = min To max-1
  If Not strValues(strValuesIndex) = strValues(strValuesIndex+1) Then
    strNewValues(strNewValuesIndex) = strValues(strValuesIndex)
    ReDim Preserve strNewValues(strNewValuesIndex + 1)
    strNewValuesIndex = strNewValuesIndex + 1
  End If
Next
strNewValues(strNewValuesIndex) = strValues(max)

End Sub
```

Room for improvement

Although *ShowUsers.vbs* is useful, this utility is lacking in one area: users can legitimately use two connection slots if their IADsSession::Computer names are different, but the utility counts the user only once. For example, user1 might log on to the domain twice, once on *COMPUTER1* and once on *SERVER1*, but our script counts user1 only once because of the RemoveDuplicates subprocedure. If you want to make the script even better, you can create an extension to the utility that remedies this situation. For example, the extension might log all user counts to a file every five minutes for later analysis.

Manipulating Print Queues and Print Jobs

So far we've shown you how to use ADSI to manipulate persistent and dynamic objects, such as shares, sessions, and resources. Now we're going to examine printer queues and jobs. In this section, we're going to lead you through creating scripts to do the following:

- Identify print queues in Active Directory
- Bind to a print queue* and access its properties
- List the print jobs in a print queue and manipulate them

 All the code in these scripts for managing printers is done using the WinNT provider, so it will work on Windows NT as well as Active Directory. The LDAP searches will not work on Windows NT.

---

* Print queues are logical ADSI names for printers installed on a computer.

One point before we go on: at the end of Chapter 20, we detail a function called SearchAD. We need to use it now to search Active Directory for the printer's ADs-Path and store it in arrSearchResults(0,0).

Identifying Print Queues in Active Directory

List-Print-Queue.vbs in Example 22-2 is a heavily commented script, so it should be easy to follow.

Example 22-2. List-Print-Queue.vbs identifies print queues in Active Directory

```
Option Explicit
On Error Resume Next


'*********************************************************************
'Active Directory path to start the search from
'*********************************************************************
Const strDomainToSearch = "LDAP://dc=mycorp,dc=com"


'*********************************************************************
'Maximizes the Notepad screen when started
'*********************************************************************
Const vbMaximizedFocus   = 3


'*********************************************************************
'Sets the location of the temporary file
'*********************************************************************
Const TEMPFILE = "C:\PRINTERLIST-TEMP.TXT"


'*********************************************************************
'Opens a file and lets you start writing from the beginning of the file
'*********************************************************************
Const ForWriting = 2

Dim arrPaths(), fso, ts, strItem, intRC, objShell, intIndex

If Not SearchAD(strDomainToSearch,"(objectClass=printQueue)","SubTree",arrPaths) Then
  MsgBox "Printer listing failed!"
Else
  '*******************************************************************
  'Opens the temporary text file for writing. If the text file already
  'exists, overwrite it.
  '*******************************************************************
  Set fso = CreateObject("Scripting.FileSystemObject")
  Set ts = fso.OpenTextFile(TEMPFILE, ForWriting, True)


  '*******************************************************************
  ' Writes out the printer ADsPaths
  '*******************************************************************
  ts.WriteLine "Total printers in Active Directory: " & UBound(arrPaths)+1
  ts.WriteLine
  For intIndex=0 To UBound(arrPaths)
```

```
    ts.WriteLine arrPaths(intIndex,1)
    ts.WriteLine vbTab & arrPaths(intIndex,0)
  Next
  ts.Close

  '**********************************************************************
  'Sets the third parameter of the Shell::Run method to TRUE, which
  'allows the script to open up the file in Notepad and maximize the
  'screen. The script stops executing until you close Notepad, which
  'places a return code into intRC. When Notepad is closed, the script
  'deletes the file.
  '**********************************************************************
  Set objShell = CreateObject("WScript.Shell")
  intRC = objShell.Run ("notepad.exe " & TEMPFILE, vbMaximizedFocus, TRUE)
  fso.DeleteFile(TEMPFILE)
End If
```

The script uses the search function to search Active Directory for all objects of class printQueue, writes their ADsPath and cn attributes out to a temporary file, displays the file for you in Notepad, and then erases the file when Notepad is closed. The code for opening and closing files and displaying them with Notepad is the same as that in the *ShowUsers.vbs* script earlier in the chapter. Here is an example of the output from this program:

```
Total printers in Active Directory: 3

DC1-ph_stores_hp4000
    LDAP://CN=DC1-stores_hp4000,CN=DC1,OU=Domain Controllers,DC=mycorp,DC=com
SS-0001-Alex&Mark
    LDAP://CN=COMPUTER-0789-Alex&Mark,CN=COMPUTER-0789,OU=Finances, _
      OU=Finance Clients,OU=Clients,DC=mycorp,DC=com
ZZ-NT0089-HP LaserJet 4M Plus
    LDAP://CN=ZZ-0089-HP LaserJet 4M Plus,CN=ZZ-0089,OU=Finances, _
      OU=Finance Clients,OU=Clients,DC=mycorp,DC=com
```

 The lines are too long to fit on the page, so we have broken them up with underscores as we would do if this were a script. They normally would be unbroken.

Let's take a look at the output for a moment. The first PrintQueue object is called "DC1-stores_hp4000" and is held within the DC1 domain controller, as if that DC were itself a container object. Computer objects are a special case and can act as containers and hold other objects beneath them. The computer called DC1 (actually an Active Directory domain controller) is actually the parent of this printQueue object. We could go through listing the properties of the PrintQueue objects for you in a script, but this is very easy to do, and to save this chapter from getting any longer, you can find the print queue properties yourself on MSDN.

Binding to a Print Queue

Unfortunately, we cannot connect to this printQueue object and list the jobs because the Active Directory object that we have connected to is only the advertisement or publication that such a queue exists. To connect to the printer object that holds the jobs and that we can manipulate, we need to use the WinNT namespace.

While we could provide a simple piece of code to connect to a queue, we'd like to modify the previous script to show you how that could be accomplished. We'll list the queues as before, but this time, we'll also bind to the first queue that we find (and only the first) and print out some properties.

To see what we need to do, let's take a look at the first queue in the previous output. The actual printer path that we need to connect to is:

```
WinNT://MYCORP/DC1/stores_hp4000
```

We need to massage the data returned by the SearchAD function to produce the information about the computer name and the printer name. *List-Print-Queue-2.vbs* is the result, a modified version of *List-Print-Queue.vbs* with two extra sets of information provided. The first is a new constant to define the workgroup or domain; the second we'll go through after the script in Example 22-3.

Example 22-3. List-Print-Queue-2.vbs binds to the print queue

```
Option Explicit
On Error Resume Next

'************************************************************************
' Sets the domain or workgroup that the servers or workstations reside in
'************************************************************************
Const strDomainOrWorkGroup = "MYCORP"

'************************************************************************
'Active Directory path to start the search from
'************************************************************************
Const strDomainToSearch = "LDAP://dc=mycorp,dc=com"

'************************************************************************
'Maximizes the Notepad screen when started
'************************************************************************
Const vbMaximizedFocus   = 3

'************************************************************************
'Sets the location of the temporary file
'************************************************************************
Const TEMPFILE = "C:\PRINTERLIST-TEMP.TXT"

'************************************************************************
'Opens a file and lets you start writing from the beginning of the file
'************************************************************************
Const ForWriting = 2
```

Example 22-3. List-Print-Queue-2.vbs binds to the print queue (continued)

```
Dim arrPaths( ), fso, ts, strItem, intRC, objShell, intIndex, strComputer
Dim strPrinter, objPrinter

If Not _
  SearchAD(strDomainToSearch,"(objectClass=printQueue)","SubTree",arrPaths) Then
    MsgBox "Printer listing failed!"
Else
  '*********************************************************************
  'Opens the temporary text file for writing. If the text file already
  'exists, overwrite it
  '*********************************************************************
  Set fso = CreateObject("Scripting.FileSystemObject")
  Set ts = fso.OpenTextFile(TEMPFILE, ForWriting, True)

  '*********************************************************************
  ' Writes out the printer ADsPaths
  '*********************************************************************
  ts.WriteLine "Total printers in Active Directory: " & UBound(arrPaths)+1
  ts.WriteLine
  For intIndex=0 To UBound(arrPaths)
    ts.WriteLine arrPaths(intIndex,1)
    ts.WriteLine vbTab & arrPaths(intIndex,0)
  Next
  ts.WriteLine

  '*********************************************************************
  'Bind to the first printer and list the properties
  '*********************************************************************
  strComputer = Split(arrPaths(0,0),",")(1)
  strComputer = Right(strComputer,Len(strComputer) - 3)
  strPrinter = Right(arrPaths(0,1),Len(arrPaths(0,1)) - Len(strComputer) - 1)
  Set objPrinter = GetObject("WinNT://" & strDomainOrWorkGroup & "/" _
    & strComputer & "/" & strPrinter)
  ts.WriteLine "Name        : " & objPrinter.Name
  ts.WriteLine "Status      : " & objPrinter.Status
  ts.WriteLine "Model       : " & objPrinter.Model
  ts.WriteLine "Location    : " & objPrinter.Location
  ts.WriteLine "PrinterPath : " & objPrinter.PrinterPath
  ts.Close

  '*********************************************************************
  'Sets the third parameter of the Shell::Run method to TRUE, which
  'allows the script to open up the file in Notepad and maximize the
  'screen. The script stops executing until you close Notepad, which
  'places a return code into intRC. When Notepad is closed, the script
  'deletes the file.
  '*********************************************************************
  Set objShell = CreateObject("WScript.Shell")
  intRC = objShell.Run ("notepad.exe " & TEMPFILE, vbMaximizedFocus, TRUE)
  fso.DeleteFile(TEMPFILE)
End If
```

To bind to the printer and list the properties, the script first splits the entire LDAP path of the first array element, using the comma as the delimiter. It then immediately retrieves the second item (indexed as 1 because item numbers start at 0) and adds it to strComputer. You use VBScript's Split function like this:

```
arrResults = Split("Moose 1,Moose 2,Penguin,Banana,Squirrel,Hamster",",")
```

This results in arrResults(0) containing Moose 1 and arrResults(5) containing Hamster. Instead of passing the results out to an array, we can directly retrieve one value from that array by passing the index value to the Split function. To retrieve and print Squirrel from the preceding string, we use the following code:

```
MsgBox Split("Moose 1,Moose 2,Penguin,Banana,Squirrel,Hamster",",")(4)
```

You can see that here we don't need arrResults at all. That's how Split works in the previous code.

The first item returned is "CN=DC1". We can then use the VBScript Right function to take the righthand part of that string—ignoring the first three characters, i.e., DC1—and put the result back into the strComputer variable. We now need the printer name. This is done by taking the right-hand part of the cn attribute returned (DC1- stores_hp4000) and ignoring the number of characters equal to the length of the computer name. That yields "stores_hp4000". We then can assemble all the pieces and bind to the printer object on that computer. We finally print out five attributes (IADs::Name, IADsPrintQueueOperations::Status, IADsPrintQueue::Model, IADsPrintQueue::Location, and IADsPrintQueue::PrinterPath) of that printer to confirm that the printer exists.

IADsPrintQueueOperations and Print Queues

Having successfully connected to a print queue, you can then use the IADsPrint-QueueOperations interface to its full extent. This interface has methods with names like Pause, Resume, and Purge that you should recognize; they correspond to specific print queue functions. There is one important property status that is also available and allows you to query the status of the printer. While *List-Print-Queue-2.vbs* just prints out this value as an integer, *Display-Print-Queue-Status.vbs* is a script that binds to the same printer and uses a Select Case statement to print the status out using the MsgBox function. This script is listed in Example 22-4.

Example 22-4. Display-Print-Queue-Status.vbs uses MsgBox to display printer status

```
'************************************************************
'IADsPrintQueueOperations::Status values
'************************************************************
Const ADS_PRINTER_PAUSED = &H00000001
Const ADS_PRINTER_PENDING_DELETION = &H00000002
Const ADS_PRINTER_ERROR = &H00000003
Const ADS_PRINTER_PAPER_JAM = &H00000004
Const ADS_PRINTER_PAPER_OUT = &H00000005
```

Example 22-4. Display-Print-Queue-Status.vbs uses MsgBox to display printer status (continued)

```vbscript
Const ADS_PRINTER_MANUAL_FEED = &H00000006
Const ADS_PRINTER_PAPER_PROBLEM = &H00000007
Const ADS_PRINTER_OFFLINE = &H00000008
Const ADS_PRINTER_IO_ACTIVE = &H00000100
Const ADS_PRINTER_BUSY = &H00000200
Const ADS_PRINTER_PRINTING = &H00000400
Const ADS_PRINTER_OUTPUT_BIN_FULL = &H00000800
Const ADS_PRINTER_NOT_AVAILABLE = &H00001000
Const ADS_PRINTER_WAITING = &H00002000
Const ADS_PRINTER_PROCESSING = &H000040000
Const ADS_PRINTER_INITIALIZING = &H00008000
Const ADS_PRINTER_WARMING_UP = &H00010000
Const ADS_PRINTER_TONER_LOW = &H00020000
Const ADS_PRINTER_NO_TONER = &H00040000
Const ADS_PRINTER_PAGE_PUNT = &H00080000
Const ADS_PRINTER_USER_INTERVENTION = &H00100000
Const ADS_PRINTER_OUT_OF_MEMORY = &H00200000
Const ADS_PRINTER_DOOR_OPEN = &H00400000
Const ADS_PRINTER_SERVER_UNKNOWN = &H00800000
Const ADS_PRINTER_POWER_SAVE = &H01000000


'**********************************************************************
' Bind to the printer
'**********************************************************************
Set objPrinter = GetObject("WinNT://MYCORP/DC1/stores_hp4000")


'**********************************************************************
' Print out the queue status
'**********************************************************************
Select Case objPrinter.Status
  Case 0
    MsgBox "On line"
  Case ADS_PRINTER_PAUSED
    MsgBox "Paused"
  Case ADS_PRINTER_PENDING_DELETION
    MsgBox "Pending deletion"
  Case ADS_PRINTER_ERROR
    MsgBox "Printer error"
  Case ADS_PRINTER_PAPER_JAM
    MsgBox "Paper jam"
  Case ADS_PRINTER_PAPER_OUT
    MsgBox "Out of paper"
  Case ADS_PRINTER_MANUAL_FEED
    MsgBox "Manual feed pending"
  Case ADS_PRINTER_PAPER_PROBLEM
    MsgBox "Paper trouble"
  Case ADS_PRINTER_OFFLINE
    MsgBox "Offline"
  Case ADS_PRINTER_IO_ACTIVE
    MsgBox "We/O active"
  Case ADS_PRINTER_BUSY
    MsgBox "Printer busy"
```

```
  Case ADS_PRINTER_PRINTING
    MsgBox "Printing"
  Case ADS_PRINTER_OUTPUT_BIN_FULL
    MsgBox "Output bin full"
  Case ADS_PRINTER_NOT_AVAILABLE
    MsgBox "Not available"
  Case ADS_PRINTER_WAITING
    MsgBox "Waiting"
  Case ADS_PRINTER_PROCESSING
    MsgBox "Processing"
  Case ADS_PRINTER_INITIALIZING
    MsgBox "Initializating"
  Case ADS_PRINTER_WARMING_UP
    MsgBox "Warming up"
  Case ADS_PRINTER_TONER_LOW
    MsgBox "Toner low"
  Case ADS_PRINTER_NO_TONER
    MsgBox "Without toner"
  Case ADS_PRINTER_PAGE_PUNT
    MsgBox "Page punt"
  Case ADS_PRINTER_USER_INTERVENTION
    MsgBox "User intervention required"
  Case ADS_PRINTER_OUT_OF_MEMORY
    MsgBox "Out of memory"
  Case ADS_PRINTER_DOOR_OPEN
    MsgBox "Door open"
  Case ADS_PRINTER_SERVER_UNKNOWN
    MsgBox "Server unknown"
  Case ADS_PRINTER_POWER_SAVE
    MsgBox "Power save"
  Case Else
    MsgBox "UNKNOWN"
End Select
```

The final important IADsPrintQueueOperations method that is available to you is IADsPrintQueueOperations::PrintJobs, which returns a collection of print jobs that you can interact with using IADsCollection.

Print Jobs

The IADsPrintQueueOperations::PrintJobs method allows you to obtain a collection object that you then can use in a For Each...Next loop. You can pause and resume the jobs using methods of the same name from the IADsPrintJobOperations interface. In addition, as the collection represents the underlying print jobs, you also can use the IADsCollection::Add and IADsCollection::Remove methods to add and remove print jobs from the collection. The Add method is not of much use here, but the Remove method is, since this allows you to delete jobs from the queue. Assuming we had bound successfully to the queue as before, this section of code would purge the queue manually. The following code gives you some idea of what you can do:

```
For Each objJob in objPrinter.PrintJobs
  objPrinter.PrintJobs.Remove (objJob.Name)
Next
```

Example 22-5 demonstrates that each job has a number of attributes from IADs-PrintJob and IADsPrintJobOperations you can print. This is not the definitive list, and we urge you to check out MSDN for the full set.

Example 22-5. Display some properties and the status of each print job

```
'***********************************************************************
'IADsPrintJobOperations::Status values
'***********************************************************************
Const ADS_JOB_PAUSED = &H00000001
Const ADS_JOB_ERROR = &H00000002
Const ADS_JOB_DELETING = &H00000004
Const ADS_JOB_PRINTING = &H00000010
Const ADS_JOB_OFFLINE = &H00000020
Const ADS_JOB_PAPEROUT = &H00000040
Const ADS_JOB_PRINTED = &H00000080
Const ADS_JOB_DELETED = &H00000100


'***********************************************************************
' Bind to the printer
'***********************************************************************
Set objPrinter = GetObject("WinNT://MYCORP/DC1/stores_hp4000")


'***********************************************************************
'Print out some properties and the status of each job
'***********************************************************************
For Each objJob in objPrinter.PrintJobs
  str = "Name: " & objJob.Name & vbCrLf
  str = str & "Position: " & objJob.Position & vbCrLf
  str = str & "Size: " & objJob.Size & vbCrLf
  str = str & "Total Pages: " & objJob.TotalPages & vbCrLf
  str = str & "Pages Printed: " & objJob.PagesPrinted & vbCrLf
  Select Case objJob.Status

    Case 0
      str = str & "Status : " & "OK"
    Case ADS_JOB_PAUSED
      str = str & "Status : " & "Paused"
    Case ADS_JOB_ERROR
      str = str & "Status : " & "Error"
    Case ADS_JOB_DELETING
      str = str & "Status : " & "Deleting"
    Case ADS_JOB_PRINTING
      str = str & "Status : " & "Printing"
    Case ADS_JOB_OFFLINE
      str = str & "Status : " & "Offline"
    Case ADS_JOB_PAPEROUT
      str = str & "Status : " & "Paper Out"
    Case ADS_JOB_PRINTED
      str = str & "Status : " & "Printed"
```

```
      Case ADS_JOB_DELETED
        str = str & "Status : " & "Deleted"
      Case Else
        str = str & "Status : " & "Unknown"
    End Select

    MsgBox str
Next
```

Again, just as in *Display-Print-Queue-Status.vbs*, the IADsPrintJobOperations:: Status property method has a defined set of constants that can be used to tell you about a job. One thing to note is that IADsPrintJobOperations::Position is a read/ write value, so you can use this to move jobs around in the queue print sequence. Actually, a number of IADsPrintJob property methods are also read/write: IADsPrint-Job::StartTime and IADsPrintJob::UntilTime (to set a future time before which the job can be printed), IADsPrintJob::Priority, IADsPrintJob::Description, and IADsPrintJob::Notify, plus IADsPrintJob::NotifyPath (the user is contacted when the job is printed).

Summary

While the future of automating systems management–related tasks lies with WMI, you can still use ADSI very effectively to accomplish a number of key tasks. In this chapter, we took a look at how you can use ADSI to manipulate persistent objects (like a computer's shares and services) and dynamic objects (computers' open resources, users' active sessions, and print jobs that users initiate) in Active Directory or Windows NT SAM.

CHAPTER 23

Permissions and Auditing

Security descriptors (SDs), access control lists (ACLs), and access control entries (ACEs) have been used for files and directories on NTFS filesystems for years. The same concepts apply to securing Active Directory objects as well. While the information in this chapter is focused on Active Directory, the principles of creating an SD that contains a discretionary access control list (DACL) and system access control list (SACL) can map exactly over to NTFS files and directories.

ADSI provides four main interfaces we can use:

IADsAccessControlEntry
> Manipulates individual ACEs that represent access or audit permissions for specific users or groups to objects and properties in Active Directory.

IADsAccessControlList
> Manages collections of ACEs for an object.

IADsSecurityDescriptor
> Manages the different sets of ACLs to an object.

IADsSecurityUtility
> Gets, sets, and retrieves security descriptors for an object.

All of the ADSI security interfaces can be found in the MSDN Library (*http://msdn. microsoft.com/library/*) under Networking and Directory Services → Active Directory, ADSI and Directory Services → SDK Documentation → Directory Services → Active Directory Service Interfaces → Active Directory Service Interfaces Reference → ADSI Interfaces → Security Interfaces.

> Microsoft provides a DLL (*ADsSecurity.dll*) with the Platform SDK that contains several interfaces that you can use to manage security descriptors, ACLs, and ACEs. It isn't covered in this chapter because it doesn't come installed with Windows 2000 or Windows Server 2003, but we encourage you to check it out and take a look at the example source code that comes with it for more information. Remember that the DLL will need to be installed and registered using REGSVR32.EXE ADSecurity.dll on every client that would use it.

How to Create an ACE Using ADSI

Microsoft has a habit of calling a shovel a ground insertion earth management device, that is, they like to give names that are not always intuitive to the average person. The contents of the five properties of the ACE object are not all immediately obvious from the names. In addition, as Microsoft uses the ACE for system-audit and permissions entries, a number of values that can go into the properties make sense only in a particular context. To complicate matters further, one property (AceFlags) is a catchall area that currently is the location for two completely different sets of information.

Creating an ACE is a simple matter. To set up an ACE, you need the following basic pieces of information:

AccessMask
> What permissions you want to set

AceType
> Whether you are setting allow/deny permissions or auditing for an object or property

Trustee
> Who to apply the permissions to

AceFlags
> What inheritance options you want and, if it is an audit entry, whether you are monitoring successes or failures

Flags, ObjectType, InheritedObjectType
> What the ACE applies to if not just the entire object

We will now go through several examples to show you what the five properties of an ACE will contain based on certain security settings. Let's start with the simple example: giving a user full control permissions to an Organizational Unit. That means the information in Table 23-1 gets stored as an ACE on the SD of the Organizational Unit itself.

Table 23-1. Contents of the ACE properties when giving a user full control permissions to an Organizational Unit

Name of the property	Value to be stored
Trustee	Names the user who is to have the permission.
AccessMask	Gives full control (i.e. give every permission).
AceType	This is an allow permission.
AceFlags	The permission applies to this object. Child objects inherit this ACE.
Flags	Neither ObjectType nor InheritedObjectType is set.
ObjectType	Null.
InheritedObjectType	Null.

The user (Trustee) is allowed (AceType) full control (AccessMask) to the current object and all objects down the tree (AceFlags). The last three are not used here, as the permission is a simple one to an entire object.

If we were auditing successful and failed modifications to the entire Organizational Unit by the user, the contents of the audit ACE on the Organizational Unit would look like Table 23-2.

Table 23-2. Contents of the ACE properties when auditing successful modifications to an Organizational Unit and all children by a user

Name of the property	Value to be stored
Trustee	Names the user who is to be audited.
AccessMask	Gives full control (i.e., audit every action).
AceType	This is an audit ACE.
AceFlags	The auditing applies to this object. Child objects inherit this ACE. This ACE audits successes and failures.
Flags	Neither ObjectType nor InheritedObjectType is set.
ObjectType	Null.
InheritedObjectType	Null.

In this case we are auditing (AceType) successful and failed (AceFlags) modifications of all types (AccessMask) by a user (Trustee) for this object and all children (AceFlags).

 Note the changes to AceFlags as compared to the previous permissions entry. While a permissions entry uses AceType to indicate whether it is allow or deny, an auditing entry uses AceFlags to indicate whether it is auditing successes or failures.

Let's take a look at a more complex example: giving the same user the ability to set the password for user objects within the entire branch beneath an Organizational Unit, as shown in Table 23-3. Again, this ACE is set on the SD of the Organizational Unit, yet it doesn't actually apply to the Organizational Unit itself. This ACE applies to passwords of user objects, so the Organizational Unit acts only as a carrier. The ACE is inherited down the tree by all containers that could ever contain users. As soon as a user is created in one of those containers, the ACE is instantly added as an ACE on the SD of the user via inheritance rules.

Table 23-3. Contents of the ACE properties for a more complex example

Name of the property	Value to be stored
Trustee	Names the user who is to have the permission.
AccessMask	Gives write access to a specific property.

Table 23-3. Contents of the ACE properties for a more complex example (continued)

Name of the property	Value to be stored
AceType	This is an allow permission.
AceFlags	The permission is inherited only and does not apply to this object. Child objects inherit this ACE.
Flags	Both ObjectType and InheritedObjectType are set.
ObjectType	This is the GUID of the userPassword attribute.[a]
InheritedObjectType	This is the GUID of the User class.

[a] Globally Unique Identifiers (GUIDs) are used in the schema to distinguish objects and object attributes uniquely across your forest. Specifying that a GUID is used somewhere means that you are using a unique identifier for that item.

The user (Trustee) is allowed (AceType) write access (AccessMask) to a specific attribute of a specific object class (AccessMask and Flags), namely, the password (ObjectType) of user objects (InheritedObjectType). The ACE does not apply to the current object (AceFlags), so the current object is acting only as a propagator of the ACE down the tree (AceFlags).

To audit successful and failed modifications to the passwords of user objects within the entire branch beneath an Organizational Unit, the contents of the audit ACE on the Organizational Unit would look like Table 23-4.

Table 23-4. Contents of the ACE properties when auditing successful modifications to an Organizational Unit and all children by a user

Name of the property	Value to be stored
Trustee	Names the user who is to be audited.
AccessMask	Gives write access to a specific property.
AceType	This is an audit ACE.
AceFlags	The auditing is inherited only and does not apply to this object. Child objects inherit this ACE. This ACE audits successes and failures.
Flags	Both ObjectType and InheritedObjectType are set.
ObjectType	This is the GUID of the userPassword attribute.
InheritedObjectType	This is the GUID of the User class.

We are auditing (AceType) successful and failed (AceFlags) write access (AccessMask) to a specific attribute of a specific object class (AccessMask and Flags) by a user (Trustee), namely, the password (ObjectType) of user objects (InheritedObjectType). The ACE does not apply to the current object (AceFlags), so the current object is acting only as a propagator of the ACE down the tree (AceFlags).

Each ACE property uses a set of values that correspond to the text populating the tables. In the last example, AceFlags is held by the system as the integer 202 that is interpreted as a bit flag.* As you saw in Chapter 21, bits in specified positions on an integer represent each of the flags.

 Many companies and programmers that publish sets of values like these do not always keep the sequences as simple as this. Sometimes the values make no sense as binary values. For example, under the later section "AceType," we'll show you that Microsoft has values of 0,1,2,5,6, and 7 for AceType. This may seem daft, since you won't know if the integer 7 represents 7 on its own or 5+2. Not only that, but surely every value can include 0, so how do you check for it? The simple answer is that in this case, each integer represents one and only one value at any one time, so there is no need to check for multiple bits.

Let's consider each of the properties of an ACE in turn to examine the values that can be stored within.

Trustee

The Trustee is the group or user receiving the permissions defined in the AccessMask and AceType fields or the user or group that is being audited. The Trustee can take any of the following forms:

Domain accounts
> These are the logon names used in previous versions of Windows NT, in the form *domain\useraccount*, where *domain* is the name of the Windows NT domain that contains the user and *useraccount* is the sAMAccountName property of the specified user. An example is AMER\jsmith. This is still valid for Windows 2000 and Windows Server 2003 domains.

Well-known security principals
> These represent special identities defined by the Windows NT/Windows 2000/ Windows Server 2003 security system, such as Everyone, Authenticated Users, System, Creator Owner, etc. The objects representing the security principals are stored in the WellKnown Security Principals container beneath the Configuration container.

Built-in groups
> These represent the built-in user groups defined by the Windows NT security system. They have the form BUILTIN*groupname* where *groupname* is the name of the built-in user group. The objects representing the built-in groups are stored in the Builtin container beneath the domain container. An example is BUILTIN\\ Administrators.

---

* We're using flags here as a general term (*lowercase*) to distinguish it from the ACE property called Flags (*uppercase*).

Security Identifiers (SIDs)

These are specified in string format and represent the objectSID property of the specified user or group in Active Directory. An example is S-1-5-99-427-9.

Distinguished Name (DN)

This is the distinguishedName property of the specified user or group in Active Directory. An example is cn=Tracy Poodles,ou=Finance,dc=mycorp,dc=com.

AccessMask

The AccessMask specifies the single or multiple permissions you are setting or auditing for the ACE. Note that this property does not determine whether you are allowing or denying the permission or whether you are auditing successful or failed access, only what the permission is.

> If you are applying the permissions to a specific object or property, you also need to specify the relevant GUID of the object or property that you are giving rights to in the ObjectType or InheritedObjectType properties.

The largest set of values applies to the AccessMask, which is probably what you would expect. See Table 23-5.

Table 23-5. AccessMask constants

ADSI name	Decimal value	Hex value	Description
ADS_RIGHT_GENERIC_ READ	2,147,483,648	&H80000000	Right to read from the Security Descriptor, to examine the object and its children, and to read all properties
ADS_RIGHT_GENERIC_ WRITE	1,073,741,824	&H40000000	Right to write all properties, write to the DACL, and add/remove the object from the tree
ADS_RIGHT_GENERIC_ EXECUTE	536,870,912	&H20000000	Right to list children of the object
ADS_RIGHT_GENERIC_ ALL	268,435,456	&H10000000	Right to create/delete children, delete the tree, read/write properties, examine the object and its children, add/remove the object from the tree, and read/write with an extended right
ADS_RIGHT_ACCESS_ SYSTEM_ SECURITY	16,777,216	&H1000000	Right to get or set the SACL in the SD of the object
ADS_RIGHT_ SYNCHRONIZE	1,048,576	&H100000	Right to use the object for synchronization (see ADSI documentation for more information)
ADS_RIGHT_WRITE_ OWNER	524,288	&H80000	Right to assume ownership of the object; no right to grant ownership to others (User must be a trustee of the object)

Table 23-5. AccessMask constants (continued)

ADSI name	Decimal value	Hex value	Description
ADS_RIGHT_WRITE_ DAC	262,144	&H40000	Right to write to the DACL of the object
ADS_RIGHT_READ_ CONTROL	131,072	&H20000	Right to read from the security descriptor of the object
ADS_RIGHT_DELETE	65,536	&H10000	Right to delete the object
ADS_RIGHT_DS_ CONTROL_ ACCESS	256	&H100	Right to perform an application-specific extension on the object (GUID=extended right)
ADS_RIGHT_DS_LIST_ OBJECT	128	&H80	Right to examine the object (if this is missing, the object is hidden from the user)
ADS_RIGHT_DS_ DELETE_TREE	64	&H40	Right to delete all children of this object, regardless of the permission on the children
ADS_RIGHT_DS_ WRITE_PROP	32	&H20	Right to write properties of the object (GUID=specific property; no GUID=all properties)
ADS_RIGHT_DS_READ_ PROP	16	&H10	Right to read properties of the object (GUID=specific property; no GUID=all properties)
ADS_RIGHT_DS_SELF	8	&H8	Right to modify the group membership of a group object
ADS_RIGHT_ACTRL_ DS_LIST	4	&H4	Right to examine children of the object
ADS_RIGHT_DS_ DELETE_CHILD	2	&H2	Right to delete children of the object (GUID=specific child object class; no GUID=all child object classes)
ADS_RIGHT_DS_ CREATE_CHILD	1	&H1	Right to create children of the object (GUID=specific child object class; no GUID=all child object classes)
No name defined	−1	&HFFFFFFFFFFFFFFFF	Full control

These values were taken from the ADSI documentation for the ADS_RIGHTS_ ENUM enumerated type available from the MSDN Library under the section described at the beginning of the chapter.

The value in the first column is the constant name that Microsoft defined for ADSI. This works fine if you are programming in VB or VC++ or scripting in a language that can make use of the available ADSI libraries, but with VBScript these constants are not defined. In other words, you have to define them in each script you use. To save you time, just copy the Const definitions from any of the ACE scripts provided on the O'Reilly web site for this book. We've included the values in decimal and in hex for two reasons. First, we will be using hex in the scripts; the decimal values are there in case you want to use them for your own preference. Second, Microsoft defines all their constants in hexadecimal, so that is what you will see in the ADSI documentation. &H is the prefix for a hex number in VBScript, so if you want to specify that a group can list, create, and delete all children, you would use the value &H7, consisting of the rights ADS_ RIGHT_ACTRL_DS_LIST + ADS_RIGHT_DS_ DELETE_CHILD + ADS_RIGHT_DS_ CREATE_CHILD.

The last value has no name and is what you use if you want to define full control permissions. Note that in this case most programmers tend to use the integer value –1 even if they have used hex elsewhere.

The GUIDs relating to properties and children are discussed further under the ACE Flags property.

AceType

This property dictates whether the ACE denies permissions, allows permissions, or audits use of permissions (whether success or failure is defined in AceFlags). The values set here depend on whether the ACE applies to a specific object/property or just applies generally. See Table 23-6.

 Only one value can be set at any one time. This is why the values are not 1, 2, 4, and so on.

Table 23-6. Constants

ADSI name	Decimal value	Hex value	Description
ADS_ACETYPE_SYSTEM_ ALARM_OBJECT	8	&H8	Not used.
ADS_ACETYPE_SYSTEM_ AUDIT_OBJECT	7	&H7	This is a system-audit entry ACE using a GUID.
ADS_ACETYPE_ACCESS_ DENIED_OBJECT	6	&H6	This is an access-denied ACE using a GUID.
ADS_ACETYPE_ACCESS_ ALLOWED_OBJECT	5	&H5	This is an access-allowed ACE using a GUID.
ADS_ACETYPE_SYSTEM_ AUDIT	2	&H2	This is a system-audit entry ACE using a Windows NT Security Descriptor.
ADS_ACETYPE_ACCESS_ DENIED	1	&H1	This is an access-denied ACE using a Windows NT Security Descriptor.
ADS_ACETYPE_ACCESS_ ALLOWED	0	&H0	This is an access-allowed ACE using a Windows NT Security Descriptor.

These values were taken from the ADSI documentation for the ADS_ACETYPE_ ENUM enumerated type available from the MSDN Library under the section described at the beginning of the chapter.

Those ACEs that have a GUID in ObjectType or InheritedObjectType use the top three _OBJECT values. Any ACEs that do not refer to a specific GUID use the bottom three.

AceFlags

This catchall location stores two sets of information: inheritance and auditing. First it stores whether its children can inherit this ACE, whether the ACE applies to this object or is only acting as a propagator to pass it on to other objects, and whether the ACE is itself inherited. Second, for system-audit ACEs, this property indicates whether audit events are generated for success, failure, or both of the AccessMask permissions. See Table 23-7.

Table 23-7. AceFlags constants

ADSI name	Decimal value	Hex value	Description
ADS_ACEFLAG_FAILED_ACCESS	128	&H80	Used in the SACL only; indicates to generate audit messages for failed access attempts.
ADS_ACEFLAG_SUCCESSFUL_ ACCESS	64	&H40	Used in the SACL only; indicates whether to generate audit messages for successful access attempts.
ADS_ACEFLAG_VALID_INHERIT_ FLAGS	31	&H1F	Indicates whether the inherit flags for this ACE are valid (set only by the system).
ADS_ACEFLAG_INHERITED_ACE	16	&H10	Indicates whether this ACE was inherited (set only by the system).
ADS_ACEFLAG_INHERIT_ONLY_ ACE	8	&H8	Indicates an inherit-only ACE that does not exercise access controls on the object to which it is attached.
ADS_ACEFLAG_NO_ PROPAGATE_ INHERIT_ACE	4	&H4	Child objects will not inherit this ACE.
ADS_ACEFLAG_INHERIT_ACE	2	&H2	Child objects will inherit this ACE.

These values were taken from the ADSI documentation for the ADS_ACEFLAG_ ENUM enumerated type available from the MSDN Library under the section described at the beginning of the chapter.

There are three unusual aspects to this property:

- The two SACL flags should surely be in AceType, not AceFlags, since AceType already indicates the allow or deny aspects of a DACL ACE. Strangely, they are here instead.

- The ADS_ACEFLAG_INHERIT_ONLY_ACE indicates that the object that this ACE is attached to is acting only as a carrier for the object, rather than being affected by the ACE itself. This normally applies to containers, where the container acts as a placeholder for the ACE and applies it to whatever specific objects it is targeted to when they are created. If appropriate, the ACE will be propagated to containers below so they can act as carriers themselves.

- Flags of this nature in ADSI normally are intended to indicate the presence or absence of something. The flag is set or it is not, giving us two states for what-

ever the flag refers to. Take a look at the last two flags in the table. The ADS_
ACEFLAG_INHERIT_ACE flag indicates that the ACE will be propagated down
to child objects throughout the section of the tree below this object. If the ADS_
ACEFLAG_INHERIT_ACE flag is set, ADS_ACEFLAG_NO_PROPAGATE_
INHERIT_ACE will not be set. If ADS_ACEFLAG_NO_PROPAGATE_
INHERIT_ACE is set, ADS_ACEFLAG_INHERIT_ACE is not, and this pre-
vents the ACE from being inherited by subsequent generations of objects. Don't
try to set both at the same time.

Flags, ObjectType, and InheritedObjectType

For the ACE to know whether it contains an ObjectType or InheritedObjectType
field, it contains a Flags property. This can have only four values. If the value is 0,
neither object is present in the ACE. The other three values (1, 2, and 3) are made up
from the two constants displayed in Table 23-8.

Table 23-8. Flag type constants

ADSI name	Decimal value	Hex value	Description
ADS_FLAG_ INHERITED_OBJECT_ TYPE_PRESENT	2	&H2	Indicates that an InheritedObjectType is present in the ACE and that an ObjectType is not present
ADS_FLAG_OBJECT_ TYPE_PRESENT	1	&H1	Indicates that an ObjectType is present in the ACE and that an InheritedObjectType is not present

These values were taken from the ADSI documentation for the ADS_FLAGTYPE_
ENUM enumerated type available from the MSDN Library under the section
described at the beginning of the chapter.

The ObjectType and InheritedObjectType fields store GUIDs or null values that indicate what the ACE actually applies to. Table 23-9 explains it much better.

Table 23-9. How to use ObjectType and InheritedObjectType

ACE requirement	AceFlags	Flags	ObjectType	Inherited ObjectType
Permissions are to apply to entire current object.	Effective on current object; not inherited by child objects.	Neither	Null (ignored but still set)	Null (ignored but still set)
Permissions are to apply to a specific attribute of the current object.	Effective on current object; not inherited by child objects.	ObjectType only	schemaIDGUID of the attribute-Schema object that defines the attribute in the schema	Null (ignored but still set)
Permissions are to apply to all child objects.	Not effective on current object; inherited by children.	ObjectType only	Null[a]	Null (ignored but still set)

Table 23-9. How to use ObjectType and InheritedObjectType (continued)

ACE requirement	AceFlags	Flags	ObjectType	Inherited ObjectType
Permissions are to apply to child objects that are of a specific class.	Not effective on current object; inherited by children.	`ObjectType` only	`schemaIDGUID` of the `classSchema` object that defines the class in the schema	Null (ignored but still set)
Permissions are to apply to a specific attribute of specific child objects.	Not effective on current object; inherited by children.	Both	`schemaIDGUID` of the `attribute-Schema` object that defines the attribute in the schema	`schemaIDGUID` of the `classSchema` object that defines the class in the schema

ᵃ Setting null for the `ObjectType` field in the third entry signifies that this ACE applies to all child objects; this is the only time that you do not use a GUID in this property. The system understands that a null value for a required `ObjectType` field is the same as providing the GUIDs for every possible child object all at once.

You do not need to set null items that are ignored; they will be set to null by the system on creation of the ACE.

Note that `Flags`, `ObjectType`, and `InheritedObjectType` have defaults of 0, null, and null, respectively.

A Simple ADSI Example

All of the seven ACE properties are set using property methods of the same names as those in an ADSI interface called `IADsAccessControlEntry`. The ACEs that are created using this are then modified using `IADsAccessControlList` and `IADsSecurity-Descriptor`.

Let's go through an example now so you can see how it all fits together. Example 23-1 shows a section of VBScript code that creates an ACE that allows ANewGroup full access to the myOU organizational unit and all its children.

Example 23-1. A simple ADSI example

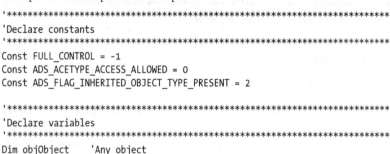

```
'*************************************************************************
'Declare constants
'*************************************************************************
Const FULL_CONTROL = -1
Const ADS_ACETYPE_ACCESS_ALLOWED = 0
Const ADS_FLAG_INHERITED_OBJECT_TYPE_PRESENT = 2


'*************************************************************************
'Declare variables
'*************************************************************************
Dim objObject      'Any object
```

Example 23-1. A simple ADSI example (continued)

```
Dim objSecDesc    'SecurityDescriptor
Dim objDACL       'AccessControlList
Dim objNewACE     'AccessControlEntry

'**************************************************************************
'Create the new ACE and populate it
'**************************************************************************
Set objNewACE = CreateObject("AccessControlEntry")
objNewACE.Trustee = "AMER\ANewGroup"
objNewACE.AccessMask = FULL_CONTROL
objNewACE.AceType = ADS_ACETYPE_ACCESS_ALLOWED
objNewACE.AceFlags = ADS_FLAG_INHERITED_OBJECT_TYPE_PRESENT

'**************************************************************************
'Add the new ACE to the object and write it to the AD
'**************************************************************************
Set objObject = GetObject("LDAP://ou=myOU,dc=amer,dc=mycorp,dc=com")

'**************************************************************************
'Use IADs::Get to retrieve the SD for the object
'**************************************************************************
Set objSecDesc = objObject.Get("ntSecurityDescriptor")

'**************************************************************************
'Use IADsSecurityDescriptor:: DiscretionaryAcl to retrieve the existing DACL
'**************************************************************************
Set objDACL = objSecDesc.DiscretionaryAcl

'**************************************************************************
'Use IADsAccessControlList::AddACE to add an ACE to an existing DACL
'**************************************************************************
objDACL.AddAce objNewACE

'**************************************************************************
'Use IADsSecurityDescriptor:: DiscretionaryAcl to put back the modified DACL
'**************************************************************************
objSecDesc.DiscretionaryAcl = objDACL

'**************************************************************************
'Use IADs::Put to replace the SD for the object
'**************************************************************************
objObject.Put "ntSecurityDescriptor", Array(objSecDesc)

'**************************************************************************
'Write out the property cache using IADs::SetInfo
'**************************************************************************
objObject.SetInfo
```

First we create the new ACE. This requires use of a CreateObject function call to create a new empty instance of an ACE object. We then have to set the four fields that
we need. The Trustee is the user or group that will have the permission to the myOU

object. The AccessMask value set to −1 indicates that full permission is being set. To say whether the full permissions are allowed or denied, we use a 0 in the AceType field, which indicates that the ACE is a permissions-allowed ACE. Finally, the AceFlags field is set to 2 so that child objects will inherit this ACE. This means that the ACE now allows ANewGroup full access to the myOU organizational unit and all its children.

We then go through binding to the object to get the security descriptor and ultimately the DACL so that we can add the new ACE to the DACL. Once that is done, we reverse the steps and set the security descriptor for the object, writing out the property cache as the last step.

A Complex ACE Example

Example 23-2 shows two further ACEs being created. This time we have included all the constants. This example sets the following ACEs on myOU:

- No permissions even to see the object for members of DenyGroup.
- Ability to create, delete, and examine all children of the object for AllowChild-Group.
- Ability for user Vicky Launders to assume ownership of the Organizational Unit only and not any children.
- Permission for the user Lee Flight to read and write this OU's description.
- Permission for the Chris Heaton account to read and write all users' passwords
- Generation of audit messages for failed access by Everyone to delete the object itself.
- Generation of audit messages for all modifications to Active Directory by Brian Kerr below this Organizational Unit, but not including this Organizational Unit.

Example 23-2. A complex ACE example

```
'***************************************************************************
'AccessMask constants
'***************************************************************************
Const ADS_RIGHT_GENERIC_READ = &H80000000
Const ADS_RIGHT_GENERIC_WRITE = &H40000000
Const ADS_RIGHT_GENERIC_EXECUTE = &H20000000
Const ADS_RIGHT_GENERIC_ALL = &H10000000
Const ADS_RIGHT_SYSTEM_SECURITY = &H1000000
Const ADS_RIGHT_SYNCHRONIZE = &H100000
Const ADS_RIGHT_WRITE_OWNER = &H80000
Const ADS_RIGHT_WRITE_DAC = &H40000
Const ADS_RIGHT_READ_CONTROL = &H20000
Const ADS_RIGHT_DELETE = &H10000
Const ADS_RIGHT_DS_CONTROL_ACCESS = &H100
Const ADS_RIGHT_DS_LIST_OBJECT = &H80
```

Example 23-2. A complex ACE example (continued)

```
Const ADS_RIGHT_DS_DELETE_TREE = &H40
Const ADS_RIGHT_DS_WRITE_PROP = &H20
Const ADS_RIGHT_DS_READ_PROP = &H10
Const ADS_RIGHT_DS_SELF = &H8
Const ADS_RIGHT_ACTRL_DS_LIST = &H4
Const ADS_RIGHT_DS_DELETE_CHILD = &H2
Const ADS_RIGHT_DS_CREATE_CHILD = &H1
Const FULL_CONTROL = -1


'*************************************************************************
'AceType constants
'*************************************************************************
Const ADS_ACETYPE_SYSTEM_AUDIT_OBJECT = &H7
Const ADS_ACETYPE_ACCESS_DENIED_OBJECT = &H6
Const ADS_ACETYPE_ACCESS_ALLOWED_OBJECT = &H5
Const ADS_ACETYPE_SYSTEM_AUDIT = &H2
Const ADS_ACETYPE_ACCESS_DENIED = &H1
Const ADS_ACETYPE_ACCESS_ALLOWED = &H0


'*************************************************************************
'AceFlags constants
'*************************************************************************
Const ADS_ACEFLAG_FAILED_ACCESS = &H80
Const ADS_ACEFLAG_SUCCESSFUL_ACCESS = &H40
Const ADS_ACEFLAG_VALID_INHERIT_FLAGS = &H1F
Const ADS_ACEFLAG_INHERITED_ACE = &H10
Const ADS_ACEFLAG_INHERIT_ONLY_ACE = &H8
Const ADS_ACEFLAG_NO_PROPAGATE_INHERIT_ACE = &H4
Const ADS_ACEFLAG_INHERIT_ACE = &H2


'*************************************************************************
'Flags constants
'*************************************************************************
Const ADS_FLAG_INHERITED_OBJECT_TYPE_PRESENT = &H2
Const ADS_FLAG_OBJECT_TYPE_PRESENT = &H1


'*************************************************************************
'Constants representing paths to classes and attributes in the schema
'*************************************************************************
Const USER_PASSWORD_ADSPATH = _
  "LDAP://cn=User-Password,cn=Schema,cn=Configuration,dc=mycorp,dc=com"
Const DESCRIPTION_ADSPATH = _
  "LDAP://cn=Description,cn=Schema,cn=Configuration,dc=mycorp,dc=com"
Const USER_ADSPATH = "LDAP://cn=User,cn=Schema,cn=Configuration,dc=mycorp,dc=com"


'*************************************************************************
'Declare general variables
'*************************************************************************
Dim objObject             'The Organizational Unit to bind to
Dim objSecDesc            'SecurityDescriptor
Dim objDACL               'AccessControlList object containing permission ACEs
Dim objSACL               'AccessControlList object containing audit ACEs
```

Example 23-2. A complex ACE example (continued)

```
Dim objNewACE                   'AccessControlEntry
Dim objAttributeSchemaObject 'An object representing an attribute in the schema

'**************************************************************************
'Get a handle to the DACL of the OU
'**************************************************************************
Set objObject = GetObject ("LDAP://ou=myOU,dc=mycorp,dc=com")
Set objSecDesc = objObject.Get("ntSecurityDescriptor")
Set objDACL = objSecDesc.DiscretionaryAcl
Set objSACL = objSecDesc.SystemAcl


'**************************************************************************
'Set no permission to view the object for members of DenyGroup
'**************************************************************************
Set objNewACE = CreateObject("AccessControlEntry")
objNewACE.Trustee = "AMER\DenyGroup"
objNewACE.AccessMask = ADS_RIGHT_DS_LIST_OBJECT
objNewACE.AceType = ADS_ACETYPE_ACCESS_DENIED
objNewACE.AceFlags = ADS_ACEFLAG_INHERIT_ACE
objDACL.AddAce objNewACE
Set objNewACE = Nothing


'**************************************************************************
'Ability to create, delete, and examine all children of the object for
'AllowChildGroup
'**************************************************************************
Set objNewACE = CreateObject("AccessControlEntry")
objNewACE.Trustee = "AMER\AllowChildGroup"
objNewACE.AccessMask = ADS_RIGHT_ACTRL_DS_LIST + ADS_RIGHT_DS_DELETE_CHILD _
    + ADS_RIGHT_DS_CREATE_CHILD
objNewACE.AceType = ADS_ACETYPE_ACCESS_ALLOWED
objNewACE.AceFlags = ADS_ACEFLAG_INHERIT_ACE
objDACL.AddAce objNewACE
Set objNewACE = Nothing


'**************************************************************************
'Ability for user Vicky Launders to assume ownership of the Organizational
'Unit only and not any children
'**************************************************************************
Set objNewACE = CreateObject("AccessControlEntry")
AdsACE.Trustee = "cn=Vicky Launders,cn=Users,dc=amer,dc=mycorp,dc=com"
objNewACE.AccessMask = ADS_RIGHT_WRITE_OWNER
objNewACE.AceType = ADS_ACETYPE_ACCESS_ALLOWED
objNewACE.AceFlags = ADS_ACEFLAG_NO_PROPAGATE_INHERIT_ACE
objDACL.AddAce objNewACE
Set objNewACE = Nothing


'**************************************************************************
'Allowing the Lee Flight account to read and write this OU's description
'**************************************************************************
Set objNewACE = CreateObject("AccessControlEntry")
AdsACE.Trustee = "cn=Lee Flight,cn=Users,dc=amer,dc=mycorp,dc=com"
```

Example 23-2. A complex ACE example (continued)

```
objNewACE.AccessMask = ADS_RIGHT_DS_WRITE_PROP + ADS_RIGHT_DS_READ_PROP
objNewACE.AceType = ADS_ACETYPE_ACCESS_ALLOWED_OBJECT
objNewACE.AceFlags = ADS_ACEFLAG_NO_PROPAGATE_INHERIT_ACE
objNewACE.Flags = ADS_FLAG_OBJECT_TYPE_PRESENT
'*****************************************************************************
'Retrieve the GUID of the Description class from the schema and place the
'result in the ObjectType property
'*****************************************************************************
Set objAttributeSchemaObject = GetObject(DESCRIPTION_ADSPATH)
objNewACE.ObjectType = objAttributeSchemaObject.GUID

objDACL.AddAce objNewACE
Set objNewACE = Nothing


'*****************************************************************************
'Allowing the Chris Heaton account to read and write users' passwords
'*****************************************************************************
Set objNewACE = CreateObject("AccessControlEntry")
objNewACE.Trustee = "AMER\Chris Heaton"
objNewACE.AccessMask = ADS_RIGHT_DS_WRITE_PROP + ADS_RIGHT_DS_READ_PROP
objNewACE.AceType = ADS_ACETYPE_ACCESS_ALLOWED_OBJECT
objNewACE.AceFlags = ADS_ACEFLAG_INHERIT_ACE + ADS_ACEFLAG_INHERIT_ONLY_ACE
objNewACE.Flags = ADS_FLAG_OBJECT_TYPE_PRESENT _
  + ADS_FLAG_INHERITED_OBJECT_TYPE_PRESENT
'*****************************************************************************
'Retrieve the GUID of the User-Password class from the schema and place
'the result in the ObjectType property
'*****************************************************************************
Set objAttributeSchemaObject = GetObject(USER_PASSWORD_ADSPATH)
objNewACE.ObjectType = objAttributeSchemaObject.GUID
'*****************************************************************************
'Retrieve the GUID of the User class from the schema and place the result
'in the InheritedObjectType property
'*****************************************************************************
Set objAttributeSchemaObject = GetObject(USER_ADSPATH)
objNewACE.InheritedObjectType = objAttributeSchemaObject.GUID

objDACL.AddAce objNewACE
Set objNewACE = Nothing


'*****************************************************************************
'Generation of audit messages for failed access by Everyone to delete the
'object itself
'*****************************************************************************
Set objNewACE = CreateObject("AccessControlEntry")
objNewACE.Trustee = "AMER\Everyone"
objNewACE.AccessMask = ADS_RIGHT_DELETE
objNewACE.AceType = ADS_ACETYPE_SYSTEM_AUDIT
objNewACE.AceFlags = ADS_ACEFLAG_FAILED_ACCESS _
  + ADS_ACEFLAG_NO_PROPAGATE_INHERIT_ACE
objSACL.AddAce objNewACE
Set objNewACE = Nothing
```

Example 23-2. A complex ACE example (continued)

```
'**************************************************************************
'Generation of audit messages for successful and failed modifications by
'Brian Kerr to Active Directory below this Organizational Unit, but
'not including this Organizational Unit
'**************************************************************************
Set objNewACE = CreateObject("AccessControlEntry")
AdsACE.Trustee = "cn=Brian Kerr,cn=Users,dc=amer,dc=mycorp,dc=com"
objNewACE.AccessMask = FULL_CONTROL
objNewACE.AceType = ADS_ACETYPE_SYSTEM_AUDIT_OBJECT
objNewACE.AceFlags = ADS_ACEFLAG_FAILED_ACCESS + ADS_ACEFLAG_SUCCESSFUL_ACCESS _
    + ADS_ACEFLAG_INHERIT_ONLY_ACE + ADS_ACEFLAG_INHERIT_ACE
objNewACE.Flags = ADS_FLAG_OBJECT_TYPE_PRESENT
objNewACE.ObjectType = vbNull
objSACL.AddAce objNewACE
Set objNewACE = Nothing


'**************************************************************************
'Write the newly expanded DACL and SACL to the SD and then out to the AD
'**************************************************************************
objSecDesc.DiscretionaryAcl = objDACL
objSecDesc.SystemAcl = objSACL
objObject.Put "ntSecurityDescriptor", Array(objSecDesc)
objObject.SetInfo
```

Note that the last two items modify the SACL and not the DACL as they are audit
ACEs and not permissions ACEs. You can also see that we have chosen to use DNs
and domain accounts for the trustees in the script. Again, as usual in these scripts,
there is no error handling. As the SD is not being written until the end of the code,
an error causes the entire script to fail.

Creating Security Descriptors

If you are creating an object from scratch, and you don't want it to get the default
DACL and SACL that due to inheritance would normally be applied to objects created at that location in the tree, you can write your own DACL and SACL for an
object. As you would expect, there are a number of properties associated with security descriptors and ACLs that you need to set. SDs and ACLs can be manipulated
with the IADsAccessControlList (see Table 23-10) and IADsSecurityDescriptor (see
Table 23-11) interfaces. We'll go through these briefly now and then move on to
some more examples.

Table 23-10. IADsAccessControlList methods and properties

IADsAccessControlList methods and properties	Action
AddAce method	Adds an ACE to an ACL
RemoveAce method	Removes an ACE from an ACL
CopyAccessList method	Copies the current ACL

Table 23-10. IADsAccessControlList methods and properties (continued)

IADsAccessControlList methods and properties	Action
AclRevision property	Shows the revision of the ACL (always set to 4; see later text)
AceCount property	Indicates the number of ACEs in the ACL

The revision level is a static version number for every ACE, ACL, and SD in Active Directory. It is defined in the ADS_SD_REVISION_ENUM enumerated type, which contains a single constant definition as follows:

```
Const ADS_SD_REVISION_DS = 4.
```

Having a revision allows Active Directory to know which elements of an ACE could exist. Later, if new properties and concepts are added to the ACE so that it has a more extended definition, the revision would increment. Active Directory would then know that old revision-4 ACEs could not support the new extensions and could upgrade them or support them with lesser functionality.

Table 23-11. IADsSecurityDescriptor methods and properties

IADsSecurityDescriptor methods and properties	Action
CopySecurityDescriptor method	A copy of an existing SD.
Revision property	The revision of the SD (always set to 4, as noted earlier).
Control property	A set of flags indicating various aspects of the SD (see later text).
Owner property	The SID of the owner. If this field is null, no owner is set.
OwnerDefaulted property	A Boolean value indicating whether the owner is derived by the default mechanism when created (i.e., assembled out of all the inherited ACEs passed down by its parents) rather than explicitly set by the person or application that created the SD in the first place.
Group property	The SID of the object's primary group if appropriate. If this field is null, no primary group exists.
GroupDefaulted property	A Boolean value indicating that the group is derived by the default mechanism rather than explicitly set by the person or application that created the SD in the first place.
DiscretionaryAcl property	The discretionary ACL that holds permissions ACEs. The SE_DACL_PRESENT flag must be set in the Control property if a DACL exists. If the flag is set and yet this field is null, full access is allowed to everyone.
DaclDefaulted property	A Boolean value indicating that the DACL is derived by the default mechanism rather than explicitly set by the person or application that created the SD in the first place. This is ignored unless SE_DACL_PRESENT is set.
SystemAcl property	The system ACL that holds auditing ACEs. The SE_SACL_PRESENT flag must be set in the Control property if a SACL exists.
SaclDefaulted property	A Boolean value indicating that the SACL is derived by the default mechanism rather than explicitly set by the person or application that created the SD in the first place. This is ignored unless SE_SACL_PRESENT is set.

The Control property can take a number of flags that help to define the properties of an SD. See Table 23-12 for a full description.

Table 23-12. Control constants

ADSI name	Decimal value	Hex value	Description
ADS_SD_CONTROL_SE_OWNER_ DEFAULTED	1	&H1	This Boolean flag, when set, indicates that the SID pointed to by the Owner field was provided by the default mechanism rather than set by the person or application that created the SD in the first place. This may affect the treatment of the SID with respect to inheritance of an owner.
ADS_SD_CONTROL_SE_GROUP_ DEFAULTED	2	&H2	This Boolean flag, when set, indicates that the SID in the Group field was provided by the default mechanism rather than explicitly set by the person or application that created the SD in the first place. This may affect the treatment of the SID with respect to inheritance of a primary group.
ADS_SD_CONTROL_SE_DACL_ PRESENT	4	&H4	This Boolean flag, when set, indicates that the security descriptor contains a DACL. If this flag is set and the DiscretionaryAcl field of the SD is null, an empty (but present) ACL is explicitly being specified.
ADS_SD_CONTROL_SE_DACL_ DEFAULTED	8	&H8	This Boolean flag, when set, indicates that the DiscretionaryAcl field was provided by the default mechanism rather than explicitly set by the person or application that created the SD in the first place. This may affect the treatment of the ACL with respect to inheritance of an ACL. This flag is ignored if the SE_DACL_PRESENT flag is not set.
ADS_SD_CONTROL_SE_SACL_ PRESENT	16	&H10	This Boolean flag, when set, indicates that the security descriptor contains a SACL.
ADS_SD_CONTROL_SE_SACL_ DEFAULTED	32	&H20	This Boolean flag, when set, indicates that the ACL pointed to by the SystemAcl field was provided by the default mechanism rather than explicitly set by the person or application that created the SD in the first place. This may affect the treatment of the ACL with respect to inheritance of an ACL. This flag is ignored if the SE_SACL_PRESENT flag is not set.
ADS_SD_CONTROL_SE_DACL_ AUTO_INHERIT_REQ	256	&H100	The DACL of the SD must be inherited.
ADS_SD_CONTROL_SE_SACL_ AUTO_INHERIT_REQ	512	&H200	The SACL of the SD must be inherited.
ADS_SD_CONTROL_SE_DACL_ AUTO_INHERITED	1,024	&H400	The DACL of the SD supports auto-propagation of inheritable ACEs to existing child objects.
ADS_SD_CONTROL_SE_SACL_ AUTO_INHERITED	2,048	&H800	The SACL of the SD supports auto-propagation of inheritable ACEs to existing child objects.
ADS_SD_CONTROL_SE_DACL_ PROTECTED	4,096	&H1000	The DACL of the SD is protected and will not be modified when new rights propagate through the tree.
ADS_SD_CONTROL_SE_SACL_ PROTECTED	8,192	&H2000	The SACL of the SD is protected and will not be modified when new rights propagate through the tree.
ADS_SD_CONTROL_SE_SELF_ RELATIVE	32,768	&H8000	The SD is held in a contiguous block of memory.

These values were taken from the ADSI documentation for the ADS_SD_ CONTROL_ENUM enumerated type available from the MSDN Library under the section described at the beginning of the chapter.

 In your ADSI code, it is possible to specify that the DACL or SACL is either null or empty. While in both cases each ACL contains no ACEs, there is a big difference between the effects of each setting. Specifically, any ACL that has been set to null (vbNull) grants full permissions to everyone while an ACL that exists but contains no ACEs (i.e., is empty) grants no permissions to anyone at all.

Now we have enough information to be able to create our own SD. Example 23-3 does exactly that. While we have defined all of the SD constants, to save space we have defined only the ACE constants that we are using. Also note that this code is not 100% complete; the object creation code is not included.

Example 23-3. Creating your own security descriptor

```
'*************************************************************************
'AccessMask constants
'*************************************************************************
Const ADS_RIGHT_DS_LIST_OBJECT = &H80


'*************************************************************************
'AceType constants
'*************************************************************************
Const ADS_ACETYPE_ACCESS_DENIED = &H1


'*************************************************************************
'AceFlags constants
'*************************************************************************
Const ADS_ACEFLAG_INHERIT_ACE = &H2


'*************************************************************************
'Security Descriptor constants
'*************************************************************************
Const ADS_SD_CONTROL_SE_OWNER_DEFAULTED = &H1
Const ADS_SD_CONTROL_SE_GROUP_DEFAULTED = &H2
Const ADS_SD_CONTROL_SE_DACL_PRESENT = &H4
Const ADS_SD_CONTROL_SE_DACL_DEFAULTED = &H8
Const ADS_SD_CONTROL_SE_SACL_PRESENT = &H10
Const ADS_SD_CONTROL_SE_SACL_DEFAULTED = &H20
Const ADS_SD_CONTROL_SE_DACL_AUTO_INHERIT_REQ = &H100
Const ADS_SD_CONTROL_SE_SACL_AUTO_INHERIT_REQ = &H200
Const ADS_SD_CONTROL_SE_DACL_AUTO_INHERITED = &H400
Const ADS_SD_CONTROL_SE_SACL_AUTO_INHERITED = &H800
Const ADS_SD_CONTROL_SE_DACL_PROTECTED = &H1000
Const ADS_SD_CONTROL_SE_SACL_PROTECTED = &H2000


'*************************************************************************
'Security Descriptor Revision
```

Example 23-3. Creating your own security descriptor (continued)

```
'**************************************************************************
Const ADS_SD_REVISION_DS = 4


'**************************************************************************
'Declare general variables
'**************************************************************************
Dim objObject                  'The object to bind to
Dim objSecDesc                 'SecurityDescriptor
Dim objDACL                    'AccessControlList object containing permission ACEs
Dim objSACL                    'AccessControlList object containing audit ACEs
Dim objNewACE                  'AccessControlEntry
Dim objAttributeSchemaObject   'An object representing an attribute in the schema


'**************************************************************************
'Create the objObject first [this code is not included here]
'**************************************************************************


'**************************************************************************
'Set no permission to view the object for members of DenyGroup
'**************************************************************************
Set objNewACE = CreateObject("AccessControlEntry")
AdsACE.Trustee = "cn=VickyLaunders,cn=Users,dc=amer,dc=mycorp,dc=com"
objNewACE.AccessMask = ADS_RIGHT_DS_LIST_OBJECT
objNewACE.AceType = ADS_ACETYPE_ACCESS_DENIED
objNewACE.AceFlags = ADS_ACEFLAG_INHERIT_ACE


'**************************************************************************
'Create a new DACL and add the ACE as the sole entry
'**************************************************************************
Set objDACL = CreateObject("AccessControlList")
ObjDACL.AceCount = 1
ObjDACL.AclRevision = ADS_SD_REVISION_DS
ObjDACL.AddAce objNewACE
Set objNewACE = Nothing


'**************************************************************************
'Create the SD for the object. Set the SD to use the DACL supplied rather
'than the default one. Set the SD to use the default SACL that will be
'generated from all the inherited ACEs from parents further up the hierarchy.
'**************************************************************************
Set objSecDesc = CreateObject("SecurityDescriptor")
objSecDes.Revision = ADS_SD_REVISION_DS
objSecDes.Control = ADS_SD_CONTROL_SE_SACL_PRESENT _
  + ADS_SD_CONTROL_SE_SACL_PRESENT + ADS_SD_CONTROL_SE_SACL_DEFAULTED _
  + SE_OWNER_DEFAULTED + SE_GROUP_DEFAULTED
objSecDes.OwnerDefaulted = True
objSecDes.GroupDefaulted = True
objSecDes.DiscretionaryAcl = objDACL
objSecDes.DaclDefaulted = False
objSecDes.SaclDefaulted = True


'**************************************************************************
```

Example 23-3. Creating your own security descriptor (continued)

```
'Assign the SD to the existing object
'***********************************************************************
objObject.Put "ntSecurityDescriptor", objSecDes
obj Object.SetInfo
```

Listing ACEs to a File for All Objects in an OU and Below

A good example of a useful real-world task is when you are curious to see what ACEs have been set on all objects below a container, such as a domain or Organizational Unit. Example 23-4 is a piece of code that can be used as the basis for checking through an Active Directory forest looking for irregularities.

This code also could be used on the root of Active Directory when dealing with the problem outlined in "Bringing Order Out of Chaos" in Chapter 11. The code is fairly simple but very long, due to the fact that it has to check every constant for both the SACL and DACL of each object.

Example 23-4. Examining the ACEs on all objects below a container

```
On Error Resume Next


'***********************************************************************
'If the GUID corresponds to a schema object or attribute, then print the
'schema attribute/object name and the GUID. Otherwise just print the GUID.
'***********************************************************************
Sub PrintGUID(ByVal objType)

  Dim strACEGUID, bolFound, intIndex

  '***********************************************************************
  'Convert a GUID that starts and ends with {} and has dashes within to a
  'simple string of text
  '***********************************************************************
  strACEGUID = Replace(Mid(objType,2,Len(objType)-2),"-","")

  '***********************************************************************
  'Scan the array of schema values for a matching GUID (after converting both
  'GUIDs to uppercase first). If a GUID is found, the name is printed.
  '***********************************************************************
  ts.WriteLine vbTab & vbTab & "GUID: " & objType
  For intIndex=0 To UBound(arrSchema,2)
    If (UCase(strACEGUID) = UCase(arrSchema(0,intIndex))) Then
      ts.WriteLine vbTab & vbTab & "Name: " & arrSchema(1,intIndex)
    End If
  Next
End Sub


'***********************************************************************
'This function checks to see if the first integer value contains the constant
```

```
'passed in as the second integer value. If it does, then the third parameter
'is written out to the file, and the first value is decremented by the amount
'of the constant.
'***************************************************************************
Sub CheckValue(ByRef lngValueToCheck, ByVal lngConstant, ByVal strConstantName)
  If ((lngValueToCheck And lngConstant) = lngConstant) Then
    ts.WriteLine vbTab & strConstantName
    lngValueToCheck = lngValueToCheck Xor lngConstant
  Else
    lngValueToCheck = lngValueToCheck
  End If
End Sub


'***************************************************************************
'AccessMask constants
'***************************************************************************
Const ADS_RIGHT_GENERIC_READ = &H80000000
Const ADS_RIGHT_GENERIC_WRITE = &H40000000
Const ADS_RIGHT_GENERIC_EXECUTE = &H20000000
Const ADS_RIGHT_GENERIC_ALL = &H10000000
Const ADS_RIGHT_SYSTEM_SECURITY = &H1000000
Const ADS_RIGHT_SYNCHRONIZE = &H100000
Const ADS_RIGHT_WRITE_OWNER = &H80000
Const ADS_RIGHT_WRITE_DAC = &H40000
Const ADS_RIGHT_READ_CONTROL = &H20000
Const ADS_RIGHT_DELETE = &H10000
Const ADS_RIGHT_DS_CONTROL_ACCESS = &H100
Const ADS_RIGHT_DS_LIST_OBJECT = &H80
Const ADS_RIGHT_DS_DELETE_TREE = &H40
Const ADS_RIGHT_DS_WRITE_PROP = &H20
Const ADS_RIGHT_DS_READ_PROP = &H10
Const ADS_RIGHT_DS_SELF = &H8
Const ADS_RIGHT_ACTRL_DS_LIST = &H4
Const ADS_RIGHT_DS_DELETE_CHILD = &H2
Const ADS_RIGHT_DS_CREATE_CHILD = &H1
Const FULL_CONTROL = -1


'***************************************************************************
'AceType constants
'***************************************************************************
Const ADS_ACETYPE_SYSTEM_AUDIT_OBJECT = &H7
Const ADS_ACETYPE_ACCESS_DENIED_OBJECT = &H6
Const ADS_ACETYPE_ACCESS_ALLOWED_OBJECT = &H5
Const ADS_ACETYPE_SYSTEM_AUDIT = &H2
Const ADS_ACETYPE_ACCESS_DENIED = &H1
Const ADS_ACETYPE_ACCESS_ALLOWED = &H0


'***************************************************************************
'AceFlags constants
'***************************************************************************
Const ADS_ACEFLAG_FAILED_ACCESS = &H80
Const ADS_ACEFLAG_SUCCESSFUL_ACCESS = &H40
```

Example 23-4. Examining the ACEs on all objects below a container (continued)

```
Const ADS_ACEFLAG_VALID_INHERIT_FLAGS = &H1F
Const ADS_ACEFLAG_INHERITED_ACE = &H10
Const ADS_ACEFLAG_INHERIT_ONLY_ACE = &H8
Const ADS_ACEFLAG_NO_PROPAGATE_INHERIT_ACE = &H4
Const ADS_ACEFLAG_INHERIT_ACE = &H2


'**************************************************************************
'Security Descriptor constants
'**************************************************************************
Const ADS_SD_CONTROL_SE_OWNER_DEFAULTED = &H1
Const ADS_SD_CONTROL_SE_GROUP_DEFAULTED = &H2
Const ADS_SD_CONTROL_SE_DACL_PRESENT = &H4
Const ADS_SD_CONTROL_SE_DACL_DEFAULTED = &H8
Const ADS_SD_CONTROL_SE_SACL_PRESENT = &H10
Const ADS_SD_CONTROL_SE_SACL_DEFAULTED = &H20
Const ADS_SD_CONTROL_SE_DACL_AUTO_INHERIT_REQ = &H100
Const ADS_SD_CONTROL_SE_SACL_AUTO_INHERIT_REQ = &H200
Const ADS_SD_CONTROL_SE_DACL_AUTO_INHERITED = &H400
Const ADS_SD_CONTROL_SE_SACL_AUTO_INHERITED = &H800
Const ADS_SD_CONTROL_SE_DACL_PROTECTED = &H1000
Const ADS_SD_CONTROL_SE_SACL_PROTECTED = &H2000


'**************************************************************************
'Flags constants
'**************************************************************************
Const ADS_FLAG_INHERITED_OBJECT_TYPE_PRESENT = &H2
Const ADS_FLAG_OBJECT_TYPE_PRESENT = &H1


'**************************************************************************
'Two example paths. You need to specify your own path here in the constant or
'obtain it from an argument to the script or an InputBox.
'**************************************************************************
'Const LDAP_PATH = "LDAP://cn=Mike Felmeri,ou=Sales,dc=amer,dc=mycorp,dc=com"
'Const LDAP_PATH = "LDAP://dc=amer,dc=mycorp,dc=com"
Const SCHEMA_ROOT="LDAP://cn=Schema,cn=Configuration,dc=mycorp,dc=com"


' **************************************************************************
' Opens a file, and lets you start writing from the beginning of the
' file.
' **************************************************************************
Const ForWriting = 2


' **************************************************************************
' Sets the location of the temporary file
' **************************************************************************
Const TEMPFILE = "C:\SD-LIST-TEMP.TXT"


'**************************************************************************
'Declare the variables
'**************************************************************************
Dim objUser, objSecDesc, objSecDescControl, objACE, objDACL
Dim objSACL, objACEAccessMask, objACEAceType, objACEAceFlags
```

Example 23-4. Examining the ACEs on all objects below a container (continued)

```
Dim lngBeforeChange, intCount, fso, ts, strCriteria, objObject
Dim arrSchema( ), objSchema, intIndex

'***************************************************************************
'Fill an array with GUIDs and CNs from all the objects in the schema. As we
'don't know the maximum number of elements in advance, the array is gradually
'redimensioned (i.e.,  has its size increased) each time we wish to add a new value.
'
'So, if there are 4,000 values in the schema, then the array will look like
'this:
'
'  arrSchema(0,0) = 1st schema object GUID
'  arrSchema(1,0) = 1st schema object cn
'  arrSchema(0,1) = 2nd schema object GUID
'  arrSchema(1,1) = 2nd schema object cn
'  arrSchema(0,2) = 3rd schema object GUID
'  arrSchema(1,2) = 3rd schema object cn
'    etc.
'  arrSchema(0,3999) = 4,000th schema object GUID
'  arrSchema(1,3999) = 4,000th schema object cn
'
'UBound(arrSchema,1) gives the max-size of the first dimension (i.e., 1)
'UBound(arrSchema,2) gives the max-size of the second dimension (i.e., 3999)
'***************************************************************************
Set objSchema = GetObject(SCHEMA_ROOT)
intIndex = 0
For Each objObject in objSchema
   'Increase the size of the array while preserving values
   ReDim Preserve arrSchema(1,intIndex)
   arrSchema(0,intIndex) = objObject.GUID
   'Set the name to be everything except the "cn=" on the front
   arrSchema(1,intIndex) = Right(objObject.cn, Len(objObject.Name)-3)
   intIndex = intIndex + 1
Next

'***************************************************************************
'Opens the temporary text file for writing. If the text file already
'exists, overwrite it.
'***************************************************************************
Set fso = CreateObject("Scripting.FileSystemObject")
Set ts = fso.OpenTextFile(TEMPFILE, ForWriting, True)

'***************************************************************************
'Get the security descriptor of the object
'***************************************************************************
Set objObject = GetObject(LDAP_PATH)
Set objSecDesc = objObject.Get("nTSecurityDescriptor")

'***************************************************************************
'Write out the SD general information
'***************************************************************************
ts.WriteLine "----------------------------------------------------------------"
```

Example 23-4. Examining the ACEs on all objects below a container (continued)

```
ts.WriteLine "SD revision is: " & objSecDesc.Revision
ts.WriteLine "SD Owner is: " & objSecDesc.Owner
ts.WriteLine "SD Group is: " & objSecDesc.Group
ts.WriteLine "SD GroupDefaulted is: " & objSecDesc.GroupDefaulted
ts.WriteLine "SD OwnerDefaulted is: " & objSecDesc.OwnerDefaulted
ts.WriteLine "SD DaclDefaulted is: " & objSecDesc.DaclDefaulted
ts.WriteLine "SD SaclDefaulted is: " & objSecDesc.SaclDefaulted
ts.WriteLine "----------------------------------------------------------------"

'****************************************************************************
'Write out the SD control flags
'****************************************************************************
ts.WriteLine "SD Control is: "
objSecDescControl = objSecDesc.Control
CheckValue objSecDescControl, ADS_SD_CONTROL_SE_SELF_RELATIVE, _
   "The SD is held in a contiguous block of memory."
CheckValue objSecDescControl, ADS_SD_CONTROL_SE_SACL_PROTECTED, "The SACL of " _
   & "the SD is protected and will not be modified when new rights propagate " _
   & "through the tree."
CheckValue objSecDescControl, ADS_SD_CONTROL_SE_DACL_PROTECTED, "The DACL of " _
   & "the SD is protected and will not be modified when new rights propagate " _
   & "through the tree."
CheckValue objSecDescControl, ADS_SD_CONTROL_SE_SACL_AUTO_INHERITED, "The SACL" _
   & " of the SD supports auto-propagation of inheritable ACEs to existing " _
   & " child objects."
CheckValue objSecDescControl, ADS_SD_CONTROL_SE_DACL_AUTO_INHERITED, "The DACL" _
   & " of the SD supports auto-propagation of inheritable ACEs to existing " _
   & "child objects."
CheckValue objSecDescControl, ADS_SD_CONTROL_SE_SACL_AUTO_INHERIT_REQ, "The " _
   & "SACL of the SD must be inherited."
CheckValue objSecDescControl, ADS_SD_CONTROL_SE_DACL_AUTO_INHERIT_REQ, "The " _
   & "DACL of the SD must be inherited."
CheckValue objSecDescControl, ADS_SD_CONTROL_SE_SACL_DEFAULTED, "The ACL " _
   & "pointed to by the SystemAcl field was provided by the default mechanism " _
   & "rather than explicitly set by the person or application that created the " _
   & "SD in the first place."
CheckValue objSecDescControl, ADS_SD_CONTROL_SE_SACL_PRESENT, "The security " _
   & "descriptor contains a SACL."
CheckValue objSecDescControl, ADS_SD_CONTROL_SE_DACL_DEFAULTED, "The " _
   & "DiscretionaryAcl field was provided by the default mechanism rather than " _
   & "explicitly set by the person or application that created the SD in the " _
   & "first place."
CheckValue objSecDescControl, ADS_SD_CONTROL_SE_DACL_PRESENT, "The security " _
   & "descriptor contains a DACL."
CheckValue objSecDescControl, ADS_SD_CONTROL_SE_GROUP_DEFAULTED, "The SID in " _
   & "the Group field was provided by the default mechanism rather than " _
   & "explicitly set by the person or application that created the SD in the " _
   & "first place."
CheckValue objSecDescControl, ADS_SD_CONTROL_SE_OWNER_DEFAULTED, "The SID " _
   & "pointed to by the Owner field was provided by the default mechanism " _
   & "rather than set by the person or application that created the SD in the " _
   & "first place."
```

Example 23-4. Examining the ACEs on all objects below a container (continued)

```
'*************************************************************************
'Write out the DACL general information
'*************************************************************************
Set objDACL = objSecDesc.DiscretionaryAcl    'Permissions List

ts.WriteLine "-----------------"
ts.WriteLine "-----------------"
ts.WriteLine "Discretionary ACL"
ts.WriteLine "-----------------"
ts.WriteLine "-----------------"
ts.WriteLine "There are " & objDACL.AceCount & " ACEs in the DACL."
ts.WriteLine "DACL revision is: " & objDACL.AclRevision

intCount = 1
For Each objACE In objDACL
  ts.WriteLine "--------------------------------------------------------------------"
  ts.WriteLine "ACE Trustee " & intCount & " of " & objDACL.AceCount & " is: " _
    & objACE.Trustee

  '*********************************************************************
  'Write out the ACEType details
  '*********************************************************************
  objACEAceType = objACE.AceType
  ts.WriteLine "AceType: "

  If (objACEAceType <> 0) Then
    CheckValue objACEAceType, ADS_ACETYPE_SYSTEM_AUDIT_OBJECT, "This is a " _
      & "System Audit Entry ACE using a GUID"
    CheckValue objACEAceType, ADS_ACETYPE_ACCESS_DENIED_OBJECT, "This is an " _
      & "Access Denied ACE using a GUID"
    CheckValue objACEAceType, ADS_ACETYPE_ACCESS_ALLOWED_OBJECT, "This is an " _
      & "Access Allowed ACE using a GUID."
    CheckValue objACEAceType, ADS_ACETYPE_SYSTEM_AUDIT, "This is a System " _
      & "Audit Entry ACE using a Windows NT Security Descriptor."
    CheckValue objACEAceType, ADS_ACETYPE_ACCESS_DENIED, "This is an Access " _
      & "Denied ACE using a Windows NT Security Descriptor."
  Else
    ts.WriteLine vbTab & "This is an Access Allowed ACE using a Windows NT " _
      & "Security Descriptor."
  End If

  '*********************************************************************
  'Write out the AccessMask details
  '*********************************************************************
  objACEAccessMask = objACE.AccessMask
  ts.WriteLine "Access Mask: "

  If objACEAccessMask = FULL_CONTROL Then
    ts.WriteLine vbTab & "Full Control"
  ElseIf (objACEAccessMask <> 0) Then
    CheckValue objACEAccessMask, ADS_RIGHT_GENERIC_READ, "Right to read from " _
      & "the security descriptor, to examine the object and its children, and " _
```

Example 23-4. Examining the ACEs on all objects below a container (continued)

```
            & "to read all properties."
        CheckValue objACEAccessMask, ADS_RIGHT_GENERIC_WRITE, "Right to write all " _
            & "properties and write to the DACL. User can also add/remove the " _
            & "object from the tree."
        CheckValue objACEAccessMask, ADS_RIGHT_GENERIC_EXECUTE, "Right to list " _
            & "children of the object."
        CheckValue objACEAccessMask, ADS_RIGHT_GENERIC_ALL, "Right to " _
            & "create/delete children, delete the tree, read/write properties, " _
            & "examine the object and its children, add/remove the object from the " _
            & "tree, and read/write with an extended right."
        CheckValue objACEAccessMask, ADS_RIGHT_ACCESS_SYSTEM_SECURITY, "The right " _
            & "to get or set the SACL in the SD of the object."
        CheckValue objACEAccessMask, ADS_RIGHT_SYNCHRONIZE, "The right to use the " _
            & "object for synchronization."
        CheckValue objACEAccessMask, ADS_RIGHT_WRITE_OWNER, "Right to assume " _
            & "ownership of the object; no right to grant ownership to others. " _
            & "[User must be a trustee of the object]."
        CheckValue objACEAccessMask, ADS_RIGHT_WRITE_DAC, "Right to write to the " _
            & "DACL of the object."
        CheckValue objACEAccessMask, ADS_RIGHT_READ_CONTROL, "Right to read from " _
            & "the security descriptor of the object."
        CheckValue objACEAccessMask, ADS_RIGHT_DELETE, "Right to delete the object."

        lngBeforeChange = objACEAccessMask
        CheckValue objACEAccessMask, ADS_RIGHT_DS_CONTROL_ACCESS, "Right to " _
            & "perform an application specific extension on the object."
        If (objACEAccessMask <> lngBeforeChange) Then
            PrintGUID objACE.ObjectType
        End If

        CheckValue objACEAccessMask, ADS_RIGHT_DS_LIST_OBJECT, "Right to examine " _
            & "the object. [If this is missing the object is hidden from the user]."
        CheckValue objACEAccessMask, ADS_RIGHT_DS_DELETE_TREE, "Right to delete " _
            & "all children of this object, regardless of the permission on the " _
            & "children."

        lngBeforeChange = objACEAccessMask
        CheckValue objACEAccessMask, ADS_RIGHT_DS_WRITE_PROP, "Right to write " _
            & "properties of the object."
        If (objACEAccessMask <> lngBeforeChange) Then
            If objACE.ObjectType = "" Then
                ts.WriteLine vbTab & vbTab & "All properties can be written."
            Else
                PrintGUID objACE.ObjectType
            End If
        End If

        lngBeforeChange = objACEAccessMask
        CheckValue objACEAccessMask, ADS_RIGHT_DS_READ_PROP, "Right to read " _
            & "properties of the object."
        If (objACEAccessMask <> lngBeforeChange) Then
            If objACE.ObjectType = "" Then
```

```
      ts.WriteLine vbTab & vbTab & "All properties can be read."
    Else
      PrintGUID objACE.ObjectType
    End If
  End If

  CheckValue objACEAccessMask, ADS_RIGHT_DS_SELF, "Right to modify the " _
    & "group membership of a group object."
  CheckValue objACEAccessMask, ADS_RIGHT_ACTRL_DS_LIST, "Right to examine " _
    & "children of the object."

  lngBeforeChange = objACEAccessMask
  CheckValue objACEAccessMask, ADS_RIGHT_DS_DELETE_CHILD, "Right to delete " _
    & "children of the object"
  If (objACEAccessMask <> lngBeforeChange) Then
    If objACE.ObjectType = "" Then
      ts.WriteLine vbTab & vbTab & "All Children inherit this right."
    Else
      PrintGUID objACE.ObjectType
    End If
  End If

  lngBeforeChange = objACEAccessMask
  CheckValue objACEAccessMask, ADS_RIGHT_DS_CREATE_CHILD, "Right to create " _
    & "children of the object"
  If (objACEAccessMask <> lngBeforeChange) Then
    If objACE.ObjectType = "" Then
      ts.WriteLine vbTab & vbTab & "All Children inherit this right."
    Else
      PrintGUID objACE.ObjectType
    End If
  End If

Else
  ts.WriteLine vbTab & "ACE Access Mask is 0, therefore no permissions " _
    & "exist for this ACE!"
End If

'****************************************************************************
'Write out the ACEFlags details
'****************************************************************************
objACEAceFlags = objACE.AceFlags
ts.WriteLine "ACEFlags: "

If (objACEAceFlags <> 0) Then
  CheckValue objACEAceFlags, ADS_ACEFLAG_FAILED_ACCESS, "SACL: Generates " _
    & "audit messages for failed access attempts."
  CheckValue objACEAceFlags, ADS_ACEFLAG_SUCCESSFUL_ACCESS, "SACL: " _
    & "Generates audit messages for successful access attempts."
  CheckValue objACEAceFlags, ADS_ACEFLAG_VALID_INHERIT_FLAGS, "Indicates " _
    & "whether the inherit flags are valid. [Set only by the system]."
  CheckValue objACEAceFlags, ADS_ACEFLAG_INHERITED_ACE, "Indicates whether " _
```

Example 23-4. Examining the ACEs on all objects below a container (continued)

```
         & "or not the ACE was inherited. [Set only by the system]."
       CheckValue objACEAceFlags, ADS_ACEFLAG_INHERIT_ONLY_ACE, "Indicates an " _
         & "inherit-only ACE that does not exercise access controls on the " _
         & "object to which it is attached."
       CheckValue objACEAceFlags, ADS_ACEFLAG_NO_PROPAGATE_INHERIT_ACE, "Child " _
         & "objects will not inherit this ACE."
       CheckValue objACEAceFlags, ADS_ACEFLAG_INHERIT_ACE, "Child objects will " _
         & "inherit this ACE."
     Else
       ts.WriteLine vbTab & "ACE is not inherited by children."
     End If

     '****************************************************************************
     'Write out the Flags details
     '****************************************************************************
     ts.WriteLine "Flags: "

     If (objACE.Flags = 0) Then
       ts.WriteLine vbTab & "Object Type and Inherited Object Type aren't present."
     ElseIf (objACE.Flags = ADS_FLAG_INHERITED_OBJECT_TYPE_PRESENT) Then
       ts.WriteLine vbTab & "Inherited Object Type present: "
       PrintGUID objACE.InheritedObjectType
     ElseIf (objACE.Flags = ADS_FLAG_OBJECT_TYPE_PRESENT) Then
       ts.WriteLine vbTab & "Object Type present: "
       PrintGUID objACE.ObjectType
     ElseIf (objACE.Flags = (ADS_FLAG_OBJECT_TYPE_PRESENT + _
       ADS_FLAG_INHERITED_OBJECT_TYPE_PRESENT)) Then
       'Both present, so print the GUIDs

       ts.WriteLine vbTab & "Inherited Object Type present: "
       PrintGUID objACE.InheritedObjectType

       ts.WriteLine vbTab & "Object Type present: "
       PrintGUID objACE.ObjectType
     End If

     intCount = intCount + 1
   Next

   '****************************************************************************
   'Write out the SACL general information
   '****************************************************************************
   Set objSACL = objSecDesc.SystemAcl        'System Auditing List

   ts.WriteLine "----------"
   ts.WriteLine "----------"
   ts.WriteLine "System ACL"
   ts.WriteLine "----------"
   ts.WriteLine "----------"
   ts.WriteLine "There are " & objSACL.AceCount & " ACEs in the SACL."
   ts.WriteLine "SACL revision is: " & objSACL.AclRevision
```

Example 23-4. Examining the ACEs on all objects below a container (continued)

```
intCount = 1
For Each objACE In objSACL
  ts.WriteLine "----------------------------------------------------------------"
  ts.WriteLine "ACE Trustee " & intCount & " of " & objSACL.AceCount & " is: " _
  & objACE.Trustee

  '*************************************************************************
  'Add the ACEType, AccessMask, ACEFlags, and Flags code here from the preceding.
  'The code has been cut to save wasting space by duplicating it in the book.
  'You could even move the entire section of code to a Sub rather than including
  'it twice.
  '*************************************************************************

  intCount = intCount + 1
Next

ts.WriteLine "----------------------------------------------------------------"
ts.Close

MsgBox "End!"
```

Summary

This chapter took a very detailed look at the four main interfaces that you can use to manipulate and iterate over permissions and auditing entries for objects and attributes in your organization:

- IADsAccessControlEntry
- IADsAccessControlList
- IADsSecurityDescriptor
- IADsSecurityUtility

You should now have the tools in your programming belt necessary to modify the permissions in Active Directory as needed.

CHAPTER 24

Extending the Schema and the Active Directory Snap-Ins

This chapter takes a look at two different areas: programmatically extending the schema and customizing the functionality of the Active Directory administrative MMC snap-ins. While these topics may seem very different, they share the common thread of storing and presenting information beyond what Active Directory is configured to do by default. They are also related because you will often want to include new schema extensions in the Active Directory snap-ins.

In the first half of the chapter, we take a look at how you can manipulate the schema to include new attributes and classes. In the second half, we describe how to modify the various components of the Active Directory Users and Computers (ADUC) snap-in to include customized display names and menus. While we will focus on ADUC, the techniques presented in this chapter can be used to modify any of the Active Directory administrative snap-ins.

Modifying the Schema with ADSI

We've shown you how the schema works in Chapter 4, and how to design extensions in Chapter 12. Now let's take a look at how to query and manipulate the schema using ADSI.

IADsClass and IADsProperty

In addition to being able to query and update schema objects as you can any other type of object with the *IADs* interface, there are two main schema-specific interfaces available: *IADsClass* and *IADsProperty*. Each of these interfaces has a variety of useful methods and property methods to allow you to set mandatory properties for classes, optional properties for classes, maximum values for attributes, and so on. If you look at these interfaces, you will see that they are very simple to understand.

First, let's compare accessing and modifying the schema by using the attributes we are interested directly in versus using the *IADsClass* and *IADsProperty* methods. This first code section uses attributes directly:

```
objAttribute.Put "isSingleValued", False
objAttribute.Put "attributeId", "1.3.6.1.4.1.999999.1.1.28"

arrMustContain = objSchemaClass.Get("mustContain")
arrMayContain = objSchemaClass.Get("mayContain")
```

Now we will use the ADSI schema interfaces to do the same thing:

```
objAttribute.MultiValued = True
objAttribute.OID = "1.3.6.1.4.1.999999.1.1.28"

arrMustContain = objSchemaClass.MandatoryProperties
arrMayContain = objSchemaClass.OptionalProperties
```

This makes use of *IADsProperty::MultiValued*, *IADsProperty::OID*, *IADsClass::Man-datoryProperties*, and *IADsClass::OptionalProperties*. As you can see, it's not hard to convert the code. However, we feel that including code that directly modifies the properties themselves gives you some idea of what you are actually changing and helps you to refer back to the definitions presented in Chapter 4.

More details on these three interfaces can be found in the MSDN Library (*http://msdn.microsoft.com/library/*) under Networking and Directory Services → Active Directory, ADSI and Directory Services → SDK Documentation → Directory Services → Active Directory Service Interfaces → ADSI Reference → ADSI Interfaces → Schema Interfaces.

Creating the Mycorp-LanguagesSpoken attribute

We will create an example attribute called *Mycorp-LanguagesSpoken*. It is to be a multivalued, indexed attribute that can hold an array of case-sensitive strings of between 1 and 50 characters. The name is prefixed with Mycorp so it is obvious that Mycorp created the attribute.

Mycorp's Schema Manager has decided that the OID for this attribute is to be 1.3.6. 1.4.1.999999.1.1.28. This is worked out as follows:

- Mycorp's root OID namespace is 1.3.6.1.4.1.999999.
- Mycorp's new attributes use 1.3.6.1.4.1.999999.1.1.*xxxx* (where *xxxx* increments from 1).
- Mycorp's new classes use 1.3.6.1.4.1.999999.1.2.*xxxx* (where *xxxx* increments from 1).
- The attribute is to be the 28th new attribute created by Mycorp.

The code to create such an attribute is included in Example 24-1.

Example 24-1. Creating the MyCorp-LanguagesSpoken attribute

```
Dim objAttribute
Dim objSchemaContainer

Set objSchemaContainer = _
  GetObject("LDAP://cn=Schema,cn=Configuration,dc=mycorp,dc=com")

Set objAttribute = objSchemaContainer.Create("attributeSchema", _
                                   "cn=Mycorp-LanguagesSpoken")

'Write out mandatory attributes
objAttribute.Put "attributeId", "1.3.6.1.4.1.999999.1.1.28"
objAttribute.Put "oMSyntax", 20
objAttribute.Put "attributeSyntax", "2.5.5.3"
objAttribute.Put "isSingleValued", False
objAttribute.Put "lDAPDisplayName", "myCorp-LanguagesSpoken"

'Create the attribute
objAttribute.SetInfo

'Write out optional attributes
objAttribute.GetInfo
objAttribute.Description = "Indicates the languages that " & _
                      "a user speaks"
objAttribute.Put "rangeLower", 1
objAttribute.Put "rangeUpper", 50
objAttribute.Put "searchFlags", True
objAttribute.SetInfo
```

That was fairly straightforward. Remember to change the *attributeID* to correspond to your own OID namespace if you use the code. Figure 24-1 shows the newly created attribute using the Schema Manager snap-in.

Creating the FinanceUser class

We will now create a new class called *Mycorp-FinanceUser*. It is to be a structural class so that others can create instances of it within containers. It will have the new *Mycorp-LanguagesSpoken* as an attribute, as well as inheriting from the User class. The OID for the class will be 1.3.6.1.4.1.999999.1.2.4, representing the fourth class

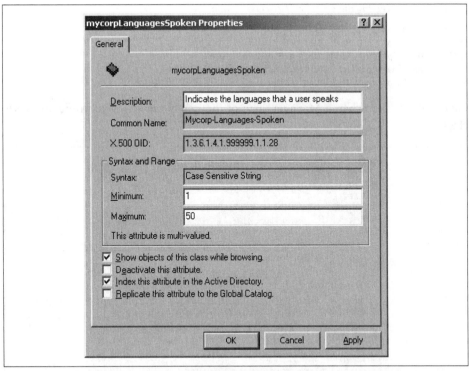

Figure 24-1. The Mycorp-LanguagesSpoken attribute viewed using the Schema Manager snap-in

we've created under our base OID. Example 24-2 contains the code to create the class.

Example 24-2. Creating the FinanaceUser class

```
Const ADS_PROPERTY_APPEND = 3

Dim objAttribute
Dim objSchemaContainer

Set objSchemaContainer = _
  GetObject("LDAP://cn=Schema,cn=Configuration,dc=mycorp,dc=com")

Set objClass = objSchemaContainer.Create("classSchema", _
                                         "cn=Mycorp-FinanceUser")

'Write out mandatory attributes
objClass.Put "cn", "Mycorp-FinanceUser"
objClass.Put "governsId", "1.3.6.1.4.1.999999.1.2.4"
objClass.Put "objectClassCategory", 1 'Structural Class
objClass.Put "subClassOf", "user"
objClass.Put "lDAPDisplayName", "mycorp-FinanceUser"

'Create the class
objClass.SetInfo
```

Example 24-2. Creating the FinanaceUser class (continued)

```
'Write out optional attributes
objClass.GetInfo
objClass.Description = "Indicates a Financial User"
objClass.Put "mustContain", "1.3.6.1.4.1.999999.1.1.28"
objClass.SetInfo
```

Figure 24-2 is the Schema Manager view of the newly created Mycorp-FinanceUser class.

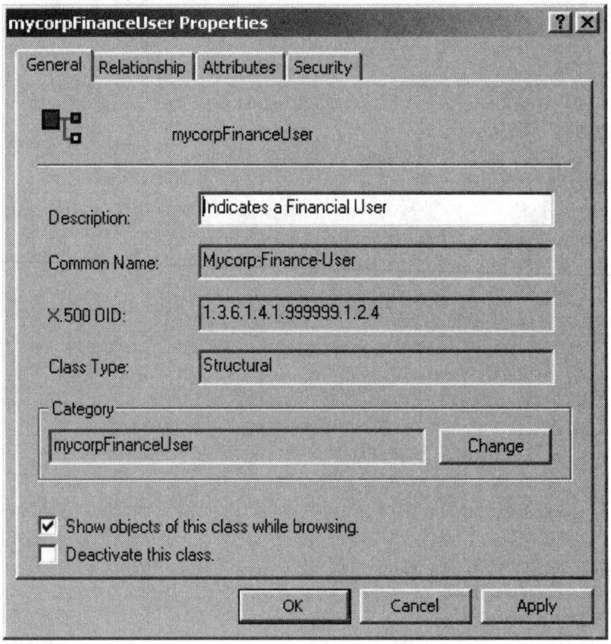

Figure 24-2. The Mycorp-FinanceUser class viewed using the Schema Manager snap-in

Creating instances of the new class

Finally, we want to create a new *Mycorp-FinanceUser* object. First, we have to get a reference to the Schema Container and create the object with all the mandatory attributes. Example 24-3 shows what this would look like.

Example 24-3. Creating a reference to the Schema Container

```
Dim objContainer
Dim objMycorpFinanceUser

Set objContainer = _
  GetObject("LDAP://ou=Finance Users,dc=Mycorp,dc=com")

'Create the new Mycorp-FinanceUser object
```

Example 24-3. Creating a reference to the Schema Container (continued)

```
Set objMycorpFinanceUser = objContainer.Create("Mycorp-FinanceUser", _
  "cn=SimonWilliams")

'Set the mandatory properties
objMycorpFinanceUser.Put "sAMAccountName", "SimonWilliams"
objMycorpFinanceUser.Put "userPrincipalName", "SimonWilliams@mycorp.com"
objMycorpFinanceUser.Put "Mycorp-LanguagesSpoken", _
  Array("English", "French", "German")

'Write the object to the AD
objMycorpFinanceUser.SetInfo
```

Note that the mandatory properties include *Mycorp-LanguagesSpoken* from the *Mycorp-FinanceUser* class and *sAMAccountName* from the User class, which the *Mycorp-FinanceUser* class inherits from. *UserPrincipalName* is also included for completeness.

Finding the Schema Container and Schema FSMO

In your scripts or applications, it is good practice to locate the Schema Container and Schema FSMO dynamically instead of hardcoding those values. By finding those values programmatically, your scripts become much more forest-independent, which makes it much easier to transport to other forests in the future.

The solution to find the Schema Container is an easy one. The DN of the Schema Container for a forest can be found by querying the schemaNamingContext value of the RootDSE on any domain controller in the forest. The following code shows how to do that:

```
Dim objRootDSE
Dim objSchemaContainer
Dim strSchemaPath

'Get the Root DSE from a random DC
Set objRootDSE = GetObject("LDAP://RootDSE")

'Get the Schema NC path for the domain
strSchemaPath = objRootDSE.Get("schemaNamingContext")

'Connect to the schema container on a random DC
Set objSchemaContainer = GetObject("LDAP://" & strSchemaPath)
```

The first *GetObject* call retrieves the RootDSE. Next we simply get the *schema-NamingContext* attribute and pass that to another *GetObject* call (or the *IADs-OpenDSObject::OpenDSObject* method if you prefer to authenticate), which will return a reference to the Schema Container on a random domain controller. If you want to make changes without forcing the FSMO role to your currently connected server, you need to change the last line to connect to the server currently holding the Schema FSMO. This can be done in three additional steps:

```
Set objSchemaContainer = GetObject("LDAP://" & strSchemaPath)
strFSMORoleOwner =  objSchemaContainer.Get("fSMORoleOwner")

Dim objNTDS, objServer
Set objNTDS = GetObject("LDAP://" &  objSchemaContainer.Get("fSMORoleOwner") )
Set objServer = GetObject( objNTDS.Parent )
strFSMORoleOwner = objServer.Get("dNSHostName")

'Connect to the schema container on the server holding the FSMO Schema
'Master role
Set objSchemaContainer = _
  GetObject("LDAP://" & strFSMORoleOwner & "/" & strSchemaPath)
```

The *fSMORoleOwner* attribute of the Schema Container actually contains the NTDS Settings DN (e.g., *cn=NTDS Settings,cn=MOOSE,cn=Servers,cn=Main-Headquarters-Site,cn=Sites,cn=Configuration,dc=mycorp,dc=com*) of the domain controller holding the Schema FSMO. From this you can retrieve the *ADsPath* of the parent container which holds an attribute called *dNSHostName* that contains the DNS host name of the domain controller that object represents.

Transferring the Schema FSMO Role

If you want to transfer the Schema FSMO role to a specific server, just set the *becomeSchemaMaster* attribute to 1 on the RootDSE for that server. The script will need to either run under the credentials of someone in the Schema Admins group to perform this transfer or use *IADsOpenDSObject::OpenDSObject* and authenticate as someone in Schema Admins. The moment we write out the property cache, the proposed master contacts the current master and requests the role and any updates to the Schema NC that it has yet to see. Here is the code to do the transfer:

```
Const DC_TO_TRANSFER_FSMO_TO = "niles.mycorp.com"

Dim objRootDSE
Dim objSchemaContainer
Dim strSchemaPath

'Get the Root DSE from a random DC
Set objRootDSE = GetObject("LDAP://" & DC_TO_TRANSFER_FSMO_TO & _
                           "/RootDSE")

'Request a Schema Master transfer
objRootDSE.Put "becomeSchemaMaster", 1
objRootDSE.SetInfo
```

At this point, the transfer has been requested. We now need to connect to the Schema NC and wait until the *fSMORoleOwner* attribute points to our new server:

```
'Get the Schema NC path for the domain
strSchemaPath = objRootDSE.Get("schemaNamingContext")
```

```
'Connect to the schema container on my DC
Set objSchemaContainer = GetObject("LDAP://" & DC_TO_TRANSFER_TO _
  & "/" & strSchemaPath)

'Initialize the while loop by indicating that the server is not the one
'I am looking for
strServerName = ""

'While the Server Name is not the one we are looking for, keep searching
While Not strServerName = DC_TO_TRANSFER_FSMO_TO
  'Get the FSMO Role Owner attribute
  strFSMORoleOwner = objSchemaContainer.Get("fSMORoleOwner")

  Set objNTDS = GetObject("LDAP://" & strFSMORoleOwner )
  Set objServer = GetObject( objNTDS.Parent )
  strServerName = objServer.Get("dNSHostName")

  objNTDS = Nothing
  objServer = Nothing
Wend

'At this point in the code, the role has been transferred, so I can continue
```

You shouldn't use the code exactly as written here because no error checking is being done. Without error checking, there is no guarantee that the original writing of the *becomeSchemaMaster* attribute actually worked. There is also no guarantee that the attachment to the DC_TO_TRANSFER_FSMO_TO server actually worked, either. So if either of these or anything else went wrong, we may never exit the while loop. Even if both of these conditions worked, we may set the value, and the DC may attempt to contact the current Schema FSMO to find that it is unavailable. Again, we go into an infinite loop and the code never terminates. You certainly should include a timeout value as a second condition to the while loop to trap an occurrence of this problem.

Forcing a Reload of the Schema Cache

If you need to reload the schema cache, Microsoft recommends that you do so once you've finished all your writes. While the cache is being reloaded, any new queries are served from the old cache and will continue to be served by the old cache until the new one comes online. Microsoft specifically states that working threads that are referencing the old cache once a reload is finished will continue to reference the old cache. Only new threads will reference the new cache. As a worst-case (and really daft) scenario, if you were to create 100 new attributes, start a process that queried the schema cache, and then reload the schema cache before continuing on to the next attribute, you potentially have 101 sets of schema caches (the original plus 100 new ones) being maintained by the DC acting as the Schema FSMO. This would cause the DC to have 101 times the amount of normal schema cache memory in use for caching. This is likely to cause a drain on your DC. In this scenario, things will only improve as the working threads cease referencing the old caches on the DC, allowing it to free up the memory.

Reloading the cache using ADSI is very simple. All you have to do is set the *schemaUpdateNow* attribute to 1 on the RootDSE of a DC. The following code shows how to do this:

```
Dim objRootDSE
Dim strDC

strDC = "dc01"

'Get the Root DSE
Set objRootDSE = GetObject("LDAP://" & strDC & "RootDSE")

'Reload the cache on that DC
objRootDSE.Put "schemaUpdateNow", 1
```

Note that just because you have requested a change doesn't mean it's going to happen instantaneously, although your code will continue executing. You should check the schema to see if your new objects are there, and if they are not, wait until they are before proceeding.

Finding Which Attributes Are in the GC for an Object

In Chapter 4, we described a desire to programmatically query all attributes directly defined on an object class in the schema to find out which ones are in the GC. It now should be possible to see how simple it is to write this code. First, you know that you can find out which attributes a *classSchema* object can have by looking in the *mayContain*, *systemMayContain*, *mustContain*, and *systemMustContain* attributes. Once you have the entire list of attributes, you can use the *lDAPDisplayName* that you will have retrieved to reference the attributeSchema class in the Schema Container. Lastly, you need to check to see whether each *attributeSchema* object has an attribute called *isMemberOfPartialAttributeSet*. Example 24-4 contains the code.

Example 24-4. Checking for the isMemberOfPartialAttributeSet attribute

```
'Check the User class, via the administrator user
Const OBJECT_TO_CHECK = _
  "LDAP://cn=administrator, cn=Users, dc=Mycorp, dc=com"

Dim objObject, objSchemaClass, arrMustContain, arrMayContain
Dim strListOfAttributesinGC, objAttribute, strAttribute

'Connect to object and get IADs::Schema on an object instance
Set objObject = GetObject(OBJECT_TO_CHECK)

Set objSchemaClass = GetObject(objUser.Schema)

'Get May-Contain and Must-Contain attributes directly on the class
arrMustContain = objSchemaClass.Get("mustContain")
arrMayContain = objSchemaClass.Get("mayContain")
```

```
'Initialize the output string
strListOfAttributesinGC = "The list of attributes for the class: " & vbCrLf _
    & vbCrLf & vbTab & objUser.Schema & vbCrLf & vbCrLf & "is:"_
    & vbCrLf & vbCrLf

'Use the array of LDAP names to connect to each attribute in turn
'and read whether it is in the GC or not. If it is, then add it to the string
For Each strAttribute In arrMustContain
    Set objAttribute = GetObject("LDAP://" & strAttribute & _
        ",cn=Schema,cn=Configuration,dc=Mycorp,dc=com")
    If objAttribute.Get("isMemberOfPartialAttributeSet") Then
        strListOfAttributesinGC = strListOfAttributesinGC & _
                                  strAttribute & vbCrLf
    End If

    'Stop referencing the current attribute
    Set objAttribute = Nothing
Next

For Each strAttribute In arrMayContain
    Set objAttribute = GetObject("LDAP://" & strAttribute & _
        ",cn=Schema,cn=Configuration,dc=Mycorp,dc=com")
    If objAttribute.Get("isMemberOfPartialAttributeSet") Then
        strListOfAttributesinGC = strListOfAttributesinGC & _
                                  strAttribute & vbCrLf
    End If

    'Stop referencing the current attribute
    Set objAttribute = Nothing
Next

Wscript.Echo strListOfAttributesinGC
```

This will print out a list of all attributes that are held in the GC and defined directly on the object. Of course, to be very thorough and find every attribute that the *class-Schema* object could have in the GC, you also would need to look inside *auxiliary-Class*, *systemAuxiliaryClass*, and *subClassOf* to retrieve any class names and then iterate back up the tree to find the *mayContain*, *systemMayContain*, *mustContain*, and *systemMustContain* from any inherited classes.

Adding an Attribute to the GC

If you identify an attribute that you would like to be part of the GC, but it is not, it is straightforward to add it. Typically, an attribute that is part of the GC should be "globally interesting," meaning more than one application would find use for it. The data for the attribute also should not be very volatile or very large since it will be replicated to every GC server in the forest. To add an attribute, the *isMemberOf-PartialAttributeSet* attribute for the *attributeSchema* object must be set to true.

Example 24-5 shows how to enable the *myCorp-SpokenLanguages* attribute in the GC.

Example 24-5. Enabling the myCorp-SpokenLanguages attribute

```
Const ATTR_TO_GC = "myCorp-LanguagesSpoken"

Dim objRootDSE, objSchemaContainer
Dim strFSMORoleOwner, strSchemaPath

'Get the Root DSE from a random DC
Set objRootDSE = GetObject("LDAP://RootDSE")

'Get the Schema NC path for the domain
strSchemaPath = objRootDSE.Get("schemaNamingContext")

'Connect to the schema container on a random DC
Set objSchemaContainer = GetObject("LDAP://" & strSchemaPath)
strFSMORoleOwner =  objSchemaContainer.Get("fSMORoleOwner")

'Get the Schema FSMO DNS name
Dim objNTDS, objServer
Set objNTDS = GetObject("LDAP://" &  objSchemaContainer.Get("fSMORoleOwner") )
Set objServer = GetObject( objNTDS.Parent )
strFSMORoleOwner = objServer.Get("dNSHostName")

'Get the attribute
Set objSchemaContainer = _
  GetObject("LDAP://" & strServerIPName & "/" & strSchemaPath)

Dim objAttr
Set objAttr = GetObject("LDAP://" & strFSMORoleOwner & "," & _
                "cn=" & ATTR_TO_GC & "," & strSchemaPath

'Set the property to true
objAttr.Put "isMemberOfPartialAttributeSet", True
objAttr.SetInfo
```

 Under Windows 2000, anytime an attribute is added to the GC, a full sync of the GC contents is initiated to all GC servers in the forest. Since this can have a significant impact on replication and network performance, it should be done with caution. This limitation was removed in Windows Server 2003.

Customizing the Active Directory Administrative Snap-ins

For those who have worked with Windows NT domains, you are undoubtedly familiar with two GUI tools: User Manager (*usrmgr.exe*) and Server Manager (*srvmgr.exe*). User Manager allows administrators to manipulate the properties of users and groups, while Server Manager can manipulate computer accounts. In Active Directory, a Microsoft Management Console (MMC) snap-in called Active Directory Users and Computers (ADUC) has taken the place of both these tools.

While ADUC is built primarily to manage users, groups, and computers as the previous User Manager and Server Manager did, you can actually use it to manage any type of object within a Domain Naming Context. You can create an entire hierarchy of Organizational Units, user accounts, computer accounts, groups, printers, and so on and manage them with ADUC. The tool, however, is limited in what it provides "out of the box." While ADUC can display a lot of attributes for objects, you cannot view every attribute, as you can with ADSI Edit. Figure 24-3 shows the various groupings of attributes (e.g., Organization) that can be viewed by clicking the appropriate tab. Each tab represents a property page, which contains a logical grouping of attributes to display.

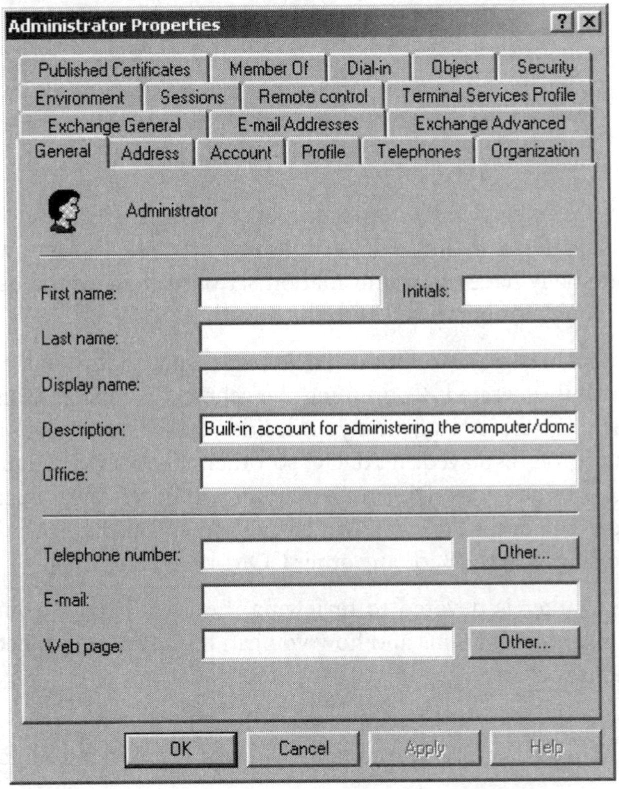

Figure 24-3. Numerous property pages for a user object

Now compare Figure 24-3 with Figure 24-4, which shows the property pages for a computer object.

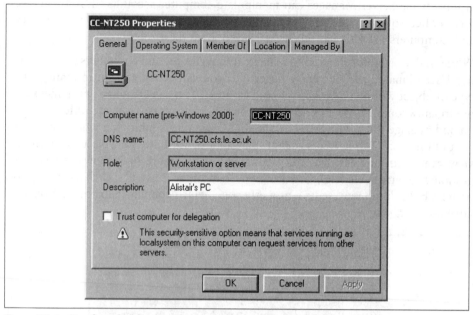

Figure 24-4. Significantly fewer property pages for a computer obj

Figure 24-4 contains considerably fewer property pages. A computer object inherits from the user class and contains a few additional attributes of its own. So a computer could potentially have more information set on it than even a user object, but those attributes could not be viewed with the default ADUC.

In many cases, you may want to modify ADUC to display additional attributes, perhaps even ones you've created. Continuing the schema extension example from the beginning of the chapter, let's say that you decide you want the *myCorp-Languages-Spoken* attribute to be displayed in ADUC so others can view the languages a user speaks. Fortunately, the Active Directory snap-ins are largely customizable by modifying one or more attributes in Active Directory. You can also extend the functionality of a snap-in using WSH, VB, or any other COM-based language.

The rest of the chapter is devoted to reviewing the components behind the Active Directory administrative snap-ins and how you can modify them to meet your needs. These components include:

Display specifiers
Objects in Active Directory that contain localized user interface information

Property ages
Tabbed dialog box that displays information

Context menus
Menu displayed after right-clicking an object (e.g., user)

Icons
> Image displayed when viewing a particular class

Display Names
> User-friendly names displayed for attributes and classes (e.g., Last Name)

Creation Wizard
> Wizard interface used to create an object

Display Specifiers

Display specifiers are objects stored in Active Directory that contain information on how to display and manage objects for a specific object class through the Active Directory snap-ins. These display specifiers are held in the Configuration Naming Context under the DisplaySpecifiers container. Within the DisplaySpecifiers container, there is a container for each supported locale, in a path similar to this:

```
LDAP://cn=409,cn=DisplaySpecifiers,cn=Configuration,dc=mycorp,dc=com
```

The preceding container contains the display specifiers for the U.S./English locale of 409. If you wanted to create or manage display specifiers for a different locale, you just create a new container with the relevant hexadecimal code for the locale and populate it with the relevant display specifier objects. For example, 409 in hex represents 1,033 in decimal, and 1,033 is the U.S./English locale. If we created 809 (2,057 in decimal), we would get the U.K./English locale, and if we created 40C (1,036 in decimal), we would get the French locale. The currently installed locale values can be found in the registry at HKLM\SYSTEM\CurrentControlSet\Control\ContentIndex\Language. Having display specifiers per locale enables you to support a wide variety of languages for a geographically disperse client base.

Each of the locale-specific containers contains a series of objects of the *display-Specifier* class. The object names are in the form of *ObjectClass-Display*. The user class has one called *User-Display*, the computer class has one called *Computer-Display*, and so on. To extend the interface for a specific object class for a particular language, you just need to modify the appropriate attributes on the *displaySpecifier* object that represents the class in that container.

Here's a simple example. The *classDisplayName* attribute exists on all *display-Specifier* objects. Let's say we use the ADSI Edit tool from the Support Tools to open up the *Group-Display* object and change this attribute from Group to *Moose*. If we right-click on any container in the ADUC tool, a context menu normally appears, allowing us to create a new user, group, or Organizational Unit (among other things). After making the edit and reopening ADUC, it allows us to create a new User, *Moose*, or Organizational Unit. The way that the *Group* class was displayed in the interface has been changed. If we wanted to change the display specifier for the French locale as well as or instead of the U.S./English locale, we would go to (or create) the 40C container and apply the change to the *Group-Display* object.

Let's now review some of the other customizations you can make.

Property Pages

You can see the array of property pages that exist for two objects in Figures 24-3 and 24-4. You can add property pages to these and display your own here. For this to work, though, the property page has to exist as a Component Object Model (COM) object that supports the *IShellExitInit* and *IShellPropSheetExt* interfaces. This means that the property page has to be created first in Visual Basic, Visual C++, or something similar.

Creating the object is the hardest part. Actually telling the system to use it is easy. Once the property page COM object exists, it will have a Universally Unique Identifier (UUID). You then use ADSI Edit to go to the display specifier object representing the class that you wish to modify and alter the *adminPropertyPages* or *shellPropertyPages* attributes. These attributes are multivalued and store data in the following form:

```
2, {AB4909C2-6BEA-11D2-B1B6-00C04F9914BD}
1, {AB123CDE-ABCD-1124-ABAB-00CC4DD11223}
```

The first item represents the order number in which the sheets should appear. The second represents the UUID. A third optional parameter can be used to store extended information, such as data passed to the property page as it is displayed.

To add your own property page to a class, you edit either the *Shell* or *Admin* property page attribute, depending on whether you want the default (shell) or administrator UI to be modified, and add in a line like the preceding form. It really is that simple. You can even modify the existing pages, if any exist, and resequence them to your liking.

Context Menus

When you right-click an object in the ADUC tool, a context menu pops up. You can add your own entries to this context menu. Context menu items are held in the *shellContextMenu* attribute for the default UI and *adminContextMenu* attribute for the admin UI in each *displaySpecifier* object. Items that should appear in both go into the *contextMenu* attribute.

The items that you add to the context menus can launch an application or create an instance of a COM object. The data takes the following form in the relevant attributes:

```
1,Extra &Data..., E:\MYPROG.EXE
2,&Extended Attributes...,C:\MYSCRIPT.VBS
3,{DB4909C2-6BEA-11D2-B1B6-00C04F9914BD}
```

Notice that the last item is a COM object. It is denoted by its UUID. The COM object must have been created to support the *IShellExtInit* and *IContextMenu* interfaces. Extra data can be passed to the COM object by including it as a third parameter on the line. The former two items are much more important to administrators.

Here you can see that we added two extra items to the menu. These items are an executable program and a VBScript script. Any type of application is valid. The second parameter is the string you want to appear on the context menu. Use of an ampersand (&) character before a letter denotes that letter as the menu selector. Thus, when the menu is being displayed, typing "d" selects the first option, and "e" selects the second.

Being able to add scripts and programs to a context menu is a very powerful capability. Couple these scripts and programs with ADSI, and you have a way of extending the snap-ins Microsoft provides to deliver completely customized functionality based on your business or organizational needs. For example, let's say that you wish to extend the schema and include a new, optional *myCorp-LanguagesSpoken* attribute for the User class. You can go to the *User-Display* object for the appropriate locale and modify the *Context-Menu* attribute (so it is available to both users and administrators) to include an ADSI script that displays that attribute in a message box. The following code is all that is needed:

```
Set wshArgs = WScript.Arguments

Set objUser = GetObject(wshArgs(0))
MsgBox objUser.Get("myCorp-LanguagesSpoken"),,"Languages Spoken"
```

The script does nothing more than bind to the object's *ADsPath* that is passed in as an argument to the program, and print out the attribute in a *MsgBox* with an appropriate title, as shown in Figure 24-5.

The Guest user object was right-clicked, which popped up a context menu that includes Languages Spoken. You can see that it is actually the string "&Languages Spoken..." being displayed if you look at the text in the bottom left-hand corner of the window. When we click the item or press the L key, a dialog box generated by the script is displayed on the screen. Normally the dialog box and the context menu would not be displayed together, but we have done so in this screen to show you the process.

You could also write a script or program that allowed you to modify the Languages-Spoken attribute and have it appear only on the administrator's context menus. Then you can use the ADUC tool to manage your users and this extra attribute, without ever needing to actually develop an entirely new interface if you don't want to.

Icons

When you look at a container of objects in ADUC, it shows you an icon for each object appropriate to the specific object class for that object. The icons for Organizational Units look different than those for containers, users, and printers, for example. The icon can actually be used to represent different states of that object. For example, if you disable a user or computer object, the icon is changed to indicate that the object is disabled. All in all, 16 different state icons can be defined for any

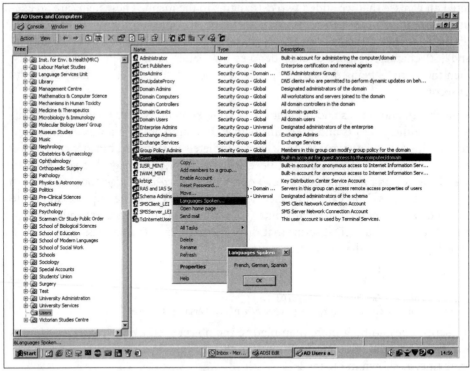

Figure 24-5. Looking at the languages spoken for a user

object class. The first three represent the states closed (the default state), open, and disabled; the last 13 are currently undefined and left for your own use.

To modify the icon for an object class, simply use the *Icon-Path* attribute to store multivalued data of the following form:

```
0, c:\windows\system32\myicon.ico
1, c:\windows\system32\myicons.dll, 0
2, c:\windows\system32\myicons.dll, 2
3, c:\windows\system32\myicons.dll, 7
```

This sets the first four icon values. Remember that 0 is closed, 1 is open, and 2 is disabled; 3 through 15 are undefined. The first one uses a proper icon file with an ICO extension and so doesn't need a third parameter. The last three use the first (0), third (2), and eighth (7) icons from *MYICONS.DLL,* using an index for the set of icons held in the DLL, starting at 0. The icon path has to exist on the local machine for any client to properly display the icon. Remember to take that into account, since you may need to deploy the icon files to all clients in an enterprise if they are to display the icons properly.

Display Names

As shown earlier, you can alter the way that both class and attribute names appear within a GUI. If you want to change the class name, change the text in the *class-DisplayName* property of the relevant *displaySpecifier* object. If you want to change what attributes names appear as, then you need to modify the multivalued attribute *attributeDisplayNames*. Attribute values take the form of a comma-delimited string as follows:

```
mobile,Mobile Number
physicalDeliveryOfficeName,Office Location
extensionAttribute1,My First Extended Attribute
```

The first value is the LDAP name corresponding to the attribute in the schema, and the second is the name that it is to be displayed as. Note that you shouldn't insert a space between the comma and the second value unless you want the name to be preceded by a space.

Leaf or Container

When you view objects in the ADUC, some display as containers and some display as leaf objects. Most objects that you are concerned with actually act as containers, even if you see them displayed as leaf objects. Take a printer on a computer, for example. If that printer is published as a *printQueue* object to Active Directory, the object is located as a leaf object within the computer object that it is published on. The computer object acts as a container for any print queues that it publishes. User, computer, and group objects by default do not display themselves as containers. ADUC in fact has an option on the View menu to change this, called "View users, groups, and computers as containers." However, all objects get treated in this fashion, and you can modify any object's default setting by going to the *displaySpecifier* and changing the Boolean value of *treatAsLeaf* to true or false as required.

Object Creation Wizard

When you create a user, group, or Organizational Unit, ADUC presents a simple wizard to allow you to specify the relevant data for that object. It is possible for administrators to modify the default behavior in one of two ways. Administrators can replace the existing wizard entirely, if one exists, or they can just add extra pages to the wizard. Only one wizard can ever exist, so you either create a new one or modify the existing one. Let's say that you made the *myCorp-LanguagesSpoken* attribute a mandatory attribute for the User class. This forces you to define a value for *myCorp-LanguagesSpoken* for all new users at creation time. As the existing User creation wizard does not allow data to be input for this attribute, you can replace the entire wizard with a new one of your own, or you can place a new page into the wizard to receive data on this attribute. With property pages we need to create new wizards or creation wizard extensions (extra pages to existing wizards) as COM objects that support the *IDsAdminNewObjExt* interface. New wizards that replace the default wizards in use by the system are known as primary extensions, and they replace the core set of pages that would be used to create the object. Primary extensions support creation wizard extensions; you can define a primary extension for all users, for example, and later add a couple of extra pages using a creation wizard extension if you require.

If you are replacing the wizard entirely with a primary extension, modify the *creationWizard* attribute of the relevant *displaySpecifier* object to hold the UUID of the COM object. If you are just providing creation wizard extensions, you specify the order that the pages should appear, followed by the UUID in the *createWizardExt* multivalued attribute. The format is the same as for property pages.

Summary

In this chapter, we covered how to query and manipulate the Active Directory Schema, including how to locate and transfer the Schema FSMO. The schema cache and its importance was also briefly touched on, along with information on how to determine which attributes of an object are in the GC and how to add an attribute to the GC if necessary.

The second part of the chapter focused on how to customize the Active Directory administrative MMC snap-ins by modifying *displaySpecifier* objects. We described how to manipulate each of the major snap-in components, including property pages, context menus, icons, display names and the object creation wizard. For more information about customizing snap-ins, check out the following locations in the MSDN Library (*http://msdn.microsoft.com/library/*):

- Networking and Directory Services → Active Directory, ADSI, and Directory Services → SDK Documentation → Directory Services → Active Directory → Using Active Directory → Extending the User Interface for Directory Objects
- Networking and Directory Services → Active Directory, ADSI, and Directory Services → SDK Documentation → Directory Services → Active Directory → Active Directory Reference → Active Directory Interfaces → Active Directory Admin Interfaces
- User Interface Design and Development → Windows Shell → Shell Programmers Guide

CHAPTER 25

Using ADSI and ADO from ASP or VB

Two important features of Active Directory require administrators to create their own tools:

- The ability to extend the Active Directory schema with your own classes and attributes, which allows you to store additional data with objects

- The ability to delegate control of administration of Active Directory in a very detailed manner

If you take advantage of these, there is a large chance that you will want to provide customized tools for administration.

For example, you might decide that a group of users is to manage only certain properties of certain objects, say which users can go into a group. There is no point in giving them Active Directory Users and Computers snap-in; that's like using a sledgehammer to crack a nut. Why not create a tool of your own that only allows them to manipulate the values that they have permission to? If you then incorporate logging into a file or database within this application, you have a customized audit trail as well.

Tools of this nature do not lend themselves to VBScript since they tend to require a much more enhanced GUI interface. Consequently, you are left with three choices:

- Write code in a compiled language like Visual Basic or VB.NET that supports complex GUI routines.

- Write code for a web-based interface using HTML and Active Server Pages (ASPs) or using ASP.NET.

- Write code in another scripting language such as Perl that supports complex graphical controls.

We will concentrate on the first two in this chapter.

VBScript Limitations and Solutions

Using ADSI from within WSH is very useful, but it does have certain limitations. For one thing, you cannot display output on screen in anything other than a MsgBox or request information from users without using the InputBox. It is easy to show how these are lacking. Consider that we wish to write a general script that adds a user to a single group selected from a list. If we wrote this under WSH, we would have to list all the groups to the screen in a large MsgBox (or via a file using Notepad) with incremental numbers so that each group could be identified. Then the person running the script would have to remember the number and type it into an InputBox later so that the request could be serviced. If there were more than a few dozen groups in Active Directory, the person running the script would have to go through a number of screens of groups before being able to see them all. It would be much simpler just to display a drop-down list box of all groups and have the user select one. This is not possible under WSH using VBScript, but it is possible under VB and Active Server Pages (ASP).

VB provides a full programming environment for your ADSI applications. ASP provides VBScript with the user-interface facilities that HTML allows, effectively making your scripts more user friendly. ASPs are useful for two important reasons. First, there is a single copy maintained in the organization. Hence, if the single copy is updated, everyone gets the latest copy on the next use. This also saves you from version hell—having multiple versions of a program floating around. Second, no run-time or design-time licenses are required in the development of such pages, as is the case when you develop VB applications.

Also, if we publish the web pages on an Internet server rather than an intranet server, we can make the scripts available to anyone who has the correct privilege to the script whether he is on our local network or not. At present you may find it hard to see a need for being able to manipulate Active Directory from outside the organization. As Active Directory becomes a larger store for complex objects, you may find yourself writing pages to interrogate company databases as well as Active Directory, bringing both sets of information forward to the user. Web pages also allow you to prototype or identify a need for a future application. If you find that your users are making heavy use of the web interface, perhaps it is time to consider rolling out a proper application. It all depends on what sort of mechanism you prefer to develop and maintain to let your users access your Active Directory.

This chapter will describe in detail how to create ASPs using HTML and ADSI and how to migrate VBScript scripts to simple VB applications.

While incorporating ADSI scripts into ASPs via HTML is fairly easy, anyone who is considering using VBScript with HTML pages needs to do some background reading. This chapter alone barely scratches the surface and in no way covers HTML in any real depth.

How to Avoid Problems When Using ADSI and ASP

There is one very large pitfall with ADSI scripts under ASP that is very easy to fall into. ADSI scripts running under ASP work only when served from IIS. This is because IIS understands ADSI, and IE on its own does not. So whenever you want to test-run an ASP incorporating an ADSI script, make sure that you are obtaining it from the server. This problem tends to occur in two main ways:

- When developing scripts on the machine that IIS is running on
- When developing scripts on a machine that has a drive mapped to the directory on IIS where you are storing the scripts

In both of these cases, it is just as easy to open a file called *C:\INETPUB\ WWWROOT\MYTEST.ASP* as it is to open *http://www.mycorp.com/mytest.asp* from within IE. Both files will open correctly, but only the IIS-served page will correctly work with ADSI. If you start getting unexplained errors with code that you know should be working, just check the URL of the ASP that you are opening.

The second annoying pitfall occurs when you are constantly updating pages, testing them with a browser, and then updating them again. If you are developing in this cycle, remember to keep refreshing the page. It becomes really annoying to find that the bug you have been trying to solve is due to the fact that your browser thoughtfully cached a page 15 minutes ago, and you have been forgetting to press the Shift key when clicking the Refresh button.[*]

Combining VBScript and HTML

HTML pages are written as text files in the same way as VBScripts. HTML pages display information according to a series of tags, which you use to turn certain formatting on and off. The tags you normally use to construct a basic page look like this:

```
<HTML>

<HEAD>
<TITLE>Hello World Page</TITLE>
</HEAD>

<BODY>
Hello World
<P>Hello again
</BODY>

</HTML>
```

---

[*] Another option if you are using Internet Explorer is to open up the Internet Options from the Tools menu and set the Temporary Internet Files to check for newer versions of stored pages on every visit to the page.

The <HTML> tag denotes it as an HTML document. The <HEAD> and </HEAD> pair denote everything within those tags as belonging to the header description part of the document. The <TITLE> tag denotes the start of the page title and </TITLE> turns it off again. The <BODY> tag denotes the main part of the page, which contains a simple text string, a newline or paragraph marker <P>, and then another line of text. This is the bare bones of writing HTML documents. You can create lists, set colors, make and populate tables, display images, and so on. However, you do not need to go into all of that to demonstrate incorporating ADSI VBScripts into HTML pages. You only need to be aware of the following major sets of tags: <FORM>...</FORM>, <OBJECT>...</OBJECT>, <%...%>, and <SCRIPT>...</SCRIPT>.

Incorporating Scripts into Active Server Pages

Two sorts of scripts can be created within ASPs: client-side scripts and server-side scripts. Client-side scripting is used to access all the objects in a web page (e.g., text, images, tags), browser objects (e.g., frames, windows), and local ActiveX components. Server-side scripting is used to create a web page dynamically via parameters, forms, and code that is then passed to a browser.

Because the two types of scripts are executed at different locations, each has a separate set of interfaces. You place your ADSI scripts in server-side scripting, not client-side scripting. We'll go through the major differences now so that you will be less likely to make annoying mistakes.

Client-side scripting

You can use the <SCRIPT> tags to add client-side VBScript code to an HTML page. Whenever the browser encounters the tags, the enclosed script is executed as if it were being issued from the client. You can use blocks of scripting in both the BODY and HEAD sections of an ASP if you want to. If you put your code in the HEAD section, it will be read and executed before any item in the BODY section is accessed. As an example, here is a procedure to display a line of text:

```
<SCRIPT LANGUAGE="VBScript">

    Document.Write "This is a line of text<P>"

</SCRIPT>
```

The LANGUAGE attribute indicates that this is VBScript rather than one of the other languages. As this is not running under the WSH, you do not have a VBS or JS extension to denote the language. The *Document::Write* method writes the line to the web page. It is only one of a number of properties and methods from interfaces available to you as an ASP developer. You also can use MsgBox and InputBox within client-side scripts.

The important thing about client-side scripts from this chapter's point of view is that ADSI functions and methods cannot be included in these scripts. This is an important limitation, one that we will show you how to get around later.

Server-side scripting

You also can use the SCRIPT tags to denote server-side scripting in ASPs. To distinguish server-side SCRIPT tags from client-side tags, you use the RUNAT attribute as follows:

```
<SCRIPT LANGUAGE="VBScript" RUNAT="SERVER">
Set objGroup = GetObject("LDAP://cn=Managers,ou=Sales," _
  & "dc=mycorp,dc=com")

Response.Write objGroup.Description
</SCRIPT>
```

 The RUNAT="SERVER" tag is used as is. It does not require you to substitute an actual server name.

Server-side scripting can also go in either the BODY or HEAD sections. As you can see from the example, server-side scripting can include ADSI calls without any problem. The Response::Write method is used to write lines of text out to a page by code that is processed on the web server. You cannot use Document::Write in server-side scripts as the Document interface is unavailable to the server; it is available only to the browser.

There is also another and more common short form to denote server-side scripting, the <% . . .%> tags. Any code between this set of tags is automatically treated as server-side scripting code. Here is the previous example again, using these tags:

```
<%
  Set objGroup = GetObject("LDAP://cn=Managers,ou=Sales," _
    & "dc=mycorp,dc=com")

  Response.Write objGroup.Description
%>
```

Throughout the rest of the chapter, we will use the <%. . .%> tags to indicate server-side scripting and the SCRIPT tag to indicate client-side scripting. The <%. . .%> tags allow you to create quite complex scripts that switch back and forth between HTML on every line if you like. For example, here is a simple server-side script:

```
<%
  If myCondition = True Then
    Response.Write "The Condition is TRUE<P>"
  Else
    Response.Write "The Condition is FALSE<P>"
  End If
%>
```

Here is the same script again using the <%. . .%> tags more heavily so that we can make use of HTML whenever we want to:

```
<% If myCondition = True Then %>
     The Condition is TRUE<P>
<% Else %>
     The Condition is FALSE<P>
<% End If %>
```

Setting the Default Language

If you choose to use the <%. . .%> tags, you can change the primary scripting language for a single page by adding a command line to the beginning of your ASP. The syntax for this command is the following if you are using JScript, VBScript, or any other language that supports *Object.Method* syntax:

```
<%@ LANGUAGE="VBSCRIPT" %>
```

```
<%@ LANGUAGE="JSCRIPT" %>
```

You should make this line the first line of the ASP and make sure that you have a blank space between the @ character and the LANGUAGE keyword.

If you are writing ASPs using VBScript as your language, you can omit this line from all your ASPs, as VBScript is set as the default language anyway.

ActiveX Controls and ASPs

Anyone who has developed ASPs before or who reads any ASP book will find out about embedding ActiveX controls into web pages. The OBJECT tag is used to add extra functionality to an HTML document by allowing the insertion of various ActiveX controls onto web pages. Included in these are items such as buttons you can press, drop-down list boxes from which you can select items, text entry and display fields, and so on. When you insert an object into your web page using the OBJECT tag, you can specify its initial contents, its position, its caption, its color, and so on. Most people who create web pages using ActiveX controls do not type all this data in by hand. Instead, developers normally use a tool to select from the available options when creating the tag.

If you want to buy a tool, you could use Microsoft FrontPage, which was designed for people who are not used to scripting and would prefer an Office-type interface. Alternatively, you could use Microsoft InterDev, which was designed to have the same interface as all of Microsoft's other development products, such as VB. Various other free web-development tools also exist that will insert these tags. Here is the clickable code for a command button in a web page:

```
<HTML>
<HEAD>
<TITLE>Simple Command Button</TITLE>
</HEAD>
<BODY>

<OBJECT ID="CommandButton1" WIDTH=93 HEIGHT=33
  CLASSID="CLSID:D7053240-CE69-11CD-A777-00DD01143C57">
    <PARAM NAME="ForeColor" VALUE="2147483670">
    <PARAM NAME="BackColor" VALUE="2147483668">
    <PARAM NAME="VariousPropertyBits" VALUE="23">
    <PARAM NAME="Caption" VALUE="Click me!">
    <PARAM NAME="Size" VALUE="2469;882">
    <PARAM NAME="MousePointer" VALUE="1">
    <PARAM NAME="FontCharSet" VALUE="0">
    <PARAM NAME="FontPitchAndFamily" VALUE="2">
    <PARAM NAME="ParagraphAlign" VALUE="3">
    <PARAM NAME="FontWeight" VALUE="0">
</OBJECT>

</BODY>
</HTML>
```

ActiveX controls are very useful, but they do have their limits with respect to ADSI. For example, the object specified in the preceding script is a client-side ActiveX control. If you wanted to attach an event to it, say a procedure that is executed when the button is pressed, you couldn't use ADSI code within that procedure. For example, while this looks like great code, it will not work:

```
<SCRIPT LANGUAGE="VBScript">
Sub CommandButton1_Click( )
  Set objGroup = GetObject("LDAP://cn=Managers,ou=Sales," _
    & "dc=mycorp,dc=com")

  Document.Write objGroup.Description
</SCRIPT>
```

You can, however, easily populate list boxes and other controls with the results of ADSI calls. This is great for display purposes, but you can't manipulate the contents. Let's lay out an example to show you the problem.

Let's say that we have an ASP with two list box ActiveX controls. When the page is loaded, we can trigger the population of the first list box with all the users in Active Directory. We can do the same for the second list box with all the groups in Active Directory. We now can click and select values from each of the list boxes, although nothing happens when we do so. Now we need to add a command button ActiveX control to the ASP. We wish to attach an event to that button so that an ADSI call is made that attempts to add the user to the group and print out the result. Unfortunately, we can't do that, since the ActiveX control event procedure is client-side and ADSI code must be server-side.

While ActiveX controls may be very powerful, they can't incorporate ADSI directly from triggered events.

Forms

If ActiveX control events are not available, you can use HTML forms to create simple ASPs. Here is an example:

```
<FORM ACTION = "simple_form_demo.asp" METHOD = "POST">
  <P>A simple input field: <INPUT NAME = "myfield1" SIZE = 48>
  <P>Here is a list of all the users in the default Users container:
  <SELECT NAME = "user">
    <% Set objUsers = GetObject("LDAP://cn=Users,dc=mycorp,dc=com")
       For Each objObject in objUsers
         If objObject.Class = "user" Then %>
           <OPTION><% = objObject.Name %>
    <%   End If
       Next %>
  </SELECT>
  <P><INPUT TYPE = SUBMIT>
</FORM>
```

This form incorporates an alphanumeric input field, a list box populated by users from the default Users container and a button labeled Submit Query. The list box is populated via the OPTION tag between a <SELECT>. . .</SELECT> tag pair. Clever use of server-side scripts here between the SELECT tag pair means that you can populate the list box using ADSI calls.

More importantly, once the form is submitted, server-side scripts can retrieve the values typed into the input fields by passing the name of the form to the *Request::Form* method. If the previous form were submitted, you could retrieve the value selected in the list box by using the following code:

```
Request.Form("user")
```

One important point needs noting here. It is possible to attach scripts to form-field events, such as clicking a button or tabbing out of a field. Unfortunately, as the form is client-side, the script attached to the event has to be client-side. That precludes the use of ADSI in these sorts of scripts. Here is an example:

```
<HTML>
<HEAD>
<TITLE>Display Description</TITLE>
</HEAD>
<BODY>
<FORM NAME="Form1">
  <INPUT TYPE="Button" NAME="Button1" VALUE="Click me for Description!">
  <SCRIPT FOR="Button1" EVENT="onClick" LANGUAGE="VBScript">
    MsgBox "Clicked!"
  </SCRIPT>
</FORM>
</BODY>
</HTML>
```

Since the scripts are only client-side we will not be using these types of scripts within this chapter.

Binding to Objects Via Authentication

Whenever we need to access the properties of an object in Active Directory, we bind to it using VBScript's *GetObject* function or the ADSI method *IADsOpenDSObject:: OpenDSObject*. The circumstances in which each method should be used to access Active Directory is very clear-cut but deserves to be outlined here, as it will be important whenever you construct ASPs.

When to Use VBScript's GetObject Function

By default, many of the objects and properties within Active Directory can be read by any authenticated user of the forest. As an example, here is some code to connect to an Organizational Unit called Sales under the root of the domain. This code works under the WSH:

```
Set objSalesOU = GetObject("LDAP://ou=Sales,dc=mycorp,dc=com")
Wscript.Echo objSalesOU.Description
```

Here is the same script incorporated into an ASP:

```
<HTML>
<HEAD>
<TITLE>Binding to an existing Organizational Unit</TITLE>
</HEAD>

<BODY>
<%
  Set objSalesOU = GetObject("LDAP://ou=Sales,dc=mycorp,dc=com")
  Response.Write "The Sales OU description is: " & objSalesOU.Description
%>
</BODY>
</HTML>
```

This mechanism works perfectly when you wish to have read-only access to properties of objects that can be read without special privileges. Using GetObject is not appropriate in the following cases:

- You want to write properties of an object.
- The object you are attempting to bind to requires elevated privileges to access.

While it may make little sense, it is perfectly feasible to restrict read access to the description of the Sales Organizational Unit, or more commonly the Sales Organizational Unit itself. If the Sales Organizational Unit is restricted, a GetObject will fail to bind to it. If only the description is restricted, a GetObject will successfully bind to the Sales Organizational Unit, but access to the description property will be denied.

To gain access to a restricted object or impersonate another user, you must authenticate using *IADsOpenDSObject::OpenDSObject*.

When to Use IADsOpenDSObject::OpenDSObject

Here is a simple Organizational Unit creation script that works under the WSH when an administrator is logged in:

```
Set objRoot=GetObject("LDAP://dc=mycorp,dc=com")

Set objSalesOU = objRoot.Create("organizationalUnit","ou=Sales")
objSalesOU.Description = "My new description!"
objSalesOU.SetInfo
```

We cannot transfer the script to an ASP as it stands. To make the script work, we must use the *IADsOpenDSObject::OpenDSObject* method, which does allow authentication. Here is the same example using authentication within an ASP:

```
<HTML>
<HEAD>
<TITLE>Successful Organizational Unit Creation</TITLE>
</HEAD>

<BODY>
<%
    strPath = "LDAP://dc=mycorp,dc=com"
    strUsername = "cn=Administrator,cn=Users,dc=mycorp,dc=com"
    strPassword = "my-admin-password"

    Set objNamespace = GetObject("LDAP:")
    Set objRoot = objNamespace.OpenDSObject(strPath, strUsername, strPassword, 0)

    Set objSalesOU = objRoot.Create("organizationalUnit","ou=Sales")
    objSalesOU.Description = "My new description!"
    objSalesOU.SetInfo

    Response.Write "The Sales OU has been created in the " & strPath & " domain."
%>
</BODY>
</HTML>
```

If we wanted to manipulate any of the properties of the new Sales Organizational Unit during that script, we could continue to use the *objSalesOU* variable to do so. If we write a new script that needs to access that Organizational Unit and to print the description, we now can use either *GetObject* or authenticate directly to that Organizational Unit in the same way as we did to the root of the tree:

```
<HTML>
<HEAD>
<TITLE>Binding to an existing Organizational Unit</TITLE>
</HEAD>

<BODY>
```

```
<%
    adsOUPath = "LDAP://ou=Sales,dc=mycorp,dc=com"
    strUsername = "cn=Administrator,cn=Users,dc=mycorp,dc=com"
    strPassword = "my-admin-password"

    Set objNamespace = GetObject("LDAP:")
    Set objSalesOU = objNamespace.OpenDSObject(adsOUPath,strUsername,strPassword,0)

    Response.Write "The Sales OU description is: " & objSalesOU.Description
%>
</BODY>
</HTML>
```

What may seem strange is that you can authenticate to the root of the tree and access objects there, but you still need to authenticate again to other areas of the tree if you need to bind to them. One authentication to a point in the tree does not allow you to use GetObject happily throughout the rest of the script for all objects and containers below that point. If you need authentication, for whatever reason, to access objects in disparate areas of the tree, you need to authenticate each binding separately. As an example, this next script creates the Organizational Unit again and then sets the description for a user named Ian Harcombe in the Users container. In this example, both need authentication because we wish to update properties in both cases:

```
<HTML>
<HEAD>
<TITLE>Example use of Complex Authentication</TITLE>
</HEAD>

<BODY>
<%
    strRootPath = "LDAP://dc=mycorp,dc=com"
    strUserPath  = "LDAP://cn=Ian Harcombe,cn=Users,dc=mycorp,dc=com"
    strUsername = "cn=Administrator,cn=Users,dc=mycorp,dc=com"
    strPassword = "my-admin-password"

    Set objNamespace = GetObject("LDAP:")
    Set objRoot = objNamespace.OpenDSObject(strRootPath,strUsername,strPassword,0)

    Set objSalesOU = objRoot.Create("organizationalUnit","ou=Sales")
    objSalesOU.Description = "My new description!"
    objSalesOU.SetInfo

    Set objUser = objNamespace.OpenDSObject(strUserPath,strUsername,strPassword,0)
    objUser.Description = "My new description!"
    objUser.SetInfo
%>
</BODY>
</HTML>
```

When to Use IADsContainer::GetObject

We've shown that we cannot use the VBScript `GetObject` function to authenticate a connection to objects in Active Directory from an ASP. However, there is a method called *IADsContainer::GetObject* that can be used to bind to objects from a container using the preexisting authenticated connection for the container. While both *GetObjects* have identical names and similar functions, to save confusion, we will use the fully qualified *IADsContainer::GetObject* when talking about the method and *GetObject* when talking about VBScript's function.

The *IADsContainer::GetObject* method is used to retrieve items from a container. It takes two parameters, the class of the object to retrieve and the object's RDN. The fact that *IADsContainer::GetObject* retrieves objects using the RDN means that you do not have to bind to individual objects below a container. This saves authenticating a connection to each object if you need to work on multiple objects in a container. If the Sales Organizational Unit now has three users below it, we can authenticate to the container and then use the *IADsContainer::GetObject* method to manipulate the three users. Here is an example:

```
<HTML>
<HEAD>
<TITLE>Use of IADsContainer::GetObject</TITLE>
</HEAD>

<BODY>
<%
    adsOUPath = "LDAP://ou=Sales,dc=mycorp,dc=com"
    strUsername = "cn=Administrator,cn=Users,dc=mycorp,dc=com"
    strPassword = ""

    Set objNamespace = GetObject("LDAP:")
    Set objSalesOU = objNamespace.OpenDSObject(adsOUPath,strUsername,strPassword,0)

    Set objUser1 = objSalesOU.GetObject("User","cn=Simon Williams")
    Set objUser2 = objSalesOU.GetObject("User","cn=Markie Newell")
    Set objUser3 = objSalesOU.GetObject("User","cn=Jason Norton")

    Response.Write "Simon Williams' description is: " & objUser1.Description
    Response.Write "Markie Newell's description is: " & objUser2.Description
    Response.Write "Jason Norton's description is: " & objUser3.Description
%>
</BODY>
</HTML>
```

This works under WSH in exactly the same way as it does here. However, it is something that you may make much more use of in an ASP to save you from a lot of unnecessary authentication. If the class is null with *IADsContainer::GetObject*, the first item matching the RDN of any class is returned.

Authenticating from Passwords Input Via Forms

When you need to force authentication in a script, the last thing you want to do is hardcode a password into the script as we have been doing previously. That's not to say that the ASP isn't secure; it is. The script is visible only to users of the computer in which IIS is running and not to web client users, because it is parsed before being displayed. Also, if the permissions are secured, even this is not visible. However, you have to keep in mind that you will have to change the embedded password in all the ASPs every time the real password is changed. The simplest solution is to use an HTML form with a field for the password in your ASP and prompt for a password from the user. An example would look like this:

```
<HTML>
<HEAD>
<TITLE>Authentication Request</TITLE>
</HEAD>

<BODY>
<FORM ACTION="restricted.asp" METHOD=POST>

  <P>Name <BR><INPUT
    NAME="Name"
    TYPE=TEXT
    VALUE="cn=Administrator,cn=Users,dc=mycorp,dc=com"
    SIZE="60">

  <P>Password<BR><INPUT
    TYPE="PASSWORD"
    NAME="Password">

  <P><INPUT TYPE="SUBMIT" VALUE="OK"><INPUT TYPE="RESET" VALUE="Reset">
</FORM>

</BODY>
</HTML>
```

This eliminates the problem of having to embed the username and password in a script. The <INPUT TYPE="PASSWORD"> tag places asterisk (*) characters in the field whenever a character is entered. In this instance, the username and password are passed from this authentication page to your page entitled *restricted.asp*, which will use the credentials to perform the authentication and continue on.

However, it is still extremely cumbersome for you to have to type in the full DN you want to authenticate with. It would be much better for it to accept the simple username (i.e., Administrator) in the username box. For this script to do that, it would need to use ADO to search Active Directory for the user object with the RDN made up of the prefix CN= and the username. You know it is CN= as all users use this prefix, and you only authenticate to the tree with user objects. This example will be left until later, in the "Incorporating Searches into Active Server Pages" section of this chapter.

A Simple Password Changer

A simple ASP example to show both server-side ADSI scripts and the use of the password attribute of the FORM tag is a password changer. Users load the page, type their usernames along with their old and new passwords into a form, and click the Submit button. Submitting the form triggers an authentication access to the user object supplied, using the user object itself and the old password. Provided that the user successfully authenticated to the user's own object, the password is then changed using the *IADsUser::ChangePassword* method.

This script consists of two parts: the form itself, which sits in the body of the page, and the code that interprets the submission of the form, which is located in the header. Let's start with the makeup of the form, which needs six fields:

- A text input field for the name
- A password input field for the current password
- A password input field for the new password
- A password input field to confirm the new password
- A Submit button
- A Reset button that sets all the input fields back to their default values

Here is the form:

```
<FORM ACTION="psw_changer1.asp" METHOD=POST>

    <P>Name <BR><INPUT
      NAME="Name"
      TYPE=TEXT
      VALUE="cn=xxxxx,cn=Users,dc=mycorp,dc=com"
      SIZE="60">

    <P>Old Password<BR><INPUT
      TYPE="PASSWORD"
      NAME="OldPassword">

    <P>New Password<BR><INPUT
      TYPE="PASSWORD"
      NAME="NewPassword1">
    <P>Confirm Password<BR><INPUT
      TYPE="PASSWORD"
      NAME="NewPassword2">

    <P><INPUT TYPE="SUBMIT" NAME="SetPass" VALUE="Change Password!">
    <INPUT TYPE="RESET" VALUE="Reset">
  </FORM>
```

The username field has been given a default value that will appear in the entry box to save typing. Obviously this would be much improved if the user could just type his username and an ADO search was initiated.

Whenever the Submit button is clicked, the page is reloaded according to the value associated with the ACTION parameter. In addition, the form's fields have been set. This differs from the normal loading of a page when the fields will be empty. In the server-side code, we need to make sure that the code is triggered only when the page is loaded via the submission of the form. To do this, we can surround the code with the following section:

```
<%
  On Error Resume Next
  If Request.Form("SetPass") = "Change Password!" Then
    'Code goes here
  End If
%>
```

Once the form is submitted, the value of the SetPass button will be the button's label. Until that happens, the value is blank. This is a good way to check for the submission of a form.

Assuming that this code is being executed properly after submission, we need to check that the new passwords match. We will be using only one of the values to set the new password, so we have to make sure that both passwords are as the user intended. To do that, we can use *Request::Form* again to check both passwords:

```
<%
  On Error Resume Next
  If Request.Form("SetPass") = "Change Password!" Then
    If Request.Form("NewPassword1") = Request.Form("NewPassword2") Then
      'code goes here
    Else
      Response.Write "The two new passwords do not match. Please try again."
    End If
  End If
%>
```

We are now ready to fill in the rest of the code, which is fairly straightforward. First, we need to authenticate to the user, and if that is successful, attempt to change the password. Example 25-1 lists the completed ASP code incorporating the ADSI calls, which have been highlighted.

Example 25-1. ASP code incorporating the ADSI calls

```
<HTML>
<HEAD>
<TITLE>Simple Password Changer</TITLE>
<%
  On Error Resume Next
  If Request.Form("SetPass") = "Change Password!" Then
    If Request.Form("NewPassword1") = Request.Form("NewPassword2") Then

      strUsername = "LDAP://" & Request.Form("Name")
      Set objNamespace = GetObject("LDAP:")
      'Attempt to authenticate to the user object in the tree using
```

Example 25-1. ASP code incorporating the ADSI calls (continued)

```
            'the username and the current password
            Err.Clear
            Set objUser = objNamespace.OpenDSObject(strUsername, _
              Request.Form("Name"), Request.Form("OldPassword"), 0)
            If Err=0 Then

                'Attempt to change the password
                Err.Clear
                objUser.ChangePassword _
                  CStr(Request.Form("OldPassword")), _
                  CStr(Request.Form("NewPassword1"))
                If Err=0 Then
                  Response.Write "Password has been changed."
                Else
                  Response.Write "Error: the Password has not been changed."
                End If
            Else
              Response.Write "Unable to authenticate. Password or Username incorrect."
            End If
          Else
            Response.Write "The two new passwords do not match. Please try again."
          End If
      End If
%>
</HEAD>

<BODY>
<FORM ACTION="psw_changer1.asp" METHOD=POST>

    <P>Name <BR><INPUT
      NAME="Name"
      TYPE=TEXT
      VALUE="cn=xxxxx,cn=Users,dc=mycorp,dc=com"
      SIZE="60">

    <P>Old Password<BR><INPUT
      TYPE="PASSWORD"
      NAME="OldPassword">

    <P>New Password<BR><INPUT
      TYPE="PASSWORD"
      NAME="NewPassword1">
    <P>Confirm Password<BR><INPUT
      TYPE="PASSWORD"
      NAME="NewPassword2">

    <P><INPUT TYPE="SUBMIT" NAME="SetPass" VALUE="Change Password!">
    <INPUT TYPE="RESET" VALUE="Reset">
</FORM>
</BODY>
</HTML>
```

As you can see, this is not particularly difficult. You also could add an Else clause and print out *Hex(Err.Number)* and *Err.Description* if you wished.

Adding Users to Groups

A password changer is a good example for a simple form, but more complex forms can sometimes be necessary. In this example, we want to populate two list boxes with users and groups from the default Users container. If we select a user and a group from the two list boxes and enter a username/password that has permissions, we should be able to click the Submit button to add the user to the group.

Once again, like most ADSI ASPs that use forms, this page is split into two parts: the form itself and the server-side script. The form is a fairly simple extension of the one that we outlined earlier and it is listed in Example 25-2. Population of the list boxes is done using two sets of server-side scripts that enumerate all values in the Users container and add any items to the list box of the appropriate class. The important population code is emphasized.

Example 25-2. Adding a user to a group

```
<FORM ACTION = "userlist2.asp" METHOD = "POST">
  <P>Users:
  <SELECT NAME = "user">
<%  Set objUsersContainer = _
      GetObject("LDAP://cn=Users,dc=mycorp,dc=com")
    For Each objObject in objUsersContainer
      If objObject.Class = "user" Then %>
        <OPTION><% = objObject.Name %>
<%    End If
    Next %>
  </SELECT>
  Groups:
  <SELECT NAME = "group">
<%  For Each objObject in objUsersContainer
      If objObject.Class = "group" Then %>
        <OPTION><% = objObject.Name %>
<%    End If
    Next %>
  </SELECT></P>

  <P>Username: <INPUT
    NAME="Name"
    TYPE=TEXT
    VALUE="cn=Administrator,cn=Users,dc=mycorp,dc=com"
    SIZE="60">

  <P>Password<INPUT
    TYPE="PASSWORD"
    NAME="Password">

  <P><INPUT TYPE=SUBMIT NAME="Submit" VALUE="Add User To Group!">
</FORM>
```

The server-side script that interprets the results needs to make sure that the script is executed only when the form has been submitted. Once that condition is true, the script has to attempt to authenticate to the selected group using the username and password supplied in the form. Example 25-3 lists the whole script with the major ADSI calls in the server-side script emphasized.

Example 25-3. Authenticating the new user to the selected group

```
<HTML>
<HEAD>
<TITLE>Adding Users to Groups from the default Users Container</TITLE>

<%
  On Error Resume Next
  If Request.Form("Submit") <> "" Then
    strGroupPath = "LDAP://" & Request.Form("group") _
      & ",cn=Users,dc=mycorp,dc=com"
    strUserPath = "LDAP://" & Request.Form("user") _
      & ",cn=Users,dc=mycorp,dc=com"

    Set objNamespace = GetObject("LDAP:")
    Err.Clear
    Set objGroup = objNamespace.OpenDSObject(strGroupPath, _
                  CStr(Request.Form("Name")), _
                  CStr(Request.Form("Password")),0)
    If Err=0 Then
      If objGroup.IsMember(strUserPath) Then
        Response.Write "User is already a member of the group"
      Else
        Err.Clear
        objGroup.Add(strUserPath)
        If Err=0 Then
          Response.Write "User is now a member of the group"
        Else
          Response.Write "An error occurred when adding the user to the group."
        End If
      End If
    Else
      Response.Write "Authentication failed."
    End If
  End If
%>
</HEAD>

<BODY>
<P>
<FORM ACTION = "userlist2.asp" METHOD = "POST">
  <P>Users:
  <SELECT NAME = "user">
<%  Set objUsersContainer = _
      GetObject("LDAP://cn=Users,dc=mycorp,dc=com")
    For Each objObject in objUsersContainer
      If objObject.Class = "user" Then %>
        <OPTION><% = objObject.Name %>
```

```
<%    End If
    Next %>
  </SELECT>
  Groups:
  <SELECT NAME = "group">
<% For Each objObject in objUsersContainer
        If objObject.Class = "group" Then %>
          <OPTION><% = objObject.Name %>
<%    End If
    Next %>
  </SELECT></P>

  <P>Username: <INPUT
    NAME="Name"
    TYPE=TEXT
    VALUE="cn=Administrator,cn=Users,dc=mycorp,dc=com"
    SIZE="60">

  <P>Password<INPUT
    TYPE="PASSWORD"
    NAME="Password">

  <P><INPUT TYPE=SUBMIT NAME="Submit" VALUE="Add User To Group!">
</FORM>
</BODY>
</HTML>
```

We checked to see if the user was a member just so that the script is more user friendly. You also can see in this script that we use the *GetObject* function to populate the initial list boxes, but we then switch to *IADsOpenDSObject::OpenDSObject* as soon as we need to update Active Directory.

Incorporating Searches into ASP

ADO searches can be easily incorporated into ASPs using the information in this chapter and Chapter 20. In this first example, we will navigate through a resultset using server-side scripts in order to populate a table that gets created dynamically. To make it easier to understand, Figure 25-1 is what the final result should look like for a new server with very few users.

This ASP includes all its code in the body of the web page. To begin with, we must retrieve the resultset:

```
    <%
    Set objConn = CreateObject("ADODB.Connection")
    objConn.Provider = "ADSDSOObject"
    objConn.Open "", _
      "CN=Administrator,CN=Users,dc=mycorp,dc=com", ""
```

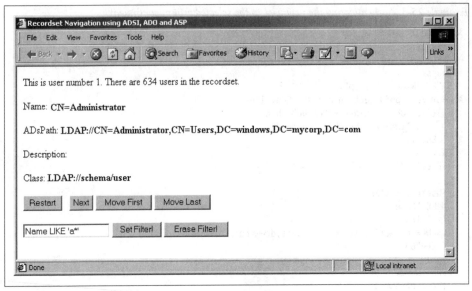

Figure 25-1. A navigable table on a web page populated by ADO

```
    Set objRS = objConn.Execute _
      ("<LDAP://dc=mycorp,dc=com>;" _
        & "(objectClass=User);Name,ADsPath;SubTree")
%>
```

Having done this, we can now begin to create the table. The table definition must include the number of columns. Even though we know that we are retrieving two columns, we will include the value returned from the query rather than hardcoding a value of 2 into the table so that we can extend the page later. The table definition then looks like this:

```
    <TABLE BORDER=1 COLS=<% = objRS.Fields.Count%>>
```

Now we need to include column headings. Again, if we take these directly from the query, then we can expand the query much more easily later:

```
    <TR>
      <% For Each adoField In objRS.Fields %>
          <TH> <% = adoField.Name %> </TH>
      <% Next %>
    </TR>
```

Now we can navigate through the actual resultset and populate the table. Each row is created via the <TR>...</TR> pair of tags by navigating through the resultset using a *Do While...Loop* construct. As soon as we go past the end of the loop, the table closing tag is sent. Each individual row is populated using a *For...Each* loop:

```
    <% Do While Not objRS.EOF %>
      <TR>
        <% For Each adoField In objRS.Fields %>
```

```
              ' Populate the cells here
          <% Next
          objRS.MoveNext %>
        </TR>
      <% Loop %>
    </TABLE>
```

Each cell within each column of that row is created using the <TD> tag within that
For loop, like so:

```
<TD ALIGN=LEFT>
<% If IsNull(adoField) Then
      Response.Write ""
    Else
      Response.Write adoField.Value
    End If %>
</TD>
```

The whole section of code comes together in Example 25-4. Ignore the first line for
now; we'll come back to it in a minute.

Example 25-4. Incorporating searches into ASP

```
<!--#include file="adovbs.inc" -->
<html>
<HEAD>
<TITLE>Navigating a simple resultset using ADSI, ADO and ASP</TITLE>
</HEAD>

<BODY>
<%
  On Error Resume Next

  Set objConn = CreateObject("ADODB.Connection")
  objConn.Provider = "ADSDSOObject"
  objConn.Open "", _
    "CN=Administrator,CN=Users,dc=mycorp,dc=com", ""

  Set objRS = objConn.Execute _
    ("<LDAP://dc=mycorp,dc=com>;" _
      & "(objectClass=User);Name,ADsPath;SubTree")
%>

<TABLE BORDER=1 COLS=<% = objRS.Fields.Count%>>
  <TR>
    <% For Each oField In objRS.Fields %>
        <TH> <% = oField.Name %> </TH>
    <% Next %>
  </TR>
  <% Do While Not objRS.EOF %>
    <TR>
      <% For Each oField In objRS.Fields %>
          <TD ALIGN=LEFT>
          <% If IsNull(oField) Then
              Response.Write " "
```

Example 25-4. Incorporating searches into ASP

```
            Else
                Response.Write oField.Value
            End If %>
        </TD>

    <% Next
    objRS.MoveNext %>
    </TR>
  <% Loop %>
</TABLE>

<%
  objConn.Close
  Set objRS = Nothing
%>

</BODY>
</HTML>
```

ASP Searches Allowing User Navigation of a Resultset

We'll now go through a rather more complex example so that you can see how to
allow users to navigate through a resultset. This example came from a need to be able
to display the name, description, and ADsPath of every object in the tree in a simple
fashion on a web page. The most obvious solution was to use an ADO resultset with
Move First, Move Last, Previous, and Next buttons to step through it. Once the simple example is assembled, we will expand it to include a demonstration of filters.

The ASP is split up as usual between the server-side script and the HTML of the web
page itself. The resultset is retrieved as part of the server-side script and looks identical to those we considered earlier:

```
<%
  Set objConn = CreateObject("ADODB.Connection")
  objConn.Provider = "ADSDSOObject"
  objConn.Open "", _
    "CN=Administrator,CN=Users,dc=mycorp,dc=com", ""

  Set objRS = objConn.Execute _
    ("<LDAP://dc=mycorp,dc=com>;(objectClass=User);ADsPath;SubTree")
%>
```

 You may need to add either Microsoft Data Access Components
(MDAC) or ADO components to your installation of IIS before IIS will
accept ADO on web pages. If you find that you are getting continual
errors with simple ADO queries, you may have forgotten to install the
relevant components so that IIS can interpret ADO code.

We'll leave the server-side script for now and concentrate on the HTML elements. The web page needs to display the name, description, and ADsPath of the user. To do that, we need to bind to the user via the ADsPath of the current record of the resultset. We will use *IADsOpenDSObject::OpenDSObject* here, although GetObject would do just as well:

```
<%
  strUsername = "cn=Administrator,cn=Users,dc=mycorp,dc=com"
  strPassword = ""

  Set objNamespace = GetObject("LDAP:")
  Set objUser = objNamespace.OpenDSObject(objRS("ADsPath"), _
    strUsername,strPassword,0)

  Response.Write "Name: <B>" & objUser.Name & "</B><P>"
  Response.Write "ADsPath: <B>" & objUser.ADsPath & "</B><P>"
  Response.Write "Description: <B>" & objUser.Description & "</B><P>"
%>
```

For the form itself, we've made sure that the Previous button is not displayed at the first resultset record and that the Next button is not displayed at the final resultset record. This prevents the resultset from going out of range, and is simple to do using server-side scripting within the HTML code by checking the *Recordset::Absolute-Position* and *Recordset::RecordCount* properties:

```
<FORM METHOD="POST" ACTION="rs_demo.asp">
  <% If objRS.AbsolutePosition = objRS.RecordCount Then %>
    <INPUT TYPE="SUBMIT" NAME="Previous" VALUE="Previous">
  <% ElseIf objRS.AbsolutePosition = 1 Then %>
    <INPUT TYPE="SUBMIT" NAME="Next" VALUE="Next">
  <% Else %>
    <INPUT TYPE="SUBMIT" NAME="Previous" VALUE="Previous">
    <INPUT TYPE="SUBMIT" NAME="Next" VALUE="Next">
  <% End If %>

  <INPUT TYPE="SUBMIT" NAME="First" VALUE="Move First">
  <INPUT TYPE="SUBMIT" NAME="Last" VALUE="Move Last">
</FORM>
```

This is essentially it for the client HTML code. Before looking at the server-side code, there is one HTML line we have to add for ADO prior to anything else on the page:

```
<!--#include file="adovbs.inc" -->
```

This line is known as a Server-side Include (SSI) and is used to include all the ADO constants you may wish to use in your ASP without having to redeclare them yourself. This file is installed with the ADO component of IIS in the *\Program Files\ Common Files\System\ado* directory as a text file so you can easily open it and look through the constants that are available to you. If you are using JScript, you need to use *adojavas.inc* instead.

After including the code to retrieve the resultset, we now need to include the code to navigate that resultset according to which buttons are clicked on the form. However, at this point we have a problem. Because the page reloads the resultset every time, the current record will always be the first no matter what button is selected. For this web page to properly navigate a resultset, we will have to maintain some sort of indicator to the current record between refreshes of each page. This is very easy to do using the HIDDEN attribute of fields on the existing form. All we need to do is set up an extra entry anywhere on the form that includes a reference to the current record. We can do this using the *Recordset::AbsolutePosition* of the resultset:

```
<INPUT TYPE="HIDDEN" NAME="AbsPosition"
  VALUE="<% = objRS.AbsolutePosition %>">
```

If we do this, whenever the form is submitted, the current record's position is transmitted with the form.

 There is one problem with using *Recordset::AbsolutePosition* in this example: the resultset may not be static throughout every query. If users are being created and deleted while the page is being accessed, there is a chance, however small, that the current record may disappear between page refreshes or that a navigation moves to a new record that did not previously exist. Solutions to this problem are discussed later in the chapter.

Assuming that we do this, we can navigate through the new resultset using the following code:

```
<%
  If Request.Form("Next") <> "" Then
    objRS.AbsolutePosition = Request.Form("AbsPosition") + 1
  ElseIf Request.Form("Previous") <> "" Then
    objRS.AbsolutePosition = Request.Form("AbsPosition") - 1
  ElseIf Request.Form("First") <> "" Then
    objRS.MoveFirst
  ElseIf Request.Form("Last") <> "" Then
    objRS.MoveLast
  End If
%>
```

At this point, the code is essentially complete. Example 25-5 shows it in its entirety.

Example 25-5. Navigating through a Resultset

```
<!--#include file="adovbs.inc" -->
<%
  Set objConn = CreateObject("ADODB.Connection")
  objConn.Provider = "ADSDSOObject"
  objConn.Open "", _
    "CN=Administrator,CN=Users,dc=mycorp,dc=com", ""

  Set objRS = objConn.Execute _
    ("<LDAP://dc=mycorp,dc=com>;(objectClass=User);ADsPath;SubTree")
```

Example 25-5. Navigating through a Resultset (continued)

```
  If Request.Form("Next") <> "" Then
    objRS.AbsolutePosition = Request.Form("AbsPosition") + 1
  ElseIf Request.Form("Previous") <> "" Then
    objRS.AbsolutePosition = Request.Form("AbsPosition") - 1
  ElseIf Request.Form("First") <> "" Then
    objRS.MoveFirst
  ElseIf Request.Form("Last") <> "" Then
    objRS.MoveLast
  End If
%>

<! Start the main page>
<html>
<HEAD>
<TITLE>Recordset Navigation using ADSI, ADO and ASP</TITLE>
</HEAD>

<BODY>
<%
  strUsername = "cn=Administrator,cn=Users,dc=mycorp,dc=com"
  strPassword = ""

  Set objNamespace = GetObject("LDAP:")
  Set objUser = objNamespace.OpenDSObject(objRS("ADsPath"), _
    strUsername,strPassword,0)

  Response.Write "Name: <B>" & objUser.Name & "</B><P>"
  Response.Write "ADsPath: <B>" & objUser.ADsPath & "</B><P>"
  Response.Write "Description: <B>" & objUser.Description & "</B><P>"
%>
<FORM METHOD="POST" ACTION="rs_demo.asp">
  <INPUT TYPE="HIDDEN" NAME="AbsPosition"
    VALUE="<% = objRS.AbsolutePosition %>">
  <% If objRS.AbsolutePosition = objRS.RecordCount Then %>
    <INPUT TYPE="SUBMIT" NAME="Previous" VALUE="Previous">
  <% ElseIf objRS.AbsolutePosition = 1 Then %>
    <INPUT TYPE="SUBMIT" NAME="Next" VALUE="Next">
  <% Else %>
    <INPUT TYPE="SUBMIT" NAME="Previous" VALUE="Previous">
    <INPUT TYPE="SUBMIT" NAME="Next" VALUE="Next">
  <% End If %>

  <INPUT TYPE="SUBMIT" NAME="First" VALUE="Move First">
  <INPUT TYPE="SUBMIT" NAME="Last" VALUE="Move Last">
</FORM>

</BODY>
</HTML>
```

Enhancing the User Navigation ASP

There are a number of enhancements that you can make to the code, not only to make it more user friendly but also to demonstrate the use of filtering an existing resultset. We'll deal with these enhancements individually and then combine them all at the end into an expanded ASP incorporating all of the enhancements.

Empty resultsets

Occasionally, you will write an ASP that generates an empty resultset. If that is the case, we should make sure that the page handles this properly. We could print a simple message and stop processing the page any further. In addition, we could provide a Restart button that could reload the page from scratch if desired. Here is the section of code to accomplish this:

```
<%
  If objRS.EOF Then
    Response.Write("No users found!")
%>
    <FORM METHOD="POST" ACTION="rs_demo.asp">
      <INPUT TYPE="SUBMIT" NAME="Restart" VALUE="Restart">
    </FORM>
<%
    objConn.Close
    Set objRS = Nothing
    Set objConn = Nothing
    Response.End
  End If
%>
```

Starting from scratch

Occasionally, it would be nice to wipe the resultset clean and start again from scratch at the first item. This is easy to achieve using another button on the form:

```
<INPUT TYPE="SUBMIT" NAME="Restart" VALUE="Restart">
```

If the page is opened using the Restart button, we reload the page from scratch by using the trick of redirecting the browser to the page. This triggers the browser to get a new copy of the page, clearing all the values set by the form on previous pages. The server-side code looks like this:

```
<%
  If Request.Form("Restart") = "Restart" Then
    Response.Redirect("rs_demo.asp")
    Response.End
  End If
%>
```

Filters

To include filters on an existing resultset, we need to monitor two extra values when the form is submitted. First, we need to know that a filter is being applied to the resultset, so that we can reapply it when the page is refreshed after the submission of a form. Second, we need to keep a copy of the actual filter itself. The first is easily taken care of by another hidden field in the form:

```
<INPUT TYPE="HIDDEN" NAME="IsFilterOn" VALUE="<% = bolFilter %>">
```

To set this value, we need to include some server-side code to cope with the fact that the value will not be set for the first-ever access to the page. We can do it like this:

```
<%
  If Request.Form("IsFilterOn") = "FALSE" Then
    bolFilter = "FALSE"
  ElseIf Request.Form("IsFilterOn") = "TRUE" Then
    bolFilter = "TRUE"
  Else
    bolFilter = "FALSE"
  End If
%>
```

We could just as easily use an INPUT field of type CHECKBOX here if desired. This is a Boolean input and would work just as well.

The second requirement can be taken care of by an INPUT field on the form:

```
<INPUT TYPE="TEXT" NAME="FilterText" VALUE= "<% = strFilter %>">
```

We would also like to include a default value for this filter, so strFilter needs to be set somewhere prior to the form itself. After the page has been accessed once, the value of this field entry will have been set. From then on, we should be able to use the existing value of this field as the base for the input field. Here is the code:

```
<%
  If CStr(Request.Form("FilterText")) = "" Then
    strFilter = "Name LIKE 'a*'"
  Else
    strFilter = CStr(Request.Form("FilterText"))
  End If
%>
```

We also need some way of being able to set and remove the filter on the resultset. As there will always be a value in the filter field, we cannot use this to trigger the addition of a filter to the resultset. Once again, the simplest solution is to use two more buttons on the form:

```
<INPUT TYPE="SUBMIT" NAME="SetFilter" VALUE="Set Filter!">
<INPUT TYPE="SUBMIT" NAME="EraseFilter" VALUE="Erase Filter!">
```

We now can write the code that actually applies and removes the filter using these two buttons:

```
ElseIf Request.Form("SetFilter") <> "" Then
  objRS.Filter = CStr(Request.Form("FilterText"))
```

```
      bolFilter = "TRUE"
   ElseIf Request.Form("EraseFilter") <> "" Then
     objRS.Filter = adFilterNone
     bolFilter = "FALSE"
```

There is still one small piece of code missing. While we can set a filter using the appropriate button, as soon as we begin to navigate the filtered resultset, we will be clicking other buttons. We need to make sure that the filter is applied while the `IsFilterOn` field is true. To do this, we add an extra line to the code that sets *bolFilter*, which we laid out earlier. The code should now look like this:

```
   If Request.Form("IsFilterOn") = "FALSE" Then
     bolFilter = "FALSE"
   ElseIf Request.Form("IsFilterOn") = "TRUE" Then
     objRS.Filter = CStr(Request.Form("FilterText"))
     bolFilter = "TRUE"
   Else
     bolFilter = "FALSE"
   End If
```

This makes sure that the filter is always applied after it has been initially set.

Displaying the location of individual records

We will add two other lines of code to the ASP. While they are not strictly necessary, these two lines serve to demonstrate how resultsets work:

```
   This is user number <% = objRS.AbsolutePosition %>.
   There are <% = objRS.RecordCount %> users in the recordset.<P>
```

The last line will always tell you how many records you can currently navigate through in the resultset. If there are 12 records and you have no filter, the result will be 12. If you have 12 records but have a filter that limits it to 4, the result will be 4. However, the first line always refers to the record number out of the entire recordset total, regardless of whether a filter has been set.

This means that including the following code can lead to undesired results:

```
   <P>This is user <% = objRS.AbsolutePosition %> out of a total of
   <% = objRS.RecordCount %> users in the recordset.</P>
```

If a filter were applied to a resultset that limited the resultset to the entries 1, 3, 8, and 9, when you navigated between the four results, you would receive the following responses:

```
   This is user 1 out of a total of four users in the recordset.
   This is user 3 out of a total of four users in the recordset.
   This is user 8 out of a total of four users in the recordset.
   This is user 9 out of a total of four users in the recordset.
```

It is important to understand this distinction.

The enhanced ASP search

Example 25-6 lists the code for the enhanced version of the ASP ADO search.

Example 25-6. The enhanced version of the ASP ADO search

```
<!--#include file="adovbs.inc" -->
<%
  ' If the page is opened using the Restart button then reload the page
  ' from scratch by redirecting to the page itself
  If Request.Form("Restart") = "Restart" Then
    Response.Redirect("rs_demo.asp")
    Response.End
  End If

  ' Retrieve the Resultset
  Set objConn = CreateObject("ADODB.Connection")
  objConn.Provider = "ADSDSOObject"
  objConn.Open "", _
    "CN=Administrator,CN=Users,dc=mycorp,dc=com", ""

  Set objRS = objConn.Execute _
    ("<LDAP://dc=mycorp,dc=com>;(objectClass=User);ADsPath;SubTree")

  If Request.Form("IsFilterOn") = "FALSE" Then
    bolFilter = "FALSE"
  ElseIf Request.Form("IsFilterOn") = "TRUE" Then
    objRS.Filter = CStr(Request.Form("FilterText"))
    bolFilter = "TRUE"
  Else
    bolFilter = "FALSE"
  End If

  If Request.Form("Next") <> "" Then
    objRS.AbsolutePosition = Request.Form("AbsPosition") + 1
  ElseIf Request.Form("Previous") <> "" Then
    objRS.AbsolutePosition = Request.Form("AbsPosition") - 1
  ElseIf Request.Form("First") <> "" Then
    objRS.MoveFirst
  ElseIf Request.Form("Last") <> "" Then
    objRS.MoveLast
  ElseIf Request.Form("SetFilter") <> "" Then
    objRS.Filter = CStr(Request.Form("FilterText"))
    bolFilter = "TRUE"
  ElseIf Request.Form("EraseFilter") <> "" Then
    objRS.Filter = adFilterNone
    bolFilter = "FALSE"
  End If

  ' If no results were returned, then end the session
  ' but provide a restart button
  If objRS.EOF Then
    Response.Write("No users found!")
%>
    <FORM METHOD="POST" ACTION="rs_demo.asp">
      <INPUT TYPE="SUBMIT" NAME="Restart" VALUE="Restart">
```

Example 25-6. The enhanced version of the ASP ADO search (continued)

```
    </FORM>
<%
    objConn.Close
    Set objRS = Nothing
    Set objConn = Nothing
    Response.End
  End If
%>

<! Start the main page>
<html>
<HEAD>
<TITLE>Recordset Navigation using ADSI, ADO and ASP</TITLE>
</HEAD>

<BODY>
This is user number <% = objRS.AbsolutePosition %>.
There are <% = objRS.RecordCount %> users in the recordset.<P>

<%
  If CStr(Request.Form("FilterText")) = "" Then
    strFilter = "Name LIKE 'a*'"
  Else
    strFilter = CStr(Request.Form("FilterText"))
  End If
  strUsername = "cn=Administrator,cn=Users,dc=mycorp,dc=com"
  strPassword = ""

  Set objNamespace = GetObject("LDAP:")
  Set objUser = objNamespace.OpenDSObject(objRS("ADsPath"), _
    strUsername,strPassword,0)

  Response.Write "Name: <B>" & objUser.Name & "</B><P>"
  Response.Write "ADsPath: <B>" & objUser.ADsPath & "</B><P>"
  Response.Write "Description: <B>" & objUser.Description & "</B><P>"
  Response.Write "Class: <B>" & objUser.Schema & "</B><P>"
%>

<FORM METHOD="POST" ACTION="rs_demo.asp">
  <INPUT TYPE="SUBMIT" NAME="Restart" VALUE="Restart">
  <INPUT TYPE="HIDDEN" NAME="AbsPosition"
    VALUE="<% = objRS.AbsolutePosition %>">
  <INPUT TYPE="HIDDEN" NAME="IsFilterOn" VALUE="<% = bolFilter %>">

  <% If objRS.AbsolutePosition = objRS.RecordCount Then %>
    <INPUT TYPE="SUBMIT" NAME="Previous" VALUE="Previous">
  <% ElseIf objRS.AbsolutePosition = 1 Then %>
    <INPUT TYPE="SUBMIT" NAME="Next" VALUE="Next">
  <% Else %>
    <INPUT TYPE="SUBMIT" NAME="Previous" VALUE="Previous">
    <INPUT TYPE="SUBMIT" NAME="Next" VALUE="Next">
  <% End If %>
```

Example 25-6. The enhanced version of the ASP ADO search (continued)

```
    <INPUT TYPE="SUBMIT" NAME="First" VALUE="Move First">
    <INPUT TYPE="SUBMIT" NAME="Last" VALUE="Move Last">
    <P>
    <INPUT TYPE="TEXT" NAME="FilterText" VALUE= "<% = strFilter %>">
    <INPUT TYPE="SUBMIT" NAME="SetFilter" VALUE="Set Filter!">
    <INPUT TYPE="SUBMIT" NAME="EraseFilter" VALUE="Erase Filter!">
</FORM>

</BODY>
</HTML>
```

Problems with this example

As mentioned earlier, there is the problem that the resultset may not be static throughout every query. One way around this is to pass the ADsPath of the user back in a hidden field, and once the query is executed, confirm that the current record of the new query is the same current record of the old query prior to performing any actions from the buttons. If there were a problem, you could pop up a MsgBox or write some text to the screen to that effect.

We have not integrated the use of bookmarks into this code, since Microsoft specifically warns against moving to a record in a resultset using a bookmark from another query. Because the query is executed again each time the page is loaded, the use of bookmarks is not appropriate. While the bookmarks for the ADSI OLE DB provider are currently only a copy of the *Recordset::AbsolutePosition* field, it would be wise to follow Microsoft's advice in case they change the format in the future.

Other Ideas for Expansion

There are many other ways that you could extend the look and functionality of the existing code. For example, you could place Previous and Next buttons on each page even if you were at the first or last record. If you did this, you could use the following section of code to cycle around the resultset. If you click Next from the last record, you will go to the first; if you click Previous from the first you will get to the last:

```
    If Request.Form("Next") <> "" Then
      objRS.AbsolutePosition = Request.Form("AbsPosition") + 1
      If objRS.EOF Then
        objRS.MoveFirst
      End If
    ElseIf Request.Form("Previous") <> "" Then
      If Request.Form("AbsPosition") = 1 Then
        objRS.MoveLast

      Else
        objRS.AbsolutePosition = Request.Form("AbsPosition") - 1  End If
    End If
```

You can actually modify the descriptions on the buttons themselves using a script if you wish. For example, while you were on Record 3, you could replace Next and Previous with Move to Record 2 and Move to Record 4.

While we bound to Active Directory using the administrator username and password, you could easily adapt the examples so that the web page had fields for both of these. That removes the authentication details from the ASP. In addition, as we have authenticated to Active Directory, you could use this fact to extend this page to manipulate the existing Active Directory information. For example, instead of displaying the description for a user as text, you could make the current description the default value for a text INPUT field in the existing form. Then you could modify this description and click another button that you included, which would write that new description back to Active Directory.

If you wanted to use the ASP to display every attribute for every mandatory and optional property that user objects have, you could walk the property list based on the schema class definition and write the results to a web page rather than a file (see Chapter 19). This is easily achieved using the *IADs::Schema* property (i.e., *objUser.Schema*).

You could modify what happens when you get an empty resultset due to an incorrect filter. Instead of just providing a Restart button and ending the session, you could put up the three filter fields and allow people to see and correct their mistakes.

Obviously, you also could expand and extend the search so that it could search for any classes of objects, possibly via a list box within a form.

Even though the HTML code on the ASPs is dynamically generated and sent to the client by server-side scripts, the HTML is static once it has been generated. This means that for a new set of data to be sent to the client, a new page has to be opened. The data on the page returned to the client has to change each time a button is pressed, so the web page is therefore reloaded with every button click. This means that the query is executed again and the resultset is retrieved afresh with every click of the button. The only way to alter the HTML code that exists on the client after it has been generated is to use Dynamic HTML or DHTML. This update to HTML does exactly what it says: it allows HTML to be updated dynamically on the client. While you could use DHTML here, it lies outside the scope of this book. The point is that there are quite a few things that you can do with ADO searches of Active Directory within Active Server Pages.

Migrating Your ADSI Scripts from VBScript to VB

If you decide you need a GUI-based application instead of a web-based application, it is time to start thinking about coding in a different language. VB is an easy language with the capabilities of great complexity. The VB language itself is very similar to VBScript, so you can port code quickly from your existing scripts. However, there is so much that you can do with VB that the bewildering array of interfaces and methods can easily get confusing. The simplest solution to this is to get a book on VB. There are many dozens of books that already exist on the complexities of writing in VB, and we do not intend to provide an introduction here. If you are seriously considering writing in VB, your best option is to pick up a book on it.

This section covers what you need to do to write ADSI code with VB after having written ADSI code in VBScript. This includes a brief look at the major differences between VBScript and VB, the options that need to be set, and the Platform SDK, which you will need to compile your code. We also briefly cover a series of examples that are available from the O'Reilly web site. The notes that we present in this section are with respect to Microsoft Visual Basic Professional Version 6.0. However, these examples should also work with future versions of VB as well.

Platform Software Development Kit

To access the ADSI interfaces and libraries, you need to be able to reference the appropriate component of the Microsoft Platform Software Development Kit (SDK) in your code. You can either download the appropriate component or obtain the full SDK, which includes all components.

The full SDK provides developers with a single, easy-to-use location from which to download current and emerging Microsoft technologies; it includes tools, headers, libraries, and sample code. The Platform SDK is the successor to the individual SDKs, such as the Win32, BackOffice, ActiveX/Internet Client, WMI, ADSI, and DirectX SDKs.

You can get the full SDK build environment or just the ADSI component in a number of ways:

- If you purchase an MSDN Professional-level subscription, you will be shipped all of the SDKs that you require.
- If you purchase an MSDN Enterprise-level subscription, you will be shipped all of the SDKs and all of the Visual Studio products, which includes Microsoft Visual Basic Enterprise Edition as well.
- If you purchase Visual Basic 6.0 Enterprise Edition, you receive the full MSDN set of CDs and the SDK build environment.

You can download the parts of the platform SDK by following going to *http://www.microsoft.com/msdownload/platformsdk/sdkupdate/*.

If you wish to make use of ADO from the next chapter, you need Microsoft Data Access Components (MDAC) as well. You can download these from the Downloads section of the Universal Data Access site: *http://www.microsoft.com/data/download.htm*.

Once the SDK has been downloaded and installed, start VB and in any new project that you write make sure that you go to Project → References and check items according to Table 25-1.

Table 25-1. When to use relevant references in VB

Reference	To use
Active DS Type Library	ADSI
Microsoft ActiveX Data Objects 2.5 Library	ADO

You can see the References window in Figure 25-2, with both items checked.

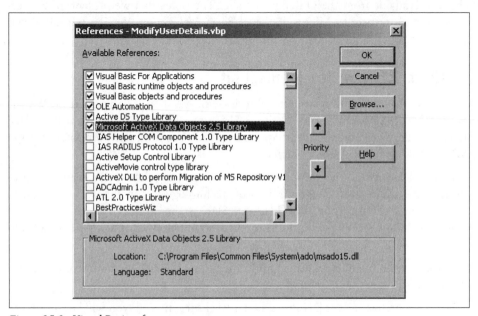

Figure 25-2. Visual Basic references

The Differences Between VB and VBScript

There are many differences between VBScript and VB, but the three major ones that you will come into contact with when porting your scripts can be quickly explained.

Screen functions

The code will not be executing under the WSH any more so *Wscript.Echo* is not appropriate. While *MsgBox* still works, these lines should be replaced either by *Debug.Print* or by directly passing results into TextBox controls.

Variables

In VBScript, every variable is of the type Variant and does not have to be declared. In VB, every variable must be declared at the beginning, just as if you were using `Option Explicit` in VBScript. In addition, each variable must be declared to be of a particular type. Here are some examples for VB:

```
'VB code
Dim objUser as IADsUser
Dim objRoot as IADsContainer
Dim objMember as IADsMember
```

In addition, `CreateObject` is not needed. Instead, you use the `New` keyword and declare the object created prior to the main code. The following VBScript code:

```
'VBScript code
Set objConn = CreateObject("ADODB.Connection")
```

is replaced with the following code in VB:

```
'VB code
Dim objConn as New ADODB.Connection
```

For another important point, look at these declarations:

```
'VB code
Dim objUser as IADsUser
Dim objUser2 as IADs
```

If we want to use the *IADsUser* methods and properties, we have to use the variable `objUser`. If we want to use the *IADs* methods and properties, we have to use `objUser2`. This is how it works:

```
'VB code
Dim objUser as IADsUser
Dim objUser2 as IADs

Set objUser = GetObject("LDAP://cn=Administrator,cn=Users,dc=mycorp,dc=com")
Set objUser2 = objUser
Debug.Print objUser.Description
Debug.Print objUser2.Class
```

The first *Debug::Print* statement prints the *IADsUser::Description* property, and the second prints the *IADs::Class* property. We have to include the second Set command to make sure that `objUser2` points to the same object as `objUser`.

Loop constructs

The syntax for loops changes slightly. Here, for example, are two loops in VBScipt:

```
'VBScript code
While (condition)
  'Do something
Wend

For Each objMember In objGroup.Members
```

```
      WScript.Echo objMember.Name & vbCrLf & objMember.ADsPath
   Next
```

Here they are again in VB:

```
'VB code
While (condition) Do
   'Do something
Wend

For Each objMember In objGroup.Members
   Debug.Print objMember.Name & vbCrLf & objMember.ADsPath
Next objMember
```

We now can move on to some proper VB coding.

Getting Help from VB When Coding in ADSI

When you begin to code in VB, the interface tries to help you code by providing you with the appropriate methods and properties for the object you are manipulating.

For example, if we started declaring a variable in VB, then as soon as we had stated something like this:

```
'Declare use variable
Dim objUser As
```

the interface would pop up a box displaying all the variable types so we could pick one. We'll say that we chose *IADsUser* from the list at this point. Now in my code we wish to use a method on the object, so we start typing:

```
'Declare use variable
Dim objUser As IADsUser

'Use IADsUser method
objUser.
```

As soon as we have typed the dot, VB knows we wish to use a method, so it pops up all the possible methods that we could use at this point. This is a great help, so that you do not have to remember the names of the methods and properties all the time.

You also can use View → Object Browser (or use the F2 key), which shows you all the possible methods and properties available in any SDKs that are currently included as references to your project.

A Simple Password Changer in VB

This is a variation on the password changer we introduced earlier. This changer is for use by a help desk to set a user's password and automatically unlock the account if it is locked. All the users are presumed to be in the Users container for this simple project, which makes use of one form, shown in Figure 25-3.

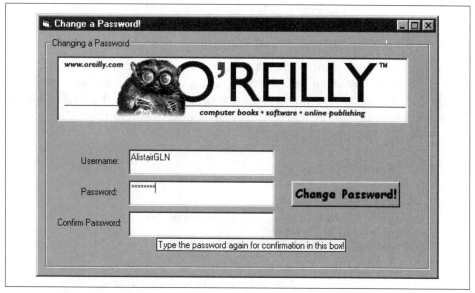

Figure 25-3. The change password script result

 The entire project can be downloaded from the O'Reilly web site.

The form (the window) contains the following controls (objects that sit on the window):

- One PictureBox control, the O'Reilly logo
- Three Label controls, the text fields that cannot be edited
- Three TextBox controls (txtUsername, txtPass1, and txtPass2), the three data entry fields
- One CommandButton control (cmdChangePassword), the Change Password button

Some of the properties for fields have been set as follows:

- To make sure that using the Tab key cycles properly through the three TextBox controls and the CommandButton control, the *TabIndex* property is set for each control in the order that the Tab key is to cycle through, e.g., txtUsername=1, txtPass1=2, txtPass2=3, cmdChangePassword=4.
- The two password boxes have the *PasswordChar* property set to "*" so that the password is not displayed in plain text on the form.

- The *ToolTipText* property specifies the text that will appear when the cursor hovers over each TextBox and CommandButton. The text for the second password field is displayed in Figure 25-3.

The command button needs some code to tell it what to do when the button is clicked. This is known as an event procedure, as it is triggered when an event (clicking the button) occurs. No code is attached to anything other than the command button. The code that sits behind the command button looks like this:

```
Private Sub cmdChangePassword_Click( )

Dim objUser As IADsUser

If txtUsername.Text <> "" Then
  If txtPass1.Text = txtPass2.Text Then
    Set objUser = GetObject("LDAP://cn=" + txtUsername.Text _
      + ",cn=Users,dc=mycorp,dc=com")

    objUser.SetPassword txtPass1.Text
    objUser.pwdLastSet = 0
    If objUser.IsAccountLocked Then objUser.IsAccountLocked = False

    objUser.SetInfo


    'Reset everything
    txtUsername.Text = ""
    txtPass1.Text = ""
    txtPass2.Text = ""

    MsgBox "Password changed!"
  Else
    MsgBox "Passwords are not the same, please try again!"
  End If
Else
  MsgBox "A username must be specified!"
End If
```

You can see that we are using the text typed into the *TextBox::Text* property for each TextBox control as necessary. We don't declare these controls as we do with variables, as the very fact that they're on the form is enough to declare them.

There is a procedure that is attached to the CommandButton called cmdChangePassword, and it is executed when a single-click event occurs on that button. When that button is clicked, we check that the txtUsername field has had a username typed in, and if it has, then we check that the two passwords are the same. If they are, we concatenate the username with the domain string and get a handle to the user object. We then use the *IADsUser::SetPassword* method with one of the two passwords as the parameter and also set the *pwdLastSet* property to 0 to indicate that the password is expired. This means the user has to change it when he next logs on. We then unlock the account if it was locked, because otherwise the user will be unable to make use of the new password. We then write out the property cache. You can also see that we are not checking that the password was set properly or later that the other properties were set. It would be simple to put in if desired.

The ModifyUserDetails Program in VB

Let's take one more example by extending the previous one to modify a variety of user details. Take a look at Figure 25-4.

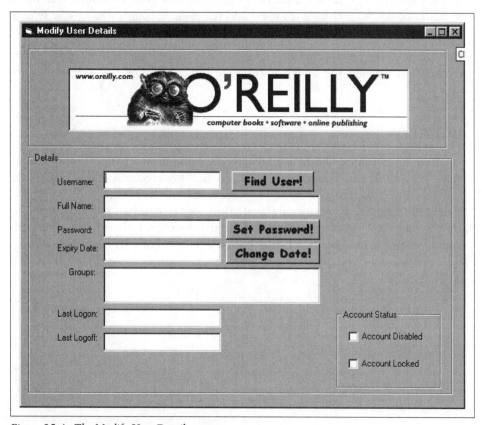

Figure 25-4. The Modify User Details screen

Figure 25-4 is another simple user querying and modification tool. This one has a number of different features. To start with, the username is typed into the top Text-Box. When the user clicks on the Find User! command button, an ADO search function retrieves the full ADsPath of the user. This ADsPath then is used to bind to the user and to retrieve the full name, the expiry date, the group memberships, the last logon and last logoff times, and whether the account is disabled or locked. The group membership's TextBox automatically displays vertical scrollbars if the results cannot be displayed in the space available.

The administrator then can use the Set Password! button to set the password. This time, no confirmation is requested; the password is just accepted as is. The Change Date! button can set the expiration date. The two account status checkboxes in the bottom right can enable/disable the account or unlock it if it gets locked.

Actually, the unlock checkbox should never give the option to lock an account; instead, it should be grayed out (disabled) by default. Then it can be enabled only when an account is locked. Clicking the checkbox on a locked account would unlock the account and then disable the checkbox again immediately. Obviously this means that a user could never change his mind and relock an account, which is fairly non-sensical, but in that case it can simply be disabled instead.

While the code is not particularly complex, it is quite long, and for that reason, we've made it available for download from the companion O'Reilly web site for this book.

Summary

Being able to customize the Active Directory schema means that you may end up using a number of new classes and attributes that you create. As these classes and attributes can be manipulated using the same ADSI interfaces that you have seen in the previous chapters, you can easily create your own customized tools to operate on these new objects. This allows you free rein in developing solutions that are perfectly tailored for your requirements, whether from a web-based or GUI-based interface.

CHAPTER 26

Scripting with WMI

The Windows Management Instrumentation (WMI) API was developed by Microsoft in 1998 in response to the ever-growing need for developers and system administrators to have a common, scriptable API to manage the components of the Windows operating systems. Before WMI, if you wanted to manage some component of the operating system, you had to resort to using one of the component specific Win32 API's, such as the Registry API or Event Log API. Each API typically had its own implementation quirks and required way too much work to do simple tasks. The other big problem with the Win32 APIs is that scripting languages such as VBScript could not use them. This really limited how much an inexperienced programmer or system administrator could do to programmatically manage systems. WMI changes all this by providing a single API that can be used to query and manage the Event Log, the Registry, processes, the filesystem, or any other operating system component.

So you may be wondering at this point: this is a book on Active Directory, so why do I need to care about a system management API? Even if your sole job in life is to manage Active Directory, WMI can benefit you in at least two ways. First, Active Directory runs on top of Windows 2000 or Windows Server 2003. These servers need to be managed (i.e., Event Log settings configured, Registry modified, applications installed, etc.) and monitored (i.e., filesystem space, services running, etc.). You can choose to do all of those tasks manually, or you can use WMI to automate them. For each task you automate, the total cost of ownership to support Active Directory is reduced, and you help ensure your servers stay consistent. The other reason why WMI is important to Active Directory is the direction Microsoft is taking WMI with respect to monitoring and managing any system or application under the Microsoft umbrella. That's right, not only does Microsoft want WMI to be the primary interface to manage and monitor Windows systems, but also any Windows application, including Active Directory. Currently, ADSI provides the primary management interface into Active Directory, but in the Windows Server 2003 release, there are several new WMI hooks into Active Directory to monitor things such as trusts and replication.

In this chapter, we will give a brief introduction to the concepts and terminology behind WMI and then delve into several sample scripts showing how to make use of it. We will cover some system-specific tasks, such as managing services, the Event Log, and the Registry, which should give you a good grounding in some of the fundamentals of WMI. In the second half of the chapter, we will review how WMI can be used to access and monitor Active Directory.

In a single chapter we can only go into so much detail about the internals of WMI. We won't be covering some of the more advanced topics. If you are interested in more information than what this chapter provides, we recommend checking out the MSDN Library or one of the WMI books available on the market. At the time this book was published, you could access the WMI SDK documentation by going to the MSDN Library (*http://msdn.microsoft.com/library*) and visiting Setup and System Administration → Windows Management Instrumentation (WMI) → SDK Documentation or by going to the following web page: *http://msdn.microsoft.com/library/en-us/wmisdk/wmi/wmi_start_page.asp*.

Origins of WMI

There have been several industry initiatives over the years to develop a model for managing systems and devices that would be robust enough to meet the needs of most vendors. Several protocols and frameworks have been developed to address the problem. The Simple Network Management Protocol (SNMP) is probably the most notable, but is pretty simple in its implementation and does not provide many features most vendors need for a single management framework.

The Distributed Management Task Force (DMTF) was created in the early 1990s to address the management framework problem. They developed the Web Based Enterprise Management (WBEM) standard, which attempts to unify the management frameworks utilizing web technologies. As part of the WBEM standard, they also created the Common Information Model (CIM), which is the language used for describing management data in an object-oriented way. The WBEM/CIM standards have garnered a lot of industry support in recent years and provide the basis for WMI.

For more information on WBEM/CIM, check out the DMTF website: *http://www.dmtf.org*.

WMI Architecture

The WMI architecture is composed of two primary layers: the CIM infrastructure, which includes the CIMOM and CIM Repository, and the WMI providers. While the concepts Microsoft uses are very similar to the WBEM/CIM standards, they did not implement one very important component: the use of web technologies for the transport mechanism. Instead of using HTTP to transport messages between the WMI infrastructure and clients, Microsoft uses COM and DCOM, two Microsoft-specific technologies. This limits the use of WMI to only Microsoft platforms.

That being said, the capabilities to manage Microsoft-based platforms with WMI are nearly unlimited. More and more vendors are utilizing WMI not only to manage components of the Microsoft OS but also to manage their own applications. NMicrosoft has also become heavily invested in WMI by providing WMI providers for nearly all of its major applications, including Active Directory, Exchange 2000, DNS, and even Microsoft Office.

CIMOM and CIM Repository

The CIM Repository is the primary warehouse for management data. It contains the static data that does not change very frequently, such as memory or disk size. The CIMOM or CIM Object Manager handles requests from clients, retrieves data from the CIM Repository, and returns it to the client. The CIMOM also provides an event service, so that clients can register for events and be notified dynamically when they occur. For dynamic data, such as performance monitor counters, the CIMOM will interact directly with a WMI provider instead of retrieving the data directly from the CIM Repository. The CIM Repository cannot store all possible data that is needed by the various WMI providers. The storage requirements would be significant, not to mention that a lot of the data would become out-of-date almost immediately after it was stored.

WMI Providers

The WMI providers contain much of the intelligence behind WMI. Typically a provider will be implemented for each individual managed component, such as the Event Log or Active Directory Trusts. Each provider is responsible for interacting with its managed component and can perform certain functions implemented by methods on classes representing that component. Also, as described earlier, some providers interact with the CIMOM to provide dynamic data that cannot be held in the CIM Repository.

Each WMI provider is also associated with a namespace. The namespace is used to segregate where WMI providers store their data and class definitions. Think of it as a file system. You could store all of your files in a single directory, but it would be hard to manage. By storing data and class definitions for providers under different namespaces, you don't have to worry about confusing the EventLog provider with the Active Directory Trust provider. Table 26-1 contains the more commonly used and AD-related WMI providers and the associated namespace.

Table 26-1. Some of the commonly used and AD-related WMI providers

Provider	Namespace
Win32 provider	root\cimv2
EventLog provider	root\cimv2
Registry provider	root\default
Active Directory provider	root\directory\LDAP
Replication provider	root\MicrosoftActiveDirectory
Trustmon provider	root\MicrosoftActiveDirectory
DNS provider	root\MicrosoftDNS

Getting Started with WMI Scripting

Once you have a basic understanding of the WMI architecture, scripting with WMI is easy. In fact, once you understand how to reference, enumerate and query objects of a particular class with WMI, it is straightforward to adapt the code to work with any managed component.

Referencing an Object

To reference objects in WMI, you use a UNC-style path name. An example of how to reference the C: drive on a computer looks like the following:

```
\\dc1\root\CIMv2:Win32_LogicalDisk.DeviceID="C:"
```

The format should be easy to follow. The first part of the path (\\dc1\) is a reference to the computer on which the object resides. To reference the computer on which the script is running, you can use a "." for the computer name. The second part (root\CIMv2) is the namespace the object resides in. The third part (Win32_LogicalDisk) is the class of the object to reference. The fourth part is the key/value pairs representing the object. Generically, the path can be shown as follows:

```
\\ComputerName\NameSpace:ClassName.KeyName="KeyValue"[,KeyName2="KeyValue2"...]
```

Now that we know how to reference WMI objects, let's go ahead and instantiate an object using VBScript's GetObject function. For GetObject to understand that we are referencing WMI objects, we have to include one additional piece of information: the moniker. Just as we've been using the LDAP: and WinNT: progIDs to reference Active Directory and SAM-based objects in ADSI, we need to use the winmgmts: moniker when we are dealing with WMI objects:

```
Set objDisk = GetObject("winmgmts:\\dc1\root\CIMv2:Win32_LogicalDisk.DeviceID='C:'")
```

Note that if you want to reference the C: logical drive on the local computer, you can leave off the computer name and namespace path. The GetObject call would then look like this:

```
Set objDisk = GetObject("winmgmts:Win32_LogicalDisk.DeviceID='C:'")
```

You can leave out the namespace path because root\CIMv2 is the default namespace. When accessing a provider that uses any other namespace, you need to include the namespace path. Also, if you are referencing a remote object, you need to include the namespace path even if it is root\CIMv2.

Enumerating Objects of a Particular Class

Now let's look at an example. We want to view all logical disks on a machine, not just a particular disk. To do so, we need to use the InstancesOf method on a WMI object pointing to the namespace of the provider that contains the class. Perhaps an example will make this clear:

```
strComputer = "."
Set objWMI = GetObject("winmgmts:\\" & strComputer & "\root\cimv2")
Set objDisks = objWMI.InstancesOf("Win32_LogicalDisk")
for each objDisk in objDisks
    Wscript.Echo "DeviceID: " &  objDisk.DeviceID
    Wscript.Echo "FileSystem: " &  objDisk.FileSystem
    Wscript.Echo "FreeSpace: " & objDisk.FreeSpace
    Wscript.Echo "Name: " & objDisk.Name
    Wscript.Echo "Size: " & objDisk.Size
    WScript.Echo ""
next
```

Here we get a WMI object pointing to the root\CIMv2 namespace, after which we call the InstancesOf method and pass the Win32_LogicalDisk class. That method returns a collection of Win32_LogicalDisk objects which we then iterate over with a For Each loop.

As you can imagine, this is very powerful and allows you to easily retrieve a list of all the logical disks, services, or processes on a computer. The only issue with the last example is that we needed to know which property methods of the Win32_LogicalDisk class we wanted to see. We can instead retrieve all properties of the Win32_LogicalDisk class using the Properties_ method on each object.

```
strComputer = "."
strWMIClass = "Win32_LogicalDisk"

Set objWMI = GetObject("winmgmts:\\" & strComputer & "\root\cimv2")
Set objDisks = objWMI.InstancesOf(strWMIClass)
for each objDisk in objDisks
    for each objProp in objDisk.Properties_
        ' Print out NULL if the property is blank
        if IsNull(objProp.Value) then
            Wscript.Echo " " & objProp.Name & " : NULL"
        else
        ' If the value is an array, we need to iterate through each element
        ' of the array
            if objProp.IsArray = TRUE then
                For I = LBound(objProp.Value) to UBound(objProp.Value)
```

```
            wscript.echo " " & objProp.Name & " : " & objProp.Value(I)
         next
       else
       ' If the property was  not NULL or a an array, we will print it
           wscript.echo " " & objProp.Name & " : " & objProp.Value
       end if
      end if
   next
   WScript.Echo ""
next
```

Searching with WQL

So far we've shown how to instantiate specific objects, such as a logical drive, and also how to enumerate all the objects of a particular class using the InstancesOf method. Knowing how to do both of these functions will take us a long way with WMI, but we are missing one other important capability: the ability to find objects that meet certain criteria.

The creators of WMI found an elegant way to handle this problem. They implemented a subset of the Structured Query Language (SQL) known as the WMI Query Language (WQL). WQL greatly increases the power of WMI by giving the programmer ultimate control over locating objects.

With WQL, we can even perform the same function as the InstancesOf method we used earlier. The following query will retrieve all the Win32_LogicalDisk objects on the system:

```
"select * from Win32_LogicalDisk"
```

We can use any property available on Win32_LogicalDisk objects as criteria in our search. As an example, lets say we wanted to find all NTFS logical disks that have less than 100 MB of available space. The query would look like the following:

```
select * from Win32_LogicalDisk
where FreeSpace < 104857600
and    filesystem = 'NTFS'
```

Pretty easy, right? Now let's put WQL to use. We first need to get a WMI object to the namespace we want to query. After we've done that, we can call the ExecQuery method on that object and pass the WQL query to use. The next example uses the "less than 100 MB" query we just described to print out all logical disks on the local computer that match that criterion:

```
strComputer = "."
Set objWMI = GetObject("winmgmts:\\" & strComputer & "\root\cimv2")
Set objDisks = objWMI.ExecQuery _
            ("select * from Win32_LogicalDisk " & _
             "where FreeSpace < 104857600 " & _
             "and filesystem = 'NTFS' ")
For each objDisk in objDisks
    Wscript.Echo "DeviceID: " & objDisk.DeviceID
    Wscript.Echo "Description: " & objDisk.Description
```

```
        Wscript.Echo "FileSystem: " & objDisk.FileSystem
        Wscript.Echo "FreeSpace: " & objDisk.FreeSpace
    Next
```

Authentication with WMI

So far, the examples we've shown assume that the caller of the script has the necessary rights to access the WMI information on the target machine. In most cases in which you are trying to automate a task, that may not be the case. Luckily, using alternate credentials in WMI is very straightforward.

Previously, to connect to a WMI namespace, we would have used the following:

```
strComputer = "dc1"
Set objWMI = GetObject("winmgmts:\\" & strComputer & "\root\cimv2")
```

But let's say that the person calling the script does not have any privileges on the *dc1* computer. We must now use the following:

```
strComputer = "dc1.mycorp.com"
strUserName = "administrator"
strPassword = "password"

Set objLocator = CreateObject("WbemScripting.SWbemLocator")
Set objWMI = objLocator.ConnectServer(strComputer, "root\cimv2", _
                                      strUserName, strPassword)
```

We've replaced the single call to GetObject with a call to CreateObject to instantiate a WbemScripting.SWbemLocator object. The SWbemLocator object has a method called ConnectServer, which allows us to specify the target machine, username, and password to authenticate with. You can then use the object returned from ConnectServer to get the instances of a class, perform a WQL search, or any other function.

This was quick introduction to WMI scripting. We will be covering additional tasks, such as invoking an action or modifying properties of an object, as we walk through specific examples later in the chapter.

WMI Tools

There are several tools available to query and browse WMI information. These tools can be very useful in situations in which you want to access WMI information but do not want to write a script to do it.

WMI from a Command line

The WMI command-line tool (WMIC) is a powerful tool that can expose virtually any WMI information you want to access. It is available in Windows XP and Windows Server 2003. Unfortunately, WMIC does not run on Windows 2000, but it can still be used to query WMI on a Windows 2000 machine.

WMIC maps certain WMI classes to "aliases." Aliases are used as shorthand so that you only need to type "logicaldisk" instead of "Win32_LogicalDisk". An easy way to get started with WMIC is to type the alias name of the class you are interested in. A list of all the objects that match that alias/class will be listed.

```
wmic:root\cli>logicaldisk list brief
DeviceID  DriveType  FreeSpace      ProviderName  Size           VolumeName
A:        2
C:        3          1540900864                   4296498688     W2K
D:        3          15499956224                  15568003072
Z:        5          0                            576038912      NR1EFRE_EN
```

Most aliases have a `list brief` subcommand that will display a subset of the properties for each object. You can run similar queries for services, CPUs, processes, and so on. For a complete list of the aliases, type `alias` at the WMIC prompt.

The creators of WMIC didn't stop with simple lists. You can also utilize WQL to do more complex queries. This next example displays all logical disks with a drivetype of 3 (local hard drive):

```
wmic:root\cli>logicaldisk where (drivetype = '3') list brief
DeviceID  DriveType  FreeSpace      ProviderName  Size           VolumeName
C:        3          1540806144                   4296498688     W2K
D:        3          15499956224                  15568003072
```

We have just touched the surface of the capabilities of WMIC. You can invoke actions, such as creating or killing a process or service, and modify WMI data through WMIC as well. For more information, check out the Support WebCast "WMIC: A New Approach to Managing Windows Infrastructure from a Command Line," available at *http://support.microsoft.com/default.aspx?scid=/webcasts/*. Help information is also available on Windows XP and Windows Server 2003 computers by going to Start → Help, and search on WMIC.

WMI from the Web

Included as sample applications with the original WMI SDK, the WMI CIM Studio and WMI Object browser are web-based applications that provide much more benefit than just being example applications provided in the SDK. The following is a list of the tools and their purpose:

- The WMI CIM Studio is a generic WMI management tool that allows you to browse namespaces, instantiate objects, view the instances of a class, run methods, edit properties, and even perform WQL queries.

- The WMI Object Browser allows you to view the properties for a specific object, look at the class hierarchy, view any associations, run methods, and edit properties for an object.

- The WMI Event Registration allows you to create, view, and configure event consumers.

- The WMI Event Viewer displays events of configured event consumers.

The web-based WMI tools can be obtained separately from the WMI SDK at: *http://www.microsoft.com/downloads/details.aspx?displaylang=en&FamilyID=6430F853-1120-48DB-8CC5-F2ABDC3ED314.*

WMI SDK

The WMI SDK provides the complete WMI reference documentation along with numerous sample scripts and programs. It also includes the web-based WMI tools described in the previous section. The WMI SDK can be downloaded from the Platform SDK site located at *http://www.microsoft.com/msdownload/platformsdk/sdkupdate/default.htm.*

Manipulating Services

Querying services is simple to do with WMI. The Win32_Service class is the WMI representation of a service. The Win32_Service class contains a lot of property methods that provide information about the service; the most useful ones have been listed in Table 26-2.

Table 26-2. Useful Win32_Service properties

Property	Description
AcceptPause	Returns a Boolean indicating whether the service can be paused.
AcceptStop	Returns a Boolean indicating whether the service can be stopped.
Description	Description of the service.
DisplayName	Display name of the service.
Name	Unique string identifier for the service.
PathName	Fully qualified path to the service executable.
Started	Boolean indicating whether the service has been started.
StartMode	String specifying the start mode of the service. Will be one of Automatic, Manual, or Disabled.
StartName	Account under which the service runs.
State	Current state of the service. Will be one of Stopped, Start Pending, Stop Pending, Running, Continue Pending, Pause Pending, Paused, or Unknown.

The following script retrieves all the running services on a machine. All we need to do is use a WQL query that finds all Win32_Service objects that have a state of "Running":

```
strComputer = "."

Set objWMI = GetObject("winmgmts:\\" & strComputer & "\root\cimv2")
Set objServices = objWMI.ExecQuery _
         ("SELECT * FROM Win32_Service WHERE State = 'Running'")
For Each objService in objServices
```

```
    Wscript.Echo objService.DisplayName
    Wscript.Echo " Name: " & objService.Name
    Wscript.Echo " PathName: " & objService.PathName
    Wscript.Echo " Started: " & objService.Started
    Wscript.Echo " StartMode: " & objService.StartMode
    Wscript.Echo " StartName: " & objService.StartName
    Wscript.Echo " State: " & objService.State
    Wscript.Echo ""
next
```

Before you can start to manipulate the status of a service, you have to be able to find any dependent services. A dependent service requires the parent service to be running while it is running. If you try to stop the parent service without first stopping all dependent services, you will get an error. The following example shows how to find all dependent services for the IIS Admin service:

```
strService  = "IISADMIN"
strComputer = "."

Set objWMI = GetObject("winmgmts:\\" & strComputer & "\root\cimv2")
Set objServiceList = objWMI.ExecQuery( _
            "Associators of {Win32_Service.Name='" & strService & "'} " & _
            "Where AssocClass=Win32_DependentServiceRole=Antecedent" )
WScript.Echo "List of dependent services for " & strService & ":"
For each objService in objServiceList
    WScript.Echo " " & objService.DisplayName
Next
```

You may have noticed the WQL query in this example is a little different than the ones we've used so far. We used something called the Associators for a class. One of the fundamental concepts within WMI is class association, which allows you to perform queries to retrieve objects that have dependencies or associations to a given object. Associators come into play in lot of situations, but a great example of them is with service dependencies. Some services are dependent on others in order to run. Using the Associators of clause within a WQL query allows you to find each dependent service.

Now that we can get a list of a service's dependent services, we can write scripts to stop, start, and restart a service. Table 26-3 lists the useful methods available to the Win32_Service class.

Table 26-3. Useful Win32_Service methods

Property	Description
ChangeStartMode	Changes the start mode for the service. Pass in Automatic, Manual, or Disabled.
PauseService	Pause a service.
ResumeService	Resume a service.
StartService	Start a service.
StopService	Stop a service.

Example 26-1 shows how to restart a service. Since there is no `RestartService` method available in WMI, you have to simulate a restart by stopping all dependent services, stopping the target service, then starting the target service and any dependent services.

Example 26-1. Using Win32_Service methods to simulate a RestartService method

```
strService  = "IISADMIN"
strComputer = "."

WScript.Echo "Restarting " & strService & "..."

' Stop dependent services
Set objWMI = GetObject("winmgmts:\\" & strComputer & "\root\cimv2")
Set objServiceList = objWMI.ExecQuery("Associators of " _
                & "{Win32_Service.Name='" & strService & "'} Where " _
                & "AssocClass=Win32_DependentService " & "Role=Antecedent" )
for each objService in objServiceList
    WScript.Echo " Stopping " & objService.Name
    objService.StopService( )
next
Wscript.Sleep 10000

' Stop target service
Set objService = objWMI.Get("Win32_Service.Name='" & strService & "'")
WScript.Echo " Stopping " & objService.Name
objService.StopService( )
Wscript.Sleep 10000

' Start target service
Set objService = objWMI.Get("Win32_Service.Name='" & strService & "'")
WScript.Echo " Starting " & objService.Name
objService.StartService( )
Wscript.Sleep 10000

' Start dependent services
Set objServiceList = objWMI.ExecQuery("Associators of " _
                & "{Win32_Service.Name='" & strService & "'} Where " _
                & "AssocClass=Win32_DependentService " & "Role=Antecedent" )
for each objService in objServiceList
    WScript.Echo " Starting " & objService.Name
    objService.StartService( )
next
```

Querying the Event Logs

The Event Logs are typically a system administrator's first line of inquiry when trying to troubleshoot problems. Since they are so important, it is also important to see how we can make use of them with WMI. The two major components that we need to be concerned with are the Event Logs themselves and the events contained within each Event Log. We will first focus on properties of Event Logs.

The `Win32_NTEventLogFile` class represents an Event Log. Table 26-4 contains several `Win32_NTEventLogFile` properties that can be used to query or modify properties of a Event Log.

Table 26-4. Useful Win32_NTEventLogFile properties

Property	Description
FileSize	Size of the Event Log file in bytes.
LogFileName	Standard name used for describing the Event Log (e.g., Application).
MaxFileSize	Max size in bytes that the Event Log file can reach. This is a writeable property.
Name	Fully qualified path to the Event Log file.
NumberOfRecords	Total number of records in the Event Log.
OverwriteOutDated	Number of days after which events can be overwritten. This is a writeable property with 0 indicating to overwrite events as needed, 1-365 being the number of days to wait before overwriting, and 4294967295 indicating that events should never be overwritten.
OverwritePolicy	Text description of the overwrite policy (as specified by the OverwriteOutDated property). Can be one of WhenNeeded, OutDated, or Never.
Sources	Array of registered sources that may write entries to the Event Log.

Let's look at an example that displays all of the properties listed in Table 26-4 for each Event Log and sets the `MaxFileSize` and `OverwriteOutDated` properties if they have not already been set to the correct values. Since we want to iterate over all Event Logs, we will pass `Win32_NTEventLogFile` to the `InstancesOf` method. Example 26-2 shows how to accomplish this.

Example 26-2. Displaying properties of the Event Log using Win32_NTEventLogFile

```
strComputer = "."
intMaxFileSize = 10 * 1024 * 1024    ' << 10MB
intOverwriteOutDated = 180           ' << 6 months

Set objWMI = GetObject("winmgmts:\\" & strComputer & "\root\cimv2")
Set objELF = objWMI.InstancesOf("Win32_NTEventLogFile")
' Iterate over each Event Log
for each objEL in objELF
   WScript.Echo objEL.LogFileName & " Log:"
   WScript.Echo " FileSize: " & objEL.FileSize

   ' If the size has not been set yet, set it
   if objEL.MaxFileSize <> intMaxFileSize then
      WScript.Echo " ** Setting MaxFileSize: " & intMaxFileSize & " (new) " & _
                   objEL.MaxFileSize & " (current)"
      objEL.MaxFileSize = intMaxFileSize
      objEL.Put_
   else
      WScript.Echo " MaxFileSize: " & objEL.MaxFileSize
   end if
```

```
WScript.Echo " Name: " & objEL.Name
WScript.Echo " NumberOfRecords: " & objEL.NumberOfRecords

' If the overwrite date has not been set, set it
WScript.Echo " OverwritePolicy: " & objEL.OverwritePolicy
if objEL.OverwriteOutDated <> intOverwriteOutDated then
    WScript.Echo " ** Setting OverwriteOutDated: " & _
                intOverwriteOutDated & " (new) " & _
                objEL.OverwriteOutDated & " (current)"
    objEL.OverwriteOutDated = intOverwriteOutdated
    objEL.Put_
else
    WScript.Echo " OverwriteOutDated: " & objEL.OverwriteOutDated
end if

    WScript.Echo ""
next
```

Note that for the `MaxFileSize` and `OverwriteOutDated` properties, we set them only if they haven't been set already. To set properties, simply set the property method equal to the new value. To commit the change, you must use the `Put_` method. Using `Put_` is very similar to `SetInfo` in ADSI. WMI implements a caching mechanism very similar to the Property Cache described in Chapter 19. If we did not call `Put_`, the new values would never have been written back to the system.

The Event Logs contain a wealth of information about the health and status of the system and hosted applications. With WMI, system administrators can write simple to complex queries to find specific events in any of the Event Logs. The `Win32_NTLogEvent` class represents individual event entries in an Event Log. Table 26-5 contains several useful properties that are available for `Win32_NTLogEvent` objects.

Table 26-5. Useful Win32_NTLogEvent properties

Property	Description
CategoryString	Category name if present.
EventCode	The event number (or id) for the event.
EventType	Numeric value representing severity of the event. See Type for the string version.
LogFile	Event Log name the event is contained in. LogFile and RecordNumber are used as keys to uniquely identify an event.
Message	Event message text.
RecordNumber	The number associated with the event. RecordNumber is unique within an Event Log.
SourceName	Name of source that generated the error.
Type	String representing the severity of the event. Will be one of Error, Warning, Informational, Security audit success, or Security audit failure.
User	User that was logged on when event was generated.

In the next example, we will retrieve all events that match certain criteria. Let's say that we want to find all Information events in the System Event Log that have an event code of 5778 and were generated after November 1, 2002. The WQL for this query works out to be:

```
Select * from Win32_NTLogEvent
  Where Type = 'Information'
  And Logfile = 'System'
  and EventCode = 5778
  and TimeGenerated > '2002/11/01'
```

Once we have the WQL query, the rest of the code is very similar to many of the previous examples.

```
strComputer = "."

Set objWMI = GetObject("winmgmts:\\" & strComputer & "\root\cimv2")
Set objEvents = objWMI.ExecQuery _
        ("Select * from Win32_NTLogEvent Where Logfile = 'System' " & _
         "and EventCode = 5778 and Type = 'Information' " & _
         "and TimeGenerated > '2002/11/01' ")

WScript.Echo "Total events that match criteria: " & objEvents.Count
for each objEvent in objEvents
    WScript.Echo " CategoryString: " & objEvent.CategoryString
    WScript.Echo " EventType: " & objEvent.EventType
    WScript.Echo " LogFile: " & objEvent.LogFile
    WScript.Echo " Message: " & objEvent.Message
    WScript.Echo " RecordNumber: " & objEvent.RecordNumber
    WScript.Echo " SourceName: " & objEvent.SourceName
    WScript.Echo " TimeGenerated: " & objEvent.TimeGenerated
    WScript.Echo " Type: " & objEvent.Type
    WScript.Echo " User: " & objEvent.User
    WScript.Echo ""
next
```

Querying AD with WMI

Up to now, we've shown how WMI can be a powerful resource to aid in managing components of individual computers. You may be wondering what impact WMI will have on Active Directory? It can, in fact, play as big a role in automating the management of Active Directory as you want. Also, over time, WMI's importance with respect to monitoring Active Directory will continue to grow as Microsoft develops new providers.

First we are going to review how you can use WMI and the Active Directory provider to access and query objects in Active Directory. We will then cover some specific WMI providers that Microsoft has made available in Windows Server 2003; these providers help you monitor certain aspects of Active Directory, such as trusts and replication. In the next chapter, we will cover the WMI DNS provider and how you can manage Microsoft DNS servers with it. To start with, let's look at the Active Directory provider.

The Active Directory provider uses the root\directory\ldap namespace. Within that namespace, every Active Directory schema class and attribute is mapped to corresponding WMI classes or properties. Each abstract class (e.g., top) is mapped to a WMI class with "ds_" prefixed on the name. Each nonabstract class (e.g., structural and auxiliary) is mapped to two classes. One has "ads_" prefixed, and the other has "ds_" prefixed. The "ads_" classes conform to the class hierarchy defined by the subClassOf attribute for each class. The "ds_" classes for nonabstract (e.g., structural) classes are descendants of their cooresponding "ads_" class. Perhaps an example would help illustrate this hierarchy:

```
ds_top
    ads_person
        ads_organizationalperson
            ads_user
                ads_computer
                    ds_computer
```

In this example, we showed the class hierarchy for the Active Directory "computer" object class as it is mapped to WMI. The attribute mappings are more straightforward. Each Active Directory attribute has a corresponding property in WMI with "ds_" prefixed. So the description attribute would map to the ds_description property in WMI. An additional property was added called ADSIPath, which is the ADsPath, and is the key for each Active Directory object in WMI. We highly recommend installing and using the WMI CIM Studio to browse the root\directory\ldap namespace. The organization of classes and objects will become apparent.

We can use the techniques shown so far to query and manipulate Active Directory objects. We can retrieve all the instances of a particular Active Directory class (via InstancesOf) or perform WQL query based on certain criteria. In the following example, we search for all user objects that have a last name equal to "Allen".

```
strComputer = "."

Set objWMI = GetObject("winmgmts:\\" & strComputer & "\root\directory\LDAP")
Set objUsers = objWMI.ExecQuery("SELECT * FROM ds_user where ds_sn = 'Allen' ")

if objUsers.Count = 0 then
    Wscript.Echo "No matching objects found"
else
    for each objUser in objUsers
        WScript.Echo "First Name: " & objUser.ds_givenName
        WScript.Echo "Last Name: " & objUser.ds_sn
        WScript.Echo ""
    next
end if
```

Since WMI is typically used to manage computers, we can leverage Active Directory as a repository of computer objects and perform certain functions on a set of computers that match our criteria. In the next code sample, we do a WQL query for all computers that are running "Windows Server 2003", connect to each one, and print the date each machine was last rebooted.

```
on error resume next

strComputer = "."

Set objWMI = GetObject("winmgmts:\\" & strComputer & "\root\directory\LDAP")
Set objComps = objWMI.ExecQuery("SELECT * FROM ds_computer " & _
                            "where ds_OperatingSystem = 'Windows Server 2003' ")

if objComps.Count = 0 then
    Wscript.Echo "No matching objects found"
else
    for each objComp in objComps
        WScript.Echo objComp.ds_name
        Set objRemoteWMI = GetObject("winmgmts:\\" & objComp.ds_name & "\root\cimv2")
        if Err <> 0 then
            WScript.Echo "  Could not connect"
            Err.Clear
        else
            ' Perform whatever functions necessary on objRemoteWMI
            Set objOSes = objRemoteWMI.InstancesOf("Win32_OperatingSystem")

            for each objOS in objOSes
                strTime = objOS.LastBootUpTime
                strYear = Left(strTime, 4)
                strMon = Mid(strTime, 5, 2)
                strDay = Mid(strTime, 7, 2)

                WScript.Echo "  Last Reboot: " & strYear & "/" & strMon & "/" & strDay
            next
        end if
        WScript.Echo ""

        Set objRemoteWMI = Nothing
    next
end if
```

In the code, we retrieve each matching computer object and then construct a WMI moniker to connect to that machine. From there, we enumerate the Win32_ OperatingSystem object and print out the LastBootUpTime property. Note that we could perform essentially any function we want, including querying disks and the event log, modifying the registry, and so on. Also, we could instantiate a WbemScripting.SWbemLocator object if we need to log on to the computers with alternate credentials other than those the script is running under.

Monitoring Trusts

New to Windows Server 2003 is the Trustmon WMI provider. The Trustmon provider allows you to query the list of trusts supported on a domain controller and determine if they are working correctly. The Trustmon provider consists of three classes, but the primary one is the `Microsoft_DomainTrustStatus` class, which represents each trust the domain controller knows about. The Trustmon provider is contained under the root\MicrosoftActiveDirectory namespace. Note that this namespace is different than for the Active Directory provider, which is contained under root\directory\ldap.

Table 26-6 provides a list of the property methods available to this class.

Table 26-6. Microsoft_DomainTrustStatus properties

Property	Description
Flatname	NetBIOS name for the domain.
SID	SID for the domain.
TrustAttributes	Flag indicating special properties of the trust. Can be any combination of the following: • 0x1 (Nontransitive) • 0x2 (Uplevel clients only) • 0x40000 (Tree parent) • 0x80000 (Tree root)
TrustDCName	Name of the domain controller the trust is set up with.
TrustDirection	Integer representing direction of the trust. Valid values include: • 1 (Inbound) • 2 (Outbound) • 3 (Bidirectional)
TrustedDomain	Naming of trusted domain.
TrustIsOK	Boolean indicating whether the trust is functioning properly.
TrustStatus	Integer representing the status for the trust. 0 indicates no failure.
TrustStatusString	Textual description of status for the trust.
TrustType	Integer representing the type of trust. Valid values include: • 1 (Downlevel) • 2 (Uplevel) • 3 (Kerberos realm) • 4 (DCE)

As you can see from Table 26-6, the `Microsoft_DomainTrustStatus` class provides just about all the information you'd want to know concerning a trust. The following example shows how easy it is to enumerate all the trusts using this class:

```
strComputer = "."

Set objWMI = GetObject("winmgmts:\\" & strComputer & _
                        "\root\MicrosoftActiveDirectory")
Set objTrusts = objWMI.ExecQuery("Select * from Microsoft_DomainTrustStatus")

for each objTrust in objTrusts
    Wscript.Echo objTrust.TrustedDomain
    Wscript.Echo " TrustedAttributes: " & objTrust.TrustAttributes
    Wscript.Echo " TrustedDCName: "     & objTrust.TrustedDCName
    Wscript.Echo " TrustedDirection: "  & objTrust.TrustDirection
    Wscript.Echo " TrustIsOk: "         & objTrust.TrustIsOK
    Wscript.Echo " TrustStatus: "       & objTrust.TrustStatus
    Wscript.Echo " TrustStatusString: " & objTrust.TrustStatusString
    Wscript.Echo " TrustType: "         & objTrust.TrustType
    Wscript.Echo ""
next
```

Next, let's illustrate a script that finds any trust that has some kind of failure. All we need to do is modify the WQL query in the previous example to include a where TrustIsOk = False clause. We then print out the TrustStatusString property, which will return a description of the failure.

```
strComputer = "."

Set objWMI = GetObject("winmgmts:\\" & strComputer & _
                        "\root\MicrosoftActiveDirectory")
Set objTrusts = objWMI.ExecQuery("Select * from Microsoft_DomainTrustStatus " & _
                                 "where TrustIsOk = False ")

if objTrusts.Count = 0 then
    Wscript.Echo "There are no trust failures"
else
    for each objTrust in objTrusts
        Wscript.Echo objTrust.TrustedDomain & " - " & objTrust.TrustStatusString
        Wscript.Echo ""
    Next
end if
```

One of the neat features of the Trustmon provider is that it is configurable. Through WMI you can modify what type of checks it does to determine trust failures and also how long to cache information it retrieves. All of this is done with the Microsoft_TrustProvider class. Table 26-7 contains a list of all property methods for this class.

Table 26-7. Microsoft_TrustProvider properties

Property	Description
TrustListLifetime	Number of minutes to cache the last trust enumeration (20 is the default).
TrustStatusLifetime	Number of minutes to cache the last trust status request (3 is the default).

Table 26-7. Microsoft_TrustProvider properties (continued)

Property	Description
TrustCheckLevel	Number representing the type of check to perform against each trust during enumeration (2 is the default). Valid values include: • 0 (Enumerate only) • 1 (Enumerate with SC_QUERY) • 2 (Enumerate with password check) • 3 (Enumerate with SC_RESET)
ReturnAll	Boolean indicating whether both trusting and trusted domains are enumerated. True is the default, which indicates to check both trusting and trusted domains.

Now we will show a simple script that changes the default settings for the Trustmon provider. In the following example, we set the `TrustListLifetime` to 15 minutes, the `TrustStatusLifetime` to 5 minutes, and the `TrustCheckLevel` to 1.

```
strComputer = "."

Set objTrustProv = GetObject("winmgmts:\\" & strComputer & _
                   "\root\MicrosoftActiveDirectory:Microsoft_TrustProvider=@")

objTrustProv.TrustListLifetime   = 15   ` 15 minutes
objTrustProv.TrustStatusLifetime = 5    ` 5 minutes
objTrustProv.TrustCheckLevel     = 1    ` Enumerate with SC_QUERY
objTrustProv.Put_
```

The Trustmon provider is a great example of how to utilize WMI in the Active Directory space. What previously could only have been done with command-line utilities or MMC snap-ins can now be done programmatically very easily.

Monitoring Replication

The WMI Replication provider is another good example of how Microsoft is leveraging WMI to help with monitoring Active Directory. Like the Trustmon provider, the Replication provider is only available with Windows Server 2003 and is contained under the root\MicrosoftActiveDirectory namespace. It provides classes to list the replication partners for a domain controller, view the supported Naming Contexts for a domain controller, and also see the pending replication operations.

 As of the time of this writing, Microsoft had not published any documentation on the Replication provider. Most of the information contained in this section was observed by one of the authors and is likely not to be the complete story!

Table 26-8 contains some of the more useful properties for the `MSAD_ReplNeighbor` class, which represents a replication partner (or neighbor) for a given domain controller.

Table 26-8. Useful MSAD_ReplNeighbor properties

Property	Description
IsDeletedSourceDsa	Boolean indicating whether the source DC has been deleted.
LastSyncResult	Number representing the result of the last sync operation with this neighbor. A value of 0 indicates success.
NamingContextDN	DN of the Naming Context for which the partners replicate.
NumConsecutiveSyncFailures	Number of consecutive sync failures between the two neighbors.
SourceDsaCN	CN of the replication neighbor.
SourceDsaSite	Site the replication neighbor is in.
TimeOfLastSyncAttempt	Time of the last sync attempt.
TimeOfLastSyncSuccess	Time of last successful sync attempt.

There are actually several property methods available other than what is shown in Table 26-8, so in the following example, we will enumerate all the replication neighbors and print out every property available to the `MSAD_ReplNeighbor` class.

```
strComputer = "."

Set objWMI = GetObject("winmgmts:\\" & strComputer & _
                       "\root\MicrosoftActiveDirectory")
Set objReplNeighbors = objWMI.ExecQuery("Select * from MSAD_ReplNeighbor")

for each objReplNeighbor in objReplNeighbors

    Wscript.Echo objReplNeighbor.SourceDsaCN & "/" & _
                 objReplNeighbor.NamingContextDN & ":"

    for each objProp in objReplNeighbor.Properties_
        if IsNull(objProp.Value) then
            Wscript.Echo " " & objProp.Name & " : NULL"
        else
            wscript.echo " " & objProp.Name & " : " & objProp.Value
        end if
    next

    Wscript.echo ""
next
```

Now that we can find all of the replication neighbors for a given domain controller, we will take a look at any outstanding replication operations. The `MSAD_ReplPendingOp` class represents a pending replication operation. The class has several property methods, and some of the more useful ones are listed in Table 26-9.

Table 26-9. Useful MSAD_ReplPendingOp properties

Property	Description
DsaDN	DN of replication neighbor.
NamingContextDN	DN of Naming Context that holds the object being sync'd.

Table 26-9. Useful MSAD_ReplPendingOp properties (continued)

Property	Description
PositionInQ	Number representing the position in the replication queue.
TimeEnqueued	Date representing when operation was put in the queue.

The next example is not much different from most of our others. We simply query all `MSAD_ReplPendingOp` objects for a particular host. If zero are returned, that signifies there are no pending replication operations on the host.

```
strComputer = "."

Set objWMI = GetObject("winmgmts:\\" & strComputer & _
                       "\root\MicrosoftActiveDirectory")
Set objRepOps = objWMI.ExecQuery("Select * from MSAD_ReplPendingOp")

if objRepOps.Count = 0 then
    Wscript.Echo "There are no pending replication operations"
else
    for each objRepOp in objRepOps
        Wscript.Echo objRepOp.DsaDN
        Wscript.Echo objRepOp.NamingContextDN
        Wscript.Echo objRepOp.PositionInQ
        Wscript.Echo objRepOp.TimeEnqueued
    next
end if
```

Summary

In this chapter we gave a quick introduction into the WMI architecture and the concepts behind it. We then covered some of the tools available for querying and modifying WMI data. Next we went through several examples for querying and manipulating services and the Event Logs. The last part of the chapter covered the WMI hooks into Active Directory, including the WMI providers for Trustmon and Replication monitoring.

In the next chapter we will put our WMI knowledge to use as we work with the WMI DNS Provider. We will use WMI to configure Microsoft DNS server settings programmatically and manipulate zones and resource records.

CHAPTER 27

Manipulating DNS

DNS is a core technology of Active Directory that cannot be overlooked. While features such as Active Directory Integrated DNS can take a lot of the hassle of managing DNS servers and zones out of your hands, you still have to set up the initial zone configurations. Unfortunately, lack of a good DNS API has always been a big gap for managing a Microsoft DNS server environment. The only way to automate maintenance and management of Microsoft DNS has been by executing Dnscmd commands from within a batch, VBScript, or Perl script. Over time, Microsoft has continued to improve Dnscmd, and as of Windows 2000, it provides just about every option you need to manage DNS server configuration, zones, and resource records using a command line. In Windows Server 2003, it even allows you to manage Application Partitions! Microsoft also provides the DNS MMC snap-in for those that want to manage DNS via a GUI, although it is not very suitable for managing large environments.

Microsoft's answer to the DNS API issue is WMI. As explained in the Chapter 26, WMI is Microsoft's API of choice for managing and monitoring systems and services. With the WMI DNS provider, you have complete programmatic control over a Microsoft DNS environment, much as you do with Dnscmd from a command line.

In this chapter, we will cover the WMI DNS provider at length, including the properties and methods available for the primary WMI DNS classes. Several sample scripts will be shown, which will give you a head start on developing scripts to manage your own DNS environment.

DNS Provider Overview

The WMI DNS provider was first released as part of the Windows 2000 Resource Kit Supplement 1, but unfortunately it was not ready for prime time. That version was buggy, did not include all the documented features, and in several cases behaved differently than what the documentation described. Also, since the DNS provider was included as part of a Resource Kit, it was not fully supported by Microsoft, which means that if you encountered problems, you were largely on your own. That said, much of the functionality you probably need is present in the Windows 2000 version, so it may be suitable. You can download the Windows 2000 DNS provider separately from the Resource Kit via FTP from the following location: *ftp://ftp.microsoft.com/reskit/win2000/dnsprov.zip*

With Windows Server 2003, the DNS provider is fully functional and supported. It is installed automatically whenever you install the DNS Server service. You can also install it separately as described in the next section. This may be necessary when doing development with the provider on a machine that does not have the DNS Server installed.

 For our purposes, all sample code has been tested using the Windows Server 2003 DNS provider.

Installing the DNS Provider

You do not need to manually install the provider if you are installing the DNS Server service on a Windows Server 2003 server because it gets installed with the service.

If you downloaded the DNS provider files for Windows 2000 (*dnsschema.mof* and *dnsprov.dll*), you will first need to copy them to the *%SystemRoot%\System32\wbem* directory. Next, you'll need to compile the DNS managed object format (MOF) file by executing mofcomp *filename* from a command line. With Windows 2000, the DNS MOF file is named *dnsschema.mof*, and with Windows Server 2003 it is called *dnsprov.mof*. The output of the command should look like the following:

```
C:\WINDOWS\system32\wbem>mofcomp dnsprov.mof
Microsoft (R) 32-bit MOF Compiler Version 5.2.3628.0
Copyright (c) Microsoft Corp. 1997-2001. All rights reserved.
Parsing MOF file: dnsprov.mof
MOF file has been successfully parsed
Storing data in the repository...
Done!
```

The last step is to register the DNS provider DLL by executing *regsvr32 dnsprov.dll* from a command line. You should see a dialog box with the following:

```
DllRegisterServer in dnsprov.dll succeeded.
```

At this point you will be able to use the DNS provider from your scripts.

Managing DNS with the DNS Provider

The three main areas of interest when it comes to managing DNS include server configuration, zone management, and creation and deletion of resource records. The DNS provider has several classes to manipulate each of these components. With the MicrosoftDNS_Server class, you can manipulate server configuration settings, start and stop the DNS service, and initiate scavenging. The MicrosoftDNS_Zone class allows you to create, delete, and modify zone configuration. The `MicrosoftDNS_ResourceRecord` class and child classes provide methods for manipulating the various resource record types. Each of these will be explained in more detail in the next few sections.

Several additional classes are also supported by the DNS provider to manage other aspects of DNS, including the root hints (`MicrosoftDNS_RootHints`), DNS cache (`MicrosoftDNS_Cache`), and server statistics (`MicrosoftDNS_Statistics`). For more information on these classes, including sample scripts in VBScript and Perl, check out the following section in the MSDN Library (*http://msdn.microsoft.com/library/*): Networking and Directory Services → Network Protocols → Domain Name System → SDK Documentation → DNS WMI Provider

Manipulating DNS Server Configuration

There are close to 50 different settings that can be configured on a Microsoft DNS server. They range from default scavenging and logging settings to settings that customize the DNS server behavior, such as how zone transfers will be sent to secondaries and whether to round-robin multiple A record responses.

The DNS provider is mapped to the root\MicrosoftDNS namespace. A DNS server is represented by an instance of a `MicrosoftDNS_Server` class, which is derived from the `CIM_Service` class. Table 27-1 contains all the property methods available in the `MicrosoftDNS_Server` class.

Table 27-1. MicrosoftDNS_Server class properties

Property name	Property description
AddressAnswerLimit	Max number of records to return for address requests (e.g., A records).
AllowUpdate	Determines whether DDNS updates are allowed.
AutoConfigFileZones	Indicates which standard primary zones that are authoritative for the name of the DNS server must be updated when the name server changes.
AutoCacheUpdate	Indicates whether the DNS server will dynamically attempt to update its root hints (also known as cache) file.
BindSecondaries	Determines the format zone transfers (AXFR) will be sent as to non-Microsoft DNS servers.
BootMethod	Determines where the server will read its zone information.
DefaultAgingState	For AD-integrated zones, the default scavenging interval in hours.
DefaultNoRefreshInterval	For AD-integrated zones, the default no-refresh interval in hours.
DefaultRefreshInterval	For AD-integrated zones, the default refresh interval in hours.
DisableAutoReverseZones	Determines whether the server automatically creates reverse zones.
DisjointsNets	Indicates whether the default port binding for a socket used to send queries to remote DNS servers can be overridden.
DsAvailable	Indicates whether Active Directory is available on the server.
DsPollingInterval	For AD-integrated zones, the interval in seconds to poll Active Directory for updates.

Table 27-1. MicrosoftDNS_Server class properties (continued)

Property name	Property description
DsTombstoneInterval	For AD-integrated zones, the length of time in seconds that tombstoned records (i.e. deleted) should remain in Active Directory.
EdnsCacheTimeout	Length of time, in seconds, the cached EDNS version information is cached.
EnableDirectoryPartition-Support	Flag indicating whether application partition support has been enabled.
EnableEDnsProbes	When TRUE, the DNS server always responds with OPT resource records according to RFC 2671, unless the remote server has indicated it does not support EDNS in a prior exchange. If FALSE, the DNS server responds to queries with OPTs only if OPTs are sent in the original query.
EnableDnsSec	Flag indicating whether DNSSEC resource records are returned if queried.
EventLogLevel	Determines the type of events (e.g., errors or warnings) that will be logged to the DNS Event Log.
Forwarders	List of IPs the server forwards queries to.
ForwardDelegations	Determines whether queries to delegated subzones are forwarded.
ForwardingTimeout	Time in seconds to wait for a response from a forwarded query.
IsSlave	Indicates whether the DNS server is a slave.
ListenAddresses	List of addresses the DNS server can receive queries on.
LocalNetPriority	If TRUE, records for IPs on the same net are given a higher priority.
LogFileMaxSize	Max size in bytes of the DNS server log.
LogFilePath	Filename and path to DNS server log.
LogIPFilterList	List of IPs used to filter entries written to the DNS server log.
LogLevel	Determines what events should be written to the system log.
LooseWildcarding	Indicates whether the server supports wildcarding (e.g., * MX records).
MaxCacheTTL	Max time in seconds to leave a recursive query in the local cache.
MaxNegativeCacheTTL	Max time in seconds to leave a recursive query that resulted in an error in the local cache.
Name	FQDN or IP of server.
NameCheckFlag	Indicates the set of eligible characters to be used in DNS names.
NoRecursion	Flag indicating whether the server will perform recursive lookups.
RecursionRetry	Time in seconds before retrying a recursive lookup.
RecursionTimeout	Time in seconds before the DNS server gives up recursive query.
RoundRobin	Flag indicating whether the server will round-robin addresses returned from a query that returns multiple A records.
RpcProtocol	Protocol to run administrative RPC over.
ScavengingInterval	Interval in hours between initiating scavenges.
SecureResponses	Indicates whether the DNS server exclusively saves records of names in the same subtree as the server that provided them.
SendPort	Port on which the DNS server sends UDP queries to other servers.
ServerAddresses	List of IP addresses for the server.
StrictFileParsing	Indicates whether the DNS server parses zone file strictly, which means if bad data is encountered, the zone will fail to load.

Table 27-1. MicrosoftDNS_Server class properties (continued)

Property name	Property description
UpdateOptions	Flag that restricts the type of records that can be updated via DDNS.
Version	DNS server version
WriteAuthorityNS	Flag indicating whether the server includes NS and SOA records in the authority section on successful response.
XfrConnectTimeout	Number of seconds server waits for a successful TCP connection to a remote server when attempting a zone transfer.

The MicrosoftDNS_Server class also provides a few methods to initiate certain actions on the DNS server. Perhaps two of the most useful are StartService and StopService, which allow you to start and stop the DNS service. Table 27-2 contains the list of methods available to the MicrosoftDNS_Server class

Table 27-2. MicrosoftDNS_Server class methods

Method name	Method description
GetDistinguishedName	For AD-integrated zones, gets the DN of the zone.
StartScavenging	Start the scavenging process for zones that have scavenging enabled.
StartService	Start the DNS service.
StopService	Stop the DNS service.

Listing a DNS Server's Properties

The first step in programmatically managing your DNS server configuration is to see what settings you currently have and determine whether any need to be modified. With WMI, it is really easy to list all properties for the server. The following example shows how to do it:

```
Set objDNS = GetObject("winMgmts:root\MicrosoftDNS")
set objDNSServer = objDNS.Get("MicrosoftDNS_Server.Name=""."""")

Wscript.Echo objDNSServer.Properties_.Item("Name") & ":"
for each objProp in objDNSServer.Properties_
   if IsNull(objProp.Value) then
      Wscript.Echo " " & objProp.Name & " : NULL"
   else
      if objProp.IsArray = TRUE then
         For I = LBound(objProp.Value) to UBound(objProp.Value)
             wscript.echo " " & objProp.Name & " : " & objProp.Value(I)
         next
      else
         wscript.echo " " & objProp.Name & " : " & objProp.Value
      end if
   end if
next
```

After getting a WMI object for the DNS provider (root\MicrosoftDNS), we get a MicrosoftDNS_Server object by looking for the "." instance. Since there can only be one instance of MicrosoftDNS_Server running on any given computer, we do not need to worry about multiple objects. After getting a MicrosoftDNS_Server object, we iterate through all the properties of the object and print each one out. Note that we have added special checks for values that contain arrays to print each element of the array. In that case, we use Lbound and Ubound to iterate over all the values for the array.

Configuring a DNS server

Now that we can see what values have been set on our DNS server, we may want to change some of them. To do so is very straightforward. We simply need to set the property method (e.g., EventLogLevel) to the correct value. This example shows how it can be done:

```
on error resume next

Set objDNS = GetObject("winMgmts:root\MicrosoftDNS")
set objDNSServer = objDNS.Get("MicrosoftDNS_Server.Name=""."""")

Wscript.Echo objDNSServer.Name & ":"
objDNSServer.EventLogLevel = 4
objDNSServer.LooseWildcarding = True
objDNSServer.MaxCacheTTL = 900
objDNSServer.MaxNegativeCacheTTL = 60
objDNSServer.AllowUpdate = 3
objDNSServer.Put_

if Err then
    Wscript.Echo " Error occurred: " & Err.Description
else
    WScript.Echo " Change successful"
end if
```

Note that we had to call Put_ at the end. If we didn't, none of the changes would have been committed.

Restarting the DNS Service

After making changes to DNS settings, you typically will need to restart the DNS service for them to take effect. We can utilize the StopService and StartService methods as shown in the following example to do this:

```
on error resume next

Set objDNS = GetObject("winMgmts:root\MicrosoftDNS")
set objDNSServer = objDNS.Get("MicrosoftDNS_Server.Name=""."""")

objDNSServer.StopService
if Err Then
```

```
    WScript.Echo "StopService failed: " & Err.Description
    Wscript.Quit
end if

objDNSServer.StartService
if Err Then
    WScript.Echo "StartService failed: " & Err.Description
    Wscript.Quit
end if

WScript.Echo "Restart successful"
```

DNS Server Configuration Check Script

Building on the examples we've used so far in this chapter, we can now move forward with writing a robust DNS server configuration check script. A configuration check script can be very important, especially in large environments where you may have many DNS servers. Unless you have a script that routinely checks the configuration on all of your DNS servers, it is very likely that those servers will not have an identical configuration. If this is true, when problems pop up over time, you may end up spending considerably more time troubleshooting because of the discrepancies between the servers.

To accomplish the configuration checking, we will store each setting in a VBScript Dictionary object. For those coming from other languages such as Perl, a Dictionary object is the VBScript analog of a hash or associative array. It is not extremely flexible but works well in situations such as what we need. Another option would be to store the settings in a text file and read them into a Dictionary object when the script starts up. Example 27-1 contains the configuration check code.

Example 27-1. DNS Server configuration check script

```
option explicit
on error resume next

Dim arrServers
Dim strUsername, strPassword
Dim dicDNSConfig

` Array of DNS servers to check
arrServers = Array("dns1.mycorp.com","dns2.mycorp.com")

` User and password that can modify the config on the DNS servers
strUsername = "dnsadmin"
strPassword = "dnspwd"

` This dictionary object will contain the key value pairs for all the settings
` that you want to check and configure  on the DNS servers
Set dicDNSConfig = CreateObject("Scripting.Dictionary")
dicDNSConfig.Add "AllowUpdate",          1
dicDNSConfig.Add "LooseWildCarding",     True
```

Example 27-1. DNS Server configuration check script (continued)

```
dicDNSConfig.Add "MaxCacheTTL",            900
dicDNSConfig.Add "MaxNegativeCacheTTL",    60
dicDNSConfig.Add "EventLogLevel",          0
dicDNSConfig.Add "StrictFileParsing",      True
dicDNSConfig.Add "DisableAutoReverseZones", True

Dim arrDNSConfigKeys
arrDNSConfigKeys = dicDNSConfig.keys

Dim objLocator
Set objLocator = CreateObject("WbemScripting.SWbemLocator")

Dim x, y, boolRestart
For x = LBound(arrServers) to UBound(arrServers)
   boolRestart = False

   WScript.echo arrServers(x)

   Dim objDNS, objDNSServer
   Set objDNS = objLocator.ConnectServer(arrServers(x), "root\MicrosoftDNS", _
                                   strUserName, strPassword)
   set objDNSServer = objDNS.Get("MicrosoftDNS_Server.Name="".""")

   for y = 0 To dicDNSConfig.Count - 1
      Dim strKey
      strKey = arrDNSConfigKeys(y)

      WScript.Echo "  Checking " & strKey
      if dicDNSConfig.Item(strKey) <> objDNSServer.Properties_.Item(strKey) then
         objDNSServer.Properties_.Item(strKey).value = dicDNSConfig(strKey)
         objDNSServer.Put_
         boolRestart = True
         if Err Then
            WScript.Echo "    Error setting " & strKey & " : " & Err.Description
            Wscript.Quit
         else
            WScript.Echo "    " & strKey & " updated"
         end if
      end if
   Next

   if boolRestart then
      objDNSServer.StopService
      if Err Then
         WScript.Echo "StopService failed: " & Err.Description
         Wscript.Quit
      end if

      objDNSServer.StartService
      if Err Then
         WScript.Echo "StartService failed: " & Err.Description
         Wscript.Quit
```

Example 27-1. DNS Server configuration check script (continued)

```
    end if
    WScript.Echo "Restarted"
  end if

  WScript.Echo ""
next
```

Besides the use of the Dictionary object, most of the script is a combination of the other three examples shown so far in this chapter. We added a server array so that you can check multiple servers at once. Then for each server, the script simply checks each key in the Dictionary object to see whether the value for it matches that on the DNS server. If not, it modifies the server and commits the change via Put_. After it's done looping through all the settings, it restarts the DNS service if a change has been made to its configuration. If a change has not been made, it proceeds to the next server.

One enhancement that would make the process even more automated would be to dynamically query the list of DNS servers instead of hardcoding them in an array. You simply would need to query the NS record for one or more zones that your DNS servers are authoritative for. As long as an NS record is added for each new name server, the script would automatically pick it up in subsequent runs. Later in the chapter, we will show how to query DNS with the DNS provider.

Creating and Manipulating Zones

The MicrosoftDNS_Zone class provides a plethora of properties and methods to aid in managing your zones. Even if you are using AD-integrated zones, which help reduce the amount of work it takes to maintain DNS, you will inevitably need to configure settings on a zone or create additional zones. In Tables 27-3 and 27-4, the list of available properties and methods for the MicrosoftDNS_Zone class are presented.

Table 27-3. MicrosoftDNS_Zone class properties

Property name	Property description
AllowUpdate	Flag indicating whether dynamic updates are allowed.
AutoCreated	Flag indicating whether the zone was auto-created.
DataFile	Name of zone file.
DisableWINSRecordReplication	If TRUE, WINS record replication is disabled.
MastersIPAddressesArray	If zone is a secondary, this contains the list of master servers to receive updates from.
Notify	If set to 1, the master server will notify secondaries of zone updates.
NotifyIPAddressesArray	Servers that will be notified when there are updates to the zone.
Paused	Flag indicating whether the zone is paused and therefore not responding to requests.
Reverse	If TRUE, zone is a reverse (in-addr.arpa) zone. If FALSE, zone is a forward zone.

Table 27-3. MicrosoftDNS_Zone class properties (continued)

Property name	Property description
SecondariesIPAddressesArray	Servers allowed to receive zone transfers.
SecureSecondaries	Flag indicating whether zone transfers are allowed only to servers specified in `SecondariesIPAddressesArray`.
Shutdown	If TRUE, zone has expired (or shutdown).
UseWins	Flag indicating whether zone uses WINS lookups.
ZoneType	Type of zone. It will be either DS Integrated, Primary, or Secondary.

Table 27-4. MicrosoftDNS_Zone class methods

Method name	Method description
AgeAllRecords	Age part or all of a zone.
ChangeZoneType	Convert zone to one of the following types: DS integrated, Primary, Secondary, Stub, Stub-DS integrated, or Forward.
CreateZone	Create a new zone.
ForceRefresh	Forces secondary to update its zone from master.
GetDistinguishedName	Get distinguished name of the zone.
PauseZone	Causes the DNS server to not respond to queries for the zone.
ReloadZone	Reload the contents of the zone. This may be necessary after making changes to a zone that you want to take effect immediately.
ResetSecondaries	Specify list of secondaries.
ResumeZone	Causes the DNS server to start responding to queries for the zone again.
UpdateFromDS	Reloads the zone information from Active Directory. This is only valid for AD-integrated zones.
WriteBackZone	Save zone data to a file.

Creating a Zone

Creating a zone with the DNS provider is a straightforward operation. You simply need to get a WMI object for the DNS namespace, instantiate an object from the MicrosoftDNS_Zone class, and call CreateZone on that object. The next example shows how to do this:

```
on error resume next

strNewZone = "mycorp.com."

Set objDNS = GetObject("winMgmts:root\MicrosoftDNS")
Set objDNSZone = objDNS.Get("MicrosoftDNS_Zone")
strNull = objDNSZone.CreateZone(strNewZone,0,True)

if Err then
   WScript.Echo "Error occurred creating zone: " & Err.Description
else
```

```
        WScript.Echo "Zone created..."
    end if
```

The three parameters we passed into CreateZone( ) include the zone name, zone type flag, and DS-Integrated flag. A zone type of 0 means to create a primary zone. When the DS-Integrated flag is set to true, the primary zone will be AD-integrated; if it is false, it will be a standard primary. At the time of this writing, Microsoft had conflicting documentation about these parameters and their valid values. Refer to the MSDN Library for more information; hopefully they will get it right eventually.

Configuring a Zone

Configuring a zone is not too different from configuring a server. The primary difference is how you instantiate a MicrosoftDNS_Zone object. To use the Get( ) method on a WMI (SWbemServices) object, you have to specify the keys for the class you want to instantiate. For the MicrosoftDNS_Zone class, the keys include ContainerName, Dns-ServerName, and Name. In this case, ContainerName and Name are the name of the zone. The DnsServerName we retrieve by getting a MicrosoftDNS_Server object as we've done earlier in the chapter.

Example 27-2 first lists all of the properties of the *mycorp.com.* zone before it modifies the "AllowUpdate" property and commits the change.

Example 27-2. Configuring a zone

```
on error resume next

strZone = "mycorp.com."

Set objDNS = GetObject("winMgmts:root\MicrosoftDNS")
set objDNSServer = objDNS.Get("MicrosoftDNS_Server.Name="".""")
Set objDNSZone = objDNS.Get("MicrosoftDNS_Zone.ContainerName=""" & strZone & _
                    """,DnsServerName=""" & objDNSServer.Name & _
                    """,Name=""" & strZone & """")

' List all of the properties of the zone
Wscript.Echo objDNSZone.Name
for each objProp in objDNSZone.Properties_
   if IsNull(objProp.Value) then
      Wscript.Echo " " & objProp.Name & " : NULL"
   else
      if objProp.IsArray = TRUE then
         For I = LBound(objProp.Value) to UBound(objProp.Value)
             wscript.echo " " & objProp.Name & " : " & objProp.Value(I)
         next
      else
         wscript.echo " " & objProp.Name & " : " & objProp.Value
      end if
   end if
next
```

Example 27-2. Configuring a zone (continued)

```
' Modify the zone
objDNSZone.AllowUpdate = 1
objDNSZone.Put_

WScript.Echo ""
if Err then
   Wscript.Echo "Error occurred: " & Err.Description
else
   WScript.Echo "Change successful"
end if
```

Listing the Zones on a Server

The last zone example we will show lists the configured zones on a specific DNS server. To make the following example a little more robust, we've added logic to make the script configurable so it can be run against any DNS server. That is accomplished by using the ConnectServer method on the SWbemLocator object.

```
strServer = "dns1.mycorp.com"
strUsername = "dnsadmin"
strPassword = "dnspwd"

Set objLocator = CreateObject("WbemScripting.SWbemLocator")
Set objDNS = objLocator.ConnectServer(strServer, "root\MicrosoftDNS", _
                             strUsername, strPassword)
set objDNSServer = objDNS.Get("MicrosoftDNS_Server.Name=""."""")
set objZones = objDNS.ExecQuery("Select * from MicrosoftDNS_Zone " & _
                        "Where DnsServerName = '" & _
                        objDNSServer.Name & "'")
WScript.Echo objDNSServer.Name
for each objZone in objZones
   WScript.Echo " " & objZOne.Name
next
```

To retrieve the list of zones, we used a WQL query with ExecQuery to find all MicrosoftDNS_Zone objects that had a DnsServerName equal to the name of the server we are connecting to.

Creating and Manipulating Resource Records

Resource records are the basic unit of information in DNS. A DNS server's primary job is to respond to queries for resource records. Most people don't realize they are generating resource record queries with nearly every network-based operation they do, including accessing a website, pinging a host, or logging into Active Directory.

Resource records come in many different flavors or types. Each type corresponds to a certain type of name or address lookup. Each record type also has additional information encoded with the record that represents things such as the time to live of the record. The following is a textual example of what a CNAME record looks like:

```
www.mycorp.com.  1800  IN  CNAME  www1.mycorp.com.
```

Or more generically:

```
Owner  TTL  Class  Type  RR-Data
```

Now let's break the record down into its individual parts:

Owner
> The owner of the resource record. This field is typically what is specified during a query for the particular type.

TTL
> The time to live, or length of time a nonauthoritative DNS server should cache the record. After the TTL expires, a nonauthoritative server should re-query for an authoritative answer.

Class
> Resource record classification. In nearly all cases, this will be "IN" for Internet.

Type
> Name of the resource record type. Each type has a standard name that is used in zones (e.g., CNAME, A, PTR, SRV).

RR-Data
> Resource record specific data. When you perform a query, you are typically looking for the information returned as part of the RR-Data.

The WMI DNS provider fully supports querying and manipulating resource records. In Tables 27-5 and 27-6, the supported properties and methods are listed for the MicrosoftDNS_ResourceRecord class, which implements a generic interface for resource records.

Table 27-5. MicrosoftDNS_ResourceRecord class properties

Property name	Property description
ContainerName	Name of container (e.g., zone name) that holds the RR
DomainName	FQDN of the domain that contains the RR
DnsServerName	FQDN of the server that contains the RR
OwnerName	Owner of the RR
RecordClass	Class of the RR; 1 represents IN
RecordData	Resource record data
TextRepresentation	Textual representation of the RR, e.g.: www.mycorp.com. 1800 IN CNAME www1.mycorp.com.
Timestamp	Time RR was last refreshed
TTL	Time to live or maximum time a DNS server is supposed to cache the RR

Table 27-6. MicrosoftDNS_ResourceRecord class methods

Method name	Method description
CreateInstanceFromTextRepresentation	Creates a new instance of a MicrosoftDNS_ResourceRecord subclass based on the textual representation of the resource record, server name, and container or zone name. A reference to the new object is returned as an out parameter.
GetObjectByTextRepresentation	Gets an instance of the appropriate MicrosoftDNS_ResourceRecord subclass as specified by the textual representation of the resource record, server name, and container or zone name.

The MicrosoftDNS_ResourceRecord class by itself is not enough. There are over two dozen different types of resource records with many having additional fields that would not have corresponding methods in the generic interface. To solve this problem, subclasses of MicrosoftDNS_ResourceRecord were created for each supported record type. Each subclass provides specific methods to access any field supported by the resource record type. Each supported resource record has a subclass with a name in the format of MicrosoftDNS_<RR Type>Type.

To show just how different resource records can be, let's take a look at an A record:

```
www.mycorp.com.   1800  IN  A  192.10.4.5
```

Now let's compare that with an SRV record:

```
_ldap._tcp.dc._msdcs.mycorp.com 1800  IN  SRV  0 100 389 dc1.mycorp.com.
```

As you can see, the SRV record has several additional fields. By using the MicrosoftDNS_SRVType subclass, we can access each field with methods provided by the class.

The complete list of supported resource record types is provided in Table 27-7.

Table 27-7. DNS provider supported resource records

Resource record type	DNS provider class	RFC	Description
A	MicrosoftDNS_Atype	RFC1035	Name-to-IPv4 address mapping
AAAA	MicrosoftDNS_AAAAType	RFC1886	Name-to-IPv6 address mapping
AFSDB	MicrosoftDNS_AFSDBType	RFC1183	Andrew File System (AFS) Database Server record
ATMA	MicrosoftDNS_ATMAType	N/A	ATM-address-to-name mapping
CNAME	MicrosoftDNS_CNAMEType	RFC1035	Canonical (alias) name
HINFO	MicrosoftDNS_HINFOType	RFC1035	Host information
ISDN	MicrosoftDNS_ISDNType	RFC1183	Integrated services digital network (ISDN) record
KEY	MicrosoftDNS_KEYType	RFC2535	KEY record
MB	MicrosoftDNS_MBType	RFC1035	Mailbox record
MD	MicrosoftDNS_MDType	RFC1035	Mail agent
MF	MicrosoftDNS_MFType	RFC1035	Mail forwarding agent

Table 27-7. DNS provider supported resource records (continued)

Resource record type	DNS provider class	RFC	Description
MG	MicrosoftDNS_MGType	RFC1035	Mail group record
MINFO	MicrosoftDNS_MINFOType	RFC1035	Mail information record
MR	MicrosoftDNS_MRType	RFC1035	Mailbox rename record
MX	MicrosoftDNS_MXType	RFC1035	Mail exchanger
NS	MicrosoftDNS_NSType	RFC1035	Name server
NXT	MicrosoftDNS_NXTType	RFC2535	Next record
PTR	MicrosoftDNS_PTRType	RFC1035	Address-to-name mapping record
RP	MicrosoftDNS_RPTType	RFC1183	Responsible person
RT	MicrosoftDNS_RTType	RFC1183	Route through record
SIG	MicrosoftDNS_SIGType	RFC2535	Signature record
SOA	MicrosoftDNS_SOAType	RFC1035	Start of authority
SRV	MicrosoftDNS_SRVType	RFC2052	Service record
TXT	MicrosoftDNS_TXTType	RFC1035	Text record
WINS	MicrosoftDNS_WINSType	N/A	WINS server
WINSR	MicrosoftDNS_WINSRType	N/A	WINS reverse-lookup
WKS	MicrosoftDNS_WKSType	RFC1035	Well-known services
X25	MicrosoftDNS_X25Type	RFC1183	X.121 Address-to-name mapping

Finding Resource Records in a Zone

With the marriage of DNS and WMI, querying DNS has never been so easy. By using WQL, you can write complex query routines that would not have been possible previously. To list all of the resource records on a server, you simply need to execute the WQL query select * from MicrosoftDNS_ResourceRecord against the target server. The following example shows what this would look like if the script is run on a DNS server:

```
Set objDNS = GetObject("winMgmts:root\MicrosoftDNS")
set objRR = objDNS.ExecQuery("Select * from MicrosoftDNS_ResourceRecord ")

For Each objInst in objRR
   WScript.Echo objInst.TextRepresentation
Next
```

The TextRepresentation method is available to all resource record types since it is defined in MicrosoftDNS_ResourceRecord. It will return a text string representing the resource record, such as the following:

```
www.mycorp.com. IN  A  192.10.4.5
```

If you want to limit the query to only a specific zone, change the WQL query to include criteria for ContainerName, such as the following:

```
Select * from MicrosoftDNS_ResourceRecord

Where ContainerName = 'ZoneName'
```

Since Active Directory uses DNS to store all of the Global Catalog servers in a forest and domain controllers in a domain, you can write scripts to utilize DNS to access this information and integrate it into your applications. The following example does exactly this by selecting all SRV records with a particular OwnerName. To find all Global Catalog servers in a forest, you can simply query *_ldap._tcp.gc._msdcs.<ForestDNSName>*, and to find all domain controllers in a domain, query *_ldap._tcp.dc._msdcs.<DomainDNSName>*.

```
option explicit

Dim strDomain
strDomain = "mycorp.com"

Dim objDNS, objRRs, objRR
Set objDNS = GetObject("winMgmts:root\MicrosoftDNS")
set objRRs = objDNS.ExecQuery("Select * from MicrosoftDNS_SRVType " & _
                              " Where OwnerName = '_ldap._tcp.gc._msdcs." & _
                              strDomain & "'")
WScript.Echo "Global Catalogs for " & strDomain
For Each objRR in objRRs
   Wscript.Echo "  " & objRR.DomainName
Next

Wscript.Echo

set objRRs = objDNS.ExecQuery("Select * from MicrosoftDNS_SRVType " & _
                              " Where OwnerName = '_ldap._tcp.dc._msdcs." & _
                              strDomain & "'")
WScript.Echo "Domain Controllers for " & strDomain
For Each objRR in objRRs
   Wscript.Echo "  " & objRR.DomainName
Next
```

Creating Resource Records

With the DNS provider, creating resource records is also very easy to do. The MicrosoftDNS_ResourceRecord::CreateInstanceFromTextRepresentation method takes the server name to create the record on, the domain name, and the text representation of the resource record as in parameters. It also provides an out parameter which will be an object representing the newly created record.

Example 27-3 goes through the process of creating both A and PTR records. Both records are typically necessary when adding a new host to DNS.

Example 27-3. Creating A and PTR resource records

```
option explicit

Dim strRR, strReverseRR, strDomain, strReverseDomain

' A record to add
strRR = "testb.mycorp.com. IN A 192.32.64.13"
strDomain = "mycorp.com"

' PTR record to add
strReverseRR = "13.64.32.192.in-addr.arpa IN PTR testb.mycorp.com"
strReverseDomain = "192.in-addr.arpa."

Dim objDNS, objRR, objDNSServer, objRR2, objOutParam
Set objDNS = GetObject("winMgmts:root\MicrosoftDNS")
Set objRR = objDNS.Get("MicrosoftDNS_ResourceRecord")
Set objDNSServer = objDNS.Get("MicrosoftDNS_Server.Name=""."""")

' Create the A record
Dim strNull
strNull = objRR.CreateInstanceFromTextRepresentation( _
                objDNSServer.Name, _
                strDomain, _
                strRR, _
                objOutParam)

Set objRR2 = objDNS.Get(objOutParam)
WScript.Echo "Created Record: " & objRR2.TextRepresentation
Set objOutParam = Nothing

' Create the PTR record
strNull = objRR.CreateInstanceFromTextRepresentation( _
                objDNSServer.Name, _
                strReverseDomain, _
                strReverseRR, _
                objOutParam)

Set objRR2 = objDNS.Get(objOutParam)
WScript.Echo "Created Record: " & objRR2.TextRepresentation
```

Summary

The WMI DNS provider fills a much-needed gap for programmatic management of a
Microsoft DNS environment. In this chapter, we reviewed how to install the DNS
provider, including some of the caveats for using it on Windows 2000. We then covered the classes used for managing server configuration along with each of the available server settings. Next, we showed how to create and manipulate zones with the
DNS provider. Finally, we covered the various resource record types and their associated WMI classes.

CHAPTER 28

Getting Started with VB.NET and System.DirectoryServices

Unless you've been hiding in a cave in recent years, you've undoubtedly heard of Microsoft's latest initiative, called .NET. At a low level, .NET is the basis for a new programming platform, including a completely new set of APIs to manage Microsoft-based products and develop Windows applications. Microsoft even released a new programming language in conjunction with .NET called C# (C-sharp). At a higher level, Microsoft has morphed the concept of .NET to the point where it is hard to define its true boundaries. Here is the definition provided on Microsoft's website: "Microsoft .NET is a set of software technologies designed to connect your world of information, people, systems, and devices."

As far as Active Directory goes, the impact of .NET has been pretty minimal so far. Windows Server 2003 Active Directory was an evolutionary step, not revolutionary. Perhaps the biggest .NET-influenced change is with the new APIs called System.Directory-Services that were developed for Active Directory. In this chapter, we will discuss the System.DirectoryServices interfaces and cover numerous examples for how they can be used to query and manipulate data in Active Directory. Before getting into that, we first need to talk a bit about the .NET Framework.

The .NET Framework

The .NET Framework is a new set of interfaces intended to replace the old Win32 and COM APIs. A couple of the major design goals for the .NET Framework were to make programming in a Windows environment much simpler and more consistent. The .NET Framework has two major components: the common language runtime (CLR) and the .NET Framework class library.

The CLR is the sandbox from which all .NET-based code, called managed code, is executed. The CLR is in charge of things such as memory management, security management, thread management, and other code management functions. One of the great benefits of the CLR is that different programming languages can develop code that runs in the CLR and can be used by other programming languages. That means you can develop managed Perl code that can be easily used by a C# application.

The other major component of the .NET Framework is the class library, which is a comprehensive set of object-oriented interfaces that replace the traditional Win32 API. The class library is divided up into namespaces. You can think of a namespace as a grouping of classes, properties, and methods that are targeted for a specific function. For example, the System.Text namespace contains classes for representing strings in ASCII, Unicode, and other character encoding systems. The namespace that is of the most interest to us is the System.DirectoryServices namespace, which contains all the classes necessary to query and manipulate a directory, such as Active Directory, using the .NET Framework.

Using VB.NET

Since the majority of the code we've demonstrated so far in this book has been written in VBScript, you may be wondering why we are going to talk about Visual Basic. NET (VB.NET). Unfortunately, one of the drawbacks with the .NET Framework is that it currently does not provide native support for VBScript. It does support JScript, but since Visual Basic is a much more powerful language than JScript, we will use VB.NET in our examples. It is still unclear what Microsoft's future direction is in regard to providing native support for scripting languages like VBScript in .NET. Until that happens, you should get more familiar with the .NET class library and gain some experience with Visual Basic, which will ultimately increase your capabilities as a programmer. As we mentioned earlier, one of the design goals for the .NET Framework was simplicity. With the .NET Framework class library, Microsoft has made developing Windows-based applications significantly easier. As far as Active Directory goes, it will not take long at all to map your ADSI knowledge to the classes, properties, and methods in the System.DirectoryServices namespace.

To get started using VB.NET, you'll need to get an integrated development environment (IDE) such as Visual Studio.NET (VS.NET), which is available from *http:// msdn.microsoft.com/vstudio/*. Once you have VS.NET, you should download the latest .NET Framework SDK, which is available from *http://msdn.microsoft.com/ netframework/*. Once you have both of those installed, you are ready to start programming with the .NET Framework.

To start a new project in VS.NET, select File → New → Project from the menu. At that point you'll see a screen similar to the one in Figure 28-1.

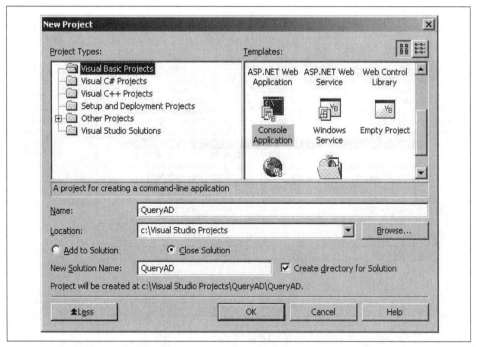

Figure 28-1. Creating a new VB.NET project

Click on Visual Basic Projects and select Console Application from the Templates window. Now you have started a new project and are ready to start writing code in a file called *Module1.vb*, which contains the following code by default:

```
Module Module1
    Sub Main( )
    End Sub
End Module
```

If you are inexperienced with VB, you can create usable programs simply by adding code to the Main( ) subroutine. Once you become more experienced, you can start creating your own classes, subroutines and functions, and reference them within Main( ).

To start using the System.DirectoryServices classes to query and manipulate Active Directory, you must add a reference to it in your project. From the menu, select Project → Add Reference, then under Component Name click on System.Directory-Services. Click the Select button and click OK. Figure 28-2 shows what this window looks like in VS.NET.

You are now ready to start writing Active Directory applications with the .NET Framework, so lets take a look at the System.DirectoryServices namespace.

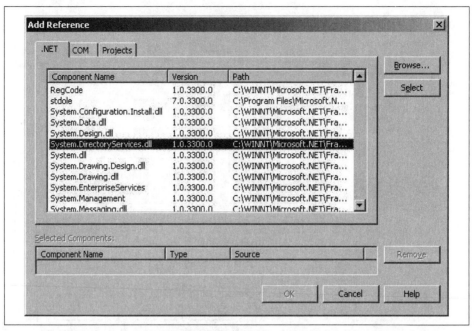

Figure 28-2. Adding a reference to System.DirectoryServices

Overview of System.DirectoryServices

The System.DirectoryServices namespace contains several classes, many of which were built on top of ADSI. If you are already familiar with ADSI, the learning curve for the System.DirectoryServices classes should be pretty minimal. Table 28-1 contains the base classes contained within the System.DirectoryServices namespace.

Table 28-1. System.DirectoryServices classes

Class name	Description
DirectoryEntries	Contains the children (child entries) of an entry in Active Directory.
DirectoryEntry	Encapsulates a node or object in the Active Directory hierarchy.
DirectorySearcher	Performs queries against Active Directory.
DirectoryServicesPermission	Allows control of code access security permissions for System.DirectoryServices.
DirectoryServicesPermissionAttribute	Allows declarative System.DirectoryServices permission checks.
DirectoryServicesPermissionEntry	Defines the smallest unit of a code access security permission set for System.DirectoryServices.
DirectoryServicesPermissionEntryCollection	Contains a strongly typed collection of DirectoryServicesPermissionEntry objects.

Table 28-1. System.DirectoryServices classes (continued)

Class name	Description
PropertyCollection	Contains the properties of a DirectoryEntry.
PropertyValueCollection	Contains the values of a DirectoryEntry property.
ResultPropertyCollection	Contains the properties of a SearchResult instance.
ResultPropertyValueCollection	Contains the values of a SearchResult property.
SchemaNameCollection	Contains a list of the schema names that the SchemaFilter property of a DirectoryEntries object can use.
SearchResult	Encapsulates a node in the Active Directory hierarchy that is returned during a search through DirectorySearcher.
SearchResultCollection	Contains the SearchResult instances that the Active Directory hierarchy returned during a DirectorySearcher query.
SortOption	Specifies how to sort the results of a search.

The list of classes in Table 28-1 was taken from the Microsoft Developer Network (*http://msdn.microsoft.com*). For more information on System.DirectoryServices and the .NET Framework, check out the .NET web site: *http://msdn.microsoft.com/netframework/*.

The two main classes within System.DirectoryServices are DirectoryEntry and DirectorySearcher. The DirectoryEntry class represents an object in Active Directory. You can create new objects and manage existing ones with DirectoryEntry. The DirectorySearcher class is the primary interface for searching Active Directory. It is an easy-to-use interface that contains properties for all the typical options you need to set when performing LDAP-based queries. We will be touching on some of the other classes as we go along, but these two are the main ones to become familiar with.

DirectoryEntry Basics

The DirectoryEntry class contains several properties to access the attributes of Active Directory objects. The following code shows how to display the currentTime attribute of the RootDSE:

```
Dim objRootDSE As New DirectoryEntry("LDAP://RootDSE")
Console.WriteLine(objRootDSE.Properties("currentTime")(0))
```

In the code, once we instantiated the DirectoryEntry object, we can access the currentTime attribute by passing it to the Properties property. The Properties property actually returns a collection of values for the attribute in the form of a PropertyCollection class, which is why we needed to specify an index of 0 to get at a specific value. If the currentTime attribute was multivalued, we could get at the other values by incrementing the index to 1 and so on.

In object-oriented parlance, a property allows you to get or set an attribute of an object. A method typically results in some kind of action being taken on the object.

Now let's look at how to display all of the values for all of the attributes of an object in Active Directory. Again we will use RootDSE as the object we want to display:

```
Dim objRootDSE As New DirectoryEntry("LDAP://RootDSE")
Dim strAttrName As String
Dim objValue As Object
For Each strAttrName In objRootDSE.Properties.PropertyNames
    For Each objValue In objRootDSE.Properties(strAttrName)
        Console.WriteLine(strAttrName & " : " & objValue.ToString)
    Next objValue
Next strAttrName
```

As you can see, the Properties property, which returns a PropertyCollection, has a PropertyNames property that returns a collection of attribute names for the Active Directory object. We loop over each attribute name and then loop over each value for that attribute to ensure we print out values for all single- and multivalued attributes. The ToString property converts whatever value is stored in the attribute to a printable string.

There are several properties available in the DirectoryEntry class. Table 28-2 contains a list of them.

Table 28-2. DirectoryEntry properties

Property name	Description
AuthenticationType	Gets or sets the type of authentication to use when accessing the directory.
Children	Gets a DirectoryEntries class that contains the child objects of this object.
Guid	Gets the GUID for the object (e.g., in Active Directory the objectGUID attribute).
Name	Gets the relative distinguished name of the object.
NativeGuid	Gets the GUID of the object as returned by the provider.
NativeObject	Gets the native ADSI object.
Parent	Gets the object's parent in Active Directory.
Password	Gets or sets the password to use when authenticating.
Path	Gets or sets the ADsPath for the object.
Properties	Gets a PropertyCollection class containing the attributes on the object.
SchemaClassName	Gets the objectclass of the object.
SchemaEntry	Gets the DirectoryEntry class of the object's objectclass.
UsePropertyCache	Gets or sets the flag indicating whether the property cache should be committed after each operation.
Username	Gets or sets the username to use when authenticating.

One interesting property to note is Children, which returns a DirectoryEntries collection containing each child object. Using the Children property, you can quickly traverse a directory tree. The following code prints out the entire directory tree rooted at dc=mycorp,dc=com:

```
Sub Main( )
    Dim objADObject As New DirectoryEntry("LDAP://dc=mycorp,dc=com")
    DisplayChildren(objADObject, " ")
End Sub
Sub DisplayChildren(ByVal objADObject As DirectoryEntry, _
                    ByVal strSpaces As String)
    Console.WriteLine(strSpaces & objADObject.Name)
    Dim objChild As New DirectoryEntry( )
    For Each objChild In objADObject.Children
        DisplayChildren(objChild, strSpaces & "  ")
    Next objChild
End Sub
```

The DisplayChildren( ) subroutine is recursive. For each child that is found, DisplayChildren( ) is called again, and so on until no child objects are found. The strSpaces variable is used to indent each child so that you can see the hierarchy when printed out.

Now let's say that we wanted to traverse the tree but print out only the Organizational Units. To do that, we can use the SchemaClassName property for each object and only print out the entry if its SchemaClassName equals organizationalUnit, which is the objectClass value for OUs.

```
Sub Main( )
    Dim objADObject As New DirectoryEntry("LDAP://dc=mycorp,dc=com")
    DisplayChildren(objADObject, " ")
End Sub
Sub DisplayChildren(ByVal objADObject As DirectoryEntry, _
                    ByVal strSpaces As String)
    If objADObject.SchemaClassName = "organizationalUnit" Then
        Console.WriteLine(strSpaces & objADObject.Name)
    End If
    Dim objChild As New DirectoryEntry( )
    For Each objChild In objADObject.Children
        DisplayChildren(objChild, strSpaces & "  ")
    Next objChild
End Sub
```

We are now going to take many of the concepts described so far and make a fully functional program. Lets expand on the first example we covered that printed the attributes and values for the RootDSE. We are going to turn it into a program that can accept a command-line argument, which should be the ADsPath of an object, and then display all of the attributes and values for that object. Example 28-1 contains the code.

Error Handling in VB.NET

One of the important new features of VB.NET is robust error handling. VB.NET supports a new Try Catch statement that allows you to easily catch exceptions as they happen and perform certain actions based on the type of exception that was thrown. Typically in .NET, if an error is encountered, an exception is thrown. Using a Try Catch statement allows you to handle errors gracefully, much as you could with the On Error directive in Visual Basic 6.0. In fact, if you use On Error with VB.NET, the compiler actually translates it into Try Catch statements.

Let's take a look at a code snippet we used earlier to print the currentTime attribute of the RootDSE:

```
Dim objRootDSE As New DirectoryEntry("LDAP://RootDSE")
Console.WriteLine(objRootDSE.Properties("currentTime")(0))
```

As you can see, there is no error handling. If there is a problem accessing the RootDSE, the program will abort gracelessly. Using a Try Catch statement, we can change the code to die gracefully or even continue execution of the rest of the program:

```
Try
    Dim objRootDSE As New DirectoryEntry("LDAP://RootDSE")
    Console.WriteLine(objRootDSE.Properties("currentTime")(0))
Catch objExp As Exception
    Console.WriteLine("Error retrieving RootDSE: " & _
                        objExp.Message)
End Try
```

One of the nice features of the Try Catch statement is you can catch different types of errors. For example, let's pretend that we wanted to write to a file after we retrieved the currentTime from the RootDSE. Interacting with a file can generate certain IO exceptions. We can insert an additional catch into the Try End Try block to catch IO exceptions as follows:

```
Try
    Dim objRootDSE As New DirectoryEntry("LDAP://RootDSE")
    Console.WriteLine(objRootDSE.Properties("currentTime")(0))
    ' write to a file
Catch objIOExp as IOException
    Console.WriteLine("File IO Error: " & objIOExp.Message)
Catch objExp As Exception
    Console.WriteLine("Error retrieving RootDSE: " & _
                        objExp.Message)
End Try
```

—continued—

You can also generate your own exceptions with the Throw statement. Here is an example:

```
Try
    If objADObject.Exists(strADsPath) = False Then
        Throw (New Exception("Object does not exist"))
    End If
Catch exp As Exception
        Console.WriteLine("Error retrieving object: " & _
                             strADsPath)
End Try
```

The Try Catch statement is very powerful and flexible. For more information on the properties and methods available to exception objects, check out the System.Exception namespace.

Example 28-1. Making a fully functional program

```
Imports System
Imports System.DirectoryServices
Module Module1
    Sub Main( )
        Dim cmd As String
        ' Read the commandline and get the number of arguments passed
        Dim intArgs As Integer
        Try
            intArgs = Environment.GetCommandLineArgs( ).Length( )
        Catch exp As Exception
            ' Set intArgs to 0 if no arguments were passed
            intArgs = 0
        End Try
        ' If an argument was specified on the commandline, set
        ' strADsPath to that, if not default to query the RootDSE
        Dim strADsPath As String
        If intArgs > 1 Then
            strADsPath = Environment.GetCommandLineArgs( )(1)
        Else
            strADsPath = "LDAP://RootDSE"
        End If
        ' We need to see if the object in strADsPath exists
        ' and if not, print an error and return
        Dim objADObject As New DirectoryEntry( )
        Try
            If objADObject.Exists(strADsPath) = False Then
                Throw (New Exception("Object does not exist"))
            End If
        Catch exp As Exception
            Console.WriteLine("Error retrieving object: " & strADsPath)
            Return
        End Try
        ' Iterate over each attribute of the object and print its values
        Dim strAttrName As String
```

Example 28-1. Making a fully functional program (continued)

```
        Dim objValue As Object
        Try
            objADObject.Path = strADsPath
            Console.WriteLine("Displaying " & objADObject.Path)
            For Each strAttrName In objADObject.Properties.PropertyNames
                For Each objValue In objADObject.Properties(strAttrName)
                    Console.WriteLine(strAttrName & " : " & objValue.ToString)
                Next objValue
            Next strAttrName
        Catch exp As Exception
            Console.WriteLine("Fatal error accessing: " & strADsPath)
            Return
        End Try
    End Sub
End Module
```

The first two lines, which use the `Imports` keyword, allow us to specify class names contained within those namespaces without fully qualifying them. For example, by using `Imports` we can use the following code:

```
New DirectoryEntry( )
```

instead of :

```
New System.DirectoryServices.Directory( )
```

For simplicity, we put the rest of the code directly in the `Main( )` subroutine. The first part of the code attempts to read the command line using the `System.Environment` namespace to see if a parameter was specified. A `Try Catch` statement was used because the call to `Environment.GetCommandLineArgs( ).Length( )` will throw an exception if no parameters are passed on the command line. For more information on error handling, see the "Error Handling in VB.NET" sidebar. Note that the `intArgs` variable will contain the number of arguments passed to the script including the script name as the first argument. To see if the user actually passed the `ADsPath` we have to check whether `intArgs > 1`. It is for this reason that we set the `strADsPath` variable to the value specified on the command line and if one wasn't, default to the `RootDSE`. Next we use the `Exists( )` method (not property) to determine if the object specified in `strADsPath` actually exists. The `DirectoryEntry` class contains a host of methods in addition to the properties we showed earlier. Table 28-3 contains a list of all the `DirectoryEntry` methods.

Table 28-3. DirectoryEntry methods

Method name	Description
Close	Closes the DirectoryEntry and releases any system resources associated with the component
CommitChanges	Saves any changes to the object in Active Directory (similar to SetInfo)
CopyTo	Creates a copy of the object

Table 28-3. DirectoryEntry methods (continued)

Method name	Description
DeleteTree	Deletes the object and any children
Equals	Determines whether two objects are the same
Exists	Determines whether the object exists in Active Directory
Invoke	Allows you to invoke a native ADSI method
MoveTo	Moves an object to a different location
RefreshCache	Refreshes the property cache for the object
Rename	Renames the relative distinguished name of the object
ToString	String representation of the object

If the Exists( ) check fails, we generate an exception using Throw( ). If the object exists, we proceed to iterate over each attribute, printing the values for it. To turn the code into an executable, you can compile the program by selecting Build → Build Solution from the VS.NET menu. If any errors are found, they are displayed in the bottom pane. If none are found, you can then execute the program. If we named the project EntryQuery, an example command line would look like the following:

```
D:\Visual Studio Projects\EntryQuery\EntryQuery\bin> entryquery.exe LDAP://
dc=mycorp,dc=com
```

Searching with DirectorySearcher

We've shown how easy it is to read individual objects from Active Directory with the DirectoryEntry class, so lets now look at how to search Active Directory with the DirectorySearcher class. The DirectorySearcher class works like many other LDAP-based search APIs. Table 28-4 contains all of the DirectorySearcher properties.

Table 28-4. DirectorySearcher properties

Property name	Description
CacheResults	Gets or sets the flag that determines whether results are cached on the client.
ClientTimeout	Gets or sets the time period the client is willing to wait for the server to answer the search.
Filter	Gets or sets the search filter string.
PageSize	Gets or sets the page size for paged searching.
PropertiesToLoad	Gets or sets the attributes to return from a search.
PropertyNamesOnly	Gets or sets the flag indicating to only return attribute names from a search.
ReferralChasing	Gets or sets whether referrals are chased.
SearchRoot	Gets or sets the base from which the search should start.
SearchScope	Gets or sets the scope of the search.
ServerPageTimeLimit	Gets or sets the time the server will wait for an individual page to return from a search.
ServerTimeLimit	Gets or sets the time the server will wait for a search to complete.

Table 28-4. DirectorySearcher properties (continued)

Property name	Description
SizeLimit	Gets or sets the maximum number of objects that can be returned by a search.
Sort	Gets or sets the attribute that is used when returning sorted search results.

Many of the properties, such as SearchScope, should look familiar. The following code shows how to search for all user objects in the *mycorp.com* domain.

```
Dim objSearch As New DirectorySearcher()
objSearch.SearchRoot = New DirectoryEntry("LDAP://dc=mycorp,dc=com")
objSearch.Filter = "(&(objectclass=user)(objectcategory=person))"
objSearch.SearchScope = SearchScope.Subtree
objSearch.PropertiesToLoad.Add("cn")
Dim colQueryResults As SearchResultCollection
colQueryResults = objSearch.FindAll()
Dim objResult As SearchResult
For Each objResult In colQueryResults
    Console.WriteLine(objResult.Properties("cn")(0))
Next
```

After a new DirectorySearcher class was instantiated, we set four properties before executing the search. The SearchRoot accepts a DirectoryEntry object representing the search base; the Filter property is the LDAP filter string; SearchScope is one of the values contained in the System.DirectoryServices.SearchScope enumeration; and PropertiesToLoad.Add() builds the attribute list to return from the query. You can specify multiple attributes in a single statement by using PropertiesToLoad.AddRange:

```
objSearch.PropertiesToLoad.AddRange(New String() {"cn", "sn", "givenname"})
```

After all of the search parameters have been set, we can use the FindAll() method to invoke the search. A System.DirectoryServices.SearchResultsCollection is returned by the FindAll() method, and you can iterate over each entry using a For Each loop. The SearchResultsCollection contains System.DirectoryServices.SearchResult objects, which are very similar to DirectoryEntry objects.

 If you want to retrieve only the first object in the search results, you can use the FindOne() method, which returns a single SearchResult object.

Manipulating Objects

Modifying objects with System.DirectoryServices can be done a couple of different ways. To modify an attribute that currently has a value, you can set it using the Properties property. For example, the following code would modify the givenName attribute:

```
objADObject.Properties("givenName")(0) = "Robert"
```

If you want to set an attribute that was previously unset, you must use the Properties.Add method. The following code would set the previously unset sn attribute:

```
objADObject.Properties("sn").Add("Robert")
```

To determine whether an attribute has been set, you can use Properties("*attributename*").Count, which will return the number of values that have been set for the attribute. Just like with ADSI, all modifications are made initially to the local property cache and must committed to the server. With ADSI you would use the IADs::SetInfo() method, and with System.DirectoryServices it is called CommitChanges(), which is available from the DirectoryEntry class.

```
objADObject.CommitChanges()
```

Now that we covered how to set an attribute, we can modify the earlier code that printed all the values of an attribute to instead set an attribute. The code in Example 28-2 expects three command line parameters: the first is the ADsPath of the object to modify, the second is the attribute name, and the third is the value to set the attribute to.

Example 28-2. Setting an attribute

```
Dim strADsPath As String
Dim strAttrName As String
Dim strAttrValue As String
Try
    Dim intArgs As Integer = Environment.GetCommandLineArgs().Length()
    If intArgs <> 4 Then
        Throw (New Exception("All parameters are required"))
    Else
        strADsPath = Environment.GetCommandLineArgs()(1)
        strAttrName = Environment.GetCommandLineArgs()(2)
        strAttrValue = Environment.GetCommandLineArgs()(3)
    End If
Catch objExp As Exception
    Console.WriteLine("Error: " & objExp.Message)
    Console.WriteLine("Usage: " & Environment.GetCommandLineArgs()(0) & _
                    " ADsPath AttributeName Attribute Value")
    Console.WriteLine()
    Return
End Try
Dim objADObject As New DirectoryEntry()
Try
    If objADObject.Exists(strADsPath) = False Then
        Throw (New Exception("Object does not exist"))
    End If
Catch objExp As Exception
    Console.WriteLine("Error retrieving object: " & strADsPath)
    Console.WriteLine("Error: " + objExp.Message)
    Return
End Try
```

Example 28-2. Setting an attribute (continued)

```
Dim strOldValue As String
Try
    objADObject.Path = strADsPath
    If objADObject.Properties(strAttrName).Count > 0 Then
        strOldvalue = objADObject.Properties(strAttrName)(0)
        objADObject.Properties(strAttrName)(0) = strAttrValue
    Else
        objADObject.Properties(strAttrName).Add(strAttrValue)
    End If
    objADObject.CommitChanges()
Catch objExp As Exception
    Console.WriteLine("Error setting object: " & strADsPath)
    Console.WriteLine("Error: " + objExp.Message)
    Return
End Try
Console.WriteLine(strADsPath)
Console.WriteLine("Attribute: " + strAttrName)
Console.WriteLine("Old value: " + strOldValue)
Console.WriteLine("New value: " + strAttrValue)
Console.WriteLine()
Console.WriteLine("Update Successful")
```

This code is not terribly different from Example 28-1 earlier in the chapter. The main difference is the check for additional command-line parameters and the determination of whether the attribute that was specified on the command line was set previously.

Adding objects with System.DirectoryServices is similar in nature to ADSI. You must first get a reference to the parent object and then add a child. You can add a child by using the Children.Add() method of a DirectoryEntry object. The following example shows how to create a user object:

```
Dim objParent As New DirectoryEntry("LDAP://ou=sales,dc=mycorp,dc=com", _
                                    "administrator@mycorp.com",_
                                    "MyPassword", _
                                    AuthenticationTypes.Secure)
Dim objChild As DirectoryEntry = objParent.Children.Add("cn=jdoe", "user")
objChild.Properties("sAMAccountName").Add("jdoe")
objChild.CommitChanges()
objChild.NativeObject.AccountDisabled = False
objChild.CommitChanges()
Console.WriteLine("Added user")
```

You may have noticed several things. First, when we instantiated the DirectoryEntry object, we passed three additional parameters that we haven't used before. The second parameter is the user to authenticate with, the third is the password for the user, and the last is any authentication options from the AuthenticationTypes enumeration (ADS_AUTHENTICATION_ENUM in ADSI). After the first CommitChanges() call, the object is created in Active Directory. After that we enable the account by calling ADSI's AccountDisabled method. System.DirectoryServices does not duplicate all of the functionality of ADSI. As we said earlier, it is primarily a wrapper

---

around ADSI. One of the reasons System.DirectoryServices is so powerful is that you can still access native ADSI interfaces by using the NativeObject method. NativeObject will return the IADs interface of the specific type of object. In our previous example, NativeObject will return an IADsUser object, which we can then call the IADsUser::AccountDisabled method on. A final CommitChanges() call will update Active Directory and enable the account.

 To use the NativeObject method, you'll need to add a reference to the *ActiveDs.dll* library. From VS.NET, select Project → Add Reference from the menu. Click the COM tab, click Active DS Type Library under Component Name, and click the Select button. Click OK to close the window.

This concludes our introduction to the .NET Framework and the System.Directory-Services namespace. The information we covered should be sufficient to get you started writing Active Directory applications with .NET, but if you need additional information, check out MSDN, which contains detailed documentation on the .NET class library, including System.DirectoryServices.

Summary

The .NET initiative is one of the biggest technology shifts at Microsoft since they embraced the Internet in the latter half of the 1990s. Microsoft is using .NET to refocus the company on new technologies such as XML web services and the .NET Framework. The .NET Framework is a completely new way to program in the Windows environment. The Common Language Runtime (CLR) helps applications share code more efficiently and securely. In addition, the .NET Framework class library is a new set of APIs that make the older Win32 APIs look antiquated. The object-oriented approach and better organization of classes make for a much more simplified programming environment.

The impact of .NET on Active Directory is pretty minimal so far. The biggest impact has been with the introduction of the System.DirectoryServices API, which builds on top of ADSI and is straightforward to use. In its current release, VBScript cannot be used natively with the .NET Framework, but due to the simplicity of .NET, using Visual Basic.NET is not much of a leap for experienced VBScript programmers. In this chapter, we covered the two main classes of System.DirectoryServices, the DirectoryEntry class and the DirectorySearcher class. By having a good understanding of these two classes, you'll be well on your way to writing robust Active Directory applications with the .NET Framework.

Index

We'd like to hear your suggestions for improving our indexes. Send email to *index@oreilly.com*.

About the Authors

Robbie Allen is a Senior Systems Architect in the Advanced Services Technology Group at Cisco Systems. He was instrumental in the deployment and automation of Active Directory, DNS, and DHCP at Cisco, and is now working on network automation tools. Robbie enjoys working on both the Unix and Windows platforms, especially when Perl is installed. He is a firm believer that all system administrators should be proficient in at least one scripting language, and most of his writings preach the benefits of automation.

Alistair G. Lowe-Norris is an Architectural Enterprise Strategy Consultant for Microsoft U.K. During the writing of the first edition of this book, he worked for Leicester University as the project manager and technical lead of the Rapid Deployment Program for Windows 2000. During his time there, Leicester University was part of Microsoft's U.K. and U.S. Rapid Deployment Programs for Windows 2000, and was responsible for rolling out what turned out to be one of the world's largest deployments of Windows 2000 preceding release of the final product. Since 1998, he has been the technical editor and a monthly columnist for *Windows Scripting Solutions* and a technical editor and author for *Windows & .Net Magazine* (previously *Windows NT Magazine* and *Windows 2000 Magazine*). In addition, he is an author and editor for various other publications and online sites worldwide. He holds various Microsoft and other accreditations and has been using Windows daily since October 1997. He lives in Leicester, U.K.

Colophon

Our look is the result of reader comments, our own experimentation, and feedback from distribution channels. Distinctive covers complement our distinctive approach to technical topics, breathing personality and life into potentially dry subjects.

The animals on the cover of *Active Directory*, Second Edition, are a domestic cat (*felis silvetris*) and her kitten. The domestic cat is a descendant of the African wild cat, which first inhabited the planet almost one million years ago. Other early forerunners of the cat existed as many as 12 million years ago.

The domestic cat is one of the most popular house pets in the world. There are hundreds of breeds of domestic cats, which weigh anywhere from five to thirty pounds, with an average of twelve pounds. The cat is slightly longer than it is tall, with its body typically being longer than its tail. Domestic cats can be any of eighty different colors and patterns. They often live to be fifteen to twenty years old; ten years for a human life is about equal to sixty years for a cat.

The cat's gestation period is approximately two months, and each litter may contain three to seven kittens. Mother cats teach their kittens to eat and to use litter boxes. Kittens ideally should not leave their mother's side until the age of twelve weeks and are considered full-grown at the age of about three years.

Darren Kelly was the production editor and Leanne Soylemez was the copyeditor for *Active Directory*, Second Edition. Mary Brady, Tatiana Apandi Diaz, Mary Anne Weeks Mayo, and Claire Cloutier provided quality control. Derek Di Matteo and Jamie Peppard provided production support. Reg Aubry wrote the index.

Hanna Dyer designed the cover of this book, based on a series design by Edie Freedman. The cover image is a 19th-century engraving from the Dover Pictorial Archive. Emma Colby produced the cover layout with QuarkXPress 4.1 using Adobe's ITC Garamond font.

Bret Kerr designed the interior layout, based on a series design by David Futato. This book was converted by Joe Wizda to FrameMaker 5.5.6 with a format conversion tool created by Erik Ray, Jason McIntosh, Neil Walls, and Mike Sierra that uses Perl and XML technologies. The text font is Linotype Birka; the heading font is Adobe Myriad Condensed; and the code font is LucasFont's TheSans Mono Condensed. The illustrations that appear in the book were produced by Robert Romano and Jessamyn Read using Macromedia FreeHand 9 and Adobe Photoshop 6. The tip and warning icons were drawn by Christopher Bing. This colophon was written by Nicole Arigo.

Related Titles Available from O'Reilly

Windows Administration

Access Database Design and Programming, *3rd Edition*

Active Directory Cookbook

DNS on Windows 2000, *2nd Edition*

DNS on Windows Server 2003

Managing Microsoft Exchange Server

Managing the Windows 2000 Registry

MCSE in a Nutshell

Securing Windows NT/2000 Servers for the Internet

Windows 2000 Administration in a Nutshell

Windows 2000 Performance Guide

Windows Server 2003 in a Nutshell

Keep in touch with O'Reilly

1. Download examples from our books

To find example files for a book, go to:

www.oreilly.com/catalog

select the book, and follow the "Examples" link.

2. Register your O'Reilly books

Register your book at *register.oreilly.com*

Why register your books?
Once you've registered your O'Reilly books you can:

- Win O'Reilly books, T-shirts or discount coupons in our monthly drawing.
- Get special offers available only to registered O'Reilly customers.
- Get catalogs announcing new books (US and UK only).
- Get email notification of new editions of the O'Reilly books you own.

3. Join our email lists

Sign up to get topic-specific email announcements of new books and conferences, special offers, and O'Reilly Network technology newsletters at:

elists.oreilly.com

It's easy to customize your free elists subscription so you'll get exactly the O'Reilly news you want.

4. Get the latest news, tips, and tools

www.oreilly.com

- "Top 100 Sites on the Web"—PC Magazine
- CIO Magazine's Web Business 50 Awards

Our web site contains a library of comprehensive product information (including book excerpts and tables of contents), downloadable software, background articles, interviews with technology leaders, links to relevant sites, book cover art, and more.

5. Work for O'Reilly

Check out our web site for current employment opportunities:

jobs.oreilly.com

6. Contact us

O'Reilly & Associates, Inc.
1005 Gravenstein Hwy North
Sebastopol, CA 95472 USA

TEL: 707-827-7000 or 800-998-9938
(6am to 5pm PST)

FAX: 707-829-0104

order@oreilly.com
For answers to problems regarding your order or our products. To place a book order online, visit:

www.oreilly.com/order_new

catalog@oreilly.com
To request a copy of our latest catalog.

booktech@oreilly.com
For book content technical questions or corrections.

corporate@oreilly.com
For educational, library, government, and corporate sales.

proposals@oreilly.com
To submit new book proposals to our editors and product managers.

international@oreilly.com
For information about our international distributors or translation queries. For a list of our distributors outside of North America check out:

international.oreilly.com/distributors.html

adoption@oreilly.com
For information about academic use of O'Reilly books, visit:

academic.oreilly.com